Richard Cantillon's *Essay on the Nature of Trade in General*

The *Essay on the Nature of Trade in General* was written in the early 1730s by Richard Cantillon, a speculator and banker who had made a vast fortune during the Mississippi and South Sea Bubbles of 1719–20. The work remained unpublished for about two decades, but when it appeared posthumously in Paris in 1755 the book was immediately recognised as a brilliant genre-defining contribution to the then emerging intellectual discipline of political economy.

A degree of mystery has always surrounded the publication of the Essay. Cantillon died under mysterious circumstances in 1734, but the work survived in various manuscript forms. This edition offers an innovative mode of presentation, displaying for the very first time all print and manuscript versions of the Essay in parallel. This allows the reader to appreciate different formulations of Cantillon's seminal contributions to a range of topics, including his circular flow analysis, monetary theory, theories of value and distribution, the role of the entrepreneur, spatial economics and international trade.

Richly annotated and accompanied by a detailed study of the historical background of Cantillon's writings, this new scholarly edition offers many fresh insights into this early masterpiece of economic theory.

Richard van den Berg is Associate Professor in the Department of Accounting, Finance and Informatics at Kingston University, UK.

Routledge Studies in the History of Economics

Richard Cantillon's *Essay on the Nature of Trade in General*

A variorum edition

By Richard Cantillon
Edited by Richard van den Berg

LONDON AND NEW YORK

First published 2015
by Routledge
2 Park Square, Milton Park, Abingdon, Oxon OX14 4RN

by Routledge
52 Vanderbilt Avenue, New York, NY 10017

First issued in paperback 2020

Routledge is an imprint of the Taylor & Francis Group, an informa business

British Library Cataloguing in Publication Data
A catalogue record for this book is available from the British Library

Library of Congress Cataloging-in-Publication Data
Cantillon, Richard, -1734.
  [Essai sur la nature du commerce en général. English & French]
  Richard Cantillon's Essay on the nature of trade in general : a variorum edition / by Richard Cantillon ; edited by Richard van den Berg.
  1. Commerce. 2. Economics. I. Berg, Richard van den.
II. Title. III. Title: Essay on the nature of trade in general.
  HB153.C313 2015
  330—dc23
  2014044535

ISBN 13: 978-0-367-66881-5 (pbk)
ISBN 13: 978-1-138-01458-9 (hbk)
ISBN 13: 978-1-315-79468-6 (ebk)

Typeset in Times New Roman
by Apex CoVantage, LLC

For my family, Daan, Amber and Deepi

Contents

Preface

The first time that Richard Cantillon was, quite literally, brought to public notice was in March 1718 when the *London Gazette* placed the following warning:

> [A]n unknown Person, who goes by the Name of Richard Cantillon, has lately been at Edinburgh, and on the 17th Instant was at Newcastle, pretending to come from France with Orders to buy several Goods, and took the Road from that Place to Shields, from thence to Sunderland, Whitby, Scarborough, Beverly, and other Places in Yorkshire, pretending that in his way to London he was to buy Horses in that County, and that he had a Credit on Sir John Lambert, Bart. By which Means he has imposed upon several People, who have taken his Bills; This publick Notice is given to prevent his doing it any farther: And whoever can discover him, so as that he may be lectured and brought to Justice, shall receive a Reward of Ten Guineas, to be paid by the said Sir John Lambert, at his House in Mincing Lane, Fenchurch-street. All the Description that has been received of this Richard Cantillon is, that of a genteel young Man, who talks very plausible of Matters of Trade.
>
> (*London Gazette* 18–22 March, 1718; issue 5626)

This notice captures in vivid detail an unknown but fairly typical episode in Cantillon's adventurous life. More than once this mercurial character was on the move and engaged in some speculative scheme. Born in Ireland sometime in the 1680s, he had worked in Spain as a 'creative accountant' to a British war profiteer, before setting up as a banker in Paris around 1714. Soon after the episode reported in the *London Gazette*, he would make a vast fortune during the Mississippi and South Sea Bubbles of 1719–20. Afterwards he would spend more than a decade moving around between London, Paris and other cities across Europe, all the while attempting to extricate himself from lawsuits. Even the circumstances surrounding the death of this elusive man in Albemarle Street, London, on 14 May 1734, are shrouded in mystery. It may have been Cantillon's final deceit, a staged death to give any pursuant the slip.

This book, however, is not about the man whose life has after all been studied in great detail in Antoin Murphy's landmark biography *Richard Cantillon. Entrepreneur and Economist* (1986). Instead it is about the manuscripts he worked on in the last years of his life. If, in the flesh, when practising one of his financial scams, Cantillon struck people as someone 'who talks very plausible of Matters of Trade', long after his death his powers as an economic theorist impressed the readers of his *Essay on the Nature of Trade in General* even more. Soon after its publication in Paris in 1755 the *Essai* was hailed as the best work that to date had been written on the theory of trade. And, despite later periods of neglect, modern students have recognised Cantillon's contribution as 'an imperishable masterpiece' (Shackle 1982: 779).

There is, however, also a considerable amount of mystery surrounding Cantillon's writings. It is not known whether the author intended to publish the work and, if so, whether by early 1734 he felt it was ready. When eventually his writings appeared in print in the 1750s, they were not published in a single form, but in three versions. This curious fact has motivated the attempt in the present edition to fit a large number of pieces together of what ultimately seems an incomplete puzzle. As my work progressed I found that some aspects of Cantillon's writings are as hard to pin down as the man himself. While my admiration for this brilliant thinker only increased as I studied the various texts more closely, I also frequently felt as if I had embarked on a vain pursuit of Cantillon's own words. I certainly do not think that this edition settles all questions about the original formulations and full extent of his various views and theories. Indeed I hope it will inspire further investigations, which perhaps will lead to new discoveries. I, for one, have thoroughly enjoyed the chase.

I would like to thank Antoin Murphy for sniffing out at a very early stage that I was on Cantillon's trail and for encouraging my pursuit, and Tony Aspromourgos, Renee Prendergast, Alex Thomas, Matteo Menegatti and Nicholas Harrison for cheering me along and offering advice on my progress. I also thank staff at the Archives Nationales in Paris, the National Archives in Kew, the Nationaal Archief in The Hague, the Municipal Library in Rouen and the Northumberland Record Office at Woodhorn for their assistance, and Emily Kindleysides, Daniel Bourner and colleagues at Routledge, for their professional support. Most of all I thank Jugdeep, my wife, for giving me time and space to roam.

October 2014

1 Introduction

The main facts of the peculiar reception history of Cantillon's writings are quite well known. After having remained in manuscript for about two decades, the *Essai sur la nature du commerce en général* appeared in print in Paris in May 1755. The work rapidly made an impression on the most significant authors of the then emerging discipline of political economy: Quesnay, Turgot, Steuart, Beccaria, Smith, Condillac and various lesser-known authors. But, after a few decades, interest in the *Essai* waned, to such an extent that after the French Revolution Cantillon's work was rarely read. Generally speaking, until the last decades of the nineteenth century all but a few economists stopped attaching any real significance to this work of somewhat mysterious provenance.[1]

A modern fascination with the *Essai* was sparked by the publication of William Stanley Jevons's article 'Richard Cantillon and the Nationality of Political Economy' in 1881. In this groundbreaking contribution Jevons proclaimed his deep admiration for the *Essai*, hailing it as 'the cradle of political economy' and 'the first systematic Treatise of Economics' (Jevons [1881] 1931: 359–60). In this manner, Jevons, himself one of the initiators of a revolution in economic theory, established the reputation of Cantillon's work as one of the foundational texts of the discipline. Of course Jevons's remarkable reappraisal of the *Essai*'s importance was not accepted at a stroke. At first especially French and German economists and historians remained somewhat lukewarm about Cantillon's importance (see Hayek [1931] 1985: 9–10). However, during the twentieth century Jevons's assessment of the *Essai* became more widely shared. In particular, influential general histories of economic thought would customarily praise the *Essai*. To give some examples, Schumpeter (1954: 217, 223) would call it 'a great work' and 'a brilliant performance'; Blaug (1997: 21): 'the most systematic, the most lucid, and at the same time the most original of all statements of economic principles before the *Wealth of Nations*'; Ekelund and Hébert (1990: 77): 'a masterpiece' and 'the state of the art of economics before Adam Smith'.

Especially in the second half of the twentieth century, there also emerged a more extensive specialist secondary literature about particular aspects of Cantillon's work. While it is hard to do justice to this literature, some important contributions were the following: Spengler (1942) wrote about Cantillon's theory of population; Ponsard (1958), Dockès (1969) and Hébert (1981) discussed his contributions to spatial economics; Brems (1978) and Brewer (1988) focussed on Cantillon's theory of value; Bordo (1983) summarised his monetary economics; Aspromourgos (1989) studied Cantillon's theory of production and distribution; Prendergast (1991) highlighted his theory of profit; and Berdell (2009) reconstructed his intersectoral analysis. General overviews of Cantillon's work were offered, for instance, by Spengler (1954) and Brewer (1992). These various studies, and others, have generated a large number of insights and a range of alternative views about Cantillon's economics. The fact that in earlier times Marx, Jevons and Hayek, originators of fundamentally different approaches to economic theory, each expressed their admiration for the author of the *Essai* attests to the broad and seminal nature of Cantillon's contribution.[2]

The modern interest in Cantillon also inspired further biographical work. For a long time the investigations of Higgs (1891, 1892, 1931) remained the most reliable sources for information about the Irish banker and speculator. But eventually Murphy's study (1986) superseded all earlier biographical research on Cantillon.

Scholarly editions that were published in the twentieth century consolidated the reputation of the *Essai* as a crucial early contribution to economic theory. The first was Henry Higgs's edition of 1931, published under the auspices of the Royal Economic Society, which presented the French text of the first print edition of 1755 alongside the first full English translation of the *Essai*. Higgs's edition became the standard text used by Anglo-Saxon readers of Cantillon for the rest of the twentieth century.[3] Also in 1931 the first German translation of the *Essai* was published, prepared by Hella Hayek and introduced by her then husband Friedrich. The modern French edition, prepared by Louis Salleron for the Institut National d'Études Démographiques, followed in 1952. It was reprinted in 1997 with some corrections and with additional introductory essays and it remains the standard modern edition in French based on the publication of 1755 (Brian and Théré 1997). The modern Italian edition by Sergio Cotta and Antonio Giolitti was published in 1955.[4]

The present work differs from all previous scholarly editions in that it includes in addition to the French print edition of 1755 other versions of Richard Cantillon's economic writings. The notion that such an edition would be desirable first suggested itself to me in the summer of 2010 when I happened across a fascinating passage in the entry 'Circulation' of Malachy Postlethwayt's massive *Universal Dictionary of Trade and Commerce* (1751–55). The passage in question, here reproduced in D134 on p. 128, came at the end of an extended fragment that roughly corresponds to Cantillon's chapter 13 of part I of the *Essai*. In this famous chapter Cantillon describes the crucial role of *entrepreneurs* in the provisioning of goods within what we would call a 'market economy'. The passage in the *Dictionary*, while summing up the preceding argument very well, did not have a direct counterpart in the French text. It spoke of the economic system as a 'grand machine' of circulation, which is 'commonly carried on with uncertainty', but in which 'every thing finds its own proportion, well or ill, according to chance or caprice, without any peculiar intellectual conduct, whereby the society of commerce and circulation is governed'.

These highly suggestive formulations piqued my interest and sent me back to Higgs's famous study, included in the edition of 1931, where he had discussed Postlethwayt's 'borrowing' of fragments of Cantillon's writings. Higgs, it turned out, seemed to play down any possible differences between the French text and the fragments found in Postlethwayt's *Dictionary*, only admitting 'occasionally some small deviations from the turn of phrase' (Higgs 1931: 384). This hardly described the quite divergent ending to the fragment I had come across. If this was true for a passage I had happened upon by chance, I wondered, could it be that similar differences between the French and English texts were more common? This led me to make an initial, more systematic comparison for which a useful starting point was Higgs's appendix of 'chief parallels between Postlethwayt's *Dictionary* and Cantillon's *Essai*'. It turned out that the variations were frequent and indeed sometimes substantial.

The most obvious explanation for any such differences, I thought initially, was that Postlethwayt had made multiple alterations and additions in the process of adopting parts of a manuscript of Cantillon's work in his *Dictionary*. My opinion changed radically, however, when I started to compare the fragments from the *Dictionary* with the other English version of Cantillon's work published in the 1750s, namely, Philip Cantillon's *The Analysis of Trade and Commerce* of 1759. Starting from the beginning of the *Analysis*, I found that, from as early as the second chapter, both English texts *shared* variations when compared to the French text. To be precise, in that chapter the sequence of paragraphs in both English texts, when compared to the order of the French text, is 1, 3, 6, 7, 4, 5, while neither has a counterpart to paragraphs 2 or 8 (see E/D/A7 to E/D/A18 in the present edition). Further along in the texts I started finding passages that occur in both English versions but which do not have an obvious counterpart in the French text (see e.g. the sequence D/A206–D/A212 or D/A257–D/A259). While French paragraphs that have counterparts in one English version only or in neither were much more common, the commonalities between the English versions in particular convinced me that the three versions were not, as has always been supposed, ultimately based on the same source.

Instead, it seems likely that the three publications were based on manuscript versions that differed from each other in substantial ways. Having arrived at this novel conclusion, and wanting to open it for examination, I presented my initial findings (in van den Berg 2012b) and decided to present the full puzzle in the form of the present work. The form of presentation chosen allows a parallel reading of the three main versions that appeared in print in the 1750s, that is to say, the French *Essai* of 1755, the English fragments from Postlethwayt's *Dictionary* of 1751–55, and large parts of Philip Cantillon's *Analysis* of 1759. In addition, the current edition attempts to record all variations between those three texts and a number of alternative versions from the same period. In the first place, there are three known French manuscript versions of the *Essai*, two partial and one complete, which all date from before the publication of the first French print edition. Second, in the years after the first print edition three more editions were published. Third, Postlethwayt plagiarised fragments taken from Cantillon in two of his other works, one published in 1749 and one from 1757. In total therefore the present edition compares eleven different texts, although with regard to any particular passage only some contain relevant content. An overview of the comparisons can be found in Table 4.1b (pp. 40–43), which also explains the coding that has been adopted to facilitate cross-referencing.

Notes

1 Perhaps the only important exception is Karl Marx (1818–83). Whilst his published writings refer to Cantillon relatively little, compared to the attention bestowed on other early authors, notebooks with extensive quotes from the *Essai* found in Marx's manuscripts show that he had a keen interest in Cantillon's work (see Ananyin 2014).
2 Of course Cantillon can neither be retrospectively called a neoclassical, nor a Marxian, nor an Austrian economist (even though some commentators have tried to do especially the latter; see e.g. Hébert (1985) and Rothbard (1995)). The temporal and spatial circulation of ideas resembles that of money and can be described with Cantillon's own favourite metaphor of a river (cf. E389). It may at times run fast or wind down, split up in different branches and fertilise different grounds. But though this may be of interest to someone downstream, it has little to do with the source.
3 Reprints of this edition were published in 1959 by F. Cass and in 1964 by A.M Kelley. Brewer (2001) provided a new introduction to a further reprint of the Higgs translation, and more recently the translation became freely accessible online at www.econlib.org/library/NPDBooks/Cantillon/cntNT.html.
4 This edition, which was in fact the second Italian translation (see p. 36), included an introduction by Luigi Einaudi. This introduction has recently been published in English translation (Einaudi 2014: 265–75).

2 Historical backgrounds to the texts

Each text has its own particular and at times incompletely known history. These histories are important for assessing the authenticity of and relations between the texts.

2.1 The French versions

2.1.1 The print editions

The first column on the verso pages reproduces the text of the renowned first print edition of the *Essai sur la nature du commerce en général*. The title page of this anonymous work (see E1), published in May 1755, set a number of puzzles that almost immediately invited various speculations. The first and most important question, as to the identity of the author, was soon put beyond dispute. The earliest reviews in Grimm's *Correspondance littéraire* (letter dated 1 July 1755) and Fréron's *L'Année Littéraire* (entry 4 August 1755) already agreed that the author had been one Richard Cantillon. The *Essai* was immediately recognised as an exceptional work and established Cantillon's early posthumous reputation as a leading economic theorist: Fréron (1755: 68) called the book 'one of the best that have been written on the subject of trade', the Marquis de Mirabeau (1756: 85), eulogised Cantillon as 'the most able man' to have written on the theory of commerce and insisted that his work was 'without equal', and Mably (1757) too styled the *Essai* 'the best work that has been written on the subject'. As a result of such endorsements the *Journal de Commerce* soon referred to the author as '*le célèbre Cantillon*' (Jan. 1760: 69). But, famous or not, beyond his name only little was known about the man: he had been *un Anglais* (Grimm [1755] 2006: 133) or *Irlandois* (Fréron 1755, v: 67) who, after having become rich at the beginning of the 1720s during the time of John Law's System, had been murdered in London in 1733 or 1734. These sparse details remained practically all that was known about Cantillon until the last decades of the nineteenth century.

The second puzzle concerned the statement on the title page that the work had been '*traduit de l'anglois*'. Both Grimm and Fréron dismissed this notion and asserted that the work had originally been composed in French, the latter further expressing the contrary opinion that 'it is the English themselves who have translated it into their language from the original of M. Cantillon' (Fréron 1755, v: 67). Soon after, however, the Marquis de Mirabeau contradicted this view in his hugely popular *L'Ami des hommes*. Clarifying the statement on the title page of the *Essai*, but without giving the source of his information, Mirabeau stated that the work had originally been written in English and subsequently translated by Cantillon himself 'for the use by one of his friends' (Mirabeau 1756: 85). Remarkably, this particular dispute between the earliest commentators on Cantillon's work has never been settled. During the last 80 years or so Mirabeau's view that the *Essai* was a translation from a text originally written in English has been the most widely accepted (see e.g. Hayek 1932; Fage [1952] 1997: xl; or Hébert 2010: 6). This is mainly due to Henry Higgs who in his famous edition of the *Essai* of 1931 argued that the presence of many plagiarised fragments in Malachy Postlethwayt's *Universal Dictionary* (1751–55) proved the existence of a (lost) English original (Higgs 1931: 383). However, not all commentators have accepted Higgs's evidence as being decisive; see e.g. Murphy (1986: 250, 2009: 77) and Brewer (2001: x).

Third, the purported place of publication, '*Londres*', and name of the publisher, '*Fletcher Gyles dans Holborn*', have been contested since the late nineteenth century. Jevons ([1881] 1931: 341) had already concluded that the work was actually produced in Paris and it has long since been agreed that a foreign origin was put on the title page as a customary method of coping with the French censor. However, which Paris publisher actually produced the book has been a more difficult question to answer. Eventually, Murphy (1986: 299–308) established that the publisher is likely to have been Pierre André Guillyn (1715–81), whose business was based at the Lis d'Or on the Quai des Augustins in Paris. As noted in the records of the Inspector of the Book Trade, Joseph d'Hémery (1722–1806), Guillyn had submitted the print edition of the *Essai* to the authorities and obtained a *permission tacite* for its publication.[1]

The final mystery concerns the identity of the person who prepared the 1755 print edition. Following an early suggestion of Higgs (1892: 452), the modern authorities Tsuda (1979) and Murphy (1986) agree that it is likely that this editor was one of the men who belonged to the group around Jacques Claude Marie Vincent de Gournay (1712–59). In the mid-1750s this group was responsible for the publication in France of a large number of works on trade (see Théré *et al.* 2011). There is, however, no concrete evidence to answer the question as to who amongst these men, if it was one of this group, may have prepared a manuscript of the *Essai* for print. The question is all the more interesting because, judging by the many variations between the 1755 print edition and the surviving manuscript versions, it is likely to be this unknown editor who made changes throughout the work.

Before discussing the nature of these changes in more detail, some brief observations must be made about the three subsequent print editions of the *Essai*. The main point here is that in all probability these later publications were based on the 1755 work and did not benefit from access to manuscripts.[2] The first subsequent edition of 1756 is more or less a straight reprint of the 1755 edition. Apart from different vignettes on the title pages and different page counts (v, 427 pages instead of vi, 430 pages), there are 13 minor corrections in the 1756a print and one newly imported printing error.[3] In the same year the *Essai* was reprinted as part of a series of *Discours Politiques*. The editor, Eléazar Mauvillon (1712–79), had produced the first volume, an edition of David Hume's *Discourses*, in 1754. The third volume, published in 1756 '*chez J. Schreuder et Pierre Mortier le jeune*', included Cantillon's *Essai* on pp. 153 to 428. Compared to the other 1756 edition, Mauvillon's alterations were more frequent and almost all of a stylistic nature.[4] In a sense, his editorial practice continued what, as we will see, the unknown editor of the 1755 edition had implemented incompletely. To give but two examples, where the first edition has '*à un ou plusieurs*', Mauvillon has '*à un ou à plusieurs*' (V13a), where the former has '*les Fermiers & Laboureurs*', the latter has '*les Fermiers & les Laboureurs*' (V13b). Such minor changes, of which there are quite a few more, while quite unsubstantial, do give an impression of the typical editorial practice of the time. A further edition of *Discourses Politiques* was published in 1769, with very few additional changes to the text of the *Essai*.[5]

2.1.2 *The French manuscript versions*

Of much greater interest than the variations in the subsequent print editions of the *Essai* are the ones found in the surviving French manuscript versions of Cantillon's writings. These manuscripts were discovered at different times. The first have been known since 1890 when Stephan Bauer reported the existence in the *Archives Nationales* in Paris of a partial transcript of the *Essai* as well as a summary of the entire work. These two manuscripts were amongst the surviving papers of Victor de Riquetti, the (fourth) marquis de Mirabeau (1715–89) and cofounder of the physiocratic movement.

The first manuscript, catalogue number M780 n° 1, with the title *Mémoire sur la Population*, consists of 107 large sheets and is considered to be an early draft of Mirabeau's *L'Ami des hommes*. Some pages into this manuscript the text starts being divided into a left-hand column, which contains a near verbatim transcript of Cantillon's *Essai*, and a right-hand column with copious, rather florid, reflections (see Figure 2.1). The handwriting of the right-hand columns is the same as on the preceding pages and is probably

Figure 2.1 Start of extract from the *Essai* in M780 no. 1 (Archives nationales de France)

that of Mirabeau. The handwriting in the left-hand columns is neater and is presumably that of one of Mirabeau's scribes. After 55 pages the extract from Cantillon's work (corresponding to the text reproduced in the present edition from E42 to E343), finishes and Mirabeau's writing continues once more over the full width of the page.

The second manuscript, catalogue number M779 n° 1, with the title *Essai sur le commerce en général*, consists of 96 smaller pages. Rather than being a transcript, it is an abridged version of Cantillon's work consisting of a mixture of paraphrases and verbatim quotations. Since it makes no attempt to follow the letter of Cantillon's writings it is in some respects less interesting than the long excerpt in M780 and for this reason only the variations between the latter manuscript and the first print edition of the *Essai* have been recorded in the present edition. However, one point that M779 proves is that, since it also covers the content of the *Essai* after M780 breaks off, Mirabeau must indeed have possessed a manuscript of the entire work (bar the elusive Supplement).[6]

While the content of M779 and M780 has been known and discussed since the late nineteenth century, a further partial transcript of the *Essai* in the Archives Nationales was located only ten years ago by Christine Théré and Loïc Charles (see Quesnay 2005: 1313). The likely reason why it was not discovered for so long is that the manuscript in which it occurs is not part of what is traditionally known as *Le fonds Mirabeau* (M778 to M785). The manuscript in question, M773 n° 2 bis, consisting of 97 sheets, is in some respects similar to M780 n° 1. That is to say, it carries the same title, *Mémoire sur la Population*, and the transcript of the *Essai* only commences after some very similar introductory pages and then is accompanied by Mirabeau's running commentary. Different from M780 is, first, that in M773 the division between transcript and commentary is not vertical, but horizontal, with Cantillon's text on the top part of the pages (see Figure 2.2). Second, the neat handwriting, both of the transcript and the commentary, appears to be of a scribe, identified by Théré and Charles as Mirabeau's faithful secretary Garçon (Quesnay 2005: 1313).[7] Third, and most importantly, M773, unlike M780, covers the whole of the first part of the *Essai* (corresponding to E1–E233 in the present edition).

The presence in Mirabeau's working papers of manuscripts that appear to be attempts to rework Cantillon's writings has led to various speculations about the former's intentions. As soon as M779 and M780 were discovered, Higgs (1891: 266–67) put forward the view that Mirabeau's motives had been 'entirely dishonourable'. Mirabeau had initially had the idea to pass off a compilation of Cantillon's ideas as his own. In Higgs's view, M779 was the result of this attempt. But when he had to return the manuscript, and feared his plagiarism would be easily detected, he tried 'to serve up the same dish in another form'. This second attempt, still according to Higgs, was M780, and Mirabeau's free commentary in this manuscript was subsequently worked into *L'Ami des hommes*. Tsuda's more recent and detailed re-examination of the textual evidence reached the same conclusion as Higgs with regard to Mirabeau's motives (see Tsuda 1979: 405–10). However, other commentators have felt they had to speak up for Mirabeau. For example, in a review of Tsuda's work, Louis Salleron (1980: 212) adamantly rejected the view that the later physiocrat would have wanted to plagiarise Cantillon as being a 'gratuitous accusation as well as an absurdity'.[8] This particular controversy is of less relevance to the current work, but let it be noted that the more recently discovered M773 may in future research throw further light on the matter.

More pertinent in the context of the present edition is the question when M779, M780 and also M773 were composed. M779 is probably the earliest and Tsuda (1979: 210) dates it to 1751 or 1752. M780, in the opinion of the same commentator, was started in 1753 or 1754 and completed by the beginning of 1756 (ibid.),[9] which is perhaps more accurate than Higgs's earlier view that it dates from 'circa 1750' (Higgs 1931: 381 n.44). M773, in turn, appears to have been written shortly after M780. My reason for saying so is that Mirabeau's well-known account about Cantillon and his writings at the beginning of M780 is repeated at the beginning of M773, but without the occasional deletions and with the corrections

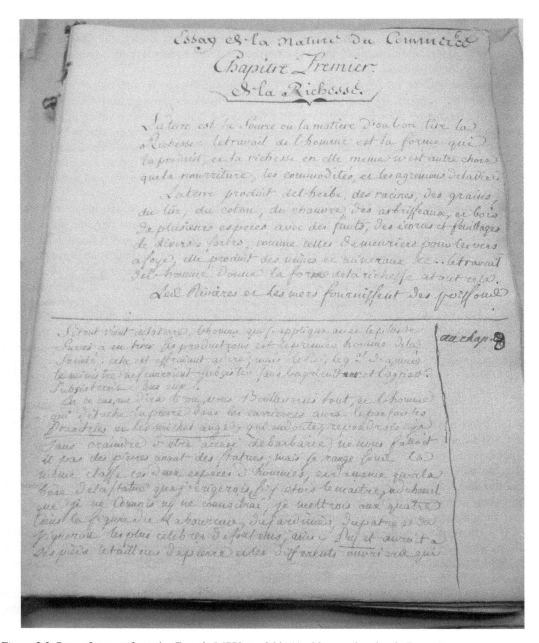

Figure 2.2 Start of extract from the *Essai* in M773 no. 2 bis (Archives nationales de France)

found in the former manuscript.[10] In any case, it seems safe to assume that all three manuscripts date from the first half of the 1750s.

It is also clear that they were all based on another manuscript version of the *Essai* not present in the Archives Nationales. A few tantalising details about this earlier source text are provided by Mirabeau himself. First, at the beginning of chap VII of *L'Ami des Hommes* he writes that [the manuscript] is but one hundredth part of the works of that illustrous man [Cantillon], which perished with him in a singular and fatal catastrophe. [The *Essai*] itself is incomplete because it lacks the Supplement to which he often refers and on which he based all his calculations. He translated the former part himself, for use by one of his friends. And *it was this manuscript that was printed* [in 1755], more than twenty years after the death of the author.

(Mirabeau 1756: 85; my translation; emphasis added)

Second, in a later letter to Jean-Jacques Rousseau, Mirabeau claimed that he had held the manuscript of '*L'Essay sur la nature de Commerce de Mr. Cantillon*' in his possession for 16 years.[11] Third, in his account in M780 Mirabeau writes: '*Ce morceau m'est tombé entre les mains par une espèce de vol, avoué depuis par la personne pour laquelle cette traduction avait été faite.*'[12] Higgs (1931: 382) translated this sentence as: 'This fragment [i.e. the manuscript] came into my hands by a kind of theft subsequently announced by the person for whom the translation was made.' This statement is rather cryptic. In the first place, what does Mirabeau mean by 'a kind of theft' and second, what does *avoué depuis par* mean precisely? Instead of Higgs's translation of the phrase as 'subsequently announced by', perhaps 'subsequently admitted by' is more literal although it still does not make the statement fully intelligible. Perhaps Mirabeau meant to write *avoué depuis à* ('subsequently admitted to') and then the statement makes sense. As it is, the sentence can arguably mean that Mirabeau initially 'borrowed' the manuscript without the owner's knowledge, but that the latter 'subsequently acknowledged' that he was allowed to do so. Or it may mean that the owner 'subsequently noticed' the absence of his manuscript and told Mirabeau so.

In any case, all commentators on this passage agree that Mirabeau was eventually asked to return the manuscript to its rightful owner, and Tsuda argues that this happened in 1754. From this he deduces that Mirabeau must have had the manuscript in his possession from the late 1730s (Tsuda 1979: 410). The identity of the supposed 'friend' of Cantillon has always remained a mystery. Higgs (1931: 383) even believed that it was 'vain to speculate who this rightful owner and intimate friend of Cantillon was'. Nevertheless, some brief speculations may be in order because in 1786 the *abbé* François-André-Adrien Pluquet (1716–90) actually claimed to have known Cantillon's mysterious friend. That is to say, in his *Traité philosophique et politique sur le luxe*, after quoting Cantillon's estimates of the average amounts of land required to maintain men at different levels of affluence (see E159–E160), Pluquet adds the following intriguing note:

This assumption [about the varying amounts of land required] is not at all arbitrary, but the result of observations M. Cantillon made in the countrysides and villages of almost all states of Europe. I was given this information by the late M. the marquis de S. Georges, *to whom the public owes the Essay on the Nature of Trade*.

(Pluquet 1786, 2, 328–29 n.; emphases added)

The 'marquis de S. George' in question was François Olivier de Saint-Georges de Vérac (1707–53). Pluquet's claim gains credibility from the separate fact that this nobleman was for many years a close friend of Mirabeau (see Montlaur 1992: 82–86). While not naming him in his manuscripts, Mirabeau, like Pluquet, also relates that 'an intimate friend' of Cantillon had told him anecdotes about the Irishman's impromptu travels throughout Europe to verify particular economic facts.[13] Originally from Poitou, de Vérac lived in Paris during the later period that Cantillon lived there as well, that is, from late 1728 until early 1733. The former still lived there in 1737 when he made his acquaintance with Mirabeau (Montlaur 1992: 82). Although we cannot be sure that de Vérac was the mutual friend of Cantillon and Mirabeau, the dates fit for a friendship between the former two and also for the moment when the marquis presumably obtained the manuscript of the *Essai*. If so, the further fact that de Vérac died on 10 July

1753 may have something to do with the request to Mirabeau to return the manuscript. One wonders whether this request came from the descendants of de Vérac.

Perhaps these speculations bring us a little closer to proving beyond any doubt the suspicion, substantiated below, that the manuscript currently preserved in the municipal library of Rouen is indeed the actual *morceau* Mirabeau was talking about.[14] What is known of the provenance of this manuscript is that the collector Jean-Michel-Constant Leber (1780–1859) acquired it, probably in Paris, in the early decades of the nineteenth century. In 1838 Leber sold his large collection to the town of Rouen for 60,000 francs (see Tsuda 1979: 410–11). Amongst this collection, the manuscript with the title *Essay de la nature du commerce en général* (collection Leber 919 (3050)) remained undiscovered until the 1970s, when professor Takumi Tsuda located it (see Figure 2.3).

Despite Tsuda's publication in 1979 of a meticulous transcript of the manuscript alongside the text of the first print edition of the *Essai* of 1755, the Rouen version has not received the recognition it deserves. It is the only known complete manuscript version of the *Essai* (to be sure, without the Supplement), consisting of 158 bound sheets measuring 187 by 130 mm, and is written in a clearly legible hand, most probably of a copyist. The orthography is very odd. Throughout the text there is an inconsistent use of capitals and punctuation, and the only diacritical mark used is the acute accent (often in a bizarre manner, for example '*entrepreneur*' is frequently written '*éntréprénéur*').[15] Perhaps more significant is the antiquated spelling. For example, the so-called preconsonantal *s* occurs frequently. In 1740 the Académie Française formalised a spelling reform whereby this letter was replaced with a circumflex on the preceding vowel in a large number of words in its dictionary. The 1755 print edition of the *Essai* consistently adhered to this new usage. Thus, to give some examples, *bâties* in the print edition is spelled *basties* in the Rouen manuscript (E33), *côté* is *costé* (E65), *mêlent* is *meslent* (E66) *paroît* is *paroist* (E77) and *conquêtes* is *conquéstes* (E77). In addition the letter *v*, apart from as the first letter of words, is not used in the Rouen manuscript. Instead, in keeping with common practice in handwritten documents before 1740, it uses the letter *u* throughout (for example *avanturier* is written *auanturier* (V129a). These antiquated spellings would suggest that the Rouen manuscript dates from before 1740. But of course it may alternatively be the case that the person who wrote it simply ignored the spelling reforms of 1740. Even if this were so, the fact that partial versions M and N drop the preconsonantal *s* and make modern use of the letter *v* surely indicates that they are of a later date than the Rouen manuscript. Another thing to note is that, in a number of places in R, peculiar homophones occur (*content* for *comptant* (V274a) or *l'aire* for *l'Ere* (V574e); for a fuller list see C274iii). As Tsuda (1979: 412) suggests, this may indicate that the manuscript was dictated. All in all the manuscript with its various peculiar imperfections in the presentation of the text and the antiquated spellings gives the impression that it was not intended for general circulation.

2.1.3 *Variations between the French versions*

Not only is R anterior to M and N, it is in fact very likely that the Rouen manuscript was the actual source text used by Mirabeau's scribes. This claim is based on the fact that there is a very close adherence of M and N to the phrasing of R. First, as can be seen at length in the main part of this edition, there are a large number of cases where the three manuscript versions differ in unison from the print edition. To take but one typical example, when compared to *Essai* I, xiv, paragraph 4 (E142), the Rouen manuscript displays 12 variations (V142a to l). Nine of these occur exactly the same in the Paris manuscripts. The remaining three variations all concern small grammatical errors in the Rouen manuscript. In two cases (V142a and l) M corrects the inconsistencies between singular and plural adverbs, nouns and verbs in the same manner as the print edition, while N follows R. Only in the other case (V142i) do both Paris manuscripts agree with the print version and differ from R.

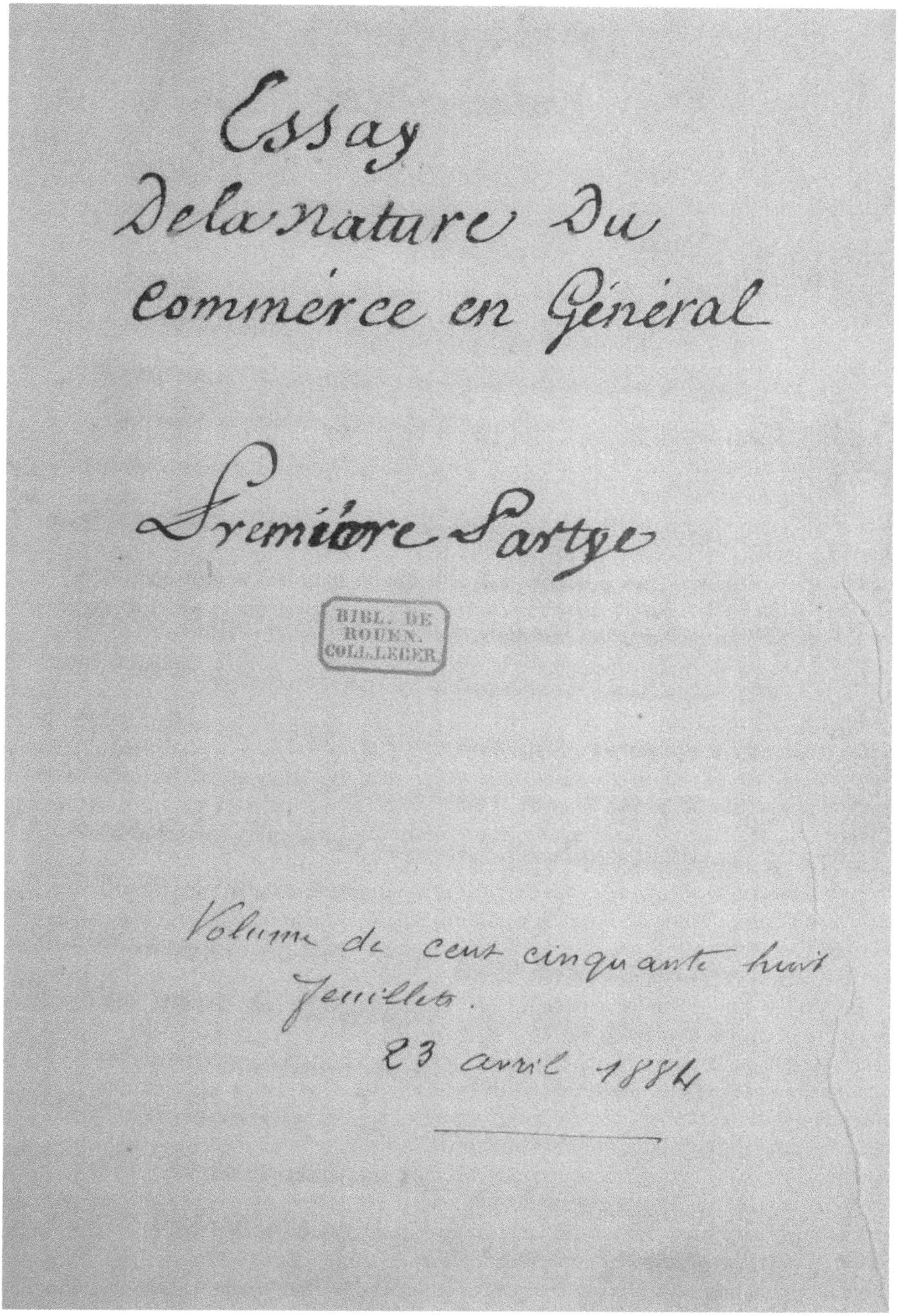
Essay
Dela Nature du
commerce en Général
Première Partye
BIBL. DE ROUEN. COLL. LEGER
Volume de cent cinquante huit feuillets.
23 avril 1884

Figure 2.3 Title page of the Rouen Manuscript (Collections de la Bibliothèque municipale de Rouen)

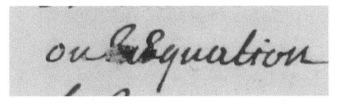

Figure 2.4a Variation 105a: Rouen Manuscript (Collections de la Bibliothèque municipale de Rouen)

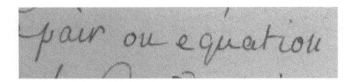

Figure 2.4b Variation 105a: M773 (Archives nationales de France)

Similar small grammatical errors are frequent in R. Sometimes, M or N provides corrections that differ from the ones found in E (see e.g. M in V120b or N in V132c). Another example is V105a where the Rouen manuscript renders what is probably originally Petty's phrase 'Par and Equation' (see C105i) as '*pair ou En Equation*'. The Paris manuscripts correct this odd expression by omitting the word *en*, and thus the expression becomes '*pair ou equation*' (see Figure 2.4a and b). The print edition, on the other hand, omits the word *ou*, and therefore has the still odd expression '*pair, en Equation*' (which, in turn, Higgs translated as 'Par, or Equation'). Similar cases are V20d and V70a, where minor ambiguities in R are solved in different ways in E, M and N.

All such minor corrections in the Paris manuscripts can, in my opinion, be explained as the somewhat hasty and incomplete editing by copyists while transcribing the Rouen text. The same is true for the frequent alterations, already noted, in the Paris manuscripts to the spellings and diacritics found in R.[16] At the same time, there are also less numerous variations that occur only in either M or N (for example V108a or V113b) and which can be explained as small copying errors.

Perhaps the most convincing evidence that R was the source text for M and N is provided by places where the handwriting of the Rouen is difficult to read. For example, the first two words of *Essai* I, xiii, 7 are scarcely legible in R (see Figure 2.5a). This may well explain why M and N have '*Le meme facturier*' (see Figure 2.5b), where E125 has '*Le Manufacturier*'. Other examples are the strange expression *notre Curgre* in the Rouen manuscript (V184c), which the copyist of N guessed to be *notre Europe*, and so it also appears in E, but which the copyist of M simply transcribed (Figure 2.6a, b and c); or the spelling of Gregory King's name as 'Xing', which is adopted in both Paris manuscripts (V175g). Such imperfections that are common between R and M and/or N are hard to explain in any way other than that the former was the actual text from which the Paris manuscripts were copied. In fact, there is not a single case in M or N that throws serious doubt on this conclusion.[17]

The significance of the finding that R was in all likelihood the source text for the partial transcripts M and N, made by Mirabeau's secretaries, is that it implies that the former was the very manuscript that the Marquis was writing about. As we saw, Mirabeau was convinced that 'it was this [same] manuscript that was printed, more than twenty years after the death of the author' (Mirabeau 1756: 85). It is, however, important not to conclude too quickly that R was also used as the source text of the famous first print edition.

Further evidence is required not only because Mirabeau may simply have been wrong, but also because various commentators have asserted that during the two decades before its publication *other* manuscript

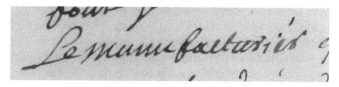

Figure 2.5a Variation 125a, Rouen Manuscript (Collections de la Bibliothèque municipale de Rouen)

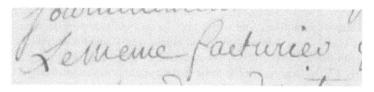

Figure 2.5b Variation 125a, M773 (Archives nationales de France)

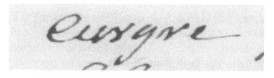

Figure 2.6a Variation 184c, Rouen Manuscript (Collections de la Bibliothèque municipale de Rouen)

Figure 2.6b Variation 184c, M780 (Archives nationales de France)

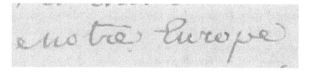

Figure 2.6c Variation 184c, M773 (Archives nationales de France)

copies of Cantillon's work were in circulation in France. A commentator who confidently expresses this opinion is Joseph Schumpeter in his magisterial *History of Economic Analysis*:

> The *Essai sur la nature du commerce en général* is supposed to have been written about 1730 and was, though in a very unconventional sense, 'published' soon after; that is to say, the manuscript circulated and exerted influence soon after. (This meant a lot in a small and highly concentrated professional circle.) The date of its actual (post-humous) publication, 1755, therefore has not the usual significance.
>
> (Schumpeter 1954: 217, n.4)

Unfortunately, Schumpeter or later commentators who express the same view (see e.g. Brian and Théré 1997: ii; Larrère 2011: 131) provide little concrete evidence. Admittedly, it is true that in the mid-eighteenth century it was not uncommon for unpublished literary works to circulate in manuscript form (see Moureau 1993). But if this were the case with Cantillon's work, one would expect to find two kinds of evidence. First, one would perhaps expect one or more neat manuscript copies of the *Essai* to have survived. As already noted, the Rouen manuscript, the only complete manuscript copy of the *Essai* known to exist, does in my opinion not look like a vehicle intended for circulation in enlightened circles. Of course all neat copies may have been lost. But in that case one would still expect a second kind of evidence, namely the mention of Cantillon's work in the writings of well-informed men or women *prior to* 1755. It is true that cases have been made for the existence of traces of Cantillon's influence prior to the publication of the *Essai*. Hayek (1931) and more fully Thornton (2007) have argued that David Hume read Cantillon in manuscript, presumably in France in the 1740s. Similarly, Larrère (2011) has argued that Montesquieu was familiar with the Irishman's ideas even in the early 1730s. However, it has to be said that neither case seems completely convincing.[18]

It seems therefore reasonable to say that Mirabeau's assumption that the print edition was based on the manuscript he had in his possession for 16 years may well be true. He also provides the following more detailed description of that manuscript:

> The author translated [a presumed English version] himself for the use by one of his intimate friends, and postponed the translation of the Supplement which perished with his other papers. But although he knew our language perfectly, what one often sees in a translation with [difficult] turns of phrases and expressions such as there are in this one, [and] since he never intended that the work should appear in French and only translated it for a friend whose solidity of mind was known to him, he paid less attention to its phrasing than he would have done if he had foreseen what happened to it today [i.e. publication].
>
> (M780 and M773; reproduced in Brian and Théré 1997: lxxi–lxxii)

The second sentence of this passage suggests that Mirabeau believed that the manuscript would benefit throughout from corrections in style and imperfect French formulations. This chimes very well with the content of the Rouen text and it is indeed this task on which the unknown editor of the print edition appears to have concentrated. Throughout E and R one finds that the majority of variations concern small improvements in French formulations. Typical are the addition of particles and small changes in word order, e.g. *les merchandises et denrees* in the manuscript, becomes *les denrées & les merchandises* in the print version (V292b). Sometimes unfamiliar terms are substituted for more commonly used ones. For example *argent sonnant* ('sounding money', i.e. coin) is, in all but one case, replaced with *argent comptant* (see C273i). In a number of cases expressions that are substituted appear to be Anglicisms: for example, *chevaux de poste* ('post horses') becomes *chevaux de carrosse* ('carriage horses') (V165a); *le manger, le boire, l'habillement* (which corresponds to 'eating, drinking, cloathing' in Postlethwayt's *Dictionary*) is replaced, in all but one case (E672), with *la nourriture, le vêtement* (see C275).[19] One is tempted to conclude from this that all such variations can be explained by assuming that the editor of the print edition made frequent stylistic corrections, more or less as Mirabeau suggested would be required before publication. At least, this seems much more likely than the alternative explanation for such variations, namely that the print edition was based on a source text other than R.

There are, admittedly, also a small number of variations that hint at this alternative possibility. For example, in E114 it is argued that, although normally the numbers of Entrepreneurs and Artisans in a state are proportioned to the amount of land available for subsistence and raw materials, in large towns such men often live by foreign trade. In the print edition then follows the clarification, missing in the manuscript versions, 'and therefore at the expense of foreign landowners' (V114a). This clarification is in keeping with Richard Cantillon's arguments about foreign trade in *Essai* III, i, which can of course also be found in the Rouen manuscript.

Therefore one might argue that it was the editor who made the addition in the light of this later discussion. Intriguingly, however, pretty much the same clarification is given in the same place in the corresponding paragraph in Philip Cantillon's *Analysis* (see A114). For this reason it would be quite a coincidence, though it is not impossible, that the editor of the *Essai* independently decided to insert the same observation at this precise point. A somewhat similar case is V442a, where no mention is made of *castor* ('beaver') while *both* E *and* D do (see C442ii). There are also a small number of other places where phrases and terms are missing in the Rouen manuscript that would have required fortuitous corrections (e.g. V304a and V143b where *Acteur* appears to be the correct version). Such differences between R and E may be explained by assuming that a (now lost) manuscript other than the one preserved in Rouen was used as the source text for the print edition. However, these cases are not numerous and in my opinion the evidence they yield in favour of this alternative explanation is not compelling. On balance, therefore, even though the evidence is not as one sided as in the case of M and N, it seems more than likely that the Rouen manuscript was the source text for the print edition of 1755 as well.[20]

This is important for the appreciation of the more substantial variations between printed text (E) and manuscript (R), that is, where real differences in meaning occur. It should be noted carefully that in some places the economic content of the Rouen manuscript is *more* intelligible than the printed version. Examples are the ratio 1:1,538,460 in R (V67a), which appears as *un, à un* in E67 (see C67i), the word *réellement* in R (V71a), which is replaced with *actuellement* in E71 (see C71), and the phrase *à la longue* in R (V286i), where E286 has *dans tous les tems* (see C286). Another example is a very telling error in the print edition where it is argued that a city where the exchange is *above* par is indebted to a city where it is *below* par: in the Rouen manuscript the words appear, correctly, the other way around (V538e and f). As Friedrich Hayek observed (see Saucier and Thornton 2010: 199 n.135), it would be unlikely that an economist of Cantillon's calibre would make such an error. Not having had the benefit of a manuscript version, Hayek speculated that a printing error had occurred, but the double variation in R suggests a more deliberate, if misconceived editorial intervention (see C538). Somewhat similar cases are V238c, where the Rouen manuscript says that the removal of quantities of goods from a local market influences market prices, while E238 states it does not, and a statement in R that, when the use of money is extended to transactions that were before concluded by means of credit, there will be a *decrease* in the velocity of money (V388d and e), as opposed to the *increase* that is said to occur in E388. In all these cases, I would argue, the manuscript text is superior to the printed text.

The most plausible explanation for the fact that the famous 1755 print edition of the *Essai* exhibits at the same time frequent, often minor, improvements on the French of the Rouen manuscript, as well as a smaller number of terms and formulations that make less economic-theoretical sense, is that the unknown editor was, in contrast to Cantillon, perhaps better versed in French but less so in political economy.

To sum up, the Rouen manuscript is, in my opinion, the most authentic French source for Cantillon's ideas that we have. All other versions, the partial manuscript versions M and N, the first printed edition and, indirectly, the subsequent print editions ultimately appear to be based on R. Still, this is not to say that Mirabeau was necessarily right to claim that the manuscript was a translation from an original English version made by Cantillon himself for the benefit of an intimate French friend. On the one hand, the fact that R is not written in the Irishman's hand does not invalidate Mirabeau's claim. R may be a copy, dictated or not, of the Irishman's translation. On the other hand, the occurrence of inelegant formulations and apparent Anglicisms in R does not have to mean it is a translation.[21] Their occurrence may be explained equally well by the supposition that the author, although writing his original in French did not quite have the literary ability of a native French man of letters. We could probably only be sure that an English original existed if such a manuscript were found. Unfortunately such a document remains elusive.

2.2 The English versions

This brings us to the English versions of Cantillon's writings that were published in the 1750s, i.e. the fragments that appeared in Malachy Postlethwayt's *Universal Dictionary* between 1752 and 1754 and

Philip Cantillon's *Analysis of Trade and Commerce* of 1759. In the current edition these versions are presented next to the French print edition in respectively the second and third columns of the verso pages. The backgrounds to these texts are the following.

2.2.1 The fragments in Postlethwayt's Universal Dictionary (column D)

Since the last decades of the nineteenth century it has been known that Malachy Postlethwayt (1707–67) had incorporated fragments of Cantillon's writings in his publications. The first fragments were found by Stanley Jevons in Postlethwayt's *Great Britain's True System* of 1757 and he did not doubt that they had been borrowed from the *Essai* of 1755 (Jevons [1881] 1931: 355–56). However, subsequent discoveries called this assumption into question. First, as reported in the *Economic Journal* of 1896, Edward Cannan identified a number of entries ('Barter', 'Cash', 'Circulation', 'Labour') in Postlethwayt's *Universal Dictionary of Trade and Commerce* (1751–55) that contained excerpts from Cantillon's work. Several decades later Friedrich Hayek ([1931] 1985: 234) established that Postlethwayt had plagiarised the Irishman even earlier, namely in his *Dissertation* of 1749, which was a kind of prospectus for the *Dictionary*.

Since Postlethwayt could not have been borrowing from the first print edition of the *Essai* six years before that work was published, he must, from the late 1740s at the latest, have had a manuscript of Cantillon's work. This text could either have been in French, perhaps a different copy from the one that was edited and published in 1755, or a version written in English. The editorial in the *Economic Journal* reporting Cannan's discovery concluded that the second possibility was the most likely and that it was desirable that a 'careful collation' be made in order 'to decide whether the *Dictionary* enables us to reconstruct any considerable portions of the original and complete English version' (*Economic Journal* 1896, 21: 165).

Henry Higgs (1864–1940), then assistant editor of the *Economic Journal* and probably responsible for the editorial note, took this considerable task to hand, not completing it until 1931 when finally his renowned French/English edition of the *Essay* was published under the auspices of the Royal Economic Society. Since then this work has remained the standard scholarly edition of the *Essay* outside the Francophone world. Higgs did not actually include any fragments from Postlethwayt's *Dictionary* in his edition, but in an accompanying essay he drew some strong conclusions about that English version. First, he concluded that the text dispersed throughout Postlethwayt's work was an accurate transcription of a (missing) original English manuscript version of the *Essay*. Commenting more specifically on a long fragment that corresponds to *Essai* III, i (see C490ii), Higgs concluded that 'Postlethwayt must have had the English original before him, and I have little doubt that in Postlethwayt's version we have Cantillon's own language with little or no variation' (Higgs 1931: 383). Second, Higgs also claimed that fragments he had found scattered throughout the *Dictionary* 'embody almost the whole substance of the *Essai*' and, third, that 'there are occasionally some small deviations from the turn of phrase when we compare the two versions [i.e., the French print edition and Postlethwayt's version] but never from the sense' (ibid. 384).

None of these three claims about the broken up version of Cantillon's writings found in Postlethwayt's *Dictionary* can be substantiated. The gross inaccuracy of the third claim, in particular, will be evident to any reader of the current edition: throughout the collated text the *Dictionary* version offers formulations that differ, in some cases substantially, from the French publication. While this makes the *Dictionary* version actually more interesting than if its content had been identical to the much better-known French work, it also raises issues of authenticity.

Unfortunately, Higgs's first claim that 'in Postlethwayt's version we have Cantillon's language with little or no variation' cannot be verified. Moreover, the second claim that 'almost the whole substance of the *Essai*' is found in the *Dictionary* is also inaccurate. Not only are whole chapters missing, but for other French chapters only partial counterparts can be recovered from the *Dictionary*. As a result only about 36 per cent of all French paragraphs have a counterpart in Postlethwayt's major publication.[22] At the same time there are also in that work a number of passages that appear to have been taken from Cantillon, but which do *not* have obvious counterparts in the *Essai*, although sometimes they do in the *Analysis*. This suggests that Postlethwayt had in his hands a version of Cantillon's work that differed in important respects from the better-known French version. However, as long as the manuscript that Postlethwayt used is not found we cannot be certain.

A second-best way of judging the authenticity and completeness of the *Dictionary* fragments is through trying to understand Postlethwayt's behaviour as an 'editor' of Cantillon's manuscript. This issue will be taken up after considering a prior question, namely how did Postlethwayt obtain a version of Cantillon's work in the first place?

Malachy Postlethwayt (1707–67) has long been a neglected author,[23] and biographical details have been scarce. Recently, however, Bennett (2011) has established that Postlethwayt was born in Stepney, East London, on 5 May 1707, the son of a victualler. Like his younger brother James (1711–61) he may have received his early education at St Paul's. But unlike the latter, who went on to study at Trinity, Cambridge, Malachy prepared for a career in business in the early 1720s by completing an apprenticeship with Charles Snell, writing master and accountant in Foster Lane. In a short autobiographical sketch he would later stress the vocational nature of his schooling, writing that 'he very early applied himself to the knowledge of figures of accountantship, and so much of the mathematical literature, and other general studies, as might not render him too contemplative, and wholly disqualify him for the man of business' (Postlethwayt 1751–55, I, xiii).

By the mid- to late 1720s Postlethwayt had started out in business as a junior partner (possibly a clerk) of 'an eminent businessman', becoming 'conversant with mercantile people in the city of London', getting engaged 'in pretty considerable mercantile concerns' and being charged with handling 'foreign correspondence, and private conduct of the business' (ibid.). Experiencing sophisticated business practice at first hand in the foremost commercial city of the world, he was soon struck by what he perceived to be 'a very great deficiency, in regard to education, among many young people of fortune, who, as merchants, had embarked pretty considerable capitals in trade' (ibid.). This insight gave him the seminal idea of establishing 'a new institution in England, for the bringing up of young British merchants with greater advantages' (ibid.). His first proposal of a Plan for such an institution was printed anonymously by the late 1730s under the title *The Accomplish'd Merchant*.[24]

Noteworthy about this Plan is that Postlethwayt envisaged an institution that went beyond the technical training of young men destined for subordinate clerical positions, as was common at the time (see Edwards 2009). What he had in mind was a school that would train wealthy youngsters to become independent men of business, or as Cantillon would call them, 'entrepreneurs':

> It is the Business of a young Gentleman of Fortune, to qualify himself to be at the Head of a *Counting-House*, that he may be able to give Directions how Business ought to be done in the best manner, suitable to the nature of his Affairs, not to make himself the Slave, the common *Sailor*, but the *Steerman*.
>
> (*The Accomplish'd Merchant*, p. 6; emphases in original)

For this reason the commercial education provided in the 'little Kind of merchantile University' (ibid. 21) that Postlethwayt wanted to establish would go beyond that of a 'meer Accountant' (ibid. 6). In addition to the by then traditional commercial subjects of business correspondence, financial arithmetic and book-keeping, '[h]ere shall we read the most judicious Writers upon merchantile Affairs' (ibid. 21).

The fact that Postlethwayt was already planning the foundation of a commercial academy in the 1730s allows us to ascribe to him a clear motivation to have been actively looking for general works on the theory of trade. Postlethwayt (1751–55, I, xiii) states that he had for 20 years been collecting a range of commercial literature and other papers relating to business practice. Many of these materials were eventually used in the *Dictionary*, but the original occasion for his collection is more likely to have been the establishment of a library for his academy. A manuscript of Cantillon's work may have ended up in this library via a number of routes.

The most direct possible route is of course that Postlethwayt received a manuscript version of the *Essay* from Richard Cantillon himself. In the early 1730s Postlethwayt was in his mid-twenties and, as was noted, 'conversant with mercantile people in the city of London'. Thus he may well have been moving in the same social circles as Cantillon. Especially since Postlethwayt had by this time already developed an interest in the theory of trade, the two men may have struck up an acquaintance. There is, however, no documentary evidence whatsoever for such an acquaintance and, therefore, unless anything in support of this possibility is found, it must remain pure speculation.[25]

Perhaps an indirect route is more plausible. Through his connections he may have obtained a manuscript through some other person in the business circles of London.[26] There is a small possibility that this person was Philip Cantillon. However, not only have I been unable to find any evidence for an acquaintance between the two men,[27] but the many differences between those parts of the *Universal Dictionary* and the *Analysis of Trade* that derive from Richard Cantillon make it unlikely that the two men shared one and the same manuscript (see p. 24).

One further fascinating possibility, for which there is some documentary support, is that Postlethwayt obtained the manuscript through the agency of no lesser person than Britain's first prime minister, Sir Robert Walpole (1676–1745). Interestingly, during most of the 1730s Postlethwayt had a second more secretive career as a literary hack writing pamphlets in support of Walpole's economic polices.[28] Bennett (2011) goes so far as to call Postlethwayt Walpole's 'spin doctor' and, even if this may overstate his significance for Walpole's ministry, it is clear that in the mid-1730s Postlethwayt had close personal contacts with the prime minister.

This may be significant in connection with the curious events that occurred in the Dutch colony of Surinam in January 1735. There a party of soldiers recovered the possessions of a mysterious 'Chevalier de Louvigny', who himself evaded capture by disappearing into the jungle.[29] On 12 January 1735 an inventory was made of these possessions which records as one item 'vierendertig boeken in Soortte' (34 books of different kinds).[30] No further details are provided, and the item may either refer to printed works or to notebooks, or a combination of the two. However, amongst them there must have been personal information about Cantillon, because on the basis of their examination the governor concluded that Louvigny 'may well be one of the domestic servants of Mr. Cantillon who murdered their master' and a new search party was sent out. This second party did not find the wanted man, but further recovered a number of papers that had belonged to Cantillon. The inventory of these papers concentrates on obligatory notes and other financial records, which partly related to considerable loans that Cantillon had made in the early 1730s.[31]

Murphy (1986: 282–98) has presented a detailed, and in my opinion convincing, case that the elusive 'Chevalier de Louvigny' may in fact have been Richard Cantillon, who had fled to Surinam after having staged his death to extricate himself from further court cases against him.[32] However, the reason to deal with this episode here in some detail is that it seems just possible that amongst the possessions of the Chevalier, either amongst his collection of books or his unlisted papers, there was a copy of Cantillon's economic essay.

Once word reached Britain that papers had been found in South America that had belonged to Cantillon, Horatio Walpole (1678–1757), British ambassador to Holland and brother of Sir Robert, requested them to be returned to England.[33] Eventually, in 1736, the papers were returned to London via Amsterdam. While Cantillon's final will of 11 April 1734 was annexed to the papers of administration of Cantillon's estate, it is unknown what happened to the other papers that were returned. Postlethwayt's connections with the Walpole government allow one to speculate that, if a manuscript of the *Essay* returned from Surinam, the prime minister may have arranged for his academically minded client to have it.

Admittedly, one cannot be confident that it was this precise route by which Postlethwayt obtained a manuscript version of Cantillon's work. A final alternative route to consider is that he received it from John and Paul Knapton, who between 1746 and 1755 were Postlethwayt's publishers.[34] In a Bill of Complaint against Postlethwayt of 1757 (NA C12/2353/64), about which more below, it is mentioned that the Knaptons, when commissioning the *Universal Dictionary of Trade and Commerce* in the late 1740s, had supplied Postlethwayt with an unspecified amount of commercial literature for incorporation in that work. The possibility exists that the *Essay* was amongst this literature. The Knaptons were established publishers who would have had good connections in London's literary circles, where a manuscript of Cantillon might possibly have been procured.[35] But, if so, this would raise other questions, like why this publishing house, which in previous decades had published all the works of Charles Davenant, would not have published this intriguing manuscript in its own right. All in all, it has to be admitted that the precise route by which Postlethwayt obtained a manuscript of Cantillon's work remains an unresolved issue.

There can, however, be no question that by the end of the 1740s at the latest Postlethwayt did possess such a manuscript and the question to consider presently is to what extent the various fragments from the *Universal Dictionary* pieced together and reproduced in column D of the main part of the present edition give us reliable insights into the content of that manuscript. Here it is important first to understand Postlethwayt's methods in composing his enormous work. The above mentioned Bill of Complaint against Postlethwayt of 1757 states that the idea to publish an English translation of Savary's *Dictionnaire de Commerce* was originally conceived by the Knaptons 'some years before' 1750.[36] Postlethwayt was then recommended to Paul Knapton 'as a person well acquainted with the accounts and with the several Branches of Trade and Commerce and very proper for the undertaking of such a work'. After some meetings it was agreed that Postlethwayt should translate as much of Savary as he thought proper and

> should from his own skill and judgement and knowledge in trade and commerce [make] such additions as to make a compleat dictionary of trade and commerce adapted to this nation and [it] should be as perfect a work in English, and for this nation, as Savary's was for France.

The Knaptons agreed to pay Postlethwayt £1,600 upon completion of the work, which was estimated to come to about 500 sheets.[37]

With some assistants, Postlethwayt set about his work, at first in a small house in Brompton, later moving to a larger place in Kensington. Initially the *Dictionary* appeared in nearly weekly instalments and Postlethwayt 'took it at his own charge and expense' to produce these. The Bill records that the first issue appeared 'on or about 1 November 1751', that by December 1752 approximately 40 issues had been published and that the final issue, number 155, appeared by November 1755.[38] As a whole the *Universal Dictionary of Trade and Commerce* is a publication of impressive length and richness of content. The scholars who have studied Postlethwayt's sources more closely agree that, despite the claim on the title page that the work was a translation of Savary's *Dictionnaire*, he actually only used parts of that French work (Mamroth-Brokman 1908: 1; Johnson 1937: 188; Fraser 1938: 28). Instead Postlethwayt crammed the nearly 1900 densely printed folio pages full with large amounts of additional materials from over 500 sources, a large number British but also many foreign (Fraser 1938: 26). While Postlethwayt, rather impressively, churned out nearly weekly issues of on average about 12 pages each for a period of four years, he does not seem to have stuck to a very strict plan of what to include. This is suggested by the fact that he picked up excerpts of works that were published even after he had started producing his weekly issues. For example, parts of David Hume's *Political Discourses*, which was published in March 1752, started to be included in the *Dictionary* from early 1753.[39]

Possibly as a result of this lack of planning, the work soon started to balloon. By December 1752 Postlethwayt had produced about 500 pages (or half the promised 500 sheets), but he had only reached

CH in the alphabet.[40] Realising that he had to be more selective, the entries later in the alphabet are less padded out with additional materials and digressions. As a result, the work as a whole is unbalanced: the first third of the alphabet (A to H) is covered in well over 900 pages; the second third (I to Q) in just over 600 pages and the final third (R to Z) in fewer than 300 pages.

These general facts about Postlethwayt's activities are of some considerable importance for understanding his use of Cantillon's manuscript. While the fragments he took from this manuscript constitute less than 1 per cent of the text of the *Dictionary*, Postlethwayt does seem to have considered the fragments as giving his work a 'solid foundation' and frequently referred his readers to the entries in which he had incorporated them (entry 'Coin', I, 531, col. 1). In the entry 'Interest' he mentioned that some crucial parts of his work were pursued 'upon one consistent plan of reasoning, we apprehend', referring to a sequence of entries that contained important fragments actually written by Cantillon (see C434).

Surely Postlethwayt used the words 'we apprehend' in the meaning of 'we conceive' but, ironically, one can also read them as meaning 'we seize', i.e. taking hold of from someone else, which of course is what really happened. In fact, in some places Postlethwayt does more than borrow without acknowledgment. He actually claimed explicitly that what we know to be Cantillon's ideas were his own (see for example D307). Such a blatant appropriation was probably considered intellectual dishonesty even in a period when the unacknowledged reproduction of ideas was more accepted, and possibly even by the standards that Postlethwayt formulated himself (see Yeo 2001). Therefore, contrary to some other commentators' views (Higgs 1931, Groenewegen 2004), it does not seem unreasonable to call Postlethwayt's use of Cantillon's work plagiarism.

At the same time, from a non-ethical point of view we may have to regret that Postlethwayt did not plagiarise Cantillon even more comprehensively than he already had. That is to say, it seems very well possible that he did not use all of the Irishman's manuscript. Clearly Postlethwayt allocated various parts of that work to different entries of his *Dictionary*, sometimes perhaps partly guided by the chapter titles he found in the manuscript (see e.g. C203ii and C239ii). Most of the fragments from Cantillon appear under subheadings like 'Further Considerations' and, as his work progressed, Postlethwayt included fewer and fewer such digressions. Indeed, it is noteworthy that all fragments that can be ascribed to Cantillon occur in entries in the first half of the alphabet. In the same place where Postlethwayt remarks that he had 'apprehended' a consistent plan of reasoning, he also states that he intends to include in the entry 'Silver' materials that would presumably have corresponded in content to *Essai* II chapter 5 (see C434). But the short entry, 'Silver' does not contain anything of the sort. Clearly Postlethwayt had changed his mind in the intervening two years (or simply forgotten what he had intended to include in his haste to finish the work).

This particular fact hints at the possibility that other significant gaps in the fragments found in the *Dictionary* when compared to the *Essai*, e.g. part I chapter 12 or part III chapter 8, may be due to Postlethwayt's failure to include further parts of the manuscript that he had at his disposal.[41] Regrettably, therefore we cannot conclude, as Higgs claimed, that the fragments found in the *Dictionary* 'embody almost the whole substance of the *Essai*'. But that does not mean that we can say that the manuscript cannibalised by Postlethwayt did not cover this whole substance (and, who knows, more).

A second fact to keep in mind, with regard to the fragments that Postlethwayt did include, is the haste with which he worked. Generally speaking, a large number of entries in the *Dictionary* consist of patchworks of borrowed materials (either acknowledged or unacknowledged) that are often adopted verbatim.[42] This is probably due to the fact that the editor laboured under a punishing publication schedule. Postlethwayt simply did not have the time to tinker extensively with the arguments of the many authors he used. With respect to the fragments from Cantillon we can get some idea of the kind of alterations Postlethwayt made by comparing those passages he plagiarised more than once. The passages occurring in both Postlethwayt's *Plan* of 1749 and the *Dictionary* (V490–V558) and in both his *Great Britain's True System* of 1757 and the *Dictionary* (V64–V75, V78–V105, V186–V200) show differences in spellings, minor alterations in phrasings and small, though in a few cases significant, omissions (see e.g. V508a).[43] While in most cases the alternatives to the *Dictionary* appear the most authentic (see e.g. C67i, C530ii, C531), the variations rarely affect the meaning of the argument. Perhaps this indicates that Postlethwayt reproduced Cantillon's text more or less faithfully. Admittedly, however, unless the actual source text for the *Dictionary* fragments is found, one can of course not confirm Higgs's view that 'in Postlethwayt's version we have Cantillon's own language with little or no variation'.

With regard to Postlethwayt's source a brief indication can be given of what may have been its subsequent fate. Judging by the fact that it figured in such a disjointed way in the *Dictionary*, it may of course no longer have been a distinct bundle of paper after Postlethwayt had finished with it. But assuming that it was still a physically coherent manuscript and Postlethwayt kept it with him until his death on 13 September 1767, then it would have been among his personal estate. He left this personal estate, which included his large collection of books and papers, to his faithful assistant and housekeeper, Catherine Johnson.[44] She will have been the beneficiary of the sale of Postlethwayt's collection, which took place in the rooms of the printers L. Davis and C. Reymers in Holborn the following year. Unsurprisingly, the sales catalogue does not make mention of 'a brilliant manuscript on economic theory with a mysterious provenance'. The entries that come closest to this description appear in a section with the heading 'Mr. Postlethwayte's *Collection of Single Tracts*' (Davis and Reymers 1768, 247–48). There we find under catalogue number 8908: tracts 'On Trade and Commerce'; and under number 8912: tracts 'On Money, Trade, Exchanges, &c.' In the case that these lots contained a manuscript of Richard Cantillon's economic writings, then an unknown buyer would have had a bargain: they were priced at 2s. 6d. and 4s., respectively. But unfortunately there is, until now, no trace of a buyer or any later sighting of the manuscript on which the *Dictionary* version was based.

2.2.2 *Philip Cantillon's* Analysis *(column A)*

The third column on the verso pages reproduces a large part of the content of Philip Cantillon's *The Analysis of Trade and Commerce*. The title page of this work, which was published in February 1759, states that its content was '[t]aken chiefly from a Manuscript of a very ingenious Gentleman deceas'd, and adapted to the present Situation of our Trade and Commerce' (see A1). Most commentators on the work, including Marx ([1867] 1977, I, 520, n.2), Jevons ([1881] 1931: 335) and Higgs (1931: 378), have dismissed the first part of this statement as a fiction, but I believe it likely to be true.

It is not clear when exactly Philip Cantillon was born. However, from the fact that at the beginning of 1725 he was named as executor of the will of his uncle Martin Harrold, by which time he must have reached the age of majority, one can infer that he cannot have been born much after the turn of the eighteenth century, and perhaps sometime before it. Possibly he learned his trade in the London banking house of his childless uncle, and he was certainly the latter's favourite nephew judging by the considerable sum of £3,000 that Harrold left him.[45] Through Harrold's London business Philip also got involved with the affairs of his kinsman Richard Cantillon. The precise blood relation between Philip and Richard is not entirely clear. A contemporary document (NA C11/1538/18) describes Philip as 'a near Relation' of Richard. Higgs (1931: 377) and Murphy (1986: 287) may well be right that they were first cousins. This would mean that Philip's father, James, and Richard's father, also Richard, were brothers, but I have not seen evidence for this. Alternatively, Hone (1944) suggests that they were second cousins, since in the family tree that he produces their grandfathers were brothers. However, Murphy (1985, 1986) has disputed this genealogy.

In any case, during the 1720s and early 1730s there was clearly a certain amount of contact between the two Cantillons. In the bubble year 1720 Martin Harrold had facilitated and benefited from Richard Cantillon's huge financial transactions between France and England (see Murphy 1986: 126, 146). Possibly in recognition of this Harrold left a 'token' of £100 to his 'friend' Richard Cantillon in his will of

1725.[46] Other sums were left to Richard Cantillon junior, the child who had been used as a figurehead in the Paris banking house of his uncle Richard Cantillon, the economist (see ibid.). Apart from £100 immediately 'for giving [Richard Cantillon Junior] three years Foreign education', Harrold stipulated that he would leave the child a further £1,000 'upon this express condition that one Thousand pounds more shall be added to it by his uncle [Richard Cantillon senior]'. The execution of this interesting arrangement, which seems designed to induce the economist to honour his responsibilities towards Richard Cantillon Junior, was left to Harrold's trusted nephew Philip.

Another thing that Philip may have been asked to do, though not in writing, was to make parts of Harrold's correspondence and the records of his financial transactions discreetly disappear. These papers, which allegedly recorded payments of over one million pounds in the single year March 1720–March 1721 (Higgs 1931: 371), were to become a bone of contention in successive court cases of Joseph Gage and Lady Mary Herbert and their family members, against Martin Harrold and Richard Cantillon and their estates, which had started in 1723 and continued into the 1740s. During this whole period Philip Cantillon was repeatedly asked for these books, which the complainants were sure contained incriminating evidence, but he persisted in staying silent about their whereabouts.[47] One gets the impression of Philip as a trusted member of the extended family who could be relied on when problems arose. This is also how one can characterise Philip's behaviour in the aftermath of the fire in Albemarle Street on 14 May 1734.

By this time Philip was 'a considerable Merchant of the City' who had in the previous year married Rebecca, the eldest daughter of William Newland (1685–1738), a city-based Tory, who from 1704 until his death was Member of Parliament for Gatton in Surrey.[48] Together with his brother David, Philip had offices at Wanford Court, Throgmorton Street, in the City of London, perhaps as early as the late 1720s.[49] There they ran a banking business as well as a wine trade, while from 1733 Philip also was an insurance broker after being elected a director of the Royal-Exchange Assurance Company.[50] In short, by 1734 Philip Cantillon was by all accounts a successful businessman.

As a result he was able to offer his support to the immediate family of Richard Cantillon just after the catastrophic events in Albemarle Street. Richard's widow, Mary Anne, and her young daughter, Henrietta, had arrived from Paris some days after the fire and we find Philip lending a hand in various ways. He offered a reward of £200, later increased to £500, for any information about the presumed murderers of Richard Cantillon.[51] He accompanied Mary Anne to the witnessing of Richard's original will on 21 January 1734 (1735 new calendar) making the oath that he 'well knew Richard Cantillon late of the Parish of St George's Hanover Square, and had often seen him write and knew his handwriting and that the will and signature were written by him' (cited in Higgs 1931, 375). Most substantially, in a legal document dated 8 November 1737 (NA C11/81/34) Francis Garvan, Richard Cantillon's friend and legal advisor,[52] testifies that after the 'unhappy Decease' of Richard Cantillon, Philip 'had advanced several considerable sums of his own money towards the maintenance and subsistence of [Richard's] widow and [his daughter] Henrietta and his Brothers [Thomas and Bernard], Nephews [Richard and Thomas] and Niece [Catherine]'. All these close family members of the economist had apparently depended on him for support and, in the first period when his financial affairs were still in disarray, Philip stepped in to take on this burden.[53] Philip even arranged the burial of the presumed remains of Richard Cantillon that took place at St Pancras Old Church on 13 July 1734.[54]

Philip's close involvement with the affairs of Richard's nearest family between May 1734 and 1736, and the fact that they trusted him and depended on him to take care of various matters, makes it quite plausible that the former had access to any surviving papers. Amongst these there may have been the 'Manuscript from a very ingenious Gentleman deceas'd' that would later form the basis of the *Analysis of Trade*. However, if this was the case, then a question is why would he have waited for about 25 years, that is, until 1759 to publish it?

One possible explanation is that the economist's widow, Mary Anne, and her new husband, François Bulkeley, may have objected to such a publication. One gets the impression that relations between Philip and Mary Anne soured after she unexpectedly remarried in October 1736.[55] During the preceding two years Philip had been looking after the financial interests of the young Henrietta, making sure for example that the income from an annuity that Richard had owned was 'laid out for her [i.e. Henrietta's] benefit & the benefit and advantage of all the Parties interested in the said Estate'. Now, however, the newly married couple declared that Philip's help was no longer required. Having recently been named administrators of the estate of Richard Cantillon they felt 'well Intituled to recover & receive the sums so received . . . for or on account of the said annuity as well as the Growing produce thereof until the complain't [i.e. Henrietta] shall attain her Age or be married'.[56] Not having been assigned any role of guardian in either of Richard's wills, Philip's involvement with the affairs of the economist's closest family appears to have come to an end with that, maybe in an acrimonious manner. And perhaps for this reason he had to wait to publish Richard's manuscript until after the executors of the economist's estate had died, first Mary Anne in 1751 and second François Bulkeley in 1756.

What may also have prevented Philip from publishing his book was that from the end of the 1730s he suffered a series of setbacks both in his personal life and in his business affairs. First, on 22 September 1738, his son of about two years died.[57] Not only was this a personal tragedy for Philip and Catherine, but it also signalled the beginning of a long and complicated fight over the Newland inheritance.[58] In addition, he appears to have made some disastrous investments at the beginning of the 1740s. In March 1743 bankruptcy proceedings were started and even though he regained his trader's certificate by the end of May, he appears to have continued in straightened circumstances.[59] In a legal report from 1755 it is noted that he

> had been a Merchant of considerable business but having met with several great misfortunes & losses he became a Bankrupt and had his Certificate in the year 1744, and that he has ever since been and now is in very low reduced Circumstances.[60]

In the same year 1755, probably as a result of his mismanagement of the Newland estate and his own business, his wife insisted on a financial separation, and perhaps a domestic one.[61] It appears that by the late 1750s Philip was a much reduced man.[62] Around the time of the publication of the *Analysis*, which Philip paid for himself, he gave up his business in London.[63] By the time he made his will in October 1766 he had only personal belongings left, besides a small amount of money which he left to his servant David Armstrong 'in Consideration of his Service to me during my illness' (NA Prob 11/984). Eventually he moved to Ghent in the then Austrian Netherlands to live with his daughter Elizabeth.[64] That is where he died in early December 1772. I have been unable to locate any surviving papers from his estate either in Britain or in Belgium.

Turning to the *Analysis*, the main thing to consider is what kind of alterations and additions Philip made to the manuscript that he had in his possession. Since no such manuscript has been found nothing can be said about this matter with certainty. But this should not prevent us from making a number of observations. First, it must be noted that the earliest advertisements for the book actually carried a somewhat extended version of the line on the title page. They read: 'Chiefly taken from a *French* Manuscript of a very ingenious Gentleman, deceased, *who resided many Years in Paris and London*' (emphases added).[65] Perhaps Philip subsequently suppressed the emphasised words in the previous sentence because they made Richard Cantillon more easily identifiable as the author of the manuscript. But the initial statement that the manuscript had been in French, raises the possibility that the parts of the *Analysis* that derived from it are actually a later English translation. Perhaps this is supported by the fact that the text appears to contain a number of Gallicisms (see e.g. C209iii). However, just like the presence of Anglicisms in the *Essai* (above p. 14) this may just as well simply show that the author had spent many years in Ireland, France and Britain. If the manuscript, as argued in some more detail below, was an early draft, then it would make some sense that it would have been in French. This is so because, as Murphy

(1986: 246–47) argues, Richard Cantillon may have originally started writing his essay in order to explain his financial operations to the French courts (Cf. C558iii).

Second, apart from the question of what the original language of the manuscript may have been, one finds that many parts of the *Analysis* are very different from both the *Essai* and the fragments from Postlethwayt's *Dictionary*. To some extent this can be explained by the editorial liberties that Philip took. As he stated on the title page of the *Analysis*, he felt the manuscript had to be 'adapted to the present Situation of our Trade and Commerce'. If the draft that Philip had at his disposal was rather sketchy in places (see below), then the fact that he perceived a need to supplement it with materials taken from other authors as well as his own further elaborations is, to an extent, understandable.

But of course the problem that Philip created in this way is that it became difficult to decide what parts are attributable to which author. Generally speaking, it seems safe to say that Richard Cantillon was responsible for those passages that have counterparts in either the *Essai* or the *Dictionary* fragments (all included in the present edition). Of course that does not mean that Philip would have adopted them verbatim, and indeed they may all be translations. But at the very least the fact that the earlier publications E and D have similar passages shows that he adopted them from an earlier source. However, those passages make up only about 40 per cent of the *Analysis*. With regard to the remaining 60 per cent, or approximately 142 pages, only some scattered passages totalling about 19 pages have been included in the present edition.[66]

This leaves another 123 pages, distributed throughout the *Analysis* as shown in Table 2.1:

Table 2.1 Parts of the *Analysis* omitted from this edition

All of the preface	iii–xix	
All of chapter xiii	34–44	See C254ii
End of chapter xv (pp. 45–51)	50–51	See C426iv
End of chapter xvi (pp. 51–62)	55–62	See C355iii
End of chapter xvii (pp. 62–68)	67–68	See C471ii
Beginning of chapter xviii (pp. 68–85)	68–74	See C530iii
End of chapter xix (pp. 86–102)	98–102	See C591ii
End of chapter xx (pp. 102–14)	112–14	See C615
Most of chapter xxiii (pp. 124–68)	124–68 (apart from isolated paragraphs on pp. 126–28)	See C118iii
End of chapter xxiv (pp. 169–94)	186–94	See C653
All of chapter xxv	194–215	See C653

Generally speaking, it is noticeable that most of the passages in Table 2.1 occur at the end of chapters. One gets the impression that in a number of cases Philip tried to round off and bulk up the content of incompletely developed sketches. In some places he was indeed obviously adapting the work 'to the present Situation of our Trade and Commerce', because they contain recent economic data or quotations from authors like David Hume (for details see the comments referred to in Table 2.1). In other cases this is more difficult to say and for this reason it should be acknowledged that some fragments of Richard's original prose may have been missed in the present edition. The preface is a particularly difficult case. It introduces themes that we know from Richard Cantillon's writings, but the style is perhaps different. To give a flavour, these are the opening lines of the *Analysis*:

The mutual Want which Mankind have of each other, and the necessary Dependance they have on each other, is the Origin of Trade, or Barter [cf. C117ii]. The tilling of the Earth, and the feeding of

Flocks, was the first Labour Men employed themselves in [cf. C8]; and 'tis probable that this Labour, at first, extended itself no farther than what was sufficient to supply the necessary Support of Life. But, as Mankind increased and multiplied, they dispersed themselves in different Parts of the Globe; and, by Degrees, as they further increased, Ambition, and the Desire of Power, crept in among them; the stronger began to invade the weaker, and the forcible Acquisitions obtained by the Conquerors could only be maintained by further Oppression and Violence [cf. E/D/A10]. This gave Birth to Submission, and this Submission is the Origin of all Government; for it does not appear to me, that the all good and gracious Providence gave the Right of Possession to one Man more than to another [cf. E/D/A77]: The Inequality of Possessions was obtained by Conquest, and supported by Power; and the Conquerors instituted Laws and Rules for the good Government of Society, to which the Conquered were, under the severest Penalties, obliged to submit: Villages, Towns, and Cities were established [cf. E/A19ff]; and Men associated together, and by Labour and Tilling the Earth supplied from thence the necessary Wants of themselves and Superiors.

(Cantillon 1759, iii–iv)

The preface goes on in a similar vein for another 16 pages. Perhaps they are Philip's general reflections based on the work of his kinsman, even though at some point he refers to 'the weak Attempt I make in these Essays . . . to convey a general Idea of Trade'. This is noteworthy because this description is very close to the title of the French work, and is not otherwise used in the 1759 publication (cf. C561ii).

However, to err on the side of caution, none of the preface has been included in the present edition. This caution is also due to the very critical assessment of previous commentators on the *Analysis* who have described it as a 'mutilated' (Higgs 1931: 378) or a 'vastly inferior and bowdlerized English version' (Murphy 2009: 77) of the *Essai*. There is certainly some truth in this assessment. But, as it is hoped the present edition will make apparent, this is not the whole story.

Notes

1 By showing that Guillyn was the publisher, Murphy contradicted the detailed case made a few years earlier by Tsuda (1979: 417–32) that Jacques Guérin published the *Essai*. Muphy's case is the more convincing due to the evidence from d'Hémery's records.
2 There are occasional agreements between variations in the later editions and what we find in the manuscripts (see e.g. V65a or V87a). However, these invariably concern quite obvious imperfections in the first print edition and the subsequent editors would not have needed access to a manuscript to make such corrections.
3 See V9a, V87b, V172a, V235o, V316g, V452d, V513e, V525e, V573c, V578e, V645a, V646d and V662a. The printing error is V218j.
4 Tsuda (1979: 417) asserts that Mauvillon's edition was based on the earlier 1756 edition rather than on the edition of 1755. Presumably this opinion is based on the fact that, of the variations in the first 1756 edition (see previous footnote), all but V218j and V235o also occur in the second 1756 edition.
5 The principal importance of the Mauvillon edition is that it seems to have been a more widely read work and in subsequent decades gave rise to confusion between the ideas of Cantillon and Hume. See p. 36.
6 M779 offers summaries and brief quotations from chapters of the *Essai* through to the end. Indeed, it provides an alternative version of the very last sentence of the work, which is the only variation in M779 recorded in the present edition. See V687b.
7 In fact the handwriting of the transcript of the *Essai* in M780 appears to be in the same hand, which suggests that Garçon was the copyist in that case too.
8 In fact, Salleron said much the same view much earlier in the INED edition of 1952, siding with Brocard (1902) who had already rejected accusations of Mirabeau. Higgs's interpretation has had its own supporters over the decades. See e.g. Legrand (1900) and Hayek ([1931] 1985: 22).
9 The first edition of *L'Ami des Hommes*, despite having the year 1756 on the title page, was not actually published until 1757.
10 In contrast, Théré and Charles (Quesnay 2005: 1313) believe M773 n°2 bis to date from about the same time as M779 n° 1 and to be earlier than M780 n° 1. It is therefore best to say that this issue is not settled and perhaps a

closer comparison between Mirabeau's copious commentaries on Cantillon in M773 and M780 will reveal developments in his thinking and arrangements and hence allow one to answer the question as to which manuscript is older.

11 Letter dated 30 July 1767 in *Correspondance générale de J.-J. Rousseau*. Paris, 1932, vol. xvii, p.176.

12 Mirabeau's account about Cantillon and his work is reproduced in Brian and Théré (1997, lxviii–lxxiii). The statement quoted above is repeated in M773, sheet 3, recto.

13 Mirabeau's account in M780 (and repeated in M773) about Cantillon and his work appears to be based on two sources. First, for some details about the Irishman's financial and legal affairs he probably relied on the record of the defence by Cantillon's lawyer Cochin (see Cochin 1822 and Murphy 1986: 82). But further anecdotes, for example that Cantillon would decide at the drop of a hat to travel across Europe to check some economic fact, must have derived from some other source.

14 A missing piece of evidence for tracing back the provenance of the Rouen manuscript to Cantillon via de Vérac would be confirmation that Leber bought the manuscript from the inheritance of one of de Vérac's descendants. Two *inventaires* of such inheritances, AN MC/RE/XLIV/15 and AN MC/ET/XCI/1229 do not seem to yield definitive evidence of this kind.

15 These variations in the orthography of the Rouen manuscript, which are very numerous indeed, are not recorded in column V of the present edition. Neither are the frequent differences in paragraph breaks recorded. Only words, phrases or word orders that differ from the print edition are noted. In these cases, if the Rouen manuscript has an orthography that differs from one or both Paris manuscripts, only the former version is given. Readers who wish to get a fuller impression of the, at times bizarre, orthography of the Rouen manuscript are referred to Tsuda (1979) who provides an impressively reliable transcript.

16 However, as pointed out in the previous footnote, the present edition does not record the variations in spellings and diacritics between the three manuscripts.

17 The only exception is, arguably, V243a, where M, like E, has '400' instead of '100' found in R. See C243. However, in my opinion this single case does not amount to convincing evidence that R cannot have been the source text of M.

18 Following Hayek ([1931] 1985: 28), Thornton (2007) offers two pieces of concrete textual evidence. The first concerns the ratio between labour and steel in the manufacture of watches. It relies on a similarity between a manuscript passage of Hume and the ratio found in Postlethwayt's *Dictionary*. However, this is *not* the ratio that would have been found in a manuscript version of the *Essai/Essay* (see C67i). The other passage concerns the presumed prevalence of infanticide in China. But this view was found in other writings of the time, and indeed the notion did not originate with Cantillon (see C151iii). Hence the fact that Hume mentions this practice too does not prove very much. For a longer discussion of the connection between the writings of Cantillon and Hume see van den Berg (2012a). Larrère's case is mostly based on textual similarities between Cantillon's account of the factors that influence the economic decline of nations and passages in Montesquieu's *Réflexions sur la monarchie universelle en Europe* of 1734. Even though some parallels are indeed striking, Montesquieu may have arrived at his ideas independently. Alternatively, such parallels might have been the result of conversations between the two men, which, given the friendship between Montesquieu and Cantillon's wife (Murphy 1986: 200–04), may well have taken place. The possibility that Montesquieu had already read the *Essai* in the beginning of the 1730s when Cantillon was still alive seems less likely.

19 The fact that E does not replace words in all cases is significant because it may be due to 'editor's fatigue'. This type of inconsistency is sometimes considered one of the strongest levels of evidence for literary dependence between texts (see Goodacre 2001: 71–76).

20 It should be noted that Tsuda (1979: 415) is less prepared to draw this conclusion, mainly because of the importance he attaches to the small mutilation (V590a, Figure 2.7) in R of the phrase *Newton m'a dit*. This does indeed pose a fascinating little puzzle (see C590), but since it cannot be said when the cutting took place, it is hard to see why this would constitute compelling evidence that the Rouen manuscript was not used as the source text of the print edition.

Figure 2.7 Variation 590a, Rouen Manuscript (Collections de la Bibliothèque municipale de Rouen)

21 Apart from the apparent Anglicisms that were corrected by the editor, mentioned before, there are also ones that slipped through his net. See for example the expression *par quartier* (C282ii).
22 For a more detailed discussion, see van den Berg (2012b: 877–80).
23 A rare exception was Johnson (1937).
24 The earliest attribution of the pamphlet to Postlethwayt is by an anonymous contributor in Brydges (1815: 5, 200), who says he had known the author personally. Over a century later, Fraser (1938) also attributed this work to Postlethwayt. However, Redlich (1970: 199–200) claimed that the pamphlet had simply been extensively plagiarised by Postlethwayt. Redlich offers very little positive evidence for his claim. Not only does he appear to be unaware of the earlier attributions, but, more importantly, he does not consider the short autobiographical sketch in the *Universal Dictionary* used here in the main body of the text. There is little reason to disbelieve Postlethwayt when he states in so many words that he was the author of 'a small tract, intitled the Accomplish'd Merchant' (1751–55, I, xiii). With regard to the dating of the pamphlet, Postlethwayt (1750: 14) writes: 'We had determined, before the late war, to establish a public design for the bringing up of young merchants. . . . To which end we drew up and printed, but never published, the sketch of a *Plan* for that purpose.' The war referred to is surely the war of the Austrian Succession, which started in 1740. Perhaps he had been contemplating the establishment of a mercantile college since the early 1730s because in the early 1750s he wrote that he first conceived this idea 'above twenty years since' (1751–55, I, xiii).
25 All I have been able to establish is that around the time of the fire in Albemarle Street, Postlethwayt lived in Lothbury a couple of miles to the east in the City (see Letter 2202 Postlethwayt to Walpole dated 10 June 1734; see n28 below).
26 For example, one particular 'mercantile person' with whom Postlethwayt was associated was the wine merchant James Royston senior. If in turn this Royston had had dealings with Richard Cantillon, who in his time had been involved in the wine trade, then they may well have discussed commercial theory. The only reason to suppose this is that Royston's will makes special mention of his large commercial library (AN Prob 11/840). This, however, is clutching at straws.
27 During the 1740s they both lived in the City, a few streets apart. Posthletwayt still lived in Coleman Street, off Lothbury (see *A Compleat Guide to all persons who have any Trade or Concern with the City of London and Parts Adjacent*. London: Osborne (3rd edn), p. 129), and Philip Cantillon and his brother David had their business in Throgmorton Street.
28 A small number of surviving letters in the Cholmondeley (Houghton) manuscripts at Cambridge University Library from Postlethwayt to Walpole show that the former's services were considerable. In one letter (2069; dated 1 November 1733) Postlethwayt notes that he has been working for Walpole's cause for two years. The first pamphlet for which Postlethwayt can be identified as the author is *Englishmen's eyes open'd* (1st edn 1733; 2nd edn 1734). This is a contribution to the excise controversy in the form of a dialogue of a 'merchant' and a 'landholder'. Postlethwayt champions the point of view of the 'landholder' (actually that of Walpole). Writing this and possibly other pamphlets came at some personal cost. In one letter to Walpole (2069; 1 November 1733) Postlethwayt complains that he had 'made several of my Friends, on whom I had dependance, my Enemies, by engageing in the Excise Controversy; which tho conceal'd as much as possible, has unluckily come to light'. A second pamphlet that can be attributed to Postlethwayt, though not with full confidence (see letter 2202; Postlethwayt to Walpole 10 June 1734), is *A series of Wisdom and Policy*. This is a forceful defence of the government's foreign policies against the criticism of William Pulteney, Earl of Bath (1684–1764) as expressed in his 1734 pamphlet *The Politicks on both sides*. The last surviving letter is dated 10 August 1739. Walpole's patronage may have come to an abrupt end with his resignation from government in 1742.
29 Dutch National Archives, section Sociëteit van Suriname, 262, fol. 1: 'On the 12th [of January] has returned here [in Fort Zeelandia] the Party that has searched for the so-called Chevalier de Louvigny. Their report is that the aforementioned Chev. had built for himself a little cabin in the upper Tampati. When the Party approached, the Chev., upon hearing the noise, fled into the forest with a matchlock, where they have pursued him for two to three days, but in vain, and then were forced to return because of lack of food and illness of most soldiers. They took with them three slaves [of the chevalier, one of whom subsequently escaped] as well as all goods they found in the little cabin. [Upon return in Fort Zeelandia] the accountant and two Counsellors have, in my presence, made an inventory of the goods . . . thereafter the two slaves were interrogated. From this information and the goods there seems to be good reason to suspect that he [i.e. 'Louvigny'] may well be one of the domestic servants of Mr. Cantillon who murdered their master and subsequently set fire to the house . . . therefore new orders were given to find him' (Author's translation).
30 Dutch National Archives, section Sociëteit van Suriname, 262, fol. 2: 'Inventory of the goods of the so-called chevalier de Louvignie', made 12 January 1735. Listed, besides the collection of books, are various items of clothing, wigs, tools, guns and ammunition. None of these would suggest a link with Cantillon, from which it can be concluded that the suspicions of the authorities were aroused by the content of the books.

31 Dutch National Archives, section Sociëteit van Suriname, 262, fol. 150–53: 'Inventory of some Papers concerning the so-called Chevalier de Louvignie, found in the Forest at the Head of the Tampaty on the 19th of this [month of January] by Albert Joosten, Director at the Woyampibo plantation'. Made 24 January 1735.

32 The last item on the inventory of papers appears to offer further support for Murphy's case that 'de Louvigny' may in fact have been Cantillon: '[item] N°. 28 Being a copy of a letter, undated, written (by whom unknown) to the Princess d'Auvergne purporting to be an apology for the murder of Mr. Cantillon and requesting the protection of said Princess'. The princess d'Auvergne was the widow of Frédéric-Jules de la Tour, Prince d'Auvergne (1672–1733). Her maiden name was Olive Trant and she was, Murphy (1986: 47) suggests, Richard Cantillon's one-time lover. Why would Cantillon's assassin ask for the protection of his victim's intimate friend?

33 During the period 1734–39 Walpole was plenipotentiary minister, i.e. ambassador, to the United Provinces. From 1736 he was actually mostly in London.

34 The first work that Postlethwayt published with the Knaptons was *The National and Private Advantages of the African Trade Considered*, which has the year 1746 on its title page. His previous publication *The African Trade, the great pillar and support of the British Plantation Trade in America* was published with J. Robinson in 1745. From this it may be inferred that his acquaintance with the Knaptons dated from the mid-1740s.

35 James Knapton (1667–1736) had traded as a bookseller near St Paul's Churchyard from 1688. In the 1720s the sons John (1697–1770) and Paul (1703–55) joined the business and after their father's death set up business at the Crown in Ludgate Street. Between 1742 and 1745 John served as master of the Stationers' Company, which attests to his standing in the London book trade.

36 Savary's *Dictionnaire Universel de Commerce*, started by Jacques Savary des Brûlons (1657–1716) and finished by his brother Louis-Philémon Savary in 1723, was a great publishing success with numerous subsequent editions and translations. For discussions of its influence, see Patalano (2001) and Perrot (1992: 97–125).

37 It is worth noting that this amount was similar to what was offered around the same time to the author of a much more famous dictionary, namely Dr Samuel Johnson (1709–84). This dictionary was commissioned in 1746 by a group of printers, amongst whom were John and Paul Knapton. Johnson delivered his work in April 1755, half a year before Postlethwayt finished his. For the making of Johnson's *Dictionary* see Reddick (1996).

38 It is sometimes thought that the dates 1751–55 refer to the years in which the two collected volumes of the *Universal Dictionary* were published, that is to say that the first volume was published in 1751 and the second in 1755. In fact those dates refer to the period during which the individual issues appeared. The first volume, which collected issues 1 to 84, was published in September 1753 and the second volume, with issues 85 to 155, was published on 22 November 1755. The schedule of work in the Bill of Complaint allows an approximate dating of the original publication of the various fragments that Postlethwayt took from Cantillon: the first, in the entry 'Arbitration', appeared in January 1752 (see C541i) and the last, in 'Money', in April or May 1754 (C338i). The intermediate dates of the first publication of the other fragments can be found in accompanying comments in the main part of this work. Britain only introduced the Gregorian calendar in September 1752, but new dates have been used also for fragments published earlier.

39 The first entry that contains a long quotation from Hume's 'Of Public Credit' is 'Credit, or public credit' (I, 576–81; see p. 580 to end). This entry appeared in issue 49, which was published in the first few months of 1753.

40 The Bill of Complaint states that at around this same time Postlethwayt 'became uneasy at the agreement because he thought the copyright would be worth much more than £1600'. Therefore on 8 December 1752 he signed an agreement with the Knaptons according to which they would equally share the profit from the sales. In current prices £1,600 is well over £100,000 and this seems a very large sum to be dissatisfied with. However, it needs to be considered that Postlethwayt was not paid up front and had to pay for all the production costs of the weekly issues. The Knaptons contributed by paying half the house rent and regularly made other advances too. However, they 'sometimes through hurry or neglect failed to obtain receipts, and they never settled quarterly accounts as they had agreed'. After Paul Knapton suddenly died on 12 June 1755, his creditors, a group of printers and stationers, took over his estate in a trust. Together with John Knapton they started a complaint against Postlethwayt for refusing to give a full account of his expenses. The trustees for their part stated they could not give an account of the profit until all copies of the *Dictionary* were sold. In the meantime they tried to get an injunction against any attempts by Postlethwayt to publish an abridged edition of his work. It is not clear how this issue was settled, but Postlethwayt does not appear to have made much money from his *Universal Dictionary*.

41 Counterparts for large parts of these two chapters are present in the *Analysis*, which arguably makes it more likely that they were available to Postlethwayt too. The same is true for *Essai* I, chapters 3 to 6, and there is an additional kind of hint that counterparts for these chapters, though absent from the *Dictionary*, would have figured in the manuscript used by Postlethwayt. See C47ii.

42 An example of an unacknowledged borrowing other than from Cantillon is from Sir Matthew Decker's *An essay on the causes of the decline of the foreign trade* of 1744. Pages 16–22 of that work are reproduced almost verbatim in the entry 'Labour' (II, 3, col. 1 to 4 col. 2), and Fraser (1938: 27) identifies further borrowings from Decker in 'Bonding', 'Coin', 'Funds', 'Ireland', 'Landed Interest' and 'Smuggling'.

43 For a more extended discussion of these variations, see van den Berg (2012b: 881–87).

44 See Postlethwayt's will (NA Prob 11/932).

45 NA PRO 11/601. This will was drawn up on 18 January 1724 (1725 new calendar) and proved soon after on 9 February, perhaps indicating a short illness. Harrold left about £17,000 in cash, and amongst the other beneficiaries were the two brothers of Philip, David (£2,000) and another, unnamed one (£2,000), as well as a number of sisters (£1,000 each).

46 In the will Richard is not described as Harrold's cousin, although Murphy (1986: 126) establishes that he was. For Philip to have been his nephew at the same time, Harrold must have married a Cantillon.

47 NA C11/331/1, *Lord* [William] *Herbert v Cantillon*. This document, dated 1 February 1738, refers to an earlier complaint against Martin Harrold and Richard Cantillon in 1723. Philip Cantillon appears not only as the person who has Harrold's 'books, papers and accounts in his custody' but also as a trustee for Richard Cantillon's widow and daughter. Also see NA C11/331/3, *Lord* [William] *Herbert v Harrold*, which has an Answer by Philip Cantillon where he, instead of volunteering to show the papers, only insists that 'there was nothing in Reality due to the Complainant upon the Bills of Exchange and Promisory Notes mentioned in the Complainants original Bill'. Further, see NA C11/123/17, [Thomas] *Gage v Bulkeley*. In the Answer to this Bill, dated 19 November 1737, Cantillon's widow and her new husband Francis Bulkeley claim ignorance. They do profess to know that Martin Harrold left papers and appointed 'the other Defendant Philip Cantillon' as one of his executors 'but what Estate, Books, Papers or Writings of the said Martin Harrold the said Philip Cantillon by Virtue thereof or otherwise possessed himself or what is become thereof these Defendants do not know'. Philip Cantillon's Answer is not found. Finally, in a Bill dated 14 February 1743 (NA C11/1594/36, *Herbert v Earl of Stafford*) Philip is accused of still withholding the notebooks and other papers of Martin Harrold.

48 *The London Evening Post*, issue 880, 19–21 July 1733, described the bride at her wedding on 14 July as 'a beautiful young Lady of very great Merit and 6000l. fortune'.

49 According to listings of London merchants, Philip and David Cantillon were based at Wanford Court, Throgmorton Street from at least 1738 (see e.g. *The Intelligencer or Merchant's Assistant* 1738: 85). After 1740 David appears to be mentioned no longer.

50 That Philip was a one-time wine trader, just like Richard, is clear from a couple of lawsuits against middlemen in the wine trade (see NA C11/81/28, which mentions a dispute over wine imports from France and Spain in January 1730 and NA C11/81/34, about 103 missing butts of sherry in February 1730).

51 Before advertising this reward in a number of newspapers, Philip had to address a petition to the King in order to be allowed to offer money to possible criminals. This petition is dated 24 May 1734 (NA SP36/32).

52 Inter alia, Garvan was also a 'very near Relation' of Philip Cantillon. At least this is how the latter describes himself in a memorial he wrote after Garvan's death (NA T1/363). In the piece Philip Cantillon points out that, in an amendment to his will, dated 25 August, Garvan had acknowledged that he owed his kinsman a balance of £2,742.7s.6d. due to investments of 'considerable sums [in] South Sea and India stock' (NA Prob 11/822).

53 In order to be reimbursed later by Garvan, the original executor of Richard's will, Philip kept a precise account, which was appended to the document cited as 'schedule A'. This shows a breakdown of advances that Philip had made to various family members: a total of £1,061.8s.9d. on behalf of Mary Anne and Henrietta 'towards their maintenance and subsistence' and other expenses; £747.18s.11d. to Richard's elder brother Thomas; £40 to his younger brother Bernard; etc. Together with various legal expenses the total amount Philip had advanced came to £2,694.2s.4d.

54 See Church of England Parish Registers 1538–1812 at the London Metropolitan Archives. St Pancras Parish burials March 1725–March 1753 (P90/PAN1, item 002). The records show that a fee of 6s. 1d. was paid (although originally 3s. 8d. had been written down). 'Schedule A' (see previous footnote) records a nearly identical sum of 6s. 2d. which Philip had paid to 'an undertaker for burying the Remains of the said Richard Cantillon'. In the eighteenth century St Pancras Old Church was regularly used for the burial of members of the Irish community in London. Despite two major disinterments due to railway building, one in 1866 and one in 2002–03, it is most likely that the body still lies in an extension to the graveyard that dates from 1727 known as the Pindle (I thank Philip A. Emery for this information. Also see Emery and Wooldridge 2011). There is no headstone. Murphy (1986: 295) speculates that Philip and other members of the family may have known that the body was not Richard's.

55 Murphy (1986: 201) suggests that Mary Anne actually started her liaison with Bulkeley a few years before her husband's death. As early as the beginning of 1735, less than a year after the fire in Albemarle Street, the couple were living together in London (ibid. 203). One can imagine that the extended Cantillon family was less than happy about this.

56 NA C11/1536/25. The nine-year-old Henrietta is called 'the complainant' because she is formally the oratrix in a bill of complaint of 1737 against her mother and stepfather. In fact it was Philip Cantillon, referred to in the papers as the girl's 'next friend', who brought the complaint on her behalf, probably to settle the question of who was looking after her financial affairs. The bill records that Francis Garvan had trusted Philip with the

annuity payment in the previous two years. But apparently by 1737 his role had been challenged, probably due to the fact that, after Richard's second will arrived from Surinam in July 1736, the latter's widow and Bulkeley were named the new administrators of the estate.

57 Before the birth of this son, James, the couple had a daughter, Martha, who was born on 9 August 1735, but she died young. A second son, William, also died young, and only the last two children, Rebecca and Elizabeth, lived to an adult age.

58 Newland died in June 1738, just a few months before his grandson, whom he had insisted was to be strictly raised in the Anglican faith (his will was almost comical for its insistence on this point: 'to the eldest Son of my eldest Daughter, Wife of Mr. Philip Cantillon, Merchant, being a Protestant, and his Heirs Male; and, for want of such Son, or his not being a Protestant, then to the eldest Son of my Second Daughter, Martha Dillon, wife of Mr. Dillon, Merchant in London, and his Heirs Male, being a Protestant; and, in Failure of such [etc.]' (Newland 1751: 1). Interestingly, his son-in-law Cantillon remained a Catholic until his death. And no surviving male heir, let alone a Protestant one, was produced by any of Newland's daughters, that is Rebecca, Martha or Elizabeth. Martha, who married Robert Dillon, died sometime before 1741, after having given birth to a daughter, and Elizabeth, who married William Binford sometime after 1738, died before 1751 only having had a daughter who died as an infant. Thus by the early 1750s the two most direct descendants of William were his daughter Rebecca Cantillon and her niece who was, unusually for a girl, called Christian. The girl would later marry Sir Edward Swinburne, the fifth Baronet of Capheaton (1733–86), whose family seat was Capheaton Hall in Northumberland. It is for this reason that a number of letters relating to the division of the Newland estate are preserved in Lady Swinburne's papers in the Northumberland Record Office. See ZWS/552/1, ZSW/552/2 and ZWS/552/3.

59 See *London Gazette*, issue 8208, 22–26 March 1743 and issue 8220, 3–7 May 1743. The second issue reported that 'Philip Cantillon hath in all things conformed himself according to the Directions of the several Acts of Parliaments made concerning Bankrupts.'

60 NA T1/363. The report, by one Mr. Sharpe, is dated 11 February 1755.

61 Philip and his wife had moved to the Gatton estate, after the death of Rebecca's uncle Dr. George Newland in October 1749. Philip turned out to be disastrously bad at running a country estate, spending more on repairs than the income of the estate. When he tried to charge half of the shortfall to his brother-in-law Robert Dillon, the latter got the lawyers involved. Philip tried to hide his poor management from his wife, writing to Dillon in a letter of 15 May 1752: 'My wife, she knows nothing of any of these little heats that have lately by letters passed between us, & I beg it may be kept from her.' Philip seems to have feared the wrath of his wife. On 27 April 1753 McCarthy, Dillon's lawyer wrote to his client: 'by what I hear Mrs. Cantillon has a good deal of money in the publick funds, and . . . she is not willing to apply any part of it to pay her Husband's Debts' (both letters in ZSW/552/2). Eventually in 1758 a buyer was found for the Gatton estate, which was sold for £23,000 to a member of the Colebrook family (ZSW/552/1; for Colebrook see C632). There were further possessions in Peckham, Passmore and Ewell. Christian Dillon and Rebecca Cantillon were thus beneficiaries of very large sums. But by this time Rebecca had separated from Philip who was left in the straightened circumstances described.

62 In 1754 Philip had obtained a small victory by making some case law (3 Burr 1553), but which at the same time may have lost him friends in the financial sector. In *Cantillon v The London Assurance Company* it was judged that if an insured ship or its cargo of 'corn, fish, salt, fruits, flour or seeds' was damaged by a vessel touching the bottom of the Thames this constituted stranding. As a result the London Assurance Company took the line about stranding out of its insurance policies and only continued to cover 'general average'.

63 The last time that Philip Cantillon was listed in *The Complete Guide to all Persons who have any Trade with the City of London* was in the 1758 edition (p. 118). By the end of that year he seems to have given up business because the title page of the *Analysis* states 'Late of the City of London'. Hence the publication of the book appears to be almost the final act of his time in London.

64 Elizabeth and her sister Rebecca had been 'well provided for in the settlement between [Philip] and their mother' (NA Prob 11/984). Sometime after 1765 Elizabeth married Chevallier O'Sullivan, who was avocat general at the Conseil supreme de Brabant. Higgs (1931: 377) may be right when he suggests that their son, Philip's grandson, Baron O'Sullivan, became an ambassador for Belgium to Austria in 1844 and in 1841 published a genealogy of the Cantillon family.

65 This is the wording that appears in the *London Evening Post* (issue 4879, 10–13 February 1759) and in the *Gazetteer and London Daily Advertiser* for 12 February 1759. Subsequent advertisements had the shorter statement as on the title page of the book.

66 These passages are reproduced in A6, A29–A30, A50, A116, A254, A288, A351, A417, A441, A449, A471, A539, A554, A560–A561, A615, A664, A675–A678, and A682. Although they do not have direct counterparts in E or D, in most cases similar arguments are found in different places. For further justification for their inclusion see the accompanying comments.

3   The Higgs translation (column H)

The first column on the recto pages contains the original English translation by Henry Higgs of the *Essai*, as reproduced in the first column on the verso pages. The main reason for including a translation is of course that it allows for an easier comparison with the other English versions. The choice for Higgs's translation requires some comment. The first reason for adopting it in this edition is that since its publication in 1931 it has remained the standard translation used invariably in the non-Francophone secondary literature on Cantillon. Even though in 2010 Thornton and Saucier published a new translation of the *Essai*, Higgs's remains the one that is generally more faithful to the original.[1]

Having said this, Higgs's translation is peculiar in a number of respects. As noted, Higgs believed that the version found in Postlethwayt's *Dictionary* was very close to the wording of Cantillon's original manuscript. Accepting Mirabeau's claim, he considered the French version to be a translation of that same English original. For this reason, in his translation of the *Essai* Higgs borrowed 'as far as justified' wordings found in the *Dictionary*. In this way, he believed, his translation 'probably goes near to a reconstruction of the English original' (Higgs 1931: 384).

This current edition allows one to appreciate Higgs's translation in a new light. One finds that it does indeed frequently use individual words and phrases that occur in the *Dictionary* fragments. Surprisingly, given the low opinion he expressed about Philip Cantillon's work, Higgs also sometimes uses the wordings of the *Analysis* (see C106ii). In many cases Higgs's borrowings from D or A explain what must have struck generations of readers as frequent odd translations. Importantly, Higgs's translation practice means that his rendering is sometimes a compromise between two versions and hence papers over, often subtle, differences between them.[2] Hopefully the nature of the current edition allows the reader to form opinions about the significance of such differences.

Notes

1 Saucier and Thornton (2010) offer a self-confessedly modernised translation for a non-academic readership. Freely available through the website of the Mises institute it threatens to influence an accurate historical reading of Cantillon. Groenewegen (2012) warns against this.
2 In order to avoid this drawback I considered at an earlier stage making a new English translation of the *Essai* that was *not* informed by knowledge of the *Dictionary* and *Analysis* versions. However, Professor Murphy then kindly showed me just such a new translation that he has made and which is to be published in the next few years. I decided that it would not be helpful to try to offer a third new translation of the *Essai* within the space of a few years.

4 The Uses of this edition

In the current edition the arrangement of the versions of Cantillon's writings that were published in the eighteenth century (that is, what is printed on the verso pages) follows the order of the *Essai*. The fragments found in Postlethwayt's *Universal Dictionary* have been arranged accordingly. Similarly, the text of Philip Cantillon's *Analysis* is, after the first 11 chapters, presented out of its original order. For a detailed overview of the rearrangements of both English versions the reader is referred to the table of correspondence on pp. 38–41.

It is not claimed that the changed order of presentation of the text of the English publications restores the original order of the manuscripts on which they were based. Rather, the reordering was done simply to allow a parallel presentation of the versions. Of course one may not want to read the versions in parallel. Instead one may prefer to concentrate on one column at a time. In particular E, until now generally considered as the sole authentic source for Cantillon's economic ideas, may be studied in this way, especially if one is interested primarily in the relations between the famous print edition of 1755 and its variations from the French manuscript versions. However, the main reason for the parallel presentation is of course to facilitate comparisons *between* corresponding passages in E, D and A, as well as providing a context for the passages that do not have counterparts in all three versions.

The frequent differences between versions are significant in at least three different ways. First, comparisons between corresponding passages afford us new insights into the specific language that Cantillon uses. While the variations in wording between versions may not, at first reading, always strike one as very substantial, it is worth remembering that we are dealing with a foundational work of economic theory. In any literary endeavour that breaks new ground, specific uses of language merit close attention. Along with pioneering new concepts, Cantillon is trying out words in new uses and contexts. This linguistic innovation is often quite subtle. But if one contemplates, for example, the varying descriptions of bargaining processes in E241, D241 and A241, one cannot fail to be struck by the importance of the language that is used. Of course readers may, for instance, differ in view as to the significance of the fact that the term 'equilibrium' (both fascinating and difficult in the light of its subsequent career in economic theory) is only used in the *Dictionary* version. But such differences of view would only confirm the importance of paying close attention to the language. Words used in new meanings, like 'economy' (see C79i) or 'altercation' (see C248i), express original economic conceptions and the use of expressions like '*cæteris paribus*' (see C49ii) and 'at the long run' (see C370) signal a conscious method of reasoning that was largely new. Sometimes the imagery is also simply beautiful, for example where the author describes the myriad of small payments in an economy as so many 'rivulets of barter' (see C284iii).

Of course attention to specific formulations in the different versions may also allow us to distinguish the original wordings that Cantillon used from later alterations by editors. As argued above, the Rouen manuscript can probably be considered as the most authentic of the French versions and sometimes its wording agrees with what we find in an English version. For a good example see C242iii, where the agreement in phrasing between the French manuscript text and the corresponding sentence from Postlethwayt's *Dictionary* strongly suggests that those versions have the original wording. While in this particular case, as in most others, the changes made by editors are of a stylistic nature, sometimes the alterations do affect the actual argument. For this reason a comparison between what precisely is said in the different versions is all the more instructive. Especially since *all* published versions were posthumous editions, comparisons may sometimes help in lending credence to or raise caution about the authenticity of specific wordings.

Second, the differences between alternative formulations of similar ideas, or the presence of passages in one or two versions but not in the other(s), sometimes invite speculations about possible developments in Richard Cantillon's thinking. Admittedly, given the fact that all three versions underwent editorial changes in the 1750s before being published, one needs to be careful with speculations of this kind. Nevertheless, it is my impression that the published versions E, D and A were each based on substantially different original drafts of Cantillon's work. Of these drafts the source text for Philip Cantillon's *Analysis* appears to have been the earliest manuscript, possibly dating from just after 1730 (see C577i).

The main reason for thinking that the *Analysis* was based on an early draft is that throughout Philip Cantillon's work the economic reasoning is often less developed than in the other two versions. For fairly typical examples compare A25 with E25 or A442 with D442. In addition one finds different emphases, for instance the perils of luxury consumption are arguably given more stress in the *Analysis* and tend to carry a more moralistic tone (see A33 or A254), something that fits with Murhpy's conjecture that in Cantillon's early attempts at economic theorising he wrote about luxury in a more traditional manner (see Murphy 1986: 50). But perhaps the most striking difference between the *Analysis* and the other two texts is the almost complete absence of the sophisticated monetary theory of part II, chapters iii to vi of the *Essai*, arguably Richard Cantillon's most innovative contribution. If one reads the paragraphs in A249 to A254, which just precede that contribution, and imagines that one does not know the other versions, one would have to conclude that the author was a somewhat crude quantity theorist in the mould of John Locke. Indeed, in the *Analysis* Locke's ideas on money, profit and interest appear to be echoed in a number of places (see C249, C442iv, C449, C463i, C471ii) and one wonders if a comparison between such passages and alternatives from the *Essai* and the *Dictionary* show us how Cantillon's monetary ideas evolved.[1] There are other striking differences in apparent influences on Cantillon of earlier authors. William Petty is named on a number of occasions in E and D, but nowhere in A (but for a likely influence see C288i, point c); Daniel Defoe is, surprisingly but undeniably, paraphrased at some length in A, but less recognisably in E (see C29, C30 and C139i).[2]

Of course it is possible to argue that all such differences between A and E, the less developed reasoning, the different emphases and the apparent influences of different authors, are all due to Philip Cantillon's particularly poor editorial judgments. Indeed, since Jevons ([1881] 1931: 335), most commentators have assumed this. However, as already argued, this cannot be the full explanation since the repeated occurrence of corresponding passages in the *Dictionary* fragments and the *Analysis* that do *not* occur in the *Essai* makes it nearly impossible that Philip Cantillon was simply a poor and partial translator of the French publication of 1755. In my opinion it is therefore legitimate to consider, with due care, what the content of the *Analysis* may tell us about developments in Richard Cantillon's thinking.

For its part the version found in Postlethwayt's *Universal Dictionary* exhibits in many respects sophisticated reasoning of a level similar to the *Essai*. It is true that essential parts are missing. For example, there is no counterpart to the whole of part I, chapter xv of the *Essai* where Cantillon develops his famous theory of population (E147–E182), or to part II, chapter v, where he elaborated on the trade and money flows between town and countryside (E318–E337). Also, in a number of places the *Essai* chapters continue after the fragments from the *Dictionary* (and the *Analysis*) break off. As indicated, in some cases these lacunae may be explained by Postlethwayt's decisions to omit them. But one could equally argue that they suggest that the manuscript that he used lacked these many passages and hence was a less accomplished draft than the one on which the French print edition was based.

At the same time, in some places one gets the impression that the fragments from the *Dictionary* are even more developed than the French version both in presentation and in argument. Commenting on the passage that is reproduced in the present edition in D265–6 and D270–D272, Murphy has recently made a similar point:

> [Postlethwayt's] presentation of the circular flow process appears so seamless, . . ., that one wonders whether in fact Cantillon had written an English version of the *Essai* which was even more complete than that produced in the French version of the *Essai* and that Postlethwayt borrowed this English rather than the French version. (Murphy 2009: 83)

Murphy's hunch can be supported by a number of other passages from the *Dictionary*, for instance the passages just preceding the ones he comments on that do not have a direct counterpart in the *Essai* (see D256–D264). Other examples are the already noted 'philosophical' ending to the chapter about entrepreneurs where it is said that due to their activities 'every thing finds its own proportion, . . ., without any peculiar intellectual conduct, whereby the society of commerce and circulation is governed' (D134); or the very clear discussion of the distinct markets for different traded goods and the distinct social groups who are the consumers of those goods (D369); or the account of a 'credit crunch' (D375); or the conception of profit as a return on capital advanced (D437).[3] These and other passages do indeed make one wonder if the source text that Postlethwayt used was a somewhat later draft than the one on which the *Essai* was based.

This, however, is far from certain. One could instead point to passages in the *Dictionary* that are closer to what we find in the *Analysis*. It might be argued that, if the latter publication was based on an earlier draft, why would the presumed later version of the *Dictionary* 'revert' to an account that appears to have been replaced in the *Essai* (see for example D/A416ff. which appear to offer an alternative to E396–E415). But there is no need here to try to impose strong views either way. The principal aim of this edition is to allow readers to judge for themselves.

A third reason why the differences between the three published versions are important is that they were read by different people in different countries. In the present edition an effort has been made to note which specific passages were quoted by, or may have exercised an influence on, later eighteenth-century authors. These references may contribute to future attempts at a fuller reconstruction of the influence of Cantillon's contribution, through its different published versions, on the formation of the new discipline of political economy in the second half of the eighteenth century and indeed other intellectual currents. Such a reconstruction cannot be offered here and it is important to emphasise, first, that the various references throughout the present edition certainly do not constitute a complete set and, second, that quotation does of course not equate with influence.

Nevertheless, it can be said with some confidence that the English publications had their own careers as vehicles for the dissemination of Cantillon's ideas. It should be noted that Postlethwayt's *Universal Dictionary* was a successful work, which by 1774 had gone through four editions and which remained the most accomplished commercial dictionary in the English-speaking world for several decades.[4] Possibly for this reason Johnson (1937: 205) concluded that '[t]he influence of Cantillon upon British economic thought can . . . be ascribed largely to Postlethwayt's writings'. One needs to be careful, however, in applying this statement to individual authors, British or otherwise. For example, some commentators have suggested that David Hume may have acquainted himself with Cantillon's ideas by reading relevant fragments in Postlethwayt's *Dictionary*. But this is simply impossible since all fragments that contain views that are, indeed, sometimes quite similar to Hume's *Political Discourses* (1752) were contained in issues of the *Dictionary* that appeared *after* the Scottish philosopher had completed his major contribution to political economy.[5]

On the other hand, we can be confident that Joseph Harris (1702–64) did derive the considerable number of passages in his *Essay upon Money and Coins* of 1757 that relied on Cantillon from no other source than Postlethwayt's *Universal Dictionary*.[6] Indeed, in almost all cases Harris's source appears to have been a single entry, namely 'Labour' (see C67iv). Another fascinating little fact that shows that some of the relevant *Dictionary* entries were actually read is that in the late 1770s Alexander Hamilton (1755 or 1757–1804) would copy out some of Cantillon's views amongst a large number of notes from Postlethwayt's *Dictionary* (see C89iii, C184v, C287iii). It is very likely that Hamilton studied the entries 'Cash' and 'Circulation', since he made special reference to them. Hence he will have come across Cantillon's theory of the entrepreneur (D118–D134) as well as the main parts of his theory of monetary circulation (D255–D317). Of course that does not necessarily imply that Cantillon, one of the most important monetary theorists of the eighteenth century, influenced Hamilton, the most significant early architect of the monetary system of the United States. But at least the existence of the 'Postlethwayt route' makes it possible to ask this question.[7] It should also be noted that the same entries 'Cash' and 'Circulation' were later reproduced verbatim in the first edition of the second most successful English commercial dictionary of the period, namely Thomas Mortimer's *A New and complete dictionary of trade and commerce* of 1766 (see C118ii and C255ii). Historians of economic and commercial ideas have long neglected the content of commercial dictionaries, but that does not mean that they were not read in their time. Through these publications Cantillon's ideas, albeit in an anonymous and disjointed form, may have had a hitherto unsuspected further impact.

Philip Cantillon's *Analysis of Trade* was a less successful publication than Postlethwayt's *Dictionary*. Nevertheless, judging by its presence in a number of libraries, it did not sell badly, something which probably also accounts for the fact that in later decades this title was the only one by an author called 'Cantillon' remembered in Britain (see McCulloch 1845: 52).[8] At least one important author carefully read the *Analysis*, namely Sir James Steuart (1713–80). This is clear from the simple fact that Steuart actually named this work twice in his *Principles of Political Economy* (see Steuart 1767, vol. 2, 17 and 48; cf. C591iii). In addition, the large majority of passages in the *Principles* that resemble arguments of Cantillon correspond more closely to formulations found in the *Analysis* than to comparable ones in the *Essai*.[9] The works of Harris and Steuart were quite well known in their time and they arguably occasioned a kind of second-hand dissemination of Cantillon's theories.

A case in point may be the way by which Adam Smith (1723–90) came to know 'Cantillon-like' views. The one actual reference to 'Cantillon' in *An Inquiry Into the Nature and Causes of the Wealth of Nations* (1776) is surely to the Cantillon of the *Essai* (see C80iii). The copy of the *Essai* that Smith is known to have had in his library he presumably picked up during his visit to France in 1765–66. However, he also owned and carefully read both Harris's *Essay* and Steuart's *Principles*[10] and it does not appear impossible that Smith in a few instances borrowed views from those authors for which they in turn were indebted to Cantillon.[11] In addition, a couple of passages in Smith's writings actually show a close resemblance with the wording of the *Analysis*. For example, only the *Analysis* uses the expression 'Haggling and Bargaining' to describe the market process, and this is of course nearly identical to Smith's famous phrase 'the higgling and bargaining of the market' (see C241v; for another example see C42iv).[12]

Perhaps some of these resemblances are simply coincidental and, even if they are not, this largely leaves unanswered the question of how fundamentally Cantillon may, directly or indirectly, have influenced Smith. Some commentators have not unreasonably suggested that this influence was quite profound (see e.g. Brewer 1992: 191–94; Murphy 2009: 161; for some important instances see C74ii and C176iii). Others have warned that, 'in Smith's case, virtually anything which could have been derived from Cantillon could have been derived in a more refined form from Quesnay or Turgot' (Aspromourgos 1996: 151). But this merely adds yet another possibility of an indirect route of influence of Cantillon on Smith.

With regard to Cantillon's readership in continental Europe the story appears to be more straightforward because there only the French *Essai* was read.[13] The influence of Cantillon on the beginnings of the physiocratic theory is hard to doubt. François Quesnay (1694–1774), like Smith, acknowledged his reliance on the *Essai* in only one place in his entire writings (see C36ii), but this most probably masks the larger extent of his indebtedness to Cantillon. Indeed, as has been noted by various commentators (e.g. Schumpeter 1954: 222; Meek 1962: 266–69; Brewer 2005), Quesnay's general ideas about circular flow and even some specific assumptions of the groundbreaking *Tableaux économiques* were in all likelihood partly inspired by Cantillon's remarkably neat conceptualisation in part II, chapter iii of the *Essai* (cf. C273ii). This was a crucial instance of the transmission of economic ideas, even though Meek (1962: 269) is of course right that 'Cantillon's inspired hints about the circulation of money and goods in a predominantly agricultural kingdom developed under their own momentum in Quesnay's mind once he had absorbed them.' Transmission of ideas almost invariably involves transmutation.

Judging by the references to the *Essai* in the last decades of the eighteenth century in works of many other French authors, the work, although not a bestseller, was quite widely read. Interestingly, some specific passages, like Cantillon's calculations of the sacrifice of the produce of 16,000 acres of land in France to pay for the luxury product lace produced in Brabant with a single acre would be cited again and again (see C498). Other passages throughout the *Essai* would attract attention and were adapted to specific later arguments. To give but two examples, Gabriel Bonnot de Mably (1709–85) used Cantillon's ideas about the cyclical decline of rich nations in his efforts to persuade his countrymen of the restorative effects of republican virtue (see Wright 1997: esp. 59–61 and 184; C401iii and C411i). His brother, Etienne Bonnot de Condillac (1714–80), claimed that the *Essai* was one of his inspirations in his attempt to offer an alternative to the physiocratic theory (see C277ii).

Beyond France, in Italy, Spain and Germany, various authors also read the *Essai*, several of whom have not been referenced in this edition. Of course since French was widely understood across Europe, readers did not have to depend on translations of the *Essai*.[14] Apparently both in Italy and Spain the Mauvillon edition was more commonly available. Since in this publication the anonymous *Essai* was part of a series of *Discours politiques*, the first volume of which carried David Hume's name, the work of the Irishman ended up being repeatedly confused with that of the Scotsman (see Becagli 1976). The appearance in Italy of a translation by one F. Scottoni, with the title *Saggio sulla natura de commercio in generale* in 1767, did little to clarify matters because the writer was identified imprecisely as an '*Autore Inglese*'. In Spain a translation, with the title *Fuentes de la riqueza pública*, did not appear until 1833, although the *Essai* had been used by a number of Spanish writers since at least the late 1770s (see Astigarraga and Zabalza 2007). The person responsible for this 'garbled translation', Antonio Domingo Porlier, having used the Mauvillon edition, believed that he had translated David Hume (see Smith 1967). Apart from this confusion, the reception of Cantillon's ideas in Italy and Spain, as indeed elsewhere, is complicated by the fact that they were deployed within different national contexts and economic and political discourses. One can only conclude this very brief sketch by noting that a full account of the various routes and receptions of Cantillon's work remains to be written.

Finally, something needs to be said about the missing Supplement that Cantillon mentions in a number of places in part I of the *Essai* (see C33ii). The content and fate of this statistical appendix have been a matter of speculation since the *Essai* was first published. Unfortunately the English versions do not yield much more information about this elusive work. The old conjecture by Cannan that Postlethwayt may have had access to the Supplement (see Higgs 1931: 385) does not have any foundation. However, the fact that the Supplement is not even mentioned anywhere in the *Dictionary* means very little because it makes perfect sense that Postlethwayt would have deleted any such reference to a work he did not have access to. More interesting is that the *Dictionary* has counterparts for most of the numerical estimates that the *Essai* says are taken from the Supplement (see C66i). In one place, the *Dictionary* even provides an estimate for the size of the international market for woollen cloth in Europe (D428), something that according to the *Essai* is an estimate provided in the Supplement (see E193). This is consistent with the hypothesis that the draft on which the *Dictionary* fragments were based was written at approximately the same time as, or perhaps a little later than, the draft that would become the source text for the first print edition of the *Essai*. By contrast the *Analysis* does not have any counterparts for passages in the *Essai* that make mention of a supplement. There is one passage that may provide an explanation for this lacuna. In the *Analysis* we find the promise that 'if these Essays have the good Fortune to merit the Approbation of the Public, I propose from a Number of Calculations by me, collected from a Course of many Years Experience, to publish a small Treatise of Arithmetic' (A561). One wonders if this was Richard Cantillon in an early draft of his work contemplating his Supplement when he had not yet written it. This is merely speculation of course, as so much surrounding this man and his writings must perhaps remain. There are, however, no compelling reasons why a copy of the Supplement, or indeed other manuscripts written by Richard Cantillon, will not someday be found. Until then may the present edition be of some use.

Notes

1   In van den Berg (2012a) I have offered a more detailed interpretation of what may be considered as Cantillon's 'early monetary theory'.

2   In van den Berg (2014b) I argue that Defoe may have had an influence on Cantillon's views about the development of human settlements.

3   A more detailed discussion of the differences between the theories of profit and interest in E, D and A is provided in van den Berg 2014a.

4   In 1819 William Anderson wrote in the introduction to his own dictionary: 'Since the large work by Postlethwayt half a century ago, which from its great excellence at the time completely superseded every former publication on the subject of Commerce, no general Dictionary, with the exception of Mortimer's has been given to the public.' Even though Anderson failed to mention less successful publications, like Rolt's *Dictionary*, his assessment appears largely correct. Arguably only McCulloch's *Dictionary* of 1832, which also still referred to Postlethwayt (McCulloch 1832: x), finally superseded the latter's work.

5   This point is made more fully in van den Berg (2012a: 6–7). As already noted, extracts from Hume's economic essays would end up joining those from Cantillon and many other authors in the fascinating haystack that is Postlethwayt's *Dictionary*.

6   Higgs (1892), Spengler (1954: 282, n4) and Hayek (1991: 177, n2) have already expressed this view.

7   Panagopoulos (1961) shows that Hamilton obtained his knowledge of a number of British economists, including Petty and Hume, at least initially, through his extensive reading in Postlethwayt's *Dictionary*. As far as I am aware, Hamilton's reading of some vital fragments of Cantillon's writings has been overlooked.

8   Apart from public libraries in Britain, the *Analysis* was in Postlethwayt's private library (Davis and Reymers 1768, item 7065) and in that of the 'Scottish physiocrat' John Gray (see van den Berg 2010). Outside Britain the work appears to have been practically unknown.

9   Earlier commentators, like Higgs (1892), Legrand (1900) and Hayek ([1931] 1985) agreed that Steuart had relied on the *Analysis*. However, some confusion was introduced into this matter by Skinner, who in his modern scholarly edition of the *Principles* left out the part where Steuart named the *Analysis* (see Skinner 1966: 2, 435) and also in his footnotes repeatedly indicated correspondences to the *Essai*, rather than the *Analysis*. Groenewegen (2001) goes to considerable length to correct the impression given by Skinner. See C19ii, C241vi, C242v, C423iii. Of course, it is not impossible that Steuart knew both publications. If he knew only the *Analysis*, then he would have studied it very soon after its appearance in February 1759, because by the end of that year he had completed an advanced draft of a large part of his *Principles* (see Skinner 1966, xli, 741–42).

10 See Mizuta (2000) for the presence of the three titles in Smith's library. Harris and Steuart are frequently referred to by the editors of the Glasgow edition of the Wealth of Nations. See Smith [1776] 1976: 1012 and 1017).

11 For the possible filtering of Cantillon's ideas through Harris, see e.g. C51ii and iii, or C70iv. The fact that there are already some passages in the lectures on jurisprudence that resemble arguments that we find in Cantillon (see also e.g. C42iv, C176iii, C232ii, C265iii) may in some cases be explained by Smith's knowledge of Harris's *Essay*, rather than Cantillon's *Essai*: the lectures were delivered in 1762–63 and 1763–64, hence before Smith's visit to France. For a possible filtering of Cantillon's ideas through Steuart's *Principles*, see C39iii, C153iii, C265ii and C265iii.

12 The *Analysis* does not figure in the catalogue of Smith's library. But neither does Postlethwayt's *Dictionary*, even though Smith appears to have purchased a copy of that work in 1767 (see Cannan 1895).

13 Philip Cantillon's book appears to have gone completely unnoticed in France and other continental European countries (see van den Berg 2012a: 3, n6). Neither does Postlethwayt's *Dictionary* appear to have had many readers there. One Anglophile Frenchman who did read it, 'attentively' even as he puts it, was André Morellet (Morellet 1769: 21–22). But the massive size of the work meant that even this connoisseur of the economic literature of his time, who knew Cantillon's *Essai* well, apparently failed to spot the fragments that Postlethwayt had plagiarised.

14 In Prussia Johann Philipp Graumann (*c.*1690–1762) read the *Essai*, in French of course, and translated Cantillon's criticism of Newton's monetary reforms into German (see C584iv). No full German translation was published until 1931.

Table 4.1a Sources used

E	*Essai sur la nature du commerce en général. Traduit de l'Anglois*. A Londres, Chez Fletcher Gyles, dans Holborn. M.DCC.LV. Pp. 1–430, plus 6 unnumbered contents pages.
1756a	*Essai sur la nature du commerce en général. Traduit de l'Anglois*. A Londres, Chez Fletcher Gyles, dans Holborn. M.DCC.LVI. Pp. 1–427, plus 5 unnumbered contents pages.
1756b	*Essai sur la nature du commerce en général. Traduit de l'Anglois*. Contained in vol. 3 of the series *Discours politiques* [edited by Eléazar Mauvillon]. Chez J.Schreuder & Pierre Mortier le jeune. [Vol. 3 does not have a place of publication but vol. 1 has 'A Amsterdam'], pp. 153–428.
1769	*Essai sur la nature du commerce en général. Traduit de l'Anglois*. This is contained in a reprint of vol. 3 of the series *Discours politiques*. Pp. 153–428.
R	*Essay de la nature du commerce en général*. Bound manuscript of 158 sheets. Collection Leber 919 (350) in the municipal library of Rouen.
M	*Mémoire sur la Population*. Consisting of five notebooks, in total 107 sheets, which form item number 1 of M780 in the Archives Nationales in Paris. The transcript from Cantillon's work starts some sheets into the manuscript, without a separate heading and continues for 55 pages.
N	*Mémoire sur la Population*. Consisting of 97 sheets forming number 2-bis of M773 in the Archives Nationales in Paris. After 9 pages there is another title page, which reads *Essay de la Nature du Commerce*. This title is repeated on the next page, where the text of Cantillon's work starts being transcribed from the beginning. The first part of the Essay ends on the verso side of sheet 96. Sheet 97 has two contents pages.
D	Postlethwayt, M. *The Universal Dictionary of Trade and Commerce, Translated from the French of the Celebrated Monsieur Savary*. London: John and Paul Knapton. Vol. 1 published in 1753, vol. 2 published in 1755. Previously published in 155 individual issues between November 1751 and November 1755. Issues containing fragments from Cantillon's writings were contained in issues that appeared between January 1752 and May 1754.
P	Postlethwayt, M. 1749. *A Dissertation on the Plan, Use, and Importance, of The Universal Dictionary of Trade and Commerce*. London: John and Paul Knapton.
T	Postlethwayt, M. 1757. *Great-Britain's True System*. London: Millar, Whiston, White and Sandby.
A	*The Analysis of Trade, Commerce, Coin, Bullion, Banks, and Foreign Exchanges. Wherein The true Principles of this useful Knowledge are fully but briefly laid down and explained, to give a clear Idea of their happy Consequences to Society, when well regulated. Taken chiefly from a Manuscript of a very ingenious Gentleman deceas'd, and adapted to the present Situation of our Trade and Commerce*. By Philip Cantillon, Late of the City of London, Merchant. London: Printed for the Author, and Sold by Mr. Lewis in Covent Garden; Mr. Goddart in Duke-Street, Lincolns-Inn-Fields; Mr. Vaillant in the Strand; Mrs. Cooper in Pater-noster-Row; and Mr. Brackestone in Cornhill. MDCCLIX.

Table 4.1b Table of the correspondence of parts

Number in the present edition	Essai 1755 edition (E)	Essai Manuscripts (M, R, N)	Postlethwayt's Dictionary (D)	Postlethwayt's other publications (T, P)	Philip Cantillon's Analysis of Trade (A)	
1 to 6	I, i, 1–2	*De la Richesse*	R, N			I, 1–5	*Riches.*
7 to 18	I, ii, 3–8	*Des Sociétés d'Hommes*	R, N	'Labour', II, 2, col. 1		II, 6–8	*How States may be formed.*
19 to 23	I, iii, 9–11	*Des Villages*	R, N			III, 8–9	*How Villages may be settled.*
24 to 30	I, iv, 12–16	*Des Bourgs*	R, N			IV, 9–12	*How Market Towns may be established.*
31 to 36	I, v, 16–20	*Des Villes*	R, N			V, 13–14	*How Cities may be established.*
37 to 39	I, vi, 21–23	*Des Villes Capitales*	R, N			VI, 14–15	*How Capital Cities may be established*
40 to 44	I, vii, 23–25	*Le travail d'un Laboureur vaut moins que celui d'un Artisan*	R, N, M (from 42)	'Labour', II, 1, col. 1		VII, 15–16	*The Labour of the Plowman is of less Value, than that of the Handy-Crafts-Man.*
45 to 52	I, viii, 25–27	*Les Artisans gagnent, les uns plus, les autres moins, selon les cas & les circonstances différentes.*	R, M, N	'Labour', II, 1, col. 1		VIII, 16–20	*Some Handy-Crafts-Men in certain Trades, earn more than others, according to the Circumstances of the Times.*
53 to 62	I, ix, 28–33	*Le nombre de Laboureurs, Artisans & autres, qui travaillent dans un état, se proportionne naturellement au besoin qu'on en a.*	R, M, N	'Labour', II, 1, col. 1–2		IX, 20–21	*The Number of Labourers and Handy-Crafts-Men, are proportioned to the Demand for them.*
63 to 75	I, x, 33–39	*Le prix & la valeur intrinsique d'une chose en général est la mesure de la terre & du travail qui entrent dans sa production.*	R, M, N	'Labour', II, 1, col. 2	T, 153–155	X, 21–22	*The Price of any Thing in general, is estimated by the Value of the Land which produces it, and the Labour and Time taken in forming it into use.*
76 to 105	I, xi, 40–55	*Du pair ou rapport de la valeur de la Terre à la valeur du travail.*	R, M, N	'Labour', II, 1, col. 2 to 2 col. 1	T, 148–153	XI, 22–25	*Of the Par and Equality between Land and Labour.*

106 to 117	I, xii, 55–61	*Tous les Ordres & tous les Hommes d'un Etat subsistent ou s'enrichissent aux dépens des Propriétaires des Terres.*	R, M, N			XXI, 114–118	*All Orders of Men in a Community or State, subsist and are enriched at the Expence of the Proprietors of Land.*
118 to 137	I, xiii, 62–75	*La circulation & le troc des denrées &des marchandises, de même que leur production, se conduisent en Europe par des Entrepreneurs, & au hazard.*	R, M, N	'Circulation', I, 498, col. 1		XXIII, 124–127	*Of Inland and Foreign Trade.*
138 to 146	I, xiv, 76–85	*Les humeurs, les modes & les façons de vivre du Prince, & principalement des Propriétaires de terre, déterminent les usages auxquels on emploie les terres dans un Etat, & causent, aux Marché, les variations des prix de toutes choses.*	R, M, N				
147 to 182	I, xv, 86–113	*La multiplication & le décroissement des Peuples dans un Etat dependent principalement de la volonté, des modes & des façons de vivre des Propriétaires de terres.*	R, M, N			XXII, 119–124	*The Increase and Decrease of the Number of People in a State, or Kingdom, principally depend on the Manner of Living of the Age, the Taste, and Luxury of the great Proprietors of Land.*
183 to 202	I, xvi, 113–126	*Plus il y a de travail dans un Etat, & plus l'Etat est cense riche naturellement.*	R, M, N	'Labour', II, 6, col. 1–2	T, 155–158		
203 to 233	I, xvii, 127–150	*Des Métaux & des Monnoies, & particulierement de l'or & de l'argent.*	R, M, N	'Mines', II, 271, col. 2		XII, 25–28 and XIX, 86–87, 97	*Of Mines and Barter.*
234 to 238	II, i, 151–155	*Du Troc*	R, M				

(Continued)

Table 4.1b (Continued)

Number in the present edition	Essai 1755 edition (E)	Essai Manuscripts (M, R, N)	Postlethwayt's Dictionary (D)	Postlethwayt's other publications (T, P)	Philip Cantillon's Analysis of Trade (A)
239 to 254	II, ii, 155–159 *Des prix des Marchés.*	R, M	'Barter', I, 222, col. 1		XII, 28–33 *Of Mines and Barter.*
255 to 298	II, iii, 159–182 *De la circulation de l'Argent*	R, M	'Cash', I, 463, col. 1–2		XIV, 42–44 *Of the Circulation of Money.*
299 to 317	II, iv, 183–196 *Autre réflexion sur la vitesse ou la lenteur de la circulation de l'argent, dans le troc.*	R, M	'Circulation', I, 498, col. 2		
318 to 337	II, v, 197–211 *De l'inégalié de la circulation de l'argent effectif dans un Etat.*	R, M			
338 to 384	II, vi, 211–231 *De l'augmentation & de la diminution de la quantié d'argent effectif dans un Etat.*	R, M (up to 343)	'Money', II, 283, col. 1 to 284, col. 2		XVI, 51–55 *Of the consequential Effect which the Increase and Decrease of the Current Coin of a Country, has on the Community.*
385 to 395	II, vii, 232–239 *Continuation du meme sujet de l'augmentation & de la diminution de la quantié d'argent effectif dans un Etat.*	R			
396 to 432	II, viii, 239–263 *Autre Reflexion sur l'augmentation & sur la diminution de la quantié d'argent effectif dans un Etat.*	R	'Labour', II, 5, col. 1 to 6, col. 1		XV, 45–49 *Of the Ways and Means by which real Species Increase and Decrease in a Kingdom.*
433 to 461	II, ix, 264–282 *De l'interêt de l'argent, & de ses causes.*	R	'Interest', I, 995, col. 2 to 996, col. 2		XVII, 62–66 *Of the Interest of Money*
462 to 485	II, x, 282–296 *Des causes de l'augmentation & de la diminution de l'interêt de l'argent, dans un Etat.*	R	'Interest', I, 996, col. 2		XVII, 66–67

486 to 526	III, i, 297–323	Du Commerce avec l'Etranger.	R	'Ballance of Trade', I, 184, col.2 to 185, col. 1	P, 41–44	
527 to 544	III, ii, 323–340	Des Changes & de leur nature.	R	'Ballance of Trade', I, 185, col. 1–2	P, 44–46	XVIII, 74–82 — Of Inland and Foreign Exchanges.
545 to 569	III, iii, 340–355	Autres éclaircissemens pour la connoissance de la nature des changes.	R	'Ballance of Trade', I, 185, col. 2 to 186, col. 1	P, 46–49	XVIII, 83–85
570 to 594	III, iv, 355–381	Des variations de la proportion des valeurs, par rapport aux Métaux qui servent de monnoie.	R	'Coin', I, 527, col. 2 to 528, col. 1		XIX, 86–96 — Of Metals and Money; particularly Gold, Silver, and Copper; their proportional Value and Variations, with respect to the Use of them as Money.
595 to 626	III, v, 381–397	De l'augmentation & de la diminution de la valeur des especes monnoïées en dénomination.	R	'Coin', I, 526, col. 1 to 527, col. 2		XX, 102–112 — Of the Increase and Decrease of Coin in Denomination.
627 to 641	III, vi, 397–406	Des Banques, & de leur crédit.	R	'Banking', I, 195, col. 2 to 196, col. 1		XXIV, 169–176 — Of Bankers and Banks.
642 to 672	III, vii, 406–423	Autres éclaircissements & recherches sur l'utilité d'une Banque nationale.	R	'Banking', I, 196, col. 1–2		XXIV, 185–186, 182–185
673 to 689	III, viii, 424–430	Des rafinemens du credit des Banques générales.	R	'Credit', I, 579, col. 1, 578, col. 2		XXIV, 176–182

1

ᵃESSAI
SURᵃ LA NATURE
DU
COMMERCE
ᵇEN GÉNÉRALᵇ

TRADUIT DE L'ANGLOIS

A LONDRES

Chez FLETCHER GYLES,
Dans Holborn

M. DCC. LV

THE
ANALYSIS
OF
TRADE,
COMMERCE,
COIN,
BULLION,
BANKS, AND
FOREIGN EXCHANGES.

WHEREIN

The true Principles of this useful Knowledge are fully but briefly laid down and explained, to give a clear Idea of their happy Consequences to Society, when well regulated.

Taken chiefly from a Manuscript of a very ingenious Gentleman deceas'd, and adapted to the present Situation of our Trade and Commerce.

By PHILIP CANTILLON
Late of the City of London, Merchant.

LONDON:

Printed for the AUTHOR, and Sold by Mr. *Lewis* in Covent Garden; Mr. *Goddart* in Duke-Street, Lincolns-Inn-Fields; Mr. *Vaillant* in the Strand; Mrs. *Cooper* in Pater-noster-Row; and Mr. *Brackstone* in Cornhill.
MDCCLIX

[Price Five Shillings]

ESSAY
ON THE NATURE
OF
TRADE IN GENERAL

[a]...[a]: R, N: 'Essay de'
[b]...[b]: N: missing

i. The word *de* instead of *sur* in the French manuscript versions (V1a) is also used in other occurrences of the title in R and M. See V234a and V486a.

ii. The spelling *Essay* (in R and N, but not further down in M, see V234a) is perhaps less significant than has been suggested. Hébert (2010: 6) assumes that the spelling is due to it being 'carelessly transcribed from an English original'. This is questionable, because the same explanation does not apply to many words in the same manuscript that are also spelled with 'y', e.g. '*etably*', '*vray*' or '*luy*'. In fact such spellings were common in early eighteenth-century French.

iii. One of the earliest advertisements for the *Analysis* has some additional words in the sentence referring to a manuscript (A1). It reads: 'Chiefly taken from a French Manuscript of a very ingenious Gentleman, deceased, who resided many Years in Paris and London, compared with the Opinions of our best English Authors, and adapted to the present Situation of our Trade and Commerce' (*London Evening Post*, issue 4879, 10–13 February 1759). See above p. 23.

1

2 [1] *PREMIERE PARTIE.*
CHAPITRE PREMIER.
De la Richesse.

RICHES.

3 |1| La Terre est la source ou la matiere d'où l'on tire la Richesse; le travail de l'Homme est la forme qui la produit: & la Richesse en elle-même, n'est autre [2] chose que la nourriture, les commodités & les agrémens de la vie.

|| The Earth is the Source or Matter from whence all Riches are produced; the Maintenance, Convenience and Superfluities of Life are properly speaking real Riches, Labour the first, and Industry the second Means, of obtaining them.

4 |2| La Terre produit de l'herbe, des racines, des grains, du lin, du coton, du chanvre, des arbrisseaux & bois de plusieurs especes, avec des fruits, des écorces & feuillages de diverses sortes, comme celles des Meuriers pour les Vers à soie; elle produit des Mines & ªMinérauxª. Le travail de l'Homme donne la forme de richesse à tout cela.

|| Land produces Herbage for all Sorts of Cattle, Corn, Flax, Timber, Coals, Mines [2] of Gold and Silver, Minerals, Mulberry-Trees; in short, every Variety to support the human Creation and to indulge their Appetites.

Chapter I.
Of Wealth

There is no counterpart for this chapter in **2**
Postlethwayt's *Universal Dictionary*.

The Land is the Source or Matter from whence all Wealth is produced. The Labour of man is the Form which produces it: and Wealth in itself is nothing but the Maintenance, Conveniencies, and Superfluities of Life.

i. For other references to labour as producing 'the form' of wealth see **3** E4, E75/D75 and E235. The distinction in E3 between the contributions of land and labour has sometimes been compared to Petty's statement in the *Treatise of Taxes* (1662a: 49) that: 'Labour is the Father and active principle of Wealth, as Lands are the Mother.' See also his *Natural and Political Observations* (1662b: 52): 'Hands being the Father as Lands are the Mother, and Womb of Wealth.'

ii. A3 uses an alternative distinction, namely between 'labour' and 'industry'. In a number of places in A the two words appear to be used almost as synonyms; see e.g. A6, A109, A114, A116. This is similar to the occurrences of the same pair in E11, E49, E91, E114, E167, E356, E414, E440, E446. However, in other places the words seem to denote distinct notions, following a usage that is perhaps more commonly found in French than in English authors of the eighteenth century. '*Travail*' was associated primarily with physical exertion, often in agriculture, while '*industrie*' tended to be used to indicate intelligent, skilful application of labour, often in manufacturing. For the use of the conceptual pair in this sense see A49, A58, A155, A181, A445.

iii. Cf. the definition of wealth in E3 with D134.

iv. These definitions of wealth are perhaps reminiscent of Boisguilbert *Le détail de la France* ([1697] 1712, II, 16): '*La Richesse au commencement du monde, & par la destination de la Nature & l'ordre du Créateur, n'étoit autre chose qu'une ample jouissance des besoins de la vie: comme ils se réduisoient uniquement à la simple nourriture & au vêtement nécessaire pour se garantir des rigueurs du temps.*'

v. Mirabeau *L'Ami des hommes* (1756: 10) clearly relies on E3: '*La nourriture, les commodités & les douceurs de la vie sont la richesse. La terre la produit, & le travail de l'homme lui donne la forme. Le fonds & la forme sont la terre & l'homme.*' Also cf. Adam Smith (1776, I, v: 1): 'Every man is rich or poor according to the degree in which he can afford to enjoy the necessaries, conveniences, and amusements of life.' On the other hand, William Tatham (1799: 74) takes his definition of wealth from A3.

Land produces Herbage, Roots, Corn, Flax, Cotton, Hemp, Shrubs and Timber of several kinds, with divers sorts of Fruits, Bark, and Foliage like that of the Mulberry-tree for Silkworms; it supplies Mines and Minerals. To all this the Labour of man gives the form of Wealth.

ᵃ...ᵃ: R, N:
'Minéraux &c'

Higgs here translates '*de l'herbe*' with **4** 'Herbage', possibly following A4. In English, as in French, 'herbage' referred to the more specific meaning of 'grassland' or 'pasture', as opposed to the more general *herbe*. The mention of cattle in A4 suggests that 'pasture' is indeed likely to be the intended meaning. The phrase in A is similar to the one used in E23.

5 |3| Les Rivieres & les Mers fournissent des Poissons, pour la nourriture de l'Homme, & plusieurs autres choses pour l'agrément. Mais ces Mers & ces Rivieres appartiennent aux Terres adjacentes, ou sont communes; & le travail de l'Homme en tire le Poisson, & autres avantages.

|| It is true the Seas abound with Fish, the Rivers and Seas belong to the adjoining Lands, Labour produces them to Light.

6 || That Labour and Industry employed in cultivating the Earth is the greatest of all wordly Advantages, the Laws which encourage the Farmer and the Husbandman are the best of all Institutions; in whatever this Encouragement is given, and the Means of Subsistence afforded, thither People will flock, and become useful and good Subjects, and by their Labour and Industry bring in a Flow of Riches.

|| Power and Government were obtained by the superior Force of Genius in the first Founder, or by the Power of the Sword; its Solidity and Duration is not to be depended upon futher than the Interest, Love and Fidelity of the Subjects carry them.

|| The Success and Stability of unjust Acquisitions are but of Short Duration, except there [3] is a very strong Mixture of political Virtue to support them.

|| Oliver Cromwell is an Instance of the great Power and Efficiacy of Political Virtue. This great but wicked Man, finished the Course of his Career in Peace; but consider him when he arrived at the Summit of all his Glory, vindicating the Honour and Reputation of his Country, procuring Redress and Satisfaction from foreign Nations, for Depredations committed on his new acquired Subjects, the great Protector of Trade and Commerce of *England* and its Colonies, the Conqueror of *Ireland* and *Scotland*, the Possessor of *Dunkirk*, the Terror of *France* and *Holland*, the Scourge of *Spain* and *Portugal*, the Author of the ᵃArt of Navigationᵃ: I say, view this surprising Man in this Light he must be seen in a Point of View supporting his Dignity by Actions worthy of the greatest Heroes, dying poor though Master of the Lives and Fortunes of his own Subjects, commanding their Submission and Obedience and the Admiration of all *Europe*.

|| Justice, Generosity, and Humanity are the Rudders by which all Government ought [4] to steer; these Principles command, nay even extort the Subjects Love and Obedience.

|| The equal Ballance of Power between the King and People ought to be most religiously observed. If the Honour, Dignity, and Prerogatives of the Crown are broke in upon, Anarchy and Confusion are the certain Consequences.

|| The greater Number of People in a State, in respect to other Countries, add superior Force and Respect to a Kingdom; an Age would carry Population to an almost incredible Series of Increase, if the Means of Subsistence are allotted to People and to their Posterity: this Support and Maintenance depends on our great Proprietors of Land, and it is to these Gentlemen the Consideration of this Matter is referred, on them depend the Increase and Decrease of Population, being the Possessors of Land, the Source and Matter from whence all Riches are produced.

|| I am of the Opinion that our Northern Colonies in *America* will in the Course of one hundred Years be in a three-fold Proportion better inhabited than their Mother Country, [5] and that arising from the Means allotted to Men to support themselves and Posterity, in the Grants daily given to them of Land, the Encouragement of clearing it, and the different Manner, Taste, and Luxury of the Inhabitants.

|| The Justice due from a Sovereign to his Subjects is Protection against the Enemies of his Country, and the Administration of impartial Justice, by just and equal Laws. The Duty of the Subject is respectful Love and Submission; this reciprocal Duty between King and People ought to extend impartially from the Seat of the Monarchy to its most distant Limits: the Prince pays his immediate Attendants about his Person, his Army, and great Ministers of State, the People pay the Taxes laid on them to support this Grandeur and Expence. The greater the Number of People are, where the Means of Subsistence are allotted to them and their Posterity, the greater Riches are, and the greater the Prince's Revenue must be, and from the Number of Inhabitants to be employed the cheaper Labour will be.

Rivers and Seas supply Fish for the food of man, and many other things for his enjoyment. But these Seas and Rivers belong to the adjacent Lands or are common to all, and the Labour of man extracts from them the Fish and other advantages.

5

ᵃ...ᵃ: *sic*. It should presumably read 'Act of Navigation'.

At this point the *Analysis* has a four-page digression that has no counterpart in E or D. Jevons ([1881] 1931: 335) may well have been right when he rejected the 'rodomontades about Oliver Cromwell' as a later insertion by Philip Cantillon. The tone and content of this extended passage as a whole are out of place when compared to the sparse language of the first chapter of E. There are, however, a few arguments that are reminiscent of what we find in E and for this reason the passage has been included. They are, first, the praise of the Navigation Acts, which is in accordance with the discussion of the need to limit Dutch naval powers in E518–E522. Second, the observations in the second half of the passage about population are strongly reminiscent of E I, xv (E147–E182). A has a counterpart for that chapter, which is much shorter than the French version (A147–A155, A173, A181). In particular, the argument in A6 that the increase in population depends 'on our great Proprietors of Land' is reminiscent of E173 (and for the phrase 'incredible Series of Increase' cf. A150). In addition, note the prediction in A6 that in 100 years the English colonies in Northern America will have three times more inhabitants than the mother country. This is not quite the same as the prediction that '[t]he English in the Colonies will become proportionately more numerous in three generations than their counterparts in England in thirty' (E176). Still, there appears to be a connection between the passages. On the other hand, the straightforward endorsement of populationist principles in the final sentence of A6 contrasts with the more reserved statement in E182. One possible explanation for these similarities and differences in argumentation is that Philip Cantillon was here paraphrasing and adapting his kinsman's manuscript.

6

7 [3] **CHAPITRE** ^aII^a.

Des Sociétés d'Hommes.

[6] **CHAP. II.**

How States may be formed.

8 |1| De quelque maniere que se forme une Société d'Hommes, la propriété des Terres qu'ils habitent, appartiendra nécessairement à un petit nombre d'entr'eux.

‖ [II, 2, col. 1] Which way soever a society of men is formed, the property of the lands must be in the hands of few men.

‖ Without examining by what Manner Societies or States were formed in the patriarchal Time, of which our Information, with regard to Riches, is very obscure,

9 |2| Dans les Sociétés errantes, comme les ^aHardes^a des Tartares ^b& les Camps^b des Indiens qui vont d'un lieu à un autre avec leurs Bestiaux & Familles, il faut que le Capitaine ^cou le Roi^c qui les conduit, regle les limites de chaque Chef de Famille, & les Quartiers d'un chacun autour du Camp. Autrement il y auroit toujours des contestations pour les Quartiers ou commodités, les bois, les herbes, l'eau, &c. mais lorsqu'on aura [4] réglé les Quartiers & les limites d'un chacun, cela vaudra autant qu'une propriété pour le tems qu'ils y séjournent.

10 |3| Dans les Sociétés plus régulieres: Si un Prince à la tête d'une Armée, a conquis un Païs, il distribuera les Terres à ses Officiers ou Favoris, suivant leur mérite, ou son bon plaisir (cas où est originairement la France); il établira des loix pour en conserver la propriété à eux & à leurs Descendans: ou bien il se réservera la propriété des Terres, & emploiera ses Officiers ou Favoris, au soin de les faire valoir; ^aou ils leur cédera^a à condition d'en païer tous les ans un certain cens, ou redevance; ou il leur cédera en se réservant la liberté de les taxer tous les ans suivant ses besoins & leurs facultés. Dans tous ces cas, ces Officiers ou Favoris, ^bsoit^b qu'ils soient Propriétaires absolus, ^bsoit^b [5] dépendans, ^bsoit^b qu'ils soient Intendans ou Inspecteurs du produit des Terres, ils ne feront qu'un petit nombre par rapport à tous les Habitans.

If a prince at the head of an army conquered France, and distributed the lands amongst his officers, or favourites, according to his pleasure, or their merit, he would then establish laws for vesting the said property in them, and their descendants.

it will answer my Purpose to suppose, (what may very naturally happen) that a Prince or Conqueror at the Head of his Forces had subdued a large Country, and distributed the Lands thereof to his Favourites and Followers, according to their Merit or his Fancy, upon Conditions and Laws between Prince and People, the due Observance of which would intitle the said Lands to descend in a regular Course from Generation to Generation.

Chapter II.   a...a: R: '2e';   i. D8–D17 occur in the entry 'Labour' of Postlethwayt's   **7**
N: '2'   *Universal Dictionary* (vol. II, pp. 1–7). This entry was
Of Human Societies   originally contained in issue 85, which was first published
in September 1753. Curiously, the fragment appears in the
form of a footnote to the paragraph reproduced in D77. The
corresponding French paragraph, E77, states '*nous avons
déja remarqué*', which is clearly a reference to E7ff. That
statement is not repeated in D, but it may well have appeared
in the manuscript that Postlethwayt used, as it would have
prompted him to insert the earlier chapter between D77 and
D78. Cf. C77.

ii. The order of the paragraphs of this chapter is similar in A
and D and differs from E.

Which way soever a Society   A8 appears to deny explicitly that there is reliable knowledge   **8**
of Men is formed the ownership   about the formation of states in early, 'patriarchal', times, i.e.
of the Land they inhabit will   the epoch from Adam to Jacob in *Genesis*. The patriarchs were
necessarily belong to a small   known as pastoral people. E9 also deals with pastoral people,
number among them.   although instead of biblical references there are examples
from secular history and anthropology. D17 also mentions
patriarchial times. For another reference to *Genesis* see E211.

In wandering Societies like Hordes of Tartars and   a...a: 1756a, b, 1769:   **9**
Camps of Indians who go from one place to another   'Hordes'
with their Animals and Families, it is necessary that   b...b: R, N: 'et camps'
the Captain or King who is their Leader should fix   c...c: R, N: 'ou Roi'
the boundaries of each Head of a Family and the
Quarters of an Individual around the Camp. Otherwise
there would always be disputes over the Quarters or
Conveniencies, Woods, Herbage, Water, etc. but when
the Quarters and Boundaries of each man are settled it
is as good as ownership while they stay in that place.

In the more settled Societies: if a prince at the head of   a...a: R; 'ou le   Only D specifies that the   **10**
an Army has conquered a Country, he will distribute   leur cédéra; N: conquered country is France.
the Lands among his Officers or Favourites according   'ou [inserted: Higgs (1931: 384) argued that
to their Merit or his Pleasure (as was originally the   'les'] leur   Cantillon had omitted this from
case in France): he will then establish laws to vest   cedera';   the French translation of his
the property in them and their Descendants: or he   1756b, 1769:   work 'to avoid wounding the
will reserve to himself the ownership of the Land and   'ou il les leur   susceptibilities of his French
employ his Officers or Favourites to cultivate it: or will   cédéra'   friend'. This does not explain
grant the Land to them on condition that they pay for it   b...b: N: why there is also no mention of
an annual Quit Rent or Due: or he will grant it to them   'soient' (R: France in A. Other variations
while reserving his freedom to tax them every year   'soit')   between the texts involving
according to his needs and their capacity. In all these   geographical names also do not
cases these Officers or Favourites, whether absolute   really fit Higgs's explanation.
Owners or Dependents, whether Stewards or Bailiffs   E.g., for an occurrence of
of the produce of the Land, will be few in number in   'Paris' in D that is missing in E,
proportion to all the Inhabitants.   see C242ii, but for an opposite
example, see E/D69.

11 |4| Que si le Prince fait la distribution des Terres par portions égales à tous les Habitans, elles ne laisseront pas dans la suite de tomber en partage à un petit nombre. Un Habitant aura plusieurs Enfans, & ne pourra laisser à chacun d'eux une portion de Terre égale à la sienne: un autre mourra sans Enfans, & laissera sa portion à celui qui en a déja, plutôt qu'à celui qui n'en a pas: un troisieme sera fainéant, extravagant ou maladif, & se verra obligé de vendre sa portion à un autre qui a de la frugalité & de l'industrie, qui augmentera continuellement ses Terres par de nouveaux achats, auxquels il emploiera le travail de ceux, qui [6] n'aïant aucune portion de terre à eux, seront obligés de lui offrir leur travail, pour subsister.

12 |5| Dans le premier établissement de Rome, on donna à chaque Habitant deux Journaux de terre: cela n'empêcha pas qu'il n'y eût bientôt après une inégalité aussi grande dans les patrimoines, que celle que nous voïons aujourd'hui dans tous les Etats de l'Europe. Les Terres tomberent en partage à un petit nombre.

13 |6| En supposant donc que les Terres d'un nouvel état appartiennent à un petit nombre de personnes, chaque Propriétaire fera valoir ses Terres par ses mains, ou les donnera ᵃà un ou plusieursᵃ Fermiers: dans cette œconomie, il faut que les Fermiers ᵇ& Laboureursᵇ trouvent leur subsistance, cela est de necessité indispensable, soit qu'on fasse valoir les Terres pour le [7] compte du Propriétaire même, ou pour celui du Fermier. On donne le surplus du produit de la Terre aux ordres du Propriétaire; celui-ci en donne une partie aux ordres ᶜdu Prince ou de l'Etatᶜ, ou bien le Fermier donnera cette partie directement au Prince, en la rabattant au Propriétaire.

|| Each proprietor manages his own estate, or letts it to one or more farmers, as he thinks fit; and the farmer and his assistants must be maintained out of it, and he pays the proprietor the overplus of the produce of the estate; the proprietor pays the prince what he requires, according to the laws of society enacted or agreed upon for the maintenance of his soldiers, courtiers, armies, &c.

In this Situation, it is natural to suppose the Proprietor of such Lands would at his own proper Charge cultivate them himself, for his own and Family's Advantage; or else he would let them out on Leases to Farmers, in order to have a certain yearly Revenue; such Farmer must retain so much out of the Produce of his Land as would suffice to maintain himself and Family; the Re-[7]mainder must go to the Landlord, and he out of his Revenue must give to his Prince what the Laws of the Community charge him with, to support the Dignity of the State.

Even if the Prince distribute the Land equally among all the Inhabitants it will ultimately be divided among a small number. One man will have several Children and cannot leave to each of them a portion of Land equal to his own; another will die without Children, and will leave his portion to some one who has Land already rather than to one who has none; a third will be lazy, prodigal, or sickly, and be obliged to sell his portion to another who is frugal and industrious, who will continually add to his Estate by new purchases and will employ upon it the Labour of those who having no Land of their own are compelled to offer him their Labour in order to live.

There are counterparts for E11 in D15 and A15. **11**

At the first settlement of Rome each Citizen had two Journaux of Land allotted to him. Yet there was soon after as great an inequality in the estates as that which we see today in all the countries of Europe. The Land was divided among a few owners.

There are counterparts for E12 in D/A16. There the English versions have 'two acres' for '*deux Journaux*', a term Higgs (H12) left untranslated. *Journal* was an old French term originally used to indicate an 'area of land that can be cultivated by a man in a day' (Rey 1998: 1927). In E161 the *journal* is calculated to a little over 0.5 'Paris acres', which equals approximately 0.63 British imperial acres, or 2569 m². Cantillon may also be referring to the similarly sized Roman measurement *jugerum*, which was equivalent to 0.623 acres, or approximately 0.25 ha. Cf. C16ii, C161. Despite the difference in size, the translation of *journal* with 'acre' is consistent with early eighteenth-century practice; see e.g. Boyer, *Dictionnaire Royale François-Anglois et Anglois-François* (1719) who translates a '*journal ou journau*' as an acre of land. Cf. C88i. **12**

Supposing then that the Land of a new country belongs to a small number of persons, each owner will manage his Land himself or let it to one or more Farmers: in this case it is essential that the Farmers and Labourers should have a living whether they cultivate the Land for the Owner or for the Farmer. The overplus of the Land is at the disposition of the Owner: he pays part of it to the Prince or the Government, or else the Farmer does so directly at the Owner's expense.

ᵃ...ᵃ: 1756b, 1769: 'à un ou à plusieurs'
ᵇ...ᵇ: 1756b, 1769: '& les Laboureurs'
ᶜ...ᶜ: R, N: 'du Prince'

i. Higgs translates '*surplus*' with 'overplus' as found in D13; but A13 has 'remainder'. **13**

ii. With regard to V13c the French manuscript versions are closer to D/A13, which also only refer to 'the prince' and not to the state/government.

iii. D13 refers to 'the laws of society', A13 has 'the laws of the Community', E does not have a corresponding phrase.

iv. The phrase 'dignity of the state' in A13 perhaps reminds of the 'grandeur' of the Prince in A6.

v. For the phrase '*dans cette œconomie*' in E13, see C79i.

14 |7| Pour ce qui est de l'usage auquel on doit emploïer la terre, il est préalable d'en emploïer une partie à l'entretien & nourriture de ceux qui y travaillent & la font valoir: le reste dépend principalement des humeurs & de la maniere de vivre du Prince, des Seigneurs de l'Etat & du Propriétaire; s'ils aiment la boisson, ᵃil fautᵃ cultiver des Vignes; s'ils aiment les soieries, ᵇil fautᵇ planter des Meuriers & élever des Vers à soie; & de plus il faut emploïer une partie proportionnée de la terre, à main-[8]tenir tous ceux qu'il faut pour ce travail; s'ils aiment les Chevaux, il faut des Prairies; & ainsi du reste.

The use the land is put to depends upon the humor and fashion of living which the prince and the proprietors follow: if they delight in horses a proportionable quantity of the land must be turned to pasture and meadow; if they are fond of a great number of servants and dependents, a proportionable quantity of the land must be applied to produce wherewithal to maintain them, &c.

This Land will be employed and cultivated, to produce that which answers most to the Taste and Manner of Living of the Times; and the Consumption of this Produce is proportioned to the Demand there is for it; and its Value is ascertained by the Value of the Land, and the Value of the Labour necessarily had for this Produce.

15 || If, upon the first conquest, the lands are divided among all the inhabitants by equal portion, yet they will gradually fall into the hands of a few; one man shall die without issue, and leave his portion to whom he pleases; another shall have several children, and not wherewithal to maintain them, and so they must become dependents on such as have too much land. One man shall be sickly, lazy, or extravagant, and be obliged to sell his portion of land to another, who is frugal and industrious, and this latter shall every year add to his estate.

Let it be supposed, that at the Time of this Conquest the Lands of the Country were equally distributed amongst the Conquerors; this Distribution would not prevent but that in Time these Lands would become the Property of a few Men of Cunning: Art and Oeconomy will acquire the Property of the Unthrifty; these last fall into Want and Dependance; some die without Children, and leave their Substance as they think proper; others leave many Children, and leave their Effects to be divided amongst them: so that by degrees Land comes to be possessed by a few Persons, in proportion to the whole Communty.

16 || Of this we have an instance in the first settlement of the Roman state: each citizen had two acres of land, and yet, soon after, the property of the land fell into few hands.

[8]|| At the first Establishment of *Rome* each Citizen had but two Acres of Land allotted to him, which he was obliged to cultivate for his Subsistence; yet in Process of Time, by the Disposition of some, the Want of Oeconomy in others, great Inequality arose in such Possessions; great Possessions begat Nobility, and Power is the certain Consequence of great Property in Land.

Higgs Translation (H)	Variations and Errata (V)	Comments (C)

As for the use to which the Land should be put, the first necessity is to employ part of it for the Maintenance and Food of those who work upon it and make it productive: the rest depends principally upon the Humour and Fashion of Living of the Prince, the Lords, and the Owner: if these are fond of drink, vines must be cultivated; if they are fond of silks, mulberry-trees must be planted and silkworms raised, and moreover part of the Land must be employed to support those needed for these labours; if they delight in horses, pasture is needed, and so on.

[a]...[a]: R: 'ils font'; N: 'ils feront'

[b]...[b]: R, N: 'ils font'

14 Only A14 already has the observation that the value of produce is determined by (the value of) the land and labour entering production (cf. C65). E first discusses the theory of intrinsic value in E I, x (E63ff.).

15 There is a counterpart for D/A15 in E11.

16 i. There is a counterpart for D/A16 in E12.

ii. The 'first establishment of Rome' refers to the foundation of Rome by Romulus in 752/53BC. The source for the observation that each citizen was given two acres (*bina iugera*) may be Marcus Terentius Varro (116–27BC), *Rerum Rusticarum Libri Tres* or Dionysius of Halicarnassus (60–7BC), *Roman Antiquities*.

17

|| The most ancient accounts we have of the forming societies and states tell us, that they have been formed by conquest; how they stood in the days of the patriarchs is not very clear.

18 |8| Cependant si on ªsupposeª que les Terres n'appartiennent à personne en particulier, il n'est pas facile de concevoir qu'on y puisse former une societé d'Hommes: nous voïons dans les Terres communes, par exemple, d'un Village, qu'on regle le nombre des Bestiaux que chacun des Habitans a la liberté d'y envoïer; & si on laissoit les Terres au premier qui les occuperoit dans une nouvelle conquête, ou découverte d'un Païs, il faudroit toujours revenir à une regle pour en fixer la propriété, pour y pouvoir établir une Societé d'Hommes, soit que la force ou la Police décidât de cette regle.

Higgs Translation (H)	Variations and Errata (V)	Comments (C)

i. Cf. A8 for another mention **17**
of patriarchal times.
ii. Postlethwayt's *Dictionary*
entry 'Labour' continues with
the text reproduced in D78.

If however we suppose that the Land belongs to no one in particular, it is not easy to conceive how a Society of men can be formed there: we see, for example, in the Village Commons a limit fixed to the number of animals that each of the Commoners may put upon them; and if the Land were left to the first occupier in a new conquest or discovery of a country it would always be necessary to fall back upon a law to settle Ownership in order to establish a Society, whether the law rested upon Force or upon Policy.

ᵃ…ᵃ: R, N: 'supposoit'

There is no direct counterpart **18**
for E18 in D or A, although the
case of a 'new conquest' of a
country also occurs in D/A10.

19

[9] **CHAPITRE** ªIIIª.

CHAP. III.

Des Villages.

How Villages may be settled.

20 |1| Quelque emploi qu'on fasse de la Terre, soit pâturage, bled, ªvignesª, il faut que les Fermiers ou Laboureurs, qui en conduisent le travail, résident tout proche; autrement le tems qu'il faudroit pour aller à leurs Champs & revenir à leurs Maisons, consommeroit une trop grande partie de la journée. De ce point dépend la nécessité des Villages répandus ᵇdansᵇ toutes les Campagnes & Terres cultivées, où l'on doit avoir aussi des Maréchaux ᶜ&ᶜ Charons pour les outils, la Charue & les Charettes dont on a besoin; surtout lorsque le Village est éloigné des Bourgs & Villes. La grandeur d'un Village est naturelle-[10]ment proportionnée ᵈenᵈ nombre d'Habitans, à celui que les Terres, qui en dépendent, demandent pour le travail journalier, & à celui des Artisans qui y trouvent assez d'occupation ᵉparᵉ le service des Fermiers & Laboureurs: mais ᶠcesᶠ Artisans ne sont pas tout-à-fait si necessaires dans le voisinage des Villes où les Laboureurs peuvent aller sans perdre beaucoup de tems.

|| To whatever Cultivation Land is put, whether Pasture, Arable, &c. Labourers and Farmers, who undertake to occupy it, ought necessarily to live together near the Place of their Work; otherwise the Time taken in going and coming to and from their Fields, would take up most of the Day; so that the Necessity of establishing Villages in several Parts of the Country, is easily perceived. The Largeness of Villages is naturally proportioned to the Number of Hands wanting for the daily Culture of the Lands in their Neighbourhood:

21 |2| Si un ou plusieurs des Propriétaires des Terres de la dépendance du Village y font leur résidence, le nombre des Habitans sera plus grand, à proportion des Domestiques & Artisans qu'ils y attireront, & des Cabarets qui s'y établiront pour la commodité des Domestiques & Ouvriers qui gagneront leur vie avec ces Propriétaires.

22 |3| Si la Terre n'est propre que pour nourrir des troupeaux de Moutons, comme dans les Du-[11]nes & ªLandesª, les Villages seront plus rares & plus petits, parceque la terre ne demande qu'un petit nombre de Pasteurs.

if the Lands are only [9] proper for maintaining Sheep and black Cattle, few Hands are required. Villages in such Countries will be scarce, and less inhabited, and the Number of Inhabitants in all well cultivated Countries is proportioned to the different kind of Labour necessary for bringing the Produce of Land into Use and Consumption.

Higgs Translation (H)	Variations and Errata (V)	Comments (C)

Chapter III

Of Villages

ᵃ...ᵃ: R, N: '3.ᵉ'

i. There is no counterpart for this chapter or the next **19** three chapters in Postlethwayt's *Universal Dictionary*. But see C47ii.

ii. According to Skinner (1966, I, 56 n1) chapter ix, vol. I of Sir James Steuart's *An Inquiry* (1767) exhibits close parallels with E, I, chapters iii–vi. However, Groenewegen (2001) argues that the parallels are actually with A, chapters 3 to 6.

To whatever cultivation Land is put, whether Pasture, Corn, Vines, etc. the Farmers or Labourers who carry on the work must live near at hand; otherwise the time taken in going to their Fields and returning to their Houses would take up too much of the day. Hence the necessity for Villages established in all the country and cultivated Land, where there must also be enough Farriers and Wheelwrights for the Instruments, Ploughs, and Carts which are needed; especially when the Village is at a distance from the Towns. The size of a Village is naturally proportioned in number of inhabitants to what the Land dependent on it requires for daily work, and to the Artisans who find enough employment there in the service of the Farmers and Labourers: but these Artisans are not quite so necessary in the neighbourhood of Towns to which the Labourers can resort without much loss of time.

ᵃ...ᵃ: R, N: 'vignes &c'
ᵇ...ᵇ: R, N: 'par'
ᶜ...ᶜ: R, N: ', des'
ᵈ...ᵈ: R: the words 'en' and 'au' are written on top of each other; N: 'au'
ᵉ...ᵉ: R, N: 'pour'
ᶠ...ᶠ: R: 'les' (N: 'ces')

i. Higgs adds 'etc.' in the first sentence, **20** which happens to agree with V20a, but is possibly due to his following of A20.

ii. The second sentence of E20 appears to be paraphrasing Daniel Defoe *A Plan of the English commerce* (1728: 22–23): 'Fifty Families of Farmers must *necessarily* find Work for a Smith or *Farrier* to Shoe their Horses, and at least two *Wheel-wrights* to make and repair their *Carts*, Waggons, *Plows*, Harrows, &c.' (compare especially the italicised words). For the significance of this apparent borrowing see C29.

If one or more of the owners of the Land dependent on the Village reside there the number of inhabitants will be greater in proportion to the domestic servants and artisans drawn thither, and the inns which will be established there for the convenience of the domestic servants and workmen who are maintained by the Landlords.

Defoe (1728: 28): 'The Town going thus **21** forward, ..., comes an honest Victualler, and he sets up an Ale-house; ... he enlarges his Building, and makes his little Ale-house into a good Inn, and a second follows him, and then a third.'

If the Lands are only proper for maintaining Sheep, as in the sandy districts and moorlands, the Villages will be fewer and smaller since only a few shepherds are required on the land.

ᵃ...ᵃ: N: 'les landes' (R: 'Landes')

Only A22 mentions black cattle. This **22** is a reference to specifically British lifestock since the term black cattle was used to indicate native Welsh and Cornish cattle varieties.

23 |4| Si la Terre ne produit que des bois, ᵃdans des Terres sabloneuses, où il ne croît point d'herbeᵃ pour la nourriture des Bestiaux, & ᵇsi elleᵇ est éloignée des Villes & Rivieres, ce qui rend ces bois inutiles pour la consommation, comme l'on en voit plusieurs en Allemagne, il n'y aura de Maisons & Villages qu'autant qu'il en faut pour recueillir les Glands, & nourrir des Cochons dans la saison: mais si la Terre est entierement stérile, il n'y aura ni Villages ni Habitans

If the Lands only produce Woods in sandy soils where there is no grass for beasts, and if they are distant from Towns and Rivers which makes the timber useless for consumption as one sees in many cases in Germany, there will be only so many Houses and Villages as are needed to gather Acorns and feed Pigs in season: but if the Lands are altogether barren there will be neither Villages nor Inhabitants.

^a...^a: R, N: '(dans les terres sabloneuses) qui ne produit point dherbe'

^b...^b: R, N:'qui'

23

24   [12] **CHAPITRE** [a]**IV**[a].

Des Bourgs.

25 |1| Il y a des Villages où l'on a érigé des Marchés, par le crédit de quelque Propriétaire ou Seigneur en Cour. Ces Marchés, qui se tiennent une ou deux fois la semaine, encouragent plusieurs petits Entrepreneurs & Marchands de s'établir dans ce lieu; ou ils achetent au Marché les denrées qu'on y apporte des Villages d'alentour, pour les transporter & vendre dans les Villes; ils [a]prennent[a] en échange dans la Ville, du fer, du sel, du sucre & d'autres marchandises, qu'on vend, les jours de Marché, aux Habitans des Villages: on voit aussi plusieurs petits Artisans s'établir dans ces lieux, [b]comme des Serruriers[b], Menui-[13]siers & autres, pour les besoins des Villageois qui n'en ont pas dans leurs Villages, & enfin [c]ces[c] Villages deviennent des Bourgs. Un Bourg étant placé comme dans le centre des Villages, dont les Habitans [d]viennent[d] au Marché, il est plus naturel & plus facile que les [e]Villageois[e] y apportent leurs denrées les jours de Marché pour les y vendre, & qu'ils y achetent les marchandises dont ils ont besoin, que de voir porter ces marchandises par les Marchands & Entrepreneurs dans les Villages, pour y [f]recevoir[f] en échange les denrées des Villageois. 1°. Les circuits des Marchands dans les Villages multiplieroient la dépense des Voitures, sans necessité. 2°. Ces Marchands seroient peut-être obligés d'aller dans plusieurs Villages [g]avant que de[g] trouver la qualité & la quantité des denrées qu'ils veulent acheter. 3°. Les [14] Villageois seroient le plus souvent aux champs lors de l'arrivée de ces Marchands, &, ne sachant quelles especes de denrées il leur faudroit, ils n'auroient rien de prêt & en état. 4°. Il seroit presqu'impossible de fixer le prix des denrées & des marchandises dans les Villages, [h]entre ces Marchands & les Villageois[h]. Le Marchand refuseroit dans un Village le prix qu'on lui demande de la denrée, dans l'espérance de la trouver à meilleur marché dans un autre Village, & le Villageois refuseroit le prix que le Marchand lui offre de sa marchandise, dans l'espérance qu'un autre Marchand qui viendra, la prendra à meilleur [i]compte[i].

|| In Countries where Villages are settled, there are by the Interest of some considerable Proprietors of the Land, Charters obtained for holding once or twice a Week Markets; the Places where Markets are kept or held, are called Market Towns; at which Places People meet, and those of middling Fortunes find their Convenience to reside in, not having Substance sufficient to support the Expence of Cities; and in such Towns there are generally established Shopkeepers, Factors, and Retailers, who exchange the Goods and Merchandize of Cities for the Produce of the Land, with the Inhabitants of several Vil-[10]lages in the Neighbourhood. The Chapmen who make it their Business to buy the Produce of the Farmers Industry, assemble once or twice a Week at these Market Towns, to which Places it is more natural, that Farmers should bring the Produce of the Land, as being a certain Market or Place to find Vent, than that Chapmen should go about the Country, where they could not well agree for the Purchase of what they wanted:

Chapter IV

Of Market Towns

There are some Villages where Markets have been established by the interest of some Proprietor or Gentleman at Court. These Markets, held once or twice a week, encourage several little Undertakers and Merchants to set themselves up there. They buy in the Market the products brought from the surrounding Villages in order to carry them to the large Towns for sale. In the large Towns they exchange them for Iron, Salt, Sugar and other merchandise which they sell on market-days to the Villagers. Many small Artisans also, like Locksmiths, Cabinet makers and others, settle down for the service of the Villagers who have none in their Villages, and at length these Villages become Market Towns. A Market Town being placed in the centre of the Villages whose people come to market, it is more natural and easy that the Villagers should bring their products thither for sale on market-days and buy the articles they need, than that the Merchants and Factors should transport them to the Villages in exchange for their products. (1) For the Merchants to go round the Villages would unnecessarily increase the cost of carriage. (2) The Merchants would perhaps be obliged to go to several Villages before finding the quality and quantity of produce which they wished to buy. (3) The Villagers would generally be in their fields when the Merchants arrived and not knowing what produce these needed would have nothing prepared and fit for sale. (4) It would be almost impossible to fix the price of the produce and the merchandise in the Villages, between the Merchants and the Villagers. In one Village the Merchant would refuse the price asked for produce, hoping to find it cheaper in another Village, and the Villager would refuse the price offered for his merchandise in the hope that another Merchant would come along and take it on better terms.

[a]...[a]: R, N: '4.[e]'

[a]...[a]: R: 'achettent'; N: 'achetent'
[b]...[b]: R, N: 'comme Serruriers'
[c]...[c]: N: 'les' (R: 'Ces')
[d]...[d]: R, N: 'mènent'
[e]...[e]: R, N: 'Villages'
[f]...[f]: R: 'achetter'; N: 'acheter'
[g]...[g]: R, N: 'avant de'
[h]...[h]: R, N: missing
[i]...[i]: R: 'conte' (N: 'compte').

There is no counterpart for this chapter in Postlethwayt's *Universal Dictionary*. **24**

i. The term 'chapman' was used primarily to indicate itinerant merchants. They are contrasted in A with 'Shopkeepers, Factors and Retailers', who are settled merchants. **25**

ii. Cf. the phrase in E and A that markets are held 'once or twice a week' with the penultimate sentence of A30. That sentence paraphrases Defoe (1728: 25–26): 'after some Time, the Lords of the Manors, to carry on the Improvement, get a Patent for a Market once a Week, and a Fair perhaps twice a Year, or oftner as there is Occasion'. Note that, like Defoe, E and A both mention the involvement of local authorities with the establishment of markets. Cf. C29.

iii. Following A25, Higgs translates the phrase '*par le crédit*' in E25 with 'by the interest', although it could perhaps be better translated with 'through the influence'.

iv. For other references to people of 'middling fortunes' (A25) see A32, A599, A600 and D369.

v. The term *entrepreneur* is used for the first time in E25. For this term and its synonyms, see C119iii.

vi. The term 'Vent' in A25 is also used in A206 and D261. Even though it was more commonly used in the economic literature of the time, it is perhaps reminiscent of Locke (1692: 78): 'Vent is nothing else but the passing of Commodities from one owner to another in Exchange.' Law (1705: 5) criticised Locke for using 'Vent' instead of 'Demand', because '[t]he Vent of Goods cannot be greater than the Quantity, but the Demand may be greater …. So the Prices of Goods are not according to the Quantity in Proportion to the Vent, but in proportion to the Demand.' Cf. C206i and C237i.

26 |2| On évite tous ces inconvéniens lorsque les Villageois viennent les jours de Marché au Bourg, pour y vendre leurs denrées, & y acheter les marchandises dont [15] ils ont besoin. Les prix s'y fixent par la proportion des denrées qu'on y ªexposeª en vente & de l'argent qu'on y offre pour les acheter; cela se passe dans la même place, sous les yeux de tous les Villageois de différens Villages, & des Marchands ou Entrepreneurs du Bourg. Lorsque le prix a été déterminé avec quelques-uns, les autres suivent sans difficulté, & l'on constate ainsi le prix du Marché de ce jour-là. Le Païsan retourne dans son Village & reprend son travail.

The Market being the Centre where the Produce of the Land is proportioned to the Demand, and where the Prices of each particular Species of Goods is determined and fixed for that Day, by the different movements of the Buyers and Sellers at Market, and the Money in the Hands of such Buyers, and its Want to the Sellers.

27 |3| La grandeur du Bourg est naturellement proportionnée au nombre des Fermiers & Laboureurs qu'il faut pour cultiver les Terres qui en dépendent, & au nombre des Artisans & petits Marchands que les Villages du ressort de ce Bourg emploient, avec leurs Assistans & Chevaux, & enfin au nombre des personnes que les Propriétaires des Ter-[16]res qui y résident y font vivre.

28 |4| Lorsque les Villages du ressort d'un Bourg (c'est-à-dire dont les Habitans portent ordinairement leurs denrées au Marché de ce Bourg) sont considérables, ils ont beaucoup de produit, le Bourg deviendra considérable & gros à proportion; mais lorsque les Villages d'alentour ont peu de produit, le Bourg est aussi-bien pauvre ª& chétifª.

29

From the Manner in which Towns may be established, may be seen how the several Parts of the Community are connected together, the mutual Dependance of each Individual on the Whole, and how Trade nourishes each other; let it be supposed that a certain District of Land is granted by the King to fifty Persons, on Condition that each of them bring in a Stock of three hundred Pounds, and there settle; to each of these Farmers there is granted three hundred Acres [11] of Virgin-Land, good in Nature and well cleared, besides a Grant of Timber and other Materials for building Houses, Barns, Stables, and other Out-Houses at the King's Expence, and Rent-free for fifty Years, but on Condition that at the Expiration of that Time these Lands shall return to the Crown, or a certain stipulated Rent be paid yearly for them.

All these difficulties are avoided when the Villagers come to Town on Market-Days to sell their produce and to buy the things they need. Prices are fixed by the proportion between the produce exposed for sale and the money offered for it; this takes place in the same spot, under the eyes of all the Villagers of different Villages and of the Merchants or Undertakers of the Town. When the price has been settled between a few the others follow without difficulty and so the Market-price of the day is determined. The peasant goes back to his Village and resumes his work.

The size of the Market Town is naturally proportioned to the number of Farmers and Labourers needed to cultivate the Lands dependent on it, and to the number of artisans and small Merchants that the Villages bordering on the Market Town employ with their assistants and horses, and finally to the number of persons whom the Landowners resident there support.

When the Villages belonging to a Market Town (i.e. whose people ordinarily bring their produce to market there) are considerable and have a large output the Market Town will become considerable and large in proportion; but when the neighbouring Villages have little produce the Market Town also is poor and insignificant.

ᵃ...ᵃ: R: 'offrent'; N: 'offre'

ᵃ...ᵃ: N: 'et bien chetif' (R: 'et Chetif')

26 E/A26 anticipate the longer discussions in E/D/A239ff. Here there is already a hint at the differences in the descriptions of the market process, which is more pronounced in the later passages. Cf. C241ii.

27

28

29 A29 and A30 develop similar basic ideas of the mutual relations between market towns and their hinterland to E27 and E28. The paragraphs in A are in fact a pared-back version of pp. 20–26 of Daniel Defoe's *A Plan of the English commerce* (1728). The interesting question here is whether Philip Cantillon added these passages to a manuscript of Richard's or whether they were part of that manuscript. A few additional phrases in the French text that are reminiscent of what Defoe writes (see C20ii, C21 and C25ii) suggest that Richard Cantillon was familiar with *A Plan*. The passages in A29/A30 may then reflect a distinct influence of Defoe on Cantillon in an earlier draft of his work. See C139i for another parallel with Defoe (1728).

30

|| Thus fifty Farmers with their Families may be brought together to live within themselves, in a kind of Circle, with every one a good Farm to manage Rent-free; their Houses erected at the Extremities of their respective Farms, so as towards the Centre to leave a large Piece of Ground, which was reserved to the Crown for building a Town; and a public Proclamation is made, that whosoever should come and build on that vacant Ground, should have a certain Proportion thereof, according to the Size of the House he should build, as also for an Orchard and Garden, also Timber and other Materials for his building, all Rent-free and at the Crown's Expence, but all upon the Conditions and Stipulations before mentioned. The Farmers with their Wives, Children, and Servants, being first established, this would naturally invite two, three, or more Butchers [12] to set up among them, to supply Meat; two or more Barbers, two or more Taylors, two or more Blacksmiths, two or more Bakers; some Wheelwrights, one or two Ironmongers, a Shoemaker or two, as many Coblers, a Collar-maker or two, a Glover, a Ropemaker, two or three Master Carpenters with their Journeymen and Servants, eight or ten Lawyers, two or three Master Bricklayers with their Journeymen and Servants. A Town thus established, many other Trades would come to reside there; the Church would have a Place of Worship; all which prove that the Concourse of Tradesmen follow the Concourse of People; the Grocer, the Haberdasher of Hats, the Draper and Milliner, would pay it a Visit, and there finding Encouragement, and a Probability of Sale for their Goods, would build or take Houses and settle there. A Market would be established for once or twice a Week, and a Fair for once or twice a Year; and thus People would Trade. Trade builds Towns, and produces every temporal Good and Advantage to a Kingdom if rightly applied.

i. There can be no doubt that this passage is **30** inspired by Defoe's account (see C29). The similarities run to such an extent that one may even correct the out of place occurrence of 'eight or ten Lawyers' in A30 to 'eight or ten Sawyers', because, in a similar list of menial professions, Defoe (1728: 23) has: 'five or six Pair of Sawyers'.

ii. The interesting spatial image of the formation of a town in the centre of surrounding lands does not have a very clear counterpart in E, although it is perhaps hinted at in the statement that a market town is 'placed in the centre of the Villages whose people come to market' (E25).

iii. There is, however, a clearer evocation of the same idea in D283: 'if we suppose this land-proprietor and several others to live together *in the common center of their lands*, where they form a city, and draw thither most of the undertakers and tradesmen' (emphasis added). It is not impossible that Postlethwayt, who quotes other works of Defoe in his *Universal Dictionary*, borrowed this notion straight from the latter's *Plan*. However, the context suggests it is more likely that the sentence occurred in the manuscript of Cantillon's work that Postlethwayt had in his hands. This would therefore be an additional indication that Richard Cantillon knew Defoe's *Plan*. Cf. C29.

31 CHAPITRE ᵃVᵃ.

[13] **CHAP. V.**

Des Villes.

How Cities may be established.

32 |1| Les Propriétaires qui n'ont que de petites portions de Terre vivent ordinairement dans les Bourgs & Villages, proche de leurs Terres & Fermiers. Le transport des denrées qui leur en reviennent, dans les Villes [17] éloignées, les mettroit hors d'état de vivre commodément dans ces Villes. Mais les Propriétaires qui ont plusieurs grandes Terres ont le moïen d'aller résider loin de leurs Terres, pour jouir d'une agréable société, avec d'autres Propriétaires & Seigneurs de même espece.

|| As People of middling Fortunes take up their Residence in Market Towns, so those who have the Means of living with Ease and Splendor, generally fix together for the Pleasure and Advantage of an agreeable Society.

33 |2| Si un Prince ou Seigneur, qui a reçu de grandes concessions de Terres lors de la conquête ou découverte d'un Païs, fixe sa demeure dans quelque lieu agréable, & si plusieurs autres Seigneurs y viennent faire leur résidence pour être à portée de se voir souvent, & jouir d'une société agréable, ce lieu deviendra une Ville: on y bâtira de grandes Maisons pour la demeure des Seigneurs en question; on y en bâtira une infinité d'autres pour les Marchands, les Artisans, & Gens de toutes sortes de professions, que la résidence [18] de ces Seigneurs attirera dans ce lieu. Il faudra pour le service de ces Seigneurs, des Boulangers, des Bouchers, des Brasseurs, des Marchands de vin, des Fabriquans de toutes especes: ces Entrepreneurs bâtiront des Maisons dans le lieu en question, ou loueront des Maisons bâties par d'autres Entrepreneurs. Il n'y a pas de grand Seigneur dont la dépense pour sa Maison, son train & ses Domestiques, ᵃn'entretienneᵃ des Marchands & Artisans de toutes especes, comme on peut le voir par les calculs particuliers que j'ai ᵇfaitᵇ faire dans le Supplément de cet Essai.

These Places where People of large Fortunes reside, are called Cities; there the Rich govern, and Markets are daily kept for the Convenience of the Rich, to supply not only their Necessities, but also their Luxury and Grandeur. Encouragement is given to all Sorts of Manufacturers and Artizans to come and reside there, whose Numbers are proportioned to the Necessities of the Rich, their Taste for Luxury and Extravagance; and the Price of things is governed by the Money which the Rich have to support or squander away in their Riot, Luxury and Extravagance.

Chapter V

31

Of Cities

The Landlords who have only small estates usually reside in Market Towns and Villages near their Land and Farmers. The transport of the produce they derive from them into distant Cities would not enable them to live comfortably there. But the Landlords who have several large estates have the means to go and live at a distance from them to enjoy agreeable society with other Landowners and Gentlemen of the same condition.

For phrases similar to 'People of middling Fortunes' (in A32) see C25iv.

32

If a Prince or Nobleman who has received large grants of Land on the conquest or discovery of a country fixes his residence in some pleasant spot, and several other Noblemen come to live there to be within reach of seeing each other frequently and enjoying agreeable society, this place will become a City. Great houses will be built there for the Noblemen in question, and an infinity of others for the Merchants, Artisans, and people of all sorts of professions whom the residence of these Noblemen will attract thither. For the service of these Noblemen, Bakers, Butchers, Brewers, Wine Merchants, Manufacturers of all kinds, will be needed. These will build houses in the locality or will rent houses built by others. There is no great Nobleman whose expense upon his house, his retinue and Servants, does not maintain Merchants and Artisans of all kinds, as may be seen from the detailed calculations which I have caused to be made in the Supplement of this Essay.

ᵃ…ᵃ: R, N: 'n'entretiennent'
ᵇ…ᵇ: R: 'faits'; N: 'fais'

i. There is a greater emphasis in A33 than in E33 on the extravagance of the rich.

ii. In E33 there is the first mention of the Supplement. Other references to this missing part are in E66, E67, E88, E158, E168, E184 and E193.

iii. Not only is there no mention of a supplement anywhere in A, but in all other places where E refers to this lost part, A does not even have a counterpart paragraph. For a possible explanation, see C561i.

iv. In several cases D does have counterparts for paragraphs in E that mention the Supplement (D66, D67, D88, D184). While the calculations presented are similar to those in E, references to a supplement are missing. See C66i.

33

34 |3| Comme tous ᵃcesᵃ Artisans & Entrepreneurs se servent mutuellement, aussi-bien que les Seigneurs en droiture, on ne s'apperçoit pas que l'entretien des uns & des autres tombe finalement sur les Seigneurs & Propriétaires des Terres. On ne [19] s'apperçoit pas que toutes les petites Maisons dans une Ville, telle qu'on la décrit ici, dépendent & subsistent de la dépense des grandes Maisons. On fera cependant voir dans la suite, que tous les Ordres & Habitans d'un Etat subsistent au dépens des Propriétaires des Terres. La Ville en question s'agrandira encore, si le Roi ou le Gouvernement y établit des Cours de Justice, auxquelles les Habitans des Bourgs & Villages de la Province doivent avoir recours. Il faudra une augmentation d'entrepreneurs ᵇ& d'artisansᵇ de toutes sortes, pour l'entretien des Gens de Justice & des Plaideurs.

35 |4| Si l'on établit dans ᵃcette même Villeᵃ des Ouvrages & Manufactures au-delà de la consommation intérieure, pour les transporter & vendre chez l'Etranger, elle sera grande à proportion des Ouvriers & Artisans qui y sub-[20]sistent aux dépens de l'Etranger.

36 |5| Mais si nous écartons ᵃcesᵃ idées pour ne point embrouiller ᵇnotreᵇ sujet, on peut dire que l'assemblage de plusieurs riches Propriétaires de Terres, qui résident ensemble dans un même lieu, suffit pour former ce qu'on appelle une Ville, & que plusieurs Villes en Europe, dans l'intérieur des Terres, doivent le nombre de leurs Habitans à cet assemblage: auquel cas, la grandeur d'une Ville est naturellement proportionnée au nombre des Propriétaires des Terres, qui y résident, ou plutôt au produit des Terres qui leur appartiennent, en rabattant les frais du transport à ceux dont les Terres en sont les plus éloignées, & la part qu'ils sont obligés de fournir au Roi ou à l'Etat, qui doit ordinairement être consommée dans la Capitale.

The Polity or civil Government which is necessary in a large Community or Society, is found in Cities, as also the Administration of Justice: where this is established, thither People of all Ranks resort in order to have them-[14]selves righted by the Laws of the State, when aggrieved by any body with whom they had Dealings; it is from thence, particuar Magistrates take their Progress to the different Parts of the Kingdom, for the Ease and Convenience of its respective Inhabitants, in order to administer Justice in pursuance of the established and known Laws of the Land.

Cities ought to be built near Rivers for the Convenience of Water-carriage; it is there the Produce of the Land for many Miles about, is consumed. The Grandeur and Riches of a City are proportioned to the Proprietors of large Fortunes, who reside there; except in Cities where considerable Manufactures are established, and where more Goods are fabricated than what are consumed by the Inhabitants, in order to be exported abroad.

As all these Artisans and Undertakers serve each other as well as the Nobility it is overlooked that the upkeep of them all falls ultimately on the Nobles and Landowners. It is not perceived that all the little houses in a City such as we have described depend upon and subsist at the expense of the great houses. It will, however, be shown later that all the classes and inhabitants of a state live at the expense of the Proprietors of Land. The City in question will increase still further if the King or the Government establish in it Law Courts to which the people of the Market Towns and Villages of the province must have recourse. An increase of Undertakers and Artisans of every sort will be needed for the service of the legal officials and Lawyers.

ᵃ...ᵃ: N: 'les' (R:'ces')
ᵇ...ᵇ: R, N: 'et artisans'

i. The reference in E34 to a later discussion of the point that all orders depend on the expense of the landlords is particularly to E I, xii (E106–E117). **34**

ii. Even though in A34 there is no similar reference to a later discussion, *Analysis* chapter XXI (A106–A117) does in fact offer this discussion.

iii. It is worth noting that D lacks both this chapter and the later chapter that develops this point. Hence in D the spending of the landlords as the ultimate source of expenditure appears to be less prominent, but that may be because Postlethwayt omitted fragments in which that point was made.

If in this same City workshops and manufactories be set up apart from home consumption for export and sale abroad, the City will be large in proportion to the Workmen and Artisans who live there at the expense of the foreigner.

ᵃ...ᵃ: R, N: 'cette ville'

i. Cf. the observation in A35 that the wealth of a city is proportioned to the rich proprietors who reside there with E36. **35**

ii. Cf. A35 with Steuart 1767, I, ix (1766: I, 58–59): 'The best rule therefore is, to set down such manufactures upon the banks of navigable rivers .... From the establishment of manufactures we see hamlets swell into villages, towns, and cities.'

But if we put aside these considerations so as not to complicate our subject, we may say that the assemblage of several rich Landowners living together in the same place suffices to form what is called a City, and that many Cities in Europe, in the interior of the country, owe the number of their inhabitants to this assemblage: in which case the size of a City is naturally proportioned to the number of Landlords who live there, or rather to the produce of the Land which belongs to them after deduction of the cost of carriage to those whose Land is the furthest removed, and the part which they are obliged to furnish to the King or the Government, which is usually consumed in the Capital.

ᵃ...ᵃ: R: 'nos'; N: 'nos' and replaced with: 'ces'
ᵇ...ᵇ: R, N: 'ce'

i. This paragraph is missing in A. It appears to be inspired by the 'methodological' remark at the start that consideration of foreign trade should be put aside for now. **36**

ii. Quesnay quotes most of E36 and some of E38 in the *Encyclopédie* article 'Grains' of 1757 (see Quesnay 2005: 185). It is Quesnay's only direct reference to Cantillon. However, the latter's influence on the founder of the physiocratic school was more significant than this single acknowledgment suggests. See C273ii.

37   [21] **CHAPITRE** [a]**VI**[a].   **CHAP. VI.**

Des Villes capitales   *How a Capital City may be established.*

38 |1| Une Capitale se forme de la même maniere qu'une Ville [a]de province[a]; avec cette différence, que les plus gros Propriétaires des Terres [b]de tout l'Etat[b] résident dans la Capitale; que le Roi ou le Gouvernement suprême y fait sa demeure, & y dépense les revenus de l'Etat; que les Cours de Justice en dernier ressort y résident; que c'est ici le centre des Modes que toutes les Provinces prennent pour modele; que les Propriétaires des Terres, qui résident dans les Provinces, ne laissent pas de venir quelquefois passer quelque tems dans la Capitale, & d'y envoïer leurs Enfans pour les façonner. Ainsi toutes les Terres [22] de l'Etat contribuent plus ou moins à la subsistance des Habitans de la Capitale.

|| A Capital City is of the same Nature with another City, except that the Prince or supreme Magistrate resides and spends his Revenue there; it is there the last Appeal to [15] Justice is found, and where the Rich, and the most powerful of the State assemble. It is at the Capital of a Kingdom, that the Modes and Fashions of Living and Dress are shewn, and from thence followed and imitated by the rest of the Community;

39 |2| Si un Souverain quitte une Ville pour faire sa résidence dans une autre, la Noblesse ne manquera pas de le suivre, & de faire sa résidence avec lui dans la nouvelle Ville, qui deviendra grande & considérable aux dépens de la premiere. Nous en avons un exemple tout récent dans la Ville de Petersbourg, au désavantage de Moscou; [a]& l'on voit[a] beaucoup de Villes anciennes, qui étoient considérables, tomber en ruine, & d'autres renaître de leurs débris. On construit ordinairement les grandes Villes sur le bord de la Mer ou des grandes Rivieres, pour la commodité des transports; parce-que le transport [b]par eau[b], des denrées & marchandises nécessaires pour la subsistance & commodité des Habitans[c], est [d]à bien[d] [23] meilleur marché, que [e]les voitures & transport[e] par terre.

it has been found by Experience that a Prince retiring from his Capital to reside elsewhere, has impoverished the Capital, and enriched the Place he went to, for the Train and Number of rich People who must follow the Prince's Court is so great, that the Expence which was formerly laid out at the Capital, must in this Case, be laid out elsewhere, and which, by so much, must [f]impverish[f] the Capital and enrich that Place where the Court is kept.

Chapter VI

Of Capital Cities

A Capital City is formed in the same way as a Provincial City with this difference that the largest Landowners in all the State reside in the Capital, that the king or supreme Government is fixed in it and spends there the government revenue, that the Supreme Courts of Justice are fixed there, that it is the centre of the fashions which all the provinces take for a model, that the Landowners who reside in the provinces do not fail to come occasionally to pass some time in the Capital and to send their children thither to be polished. Thus all the Lands in the State contribute more or less to maintain those who dwell in the Capital.

ᵃ...ᵃ: R, N: 'provincialle'
ᵇ...ᵇ: R, N: 'de l'etat'

38

If a Sovereign quits a City to take up his abode in another the Nobility will not fail to follow him and to make its residence with him in the new City which will become great and important at the expense of the first. We have seen quite a recent example of this in the City of Petersburg to the disadvantage of Moscow, and one sees many old Cities which were important fall into ruin and others spring from their ashes. Great Cities are usually built on the seacoast or on the banks of large Rivers for the convenience of transport; because water-carriage of the produce and merchandise necessary for the subsistence and comfort of the inhabitants is much cheaper than Carriages and Land Transport.

ᵃ...ᵃ: R: 'et on voy'; N: 'et on voit'
ᵇ...ᵇ: R, N: 'par eau' occurs at c instead.
ᵈ...ᵈ: R, N: 'bien a'
ᵉ...ᵉ: R, N: 'les voitures'
ᶠ...f: *sic*

i. Peter the Great's decision, only mentioned in E39, to move the capital from Moscow to St Petersburg was made in 1712.

ii. The last sentence in E39 about the location of cities near water is similar to a point made in A35. Also cf. E329.

iii. Cf. this last sentence in E39 with Smith (1776, I, iii, 3): 'it is upon the sea-coast, and along the banks of navigable rivers, that industry of every kind naturally begins to subdivide and improve itself' (also see Smith 1776, III, iii, 13). However, these passages in Smith may equally owe something to Steuart (1767), who in turn appears to depend on A35. See C35ii.

39

40 **CHAPITRE ᵃVIIᵃ.**	[II, 1, col. 1] *REMARKS*	**CHAP. VII.**
Le travail d'un Laboureur vaut moins que celui d'un Artisan.	*on LABOUR in general, in relation to the natural price thereof.*	‖ *The Labour of the Plowman is of less Value, than ᵇ~~than~~ᵇ that of the Handicrafts-Man, and the Reason why it is so.*

41 |1| ᵃLe Filsᵃ d'un Laboureur, à l'âge ᵇde sept ou douzeᵇ ans, commence à aider son Pere, soit à garder les troupeaux, soit à remuer la terre, soit à d'autres ouvrages de la Campagne, qui ne demandent point d'art ni d'habileté.

‖ A labourer's son, from 7 and 12 years of age, becomes an assistant to his father, either in keeping the flocks, or manuring the ground, or in other sorts of country labour, which require no art or skill.

The Son of a Husbandman at seven Years of Age, begins to help his Father, either as a Sheperd to attend his Flocks, the Plough, or any other Country Business, [16] which does not require Ingenuity or Art.

42 |2| Si son Pere lui faisoit apprendre un métier, il perdroit à son absence pendant tout le tems de son apprentissage, & seroit encore obligé de païer son entretien & les frais de son apprentissage pendant plusieurs années: ˙voilà donc un Fils à charge à son Pere, & dont le travail ne rap-[24]porte aucun avantage qu'au bout d'un certain nombre d'années. La vie d'un Homme n'est calculée qu'à dix ou douze années; & comme on en perd plusieurs à apprendre un métier, dont la plupart demandent en Angleterre sept années d'apprentissage, ᵃunᵃ Laboureur ne voudroit jamais en faire ᵇapprendre aucun àᵇ son Fils, si les Gens de métier ne gagnoient bien plus que les Laboureurs.

‖ But, if his father puts him to a trade, he is at some expence for it, and loses his assistance besides, during the time of his apprenticeship: and, as the life of a man is commonly calculated but 10 or 12 years, his wages as a servant, mechanic, or manufacturer, must exceed his wages as a labourer, in proportion to the expence he is at, and the risque he may run in such servitude. This shews why such servant ought to earn more than a common labourer.

If the Farmer puts his Son out to a Trade, he loses his Assistance all the Time of his Apprenticeship, and is necessitated to cloath him, and perhaps obliged to advance some Money to his Master for teaching him his Trade; therefore it is natural for the Farmer to expect that his Son has a moral Certainty, by his Work at the Trade he is put to, of Earning more Money than he would be able to get by following the Plough, or other Country Business; and the more so, as the true Computation of the Life of Man is no more than ten to twelve Years Purchase. This is the Reason why the Handicrafts-Man ought, and in Fact does earn more than the Country Ploughman and Labourer: Money and Time must be had to learn a Trade.

43 |3| Ceux ᵃdoncᵃ, qui emploient des Artisans ou Gens de métier, doivent nécessairement ᵇpaïer leur travail, plus hautᵇ que celui d'un Laboureur ou ᶜManœuvre; & ce travailᶜ sera nécessairement cher, à proportion du tems qu'on perd à l'apprendre, & de la dépense & du risque qu'il faut pour s'y perfectionner.

44 |4| Les Gens de métier eux-mêmes ne font pas apprendre le leur à tous leurs Enfans; il y en au-[25]roit trop pour le besoin qu'on en a dans une Ville, ou un État, il s'en trouveroit beaucoup qui n'auroient ᵃpoint assezᵃ d'ouvrage; cependant ce travail est toujours naturellement plus cher que celui des Laboureurs.

Chapter VII

The Labour of the Husbandman
is of less Value than that of the
Handicrafts-Man

ᵃ...ᵃ: R, N: '7.ᵉ'
ᵇ...ᵇ: The deletion in A40 of
the second 'than' (by hand
in the copy of the Goldsmith
Library, London) in is
according to the instruction
on the errata page.

D40 is the title of a subsection **40**
of the entry 'Labour', *Universal*
Dictionary (vol. II, pp. 1–7). This
title appears to be Postlethwayt's.
For a dating of the first publication
of this fragment see C7.

A Labourer's Son at seven or twelve
years of age begins to help his Father
either in keeping the Flocks, digging
the ground, or in other sorts of Country
Labour which require no Art or Skill.

ᵃ...ᵃ: N starts with a
repetition of the title: 'Le
travail d'un Laboureur
vaut moins que celui d'un
Artisan. Le Fils'
ᵇ...ᵇ: R, N: 'de 7 a 12'

Note the variations with respect to **41**
the age range during which sons are
assumed to start working. E41 has
'at seven *or* twelve'; R and N: 'from
7 *to* 12'; D41: 'from 7 *and* 12' and
A41 does not mention the upper age.

If his Father puts him to a Trade
he loses his Assistance during
the Time of his Apprenticeship
and is necessitated to cloath
him and to pay the expenses
of his Apprenticeship for
some years. The Son is thus
an expense to this Father
and his Labour brings in no
advantage till the end of some
years. The [working] life of
Man is estimated but at 10 or
12 years, and as several are
lost in learning a Trade most
of which in England require
seven years of Apprenticeship,
a Husbandman would never be
willing to have a Trade taught
to his Son if the Mechanics
did not earn more than the
Husbandmen.

* at this point
the manuscript
AN M780, here
denoted with
M, starts. The
first sentence is
especially hard to
read because it is
crossed through.
ᵃ...ᵃ: R, M, N: 'le'
ᵇ...ᵇ: R,M,N:
'apprendre a'

i. Only A42 has '10 to 12 *years purchase*'. For the **42**
significance of this phrase see C80ii.
ii. Only D42 mentions the 'risque' the son runs
during the period of his apprenticeship.
iii. In light of i and ii it appears that Harris (1757,
I, i, p. 13) is paraphrasing D42 when he writes: 'To
bring up a child to a trade, there is not only expence
in fitting him out, and during his apprenticeship, but
also a risque of his dying before he is out of his times;
from which considerations a mechanic is entitled to
better wages than a common labourer.' Cf. C67iv.
iv. For his part, Smith appears to be paraphrasing
A42 in his *Lectures on Jurisprudence* of 1762–63
where it reads: 'Now the life of a young man when he
leaves his apprenticeship is worth at most but about 10
or 12 years purchase. His wages therefore afterwards
must be such as will not only maintain him, but will
in ten or 12 years time repay him this expence of his
education' (Smith 1978 (A) vi, 60). Cf. Smith (1978
(B), 225) and Smith (1776, I, x, b, 6).
v. For the possible significance of the notion of
'moral Certainty' in A42 see C49i.

Those who employ Artisans or Craftsmen
must needs therefore pay for their labour at
a higher rate than for that of a Husbandman
or common Labourer; and their labour will
necessarily be dear in proportion to the
time lost in learning the trade and the cost
and risk incurred in becoming proficient.

ᵃ...ᵃ: M:'Ceux qui' (R, N:
'Ceux donc qui')
ᵇ...ᵇ: R, M, N: 'payer plus
haut'
ᶜ...ᶜ: M: 'mannœvre: le
travail'; N:'mannœvre &c.
et ce travail; (R: 'mannœvre,
Et ce travail').

i. The content of E43 is partly **43**
covered in the preceding one
in D/A42.
ii. The writing at V43c of
the Rouen manuscript is quite
unclear and this may explain
the different solutions in E, M
and N.

The Craftsmen themselves do not make all their
Children learn their own mystery: there would be too
many of them for the needs of a City or a State; many
would not find enough work; the work, however, is
naturally better paid than that of Husbandmen.

ᵃ...ᵃ: M: 'pas'; N: 'point'
(R: 'point assés')

44

45   CHAPITRE ^aVIII^a.   CHAP. VIII.c

Les Artisans gagnent, les uns plus
les autres moins, selon le cas & les
^bcirconstances différentes.^b

^cSame^c Handicrafts-Men in
certain Trades, earn more
than others, according to the
Circumstances of the Times.

46 |1| Si deux Tailleurs font ^atous les habits^a d'un Village, l'un pourra avoir plus de Chalands que l'autre, soit par sa maniere d'attirer ^bles^b Pratiques, soit parcequ'il travaille plus proprement ou plus durablement que l'autre, soit qu'il suive mieux les modes dans la coupe des habits.

47 |2| Si l'un meurt, l'autre se trouvant plus pressé d'ouvrage, pour-[26]ra hausser le prix de son travail, en expédiant les uns préférablement aux autres, jusqu'au point que les Villageois ^atrouveront mieux^a leur compte ^bde^b porter leurs habits à faire dans ^cquelqu'autre Village, Bourg^c ou Ville, ^den perdant^d le tems d'y aller ^e& revenir^e, ou jusqu'à ce qu'il revienne un autre Tailleur pour demeurer dans ^fleur Village, & pour y partager^f le travail.

|| Let it be supposed that two taylors make the cloaths of a village, and that, the one dying, the survivor has more work than usual: this may enhance his price, by giving some preference in point of expedition to others: he may thus continue raising his price, till the countryman shall find it more advantageous to go to some taylor of another village, or market-town, or city, to have cloaths made, or till some other taylor comes into his village, to share the business of making cloaths.

|| Suppose two Tradesmen of the same Business living in a Village, of whom one dies; the Survivor will have more than usual [17] Business, until such Time as the Inhabitants find their Account in going to the next Village to accommodate themselves, or until some other Person of the same Trade comes to settle in the same Village, to divide the Custom.

48

|| If, of two taylors in a village, the one works better than the other, he may have a better price for his work; or, if he cuts his cloaths more fashionably (that is to say, if he pleases better) he shall have a better price.

49 |3| Les Métiers qui demandent le plus de tems pour s'y perfectionner, ou plus d'habileté & d'industrie, doivent naturellement être les mieux païés. Un habile Faiseur de Cabinets doit recevoir un meilleur prix de son travail qu'un Menuisier ordinaire, & un bon Horloger plus qu'un Maréchal.

|| The same reasons will hold good in market-towns and cities; those trades which require more art and capacity to learn, and more time to arrive at perfection in, earn, cæteris paribus, a better price.

Trades which require more Ingenuity and Time in attaining, earn in proportion more Wages. If one Artist works better and more in Taste than another, he certainly ought, and will be better paid for his Work; and this extraordinary Gratification creates a Desire in others to excel in their different Branches of Industry.

Higgs Translation (H)	Variations and Errata (V)	Comments (C)

Chapter VIII

Some Handicrafts-Men earn more, others less, according to the different Cases and Circumstances

^a...^a: R, N: '8.^e'; M: 'Chap.2'
^b...^b: N: 'circonstances'
^c...^c: The errata page states 'for Same read Some' and the chapter title on the contents page (xxii) also has 'Some'

From here M has a different chapter numbering. This is presumably because the extract from Cantillon's work in M only starts in the preceding chapter (E42). However, it is unclear why the first six chapters are ignored. See Introduction p. 7. **45**

Supposing two Tailors make all the cloaths of a Village, one may have more customers than the other, whether from his mode of attracting business, or because he works better or more durably than the other, or follows the fashions better in the cut of the garments.

^a...^a: R: 'Touts deux les habits'; M, N: 'tous deux les habits'
^b...^b: R, M, N: 'des'

E46 has a counterpart in D48. **46**

If one dies, the other finding himself more pressed with work will be able to raise the price of his labour, giving some customers a preference in point of expedition to others, till the Villagers find it to their advantage to have their cloaths made in another Village, Town, or City losing the time spent in going and returning, or till some other Tailor comes to live in their Village and to share in the business of it.

^a...^a: R, M, N: 'trouveront'
^b...^b: R, M, N: 'a'
^c...^c: R: 'quelq'autres villages, bourgs' M, N: 'quelque autre vilage, bourg'
^d...^d: R, M: 'et perdre'; N: 'perdre'
^e...^e: M, N: 'et de revenir' (R: 'et revenir)
^f...^f: M: 'le vilage et y partager'

i. D47 continues from D42 without a break or chapter heading. The argument is closer to A47 than to E47. **47**
ii. Note the phrase 'village, or market-town, or city' in D47. The same sequence is found in D48–D49 and in D57–D58. Even though no counterparts have been found for chapters 3 to 6 in E and A (see C19), these phrases perhaps suggest that this is more likely due to omissions by Postlethwayt rather than that they did not figure in the manuscript he used. See Introduction p. 20.

D48 corresponds to E46. A49 has a line about working more to the taste of customers. **48**

The Crafts which require the most Time in training or most Ingenuity and Industry must necessarily be the best paid. A skillful Cabinet-Maker must receive a higher price for his work than an ordinary Carpenter, and a good Watchmaker more than a Farrier.

i. E/A49 say that trades that require more time to learn 'ought to' be paid better; D49 says that they will. However, this difference may not be so substantial. This is perhaps suggested by the notion of 'moral certainty' in A42; eighteenth-century authors used the expression to denote a very likely future state of affairs. Such strong expectations lie somewhere between 'ought to' and 'will'. **49**
ii. Only D49 uses the Latin term *cæteris paribus*. For other uses of this clause see D82, D186, D198, D260; also see the English equivalents in A64, D253, A601, D618. The clause was infrequently used in English economic writings of the seventeenth and early eighteenth century. Significant examples are Petty, *A Treatise of Taxes & Contributions* (1662a), p. 32; Mandeville, *Fable of the Bees* vol. 2 (1725), pp. 188, 418. In the French text the same clause figures as '*toutes autres choses étant égales*' (see E115, E316/V316, E323, E336, E409). Even though the occurrences in E do not have direct counterparts in D and vice versa, one is tempted to ascribe all uses of the term to Cantillon since they reflect his analytical method of limiting the number of variables under consideration.

‖ I have often thought, and still do think, that with respect to the whole Community of any Kingdom or State, the exclusive Charters granted to Cities and Corporations, that nobody but such as are free, or have served their Time in such and Such Cities, or Purchase their Freedom, shall have Leave to exercise the Excellency of the Improvement they have acquired by Labour, Study, and Pains in the several Branches of their Arts: I say, I have always looked upon those kind of Charters as Prohibitions and Bars to Ingenuity and Art; all ought to be free to the industrious and ingenious Artists, as it is in the learned World [18] with Arts and Sciences; it matters not there, whether this or that Person studied at *Oxford*, *Cambridge*, *Rome*, *Geneva*, *Salamanca*, or the *Sorbonne*: the Question among the Learned is, not the Country or the University, but the Excellency of Genius in the Science and Learning of the Professor: so it ought to be with the Artist and Artizan, no matter what Country or Religion he is of; but as this is an Abuse that is in a manner sanctified by Time, I am afraid a positive Law for its Reformation would occasion great Clamour; but there is still a Remedy, (which except those who are immediately concerned in dividing the Loaves and Fishes of each Corporation, would meet with an universal Concurrence) and that is, that a Committee may be appointed by Law, to take an Account of the Revenues of each Corporation in the Kingdom, and particularly of the large Sums yearly spent by the Mayors, Aldermen, Sheriffs, Masters, &c. of each Corporation, in unnecessary Feasting; and that such Sums of unnecessary Money so spent should be applied to the Maintenance of the Poor of each City and Country adjacent. A Law of this Sort would silence the impetuous Roaring of the fat Aldermen and Common Councilmen, who rather than be deprived [19] of their fat Hanches of Venison, green Geese, Turkey-Polts, Pheasants, Partridges, &c. which they have at the public Expence, would readily consent that the Freedom of each Corporation should be granted without Fee or Reward; and this would create a Spirit of Emulation in Artists and Artizans to excel in their different Trades; as Praise near Adoration, Respect, Submission in Opinion, and Honour, does to the great Genius in the learned World. And why a good Shoemaker, who served his Time in *Bristol*, should not have the same Liberty of exerting the Ability of his Trade in *London*, without paying for this Privilege, as well as an Attorney who serves his Clerkship in *Bristol* has, is, with respect to the Advantage of a whole Community, a Mystery to me.

This extended passage in A50 has no counterpart in **50**
E or D. In A51 it is called a 'digression' and it seems
probable that Philip Cantillon added it. The strident
language is out of keeping with the more neutral tone
that Richard Cantillon tends to adopt. The passage is
included here mainly for its interesting objections
against the regulations and pomp of the guilds. Its
inclusion at this point in the *Analysis* may have been
inspired by the last sentence of A49, which makes
the point that the 'Desire [of artisans] to excel in
their different Branches of Industry' arises from
competition between them to 'work better and more
in Taste'. A conclusion that may be drawn from this
perceived effect of competition is that regulations
of corporations, which are ostensibly meant to
guarantee the quality of work, do in fact stifle 'a
Spirit of Emulation in Artists and Artizans to excel
in their different Trades'. However, it is perhaps
more likely that it was Philip Cantillon who stated
this conclusion so explicitly, rather than Richard.
The latter does hint that the numbers of artisans in
different trades does not need to be regulated (see
E62), although this is not necessarily the same as
arguing in favour of the removal of 'quality controls'
by guilds. Later authors, like Hume and Smith,
express the latter view too. See C62.

51 |4| Les Arts & Métiers qui sont accompagnés de risques & dangers, comme Fondeurs, Mariniers, Mineurs d'argent, &c. [27] doivent être païés à proportion des risques. Lorsqu'outre les dangers, il faut de l'habileté, ils doivent encore être païés d'avantage; tels sont les Pilotes, Plongeurs, Ingénieurs, &c. Lorsqu'il faut de la capacité & de la ᵃconfianceᵃ, on paie encore le travail plus cher, comme aux Jouailliers, Teneurs de compte, Caissiers, & autres.

|| The arts and employments attended with danger, as sailors, bell-founders, silver-miners, &c. earn more in proportion; and, where there must be capacity, danger, and confidence, they earn still more, as pilots, skippers, &c.

|| But to return from this Sort of Digression to the Subject of this Chapter; that Labour which is attended with great Risk, such as Mariners, Bell-Founders, Powder-Makers, Miners, ought to earn more than other Labourers: and in the like manner, those Professions, where Ingenuity, Genius, Science, and ᵇPartsᵇ are necessary, have a right to a proportionable Reward; as also such Persons of Edu-[20]cation, where Trust and Confidence must be reposed, such as Lawyers and Accountants.

52 |5| ᵃPar ces inductions, & cent autresᵃ qu'on pourrait tirer ᵇde l'expérience ordinaireᵇ, on peut voir facilement que la différence de prix qu'on paie pour le travail journalier est fondée sur des raisons naturelles & sensibles.

The Arts and Crafts which are accompanied by risks and dangers like those of Founders, Mariners, Silver miners, etc. ought to be paid in proportion to the risks. When over and above the dangers skill is needed they ought to be paid still more, e.g. Pilots, Divers, Engineers, etc. When Capacity and trustworthiness are needed the labour is paid still more highly, as in the case of Jewellers, Bookkeepers, Cashiers and others.

ᵃ...ᵃ: R, M, N: 'conscience'

ᵇ...ᵇ: *sic*; 'Arts'?

i. The terms '*confiance*' ('confidence') in E51 and '*conscience*' ('conscientiousness') in R, M, N (V51a) are interesting in relation to D51 and A51. In E51 Cantillon discusses two kinds of moral capacities that give rise to higher wages. The first is the capacity to deal with physical danger (as encountered by miners, divers, etc.). This requires a *confident* nature. Note that these professions are the only kind noted in D51. The second is the capacity to carry out one's job *conscientiously*. This is required in professions such as lawyers and accountants. At the same time, it can also be said that the clients of such men need to have *confidence* in this capacity, or 'Trust and Confidence', as stated in A51. Also cf. V79b.

ii. Harris 1757, I, i, p. 13: 'And as any trade is attended with greater risques of any sort, requires more skill, more trust, more expence in setting up &c. the artificer will be entitled to still better wages. In the like manner, those professions that require genius, great confidence, a liberal education, &c. have a right to be rewarded proportionally.' Cf. C67iv.

iii. Cf. the contents of E49 and E51 with the five 'principal circumstances' explaining wage differentials according to Adam Smith (1776, I, x, b, 1): 'first, the agreeableness or disagreeableness of the employments themselves; secondly, easiness and cheapness, or the difficulty and expence of learning them; thirdly, the constancy or inconstancy of employment in them; fourthly, the small or great trust which must be reposed in those who exercise them; and, fifthly, the probability or improbability of success in them'.

51

By these examples and a hundred others drawn from ordinary experience it is easily seen that the difference of price paid for daily work is based upon natural and obvious reasons.

ᵃ...ᵃ: missing in N (last sentence of E51 continues)

ᵇ..ᵇ: R, M, N: 'de L'expérience'

52

53   [28] **CHAPITRE ᵃIXᵃ.**

Le nombre de Laboureurs, Artisans &
autres, qui travaillent dans un état, se
proportionne naturellement au besoin
qu'on en a.

CHAP. IX.

The Number of Labourers
and Handicrafts-Men is
proportioned to the Demand
for them.

54 |1| Si tous les Laboureurs dans un Village élevent plusieurs Fils au même travail, il y aura trop de Laboureurs pour cultiver les Terres de la dépendance de ᵃce Villageᵃ, & il faut que les Surnuméraires adultes aillent ᵇquelqu'autre partᵇ chercher à gagner leur vie, comme ils font ordinairement dans les Villes: s'il en reste quelques-uns auprès de ᵇleurs Peresᵇ, comme ils ne trouveront pas tous suffisamment de l'emploi, ils vivront dans une grande pauvreté, & ne se marieront pas, faute de moïens pour élever des enfans, ou s'ils se ma-[29]rient, peu après les enfans survenus périssent par la misere avec le Pere & la Mere, comme nous le voïons journellement en France.

|| If every labourer in a village breeds up several children, there will be too many hands for the cultivation of the land belonging to the village; and so several adult sons and daughters must go to seek a livelihood elsewhere:

|| If the Labourers, Husbandmen, and Tradesmen of a Village do all educate and bring up Children, the number may be too great for the Employment: in this Case both Sexes will be obliged to go and seek their Bread elsewhere. This occasions many not to marry, until they acquire wherewith to maintain a Family; and even then, when they come to an Age to work, some of the Children of such Marriages will be obliged to go elsewhere to seek Bread,

55 |2| Ainsi si le Village continue dans la même situation de travail, & tire sa subsistance en travaillant dans la même portion de terre, il n'augmentera pas dans mille ans en nombre d'habitans.

and it will probably happen that the inhabitants of this village shall not be more numerous in 500 years than they were at first.

by which means it may happen, that a Village without some new Acquisition of Industry, may not in a hundred Years increase in the Number of its Inhabitants.

56 |3| Il est vrai que les Femmes & Filles de ce Village peuvent, aux heures qu'elles ne travaillent pas aux champs, s'occuper à filer, à tricotter, ᵃou à faireᵃ d'autres ouvrages qu'on pourra vendre dans les Villes; mais cela suffit rarement pour élever les enfans surnuméraires, qui quittent le Village ᵇpour chercherᵇ fortune ailleurs.

57 |4| On peut faire le même raisonnement des Artisans d'un Village. Si un seul Tailleur y fait tous les habits, & qu'il éleve trois [30] Fils au même métier, comme il n'y a de l'ouvrage que pour un seul qui lui succédera, il faut que les deux autres aillent chercher à gagner ᵃleur vieᵃ ailleurs: s'ils ne trouvent pas de l'emploi dans la Ville prochaine, il faut qu'ils aillent plus loin, ou qu'ils changent de profession pour gagner leur vie, qu'ils deviennent ᵇLaquais, Soldats, Mariniers, &c.ᵇ

|| The same may be said of the tradesmen of the village. If a taylor, who makes the cloaths of the whole village, breeds up three sons to the same trade, as there is but work enough for one, he will bring up one of his sons to succeed him, and the other two must seek their livelihood elsewhere. [II, 1, col.2] If they cannot find employment any where in their trade, they will go to sea, or into the army, or into foreign countries, or turn highwaymen and be hanged. But the number of tradesmen in the village in question will always proportion itself to the demand, or work there is for them.

CHAPTER IX

The Number of Labourers, Handicrafts-men and others, who work in a State is naturally proportioned to the Demand for them.

If all the Labourers in a Village breed up several Sons to the same work there will be too many Labourers to cultivate the Lands belonging to the Village, and the surplus Adults must go to seek a livelihood elsewhere, which they generally do in Cities: if some remain with their Fathers, as they will not all find sufficient employment they will live in great poverty and will not marry for lack of means to bring up children, or if they marry, the children who come will soon die of starvation with their Parents, as we see every day in France.

Therefore if the Village continue in the same situation as regards employment, and derives its living from cultivating the same portion of Land, it will not increase in population in a thousand years.

The Women and Girls of this Village can, it is true, when they are not working in the fields, busy themselves in spinning, knitting or other work which can be sold in the Cities; but this rarely suffices to bring up the extra children, who leave the Village to seek their fortune elsewhere.

The same may be said of the Tradesmen of a Village. If a Tailor makes all the cloaths there and breeds up three Sons to the same trade, as there is but work enough for one successor to him the two others must go to seek their livelihood elsewhere: if they do not find enough employment in the neighbouring Town they must go further afield or change their occupations to get a living and become Lackeys, Soldiers, Sailors, etc.

Variations and Errata (V)

[a]...[a]: R, N: '9.[e]'; M: '3[e]'

[a]...[a]: R, M, N: 'ce méme Village'
[b]...[b]: R, M, N: 'quelque part'
[c]...[c]: R, M, N: 'leur Pere'

[a]...[a]: M: 'ou faire' (R, N: 'ou a faire')
[b]...[b]: R, M, N: 'pour aller chercher'

[a]...[a]: R: 'Leurs Vies' (M, N: 'leur vie')
[b]...[b]: R, N: 'Laquais, Soldats, Mariniers, Gueux ou Voleurs, &c.'; M: 'laquais, soldats, gueux ou voleurs &c'

Comments (C)

53 The central point of this chapter is repeated in E128.

54 i. D54 continues without chapter heading or break from D51. It occurs in the entry, 'Labour' of Postlethwayt's *Dictionary*. See C7i.

ii. The expression *Surnuméraires adultes* in E54 is reminiscent of Petty's remark in *A Treatise* (1662a: 70) about 'Supernumerary Interlopers into any Trade over and above all that are necessary'. However, Cantillon does not share Petty's opinion that such interlopers *increase* the prices of goods.

55 Note the curious difference: E55 has '1000 years', D55 '500 years' and A55 '100 years'.

56 There is no counterpart for E56 in D and A. It could be argued that some of the argument of E56 is implied in A55, because it mentions more generally 'some new Acquisition of Industry'. This may be understood to include the kind of cottage industry mentioned in E56. Also note that while D/A54 assume that children of both sexes may have to leave their village, E54 and E56 imply that females are more likely to stay.

57 Unlike E57, the manuscript versions of the French text (V57b) as well as D57 mention the possibility of less respectable careers ('*gueux ou voleurs*' [beggars or thieves] and 'highwaymen' respectively). The opposite is the case in E131 where beggars and thieves are mentioned, while they do not figure in D131.

58 |5| Il est aisé de juger par la même façon de raisonner, que les Laboureurs, Artisans & autres, qui gagnent ^aleur vie^a par le travail, doivent se proportionner en nombre à l'emploi & au besoin ^bqu'on en a^b dans les Bourgs & dans les Villes.

|| It is easy to conceive, in like manner, that the number of labourers and tradesmen proportions itself to the demand for them in market-towns and cities:

It is therefore evident, that Labour and Industry is proportioned in all Places to the Demand for it from the Number of People or Inhabitants, supposing such Inha-[21]tants capable by their Commerce and Possessions of employing Numbers of Hands: otherwise such Labourers and Tradesmen will seek for Support elsewhere; which proves that Labour and Industry is proportioned to the Demand there is for it.

59 |6| Mais si quatre Tailleurs suffisent pour faire tous les habits d'un Bourg, s'il y survient un cinquieme Tailleur, il y pourra attraper de l'emploi aux dépens des ^aautres quatre^a; de maniere [31] que si l'ouvrage vient à être partagé entre les cinq Tailleurs, aucun d'eux n'aura suffisamment de l'ouvrage, & chacun en vivra plus pauvrement.

but this futher explication may be added: that, if four taylors in a market-town be able to make all the cloaths of the inhabitants, a fifth taylor may nevertheless find employment there, by the diminution of the work of the other four; and thus it happens that tradesmen often gain a livelihood, though they may not have full occupation.

60 |7| Il arrive souvent que les Laboureurs & Artisans n'ont pas suffisamment de l'emploi lorsqu'il en survient un trop grand nombre pour partager le travail. Il arrive aussi qu'ils sont privés ^ade l'emploi^a qu'ils avoient par des accidens & par une variation dans la consommation; il arrivera aussi qu'il leur surviendra trop ^bd'ouvrage^b, suivant les cas & les variations: quoi qu'il en soit, lorsqu'ils manquent d'emploi, ils quittent les Villages, Bourgs, ou Villes où ils demeurent, en tel nombre, que celui qui reste est toujours proportionné à l'emploi qui suffit pour les faire subsister; & lorsqu'il survient une augmentation constante de travail, il y a à ga-[32]gner, & il en survient assez d'autres pour partager le travail.

Higgs Translation (H)	Variations and Errata (V)	Comments (C)
By the same process of reasoning it is easy to conceive that the Labourers, Handicraftsmen and others who gain their living by work, must proportion themselves in number to the employment and demand for them in Market Towns and Cities.	ᵃ...ᵃ: R: 'leurs vies' (M, N: 'leur vie') ᵇ...ᵇ: R, M, N: 'quon a'	Like E, D here extends the reasoning from 'villages' (D57) to 'market-towns and cities' (D58). For the significance of this, see C47ii. **58**
But if four Tailors are enough to make all the cloaths for a Town and a fifth arrives he may attract some custom at the expense of the other four; so if the work is divided between the five Tailors neither of them will have enough employment, and each one will live more poorly.	ᵃ...ᵃ: N: 'quatre autres'	The view in E/D59 that 'tradesmen' may be underemployed is also found in E348. **59**
It often happens that Labourers and Handicraftsmen have not enough employment when there are too many of them to share the business. It happens also that they are deprived of work by accidents and by variations in demand, or that they are overburdened with work according to circumstances. Be that as it may, when they have no work they quit the Villages, Towns or Cities where they live in such numbers that those who remain are always proportioned to the employment which suffices to maintain them; when there is a continuous increase of work there is gain to be made and enough others arrive to share in it.	ᵃ...ᵃ: 1756b, 1769: 'd'emploi' ᵇ...ᵇ: N: 'd'ouvrages'	**60**

61 |8| Par ces inductions il est aisé de comprendre que les Ecoles de charité en Angleterre & les projets en France, pour augmenter le nombre des Artisans sont fort ªinutilesª. Si le Roi de France envoïoit cent mille Sujets à ses frais en Hollande, pour y apprendre la Marine, ils seroient inutiles ᵇà leur retourᵇ si on n'envoïoit pas plus de Vaisseaux en Mer qu'auparavant. Il est vrai qu'il seroit d'un grand avantage dans un Etat de faire apprendre aux Sujets, à faire les Manufactures qu'on a coutume de tirer de l'Etranger, & tous les autres ouvrages qu'on y achete; mais je ne considere ᶜà-présent qu'un Etat par rapportᶜ à lui-même.

62 |9| Comme les Artisans gagnent plus que les Laboureurs, ils sont plus en état ªque les derniers, d'é-[33]lever leurs enfans à des métiersª; & on ne peut jamais manquer d'artisans dans un Etat, lorsqu'il y a suffisamment de l'ouvrage pour les emploïer constamment.

From this it is easy to understand that the Charity-Schools in England and the proposals in France to increase the number of Handicraftsmen, are useless. If the King of France sent 100,000 of his Subjects at his expense into Holland to learn Seafaring, they would be of no use on their return if no more Vessels were sent to Sea than before. It is true that it would be a great advantage to a State to teach its Subjects to produce the Manufactures which are customarily drawn from abroad, and all the other articles bought there, but I am considering only at present a State in relation to itself.

[a]…[a]: R: 'ᵢₙutiles', M: 'utiles', (N: 'inutiles')
[b]…[b]: N: 'au retour'
[c]…[c]: 1756b, 1769: 'à-présent un Etat que par rapport'

i. The word *utiles* in R (V61a) has **61** been corrected to read *inutiles* by the insertion in small writing of *in*. While N and E both follow the correction, M has the uncorrected word. Whether this means that M is a copy made from R before the correction to the latter text was made cannot be said with confidence. For a similar case, see C70i.

ii. The discussion of the point that states benefit from substituting imports with products produced at home is taken up later. See C194.

As the Handicraftsmen earn more than the Labourers they are better able to bring up their children to Crafts; and there will never be a lack of Craftsmen in a State when there is enough work for their constant employment.

[a]…[a]: R, M, N: 'dElévér leurs enfans à des métiérs que Les derniers'

The argument of E62 is reminiscent of the **62** following passage from David Hume's *History of England* (1778, iii.30): 'the constant rule of the magistrate, except, perhaps, on the first introduction of any art, is, to leave the profession to itself, and trust its encouragement for those who reap the benefit of it. The artizans finding their profits to rise by the favour of their customers, increase, as much as possible, their skill and industry; and as matters are not disturbed by any injudicious tampering, the commodity is always sure to be at all times nearly proportioned to the demand.' Smith (1776, V.i.g.3) approvingly cites this passage. Cf. C50.

63   **CHAPITRE ᵃXᵃ.**

*ᵇLe prix & valeurᵇ intrinsique
d'une chose en général est la
mesure de la terre & du travail
qui entre dans sa production.*

                                                     CHAP. X.

*The Price of any Thing, in general,
is estimated by the Value of the
Land which produces it, and the
Labour and Time taken in forming
it into Use.*

64 |1| Un Arpent de terre produit plus de blé, ᵃouᵃ nourrit plus de Moutons, qu'un autre Arpent: le travail d'un homme est plus cher que celui d'un autre homme, suivant l'art & les occurrences, comme on l'a déja expliqué. Si deux Arpens de terre sont de même bonté, l'un entretiendra autant de Moutons & produira la même quantité de laine que [34] l'autre Arpent, supposant le travail le même; & la laine produite par l'un se vendra ᵇau même prixᵇ que celle qui est produite par l'autre.

|| One acre of land produces more wheat, or feeds more sheep than another acre ᶜ, and the workᶜ of one man is dearer than that of another, according to the occurrences, ᵈas we have explainedᵈ.

|| If two acres of land are of equal goodness, the wheat or wool of one is of equal value to that of the other, ᵉprovidedᵉ the work be equal that is employed about them.

|| One Acre of Land produces more Corn and feeds more Sheep, than two Acres of Land of less Goodness; and the Labour of one Man is more valuable than the Labour of another, as I have already explained, according to the superior Skill and Occurrences of the Times.

|| If two Acres of Land are of equal Goodness, and all Things equal, the Corn of the one will sell at Market at equal Price with the other; the Wool of the Sheep fed on the one, is equal to the Wool of the Sheep fed on the [22] other.

65 |2| Si l'on travaille la Laine d'un côté en un habit de gros drap, & la Laine de l'autre en un habit de drap fin; comme ce dernier habit demandera un plus grand travail, & un travail plus cher que celui de gros drap, il sera quelquefois dix fois plus cher, quoique l'un & l'autre ᵃhabitsᵃ contiennent la même quantité de Laine & d'une même bonté. La quantité du produit de la terre, & la quantité aussi-bien que la qualité du travail, entreront nécessairement dans le prix.

|| Let us suppose the wool produced by one acre to be made into a coarse suit of ᵇcloathsᵇ and the wool of the other to be made into a suit of fine cloth, containing the same quantity of wool with the coarse cloth: as the fine suit of cloth requires more, and dearer ᶜworkmanshipᶜ, it will cost ᵈmore in makingᵈ thanᵈ the coarse suit, and, ᵉproportionablyᵉ to the difference of the work, one suit of fine cloth shall sell for ten times the price of a coarse suit, containing an equal quantity of wool.

|| ᶠWherefore theᶠ price of any thing, intrinsically, ᵍseems to takeᵍ in the quantity of land with regard to the goodness of the land, and the quantity of ʰlabourʰ, with regard to the dearness of the ʰlabourʰ.

If the Wool of the one is manufactured into coarse Cloth, and the Wool of the other into fine Cloth, the Quantity of Wool being equal, but as the fine Cloth requires more Labour, and is of a dearer Nature, the Price of the fine Cloth will be by so much proportionably dearer; and the same Rule must govern in every Species of Goods and Merchandize. Therefore it is the Value of the Quantity of Land, and the Value of the Labour made Use of, to produce all Goods and Merchandize, which fixes their intrinsic Value or Worth.

Chapter X

The Price and Intrinsic Value of a Thing in general is the measure of the Land and Labour which enter into its Production

One Acre of Land produces more Corn or feeds more Sheep than another. The work of one Man is dearer than that of another, as I have already explained, according to the superior Skill and Occurrences of the Times. If two Acres of Land are of equal goodness, one will feed as many Sheep and produce as much Wool as the other, supposing the Labour to be the same, and the Wool produced by one Acre will sell at the same Price as that produced by the other.

If the Wool of the one Acre is made into a suit of coarse Cloth and the Wool of the other into a suit of fine Cloth, as the latter will require more work and dearer workmanship it will be sometimes ten times dearer, though both contain the same quantity and quality of Wool. The quantity of the Produce of the Land and the quantity as well as the quality of the Labour, will of necessity enter into the Price.

ᵃ...ᵃ: R: '10ᵉ'; N: '10'; M: '4ᵉ'

ᵇ...ᵇ: R, M, N: 'Le prix ou valeur'; 1756b, 1769: 'Le prix & la valeur'

ᵃ...ᵃ: R, M, N: 'et'

ᵇ...ᵇ: R, M, N: 'le meme prix'

ᶜ...ᶜ:T: '; the work'

ᵈ...ᵈ: T: 'as we have already explained'

ᵉ...ᵉ: T: 'if'

ᵃ...ᵃ: R, M, N, 1756b, 1769: 'habit'

ᵇ...ᵇ: T: 'cloath'

ᶜ...ᶜ: T: 'work'

ᵈ...ᵈ: T: 'more than'

ᵉ...ᵉ: T: 'proportionally'

ᶠ...ᶠ: T: 'The'

ᵍ...ᵍ: 'takes'

T: 'the Labor'

ʰ...ʰ: T: 'Labor'

---

63 i. In the entry, 'Labour' of the *Universal Dictionary*, the text in D64 continues without a (sub)heading or break from D59. See C47.

ii. Cf. V63b with V70a.

64 i. From here up to D75 we have an alternative version to the *Dictionary* text: in Postlethwayt's *Great Britain's True System* of 1757, the text starts corresponding from the bottom half of p. 153, just after its correspondence with E I, xi finishes (D105). See C78. Variations occurring in the 1757 text are designated with T. The 1757 text uses capitalisation of nouns throughout the relevant fragments but these variations have not been recorded here. In a number of cases it is clear that the 1757 version is closer to the French counterparts, and hence generally appears more authentic (though not always, see V86b). For a significant case see V67c and f.

ii. In E64 the remark 'as I have already explained' refers to I, vii and viii (E40–E52).

65 The final sentence in each of the three texts specifies the elements of intrinsic value ('land' and 'labour') in a different way. E65 has 'the quantity of the produce of land' and 'the quantity as well as the quality of the labour'; D65 has 'the quantity of land' and the 'quantity of labour' (cf. E68/D68); A65 has 'the value of the quantity of land' and 'the value of the labour' (cf. A14, A63). For similar differences with regard to the intrinsic value of slaves see E82/D82/A82 and of products in general E75/D75. Also see V220c for an interesting variation between manuscripts and printed French text of 'value' and 'quantity'. These variations may indicate that Cantillon struggled with the formulation of his theory of intrinsic value. Alternatively they may be due to tinkering with the texts by later editors.

66 |3| Une livre de Lin travaillé en Dentelles fines de Bruxelles, demande le travail de quatorze personnes pendant une année ou le travail d'une personne pen-[35]dant quatorze années, comme on peut le voir par un calcul des différentes parties du travail, dans le Supplément. On y voit aussi que le prix qu'on donne de ces Dentelles suffit pour païer l'entretien d'une personne pendant quatorze ans, & pour païer encore les profits de tous les Entrepreneurs & Marchands qui s'en mêlent.

A pound of flax wrought into [a]Brussels[a] lace, according to the computation of the different parts of [b]labour[b] it [c]may require[c], will employ the [b]labour[b] of one person for near [d]14[d] years; and [e]thus[e] the quantity of lace, [f]manufactured[f] out of a pound of flax, sells at a price which not only pays the maintenance of a woman for [d]14[d] years, or of [d]14[d] women for one year, but also to yield a profit to the merchant, or [g]principal undertaker of the lace-manufacture[g].

67 |4| Le Ressort d'acier fin, qui regle une Montre d'Angleterre, se vend ordinairement à un prix qui rend la proportion de la matiere au travail, ou de l'acier au Ressort, comme [a]un, à un[a], de maniere que le travail fait ici la valeur preque entiere de ce Ressort, voïez-en le calcul au Supplément.

|| The [b]steel spring[b] which regulates [c]a good[c] watch, [d]may sell[d] at a price [e]which[e] makes the proportion of the value of the steel to the workmanship as [f]1 to 1,000,000[f].

A pound of Flax wrought into fine Brussels Lace requires the Labour of 14 persons for a year or of one person for 14 years, as may be seen from a calculation of the different processes in the Supplement, where we also see that the price obtained for the Lace suffices to pay for the maintenance of one person for 14 years as well as the profits of all the Undertakers and Merchants concerned.

ᵃ...ᵃ: T: 'Bruxels'
ᵇ...ᵇ: T: 'Labor'
ᶜ...ᶜ: T: 'requires'
ᵈ...ᵈ: T: 'fourteen'
ᵉ...ᵉ: T: 'so'
ᶠ...ᶠ: T: 'made'
ᵍ...ᵍ: T: 'undertaker'

i. Even though there is no reference to a supplement in D66, **66** the phrase 'according to the computation' suggests some kind of precise method of estimation. Presumably Postlethwayt would have removed references to a (missing) 'Supplement', because it would not have made sense in the context of his *Dictionary*. See E/D67, E/D88, E/D184. Cf. C33ii–iv and C561i.

ii. Cf. E168 for another mention of the Supplement in connection with trade between Brussels and Paris.

iii. This is the only passage in D corresponding to part I of the *Essai* where the term 'profit' is used. The discussion appears to anticipate the more detailed exposition in E491/D491. In that and other later passages in D the word 'profit' denotes a conception that is close to 'a return on capital advanced'. See C437v.

iv. Cf. C490iii for other variations in the spelling of 'Brussels' (V66a).

The fine steel spring which regulates an English Watch is generally sold at a price which makes the proportion of material to Labour, or of Steel to Spring, one to one million so that in this case labour makes up nearly all the value of the spring. See the calculation in the Supplement.

ᵃ...ᵃ: R: 'dun a 1,538,460'; M: 'd'un a 15384 60'; N: 'd'un a 1538460'
ᵇ...ᵇ: T: 'steel-spring'
ᶜ...ᶜ: T: 'an English'
ᵈ...ᵈ: T: 'sells'
ᵉ...ᵉ: T: 'that'
ᶠ...ᶠ: T: '1 to 1, 538, 460'

i. Higgs (1931: 29 n) argued that the '*un, a un*' in E67 was a **67** printer's error or a slip of the pen and therefore adopted the ratio 1:1,000,000 of the *Dictionary*. His reason for not adopting the ratio found in Postlethwayt's *Great Britain's True System* (V67f) was a disagreement with Edward Cannan, who in 1897 had speculated that Postlethwayt might have possessed the Supplement and taken the ratio found in his 1757 publication from that source. Higgs (1931: 385) thought it more likely that 'the figure in the Supplement at least 23 years earlier approached the round million and did not exceed one and a half million'. Hence with regard to the ratio in the 1757 text he thought it 'much more probable that [Postlethwayt] worked it out up to date for himself'. However, the fact that the French manuscripts (V67a) have exactly the same ratio as Postlethwayt's 1757 text (V67f) suggests that the ratio 1:1,538,460 was the actual one used by Richard Cantillon. Note that this ratio can also be written as 13: 20 million.

ii. The editor of Cantillon (1952 [in Brian and Théré 1997: 16 n4]) suggested that there is a special significance to the fact that in V67a M does not have commas, but a space between the digits 4 and 6. However, R has commas, but no space and N has neither commas, nor space. These particular variations seem to be very inconsequential.

iii. As an additional variation the 1757 text has, instead of 'a good watch', 'an English watch' (V67c), just like E and the French manuscripts.

iv. Joseph Harris, in An *Essay upon Money and Coins* (1757, I, ch i, p. 3 n) states: 'The balance spring in a *good* watch is worth above *a million* times the value of the steel' (emphases added). Given C67i and iii, this strongly suggests that Harris borrowed this passage from the *Dictionary*. The same is likely to be true for his other borrowings. See C42iii, C51ii, C70iii, C416iv, C426v. Note that the fragments on which Harris relied all appeared in the same entry, 'Labour' of the *Universal Dictionary* (but also see C229ii and C350iii).

68　|5| D'un autre côté, le prix du Foin d'une Prairie, rendu sur les lieux, ou d'un Bois qu'on veut couper, est réglé sur la matiere, ou sur le produit de [36] la terre, suivant sa bonté.

|| On the other hand, the apples of a tree require so little ªlabourª, that their price seems to be proportioned almost to ᵇthe land only that entersᵇ into their production.

69　|6| Le prix d'une cruche d'eau de la riviere de Seine n'est rien, parceque c'est une matiere immense qui ne tarit point; mais on en donne un sol dans les rues de Paris, ªce qui estª le prix ou la mesure du travail du Porteur d'eau.

|| The price of a bucket of water at the river is nothing; ᵇbut, carried at some distance into the street, shall sellᵇ for one penny, which seems to be the measure of the ᶜlabourᶜ of the water-carrier.

70　|7| Par ces inductions & exemples, je crois qu'on comprendra que ªle prix ou la valeur intrinsequeª d'une chose, est la mesure de la quantité de terre & du travail qui entre dans sa production, eu égard à la bonté ou produit de la terre, & à la qualité du travail.

[II, 2, col.1] || From these examples and explanations ᵇit seems toᵇ appear, that the price of anything intrinsically is the measure of the land, and ᶜthe labourᶜ that enters into ᵈit'sᵈ production:

On the other hand the price of the Hay in a Field, on the spot, or a Wood which it is proposed to cut down, is fixed by the matter or produce of the Land, according to its goodness.

ᵃ...ᵃ: T: 'Labor'
ᵇ...ᵇ: T: 'the land that enters'

Apart from the fact that D68 uses apples as an example, instead of hay and wood, it also refers simply to 'the land that enters into … production' rather than the (in this context tautological) 'matter or produce of the land' in E68. Cf. C65. **68**

The price of a pitcher of Seine Water is nothing, because there is an immense supply which does not dry up; but in the Streets of Paris people give a sol for it—the price or measure of the Labour of the Water-carrier.

ᵃ...ᵃ: R, M, N: 'qui est'
ᵇ...ᵇ: T: 'but a Bucket of Water sells in the Street'
ᶜ...ᶜ: T: 'Labor'

There is no reference to Paris in D69. Cf. C10. **69**

By these examples and inductions it will, I think, be understood that the Price or intrinsic value of a thing is the measure of the quantity of Land and of Labour entering into its production, having regard to the fertility or produce of the Land and to the quality of the Labour.

ᵃ...ᵃ: R: 'Le prix ou/Et valleur intrinseque';
M: 'le prix et valeur intrinseque'; N: 'le prix ou valeur intrinseque'
ᵇ...ᵇ: T: 'I believe it will'
ᶜ...ᶜ: T: 'Labor'
ᵈ...ᵈ: T: 'its'

i. In R the word *ou* is written above *Et*, which appears to be the original wording (V70a). The latter is followed by M and the 'correction' by N and E. For a similar case see C61i. **70**

ii. V70d suggests that Postlethwayt is responsible for the rogue apostrophe in 'its' (cf. V492h). It occurs many times in the fragments reproduced here, and indeed throughout the *Universal Dictionary*.

iii. Harris (1757, I, i, 5): 'Things in general are valued, not according to their real uses in supplying the necessities of men; but rather in proportion to the land, labour and skill that are required to produce them; It is according to this proportion nearly, that things or commodities are exchanged one for another; and it is by the said scale, that the intrinsic values of most things are chiefly estimated. Water is of great use, and yet ordinarily of little or no value; because in most places, water flows spontaneously with such great plenty, as not to be with-held within the limits of private property; but all may have enough, without other expence than that of bringing or conducting it, when the case so requires. On the other hand, diamonds, being very scarce, have upon that account a great value, though they are but of little use.' This passage appears inspired by D69/D70; but there is also a curious correspondence with the phrase 'the Expence of bringing and conducting' water in A572.

iv. The fact that Harris adds the reflection about the great value of diamonds may indicate that his statement influenced Smith (LJ B II 206): 'It is only on account of the plenty of water that it is so cheap as to be got for the lifting, and on account of the scarcity of diamonds (for their real use seems not yet to be discovered) that they are so dear.'

71 |8| Mais il arrive souvent que plusieurs choses qui ont ªactuellementª cette valeur intrinseque, ne se vendent pas au Marché, suivant cette valeur: cela dépendra ᵇdes humeurs & des fantaisiesᵇ des hommes, & de la consommation qu'ils feront.

but it may happen that things which have such an intrinsic value, may not sell accordingly, with regard to the fashion and ᶜhumorsᶜ of men.

72 [37] |9| Si un Seigneur coupe des canaux & éleve des terrasses dans son Jardin, la valeur intrinseque en sera proportionnée à la terre & au travail; mais ªle prix de la veritéª ne suivra pas toujours cette proportion: s'il offre de vendre ce Jardin, il se peut faire que personne ne voudra lui en donner la moitié de la dépense qu'il y a faite; & il se peut ᵇaussi faireᵇ, si plusieurs personnes en ont envie, qu'on lui en donnera le double de la valeur intrinseque, c'est-à-dire, de la valeur du fond & de la dépense qu'il y a faite.

For example: if a gentleman cuts canals, and erects ᶜterrassesᶜ in his garden, the price of them will be intrinsically proportionable to the land and ᵈthe labour thereon employed, because they really costᵈ the gentleman in that proportion; nevertheless it may happen that nobody else will give him one quarter part of that value for them.

73 |10| Si les Fermiers dans un Etat sement plus de blé qu'à l'ordinaire, c'est-à-dire, beaucoup plus de blé qu'il n'en faut pour la consommation de l'année, la valeur intrinseque & réelle du blé correspondra à la terre & au travail qui ªentrentª dans sa production: mais comme il y en a une [38] trop grande abondance, & plus de Vendeurs que d'Acheteurs; le prix du blé au Marché tombera nécessairement au-dessous du prix ou valeur intrinseque. Si au contraire les Fermiers sement moins de blé ᵇqu'il ne fautᵇ pour la consommation, il y aura plus d'Acheteurs que de Vendeurs, & le prix du blé au Marché haussera au-dessus de sa valeur intrinseque.

Higgs Translation (H)	Variations and Errata (V)	Comments (C)

But it often happens that many things which have actually[a] this intrinsic value are not sold in the Market according to that value: that will depend on the Humours and Fancies[b] of men[c] and on their consumption.

[a]...[a]: R, M, N: 'reellémént'

[b]...[b]: R: des humeurs fantaisie'; M, N: 'des humeurs et fantaisies'

[c]...[c]: T: 'Humours'

Even though Higgs's rendering of 'actuellement' in E71 with 'actually' makes sense in the theoretical context, it is in fact a false translation. The predominant meaning in English of 'actually' is 'in reality'. By contrast, in French the word 'actuellement' had (and has) the predominant meaning of 'at present'. V71a offers an explanation for the puzzling occurrence of 'actuellement', since it suggests that it is an (ill-advised) later alteration and that the original word used was 'réellement'. This finds support in the characterisation of intrinsic value as what something 'really' costs in D72 and the phrase 'valeur intrinseque & réelle' in E73. The word 'actuellement' does occur in two other places in E (see E135 and E238/V238b), but neither use relates to the notion of intrinsic value. **71**

If a gentleman cuts Canals and erects Terraces in his Garden, their intrinsic value will be proportionable to the Land and Labour; but the Price[a] in reality will not always follow this proportion. If he offers to sell the Garden possibly no one will give him half the expense he has incurred. It is also possible that if several persons desire it he may be given double the intrinsic value, that is twice the value of the Land and the expense he has incurred.

[a]...[a]: R, M, N: 'le prix'

[b]...[b]: N: 'faire aussi'

[c]...[c]: T: 'Terasses'

[d]...[d]: T: 'the Labor they require, and they will really cost'

i. D72 has 'a quarter part', where E72 has 'half' ('la moitié'). **72**

ii. V72a suggests the phrase 'de la verité' may be an addition by the editor of the print version.

iii. E72 appears to use quite deliberately the contrasting terms 'intrinsic *value*' and 'market *price*'. Similar terminology can be found in D205. But in other places the terms 'value' and 'price' are used less distinctly, e.g. D72, E205, E207 (cf. C205i).

If the Farmers in a State sow more corn than usual, much more than is needed for the year's consumption, the real and intrinsic value of the corn will correspond to the Land and Labour which enter into its production; but as there is too great an abundance of it and there are more sellers than buyers the Market Price of the Corn will necessarily fall below the intrinsic price or Value. If on the contrary the Farmers sow less corn than is needed for consumption there will be more buyers than sellers and the Market Price of corn will rise above its intrinsic value.

[a]...[a]: R, M, N: 'entre'

[b]...[b]: 1756b, 1769: 'qu'il n'en faut'

There are no counterparts to E73 and E74 in either D or T. Skinner (1966, I, 312 n1) sees a correspondence with the notion of 'intrinsic worth' in Steuart (1767, II, xxvi), but that appears to be quite a different notion. If there is a link, in the sense of merely borrowing the term, it may just as well be with A65. **73**

74 |11| Il n'y a jamais de variation dans la valeur intrinseque des choses; mais l'impossibilité de proportionner la production des marchandises & denrées à leur consommation dans un Etat, cause une variation journaliere, & un flux & reflux perpétuel dans les prix du Marché. Cependant dans ᵃles Sociétésᵃ bien réglées, les prix du Marché des denrées & marchandises dont la consommation est assez constante & uniforme, ne s'écartent [39] pas beaucoup de la valeur intrinseque; & lorsqu'il ne survient pas des années trop steriles ou trop abondantes, les Magistrats des Villes sont toujours en état de fixer le prix du Marché de beaucoup de choses, comme du pain & de la viande, sans que personne ait de quoi s'en plaindre.

75 |12| La Terre est la matiere, & le travail la forme, de toutes les denrées & marchandises; & comme ceux qui travaillent doivent nécessairement subsister du produit de la Terre, il semble qu'on pourroit trouver un rapport de la valeur du travail à celui du produit de la Terre: ce sera le sujet du Chapitre suivant.

|| Land, which produces all commodities and goods, must necessarily maintain those who give ᵃthoseᵃ goods and commodities their form by ᵇlabourᵇ; and the ᵇlabourᵇ itself may be estimated by the quantity of land required to maintain those who ᵇlabourᵇ, as ᶜmay be further elucidated from what follows:ᶜ

There is never a variation in intrinsic values, but the impossibility of proportioning the production of merchandise and produce in a State to their consumption causes a daily variation, and a perpetual ebb and flow in Market Prices. However in well organized Societies the Market Prices of articles whose consumption is tolerably constant and uniform do not vary much from the intrinsic value; and when there are no years of too scanty or too abundant production the Magistrates of the City are able to fix the Market Prices of many things, like bread and meat, without any on having cause to complain.

ᵃ...ᵃ: N: 'les ventes'

i. The expression '*constante & uniforme*' is equivalent to 'constant and uniform' in D248. **74**

ii. Cf. Smith (1776, I, vii, 15): 'The natural price, therefore, is, as it were, the central price, to which the prices of all commodities are continually gravitating. Different accidents may sometimes keep them suspended a good deal above it, and sometimes force them down even somewhat below it. But whatever may be the obstacles which hinder them from settling in this center of repose and continuance, they are constantly tending towards it.'

Land is the matter and Labour the form of all produce and Merchandise, and as those who labour must subsist on the produce of the Land it seems that some relation might be found between the value of Labour and that of the produce of the Land: this will form the subject of the next chapter.

ᵃ...ᵃ: T: 'these'
ᵇ...ᵇ: T: 'Labor'
ᶜ...ᶜ: T: 'appears from what has been urged.'

i. Both E75 and D75 refer to labour as giving goods and commodities their 'form'. See E3, E4 and E235 for other instances. Cf. C3. **75**

ii. Postlethwayt's 1757 text carries on immediately with the text reproduced in D186–D200. Since this text borrowed fragments in an order that differs from how they are arranged in E, the reference (V75c) is backwards rather than forward. It is actually referring to the fragment reproduced here in D78–D105. See C78.

76   [40] **CHAPITRE** ^a**XI**^a.

CHAP. XI.

Du pair ou rapport de la valeur de la Terre à la valeur du travail.

Of the Par and Equality between Land and Labour.

77 |1| Il ne paroît pas que la Providence ait donné le droit de la possession des Terres à un Homme plutôt qu'à un autre. Les Titres les plus anciens sont fondés sur la violence & les conquêtes. Les Terres du Mexique appartiennent aujourd'hui à des Espagnols, ^a& celles^a de Jerusalem à des Turcs. Mais de quelque maniere qu'on parvienne à la proprieté & possession des Terres, nous avons déja remarqué ^bqu'elles échéent^b toujours à un petit nombre de personnes par rapport à tous les habitans.

|| It does not appear that providence has given the right of the possession of land to one man preferably to another; some of the most ancient titles that we have any knowledge of, came by violence and conquest, and by laws established in consequence of such conquests. The property of the lands in Mexico is vested in Spaniards, and of those at Jerusalem in Turks; but, however people come by the property of land in a state, it naturally falls into the hands of a few.

|| It does not appear, that the all good and wise Being, ever gave the Right of Possession to one Man more than to another: the most ancient Titles we know of, are those of Conquest: the Property of the Kingdoms of *Mexico* and *Peru* belongs to the *Spaniards,* and that of the Holy land to the *Turks.*

78 |2| Si un Propriétaire d'une grande Terre entreprend de la faire [41] valoir lui-même, il emploiera des Esclaves, ^aou des Gens libres^a, pour y travailler: s'il y emploie plusieurs Esclaves, il faut qu'il ait des Inspecteurs pour les faire travailler; il faut qu'il ^bait aussi des^b Esclaves Artisans, pour se procurer toutes les commodités & agrémens de la vie, & à ceux qu'il emploie; il faut qu'il fasse apprendre des métiers à d'autres pour la continuation du travail

|| Let us suppose the proprietor of an estate in land keeps it in his own hands, he will employ slaves, vassals, or servants, to work for him. If he employs slaves in great numbers, he must have overseers to keep them at work; ^che must have^c as many ^dlabourers and tradesmen, and mechanics,^d as are necessary to procure him all the conveniencies ^ehis fancy and inclinations lead him to.^e

[23] || But in supposing the Proprietor of an Estate or Plantation, we may conceive that if he himself cultivates it, he will be obliged to employ Slaves, Vassals, and Labourers: if the Number of such is considerable, Inspectors and Overseers must be employed to see the Work done:

79 |3| Dans cette œconomie, il faut qu'il donne une simple subsistance à ^ases^a Laboureurs esclaves & de quoi élever leurs Enfans. Il faut qu'il donne à leurs Inspecteurs des avantages proportionnés à la ^bconfiance^b & à l'autorité qu'ils ont; il faut qu'il maintienne les Esclaves, auxquels il fait apprendre des Métiers, pendant le tems de leur Aprentissage sans fruit, & qu'il accorde aux Esclaves artisans qui travail-[42]lent, & à leurs Inspecteurs, qui doivent être entendus dans les Métiers, ^cune subsistance plus forte^c à proportion que celle des Esclaves laboureurs, &c. à cause que la perte d'un Artisan seroit plus grande que celle d'un Laboureur, & qu'on en doit avoir plus de soin, attendu qu'il en coute toujours pour faire apprendre un métier pour ^dles^d remplacer.

|| In this œconomy, he must allow these slaves not only ^ewhat will maintain them^e, but ^falso their children; he must likewise allow^f the overseers of the slaves ^gsuch advantages^g and rewards ^has are proportionable^h to the authority ⁱwhich heⁱ gives them.

so much of the Produce of this Land must be allotted to the Slaves, as will be necessary to support them, their Wives and their Children: the Overseers and Inspectors must be allotted Advantages and Distinction, proportionable to the Authority of their Office. Slaves are not fond of Work; they must be compelled to it by the Fear of Punishment, or else flattered into it by the Hopes of Reward, over and above the bare necessary Support of Life for themselves, their Wifes and infant Children.

Chapter XI

Of the Par or Relation between the
Value of Land and Labour

It does not appear that Providence has given the Right of the Possession of Land to one Man preferably to another: the most ancient titles are founded on Violence and Conquest. The Lands of Mexico now belong to the Spaniards and those at Jerusalem to the Turks. But howsoever people come to the property and possession of Land we have already observed that it always falls into the hands of a few in proportion to the total inhabitants.

If the Proprietor of a great Estate keeps it in his own hands he will employ Slaves or free men to work upon it. If he has many Slaves he must have Overseers to keep them at work: he must likewise have Slave craftsmen to supply the needs and conveniencies of life for himself and his workers, and must have trades taught to others in order to carry on the work.

In this oeconomy he must allow his Labouring Slaves their subsistence and wherewithal to bring up their Children. The Overseers must allow Advantages proportionable to the confidence and authority which he gives them. The Slaves who have been taught a craft must be maintained without any return during the time of their Apprenticeship and the artisan Slaves and their Overseers who should be competent in the crafts must have a better subsistence than the labouring Slaves, etc. since the loss of an Artisan would be greater than that of a Labourer and more care must be taken of him having regard to the expense of training another to take his place.

ᵃ…ᵃ: N: '11.ᵉ'; M: '5ᵉ'

ᵃ…ᵃ: R, M, N: 'celles'
ᵇ…ᵇ: R, M, N: 'quil echeoit'

ᵃ…ᵃ: R, M, N: 'ou des Libres'
ᵇ…ᵇ: N: 'ait des'
ᶜ…ᶜ:T: 'and'
ᵈ…ᵈ: T: 'Labourers and Tradesmen'
ᵉ…ᵉ: T: 'and Superfluities he shall require.'

ᵃ…ᵃ: R, M, N: 'ces'
ᵇ…ᵇ: R, M: 'Consciénce'; N: 'conscience' replaced with 'confiance'
ᶜ…ᶜ: R, M, N: 'une plus forte subcistance'
ᵈ…ᵈ: R, M, N: 'le'
ᵉ…ᵉ: T: 'a necessary Maintenance'
ᶠ…ᶠ: T: 'their Children likewise. He must allow'
ᵍ…ᵍ: T: 'advantages'
ʰ…ʰ: T: 'proportionate'
ⁱ…ⁱ: T: 'he'

---

76 i. D77 continues from D75 without a chapter or section heading (entry 'Labour'). Cf. C7.

ii. In this case only (V76a) R adopts roman numerals in the chapter titles.

77 The phrase 'we have already observed' in E77 refers to the discussion in E I, ii (E7–E18 above). The counterpart in the *Universal Dictionary* is reproduced in D8 to D17, but in the entry 'Labour' that fragment actually occurs as a note, in a smaller font, inserted between D77 and D78. See C7.

78 From the beginning of D78 up to D105 we again have two versions: this fragment also appears in Postlethwayt's *Great Britian's True System* of 1757, starting bottom half of p. 148 up to the middle of p. 153. In that publication the fragment D78–D105 actually precedes the text reproduced in D64–D75. Cf. C 64i.

79 i. In E and D the phrase 'in this oeconomy'/ '*dans cette œconomie*' occurs in a number of other places (E13, E115, E490; D134, D270, D437). It is used to indicate a specific socio-economic arrangement. This modern meaning of the term is absent from A where 'œconomy' is exclusively used to indicate the tendency to save (A15, A17, A349, A422, A635). This meaning also occurs in the other two texts (D263, E311, E439, E470, E513).

ii. Only A79 refers to the 'motivations' of slaves.

iii. V79a agrees with 'these' in D79.

iv. Cf. V79b with V51a. See C51i.

80 |4| Dans cette supposition, le travail du plus vil Esclave adulte, vaut au moins & correspond à la quantité de terre que le Propriétaire est obligé d'emploïer pour ªsa nourriture & ses commoditésª nécessaires, & encore au double de la quantité de terre qu'il faut pour élever un Enfant jusqu'à l'âge du travail, attendu que la moitié des Enfans qui naissent, meurent avant l'âge de ᵇdix-septᵇ ans, suivant les calculs & observations du célebre [43] Docteur ᶜHalleyᶜ: ᵈainsiᵈ il faut élever deux Enfans pour en conserver un dans l'âge de travail, & il sembleroit que ce compte ne suppléeroit pas assez pour la continuation du travail, parceque les Hommes adultes meurent à tout âge.

|| ᵉWhereforeᵉ the ᶠlabourᶠ of a slave is worth, at least, the quantity of land ᵍthatᵍ serves to maintain him, and about double the quantity of land which serves to breed up a child till he is of age fit for ᵍlabourᵍ; for half the children ʰthatʰ are born die before ⁱ17ⁱ; so that two children must be reared up, on an average, ʲin order to haveʲ one fit for ᶠlabourᶠ, and even then their lives can be calculated but ᵏat 10 to 12 yearsᵏ.

The Labour of a Slave, is at least of as much Value, as the Worth of the Produce of so much Land, as was necessary to be cultivated for his Support, and half as much for the bringing up his Child to an Age of earning its Bread: because Experience shews, that half of the Children born, do not live to this Age: therefore, two Children must be born, to have a reasonable Probability, that one shall live to the Age of seventeen; and [24] even after so doing, his Life is not to be calculated at more than ten to twelve Years Purchase.

81 |5| Il est vrai que la moitié des Enfans qui naissent & qui meurent avant l'âge de ªdix-septª ans, décedent bien plus vite dans les premieres années de leur vie que dans les suivantes, puisqu'il meurt un bon tiers de ceux qui naissent, dès la premiere année. Cette circonstance semble diminuer la dépense qu'il faut pour élever un Enfant jusqu'à l'âge du travail: mais comme les Meres perdent beaucoup de tems à soigner leurs Enfans dans ᵇleurs infirmités & enfanceᵇ, & que les Filles mêmes adultes n'égalent pas le travail des ᶜMâlesᶜ, & gagnent à peine de quoi subsister; [44] il semble que pour conserver un de deux Enfans qu'on éleve jusqu'à l'âge de virilité ou du travail, il faut emploïer autant de produit de Terre que pour la ᵈsubsistanceᵈ d'un Esclave adulte, soit que le Propriétaire éleve lui-même dans sa maison ou y fasse élever ces Enfans, *soit que le Pere esclave les éleve dans une Maison ou ᵉHameauᵉ à part. Ainsi je conclus que le travail journalier du plus vil Esclave, correspond en valeur au double du produit de Terre dont il subsiste, soit que le Propriétaire le lui donne pour sa propre subsistance & celle de sa Famille; soit qu'il le fasse subsister avec sa Famille dans sa Maison.* C'est une matiere qui n'admet pas un calcul exact, & dans laquelle la précision n'est pas même fort nécessaire, il suffit qu'on ne s'y éloigne pas beaucoup de la réalité.

|| ᶠIt is true, thatᶠ the one half of the children who die before ᵍ17ᵍ, die faster ʰin the first years than in the followingʰ; but, as the time the mother loses in producing and ⁱtendingⁱ them, seems to make up for this computation, and the females ʲareʲ more chargeable, and less profitable ᵏwhen they grow up, than the malesᵏ; it ˡappearsˡ reasonable to think, that the ᵐlabourᵐ of the meanest slave is equal to double the produce of ⁿthe landⁿ that is required to maintain him.

|| It is true, that this Moiety of Children die more frequently in the early Years of Life. Time and Experience must be had in bringing the Survivors up: Allowances must be made for Females. All these Circumstances taken together, it is generally computed that the Labour of the able bodied Slave, is proportioned in Value to the Quantity of Land necessary to be employed for the Maintenance of two Slaves.

On this assumption the labour of an adult Slave of the lowest class is worth at least as much as the quantity of Land which the Proprietor is obliged to allot for his food and necessaries and also to double the Land which serves to breed a Child up till he is of age fit for labour, seeing half the children that are born die before the age of 17, according to the calculations and observations of the celebrated Dr Halley. So that two children must be reared up to keep one of them till working age and it would seem that even this would not be enough to ensure a continuance of Labour since adult Men die at all ages.

ᵃ…ᵃ: R, M, N: 'La Nouriture et Commodités'
ᵇ…ᵇ: R, M, N: '17'
ᶜ…ᶜ: R, M, N: 'Hallay'
ᵈ…ᵈ: M: 'mais'
ᵉ…ᵉ: T: 'Therefore'
ᶠ…ᶠ: T: 'Labor'
ᵍ…ᵍ: T: 'which'
ʰ…ʰ: T: 'who'
ⁱ…ⁱ: T: 'seventeen'
ʲ…ʲ: T: 'to have'
ᵏ…ᵏ: T: 'from ten to twelve Years'

i. The contributions of Dr. Halley referred to in E80 **80** are Edmond Halley's 'An Estimate of the Degrees of the Mortality of Mankind' and 'Some further Considerations on the Breslaw Bills of Mortality' both published in the *Philosophical Transactions*, January 1693. In the second contribution, on p. 655, commenting on his table on p. 599, Halley states: 'the one half of those that are born are dead in Seventeen years time, 1238 being in that time reduced to 616'. Cf. E172.

ii. The final statement in D80 and A80, but not E80, about the average life being 10 to 12 years (purchase) is a repetition of the statement in E/D/A42. Cf. C42i. Even though D80 and A80 do not mention Halley, it should be noted that this author calculates the values of annuities taken out at the age from early adulthood up to the early 40s as gradually declining from 12 to 10 years' purchase (ibid. 603–04).

iii. Smith (1776, I, viii, 15) paraphrases the content of E80. His reference to 'Mr. Cantillon' in the same place is Smith's only acknowledgment of a reliance on Cantillon's ideas.

It is true that the one half of the Children who die before 17 die faster in the first years after birth than in the following, since a good third of those who are born die in their first year. This seems to diminish the cost of raising a Child to working age, but as the Mothers lose much time in nursing their Children in illness and infancy and the Daughters even when grown up are not the equals of the Males in work and barely earn their living, it seems that to keep one of two Children to manhood or working age as much Land must be employed as for the subsistence of an adult Slave, whether the Proprietor raises them himself in his house or has the children raised there or that the Father brings them up in a House or Hamlet apart. Thus I conclude that the daily labour of the meanest Slave corresponds in value to double the produce of the Land required to maintain him, whether the Proprietor give it him for his subsistence and that of his Family or provides him and his Family subsistence in his own house. It does not admit of exact calculation, and exactitude is not very necessary; it suffices to be near enough to the truth.

ᵃ…ᵃ: R, M: '17'
ᵇ…ᵇ: R, M: 'les infirmites et enfances'; N: 'les infirmités delenfance'
ᶜ…ᶜ: R, M, N: 'hommes'
ᵈ…ᵈ: R, M, N: 'nourriture'
ᵉ…ᵉ: R, M, N: 'berceau'
ᶠ…ᶠ: T: ' 'Tis true,'
ᵍ…ᵍ: T: 'seventeen'
ʰ…ʰ: T: 'in the first than in the following years'
ⁱ…ⁱ: T: 'attending'
ʲ…ʲ: T: 'being'
ᵏ…ᵏ: T: 'than the Males when they grow up to Maturity'
ˡ…ˡ: T: ' seems'
ᵐ…ᵐ: T: 'Labor'
ⁿ…ⁿ: T: 'Land'

i. The assumption in **81** E81 that 'a good third' of children die in their first year does not quite agree with Halley's figure of 348 deaths in the first year out of 1,238 births.

ii. Where E81 has italics, the text in R is underlined, except that the underlining continues until the end of the sentence ('*sa maison.*'). In M only the first two words, '*soit que*', are underlined and none of the words is underlined in N.

82 |6| Si le Propriétaire emploie à [45] son travail des Vassaux ou Païsans libres, il les ᵃentretiendraᵃ probablement un peu mieux qu'il ne feroit des Esclaves, & ce, suivant la coutume du lieu; mais encore dans cette supposition, le travail du Laboureur libre doit correspondre en valeur au double du produit de terre qu'il faut pour son entretien; mais il seroit toujours plus avantageux au Propriétaire d'entretenir des Esclaves, que des Païsans libres, attendu que lorsqu'il en aura élevé un trop grand nombre pour son travail, il pourra vendre les Surnumeraires comme ses bestiaux, & qu'il en pourra tirer un prix proportionné à ᵇla dépenseᵇ ᶜqu'il auraᶜ faite pour les élever jusqu'à l'âge de virilité ou de travail; hors des cas de la vieillesse & de l'infirmité.

|| When the proprietor maintains slaves on his land, if he has more of them than his ᵈlabourᵈ requires, he sells the superfluous hands, as he does his cattle; in which case their value or price ought to answer ᵉ(cæteris paribus)ᵉ to the quantity of land employed to breed up two slaves to maturity.

|| But, if the proprietor employs in his service free servants, or vassals, instead of slaves, he may probably maintain them upon a better foot than slaves, according to the usage ᶠandᶠ [II, 2, col.2] custom of the place he lives in: yet in this case also, the labour of ᵍa day-labourerᵍ ought to correspond to about double the quantity of land that is employed to maintain him.

|| When the Planter of an Estate brings up Slaves, and their Children, and if the Increase in Number is more than sufficient for cultivating his Estate, he has a Right to dispose of his useless Hands, in the same Manner as he would of any Produce of his Land, and the Price of such a Slave ought to correspond to the Value of the Land's Produce, and the Labour attending it, allotted to support and bring him up. If the Proprietor of an Estate employs Vassals or Husbandmen, who are free, they must be supported better than absolute Slaves; and the Value of Labour of such [25] ought to correspond to double the Value of the Land allotted for their Support.

83 |7| On peut de même estimer le travail des Artisans esclaves au double du produit de terre qu'ils con-[46]sument; celui des Inspecteurs de travail, de même, suivant les douceurs & avantages qu'on leur donne au-dessus de ceux qui travaillent sous leur conduite.

84 |8| Les Laboureurs ou Artisans, lorsqu'ils ont leur double portion dans leur propre disposition, s'ils sont mariés emploient une portion pour leur propre entretien, & l'autre pour celui de leurs Enfans.

If he be married, the surplus goes to the breeding up of his children, his wife being supposed just able to maintain herself by her ᵃlabourᵃ:

85 |9| S'ils sont Garçons, ils mettront à part ᵃune petite partieᵃ de leur double portion, pour se mettre en état ᵇde se marier, & faireᵇ un petit fond pour le ménage; mais le plus grand nombre ᶜconsumeraᶜ la double portion pour leur propre entretien.

but if he be a batchelor, he will probably employ his surplus to live more at his ease:

If the Proprietor employ the Labour of Vassals or free Peasants he will probably maintain them upon a better foot than Slaves according to the custom of the place he lives in, yet in this case also the Labour of a free Labourer ought to correspond in value to double the produce of Land needed for his maintenance. But it will always be more profitable to the Proprietor to keep Slaves than to keep free Peasants, because when he has brought up a number too large for his requirements he can sell the surplus Slaves as he does his cattle and obtain for them a price proportionable to what he has spent in rearing them to manhood or working age, except in cases of old age or infirmity.

[a]...[a]: 1756b: 'entiendra'; 1769: 'entretienda'
[b]...[b]: R: 'sa depence' (M, N: 'la dépense')
[c]...[c]: 1756b, 1769: 'qu'il en aura'
[d]...[d]: T:'Labor'
[e]...[e]: T: 'cæteris paribus' (italics, no parentheses)
[f]...[f]: T: 'or'
[g]...[g]: T: 'a Day's Work'

i. For the use in D of the *cæteris paribus* clause, cf. C49ii. **82**

ii. This is the only occurrence in E of the term '*Vassaux*' (vassals). It also occurs in D/A78, D98 and D257. Cf. CD257ii.

iii. The differences in formulations in E/D/A82 with respect to the price of slaves are similar to the differences between the formulations of the concept of intrinsic price generally in E65/D65/A65. See C65.

iv. Cf. V82g with '*travail journalier*' in E97.

In the same way one may appraise the Labour of slave craftsmen at twice the produce of the Land which they consume. Overseers likewise, allowing for the favours and privileges given to them above those who work under them.

In E83, E84 and before in E79, **83** the labour of both (agricultural) labourers and artisans is discussed. In D up to D92 the discussion remains limited to agricultural labour. D92 shows similarities with E83. In A the corresponding chapter XI only mentions artisans briefly in A100.

When the Artisans or Labourers have their double portion at their own disposal they employ one part of it for their own upkeep if they are married and the other for their Children.

[a]...[a]: T: 'Labor'

84

If they are unmarried they set aside a little of their double portion to enable them to marry and to make a little store for housekeeping; but most of them will consume the double portion for their own maintenance.

[a]...[a]: R, M, N: 'une partie'
[b]...[b]: M: 'de se nourrir et de se faire' (R, N: 'de se marier et faire')
[c]...[c]: M: 'consommera' (R, N: 'consumera')

85

86 |10| Par exemple, le Païsan marié se contentera de vivre de pain, de fromage, de légumes, &c. mangera rarement de la viande, boira peu de vin ou de biere, n'aura guere que des habits vieux & [47] mauvais, qu'il portera le plus long-tems qu'il pourra: il emploiera le surplus de sa double portion à élever & entretenir ses Enfans; au lieu que le Païsan garçon mangera le plus souvent qu'il pourra de la viande, & se donnera des habits neufs, &c. & par conséquent emploiera sa double portion pour son entretien; ainsi il ᵃconsumeraᵃ deux fois plus de produit de terre sur sa personne que ne fera le Païsan marié.

for example, the married labourer will live upon bread and cheese, roots &c. ᵇeat meat, drink strong beer or wine seldomᵇ, change cloaths and linnen ᶜseldomᶜ; whereas the unmarried labourer will eat and drink better, ᵈand wearᵈ better apparel, and consequently (if we suppose their wages equal) he will consume the produce of more land for the maintenance of his own person, than the married man, if he saves nothing.

87 |11| Je ne considere pas ici la dépense de la Femme, je suppose que son travail suffit à peine pour son propre entretien, & lorsqu'on voit un grand nombre de petits Enfans dans un de ces pauvres ménages, je suppose que quelques personnes charitables contribuent ᵃquelque choseᵃ à leur subsistance, sans quoi il faut que le Mari & la Femme se privent d'une partie de leur nécessaire [48] pour faire ᵇvivteᵇ leurs Enfans.

88 |12| Pour mieux comprendre ceci, il faut savoir qu'un pauvre Païsan peut s'entretenir, au plus bas calcul, du produit d'un Arpent & demi de terre, en se nourrissant de pain & de légumes, en portant des habits de Chanvre & des sabots, &c. au lieu que s'il se peut donner du vin & de la viande, des habits de drap, &c. il pourra dépenser, sans ivrognerie ni gourmandise, & sans aucun excès, le produit de quatre jusqu'à dix Arpens de terre de moïenne bonté, comme sont la plûpart des terres en Europe, l'une portant l'autre; j'ai fait faire des calculs qu'on trouvera au Supplément, pour constater la quantité de terre dont un Homme peut consommer le produit ᵃdeᵃ chaque espece de nourriture, habillement, & autres choses nécessaires à la vie, dans une année, [49] suivant les façons de vivre de notre Europe, où les Païsans des différens Païs sont souvent nourris & entretenus assez différemment.

|| For the better understanding of ᵇthisᵇ, it is to be observed, that a poor labourer may maintain himself, at the lowest computation, upon the produce of an acre and an half of land; whereas, if he allows himself ᶜstrong beer, meat, and allᶜ other conveniencies, he may, without gluttony or excess, consume the produce of ᵈfourᵈ to 10 acres of land, ᵉof ordinary goodnessᵉ.

For example the married Labourer will content himself with Bread, Cheese, Vegetables, etc., will rarely eat meat, will drink little wine or beer, and will have only old and shabby clothes which he will wear as long as he can. The surplus of his double portion he will employ in raising and keeping his children, while the unmarried Labourer will eat meat as often as he can, will treat himself to new cloaths, etc. and employ his double portion on his own requirements. Thus he will consume twice as much personally of the produce of the Land as the married man.

[a]...[a]: M: 'consommera' (R, N: 'consumera')
[b]..[b]: T: 'eat meat seldom, avoid strong Drinks'
[c]...[c]: T: 'rarely'
[d]...[d]: T: ' wear'

i. The possibility of bachelors saving in D86 is also mentioned in E85. **86**

ii. D86 says that a bachelor has a larger personal consumption, and has the qualification 'if we suppose their wages equal', where E86 says the batchelor's consumption is 'double' that of a married man.

iii. With regard to V86b, this is the only significant instance where D is closer to E than T is.

I do not here take into account the expense of the Wife. I suppose that her Labour barely suffices to pay for her own living, and when one sees a large number of little Children in one of these poor families I suppose that charitable persons contribute somewhat to their maintenance, otherwise the Parents must deprive themselves of some of their necessaries to provide a living for their Children.

[a]...[a]: M, N: "de quelque chose' (R: 'quelque chose')
[b]...[b]: R, M, N, 1756a, 1756b and 1769: 'vivre'

The first phrase in E88 ('*Pour mieux comprendre ceci*') refers to the argument of E86, rather than E87. This suggests that the intervening E87 is something of a digression. This may be related to the fact that the corresponding paragraph in D appears in a different place (see D99). **87**

For the better understanding of this it is to be observed that a poor Labourer may maintain himself, at the lowest computation, upon the produce of an Acre and a half of Land if he lives on bread and vegetables, wears hempen garments, wooden shoes, etc., while if he can allow himself wine, meat, woollen cloaths, etc. he may without drunkenness or gluttony or excess of any kind consume the produce of 4 to 10 acres of Land of ordinary goodness, such as most of the Land in Europe taking part with another. I have caused some figures to be drawn up which will be found in the Supplement, to determine the amount of Land of which one man can consume the produce under each head of Food, Clothing, and other necessaries of life in a single year, according to the mode of living in Europe where the Peasants of divers countries are often nourished and maintained very differently.

[a]...[a]: R, M, N: 'dans'
[b]...[b]: T: 'what is meant'
[c]...[c]: T: 'constantly Wine, Beer, Meat, and'
[d]...[d]: T: '4'
[e]...[e]: T: 'of ordinary goodness, according to the different Ways of Living'

i. While a reference to a supplement is missing in D, the estimates are the same, if one takes the *arpent* to be equivalent to the acre. The *arpent* of the *ancien régime* was subject to regional variations and could be as little as about 0.8 acres and as much as 1.2 acres. **88**

ii. The expression '*notre Europe*' in E88 is also used in E184 and E461. Cf. C184iii.

89 |13| C'est pourquoi je n'ai pas déterminé à combien de Terre le travail du plus vil Païsan ou Laboureur correspond en valeur, lorsque j'ai dit qu'il vaut le double du produit de la Terre qui sert à l'entretenir; car cela varie suivant la façon de vivre dans les différens Païs. Dans quelques Provinces méridionales de France, le Païsan s'entretient du produit d'un arpent & demi de Terre, & ªon y peutª estimer son travail, égal au produit de trois arpens. Mais dans le Comté de ᵇMiddlesexᵇ, le Païsan dépense ordinairement le produit de ᶜ5 à 8ᶜ arpens de Terre, & ainsi on peut estimer son travail au double.

90 |14| Dans ªle Païsª des Iroquois, où [50] les Habitans ne labourent pas la terre, & où on vit uniquement de la chasse, le plus vil Chasseur peut consommer le produit de 50 arpens de Terre, puisqu'il faut vraisemblablement ce nombre d'arpens pour nourrir les bêtes qu'il mange dans l'année, d'autant plus que ces Sauvages n'ont pas l'industrie de faire venir de l'herbe en abbattant quelque bois, & qu'ils laissent tout au gré de la nature.

91 |15| On peut donc estimer le travail de ce Chasseur, comme égal en valeur au produit de cent arpens de Terre. Dans les Provinces méridionales de la Chine, la Terre produit du Ris jusqu'à trois fois l'année, & rapporte jusqu'à cent fois la semence, à chaque fois, par le grand soin qu'ils ont de l'Agriculture, ª& par laª bonté de la terre qui ᵇne se reposeᵇ jamais. Les Païsans, qui y travaillent presque tout nus, ne [51] vivent que de Ris, & ne boivent que de l'eau de Ris; & il y a apparence qu'un arpent y entretient plus de dix Païsans: ainsi il n'est pas étonnant que les Habitans y soient dans ᶜun nombre prodigieuxᶜ. Quoi qu'il en soit, il paroît par ces exemples, qu'il est très indifférent à la nature, que les Terres produisent de l'herbe, des bois ou des grains, & qu'elle entretienne un grand ou un petit nombre de Vegetaux, d'animaux, ou d'Hommes.

|| ᵈFrom thisᵈ may be inferred, that the ᵉlabourᵉ of a working man corresponds to more or less land in different countries, according to the different customs of living used in ᶠthe saidᶠ countries; and that, if the ᵉlabourᵉ of a peasant in France be worth the produce of three acres, that of an English country-man, who drinks beer, wears woollen cloth, eats meat pretty often, and consequently consumes the produce of more land, is worth in England from ᵍsix to eightᵍ acres.

For this reason I have not determined to how much Land the Labour of the meanest Peasant corresponds in Value when I laid down that it is worth double the produce of the Land which serves to maintain him: because this varies according to the mode of living in different countries. In some southern Provinces of France the Peasant keeps himself on the produce of one acre and a half of Land and the value of his Labour may be reckoned equal to the product of Three Acres. But in the County of Middlesex the Peasant usually spends the produce of 5 to 8 acres of Land and his Labour may be valued at twice as much as this.

ᵃ...ᵃ: R, M: 'y peut'; N: 'ɏ' and inserted: 'l'on y' peut'
ᵇ...ᵇ: R: 'Middlexx'; M: Middleux; (N: Middlesex)
ᶜ...ᶜ: R, M: 'Cinq a huit' (N: '5 a 8')
ᵈ...ᵈ: T: 'Whence it'
ᵉ...ᵉ: T: 'Labor'
ᶠ...ᶠ: T: 'such'
ᵍ...ᵍ: T: '6 to 8'

i. While E89 compares poor southern French provinces to a rich English county, D89 compares the living standards of 'countrymen' in France and England in general.

ii. The estimate of acres per head in England is slightly higher in D89.

iii. The young Alexander Hamilton paraphrased D89 in his *Pay Book*, p. 243: 'The par between land and labour is twice the quantity of land whose product will maintain the labourer. In France one acre and a half will maintain one, in England three owing to the differences in the manner of living.'

89

In the country of the Iroquois where the inhabitants do not plough the Land and live entirely by Hunting, the meanest Hunter may consume the produce of 50 Acres of Land since it probably requires so much to support the animals he eats in one year, especially as these Savages have not the industry to grow grass by cutting down the trees but leave everything to nature.

ᵃ...ᵃ: R: 'les pays' (M: 'le pays'; N: 'le pais')

There is a counterpart for E90 in D98. Also see E/A153.

90

The Labour of this Hunter may then be reckoned equal in value to the product of 100 acres of Land. In the southern Provinces of China the Land yields Rice up to three crops in one year and a hundred times as much as is sown, owing to the great care which they have of Agriculture and the fertility of the soil which is never fallow. The Peasants who work there almost naked live only on Rice and drink only Rice water, and it appears that one Acre will support there more than 10 Peasants. It is not surprising, therefore, that the population is prodigious in number. In any case it seems from these examples that Nature is altogether indifferent whether the Earth produce grass, trees, or grain, or maintains a large or small number of Vegetables, Animals, or Men.

ᵃ...ᵃ: R, M, N: 'et la'
ᵇ...ᵇ: R, M, N: 'ne repose'
ᶜ...ᶜ: R, M 'un nombre innombrable'; N: 'un nombre inombrable'

There is a counterpart for D91 in D98.

91

92

|| *'It has already been observed, that a mechanic tradesman earns more than a day-labourer, and, consequently, he is able to consume, in the maintenance of his person, the produce of more land, or he may spare his overplus, if he pleases.

93 |16| Les Fermiers en Europe semblent correspondre aux Inspecteurs des Esclaves laboureurs dans les autres Païs, & les Maîtres Artisans qui font travailler plusieurs Compagnons, aux Inspecteurs des Esclaves artisans.

|| The master-tradesmen, and superior undertakers of business, upon the footing that things are managed in Europe, correspond something to the overseers of slaves in other parts, and gain more than the journeymen tradesmen:

94 |17| Ces Maîtres Artisans savent ᵃà-peu-près combienᵃ d'ouvrage un Compagnon artisan peut faire par jour dans chaque Métier, [52] & les paient souvent à proportion de l'ouvrage qu'ils font; ᵇainsi ces Compagnonsᵇ travaillent autant qu'ils peuvent, pour leur propre intérêt, sans autre inspection.

and these master-tradesmen know how much work a journeyman can do in a day, and often pay them by the work and piece: this makes them work, for their own interest, as hard as they can, without further inspection.'*

95 |18| Comme les Fermiers & Maîtres artisans en Europe sont tous Entrepreneurs & travaillent au hasard, ᵃles unsᵃ s'enrichissent & gagnent plus qu'une double subsistance, d'autres se ruinent & font banqueroute, comme on l'expliquera plus particulierement en traitant des Entrepreneurs; mais le plus grand nombre s'entretiennent au jour la journée avec leurs Familles, & on pourroit estimer le travail ᵇouᵇ inspection de ceux-ci, à-peu-près au triple du produit de Terre qui sert pour leur entretien.

96 |19| Il est certain que ces Fermiers & Maîtres artisans, s'ils conduisent le travail de dix Laboureurs ou Compagnons, seroient éga-[53]lement capables ᵃde conduire le travail de vingtᵃ, suivant la grandeur de leurs Fermes ᵇouᵇ le nombre de leurs Chalans: ᶜce qui rend incertain la valeur de leur travail ou inspectionᶜ.

	...: D92-94 are missing in T.	i. There is a correspondence between D92 and E83. Only from this point in D are the wages of industrial labourers considered. Cf. C83. ii. The reference 'it has already been observed' is to D42.	92

Farmers in Europe seem to correspond to Overseers of labouring Slaves in other Countries, and the Master Tradesmen who employ several Journeymen to the Overseers of Artisan Slaves.

The point in D93 about 'superior undertakers' corresponding to 'overseers of slaves' under an alternative socio-economic arrangement is also made in D437 and D442. In E139 a similar point is made about the role of *inspecteurs* on an isolated estate.   **93**

These Masters know pretty well how much work a journeyman Artisan can do in a day in each Craft, and often pay them in proportion to the work they do, so that the Journeymen work for their own interest as hard as they can without further inspection.

^a...^a: R, M, N: 'Combien a peu prés'
^b...^b: R, M, N: 'au moyen de quoy ils'   **94**

As the Farmers and Masters of Crafts in Europe are all Undertakers working at a risk, some get rich and gain more than a double subsistence, others are ruined and become bankrupt, as will be explained more in detail in treating of Undertakers; but the majority support themselves and their Families from day to day, and their Labour or Superintendence may be valued at about thrice the produce of the Land which serves for their maintenance.

^a...^a: R: 'Luns' (M, N: 'les uns')
^b...^b: R, M, N: 'et'

For other cases like V95b, cf. V63a and V70a.   **95**

Evidently these Farmers and Master Craftsmen, if they superintend the Labour of 10 Labourers or Journeymen, would be equally capable of superintending the Labour of 20, according to the size of their Farms or the number of their customers, and this renders uncertain the value of their Labour or Superintendence.

^a...^a: M:'de conduire de vingt'
^b...^b: N: 'et'
^c...^c: R, M, N: 'Cequi rend La valeur de leur travail ou inspection incertaine'   **96**

97 |20| Par ces inductions, & autres qu'on pourroit faire dans le même goût, l'on voit que la valeur du travail journalier a un rapport au produit de la Terre, & que la valeur intrinseque d'une chose peut être mesurée par la quantité ᵃde Terreᵃ qui est emploïée pour sa production, & par la quantité du travail qui y entre, c'est-à-dire encore par la quantité de Terre dont on attribue le produit à ceux qui y ont travaillé; & comme toutes ces Terres appartiennent au Prince & aux Propriétaires, toutes les choses qui ont ᵇcetteᵇ valeur intrinseque, ne l'ont qu'à leurs dépens.

|| From what has been said, ᶜit seems to be pretty clear, that the parᶜ and equation of land and ᵈlabourᵈ ᵉis knownᵉ by the quantity of land, the produce whereof is given for wages to the man who labours ᶠ. Thatᶠ the ᵈlabourᵈ of a man, who earns the produce of three acres, ᵍisᵍ equal to ʰthree acresʰ; ⁱofⁱ a man who earns the produce of ʲsixʲ acres, ᵏto six acresᵏ, &c. And it seems that the same proportion allotted for ᵈlabourᵈ differs in several parts of the world, according to ˡthe differentˡ ways of living.

98 - That, in China, the ᵃlabourᵃ of a peasant may be equal to half an acre of land, since a quarter of an acre may probably maintain him after the Chinese manner. - That, among the ᵇIroquois Indiansᵇ in America, the ᵃlabourᵃ of a vassal, or slave, may be equal to 20 or 100 acres, since the maintenance of a man may require half that quantity, in regard ᶜthat they liveᶜ mostly on wild beasts, which they hunt, and that the ᵈbeasts one manᵈ consumes in a year must have many acres of pasture to feed them; especially since people there ᵉhave not the knowledge to cut down the woodsᵉ, and ᶠmake the land produce as much grass for them as it might; and it seems in this as if nature had no regard to the multiplication of men in particular, but is indifferent whether the land produces grass, corn, or trees, or whether it maintains a great or small number of birds, beasts, or men.ᶠ

99 || The females commonly consume the produce of less land than the males, or, in other words, spend less; their infancy is not only ᵃindeed expenceᵃ, but even when they are grown up, they seldom earn more than what barely maintains them. Therefore it should seem that the ᵇlabourᵇ of a peasant ought to exceed twice the quantity of land necessary to maintain him, with regard to the female children that are bred up in a state: but, as most of the day-labourers do not marry till they have saved something, ᶜsuch whoᶜ are frugal are, by that means, enabled to breed up several children.

100 || So that, if it be allowed reasonable that the ᵃlabourᵃ of a peasant is equal to twice the product of the land that serves to maintain him, the mechanic ᵇand tradesmanᵇ, who earns more, may be said to follow the same proportion.

[25 continued] All Things considered, it is calculated that the Value of the lowest Peasant's Labour, may be rated at double the Value of the Land that was necessary to support him, according to the ordinary Expence of the Place where he resides; and the Labourer of the Artizan ought to follow the same Proportion.

By these examples and others which might be added in the same sense, it is seen that the value of the day's work has a relation to the produce of the soil, and that the intrinsic value of any thing may be measured by the quantity of Land used in its production and the quantity of labour which enters into it, in other words by the quantity of Land of which the produce is allotted to those who have worked upon it; and as all the Land belongs to the Prince and the Landowners all things which have this intrinsic value have it only at their expense.

[b]...[b]: R, M, N: 'de la terre'
[c]...[c]: T: 'the par'
[d]...[d]: T: 'Labor'
[e]...[e]: T: 'may be determined'
[f]...[f]: T: '; and that'
[g]...[g]: T: 'may be said to be'
[h]...[h]: T: 'such produce'
[i]...[i]: T: 'if'
[j]...[j]: T: '6'
[k]...[k]: T: 'is equal to such Produce'
[l]...[l]: T: 'their respective'

Note that D97 does **97** not have a sentence corresponding to the last sentence of E97. That sentence alludes to the content of E I, xii, which is not found in Postlethwayt's *Dictionary*. Cf. C106iii.

[a]...[a]: T: 'Labor'
[b]...[b]: T: 'Iroquois'
[c]...[c]: T: 'they subsist'
[d]...[d]: T: 'beasts which one man'
[e]...[e]: T: 'do not clear the Lands of the Wood'
[f]...[f]: T: 'are unacquainted with the Methods of making them produce as much grass as they might.'

There is a counterpart **98** for D98 in E90–E91. For American Indians, also see E/A153.

[a]...[a]: T: 'a dead Expense'
[b]...[b]: T: 'Labor'
[c]...[c]: T: 'such as'

The argument of E87 **99** suggests that V99a is the correct version.

[a]...[a]: T: 'Labor'
[b]...[b]: T: 'or manufacturer'

i. A100 carries on **100** from A82.
ii. D/A100 and D/A101 do not seem to have a clear counterpart in E.

101

|| If we consider to what quantity of land an hundred bushels of wheat correspond in value, we must not only [a]take into consideration[a] the number of acres which produced it, but also the double of the number of acres necessary to maintain the men whose work and [b]labour produced it[b] in that form, [c]during[c] the time they were at work [d]thereupon[d]: and, if the said wheat has been brought from afar, we must also [e]take into consideration[e] the land necessary to maintain the men and beasts employed in the carriage.

If you are to calculate how much Land corresponds in Value to a hundred Quarters of Wheat, you must first find out how many Acres of Land were employed in producing this Quantity of Grain, the Expence of preparing the Land for Sowing, its Rent; then double the Value of this Land for the Payment of the Labourers, and add the Charges of carrying it to the Market.

102

Thus, to [a]judge of[a] the intrinsic value of any thing, we must consider the land, and the [b]labour[b] that enters into [c]it's productions[c]; and, since we may pretty nearly determine the par of land and [b]labour[b], we may look upon land alone [d], perhaps, to be[d] the principal measure of all values.

103

|21| [a]*L'Argent ou la Monnoie,* [b]*qui* [54] *trouve*[b] *dans le troc les proportions des valeurs, est la mesure la plus certaine pour juger du pair de la Terre & du travail, & du rapport que l'un a à l'autre dans les différens Païs ou ce Pair varie suivant le plus ou moins de produit de Terre qu'on attribue à ceux qui travaillent.*[a]

|| But as money is the medium, which finds out the proportion of all values, it is also the best medium to fix the proportion [II, 3, col.1] of land and [c]labour, in relation to[c] all goods and commodities.

104

|22| Par exemple, si un Homme gagne une once d'argent tous les jours par son travail, & si un autre n'en gagne qu'une demi-once dans le même lieu; on peut déterminer que le premier a une fois plus de produit de Terre à dépenser que le second.

|| If a workman earns half an ounce of silver per diem, and another earns an ounce, it may be [a]judged that[a] the latter has twice the quantity of land to spend, since he earns twice the quantity of money.

105

|23| Monsieur le Chevalier Petty, dans un petit Manuscrit de l'année 1685, regarde ce pair, [a]en Equation[a] de la Terre & du travail, comme la considération la plus importante dans l'Arithmétique politique; mais la recherche qu'il en a faite en passant, n'est bisarre & éloignée des re-[55]gles de la nature, que parcequ'il ne s'est pas attaché aux causes & aux principes, mais seulement aux effets; comme Messieurs [b]Locke & d'Avenant[b], & tous les autres Auteurs Anglois qui ont écrit quelque chose de cette matiere, ont fait après lui.

|| This notion of the par of land and [c]labour[c] Sir William Petty looked upon to be [d]one of the most important considerations[d] in political œconomics, as appears by a MS. of his, written in the year 1685; but the method he [e]has taken to enquire[e] into it, seems [f]to be but very indifferently grounded[f]. [g]But the principles which we have laid down seem to be very plain and natural, and may be applied to the eclaircissement of many political altercations.[g]

101

ᵃ...ᵃ: T: 'take in'
ᵇ...ᵇ: T: 'Labor produce it'
ᶜ...ᶜ: T: 'for'
ᵈ...ᵈ: T: 'about it'
ᵉ...ᵉ: T: 'take in'

After this paragraph in A the short chapter XI finishes. Up to this point the order of texts in E and A, as well as the chapter numberings, are the same. However, the subsequent chapter XII, 'Of Mines and Barter', in A corresponds with E I, xvii and with the entry, 'Mines' of the *Universal Dictionary* (see E203/D203/A203ff). Some of the intervening text in E has counterparts in later chapters of *The Analysis*. These pieces are presented here out of the order found in Philip Cantillon's book. Some consist of short fragments (see A118–A119, A123, A129, A196–A197), but there are also two longer corresponding fragments: chapter XXI of A matches very well with part of E I, xii (see A106–A117) and chapter XXII of A with part of E I, xv (see A147–A155, A162, A173, A181). It is not clear why these parts occur in different orders in E and A.

102

ᵃ...ᵃ: T: 'consider'
ᵇ...ᵇ: T: 'Labor'
ᶜ...ᶜ: T: 'its production'
ᵈ...ᵈ: T: 'to be'

103

The Money or Coin which finds the proportion of Values in exchange is the most certain measure for judging of the Par between Land and labour and the relation of one to the other in different Countries where this Par varies according to the greater or less produce of the Land allotted to those who labour.

ᵃ...ᵃ: The italics in the published French text corresponds to the underlining in R and N manuscript of the same lines. In addition, in those manuscripts part of the preceding sentence is also underlined (in E97 from *'toutes les choses'* up to the end of the sentence). In M none of the passages is underlined.
ᵇ...ᵇ: R, M, N: 'qu'on trouve'
ᶜ...ᶜ: T: 'Labor, with Respect to'

104

If, for example, one man earn an ounce of silver every day by his work, and another in the same place earn only half an ounce, one can conclude that the first has as much again of the produce of the Land to dispose of as the second.

ᵃ...ᵃ: T: 'judged'

105

Sir William Petty, in a little manuscript of the year 1685, considers this Par, or Equation between Land and Labour, as the most important consideration in Political Arithmetic, but the research which he has made into it in passing is fanciful and remote from natural laws, because he has attached himself not to causes and principles but only to effects, as Mr Locke, Mr Davenant and all the other English authors who have written on this subject have done after him.

ᵃ...ᵃ: R: 'ou En Equation', M, N: 'ou equation'
ᵇ...ᵇ: R, M, N: 'Lock, Davénant'
ᶜ...ᶜ: T: 'Labor'
ᵈ...ᵈ: T: 'the most important consideration'
ᵉ...ᵉ: T: 'took for enquiring'
ᶠ...ᶠ: T: 'very triffling and ill grounded'
ᵍ...ᵍ: missing in T.

i. The work of Petty referred to is *The political anatomy of Ireland*, written in 1672 but not published until 1691. On p. 63 of the 1691 edition Petty writes about 'the most important Consideration in Political Oeconomies, *viz.* how to make a *Par* and *Equation* between Lands and Labour'. This phrase is followed most closely in T (see V105d), although both T and D have 'political œconomics' instead of 'political œconomies'. It is not clear why Cantillon thought the work was written in 1685. Cf. C289i.

ii. Postlethwayt's 1757 publication only has the first sentence in D105. Immediately after, it continues with the text reproduced in D64. Cf. C64.

iii. After D105 the text in the *Dictionary* continues with some short passages that form a kind of bridge to Postlethwayt's next (also unacknowledged) borrowing, this time from Sir Matthew Decker's *An essay on the causes of the decline of the foreign trade* (1744: 17–22). See *Universal Dictionary* II, p. 3, col. 1 just above halfway to p. 4 col. 2, two-thirds down.

106   **CHAPITRE ᵃXIIᵃ.**

Tous les Ordres ᵇ& tous les Hommesᵇ
d'un Etat subsistent ou s'enrichissent aux
dépens des Propriétaires des Terres

[114] CHAP. XXI.

All Orders of Men in a Community or State,
subsist and are enriched at the Expence of
the Proprietors of Land.

107 |1| Il n'y a que le Prince & les Propriétaires des Terres, qui vivent dans l'indépendance; tous les autres Ordres ᵃ& tous les Habitans sont à gages ou sont Entrepreneursᵃ. On en verra plus particulierement l'induction & le détail, dans le Chapitre suivant.

|| There are none but the King, and the great Proprietors of Land, who properly can be said, to live in a Kingdom independant; all other Persons and Inhabitants are such who are supported by Hire, or are Adventurers in Trade or Business;

108 |2| Si le Prince & les Proprié-[56]taires des Terres renfermoient leurs Terres, & s'ils n'y vouloient laisser travailler personne, il est visible qu'il n'y auroit ni nourriture ni habillement pour aucun des Habitans de l'Etat: parconséquent, non-seulement tous les Habitans de l'Etat subsistent du produit de la Terre qui est cultivée pour le compte des Propriétaires, mais aussi aux dépens ᵃdes mêmesᵃ Propriétaires du fond desquels ils tirent tout ce qu'ils ont.

if the King and the Proprietors of Land once lose their Estates, and will not suffer them to be cultivated and improved, it is clear that there would be neither Food nor Rayment for any [115] of the Inhabitants; consequently all the Individuals are supported at the Expence of the said Proprietors, for whose Account, and at whose Expence these Lands are cultivated, as the Source or Stock from whence all Subsistance and Support is produced and wrought into Form for Use.

109 |3| Les Fermiers ont ordinairement les deux tiers du produit de la Terre, ᵃl'un pour les frais & le maintien de leurs Assistansᵃ, l'autre pour le profit de leur entreprise: de ces deux tiers le Fermier fait subsister généralement tous ceux qui vivent à la Campagne directement ou indirectement, & même plusieurs ᵇArtisans ou Entrepreneursᵇ dans la Ville, ᶜà cause des marchandisesᶜ [57] de la Ville qui sont consommées à la Campagne.

Farmers who rent Land generally reserve to themselves two Thirds of its Produce; one Third for the Support and Maintenance of themselves and their Labourers, and the other as the Profit and Risk of their Undertaking: these two Thirds are applied in general to the Support of those who live by their Labour and Industry in Villages near such Estates, as also to the Support of several Mechanicks or Adventurers in Towns and Cities, who dispose of their Goods and Merchandize in the Country:

Chapter XII

*All Classes and
Individuals in a State
subsist or are enriched
at the Expense of the
Proprietors of Land*

ᵃ...ᵃ: R, N: '12ᵉ';
M: '6ᵉ'

ᵇ...ᵇ: R, M, N: 'et
hommes'

i. Chapter XXI in A is here presented out of order. Not only does it form an almost complete counterpart to E I, xii, the language also appears to correspond more closely to E than in other parts.

ii. Higgs clearly made use of this chapter in A for his translation of E. Not only does he sometimes follow the capitalisation of nouns that are not capitalised in the French text, in some instances his translation is an almost verbatim reproduction of A (see e.g. H112). Higgs's use of A is surprising considering his stated belief that it was not an authentic version, but a poor translation. See also C151i and C173i.

iii. None of this chapter seems to appear anywhere in Postlethwayt's *Universal Dictionary*.

106

There are none but the Prince and the Proprietors of Land who live independent; all other Classes and Inhabitants are hired or are Undertakers. The proof and detail of this will be developed in the next Chapter.

ᵃ...ᵃ: R, N: 'et habitans sont a gages ou éntréprénéurs'; M: 'et habitans sont a gages ou entrepreneurs'.

i. The main point of E/A107 is made more fully in E/D131

ii. A here uses the term 'Adventurers' for entrepreneurs. See C119iii.

107

If the Prince and Proprietors of Land close their Estates and will not suffer them to be cultivated it is clear that there would be neither Food nor Rayment for any of the Inhabitants; consequently all the Individuals are supported not only by the produce of the Land which is cultivated for the benefit of the Owners but also at the Expense of these same Owners from whose property they derive all that they have.

ᵃ...ᵃ: M: 'meme des' (R, N: 'des mémes')

The phrase 'lose their Estates' in A108, should perhaps be 'close their Estates', as in Higgs's translation. The word '*renfermer*' in this context means something like 'taking out of cultivation'.

108

The Farmers have generally two thirds of the Produce of the Land, one for their costs and the support of their Assistants, the other for the Profit of their Undertaking: on these two thirds the Farmer provides generally directly or indirectly subsistence for all those who live in the Country, and also Mechanicks or Undertakers in the City in respect of the Merchandise of the City consumed in the Country.

ᵃ...ᵃ: R, M, N: 'lune pour le maintien de leurs assistans et les frais'

ᵇ...ᵇ: R, M, N: 'artisans'

ᶜ...ᶜ: R, M, N: 'pour les marchandises'

i. For other statements of the 'three rents' theory see E119, E/D265ff and E438–E439. It occurs nowhere else in A. Cf. C265i.

ii. V109b would suggest that the editor of the French-printed text added '*ou Entrepreneurs*'. However, the phrase 'Mechanicks or Adventurers' in A109 perhaps suggests otherwise.

iii. Higgs's translation of '*Artisans*' with 'Mechanicks' (using antiquated spelling) is probably due to its occurrence in A. This would explain his favouring of the word 'Mechanicks' in a number of other places in his translation too.

109

110 |4| Le Propriétaire a ordinairement le tiers du produit de sa Terre, & de ce tiers, il fait non-seulement subsister tous ᵃles Artisansᵃ & autres qu'il emploie dans la Ville, mais ᵇbien souvent aussiᵇ les Voituriers qui apportent les denrées de la Campagne à la Ville.

The remaining Third is reserved to the Proprietor, as the Consideration which such Farmers pay for the Liberty of cultivating his Estate; this is generally laid out by the Landlord with his Tradesmen and others whom he employs in Cities and Towns, as also with those he employs to carry the Produce of the Country to the City.

111 |5| On suppose généralement que la moitié des Habitans d'un Etat subsiste & fait sa demeure dans les Villes, & l'autre moitié à la Campagne: cela étant, le Fermier qui a les deux tiers ou quatre sixiemes du produit de la Terre, en donne directement ou indirectement un sixieme aux Habitans de la Ville en échange des marchandises qu'il en tire; ce qui avec le tiers ou deux sixiemes que le Propriétaire dépense dans la Ville, fait trois sixiemes ou une moitié du pro-[58]duit de la Terre. Ce calcul n'est que pour donner une idée générale de la proportion; car au fond, si la moitié des Habitans demeure dans la Ville, elle dépense plus de la moitié du produit de la Terre, attendu que ceux de la Ville ᵃvivent mieuxᵃ que ceux de la Campagne, & dépensent plus de produit de Terre, étant tous Artisans ou Dépendans des Propriétaires, & parconséquent mieux entretenus que les Assistans & Dépendans ᵇdes Fermiersᵇ.

|| It is generally calculated that one half of the Inhabitants of a Kingdom subsist and take [116] their Abode in Cities, and the other half live in the Country; on this Supposition, the Farmer, who reserves to himself two Rents, pays either directly or indirectly, one sixth to the Citizens, in Exchange of the Goods and Implements of Husbandry, &c. had from thence: This Sixth with the one Third reserved by the Proprietor of the Land for his Rent is laid out in the City, and make near one Half of the Produce of the whole Estate. This Calculation is only to convey a general Idea of the Proportion of Expence between Town and Country; but in fact, if half of the Inhabitants of the Kingdom live in Cities they must consume more of the Land's Produce, as they eat and drink better, and are better cloathed, than those who reside in the Country;

112 |6| Quoi qu'il en soit, qu'on examine les moïens dont un Habitant subsiste, on trouvera toujours en remontant à leur source, qu'ils sortent du fond du Propriétaire, soit dans les deux tiers du produit qui est attribué au Fermier, soit dans le tiers qui reste au Propriétaire.

but let this Matter be how it will, if we examine the Means by which an Inhabitant is supported, it will always appear, in returning back to the Fountain-Head, that these Means arise from Land, and consequently from its Proprietors, either in the two Thirds reserved by the Farmer, or from the one Third reserved for the Rent to the Landlord.

113 |7| Si un Propriétaire n'avoit que la quantité de Terre qu'il donne [59] à ᵃun seul Fermierᵃ, ce Fermier en tireroit une meilleure subsistance que lui; mais les Seigneurs & Propriétaires de grandes Terres dans les Villes, ont quelquefois plusieurs centaines de Fermiers, & ne font dans ᵇun Etatᵇ qu'un très petit nombre par rapport à tous les Habitans.

The Proprietor has usually one third of the produce of his Land and on this third he maintains all the Mechanicks and others whom he employs in the City as well, frequently, as the Carriers who bring the Produce of the Country to the City.

ᵃ...ᵃ: R, M, N: 'les autres artisans'

ᵇ...ᵇ: R, M, N: 'aussy bien souvent'

110

It is generally calculated that one half of the Inhabitants of a kingdom subsist and make their Abode in Cities, and the other half live in the Country; on this supposition the Farmer who has two thirds or four sixths of the Produce of the Land, pays either directly or indirectly one sixth to the Citizens in exchange for the Merchandise which he takes from them. This sixth with the one third or two sixths, which the Proprietor spends in the City makes three sixths or one Half of the Produce of the Land. This Calculation is only to convey a general Idea of the Proportion; but in fact, if half of the Inhabitants live in the Cities they consume more than half of the Land's Produce, as they live better than those who reside in the Country and spend more of the Produce of the Land being all Mechanicks or Dependents of the Proprietors and consequently better maintained than the Assistants and Dependents of the Farmers.

ᵃ...ᵃ: R: 'Subciste mieux'; M, N: 'subcistent mieux'

ᵇ...ᵇ: R, M, N: 'du fermier'

i. The assumption that half **111** the population lives in towns is also made in E120, E277, E319 and D284. The calculation $1/6 + 1/3 = 1/2$ is also repeated in E277.

ii. Apart from the last sentence, Higgs adopts A111 verbatim as a translation of E111.

But let this Matter be how it will, if we examine the Means by which an Inhabitant is supported it will always appear in returning back to the Fountain-Head, that these Means arise from the Land of the Proprietor either in the two thirds reserved by the Farmer, or the one third which remains to the Landlord.

i. Higgs adopts A112 nearly verbatim as **112** a translation of E112. This explains his, otherwise curious, translation of '*source*' with 'Fountain-Head'.

ii. This brief description of circular flow is given a more detailed treatment in E II, iii (especially from E273 onwards).

If a Proprietor had only the amount of Land which he lets out to one Farmer the Farmer would get a better living out of it than himself; but the Nobles and large Landowners in the Cities have sometimes several hundreds of Farmers and are themselves very few in number in proportion to all the Inhabitants of a state.

ᵃ...ᵃ: R, M, N: 'un fermier'

ᵇ...ᵇ: N: 'un ~~bon~~ etat' (R, M: 'un état')

113

114 |8| Il est vrai qu'il y a souvent dans les grandes Villes plusieurs Entrepreneurs & Artisans qui subsistent par un Commerce étranger, ª& parconséquent aux dépens des Propriétaires des Terres en Païs étranger:ª mais je ne considere Jusqu'à présent un Etat, que par rapport à son produit ᵇ& à son industrieᵇ, afin de ne pas embarasser mon sujet par des choses accidentelles.

[117] ‖ Cities abound with Merchants, Manufacturers, Artists and Mechanicks, who are aided in their Support and Subsistence by foreign Commerce; but yet this Subsistence and Support is acquired at the Expence of the Proprietors of Land, who live in foreign Countries. At present I only consider a State from its native Produce, compared with the Proportion it bears to the Labour and Industry of the inhabitants;

115 |9|ªLe fondª des Terres appartient aux Propriétaires, mais ce fond leur deviendroit inutile si on ne le cultivoit pas, & plus on y travaille, toutes autres cho-[60]ses étant égales, plus il ᵇrendᵇ de denrées ᶜ; & plus on travailleᶜ ces denrées, toutes autres choses étant égales, lorsqu'on en fait des marchandises, plus elles ont de valeur. Tout cela fait que les Propriétaires ont besoin des autres Habitans, comme ceux-ci ont besoin des Propriétaires; mais dans cette œconomie, c'est aux Propriétaires, qui ont la disposition & la direction des fonds, ᵈà donnerᵈ le tour & le mouvement le plus avantageux au tout. Aussi tout dépend dans un Etat, des humeurs, modes & façons de vivre des Propriétaires ᵉde Terresᵉ principalement, comme je tacherai de le faire voir clairement dans la suite de cet Essai.

and as the Land belongs to its Proprietors, this Land would be useless and insignificant to them if it was not cultivated; the higher this Cultivation is carried the greater and more valuable will be its Produce, when wrought up for Consumption and Use: From hence arises the mutual Advantage between the great Proprietors of Land and the other Members of the Community; and this begets a mutual Dependance, as they reciprocally stand in need of each other's Assistance;

116

it therefore becomes the essential Interest of the great Proprietors of Land, who are our Law-givers, to take the greatest Care, by just and equal Institutions, that the Farmer and Labourer may be protected, encouraged and eased of all Taxes on Labour and Industry; for the Value [118] of this Labour and Industry depends on the Modes, Fashion, Manner of Living, and Luxury of the landed Gentlemen.

117 |10| C'est le besoin & la nécessité qui font subsister dans l'Etat, ªles Fermiers & les Artisans de toute espece, les Marchands, les Officiers, les Soldats & les Matelots, les Domestiques, & tous les [61] autres Ordresª qui travaillent ou sont emploïés dans l'Etat. Tous ces Gens de travail servent non-seulement le Prince & les Propriétaires, mais se servent mutuellement les uns les autres; de maniere qu'il y en a plusieurs ᵇqui ne travaillent pas directement pour les Propriétairesᵇ de Terres, ce qui fait qu'on ne s'apperçoit pas qu'ils subsistent de leurs fonds, & qu'ils vivent à leurs dépens. ᶜQuant à ceux qui exercentᶜ des Professions qui ne sont pas ᵈnécessairesᵈ, comme ᵉles Danseurs, les Comédiens, les Peintres, les Musiciens, &c.ᵉ ils ne sont entretenus dans l'État que pour le plaisir ou l'ornement; & leur nombre est toujours très petit par rapport aux autres Habitans.

It is mutual Want and Necessity which creates Subsistence, the Farmer and all Adventurers in Trade and Business, the Merchants, the Officers, the Army, the Navy, and all other Orders of Men, serve and are useful not only to the Prince and the Proprietors of Land, but also to one another, in a reciprocal Ratio; and this nice Relation seemingly enables several to live at their own Expence, without the immediate Intervention of the Proprietors of Land: Though it is very certain, that it is from this fruitful Source all Subsistence and Riches are had; yet as this reciprocal and mutual Dependance between the Inhabitants of a Kingdom does not at first Sight strike the Imagination, a Distinction is begot between the landed and monied Interest of a Kingdom, very hurtful to the Interest of the Community in general.

True there are often in the Cities several Undertakers and Mechanicks who live by Foreign Trade, and therefore at the Expense of Foreign Landowners: but at present I am considering only a State in regard to its own Produce and Industry, not to complicate my argument by accidental circumstances.

ᵃ...ᵃ: missing in R, M, N
ᵇ...ᵇ: R, M, N: 'et Industrie'

The words that are missing in the **114** French manuscript versions (V114a) have a counterpart in A. This is somewhat surprising if R was used as the source text for the French print version: how would the editor have known to add the clarification in this place? For a similar case, see C629ii and see the Introduction p. 14.

The Land belongs to the Proprietors but would be useless to them if it were not cultivated. The more labour is expended on it, other things being equal, the more it produces; and the more its products are worked up, other things being equal, the more value they have as Merchandize. Hence the Proprietors have need of the Inhabitants as these have of the Proprietors; but in this oeconomy it is for the Proprietors, who have the disposition and the direction of the Landed capital, to give the most advantageous turn and movement to the whole. Also everything in a State depends on the Fancy, Methods, and Fashions of life of the Proprietors of Land in especial, as I will endeavour to make clear later in this Essay.

ᵃ...ᵃ: N: 'Les fonds'
ᵇ...ᵇ: R: 'vend' (M, N: 'rend')
ᶜ...ᶜ: R, M: 'plus on travail'; N: '. Plus on travaille'
ᵈ...ᵈ: R, M, N: 'de donner'
ᵉ...ᵉ: R, M, N, 1769: 'des Terres'

i. Cf. C49ii for the phrase **115** *'toutes autres choses étant égales'*.
ii. Cf.C79i for the phrase *'dans cette œconomie'*.
iii. The further discussion promised in the final sentence of E115 is specifically referring to E I, xiv (E138–E146).

E116 has no counterpart in E and is reminiscent of the **116** beginning of A6. The observation in the first sentence that the large landowners 'are our Law-givers' applies to Britain, not to France. Since the Cantillon of the *Essai* normally refrains from 'policy recommendations', one may be tempted to conclude that the remarks about creating the right political institutions and exemption from taxes were penned by Philip Cantillon.

It is need and necessity which enable Farmers, Mechanicks of every kind, Merchants, Officers, Soldiers, Sailors, Domestic Servants and all the other Classes who work or are employed in the State, to exist. All these working people serve not only the Prince and the Landowners but each other, so that there are many of them who do not work directly for the Landowners, and so it is not seen that they subsist on the capital of these Proprietors and live at their Expense. As for those who exercise Professions which are not essential, like Dancers, Actors, Painters, Musicians, etc. they are only supported in the State for pleasure or for ornament, and their number is always very small in proportion to the other Inhabitants.

ᵃ...ᵃ: R, M, N: 'Les fermiers, Laboureurs, artisans de toutes especes [M, N: toute espece] Marchands, officiers soldats matelots domestiques et autres de Touts Les ordres'
ᵇ...ᵇ: R, M, N: 'qui nont rien a faire directement aux propriétaires'
ᶜ...ᶜ: R, M, N: 'pour cequi est'
ᵈ...ᵈ: R, M, N: 'mercenaires'
ᵉ...ᵉ: R, M, N: ''des joŭeuers danseurs, commediens peintre farceurs Musiciens &c.'

i. In R the surprising word **117** *'mercenaires'* ('mercenary') (V117d) is difficult to read.
ii. The wording in A117 is reminiscent of the opening sentence of the preface of Philip Cantillon's book: 'The mutual Want which Mankind have of each other, and the necessary Dependance they have on each other, is the Origin of Trade, or Barter' (1759: iii).
iii. The final observation in A117 about the perceived opposition between the landed and monied interest of a kingdom, appears to apply in particular to the politics of Britain. Cf. C135ii.
iv. Hereafter A continues with chapter XXII (pp. 119–24). See A147 ff.

| | *Essai (E)* | *Dictionary (D)* | *Analysis (A)* |

118

| [62] **CHAPITRE ᵃXIIIᵃ.** | [I, 498, col.1] **REMARKS** | [124] **CHAP. XXIII.** |

La circulation ᵇ& le trocᵇ des denrées ᶜ& des marchandisesᶜ, de même que leur production, se conduisent en Europe par des Entrepreneurs, & au hazard.

The circulation of all the goods and commodities in a state is carried on by undertakers, and all at an uncertainty.

Of Inland and Foreign Trade.

119

|1| Le Fermier est un Entrepreneur qui promet de païer au Propriétaire, pour sa Ferme ou Terre, une somme fixe d'argent ᵃ(qu'on suppose ordinairement égale en valeur au tiers du produit de la Terre)ᵃ, sans avoir de certitude de l'avantage qu'il tirera de cette entreprise. Il emploie une partie de ᵇcetteᵇ Terre à nourrir des Troupeaux, à produire du grain, du vin, ᶜdes foins, &c.ᶜ suivant ses idées, sans pouvoir prévoir ᵈlaquelle des especes de ces denréesᵈ rapportera le meilleur prix. Ce prix des [63] denrées dépendra en partie des Saisons & en partie de la consommation; s'il y a abondance de blé par rapport à la consommation, il sera à vil prix, s'il y a rareté, il sera cher. Qui est celui qui peut prévoir le nombre des ᵉnaissances & mortsᵉ des Habitans de l'Etat, dans le courant de l'année ᶠ?ᶠ Qui peut prévoir l'augmentation ou la diminution de dépense qui peut survenir dans les Famillesᶠ?ᶠ cependant le prix des denrées du Fermier dépend naturellement de ces événemens qu'il ne sauroit prévoir, & parconséquent il conduit l'entreprise de sa Ferme avec incertitude.

||The farmer who sows his corn, and feeds his flocks upon his farm, does not know what price the commodities will bear, since they may be scarce or plenty in a state, according to the goodness or badness of the season: if there be a great plenty, there will be too much for the consumption of the year, and an overplus to serve the next year; and so the farmer's commodities will be cheaper: if there be a scarcity, they will be dear. Thus the farmer is an undertaker, who carries on his business at an uncertainty.

[126] All Individuals of a State who exercise Professions, and are Adventurers in Trade and Business, carry them on at Risk and Hazard: the Farmer contracts to pay his Landlord a certain fixed Rent, for a Term of Years, and runs the Risk of the Land's Produce, and the more or less Price of the Market. There is no absolute foreseeing them, nor that of the Increase or Decrease of the human Species, in the Course of the current Year, nor the In-[127]crease and Decrease of the Expences of Families, yet the Value of the Farmer's Produce at Market, depends on these Circumstances, and consequently his Undertaking is carried on with Uncertainty and Risk.

Chapter XIII

The circulation and exchange of goods and merchandise as well as their production are carried on in Europe by Undertakers, and at a risk

ᵃ...ᵃ: R, N: '13ᵉ'; M: '7'
ᵇ...ᵇ: R, M, N: 'et troc'
ᶜ...ᶜ: R, M, N: 'et marchandises'

i. D occurs in the entry 'Circulation' (I, 498–99). This entry appeared in issue 42 of the *Universal Dictionary*, first published in the last weeks of 1752 or the first weeks of 1753. The entry starts with the following definition: 'CIRCULATION, in it's common acceptation, signifies the act of moving round, or in a circle. The light wherin I shall consider this article, as consistent with the tenor of our work, is as follows.' Then, under the heading, Remarks, the text reproduced here (D118–D134) commences. Immediately thereafter follows a fragment that corresponds to E II, iv (D299–D317).

ii. The entry 'Circulation' as a whole (as well as 'Cash', cf. C255ii) was in turn plagiarised by Thomas Mortimer in the first edition of *A New and complete dictionary of trade and commerce* (London 1766).

iii. The long chapter XXIII in A, pp. 124–68, contains only a few paragraphs (on pp. 126–27) that show clear correspondence with E I, xiii and a couple (on pp. 127–28) that correspond with E I, xvi (see A196–A197). Amongst the remaining material, not included here, there may be other fragments that were written by Richard Cantillon. Steuart (1767, II, 48) quotes a passage from p. 133, naming his source as the *Analysis*.

118

The Farmer is an undertaker who promises to pay to the Landowner, for his Farm or Land, a fixed sum of money (generally supposed to be equal in value to the third of the produce) without assurance of the profit he will derive from this enterprise. He employs part of the land to feed flocks, produce corn, wine, hay, etc. according to his judgment without being able to foresee which of these will pay best. The price of these products will depend partly on the weather, partly on the demand; if corn is abundant relatively to consumption it will be dirt cheap, if there is scarcity it will be dear. Who can foresee the number of births and deaths of the people in a State in the course of the year? Who can foresee the increase or reduction of expense which may come about in the families? And yet the price of the Farmer's produce depends naturally upon these unforeseen circumstances, and consequently he conducts the enterprise of his farm at an uncertainty.

ᵃ...ᵃ: R, M, N: parentheses missing
ᵇ...ᵇ: R, M, N: 'la'
ᶜ...ᶜ: R: 'des foints'; M: 'du foin'; (N: 'des foins')
ᵈ...ᵈ: M: 'laquelle de ces especes de denrées'
ᵉ...ᵉ: R, M, N: 'naissants et mort'
ᶠ...ᶠ: R: question mark missing; (present in M, N).

i. The argument of A119 corresponds more closely to E119 than D119. The latter mentions neither the fixed nature of rents nor fluctuations in demand due to changes in population and spending patterns (these points, though, are made in D124).

ii. The assumption, only in E, that the value of rent is equal to a third of the produce is also found in E/A111 and E/D265ff.

iii. Where E119 has '*entrepreneur*', D119 has 'undertaker' and A119 'adventurer'. In D the term 'adventurer' also occurs a few times as a synonym for 'undertaker' (D129, D208, D367), but the latter term is much more common. In the French manuscript versions '*avanturiers*' occurs once, but the word did not make it into the print version. See V129a. In A, on the other hand, 'undertaker' occurs sometimes (A260, A420, A444, A446, A470), but 'Adventurer' is more common. Cf. C129i.

iv. Louis-Paul Abeille in *Corps d'observations 1759–60* of the *Société d'Agriculture de Commerce & des Arts de Bretagne* (1760: 98–99, Paris) refers to the estimate of the size of rents in E119 and appears to associate it with the system of *la grande culture*: '*Le produit de toute Terre bien administrée, qui n'excede pas cent cinquante journaux, & qui n'est pas audessous de cent, doit etre partagé a peu pres en trois portions; un tiers au Propriétaire, deux tiers au Fermier pour sa subsistance, ses avances; & ses frais d'exploitation.*'

119

120 |2| La Ville consume plus de la moitié des denrées du Fermier. Il les y porte au Marché, ªou il les vendª au Marché du plus prochain Bourg, ᵇou bien quelques-unsᵇ s'érigent en Entrepreneurs pour faire ce transport. [64] Ceux-ci s'obligent de païer au Fermier un prix certain de ses denrées, qui est celui du Marché du jour, pour en tirer dans la Ville un prix incertain, qui doit néanmoins les défraïer des frais de la voiture, & leur laisser un profit pour leur entreprise; cependant la variation journaliere du prix des denrées dans la Ville, quoiquelle ne soit pas considérable, rend leur profit incertain.

121 |3| L'Entrepreneur ou Marchand qui voiture les denrées de la Campagne à la Ville, n'y peut pas demeurer pour les vendre en détail lors de leur consommation: pas une des Familles de la Ville ne se chargera d'acheter tout-à-la-fois les denrées dont ªelleª pourroit faire la consommation; chaque Famille ᵇpouvantᵇ augmenter ou diminuer en nombre aussi-bien qu'en consommation, ou au moins varier [65] dans les especes de denrées quelle consommera: on ne fait guere de provisions dans les Familles que de vin. ᶜQuoi qu'il en soitᶜ, le plus grand nombre des Habitans de la Ville, qui ne subsiste qu'au jour la journée, & qui cependant fait la plus forte consommation, ne pourra faire aucune provision des denrées de la Campagne.

|| The consumption of the farmer's commodities not being in his village only, but a good part of it in the nearest city, he cannot go to the city, and sit down there, to retail his commodities, without neglecting the business of his farm: nor will the proprietors of the city, or the artisans and mechanics, and others there, buy so much of his commodities as they will consume in their families in a year; their families may increase or decrease within the year, and they may consume sometimes more, sometimes less, of each commodity, and few or none of them are able to lay up a year's provision for their families:

122 |4| Cela fait que plusieurs personnes dans la Ville s'érigent en Marchands ou Entrepreneurs, pour acheter les denrées de la Campagne de ceux qui les apportent, ou pour les faire apporter pour leur compte: ils en donnent un prix certain suivant celui du lieu où ils les achetent, pour les revendre en gros ou en détail à un prix incertain.

so that several others set up for undertakers, and give a certain price for the farmer's commodities, and resell them at an uncertain price.

123 |5| ªCesª Entrepreneurs sont les Marchands, en gros, de laine, de grains, les Boulangers, Bouchers, Manufacturiers, & tous [66] les Marchands de ᵇtoute especeᵇ qui achetent les denrées ᶜ&ᶜ matériaux de la Campagne, pour les travailler & revendre à mesure que les Habitans ont besoin de les consommer.

Such are the merchants of corn, wool, wine, butchers, tanners, &c. and all these undertakers work at an uncertainty, and bankrupcies happen frequently among them.

[127 continued] Factors, Butchers, Bakers, Corn Chandlers, Farmers, Wool Staplers, Brewers, and Retailers of all Sorts and Sizes; buy the Produce of the Land at the certain fixed Price of the Day, and must run the Risk of reimbursing themselves, at the Uncertainty of other Markets, in Cities, Towns and Villages

124 |6| Ces Entrepreneurs ne peuvent jamais savoir la quantité de la consommation dans leur Ville, ni même combien de tems leurs Chalans acheteront d'eux, vu que leurs Rivaux tacheront par toutes sortes de voies de s'en attirer les Pratiques: tout cela cause tant d'incertitude parmi tous ces Entrepreneurs, qu'on en voit qui font journellement banqueroute.

It is impossible for any of them to know the consumption of the city he is in, because he cannot know the increase or decrease of the inhabitants within the year, and because the same families consume sometimes more and sometimes less of each kind in a year; and, because of the rival undertakers in the same trade, some find more favour and confidence from their customers than others.

The City consumes more than half the farmer's produce. He carries it to Market there or sells it in the Market of the nearest Town, or perhaps a few individuals set up as Carriers themselves. These bind themselves to pay the Farmer a fixed price for his produce, that of the market price of the day, to get in the City an uncertain price which should however defray the cost of carriage and leave them a profit. But the daily variation in the price of produce in the City, though not considerable, makes their profit uncertain.

The Undertaker or Merchant who carries the products of the Country to the City cannot stay there to sell them retail as they are consumed. No City family will burden itself with the purchase all at once of the produce it may need, each family being susceptible of increase or decrease in number and in consumption or at least varying in the choice of produce it will consume. Wine is almost the only article of consumption stocked in a family. In any case the majority of citizens who live from day to day and yet are the largest consumers cannot lay in a stock of country produce.

For this reason many people set up in a City as Merchants or Undertakers, to buy the country produce from those who bring it or to order it to be brought on their account. They pay a certain price following that of the place where they purchase it, to resell wholesale or retail at an uncertain price.

Such Undertakers are the wholesalers in Wool and Corn, Bakers, Butchers, Manufacturers and Merchants of all kinds who buy country produce and materials to work them up and resell them gradually as the Inhabitants require them.

These Undertakers can never know how great will be the demand in their City, nor how long their customers will buy of them since their rivals will try all sorts of means to attract customers from them. All this causes so much uncertainty among these Undertakers that every day one sees some of them become bankrupt.

---

[a]...[a]: R, M, N: 'ou bien il les vend'
[b]...[b]: R, N: 'ou quelque uns'; M: 'ou quelqu un'

[a]...[a]: R, M, N: 'ils'
[b]...[b]: R, M, N: 'poura'
[c]...[c]: R, M, N: 'en tout cas'

[a]...[a]: R, M, N: 'Tels'
[b]...[b]: R: 'Touttes especes' (M, N: 'toute espece')
[c]...[c]: R, M, N: 'ou'

---

120 The basis for the assumption in E120 that more than half of the agricultural produce is consumed in towns is the argument in E111, which has a counterpart in A, but not D. The same assumption is repeated in E277 and E319. In D the argument that half of the population lives in towns and that more than half of the agricultural produce is consumed there, occurs in D284. Cf. C284v.

121 In the first sentence of D121 it is the farmer who, lacking time to stay in town, leaves the sale of his produce to retailers, while in E121 it is the wholesale carrying merchant. This difference is probably due to the fact that D has no counterpart to the preceding paragraph, E120, where the latter intermediary agent is introduced.

122

123 i. V123a agrees with 'such' in D123.
ii. A123 combines the argument of E122 and E123.

124 i. Cf. the mention of bankruptcy in E124 with D123.
ii. In D119 only fluctuations in supply are considered, unlike E119 and A119, which also mention fluctuations in demand. In D124, on the other hand, the consideration of fluctuations in demand is a little more extended than in E124.

125 |7| ^aLe Manufacturier^a qui a acheté la laine ^bdu Marchand ou du Fermier^b en droiture, ne peut pas savoir le profit qu'il tirera de son entreprise, en vendant ses draps & étoffes au Marchand drapier. Si celui-ci n'a pas un débit raisonnable, il ne se char-[67]gera pas des draps & étoffes du Manufacturier, encore moins si ces étoffes cessent d'être à la mode.

|| In like manner the undertaker who has bought the farmer's wool at a certain price, is not sure of the price he shall have for it from the undertaker of the woolen manufacture. That price may vary in proportion to the plenty or scarcity of wool, with regard for the demand for it's consumption; and this consumption cannot be previously known or computed. In several families they do not know themselves how long the fancy will hold them to wear the same cloaths, nor what sort of cloth they will wear next.

126 |8| Le Drapier est un Entrepreneur qui achete des draps & des étoffes du Manufacturier à un prix certain, pour les revendre à un prix incertain, parcequ'il ne peut pas prévoir la quantité de la consommation; il est vrai qu'il peut fixer un prix & s'obstiner à ne pas vendre à moins qu'il ne l'obtienne, mais si ^ases Pratiques le quittent^a pour acheter à meilleur marché de ^bquelqu'autre^b, il se consumera en frais en attendant de vendre au prix qu'il se propose, ^b& cela le ruinera autant ou plus que^b s'il vendoit sans profit.

The undertaker of the manufacture runs the same hazard, besides that of the change of mode, and fashion, which may occasion his having several unfashionable stuffs lie upon his hands, to be sold off at under prices.

127 |9| Les Marchands en boutique, ^a& les Détailleurs^a de ^btoutes especes^b, sont des Entrepreneurs qui achetent à un prix certain, ^c& qui^c revendent dans leurs Boutiques ou [68] dans les Places publiques, à un prix incertain. Ce qui encourage & maintient ces sortes d'entrepreneurs dans un Etat, c'est que les Consommateurs qui sont leurs Chalans, aiment mieux donner quelque chose de plus dans le prix, pour trouver à portée ce dont ils ont besoin dans le détail, que d'en faire provision, & que la plus grande partie n'ont pas le moïen de faire une telle provision, en achetant de la premiere main.

|| The retailers and shopkeepers of all kinds are also undertakers, and sell at an uncertainty; what encourages and maintains them in a state is, that their customers, or the consumers, chuse to give something more to find what they want ready to their hand, when they have the fancy or means to buy, than to make a provision of those things at the first hand; for, some of the customers want means to make a yearly provision beforehand, and few care to confine their fancy, which is so liable to vary, when, for a small addition of price, they may please themselves, and determine their humour in a shop, at the very time they come to the consumption. Thus no body cares to bespeak cloth for his family at the manufacturer's a year beforehand, when he may, for a small matter more, please himself, when he has occasion, at a woollen-draper's shop.

128 |10| Tous ces Entrepreneurs deviennent consommateurs & Chalans réciproquement les uns des autres; le Drapier, du Marchand de vin; ^acelui-ci^a, du Drapier: ils se ^bproportionnent^b dans l'Etat à leurs Chalans ou à leur consommation. S'il y a trop de Chapeliers dans une Ville ou dans une rue pour le nombre de personnes qui y achetent des chapeaux, il faut que quelques-uns qui se-[69]ront les plus mal achalandés fassent banqueroute; ^cs'il^c y en a trop peu, ce sera une entreprise avantageuse, qui encouragera quelques nouveaux Chapeliers d'y ouvrir boutique, & c'est ainsi que les ^dEntrepreneurs de toutes especes se proportionnent^d au hazard dans un Etat.

The undertakers become consumers and customers one in regard to the other: the woollen-draper to the wine-merchant, or brewer, and the wine-merchant to the woollen-draper; and thus is carried on the indefinite circulation of traffic in societies.

The Manufacturer who has bought wool from the Merchant or direct from the Farmer cannot foretell the profit he will make in selling his cloths and stuffs to the Merchant Taylor. If the latter have not a reasonable sale he will not load himself with the cloths and stuffs of the Manufacturer, especially if those stuffs cease to be in the fashion.

ᵃ…ᵃ: M, N: 'Le meme facturier' (R: Le manufacturier')
ᵇ…ᵇ: R, M, N: 'du fermier ou du marchand'

The words *Le manufacturier* in R (V125a) are difficult to read and this may explain the odd expression *Le meme facturier* in M and N. See Figure 2.5 on p. 13. **125**

The Draper is an Undertaker who buys cloths and stuffs from the Manufacturer at a certain price to sell them again at an uncertain price, because he cannot foresee the extent of the demand. He can of course fix a price and stand out against selling unless he gets it, but if his customers leave him to buy cheaper from another, he will be eaten up by expenses while waiting to sell at the price he demands, and that will ruin him as soon as or sooner than if he sold without profit.

ᵃ…ᵃ: R: 'Ces pratiques Le quitte' (M, N: 'ses pratiques le quittent')
ᵇ…ᵇ:R, M, N: 'quelques autres'
ᶜ…ᶜ: R, M, N: 'autant ou plus que'

i. The strategy of 'standing out' (*s'obstiner*) in E126 is perhaps reminiscent of the description of the market process in A241. **126**
ii. In D126 the expression selling at 'under prices' refers to sales prices below the costs to the supplier.

Shopkeepers and retailers of every kind are Undertakers who buy at a certain price and sell in their Shops or the Markets at an uncertain price. What encourages and maintains these Undertakers in a State is that the Consumers who are their Customers prefer paying a little more to get what they want ready to hand in small quantities rather than lay in a stock and that most of them have not the means to lay in such a stock by buying at first hand.

ᵃ…ᵃ: R, M, N: 'et detailleurs'
ᵇ…ᵇ: M, N: 'toute espece' (R: 'touttes especes'); 1756b, 1769: 'toute espéce'
ᶜ…ᶜ: R, M, N: 'et'

127

All these Undertakers become consumers and customers one in regard to the other, the Draper of the Wine Merchant and vice versa. They proportion themselves in a State to the Customers or consumption. If there are too many Hatters in a City or in a street for the number of people who buy hats there, some who are least patronised must become bankrupt: if they be too few it will be a profitable Undertaking which will encourage new Hatters to open shops there and so it is that the Undertakers of all kinds adjust themselves to risks in a State.

ᵃ…ᵃ: R, M, N: 'et celui cy'
ᵇ…ᵇ: R: 'proportionne' (M, N: 'proportionnent')
ᶜ…ᶜ: R: 'et si il'; M, N: 'et s'il'
ᵈ…ᵈ: R: 'Entrepreneurs de touttes especes se proportionne'; M, N, 1756b, 1769: 'Entrepreneurs de toute espece se proportionnent'

Similar arguments to E128 about the number of entrepreneurs of each type proportioning themselves to the consumption of their wares are made in E57–E62, D57–D59, D129 and D134. **128**

129 |11| Tous les autres Entrepreneurs, ᵃcomme ceux qui se chargent des Mines, des Spectacles, des Bâtimens, &c., les Négocians sur mer & sur terre, &c., les Rotisseurs, les Pâtissiers, les Cabaretiers, &c.ᵃ de même que les Entrepreneurs dans leur propre travail & qui n'ont pas besoin de fonds pour s'établir, comme Compagnons artisans, Chauderoniers, Ravaudeuses, Ramoneurs, ᵇPorteurs-d'eauᵇ, subsistent avec incertitude, & se proportionnent à leurs Chalans. Les Maîtres artisans, comme Cordonniers, Tailleurs, Menui-[70]siers, Perruquiers, &c. qui emploient des Compagnons à proportion de l'ouvrage qu'ils ont, vivent dans la même incertitude, puisque leurs Chalans les peuvent quitter du jour au lendemain: les Entrepreneurs de leur propre travail dans les Arts & ᶜSciences, comme Peintresᶜ, Médecins, Avocats, &c. subsistent dans la même incertitude. Si un Procureur ou Avocat gagne ᵈ5000 livres sterlinsᵈ par an, en servant ses Cliens ou ᵉpratiquesᵉ, & qu'un autre n'en gagne que ᶠ500ᶠ, on peut les considérer comme aïant autant de gages incertains de ceux qui les emploient.

|| The other undertakers, as mine-adventurers, merchants of all kinds, whether adventurers or shop-keepers, undertakers of public houses, coffee-houses, pastry-cooks, hackney coaches, &c. subsist by undertaking at an uncertainty, and proportion themselves in number to the demand of the consumers and customers. If there be too many hackney coaches with regard to the customers who employ them, some of them must break, or put down their coaches; if too few, new ones will be erected.
|| The master tradesmen, or undertakers, who keep journeymen at work, as shoemakers, taylors, peruke-makers, &c. and the undertakers of their own labours, as tinkers, chimney-sweepers, water-carriers, &c. subsist also at an uncertainty, and proportion themselves in number to the demand, and to their customers. If a water-carrier keeps an account of what he earns in one year (suppose 20 *l.*) and in another year (suppose 15 *l.*) it will answer the same thing as if he were said to have 20 *l.* wages from his customers, in one year, and 15 *l.* in another: but, as he is an undertaker, his wages are uncertain.
|| The like may be said of higher undertakers of their own labour, or science, as painters, physicians, lawyers, &c.

[127 continued] The Professors of Arts and Sciences, exercise their Professions at Hazard and Risk, such as Painters, Physicians, Lawyers, &c. and have very uncertain Stipends from the Public.

130 |12| On pourroit peut-être avancer que tous les Entrepreneurs cherchent à attraper tout ce qu'ils peuvent dans leur état, & à dupper leurs Chalans, mais cela n'est pas de mon sujet.

131 |13| Par toutes ces inductions & par [71] une infinité d'autres qu'on pourroit faire dans une matiere qui a pour objet tous les Habitans d'un Etat, on peut établir que, excepté le Prince & les Propriétaires de Terres, tous les Habitans d'un Etat sont dépendans; ᵃqu'ils peuvent se diviserᵃ en deux classes, savoir en Entrepreneurs, ᵇ& en Gens à gages; & queᵇ les Entrepreneurs sont comme à gages incertains, & tous les autres à gages certains pour le tems qu'ils en jouissent, bien que ᶜleurs fonctions & leur rangᶜ soient très disproportionnés. Le Général qui a une paie, le Courtisan qui a une pension, & le Domestique qui a des gages, ᵈtombentᵈ sous cette derniere espece. Tous les autres sont Entrepreneurs, soit qu'ils s'établissent avec un fond pour conduire leur entreprise, soit qu'ils soient Entrepreneurs de leur propre travail sans aucuns fonds, ᵉ& ils peu-[72]vent être considerés comme vivant à l'incertain; les Gueux même & les Voleursᵉ sont des Entrepreneurs de cette classe ᶠ. Enfinᶠ tous les Habitans d'un Etat tirent leur subsistance ᵍ& leurs avantagesᵍ du fond des Propriétaires de Terres, & sont dépendans.

|| From these inductions and explications, which may be applied, with a little variation, to all orders of men in society, it appears, that every body in a state is either an undertaker, or at wages, though their ranks and functions be very different. The courtier, who has a pension, the general, who has pay, and the servant, who has wages, fall under the same denomination: all others in a state are undertakers, or subsist at uncertain wages.
|| But the prince and the proprietors of land alone are independent in a state, and those from whom the subsistance and riches of all other ranks of men flow. And, whereas the land is commonly in the hands of the gentry and nobility, it is not surprizing that the notion of gentlemen and noblemen has ever had so great an influence in the world.

All the other Undertakers like those who take charge of Mines, Theatres, Building, etc., the Merchants by sea and Land, etc., Cook-shop keepers, Pastry Cooks, Innkeepers, etc. as well as the Undertakers of their own labour who need no Capital to establish themselves, like Journeymen artisans, Copper-smiths, Needlewomen, Chimney Sweeps, Water Carriers, live at uncertainty and proportion themselves to their customers. Master Craftsmen like Shoemakers, Taylors, Carpenters, Wigmakers, etc. who employ Journeymen according to the work they have, live at the same uncertainty since their customers may foresake them from one day to another: the Undertakers of their own labour in Art and Science, like Painters, Physicians, Lawyers, etc. live in the like uncertainty. If one Attorney or Barrister earn 5000 pounds sterling yearly in the service of his Clients or in his practice and another earn only 500 they may be considered as having so much uncertain wages from those who employ them.

It may perhaps be urged that Undertakers seek to snatch all they can in their calling and to get the better of their customers, but this is outside my subject.

By all these inductions and many others which might be made in a topic relating to all the Inhabitants of a State, it may be laid down that expect the Prince and the Proprietors of Land, all the Inhabitants of a State are dependent; that they can be divided into two classes, Undertakers and Hired people; and that all the Undertakers are as it were on unfixed wages and the others on wages fixed so long as they receive them though their functions and ranks may be very unequal. The General who has his pay, the Courtier his pension and the Domestic servant who has wages all fall into this last class. All the rest are Undertakers, whether they set up with a capital to conduct their enterprise, or are Undertakers of their own labour without capital, and they may be regarded as living at uncertainty; the Beggars even and the Robbers are Undertakers of this class. Finally all the Inhabitants of a State derive their living and their advantages from the property of the Landowners and are dependent.

ᵃ…ᵃ: R, M, N: 'Comme auanturiers Des mines entrepreneurs d'operas, d'enterremens de batimens &c Négocians sur mer et sur terre &c Rotisseurs Patissiers cabaretiers &c'

ᵇ…ᵇ: R,M, N: 'Porteurs deau &c'

ᶜ…ᶜ: R: 'science comme peintre' (M, N: 'sciences comme peintres')

ᵈ…ᵈ: R, M, N: 5000ˡᵇ sterling'; 1756b and 1769: '5000 livres sterling'

ᵉ..ᵉ: R: 'pratique' (M, N: 'pratiques')

ᶠ…ᶠ: N: '5000ˡᵇ'

ᵃ…ᵃ: R, M, N: 'quils se peuvent diviser'

ᵇ…ᵇ: R, N: 'ou gens a gages que'; M: ou gens a gages, et que'

ᶜ…ᶜ: R, M: 'leur Rang et fonctions'; N: 'leurs rangs et fonctions'

ᵈ…ᵈ: R, M, N: 'tombe'

ᵉ…ᵉ: R, M, N: 'et peuvent étre considerés comme subcistans par des gages incertains, mais les guéux et les voleurs'

ᶠ…ᶠ: R, M, N: 'et enfin'

ᵍ…ᵍ: 'et avantages'

---

129 i. The term 'auanturiers Des mines' (as it is spelled in R) in V129a is identical to 'mine-adventurers' in D129. It is the only place in the French manuscripts (and nowhere in the printed text) where the term 'aventurier' is used to indicate 'entrepreneur'. Cf. C119iii. In the early eighteenth century there was a London-based joint stock concern called the Mine Adventurers of England that traded tin mined in Cornwall. This activity is mentioned in D/A206. Therefore, perhaps Cantillon had these particular mine adventurers in mind. The term 'mine-adventurer' is also used in D367.

ii. See D131 and D259 for other occurrences of the term gages-incertains/'uncertain wages'.

iii. The next paragraphs in A correspond to E I, xvi, 12–13. See A196–A197.

130 This aside has no counterpart in D. It can be seen either as an indication that Cantillon does not wish to go into the morality of market behaviour, or as an indication that he does not want to discuss the issue of the establishment of reputation.

131 i. The view that beggars and robbers may be considered entrepreneurs is missing in D131. Cf. C57.

ii. The statement in the second paragraph of D131 that all 'subsistence and riches flow' from the landowners and the Prince and the similar observation at the beginning of E136 are particularly evocative of the analysis of Quesnay's Tableaux économiques. Cf. C197, C273ii.

iii. There is perhaps a correspondence with A196, which actually follows directly after the passage reproduced in A129. See C129iii.

132 |14| Il est cependant vrai que si quelqu'Habitant à gros gages ou quelqu'Entrepreneur considérable a épargné du bien ᵃou des richessesᵃ, c'est-à-dire, s'il a des magasins ᵇde blé, de laines, de cuivre, d'or ou d'argentᵇ, ou de ᶜquelque denrée ou marchandise qui soitᶜ d'un usage ou débit constant dans un Etat & qui ait une valeur intrinseque ou réelle, on pourra à juste titre le regarder comme indépendant jusqu'à la concurrence de ᵈce fondᵈ. Il peut en disposer pour s'acquérir une hypotheque, & une rente sur des Terres, & sur les fonds de l'Etat, [73] lorsqu'il fait des emprunts assurés sur les terres: il peut même vivre bien mieux que les Propriétaires de petites terres, & même acheter la propriété de quelques-unes.

|| But if any undertaker, or person at high wages, has saved wealth; that is, if any has a magazine of corn, wine, wool, lead, tin, copper, silver, gold, or any other commodities or goods that have an intrinsic value, or constant vent, he may so far be esteemed wealthy and independent, though he has no land. With these he may buy all conveniencies of life, and make a better figure than if he had a small portion of land, and may even become a land-proprietor:

133 |15| Mais les denrées & les marchandises, même l'or & l'argent, sont bien plus sujets aux accidens & aux pertes, que la propriété des terres; & de quelque façon qu'on les ait gagnées ou épargnées, on les a toujours tirées du fond des Propriétaires actuels, soit par gain, soit par épargne des gages destinés à sa subsistance.

but these goods are more variable in their value than land, and more in danger of being lost; and it should not be forgot, that they have been acquired, one way or other, by the weight and influence, or at the expence of the proprietors of lands.

134

|| From all that has been said I think it appears, that the machine of circulation of traffic in a society, which is principally concerned in eating, drinking, cloathing, and the other conveniencies of life, is carried on among us in *Europe* by undertakers, all at an uncertainty; and that, though political societies and cities seem, from the indefinite number of people of different ranks, stations and occupations which compose them, to have something wonderful and incomprehensible in their œconomy; yet it seems that the grand machine is commonly carried on with uncertainty, and that every thing finds it's own proportion, well or ill, according to chance or caprice, without any peculiar intellectual conduct, whereby the society of commerce and circulation is governed.

It is true, however, that if some person on high wages or some large Undertaker has saved capital or wealth, that is if he have stores of corn, wool, copper, gold, silver or some produce or merchandise in constant use or vent in a State, having an intrinsic or a real value, he may be justly considered independent so far as this capital goes. He may dispose of it to acquire a mortgage, and interest from Land and from Public loans secured upon Land: he may live still better than the small Landowners and even buy the Property of some of them.

But produce and merchandise, even gold and silver, are much more subject to accident and loss than the ownership of land; and however one may have gained or saved them they are always derived from the land of actual Proprietors either by gain or by saving of the wages destined for one's subsistence.

ᵃ...ᵃ: R, M, N: 'et de la richesse'

ᵇ...ᵇ: R, M, N: 'de bled, laine plomb cuivre or ou argent'

ᶜ...ᶜ: R, M: 'quelques danrees ou marchandises qui soit'; N: 'quelques denrées ou marchandises qui soient'

ᵈ...ᵈ: R, M: 'son fond'; N: 'son fonds'

---

132 i. The French manuscript versions include *plomb* (lead) (V132b), unlike E132, but like D132.

ii. Unlike any of the French versions D132 also has 'wine' and 'tin'.

133 The phrase 'weight and influence' in D133 perhaps hints at a more political way of securing wealth, compared to the more neutral formulation in E133.

---

134 i. This remarkable passage, with its philosophical ending has no counterpart in E. Yet it follows quite naturally from what has been said in the French chapter, especially about the natural proportioning of entrepreneurs of each type to the demand for their products (Cf. C128).

ii. Cf. C79i for the use of the term 'œconomie'.

iii. Cf. C275 for the phrase 'eating, drinking, cloathing'.

iv. Note the use of the term 'machine' (twice). It occurs nowhere in E. Neither does it occur anywhere else in fragments attributable to Cantillon in D. When we check the occurrences of the term 'machine' in the *Universal Dictionary* generally we find that it is used many times but almost always in the literal sense of a mechanical device. There are only three exceptions: the entry 'Mathematics' (II, 179) contains the Newtonian expression 'machine of the universe'; the entry 'Quack' (II, 560) has the Cartesian observation: 'the human body, may be properly considered, as a most perfect and noble machine'. Neither of these uses of the term is very original and it is not used as a metaphor for a social phenomenon. The only passage that hints at such a use occurs in 'People' (II, 442): 'it may be worth the consideration of such as study the prosperity and welfare of England, whether the grand engine of maintaining the poor, and finding them work and employment, may not be put in motion by giving some body of undertakers a reasonable gain to put the machine upon it's wheels'. Here 'machine' refers to a 'project' or 'design' for provision of work to the poor. It is not applied to society as a whole. But is is perhaps noteworthy that the term 'undertakers' is used in the same passage especially because Postlethwayt in fact plagiarised it from Charles Davenant, *An essay upon the probable methods of making a people gainers in the ballance of trade* (1699) p. 56. Cantillon is probably referring to the same work by Davenant in E175. Cf. C175ii.

v. After D134 the entry, 'Circulation' immediately continues with a digression that corresponds to E II, iv (below D299–D317). Cf. C118i.

135 |16| Le nombre des Propriétaires d'argent, dans un grand Etat, est souvent assez considérable; & quoique la valeur de tout l'argent qui circule dans l'Etat n'excede guere la neuvieme ou la dixieme partie de la valeur des denrées qu'on tire actuellement de la terre, néanmoins comme les Propriétaires d'argent prêtent des sommes considérables dont [74] ils tirent ᵃintérêtᵃ, soit par l'hypotheque des terres, ᵇsoit par les denrées mêmesᵇ & marchandises de l'Etat, les sommes qu'on leur doit excedent ᶜle plus souventᶜ tout l'argent réel de l'Etat, ᵈ& ilsᵈ deviennent souvent un corps si considérable, qu'ils le disputeroient dans certains cas aux Propriétaires de terres, si ceux-ci n'étoient pas souvent également des Propriétaires d'argent, & si les Propriétaires de grandes sommes en argent ne cherchoient toujours aussi à devenir Propriétaires de terres.

136 |17| Il est cependant toujours vrai que toutes les sommes qu'ils ont gagnées ou épargnées, ont été tirées du fond des Propriétaires actuels; mais comme plusieurs de ceux-ci se ruinent journellement dans un Etat, & que les autres qui ᵃacquerentᵃ la propriété de leurs terres prennent leur place, l'indépendance que donne la pro-[75]priété des terres ne ᵇregardeᵇ que ceux qui s'en conservent la possession; & comme toutes les terres ont toujours un Maître ou Propriétaire actuel, je suppose toujours que c'est du fond de ceux-ci que tous les ᶜHabitans de l'Etatᶜ, tirent leur subsistance & toutes leurs richesses. Si ces Propriétaires se bornoient tous à vivre de leurs rentes, cela ne seroit pas douteux, & en ce cas il seroit bien plus difficile aux autres Habitans de s'enrichir à leurs dépens.

137 |18| J'établirai donc pour principe que les Propriétaires de terres sont seuls indépendans naturellement dans un Etat; que tous les autres ordres sont dépendans, soit comme Entrepreneurs, ᵃou comme à gagesᵃ, & que tout le troc & la circulation de l'Etat se conduit par l'entremise de ces Entrepreneurs.

The number of Proprietors of money in a large State is often considerable enough; and though the value of all the money which circulates in the State barely exceeds the ninth or tenth part of the value of the produce drawn from the soil yet, as the Proprietors of money lend considerable amounts for which they receive interest either by mortgage or the produce and merchandise of the State, the sums due to them usually exceed all the money in the State, and they often become so powerful a body that they would in certain cases rival the Proprietors of Lands if these last were not often equally Proprietors of money, and if the owners of large sums of money did not always seek to become Landowners themselves.

It is nevertheless always true that all the sums gained or saved have been drawn from the Land of the actual Proprietors; but as many of these ruin themselves daily in a State and the others who acquire the property of their land take their place, the independence given by the ownership of Land applies only to those who keep the possession of it; and as all Land has always an actual Master or Owner, I presume that it is from their property that all the Inhabitants of the State derive their living and all their wealth. If these Proprietors confined themselves to living on their Rents it would be beyond question, and in that case it would be much more difficult for the other inhabitants to enrich themselves at their Expence.

I will then lay it down as a principle that the Proprietors of Land alone are naturally independent in a State: that all the other Classes are dependent whether Undertakers or hired, and that all the exchange and circulation of the State is conducted by the medium of these Undertakers.

ᵃ…ᵃ: R, M, N: 'un interet'

ᵇ…ᵇ: R, M, N: 'ou des denrées méme'

ᶜ…ᶜ: R, M, N: 'souvent'

ᵈ…ᵈ: R, M, N: 'ils'

ᵃ…ᵃ: R, M, N: 'acquierent'; 1756b, 1769: 'acquiérent'

ᵇ…ᵇ: M, N: 'regardent' (R: 'regarde')

ᶜ…ᶜ: N: 'habitans' (R, M: 'habitans de lEtat')

ᵃ…ᵃ: R, M, N: 'ou a gages'

135

i. There is no precise counterpart in D to E135–E137, but for a related discussion see E/D477.

ii. The discussion here about the difference between the monied interest and the landed interest is somewhat reminiscent of the final remark in A117, which mentions 'the Distinction between the landed and monied Interest of the Kingdom'. This social opposition had become an important theme in British political discourse in the early decades of the eighteenth century.

136

Cf. V136a with V390b (and V179d, V513e).

137

138   [76] **CHAPITRE** ^a**XIV**^a.

Les humeurs, ^b*les modes & les façons*^b *de vivre du Prince,* ^c*&*
principalement des Propriétaires de terres,^c *déterminent les* ^d*usages*^d
auxquels on emploie les terres dans un Etat, & causent, ^e*au Marché,*
les variations des prix de toutes choses^e.

139 |1| Si le Propriétaire d'une grande terre (que je veux considerer ici
comme s'il n'y en avoit aucune autre au monde) la fait cultiver lui-
même, il suivra sa fantaisie dans les usages auxquels il l'emploiera.
^aI°^a. Il en emploiera nécessairement une partie en grains pour la
subsistance de tous les Laboureurs, Artisans & Inspecteurs qui
doivent travailler pour lui; & une autre portion pour nourrir ^bles
Bœufs, les Mou-[77]tons & les autres Animaux nécessaires pour leur
habillement & leur nourriture, ou pour d'autres^b commodités, suivant
la façon ^cdont il^c veut les entretenir; 2°. il mettra une portion de ^dsa^d
terre en parcs, jardins & arbres fruitiers, ^eou en vignes^e, suivant son
inclination, & en prairies pour l'entretien des Chevaux dont il se
servira pour son plaisir, &c.

140 |2| Supposons maintenant que pour éviter tant de ^asoins & d'embarras^a,
il fasse un calcul avec les Inspecteurs ^bde^b ses Laboureurs; qu'il
leur ^cdonne^c des Fermes ou portions de sa terre; qu'il leur laisse le
soin d'entretenir à l'ordinaire tous ces Laboureurs dont ils avoient
l'inspection, de maniere que ces Inspecteurs, devenus ainsi Fermiers
ou Entrepreneurs, ^dcedent aux Laboureurs, pour le travail de la terre
ou ferme^d, un autre tiers du produit, tant pour leur nourriture que [78]
pour leur habillement & autres commodités, ^etelles qu'ils les avoient^e
lorsque le Propriétaire faisoit conduire le travail: supposons encore
que le Propriétaire fasse un calcul avec les Inspecteurs des Artisans,
pour la quantité de nourriture, ^f& pour les autres commodités^f qu'on
leur ^gdonnoit^g; qu'il les fasse devenir Maîtres artisans; qu'il regle
une mesure commune, comme l'argent, pour fixer le prix auquel les
Fermiers leur cederont la laine, & celui auquel ils lui fourniront le
drap, & que les calculs de ces prix ^hsoient reglés^h de maniere que les
Maîtres artisans ⁱaientⁱ les mêmes avantages ^j& les mêmes douceurs^j
qu'ils avoient à-peu-près lorsqu'ils étoient Inspecteurs, & que les
Compagnons artisans ^kaient^k aussi le même entretien ^lqu'auparavant^l:
le travail des Compagnons artisans sera reglé à la journée ou à la piece
^m; les^m [79] marchandises qu'ils auront faites, ⁿsoit chapeaux, soit bas,
souliers, habitsⁿ, &c. seront vendues au Propriétaire, ^oaux Fermiers,
aux Laboureurs^o & aux autres Artisans réciproquement à un prix qui
laisse à tous les mêmes ^pavantages dont ils jouissoient; & les Fermiers
vendront, à un prix proportionné, leurs denrées & matériaux^p.

Chapter XIV

The Fancies, the Fashions, and the Modes of Living of the Prince, and especially of the Landowners, determine the use to which Land is put in a State and cause the variations in the Market-prices of all things.

If the Owner of a large Estate (which I wish to consider here as if there were no other in the world) has it cultivated himself he will follow his Fancy in the use of which he will put it. (1) He will necessarily use part of it for corn to feed the Labourers, Mechanicks and Overseers who work for him, another part to feed the Cattle, Sheep and other Animals necessary for their Clothing and Food or other commodities according to the way in which he wishes to maintain them. (2) He will turn part of the Land into Parks, Gardens, Fruit Trees or Vines as he feels inclined and into meadows for the Horses he will use for his pleasure, etc.

Let us now suppose that to avoid so much care and trouble he makes a bargain with the Overseers of the Labourers, gives them Farms or pieces of Land and leaves to them the responsibility for maintaining in the usual manner all the Labourers they supervise, so that the Overseers, now become Farmers or Undertakers, give the Labourers for working on the land or Farm another third of the Produce for their Food, Clothing and other requirements, such as they had when the Owner employed them; suppose further that the Owner makes a bargain with the Overseers of the Mechanicks for the Food and other things that he gave them, that he makes the Overseers become Master-Craftsmen, fixes a common measure, like silver, to settle the price at which the Farmers will supply them with wool and they will supply him with cloth, and that the prices are such as to give the Master-Craftsmen the same advantages and enjoyments as they had when Overseers, and the Journeymen Mechanicks also the same as before, the Labour of the Mechanicks will be settled by the day or by the piece: the merchandise which they have made, Hats, Stockings, Shoes, Cloaths, etc. will be sold to the Landowner, the Farmers, the Labourers, and the other Mechanicks reciprocally at a price which leaves to all of them the same advantages as before; and the Farmers will sell, at a proportionate price, their produce and raw material.

[a]...[a]: R, N: '14.[e]'; M: '8'
[b]...[b]: R, M: 'Modes et façons'; N: 'modes et facon'
[c]...[c]: R, M, N: 'et des proprietaires des Terres principalement'
[d]...[d]: R, M: 'usades'
[e]...[e]: R, M, N: 'les variations des prix de toutes choses au marché'

[a]...[a]: R: 'Premierement' (M, N: '1.º')
[b]...[b]: R, M, N: 'Les moutons nécéssaires pour leurs habillements et les autres betes nécéssaires tant pour la nouriture, que pour les autres'
[c]...[c]: R, M, N: 'quil'
[d]...[d]: R, M, N: 'la'
[e]...[e]: R, M, N: 'ou vigne &c.'

[a]...[a]: N: 'soins'
[b]...[b]: R, M, N: 'et'
[c]...[c]: R, M, N: 'attribue'
[d]...[d]: R, M, N: 'attribuent pour le travail de la Terre ou ferme aux Laboureurs'
[e]...[e]: R, M, N: 'tels qu'on leur attribuoit'
[f]...[f]: R, M, N: 'et Commodités'
[g]...[g]: R, M, N: 'attribuoit'
[h]...[h]: R, M, N; 'auront été reglés'
[i]...[i]: R, M, N: 'auront'
[j]...[j]: R, M, N: 'et douceurs'
[k]...[k]: R, M, N: auront'
[l]...[l]: R, M, N: 'qu'on leur attribuoit auparavant'
[m]...[m]: R, M, N: 'et les'
[n]...[n]: R, M, N: 'soit Chappeaux souliers bas habits'
[o]...[o]: R, N: 'aux fermiers et aux laboureurs (M: 'aux fermiers, aux laboureurs')
[p]...[p]: R, M, N: 'avantages et subcistance quon leur attribuoit auparavant. Les fermiers vendent a touts leurs Danrees et materiaux a un prix proportionné'; 1756b and 1769 have for '& matériaux': '& leurs matériaux'

There is no direct counterpart for **138** this chapter in D or A. Higgs (1931, Appendix) states that counterparts occur in the entry 'Cash' of the *Universal Dictionary*. Some points in that entry do indeed recall E I, xiv (especially, cf. E139 with D257), but they are actually part of the argument of what appears to be an alternative version to E II, iii (see C255i).

i. A number of **139** elements of the contrast between the feudal economy in E139 and the commercial rural economy in E140 are also described in Defoe (1728) pp. 45–49. Cf. C29.

ii. The economy of E139 is also described in E/D/A78–E/D/A79, D257 and D437.

The beginning **140** of E140 shows parallels with the third paragraph of D264.

141 |3| Il arrivera d'abord que les Inspecteurs devenus Entrepreneurs ^adeviendront^a aussi les maîtres absolus de ceux qui travaillent ^bsous leur conduite, & qu'ils auront^b plus de soin & d'agrément en travaillant ainsi pour ^cleur compte^c. Nous supposons donc qu'après ce changement tous les Habitans de cette grande terre subsistent tout de même qu'auparavant; & par conséquent je dis qu'on emploiera toutes les portions & Fermes de cette grande terre, aux mêmes usages aux-[80]quels on les emploïoit auparavant.

142 |4| Car ^asi quelques-uns des Fermiers semoient dans leur Ferme^a ou portion de terre plus de grains qu'à l'ordinaire, ^bil faudra^b qu'ils nourrissent un plus petit nombre ^cde Moutons^c, & qu'ils aient moins de laine ^d& moins de viande de mouton à vendre;^d par conséquent il y ^eaura^e trop de grains & trop peu ^fde laine^f pour la consommation des Habitans. Il y aura donc cherté de laine, ce qui forcera les Habitans à porter leurs habits plus longtems qu'à l'ordinaire^g; & il^g y aura grand marché de grains & un surplus pour l'année suivante. Et comme nous supposons que le Propriétaire a stipulé en argent le paiement du tiers du produit de la Ferme, qu'on doit lui païer, les Fermiers qui ont trop de blé & trop peu de laine, ne seront pas en état de lui païer sa rente. S'il [81] leur fait quartier, ils auront soin l'année suivante d'avoir moins de blé & plus de laine; car les Fermiers ont toujours ^hsoin^h d'emploïer ⁱleurs terresⁱ au produit des denrées, qu'ils jugent devoir rapporter le plus haut prix au Marché. Mais si dans l'année suivante ils ^javoient^j trop de laine & trop peu de grains pour la consommation, ils ne manqueront pas de changer d'année en année l'emploi des terres, jusqu'à ce qu'ils puissent parvenir à proportionner à-peu-près leurs denrées à la consommation des Habitans. Ainsi un Fermier ^kqui a attrapé^k à-peu-près la proportion de la consommation, mettra une portion de sa ferme en Prairie, pour avoir du foin, une autre pour les grains, pour la laine, & ainsi du reste; & il ne changera pas de méthode, à moins qu'il ne voie ^lquelque variation considérable^l dans la consommation; mais [82] dans l'exemple présent nous avons supposé que tous les Habitans vivent à-peu-près de la même façon, qu'ils vivoient lorsque le Propriétaire faisoit lui-même valoir sa terre, & par conséquent les Fermiers emploieront les terres aux mêmes usages qu'auparavant.

143 |5| Le Propriétaire, qui a le tiers du produit de ^ala^a terre à sa disposition, est ^bl'Acteur^b principal dans les variations qui peuvent arriver à la consommation. Les Laboureurs & Artisans qui vivent au jour la journée, ne changent que par nécessité ^cleurs façons^c de vivre; s'il y a quelques Fermiers, Maîtres artisans, ou autres Entrepreneurs accommodés, qui varient dans ^dleur dépense^d & ^econsommation^e, ils prennent toujours pour modele les Seigneurs & Propriétaires des terres. Ils les imitent dans leur habillement, ^fdans leur cuisine, & dans leur [83] façon^f de vivre. Si les Propriétaires se plaisent à porter de beau linge, des soieries, ou de la dentelle, la consommation de ces marchandises sera plus forte que celle que les Propriétaires font sur eux.

It will then come to pass that the Overseers become Undertakers, will be the absolute masters of those who work under them, and will have more care and satisfaction in working on their own account. We suppose then that after this change all the people on this large Estate live just as they did before, and so all the portions and Farms of this great Estate will be put to the same use as it formerly was.

For if some of the Farmers sowed more corn than usual they must feed fewer Sheep, and have less Wool and Mutton to sell. Then there will be too much Corn and too little Wool for the consumption of the Inhabitants. Wool will therefore be dear, which will force the Inhabitants to wear their clothes longer than usual, and there will be too much Corn and a surplus for the next year. As we suppose that the Landowner has stipulated for the payment in silver of the third of the produce of the Farm to be paid to him, the Farmers who have too much Corn and too little Wool, will not be able to pay him his Rent. If he excuses them they will take care the next year to have less corn and more Wool, for Farmers always take care to use their land for the production of those things which they think will fetch the best price at Market. If, however, next year they have too much Wool and too little Corn for the demand, they will not fail to change from year to year the use of the land till they arrive at proportioning their production pretty well to the consumption of the Inhabitants. So a farmer who has arrived at about the proportion of consumption will have part of his Farm in grass, for hay, another for Corn, Wool and so on, and he will not change his plan unless he sees some considerable change in the demand; but in this example we have supposed that all the People live in the same way as when the Landowner cultivated the Land for himself, and consequently the Farmers will employ the Land for the same purposes as before.

The Owner, who has at his disposal the third of the Produce of the Land, is the principal Agent in the changes which may occur in demand. Labourers and Mechanicks who live from day to day change their mode of living only from necessity. If a few Farmers, Master Craftsmen or other Undertakers in easy circumstances vary their expense and consumption they always take as their model the Lords and Owners of the Land. They imitate them in their Clothing, Meals, and mode of life. If the Landowners please to wear fine linen, silk, or lace, the demand for these merchandises will be greater than that of the Proprietors for themselves.

141

a...a: R, M, N: 'deviennent'
b...b: R: 'sous leurs Conduittes et ont'; M, N: sous leur conduite et ont'
c...c: R, M, N: 'leur propre compte'

142

a...a: R: 'si quelque uns des fermiers semoit dans leur ferme'; N: 'si quelqu'un des fermiers semoit dans sa ferme' (M: 'si quelques uns des fermiers semoient dans leur ferme')
b...b: R, M, N: 'il faudroit'
c...c: R, M, N: 'de bestiaux et de Moutons'
d...d: R, M, N: 'et de viande a vendre et'
e...e: R, M, N: auroit'
f...f: R, M, N: 'de viande et de laine'
g...g: R, M, N: ', il'
h...h: R, M, N: 'le soin'
i...i: R: 'Leur terres' (M, N: 'leurs terres')
j...j: R, M, N: 'ont'
k...k: R, M, N: 'qui attrape'
l...l: R: 'quelque variations considérables'; N: 'quelques variations considérables' (M: 'quelque variation considérable')

143

a...a: R, M, N: 'sa'
b...b: R, M, N: 'l'auteur'
c...c: R, M, N: 'leur façon'
d...d: R 'Leurs depences' (M, N: 'leur depense')
e...e: 1756b and 1769: 'leur consommation'
f...f: R, N: 'dans leurs cuisines, et dans leurs façons'; M: 'dans leur cuisine, et dans leurs façons'

i. Cf. the term *'l'Acteur'* with 'Actor' in D271, D272, D280, D281, D293. However, the manuscript versions have *'l'auteur'* (V143b). If R was the source text, the editor of the French print edition perhaps made a felicitous correction. See Introduction p. 15.

ii. The phenomenon of imitative behaviour in consumption is also mentioned in E/A197. Cf. C197.

144 |6| Si un Seigneur, ou Propriétaire, qui a donné toutes ᵃsesᵃ Terres à ᵇfermeᵇ, prend la fantaisie de changer notablement sa façon de vivre; si par exemple il diminue le nombre de ses Domestiques, & augmente celui de ses Chevaux; non seulement ses Domestiques seront obligés de quitter la Terre en question, mais aussi un nombre proportionné d'artisans ᶜ& de Laboureursᶜ qui travailloient à procurer leur entretien: la portion de terre qu'on emploïoit à entretenir ces Habitans, sera emploïée en ᵈPrairiesᵈ pour les Chevaux d'augmentation, & si tous les Propriétaires d'un Etat faisoient de même, [84] ils multiplieroient bientôt le nombre des Chevaux, & diminueroient celui des Habitans.

145 |7| Lorsqu'un Propriétaire a congedié un grand nombre de Domestiques, & augmenté le nombre de ses Chevaux, il y aura trop de blé pour la consommation des Habitans, & par conséquent le blé sera à bas prix, au lieu que le foin sera cher. Cela fera que les Fermiers augmenteront leurs Prairies, & diminueront la quantité de blé pour se proportionner à la consommation. C'est ainsi que les humeurs ou façons des ᵃPropriétairesᵃ déterminent l'emploi qu'on fait des terres, ᵇ& occasionnent les variationsᵇ de la consommation qui causent celles du prix des Marchés. Si tous les Propriétaires de terres, dans ᶜun Etatᶜ, les faisoient valoir eux-mêmes, ils les emploieroient à produire ce qui leur plairoit; & comme les variations [85] de la consommation sont principalement causées par ᵈleurs façonsᵈ de vivre, les prix qu'ils offrent aux Marchés, déterminent les Fermiers à toutes les variations qu'ils font dans l'emploi & l'usage des terres.

146 |8| Je ne considere pas ici la variation des prix du Marché qui peut survenir de l'abondance ᵃou de la stérilitéᵃ des années, ni la consommation extraordinaire qui peut arriver par des Armées étrangeres ou par d'autres accidens, pour ne point embarrasser ᵇce sujet; ne considérant un Etat, que dans sa situationᵇ naturelle & uniforme.

If a Lord or Owner who has let out all his lands to farm, take the fancy to change considerably his mode of living; if for instance he decreases the number of his domestic servants and increases the number of his Horses: not only will his Servants be forced to leave the Estate in question but also a proportionate number of Artisans and of Labourers who worked to maintain them. The portion of land which was used to maintain these Inhabitants will be laid down to grass for the new Horses, and if all Landowners in a State did the like they would soon increase the number of Horses and diminish the number of Men.

^a...^a: R: 'ces'; N: 'ses' corrected to 'ces' (M: 'ses')
^b...^b: R, M: 'fermes' (N: 'ferme')
^c...^c: R, N: 'et Laboureurs' (M: 'et de laboureurs')
^d...^d: M: 'prairie' (R: 'prayries', N: 'prairies')

Mirabeau paraphrases **144** E144 in *L'Ami des hommes* (1756: 86).

When a Landowner has dismissed a great number of Domestic Servants, and increased the number of his Horses, there will be too much Corn for the needs of the Inhabitants, and so the Corn will be cheap and the Hay dear. In consequence the Farmers will increase their grass land and diminish their Corn to proportion it to the demand. In this way the Fancies or Fashions of Landowners determine the use of the Land and bring about the variations of demand which cause the variations of Market prices. If all the Landowners of a State cultivated their own estates they would use them to produce what they want; and as the variations of demand are chiefly caused by their mode of living the prices which they offer in the Market decide the Farmers to all the changes which they make in the employment and use of the Land.

^a...^a: R, M, N: 'proprietaires des terres'
^b...^b: R, M, N: 'et les variations'
^c...^c: R, M, N: 'lEtat'
^d...^d: N: 'leurs façon'; 1756b, 1769: 'leur façon' (R, M: 'leurs façons')

145

I do not consider here the variations in Market prices which may arise from the good or bad harvest of the year, or the extraordinary consumption which may occur from foreign troops or other accidents, so as not to complicate my subject, considering only a state in its natural and uniform condition.

^a...^a: R, M, N: 'et sterilité'
^b...^b: R, M, N: 'mon sujet que jay Calculé pour un état dans la scituation'

i. The effect of the arrival of **146** an army on the local price of food is considered in D245.

ii. The phrase '*naturelle & uniforme*' is reminiscent of an expression in D260.

147

[86] **CHAPITRE ªXVª.**

*La multiplication & le décroissement
des Peuples dans un Etat dépendent
principalement de la volonté,
ᵇdes modes & des façonsᵇ de vivre des
Propriétaires de Terres*

[119] **CHAP. XXII.**

*The Increase and Decrease of the
Number of People in a State or Kingdom,
principally depend on the Manner of Living
of the Age, the Taste and Luxury of the
great Proprietors of Land.*

148 |1| L'Expérience nous fait voir qu'on peut multiplier les Arbres, Plantes & autres sortes de végétaux, & qu'on en peut entretenir toute la quantité que la portion de terre qu'on y destine peut nourrir.

|| Experience has shewn, that all Sorts of Trees, Plants and other Vegetables, are to be multiplied and increased to any Quantity or Number, in Proportion to the Extent of Ground employed or laid out for raising and nourishing them.

149 |2| La même expérience nous fait voir qu'on peut également multiplier toutes les especes d'animaux, & ªlesª entretenir en telle quantité que la portion de terre qu'on y destine ᵇpeut en nourrirᵇ. Si l'on éleve des Haras, des troupeaux ᶜde Bœufs ou de Moutonsᶜ, [87] on les multipliera aisement, jusqu'au nombre que la terre qu'on destine pour cela ᵈpeut en entretenirᵈ. On peut même améliorer les Prairies qui servent pour cet entretien, en y faisant couler plusieurs petits ruisseaux & torrens, comme dans le Milanez. On peut faire du foin, & par ce moïen entretenir ᵉcesᵉ Bestiaux dans les Etables, ᶠ& lesᶠ nourrir en plus grand nombre que si on les ᵍlaissoitᵍ en liberté dans les Prairies. On peut nourrir quelquefois les Moutons avec des navets, comme on fait en Angleterre, au moïen de quoi un arpent de terre ira plus loin pour leur nourriture, que s'il ne produisoit que de l'herbe.

|| The same Experience has also shewn, that all Kinds of the Animal Creation, such as Horses, Cows, Oxen, Sheep, &c. are to be increased and multiplied to any Number or ʰQualityʰ, in Proportion to the Land allotted for their Support; and that this Land by Manure is capable of being cultivated and laid down to produce this Nourishment and Food for the four Seasons in the Year.

Chapter XV

The Increase and Decrease of the Number of People in a State chiefly depend on the taste, the fashions, and the modes of living of the proprietors of land

ᵃ...ᵃ: R: '15'; N: 15.ᵉ'; M: '9'
ᵇ...ᵇ: R, M, N: 'modes et facons'; 1756b and 1769: 'des modes & de la façon'

i. All of chapter XXIII in A is reproduced here. It is considerably shorter than its counterpart in E. In Philip Cantillon's book A147 follows directly after A117. **147**

ii. There is no direct counterpart for this chapter in Postlethwayt's *Dictionary*. Higgs (1931, Appendix) suggests that the entry, 'Manure' contains corresponding fragments, but this appears to be incorrect. The closest correspondence in subject matter is the entry, 'Population' (II, 438–42), which includes references to Davenant, King, uses the term undertaker (at the very end) and has some reference to China's large population. But there do not seem to be any passages that can be attributed to Richard Cantillon. It may be that Postlethwayt decided he did not need this chapter from Cantillon's manuscript because he had copious other materials that he used for 'Population'. Other relevant entries are: 'Annuity' (I, 68–73), where Postlethwayt discusses Halley (cf. E172) and Petty and Davenant (cf. E175), and various other authors (de Moivre, Kerseboom).

iii. This chapter appears to have influenced Steuart's theory of population (1767, I, iii; I, xiv; I, xviii). See Skinner (1966, I, 32 n5; 88 n3; 119 n5).

Experience shews that Trees, Plants and other Vegetables can be increased to any Quantity which the Extent of Ground laid out for them can support. **148**

The same Experience shews that all kinds of the Animal Creation are to be multiplied to any Quantity which the Land allotted to them can support. Horses, Cattle, Sheep can easily be multiplied up to the number that the Land will support. The fields which serve for this support may be improved by irrigation as in Milan. Hay may be saved and Cattle fed in sheds and raised in larger numbers than if they were left in the Fields. Sheep may be fed on Turnips, as in England, by which means an acre of land will go further for their nourishment than if it were pasture.

ᵃ...ᵃ: R, M, N: 'en'
ᵇ...ᵇ: R, M, N: 'peut nourir'
ᶜ...ᶜ: R, M: de bœuf ou de mouton' (N: 'de bœufs ou de moutons')
ᵈ...ᵈ: R, M, N: 'peut entretenir'
ᵉ...ᵉ: M: 'les' (R, N: 'ces')
ᶠ...ᶠ: R, M, N: 'les'
ᵍ...ᵍ: R, M, N: 'faisoit Courir'
ʰ...ʰ: sic; 'Quantity'?

The mention in E149 of the feeding of turnips to sheep appears to be a reference to a relatively new agricultural practice. The growing of turnips as winter feed for cattle and sheep was pioneered in Suffolk from about the mid-seventeenth century. By the time Cantillon wrote, the practice of fattening sheep on turnips had spread to other parts of East Anglia, but remained largely confined to the east of England. **149**

150 |3| On peut en un mot multiplier toutes sortes d'animaux, en tel nombre qu'on en veut entretenir, même à l'infini, si on pouvoit attribuer des terres propres à l'infini pour les nourrir; & la [88] multiplication des Animaux n'a d'autres bornes que le plus ᵃou moinsᵃ de moïens qu'on leur laisse ᵇpourᵇ subsister. Il n'est pas douteux que ᶜsi onᶜ emploïoit toutes les terres à la ᵈsimple nourritureᵈ de l'Homme, l'espece en multiplieroit jusqu'à la concurrence du nombre que ces terres pourroient nourrir, de la façon ᵉqu'on expliqueraᵉ.

151 |4| Il n'y a point de Païs où l'on porte la multiplication des Hommes si loin qu'à la Chine. Les pauvres gens y vivent ᵃuniquement de riz & d'eau de rizᵃ; ils y travaillent presque nus, ᵇ& dans les Provinces méridionales ils font trois moissons abondantes de riz, chaque année,ᵇ par le grand soin qu'ils ont de l'Agriculture. La terre ᶜne s'yᶜ repose jamais, & rend chaque fois, plus de cent pour ᵈunᵈ; ceux qui sont habillés, le sont pour la plûpart de coton, qui demande si peu [89] de terre pour ᵉsaᵉ production, qu'un arpent en peut ᶠvraisemblablementᶠ produire de quoi habiller cinq cens personnes adultes. Ils se marient tous par religion, & élevent autant d'enfans qu'ils en peuvent faire subsister ᵍ. Ils regardentᵍ comme un crime l'emploi des terres en Parcs ʰouʰ Jardins de plaisance, comme si on fraudoit par là les Hommes de leur nourriture. Ils portent les Voïageurs en Chaise à porteurs, & épargnent le travail des Chevaux en tout ce qui se peut faire par les Hommes. Leur nombre est incroïable, suivant les Relations, & cependant ils sont forcés de faire mourir plusieurs de leurs Enfans dès le berceau, lorsqu'ils ne se voient pas le moïen de les élever, n'en gardant que le nombre qu'ils peuvent nourrir. ⁱPar un travail rude & obstiné, ils tirent, des Rivieres, une quantité extraordinaire de [90] Poissonsⁱ, & de la Terre, tout ce qu'on en peut tirer.

152 |5| Néanmoins lorsqu'il survient des années stériles, ils meurent de faim par milliers, malgré le soin de l'Empereur, qui fait des amas de riz pour de ᵃpareils casᵃ. Ainsi tous nombreux que sont les Habitans de la Chine, ils se proportionnent ᵇnécessairement aux moïensᵇ qu'ils ont de subsister, & ne passent pas le nombre que le Païs peut entretenir, suivant la façon de vivre dont ils se contentent; & sur ce pié, un seul arpent de terre suffit pour en entretenir plusieurs.

In short, this Increase of the Animal Creation may be carried to an infinite Series, if it was possible to allot a sufficient Quantity of Land for their Maintenance; and I apprehend it is not to [120] be disputed, but the human Species may be increased and multiplied to a Series of Increase equal to the Capacity and Fertility of the Soil, capable of producing, by Labour and Agriculture, their Nourishment and Support.

There is no Country where Population is carried to a greater ʲHeighthʲ than in *China*, the common People are supported by Rice, their Cloathing is chiefly of Cloth made of Cotton, which grows in such Abundance, that it is said an Acre of Land is capable of producing a Quantity full sufficient for the Cloathing of five hundred grown-up Persons; the *Chinese* by the Principles of their Religion are obliged to marry, and to bring up as many Children as their Circumstances and Means of Subsistence will afford; they look upon it as a Crime to lay Land out in Pleasure-Gardens and Parks, defrauding the Public of so much Land capable of producing the Maintenance of so many Men; and the Number of Horses employed in the necessary Culture of the Earth is incredible, for they chuse to give their own Labour in carrying Travellers backwards and forwards, rather than to suffer these Animals to ease them of this Trouble; yet these People, if the Relation of [121] Voyages is to be depended upon, destroy their Children in the Cradle, when they apprehend themselves in such Circumstances as not to be able to support and bring them up; and yet they are indefatigable in their Labour and Industry for obtaining, both from Land and Water, every thing of Nourishment these Elements are capable of yielding.

In a word, we can multiply all sorts of Animals in such numbers as we wish to maintain even to infinity if we could find lands to infinity to nourish them; and the multiplication of Animals has no other bounds than the greater or less means allotted for their subsistence. It is not to be doubted that if all Land were devoted to the simple sustenance of Man the race would increase up to the number that the Land would support in the manner to be explained.

ᵃ...ᵃ: 1756b and 1769: 'ou le moins'
ᵇ...ᵇ: R, M, N: 'de'
ᶜ...ᶜ: N: 'si l'on' (R, M: 'si on')
ᵈ...ᵈ: R, M, N: 'Nouriture simple'
ᵉ...ᵉ: R, M, N: 'qu'on l'expliquera'

The phrase 'Series of Increase' in A150 is also used in A6. Cf. C6. For similar expressions, see A173 and A355.   **150**

There is no Country where Population is carried to a greater Height than in China. The common people are supported by Rice and Rice Water; they work almost naked and in the southern Provinces they have three plentiful harvests of Rice yearly, thanks to their great attention to Agriculture. The Land is never fallow and yields a hundredfold every year. Those who are clothed have generally Clothing of Cotton, which needs so little Land for its production that an Acre of Land, it seems, is capable of producing a Quantity full sufficient for the Clothing of five hundred grown-up Persons. The Chinese by the Principles of their Religion are obliged to marry, and bring up as many Children as their Means of Subsistence will afford. They look upon it as a Crime to lay Land out in Pleasure-Gardens or Parks, defrauding the Public of Maintenance. They carry Travellers in sedan Chairs, and save the work of Horses upon all tasks which can be performed by Men. Their number is incredible if the Relation of Voyages is to be depended upon, yet they are forced to destroy many of their Children in the Cradle when they apprehend themselves not to be able to bring them up, keeping only the number they are able to support. By hard and indefatigable Labour they draw from the Rivers an extraordinary quantity of Fish and from the Land all that is possible.

ᵃ...ᵃ: R, M, N: 'de Ris uniquémént et d'eau de Ris pour leur boisson'
ᵇ...ᵇ: R, M, N: 'et tirent dans leurs provinces meridionnalles du Ris jusqua trois fois l'an de la Terre et en grande quantité a chaque fois'
ᶜ...ᶜ: R, M, N: 'ny repose'
ᵈ...ᵈ: R, M, N: 'la seménce'
ᵉ...ᵉ: R: 'La'; M: 'la' corrected to 'sa'; (N: 'sa')
ᶠ...ᶠ: R, M, N: 'aisément'
ᵍ...ᵍ: R, M, N: ', regardant'
ʰ...ʰ: R, M, N: 'et'
ⁱ...ⁱ: R, M, N: 'ils tirent des rivieres, une quantité extraordinaire de poissons par un travail rude et obstiné'
ʲ...ʲ: sic

i. Higgs relies on A151 for his translation of E151. This also explains why he translates '*les Relations*' with 'the Relation of Voyages'.

ii. The work referred to is Eusèbe Renaudot's *Anciennes Relations des Indes et de la Chine de deux voyageurs mahométans, qui y allèrent dans le neuvième siècle; traduites d'arabe: avec des Remarques sur les principaux endroits de ces relations* (Paris: Coignard 1718). The observation that the Chinese 'often kill their children when they cannot feed them' is made on pp. 166–67.

iii. Other authors in the early decades of the eighteenth century mentioned the presumed practice of infanticide among the Chinese, for example J.B. du Halde *Description de l'empire de la Chine* (1735). Later authors commented on this and other practices due to the extreme poverty in China, e.g. Montesquieu *Esprit*, 1748: VIII, xxi; Hume 1752 'Of the Populousness of Ancient Nations' and Smith LJ (A) iii, 80–81; 1776, I, viii, 24.

iii. On China, also see E91 and D98.   **151**

Nevertheless when bad years come they starve in thousands in spite of the care of the Emperor who stores Rice for such contingencies. Numerous then as the people of China are, they are necessarily proportioned to their Means of Living and do not exceed the number the Country can support according to their standard of life; and on this footing a single Acre of Land will support many of them.

ᵃ...ᵃ: R, M, N: 'des cas pareils'
ᵇ...ᵇ: M: 'au moyens'   **152**

153 |6| D'un autre côté, il n'y a pas de Païs, où la multiplication des Hommes soit plus bornée que parmi ªles Sauvages de l'Amérique, dans l'intérieur des terres. Ils négligent l'Agriculture, ils habitent dans les Bois, & vivent de la Chasse des Animaux qu'ils y trouventª. Comme [91] les Arbres consument le suc & la substance de la terre, il y a peu d'herbe pour la nourriture de ᵇcesᵇ Animaux; & comme un Indien en mange plusieurs dans ᶜl'annéeᶜ, ᵈcinquante à cent arpens de terre ne donnent souvent que la nourriture d'un seul Indienᵈ.

‖ On the other hand, there is no Country in the World where Population is so limited, as in the interior Parts of *America*, inhabited by Savages, where Agriculture and the cultivating of the Earth is unknown: These People live in Woods and Forrests, and their Subsistence is the Flesh of wild Beasts: Their Forrests destroy the Sweetness and natural Produce of the Earth; and consequently a much greater Quantity of uncultivated Land must be had for the Support of these wild Beasts, than if this had been cleared;

154 |7| Un petit Peuple de ces Indiens aura quarante lieues quarrées ªd'étendue pourª les limites de sa Chasse. Ils se font des guerres reglées & cruelles pour ᵇcesᵇ limites, & proportionnent toujours leur nombre aux moïens qu'ils trouvent de subsister par la Chasse.

this puts these poor Savages under a Necessity very frequently of waging war against each other, to extend their hunting Districts, as they must have a proportional Quantity of Land, equal to these Means of supporting the Number of People under the Command of their several Chieftains or Kings.

155 |8| Les Habitans de l'Europe cultivent les terres, & en ªtirentª des grains pour leur subsistance. La laine des Moutons qu'ils nourrissent, leur sert d'habillement. Le froment est le grain dont le plus grand nombre se nourrit; quoique plusieurs Païsans fassent leur pain de ᵇségleᵇ, & dans le [92] Nord, d'orge & ᶜd'aveineᶜ. La subsistance des Païsans ᵈ& du Peuple n'est par la même dans tous les Païs de l'Europeᵈ, & les terres y sont souvent différentes en bonté & en fertilité.

[122] ‖ The *Europeans* by Agriculture and Industry obtain the Nourishment and Support of Life, their Land produces to them Wheat, Barley, Oats, &c. besides several ᵉwholsomeᵉ and nourishing Roots and Plants; the Wool of their Sheep is wrought into Cloathing, but the Quantity and Quality of these several Produces are different, and more or less abundant according to the Fertility and Situation of the Soil, or the Genius and Manner of Living of the Proprietors of the Land, on whom only, by the Encouragement which is in their Power to give, depend the Increase of Population, by allotting certain Quantities of their Land to the Maintenance of Posterity, and consequently to the Encouragement of Matrimony, to which Men and Women are by Nature inclined.

On the other hand there is no Country where the increase of Population is more limited than among the savages in the interior parts of America. They neglect Agriculture, live in Woods, and on the Wild Beasts they find there. As their Forests destroy the Sweetness and Substance of the Earth there is little pasture for Animals, and since an Indian eats several Animals in a year, 50 or 100 acres supply only enough food for a single Indian.

ᵃ…ᵃ: R, M, N: 'les sauvages americains [N: 'ameriquains'] en dedans des Terres, Ils habitent dans les bois negligent La Culture des terres vivent de La Chasse des Chevreuils et autres animeaux quils trouvent dans les bois'
ᵇ…ᵇ: R: 'Ses' (M, N: 'ces')
ᶜ…ᶜ: M: 'dans une année' (R, N: 'dans lannée')
ᵈ…ᵈ: R, M, N: 'il faut souvent attribuér 50 a Cent arpens de Terre pour la nouriture dun seul indien'

153 i. Cf. the estimate in E153 (but not A153) of the amount of land needed to support one Indian with the estimates in E90 and D98.
ii. Cf. V153a 'americains' with V210a.
iii. Cf. Steuart (1767, I, ix [1966, I, 56]): 'the hunting Indians are scattered in small societies, through the woods and live upon game'; Smith (1776, V.i.a.5): 'An army of hunters can seldom exceed two or three hundred men. The precarious subsistence which the chace affords could seldom allow a greater number to keep together for any considerable time. … Nothing can be more contemptible than an Indian war in North America.'

A small Tribe of these Indians will have 40 square leagues for its hunting ground. They wage regular and bitter wars over these boundaries, and always proportion their numbers to their means of support from the chase.

ᵃ…ᵃ: R, M, N: 'pour'
ᵇ…ᵇ: M: 'les' (R, N: 'ces')

154

The Europeans cultivate the Land and draw Corn from it for their subsistence. The Wool of their sheep provides them with Clothing. Wheat is the grain on which most of them are fed, but some Peasants make their Bread of Rye, and in the north of Barley and Oats. The food of the Peasants and the People is not the same in all Countries of Europe, and Land is often different in quality and fertility.

ᵃ…ᵃ: R: 'tire' (M, N: 'tirent')
ᵇ…ᵇ: R, M, N: 'seigle'; 1769: 'seigle'
ᶜ…ᶜ: R, M, N: 'davoine'; 1769: 'd'avoine'
ᵈ…ᵈ: R, M, N: 'et petites géns est differente dans Lés differents Pays de L'europpe'; 1756b and 1769: '& du Peuple n'est pas la même dans tous les Païs de l'Europe'
ᵉ…ᵉ: sic

155 Both E155 and A155 make the point that the fertility of the soil as well as the manners of living vary across Europe. E enlarges on this in the subsequent paragraphs, E156–E161, including a discussion of calculations from the Supplement in E156–E160. None of these has a counterpart in A. The point in A155 that the proprietors of land decide how land is used, and in that way influence the size of the population, is also made, slightly differently, in E162. The correspondence resumes in E162/A162. One explanation for these differences between the two texts may be that E was based on a later draft that took into account the calculations of the Supplement. Cf. C33iii and C561i.

156 |9| La plûpart des terres de Flandres, & une partie de celles de la Lombardie, rapportent dixhuit à vingt fois le froment qu'on y a semé, sans se reposer: la Campagne de Naples en rapporte encore d'avantage. Il y a quelques terres en France, en Espagne, en Angleterre & en Allemagne qui rapportent la même quantité. Ciceron nous apprend que les terres de Sicile ªproduisoientª, de son tems, ᵇdix pour unᵇ; & ᶜPline l'Ancienᶜ dit que les terres Léontines en Sicile, rapportoient cent fois la semence; que celles de Babylone ᵈla rendoientᵈ jusqu'à cent cinquante ᵉfoisᵉ; & quelques terres en Afrique, encore bien plus.

157 [93] |10| Aujourd'hui les terres en Europe peuvent rapporter, l'un portant l'autre, six fois la semence; de maniere qu'il reste cinq fois la semence pour la consommation des Habitans. Les terres ªs'y reposentª ordinairement la troisieme année, aïant rapporté du froment la premiere année, ᵇ& du petit blé, dans la secondeᵇ.

158 |11| On pourra voir dans le Supplément les calculs de la terre nécessaire pour la subsistance d'un Homme, dans les différentes suppositions de sa maniere de vivre.

159 |12| On y verra qu'un Homme qui vit ªde pain, d'ail & de racinesª, qui ne porte que ᵇdes habitsᵇ de chanvre, du gros linge, des sabots, ᶜ&ᶜ qui ne boit que ᵈde l'eau, comme c'est le cas de plusieurs Païsans dans les Parties méridionales de France,ᵈ peut subsister du produit d'un arpent & demi de terre de moïenne bonté, [94] qui rapporte six fois la semence, & qui se repose tous les trois ans.

160 |13| ªD'unª autre côté, un Homme adulte, qui porte des souliers de cuir, ᵇdes bas, du drap de laineᵇ, qui vit dans des Maisons, ᶜqui a du linge à changer, un lit, des chaises, une table,ᶜ & autres choses nécessaires, qui boit modérément de la biere, ou du vin, ᵈqui mangeᵈ de la viande tous les jours, du beurre, du fromage, du pain, des legumes, &c. le tout suffisamment, mais modérément, ne demande guere pour tout cela, que le produit de quatre à cinq arpens de terre de moïenne bonté. Il est vrai que dans ces calculs, on ne donne aucune terre pour le maintien d'autres Chevaux, que ᵉde ceuxᵉ qui sont nécessaires pour labourer la terre, & pour le transport des denrées, à dix milles de distance.

161 |14| L'Histoire rapporte que les [95] premiers Romains entretenoient chacun leur Famille, du produit de deux journaux de terre, qui ne faisoient qu'un arpent de Paris, & ª330 piés quarrésª, ou environ. Aussi ils étoient presque nus; ᵇils n'usoient ni de vin, ni d'huileᵇ, couchoient ᶜdansᶜ la paille, & n'avoient presque point de commodités; mais comme ils travaillotent beaucoup la terre, qui est assez bonne aux environs de Rome, ils en tiroient beaucoup de grains & de légumes.

Most of the Land in Flanders and part of that in Lombardy yields 18 to 20 fold without lying idle; the Campagna of Naples yields still more. There are a few Properties in France, Spain, England and Germany which yield the same amount. Cicero tells us that the Land of Sicily in his time yielded tenfold, and the Elder Pliny says that the Leontine lands in Sicily yielded a hundred fold, those of Babylon a hundred and fifty, and some African lands a good deal more.

^a...^a: R, M, N: 'raportoient'
^b...^b: R, M, N: 'dix fois la semence'
^c...^c: R, M, N: 'Pline'
^d...^d: R, M, N: 'rapportoient'
^e...^e: R, M, N: 'fois la semence'

i. The reference to Cicero is to his *Verrines*, 2.3.112 (70 B.C.): 'the [Leontine] land [in Sicily] yields eightfold when everything goes well, even tenfold when all the gods lend a hand'.

ii. The reference to Pliny the Elder is to *Natural History* book 18, 94–95: 'one modus, given suitable soil such as that on the Byzacian plain of Africa, may yield 150 modii .... Indeed, both the Leontine plains and other parts of Sicily, the whole of Baetica and particularly Egypt, yield one hundredfold.'

156

Today Land in Europe yields on the average six times what is sown, so that five times the seed remains for the consumption of the People. Land usually rests one year in three, producing wheat the first year and barley the second.

^a...^a:R, M, N: 'y reposent'
^b...^b: R, M, N; 'et la seconde du petit bled'

157

In the Supplement will be found estimates of the amount of Land required for the support of a Man according to the different assumptions of his Manner of Living.

For other mentions of the Supplement, see C33ii.

158

It will be seen that a Man who lives on Bread, Garlic and Roots, wears only hempen garments, coarse Linen, Wooden Shoes, and drinks only water, like many Peasants in the South of France, can live on the produce of an Acre and a half of Land of medium goodness, yielding a sixfold harvest and resting once in 3 years.

^a...^a: R: 'de pain aïle Racine'; M, N: 'de pain, et de racine'
^b...^b: R, M, N: 'de gros habits'
^c...^c: '&c'
^d...^d: R: 'leau Teorresme, Cest le Cas de plusieurs paysans dans les partyes meridionnales de La france'; M, N: 'de l'eau, (c'est le cas de plusieurs paisans dans les parties méridionalles de la france)'

The *abbé* Pluquet quotes the estimates of E159 and E160 and then includes an interesting footnote about the 'marquis S. Georges'. See Introduction p. 9.

159

On the other hand a grown-up Man who wears leather Shoes, Stockings, Woollen Cloth, who lives in a House and has a change of Linen, a Bed, Chairs, Table, and other necessaries, drinks moderately of Beer or Wine, eats every day Meat, Butter, Cheese, Bread, Vegetables, etc. sufficiently and yet moderately needs for all that the produce of 4 to 5 acres of land of medium quality. It is true that in these estimates nothing is allowed for the food of Horses except for the Plough and Carriage of Produce for ten Miles.

^a...^a: R, M, N: 'Que d'un'
^b...^b: R, M, N: 'des drap de laine, Chapeaux bas et du linge a Changér'
^c...^c: R, M, N: 'a des lits Chaises tables'
^d...^d: R, M, N: 'mange'
^e...^e: R, M, N: 'Ceux'

160

History records that the first Romans each maintained his family on two journaux of Land, equal to one Paris acre and 330 square feet or thereabouts. They were almost naked, had no Wine or Oil, lay in the Straw, and had hardly any Comforts, but as they cultivated intensely the Land, which is fairly good around Rome, they drew from it plenty of Corn and of Vegetables.

^a...^a: M: '330 pieds en quarré' (R, N: '330 pieds quarrez')
^b...^b: R, M, N: 'n'avoient ni vin, ni huile'
^c...^c: N: 'sur'; 1756b and 1769: 'sur' (R, M: 'dans')

Since the 'Paris acre' was 48,400 square feet, the *journal* is here calculated to be 24,350 square feet, or 2,569 metres square. This is approximately the size of the Roman *jugerum* which was equal to 2,523 metres square. Cf. C12.

161

162 |15| Si les Propriétaires de terres avoient à cœur la multiplication des Hommes, s'ils encourageoient les Païsans à se marier jeunes, & à élever des Enfans, ªpar la promesseª de pourvoir à leur subsistance, en ᵇdestinantᵇ les terres uniquement à cela, ils multiplieroient sans doute les Hommes, jusqu'au nombre que les terres pourroient entretenir; [96] & cela suivant les produits de terre qu'ils destineroient à la subsistance de chacun, soit celui d'un arpent & demi, soit celui de quatre à cinq arpens, par tête.

163 |16| Mais si au lieu de cela le Prince, où les Propriétaires de terres, les font emploïer à d'autres usages ªqu'à l'entretienª des Habitans; si, par le prix ᵇqu'ilsᵇ donnent au Marché des denrées ᶜ& marchandisesᶜ, ils déterminent les Fermiers à mettre les terres à d'autres usages, que ceux qui servent à l'entretien des Hommes (car nous avons vû que le prix que les Propriétaires offrent au Marché, & la consommation qu'ils font, déterminent l'emploi qu'on fait des terres, de la même maniere que s'ils les faisoient valoir eux-mêmes), les Habitans diminueront nécessairement en nombre. Les uns faute d'emploi seront obligés de quitter le Païs, [97] d'autres, ne se voïant pas les moïens nécessaires pour élever des Enfans, ne se marieront pas, ou ne se marieront que tard, après avoir mis quelque chose à part pour ᵈle soutien du ménageᵈ.

164 |17| Si les Propriétaires de terres, qui vivent à la Campagne, vont demeurer dans les Villes éloignées de leurs Terres, il faudra nourrir des Chevaux, tant pour le transport de leur subsistance à la Ville, que de celle de tous les Domestiques, Artisans, & autres, que leur résidence dans la Ville y ªattireª.

165 |18| La voiture des vins de Bourgogne à Paris, coute souvent plus que le vin même ne coute sur les lieux; & par conséquent la terre emploïée pour l'entretien des Chevaux de voiture, & de ceux qui en ont soin, est plus considérable que celle qui produit le vin, & qui entretient ceux qui ont eu part à sa pro-[98]duction. Plus on entretient de Chevaux dans un État, & moins il restera de subsistance pour les Habitans. L'entretien des Chevaux de ªcarrosseª, de chasse ou de parade, ᵇcouteᵇ souvent trois à quatre arpens de terre.

166 |19| Mais lorsque les Seigneurs & les Propriétaires de terres ªtirentª des Manufactures étrangeres, ᵇleurs draps, leurs soieries, leurs dentelles, &c. & s'ils les paientᵇ en envoïant chez l'Etranger le produit des denrées de l'Etat, ils diminuent par-là extraordinairement la subsistance des Habitans, & augmentent celle des Etrangers qui deviennent souvent les Ennemis de l'Etat.

[122 continued] ‖ But if the King or these great Proprietors of Land allot their Possessions otherwise than to the necessary and comfortable Support of the human Species, in order to gratify their Taste and luxuriant Appetites, they determine the Farmer to apply and cultivate this Land which they rent, to produce that which, from the great Prices given at Market, will answer the Call and Manner of Living of the Age.

If the Proprietors of Land had at heart the increase of Population, if they encouraged the Peasants to marry young and bring up Children by promising to provide them with Subsistence, devoting their Land entirely to that purpose, they would doubtless increase the Population up to the point which the Land could support, according to the produce they allotted for each person whether an Acre and a Half or Four to Five Acres a head.

a..a: R, M, N: 'en leur promettant'
b...b: R, M, N: 'employant'

Cf. E162 with the end of A155.

162

But if instead of that the Prince, or the Proprietors of Land, cause the Land to be used for other purposes than the upkeep of the People: if by the Prices they offer in the Market for produce and Merchandise they determine the Farmers to employ the Land for other purposes than the Maintenance of Man (for we have seen that the Prices they offer in the Market and their consumption determine the use made of the Land just as if they cultivated it themselves) the People will necessarily diminish in number. Some will be forced to leave the country for lack of employment, others not seeing the necessary means of raising Children, will not marry or will only marry late, after having put aside somewhat for the support of the household.

a...a: R, M, N: 'que lentretien'
b...b: R: 'quil' (M, N: 'quils')
c...c: 1756b and 1769: '& des marchandises'
d...d: R, M, N: 'soutenir le ménage'

163

If the Proprietors of Land who live in the Country go to reside in the Cities far away from their Land, Horses must be fed for the transport into the City both of their food and that of all the Domestic Servants, Mechanicks and others whom their residence in the City attracts thither.

a...a: R, M, N: 'attiréra'

164

The carriage of Wine from Burgundy to Paris often costs more than the Wine itself costs in Burgundy; and consequently the Land employed for the upkeep of the cart horses and those who look after them is more considerable than the Land which produces the Wine and supports those who have taken part in its production. The more Horses there are in a State the less food will remain for the People. The upkeep of Carriage horses, Hunters, or Chargers, often takes three or four Acres of Land.

a...a: R, M, N: 'poste'
b...b: R: 'coutent'; M, N: 'coutent'

The term *Chevaux de poste* appears to be a literal translation of 'post horses'. The editor of the print edition may have wanted to remove this apparent Anglicism.

165

But when the Nobility and Proprietors of Land draw from Foreign Manufactures their Cloths, Silks, Laces, etc. and pay for them by sending to the Foreigner their native produce they diminish extraordinary the food of the People and increase that of Foreigners who often become Enemies of the State.

a..a: R, M, N: 'Consomment'
b...b: R, M, N: 'comme draps soyeries dentelles, linge &c. et les payent'

The phrase '*Ennemis de l'Etat*' is also used in E167 and E192. D190 has a similar expression. See C190i.

166

167 |20| Si un Propriétaire, ou Seigneur Polonois, à qui ses Fermiers paient annuellement une rente égale à-peu-près au produit du tiers de ses terres, se plaît à ᵃse servir deᵃ draps, de linges, &c. d'Hollande, ᵇil donnera pour ces [99] marchandises la moitié de sa rente, & emploieraᵇ peut-être l'autre pour la subsistance de sa Famille, en d'autres denrées & marchandises du crû de Pologne: or la moitié de sa rente, dans notre supposition, répond à la sixieme partie du produit de sa terre, & cette sixieme partie sera emportée par les Hollandois, auxquels les Fermiers Polonois la ᶜdonnerontᶜ en blé, laines, chanvres & autres denrées: voilà donc une sixieme partie de la terre de Pologne qu'on ôte aux Habitans, ᵈsans comprendre la nourriture des Chevaux de voiture, de carrosse & de paradeᵈ, qu'on entretient en Pologne, par la façon de vivre que les Seigneurs y suivent; ᵉ& de plus, si surᵉ les deux tiers du produit des terres qu'on attribue aux Fermiers, ceux-ci, à l'exemple de leurs Maîtres, consument des Manufactures étrangeres, qu'ils [100] ᶠpaierontᶠ aussi aux Etrangers en denrées du crû de la Pologne, il y aura bien un bon tiers du produit des terres en Pologne qu'on ôte à la subsistance des Habitans, &, qui pis est, dont la plus grande partie est envoïée à l'Etranger, & sert souvent à l'entretien des Ennemis de l'Etat. Si les Propriétaires des terres & les Seigneurs en Pologne ne vouloient consommer que des Manufactures de leur Etat, quelque mauvaises qu'elles fussent dans leurs commencemens, ils les feroient devenir peu-à-peu meilleures, & entretiendroient un grand nombre de ᵍleurs propresᵍ Habitans à y travailler, au lieu de donner cet avantage à des Etrangers: & si tous les Etats avoient un pareil soin de n'être ʰpas les dupes des autresʰ Etats dans le Commerce, chaque Etat seroit considérable uniquement, à proportion de son produit & [101] de l'industrie de ses Habitans.

168 |21| Si les Dames de Paris se plaisent à porter des dentelles de Bruxelles, ᵃ& siᵃ la France paie ᵇcesᵇ dentelles en vin de Champagne, il faudra païer le produit d'un seul arpent de lin, par le produit de plus de seize mille arpens ᶜen vignesᶜ, si j'ai bien calculé. On expliquera cela plus particuliérement ailleurs, & on en pourra voir les calculs au Supplément. Je me contenterai de remarquer ici qu'on ôte dans ce commerce un grand produit de terre à la subsistance des François, & que toutes les denrées qu'on envoie en Païs étrangers, lorsqu'on n'en fait pas revenir en échange un produit également considérable, tendent à diminuer le nombre des Habitans de l'État.

If a Proprietor or Nobleman in Poland, to whom his Farmers pay yearly a Rent equal to about one third of the Produce of his Land, pleases to use the Cloths, Linens, etc. of Holland, he will pay for these Mechandises one half of the rent he receives and perhaps use the other half for the subsistence of his Family on other Products and rough Manufactures of Poland: but half his rent, on our supposition, corresponds to the sixth part of the Produce of his Land, and this sixth part will be carried away by the Dutch to whom the Farmers of Poland will deliver it in Corn, Wool, Hemp and other produce. Here is then a sixth part of the Land of Poland withdrawn from its people, to say nothing of the feeding of the Cart horses, Carriage Horses and Chargers in Poland, maintained by the Manner of Living of the Nobility there. Further if out of the two thirds of the Produce of the Land allotted to the Farmers there last imitating their Masters consume foreign Manufactures which they will also pay Foreigners for in raw Produce of Poland, there will be a good third of the produce of the Land in Poland abstracted from the Food of the People, and, what is worse, mostly sent to the Foreigner and often serving to support the Enemies of the State. If the Proprietors of Land and the Nobility in Poland would consume only the Manufactures of their own State, bad as they might be at the outset, they would soon become better, and would keep a great Number of their own People to work there, instead of giving this advantage to Foreigners: and if all States had the like care not to be the dupes of other States in matters of Commerce, each State would be considerable only in proportion to its Produce and the Industry of its People.

If the Ladies of Paris are pleased to wear Brussels Lace, and if France pays for this Lace with Champagne wine, the product of a single Acre of Flax must be paid for with the product of 16,000 acres of land under vines, if my calculations are correct. This will be more fully explained elsewhere and the figures are shown in the Supplement. Suffice to say here that in this transaction a great amount of produce of the Land is withdrawn from the subsistence of the French, and that all the produce sent abroad, unless an equally considerable amount of produce be brought back in exchange, tends to diminish the number of People in the State.

a...a: R, M, N: 'a consommer des'
b...b: R, M: 'il payéra la moityé de sa [N: 'la'] rente pour cés Marchandises et payera'
c...c: R, M, N: 'vendront'
d...d: R, M, N: 'et attendu les Cheveaux de Carosse de voitures de parade &c'
e...e: R, M, N: 'et que'
f...f: R, M, N: 'payent'
g...g: R, M, N: 'leurs'
h...h: R, M, N: 'plus la duppe de touts Lés autres'

167

a...a: R, M, N: 'si'
b...b: R: 'ses' (M, N: 'ces')
c...c: R, M: 'de vigne'; N: 'de vignes'

i. The promised further explanations are given in E490–E491/D490–D491. Also see E/D66.

ii. L'Abbé de Condillac, *Le commerce et le gouvernement* (1776, I, ch. 27, pp. 302–03): '*On pretend que si la France payait en vin de Champagne les dentelles de Bruxelles, elle donnerait pour le produit d'un seul arpent de lin, le produit de plus de seize mille arpens de vignes.*' In a footnote the source is given as '*Essai sur la nature du Commerce*, Part.I, ch. 15'.

iii. For other authors who quoted the same calculation, see C498ii.

iv. For other mentions of the Supplement, see C33ii.

168

169 |22| Lorsque j'ai dit que les Propriétaires de terres pourroient multiplier les Habitans à propor-[102]tion du nombre que ces terres pourroient en entretenir, j'ai supposé que le plus grand nombre des Hommes ne demande pas mieux qu'à se marier, ªsi on les metª en état d'entretenir leurs Familles de ᵇla même maniereᵇ qu'ils se contentent de vivre eux-mêmes; c'est-à-dire, que si un Homme se contente du produit d'un arpent & demi de terre, il se mariera, ᶜpourvu qu'il soit sûr d'avoirᶜ de quoi entretenir sa Famille à-peu-près de la même façon; que s'il ne se contente que du produit de ᵈcinq à dix arpensᵈ, il ne s'empressera pas de se marier, à moins qu'il ᵉne croie pouvoir faireᵉ subsister sa Famille à-peu-près de même.

170 |23| Les Enfans de la Noblesse en Europe sont élevés dans l'affluence; & comme on donne ordinairement la plus grande partie du bien aux Aînés, les Cadets ne s'empressent guere de se ma-[103]rier; ils vivent pour la plûpart garçons, soit dans les Armées, soit dans les Cloîtres, mais rarement en trouvera-t-on qui ne soient prêts à se marier si on leur offre des Héritieres ª&ª des Fortunes, c'est-à-dire, le moïen d'entretenir une Famille sur le pié de vivre qu'ils ont en vue, & sans lequel ils croiroient rendre leurs Enfans malheureux.

171 |24| Il se trouve aussi dans les classes inférieures de l'Etat plusieurs Hommes, qui, par orgueil ª&ª par des raisons semblables à celles de la Noblesse, aiment mieux vivre dans le Célibat, & ᵇdépenser sur eux-mêmes le peu de bien qu'ils ont,ᵇ que de se mettre en ménage. Mais la plupart s'y mettroient volontiers, s'ils pouvoient compter sur un entretien pour leur Famille tel qu'ils ᶜle voudroientᶜ: ils croiroient faire tort à leurs Enfans, s'ils en élevoient pour les voir tomber dans une [104] Classe inférieure à la leur. Il n'y a qu'un très petit nombre d'Habitans dans un État, qui évitent le mariage par pur esprit de libertinage: tous les bas Ordres des Habitans ne demandent qu'à vivre, & à élever des Enfans qui puissent au moins vivre comme eux. Lorsque les Laboureurs & les Artisans ne se marient pas, c'est qu'ils attendent à épargner quelque chose pour se mettre en état d'entrer en ménage, ou à trouver quelque Fille qui apporte quelque petit fond pour cela; parcequ'ils voient journellement plusieurs autres de ᵈleur especeᵈ, qui, faute de prendre de pareilles précautions, entrent en ménage & tombent dans la plus affreuse pauvreté, étant obligés de se frauder de leur propre subsistance, pour nourrir leurs Enfans.

When I said that the Proprietors of Land might multiply the Population as far as the Land would support them, I assumed that most Men desire nothing better than to marry if they are set in a position to keep their Families in the same style as they are content to live themselves. That is, if a Man is satisfied with the produce of an Acre and a half of Land he will marry if he is sure of having enough to keep his Family in the same way. But if he is only satisfied with the produce of 5 to 10 Acres he will be in no hurry to marry unless he thinks he can bring up his Family in the same manner.

In Europe the Children of the Nobility are brought up in affluence; and as the largest share of the Property is usually given to the Eldest sons, the younger Sons are in no hurry to marry. They usually live as Bachelors, either in the Army or in the Cloisters, but will seldom be fond unwilling to marry if they are offered Heiresses and Fortunes, or the means of supporting a Family on the footing which they have in view and without which they would consider themselves to make their Children wretched.

In the lower classes of the State also there are Men who from pride and from reasons similar to those of the Nobility, prefer to live in celibacy and to spend on themselves the little that they have rather than settle down in family life. But most of them would gladly set up a Family if they could count upon keeping it up as they would wish: they would consider themselves to do an injustice to their Children if they brought them up to fall into a lower Class than themselves. Only a few Men in a State avoid marriage from sheer flightiness. All the lower orders wish to live and bring up Children who can live like themselves. When Labourers and Mechanicks do not marry it is because they wait till they save something to enable them to set up a household or to find some young woman who brings a little capital for that purpose, since they see every day others like them who for lack of such precaution start housekeeping and fall into the most frightful poverty, being obliged to deprive themselves of their own food to nourish their Children.

ᵃ…ᵃ: R, M, N: 'supposé quon Veuille Les mettre'
ᵇ…ᵇ: M: 'la maniere' (R, N: 'la méme maniere')
ᶜ…ᶜ: R, M: 'pour un qui Conte avoir'; N: 'pour un/ pour vu qu'il compte avoir'
ᵈ…ᵈ: R, M, N: '4 a 5 arpens'
ᵉ…ᵉ: R: 'ne Conte de faire'; M, N: 'ne compte faire'

ᵃ…ᵃ: N: 'ou' (R, M: 'et')

ᵃ…ᵃ: R, M, N: 'ou'
ᵇ…ᵇ: R, M, N: 'depenser le peu de bien qu'ils ont sur eux memes'
ᶜ…ᶜ: R, M, N: 'les Contenteroit'
ᵈ…ᵈ: R: 'Leurs especes'; (M, N: 'leur espece')

V169c in N originally read **169** '*pour un qui compte avoir*' ('for someone who counts on having'), which is identical to what is found in R and M. This was then overwritten to read '*pour vu qu'il compte avoir*' ('if he counts on having'), which approximates to the expression in E169.

170

171

172 |25| Par les observations de M. Halley à Breslaw en Silésie, on remarque que de toutes les Fe-[105]melles qui sont en état de porter des enfans, depuis l'âge de seize jusqu'à quarante cinq ans, il n'y en a pas une, en six, qui porte effectivement un enfant tous les ans; au lieu, dit M. Halley, qu'il devroit y en avoir au moins ᵃquatre ou sixᵃ qui accouchassent tous les ans, ᵇsans y compterᵇ celles qui peuvent être stériles, ᶜou quiᶜ peuvent avorter. Qui est ce qui empêche que quatre Filles en six ne portent tous les ans des Enfans, c'est qu'elles ne peuvent pas se marier à cause des découragemens & empêchemens qui s'y trouvent. Une Fille prend soin ᵈde ne pas devenir Mereᵈ, si elle n'est mariée; elle ne se peut marier si elle ne trouve un Homme qui veuille ᵉen courir les risquesᵉ. ᶠLa plus grande partie des Habitansᶠ dans un Etat sont à gages ou Entrepreneurs; la plûpart sont dépendans, ᵍla plûpart sont dansᵍ l'incertitude, s'ils trou-[106]veront par leur travail ou par leurs entreprises, le moïen de faire subsister leur ménage sur le pié qu'ils l'envisagent; cela fait qu'ils ne se marient pas tous, ou qu'ils se marient si tard, ʰque de sixʰ Femelles, ou du moins de quatre, qui devroient tous les ans produire un Enfant, il ne s'en trouve effectivement qu'une, en six, qui ⁱdevienne Mereⁱ.

173 |26| Que les Propriétaires de terres aident à entretenir les ménages, il ne faut qu'une génération pour porter la multiplication des Hommes aussi loin que les produits des terres peuvent fournir de moïens de ᵃsubsisterᵃ. Les Enfans ne demandent pas tant de produit de terre que les personnes adultes. ᵇLes uns & les autresᵇ peuvent vivre de plus ou de moins de produit de terre, suivant ce qu'ils consument. On a vu des Peuples du Nord, où les terres produisent peu, vivre de si peu [107] de produit de terre, qu'ils ont envoïé des Colonies & des essaies d'Hommes envahir les terres du Sud, & en détruire les Habitans, pour s'approprier leurs terres. Suivant les différentes façons de vivre, quatre cens mille Habitans pourroient subsister sur le même produit de terre, qui n'en entretient régulierement que cent mille. Et celui qui ne dépense que le produit d'un arpent & demi de terre sera peut-être plus robuste & plus brave que celui ᶜqui dépenseᶜ le produit de cinq à ᵈdixᵈ arpens. Voilà, ce me semble, assez d'inductions pour faire sentir que le nombre des Habitans, dans un État, dépend des moïens de subsister; & comme les moïens de subsistance dépendent de l'application & des usages qu'on fait des terres, & que ᵉcesᵉ usages dépendent des volontés, ᶠdu goût & de la façonᶠ de vivre des Propriétaires de terres [108] principalement, il est clair que la multiplication ou le décroissement des Peuples dépendent d'eux.

[123] ‖ If the Proprietors of Land laid out the Means of Support and Maintenance for Posterity, an Age would carry Population to a very great Series of Extent, and in Proportion to the Quantity of Land capable from its Produce to support the Number of Inhabitants: In the Northern Parts of the World the Land is less fruitful than in the South, yet it is known, that these Northern People have swarmed in Multitudes, and obtained by Conquest Southern Possessions; it is the Manner of Living of the People which determines the Point, and the Quantity of Land allotted to them for procuring this Living: It is calculated that four hundred Thousand Souls are to be maintained with the Produce of as much Land as in the present Method of Living in this Country is applied to the support of one hundred Thousand. A Man who lives upon the Produce of an Acre and an half of Land, may be stronger and stouter than he who spends the Produce of five or ten Acres of Land; it therefore seems pretty clear, that the Number of Inhabitants of a State depend on the Means allotted them of obtaining their Support; and as this Means of Subsistence arises from the Methods and Manner of cul-[124]tivating the Earth, and this Method depends principally on the Pleasure, Custom, Taste, and Manner of Living of the great Proprietors of Land, the Increase and Decrease of Population, also stand on the same Foundation.

From the observations of M. Halley, at Breslaw in Silesia, it is found that of all the Females capable of child-bearing, from 16 to 45 years of age, not one in six actually bears a child every year, while, says M. Halley, there ought to be at least 4 or 6 who should have children every year, without including those who are barren or have still-births. The reason why four Women out of six do not bear children every year is that they cannot marry because of the discouragements and difficulties in their way. A young Woman takes care not to become a Mother if she is not married; she cannot marry unless she finds a Man who is ready to run the risk of it. Most of the People in a State are hired or are Undertakers; most are dependent and live in uncertainty whether they will find by their Labour or their Undertakings the means of supporting their household on the footing they have in view. Therefore they do not all marry, or marry so late that of six Women, or at least four, who should produce a child every year there is actually only one in six who becomes a Mother.

If the Proprietors of Land help to support the Families, a single generation suffices to push the increase of population as far as the Produce of the Land will supply means of subsistence. Children do not require so much of this produce as grown-up persons. Both can live on more or less according to their consumption. The Northern People, where the Land produces little, have been known to live on so little produce that they have sent out Colonists and swarms of Men to invade the Lands of the South and destroy its Inhabitants to appropriate their Land. According to the different Manner of Living, 400,000 people might subsist on the same produce of the Land which ordinarily supports but 100,000. A Man who lives upon the Produce of an Acre and a half of Land, may be stronger and stouter than he who spends the Produce of five or ten Acres; it therefore seems pretty clear that the Number of Inhabitants of a State depends on the Means allotted them of obtaining their Support; and as this Means of Subsistence arises from the Method of cultivating the soil, and this Method depends chiefly on the Taste, Humours and Manner of Living of the Proprietors of Land, the Increase and Decrease of Population also stand on the same Foundation.

[a]...[a]: R, M, N, 1756a, 1756b, 1769: 'quatre en six'
[b]...[b]: R, M, N: 'faisant abstraction de' [c]...[c]: R, M, N: 'et' [d]...[d]: R, M, N: 'de ne point enfantér' [e]...[e]: R, M, N: 'sy livrér' [f]...[f]: R, M, N: 'La plus part des ordres d'Habitans' [g]...[g]: R, M: 'la plus part est dans'; N: la plus part dans'
[h]...[h]: R, M: 'que six' (N: 'que de six')
[i]...[i]: R, M, N: 'Enfante'

[a]...[a]: R, M, N: 'sucistance'
[b]...[b]: M: 'les uns ou les autres' (R, N: 'Les uns et Les autres')
[c]...[c]: R, M, N: 'qui en depense'
[d]...[d]: R has 'six' and 'dix' written above one another; M has '6'; N has 'six'
[e]...[e]: M: 'les' (R, N: 'ces')
[f]...[f]: R, M, N: 'gouts et façons'

See C80i for Halley's **172** contribution. Cantillon here closely follows Halley's argument in 'Some further Considerations on the Breslaw Bills of Mortality' (1693b: 655): 'I find that there are [in Breslau] nearly 15000 Persons above 16 and under 45, of which at least 7000 are Women capable to bear Children. Of these notwithstanding there are but 1238 born yearly, which is but little more than a sixth part. So that about one in six of these Women do breed yearly; whereas were they all married, it would not appear strange or unlikely, that four of six should bring a Child every year.'

i. Note that from 'A Man who **173** lives', Higgs follows A173 almost verbatim for several sentences even adopting the capitalisation. Cf. C106ii.

ii. Mirabeau *L'Ami des hommes* (1756: 85) quotes the last sentence from '*le nombre des habitans*'. The fact that he follows V173f (though not V173e) suggests that he used the manuscript version. Cf. C200ii and see Introduction p. 7.

iii. A173 is the only instance in A where calculations are given that correspond to E. Perhaps significantly, the French text does not mention that these calculations are contained in the Supplement. Cf. C155 and C561i.

iv. For the expression 'Series of Extent' in A173, see C150.

174 |27| La multiplication des Hommes peut être portée ᵃau plus loinᵃ dans les Païs où les Habitans se contentent de vivre le plus pauvrement & de dépenser le moins de produit de la terre; mais dans les Païs où tous les Païsans & Laboureurs sont dans l'habitude de manger souvent de la viande, & de boire du vin, ou de la biere, &c. on ne sauroit entretenir tant d'Habitans.

175 |28| Le Chevalier ᵃGuilleᵃ Petty, & après lui M. ᵇDaventᵇ, Inspecteurs des Douanes en Angleterre, semblent s'éloigner beaucoup des voies de la nature, lorsqu'ils tâchent de calculer la propagation des Hommes, par des progressions de génération depuis ᶜle premierᶜ Pere Adam. Leurs calculs semblent être purement [109] imaginaires, & dressés au hasard. Sur ce qu'ils ont pu observer de la propagation réelle dans certains cantons, comment pourroient-ils rendre raison de la diminution de ces Peuples innombrables qu'on ᵈvoïoit autrefois en Asieᵈ, en Egypte, &c. ᵉmêmeᵉ de ᶠcelle des Peuplesᶠ de l'Europe? Si l'on voïoit, il y a dix-sept siecles, vingt-six millions d'Habitans en Italie, qui présentement est réduite à six millions pour le plus, comment pourra-t-on déterminer par les progressions de ᵍM. Kingᵍ, que l'Angleterre qui contient aujourd'hui cinq à six millions d'Habitans, en aura probablement treize millions dans un certain nombre d'années? Nous voïons tous les jours que les Anglois, en général, consomment plus de produit de terre que ʰleurs Peresʰ ne faisoient; c'est le vrai moïen ⁱqu'il y aitⁱ [110] moins d'Habitans que par le passé.

176 |29| Les Hommes se multiplient comme des Souris dans une grange, s'ils ont le moïen de subsister sans limitation; & les Anglois dans les Colonies ᵃdeviendrontᵃ plus nombreux, à proportion, dans trois générations, qu'ils ne ᵇferontᵇ en Angleterre en trente; parceque dans les Colonies ils trouvent ᶜà défricher de nouveaux fonds de terre dont ilsᶜ chassent les Sauvages.

177 |30| ᵃDans tous les Païs les Hommes ont eu en tout temsᵃ des guerres pour les terres, ᵇ& pourᵇ les moïens de subsister. ᶜLorsque les guerres ont détruit ou diminué les Habitans d'un Païs, les Sauvages, & les Nations policées, le repeuplent bientôt en tems de paix;ᶜ surtout lorsque le Prince & les Propriétaires de terres ᵈy donnentᵈ de l'encouragement.

178 |31| Un Etat qui a conquis plu-[111]sieurs Provinces, peut acquerir, ᵃpar les tributs qu'il imposeᵃ à ses Peuples vaincus, une augmentation de subsistance pour ses Habitans. Les Romains tiroient une grande partie de la leur, d'Egypte, de Sicile & d'Afrique, & c'est ce qui faisoit que l'Italie ᵇcontenoit tant d'Habitans alorsᵇ.

The Increase of Population can be carried furthest in the Countries where the people are content to live the most poorly and to consume the least produce of the soil. In Countries where all the Peasants and Labourers are accustomed to eat Meat and drink Wine, Beer, etc. so many Inhabitants cannot be supported.

ᵃ…ᵃ: R, M: 'Le plus Loin'; (N: 'au plus loin')

174

Sir Wm Petty, and after him Mr Davenant, Inspector of the Customs in England, seem to depart from nature when they try to estimate the propagation of the race by progressive generations from Adam, the first Father. Their calculations seem to be purely imaginary and drawn up at hazard. On the basis of what they have seen of the actual birth rate in certain districts, how could they explain the Decrease of those innumerable People formerly found in Asia, Egypt, etc. and even in Europe? If seventeen centuries ago there were 26 millions of people in Italy, now reduced to 6 millions at most, how can it be determined by the progressions of Mr King that England which today contains 5 or 6 millions of Inhabitants will probably have 13 millions in a certain number of years? We see daily that Englishmen, in general, consume more of the produce of the Land than their Fathers did, and this is the real reason why there are fewer Inhabitants than in the past.

ᵃ…ᵃ: R, M, N: 'Guillaume'; 1769: 'Guill.'
ᵇ…ᵇ: N: 'D'avinint' (R, M: 'Davenent')
ᶜ…ᶜ: R, M, N: 'le soit dit premier'
ᵈ…ᵈ: R, M, N: 'voyoit en asie'
ᵉ…ᵉ: R, M, N: 'ny meme'
ᶠ…ᶠ: R, M, N: 'ceux'
ᵍ…ᵍ: R, N: 'monsieur Xing'; M: 'M. Xing'
ʰ…ʰ: R: 'leur pere' (M, N: 'leurs peres')
ⁱ…ⁱ: R, M, N: 'd'y avoir'

i. The work of Petty referred to is probably *Natural and political observations* (1662b: 63): 'According to this proportion [of two growing to five in 56 years] one couple, *viz. Adam* and *Eve*, doubling themselves every 64 years of the 5610 years, which is the age of the World according to the *Scriptures*, shall produce far more People, then are now in it. Wherefore the World is not above 100 thousand years old as some vainly Imagine, nor above what the *Scripture* made it.'

ii. Gregory King's calculations are taken from Davenant's *An essay on the probable methods of making a people gainers in ballance of trade* (1699). In particular on p. 18 King presents a progression of population in which he estimates the population of England in 1700 to be 5.5 million and calculates that by the year 2300 it may grow to 11 million.

175

Men multiply like Mice in a barn if they have unlimited Means of Subsistence; and the English in the Colonies will become more numerous in proportion in three generations than they would be in thirty in England, because in the Colonies they find for cultivation new tracts of land from which they drive the Savages.

ᵃ…ᵃ: M: 'deviendroient' (R, N: 'deviendront')
ᵇ…ᵇ: R: 'seront' (M, N: 'feront')
ᶜ…ᶜ: R, M, N: 'de nouveaux fonds de Terres a deffricher en'

i. Cf. A6 for the prediction about population growth in the colonies.

ii. Mirabeau (1756: 16): '*Les hommes multiplient comme les rats dans une grange; si ils ont les moyens de subsister. C'est un axiome que je n'ai pas inventé, & qu'il est temps qu'on prenne pour base de tout calcul en ce genre.*'

iii. Smith (1776, I, xi, b1): 'men, like all other animals, naturally multiply in proportion to the means of their subsistence'. Also see Smith LJ (A) iii, 47.

176

In all Countries at all times Men have waged wars for the Land and the Means of subsistence. When wars have destroyed or diminished the Population of a Country, the Savages and civilised Nations soon repopulate it in times of peace; especially when the Prince and the Proprietors of Land lend their encouragement.

ᵃ…ᵃ: R, M, N: 'Les hommes dans Touts Les pays ont eu dans touts les temps'
ᵇ…ᵇ: R, M, N: 'et'
ᶜ…ᶜ: R, M, N: 'Les sauvages aussi bien que Ceux qui ne le sont pas, lors que les guerres ont detruit ou diminué les habitans dun etat Les repeuplent bien viste dans La paix'
ᵈ…ᵈ: M: 'se donnent' (R, N: 'y donnent')

177

A State which has conquered several Provinces may, by Tribute imposed on the vanquished, acquire an increase of subsistence for its own People. The Romans drew a great part of their subsistence from Egypt, Sicily and Africa and that is why Italy then contained so many Inhabitants.

ᵃ…ᵃ: R, M, N: 'en imposant des tributs'
ᵇ…ᵇ: 1756b, 1769: 'contenoit alors tant d'Habitans'

178

179 |32| Un Etat, ªoù il se trouve des Mines, qui a des Manufactures où il se fait des ouvragesª qui ne demandent pas beaucoup de produit de terre pour leur envoi ᵇdans lesᵇ Païs étrangers, & qui en retire, en échange, beaucoup de denrées ᶜ& deᶜ produit de terre, ᵈacquertᵈ une augmentation de fond pour la subsistance de ses Sujets.

180 |33| Les Hollandois échangent leur travail, soit dans la Navigation, ªsoit dans la Pèche ou les Manufacturesª, avec les Etrangers généralement, contre le produit [112] des terres. La Hollande sans cela ne ᵇpourroitᵇ entretenir de son fond la moitié de ses Habitans. L'Angleterre tire de l'Etranger ᶜdes quantités considérables de Bois, de Chanvres, & d'autres matériauxᶜ ou produits de terre, & consomme beaucoup de vins qu'elle paie en Mines, Manufactures, &c. Cela épargne chez eux une grande quantité de produits de terre; & sans ces avantages, les Habitans en Angleterre, sur le pié de la dépense qu'on y fait pour l'entretien des Hommes, ne pourroient être si nombreux qu'ils le sont. Les Mines de Charbon y épargnent plusieurs millions d'arpens de terre, qu'on seroit obligé ᵈsans cela d'emploïer à produire desᵈ Bois.

181 |34| Mais tous ces ªavantages sont des raffinemensª & des cas accidentels, que je ne considere ici qu'en passant. La voie naturelle [113] & constante, d'augmenter les Habitans d'un Etat, ᵇc'estᵇ de leur y donner de l'emploi, ᶜ& de faire servir les terresᶜ à produire de quoi les entretenir.

|| [124 continued] In short, the true and natural Way of encreasing Population in a State, is to find Employment for its inhabitants, and to appropriate a sufficient Quantity of Land, from which by Labour, Agriculture, and Industry, they may obtain the Means of their Support and secure it to their Posterity.

182 |35| C'est aussi une question qui n'est pas de mon sujet de savoir s'il vaut mieux avoir une grande multitude d'Habitans pauvres & mal entretenus, ªqu'un nombreª moins considérable, ᵇmais bien plus à leur aiseᵇ; un million d'Habitans qui consomment ᶜle produit de six arpensᶜ par tête, ou quatre millions ᵈqui vivent de celui d'un arpent & demiᵈ.

A State where Mines are found, having Manufactures which do not require much of the produce of the land to send them into foreign Countries, and drawing from them in exchange plentiful merchandise and produce of the land, acquires an increased fund for the subsistence of its Subjects.

^a...^a: R, M, N: 'qui fournit des mines, manufactures et ouvrages'
^b...^b: R, M, N: 'aux'
^c...^c: R, M, N: 'et'
^d...^d: R, M, N: 'aquiert'; 1756b ,1769: 'acquiert'

Cf. V179d with V513e and V136a/ V390b. **179**

The Dutch exchange their Labour in Navigation, Fishing or Manufactures principally with Foreigners, for the products of their Land. Otherwise Holland could not support of itself half its Population. England buys from abroad considerable amounts of Timber, Hemp and other materials or products of the soil and consumes much Wine for which she pays in Minerals, Manufactures, etc. That saves the English a great quantity of the products of their soil. Without these advantages the People of England, on the footing of the expense of living there, could not be so numerous as they are. The Coal Mines save them several millions of Acres of Land which would otherwise be needed to grow timber.

^a...^a: R, M: 'La peche, que les manuf.^{res}'; N: 'la peche, les manufactures'
^b...^b: R, M, N: sçauroit'
^c...^c: R, M, N: 'Une quantité considérable de bois, Chanvres, et autres materiaux'
^d...^d: R, M: 'demployer sans Cela a produire des'; N: 'sans cela a produire du'

180

But all these advantages are refinements and exceptional cases which I mention only incidentally. The natural and constant way of increasing Population in a State is to find employment for the People there, and to make the Land serve for the production of their Means of Support.

^a...^a: R, M, N: 'avantages des raffinements'
^b...^b: R, N: 'est'; M: 'et'
^c...^c: R, M, N: 'et demployer les terres'

i. In R the word '*sont*' as well as the full stop are missing from the first sentence of this paragraph. M simply copies the imperfect sentence. N remedies the problem by joining both sentences with a comma and inserts '*lors de*' (i.e. '*alors de*' ['whereas']) between '*Mais*' and '*tous*'. E does it by adding '*sont*' and the full stop.

ii. Chapter XXII in A finishes after A181. The following chapter only contains a few short passages that have clear counterparts in E I, xiii (see C118iii) and E I, xvi (see A196–A197). **181**

It is also a question outside of my subject whether it is better to have a great multitude of Inhabitants, poor and badly provided, than a smaller number, much more at their ease: a million who consume the produce of 6 acres per head or 4 millions who live on the product of an Acre and a half.

^a...^a: R, M, N: 'ou bien un Nombre'
^b...^b: R, M, N: 'bien entretenus'
^c...^c: R, M, N: 'six arpens'
^d...^d: R, M, N: 'qui ne depense qu'un arpent et demy par tete'

182

183   [113] **CHAPITRE ªXVIª.**

Plus il y a de travail dans un Etat, & plus l'Etat   [II, 6, col. 1] *The more labour there is in*
est censé riche naturellement.   *a state, the richer the state is esteemed.*

184 |1| ªPar un long calcul fait dans le Supplément, il est facile à [114] voirª que le travail de vingt-cinq personnes adultes suffit pour procurer ᵇà cent autres, aussi adultes, toutes les chosesᵇ nécessaires à la vie, suivant la consommation de ᶜnotre Europeᶜ. ᵈDans ces calculs, il est vrai, la nourritureᵈ, l'habillement, ᵉle logement, &c.ᵉ sont grossiers ᶠ& peu travaillésᶠ; mais l'aisance & l'abondance s'y trouvent. On peut présumer qu'il y a un bon tiers des Habitans d'un Etat trop jeunes ou trop vieux pour le travail journalier, & encore une sixieme partie composée de Propriétaires de terres, de Malades, ᵍ& de différentes espéces d'Entrepreneursᵍ, qui ne contribuent ʰpointʰ, par le travail de leurs mains, ⁱaux différens besoinsⁱ des Hommes. Tout cela fait une moitié des Habitans qui sont sans travail, ou du moins sans le travail dont il s'agit. Ainsi, si vingt-cinq per-[115]sonnes font tout le travail nécessaire pour l'entretien ʲde cent autres, il restera vingt-cinq personnes, en cent,ʲ qui sont en état de travailler & qui n'auront rien à faire.

|| It has been judged, by experience, that the labour of 25 persons is nearly sufficient to provide meat, drink, apparel, housing, and, generally, all the necessaries of life for 100 persons: upon this supposition, the fare and cloathing are coarse, but easy and plentiful: yet, as above one third of the inhabitants are either too old or too young to work, or sick, or infirm, and that full one half are necessarily idle, or free from common labour: there would be still, on this supposition, 25 adult working persons, or those capable of working, who would have nothing to do.

185 |2| Les Gens de guerre, & les Domestiques dans les Familles aisées, feront une partie ªde ces vingt-cinq personnesª; & si on emploie tous les autres à raffiner, par un travail additionnel, les choses nécessaires à la vie, comme à faire du linge fin, ᵇdesᵇ draps fins, &c. l'Etat sera censé riche à proportion de cette augmentation de travail, ᶜquoiqu'elleᶜ n'ajoute rien à la quantité ᵈdes choses nécessairesᵈ à la subsistance & à l'entretien des Hommes.

|| If the most part of these 25 persons in 100 are employed to draw metals out of the earth, or to work fine cloth and fine linnen, and to refine, by greater labour, the houses, the utensils, and other conveniencies of life, though they add nothing to the quantity of food of themselves, nor to the quantity and necessary uses of the cloathing; yet the state will be esteemed the richer for their labour: labour adds to the relish of food and drink, and to the ornament and conveniency of cloathing.

186 |3| Le travail donne un surcroît de goût à la nourriture & à la boisson. ªUne Fourchette, un Couteau, &c.ª travaillés finement ᵇsontᵇ plus estimés que ᶜceuxᶜ [116] ᵈqui sont travaillésᵈ grossierement & à la hâte: on en peut dire autant d'une Maison, d'un lit, d'une table, & généralement de tout ce qui est nécessaire aux commodités de la vie.

|| The more ᵉlabourᵉ is employed in a suit of cloaths, the dearer it sells, and the richer it is esteemed. A knife and fork that ᶠareᶠ nicely wrought, ᵍtakingᵍ up more ᵉlabourᵉ, ᶠareᶠ dearer, and esteemed richer, cæteris paribus.

Chapter XVI

The more Labour there is in a State the more naturally rich the State is esteemed

In a long calculation worked out in the Supplement it is shewn that the Labour of 25 grown persons suffices to provide 100 others, also grown up, with all the necessaries of life according to the European standard. In these estimates it is true the Food, Clothing, Housing, etc. are coarse and rather elementary, but there is ease and plenty. It may be assumed that a good third of the People of a State are too young or too old for daily work and that another sixth are Proprietors of Land, Sick, or Undertakers of different sorts who do not by the Labour of their hands, contribute to the different needs of Men. That makes half the People without work, or at least without the work in question. So if 25 persons do all the work needed for the maintenance of a hundred others, there remain 25 persons out of the hundred who are capable of working but would have nothing to do.

The Soldiers, and the Domestic Servants in well-to-do families, will form part of these 25; and if all the others are busied in working up by additional labour the things necessary for life, like making fine linen, fine cloth, etc. the State will be deemed rich in proportion to this increase in work, though it add nothing to the quantity of things needed for the subsistence and maintenance of Man.

Labour gives an additional relish to food and drink. A fork, a knife, etc. nicely wrought, are more esteemed than those roughly and hastily made. The same may be said of a House, a Bed, a Table and everything needed for the comfort of life.

ᵃ…ᵃ: R, N: '16ᵉ'; M: '10ᵉ'

ᵃ…ᵃ: R, M, N: L'on peut voir par un Long Calcul Dans Le Supplement'
ᵇ…ᵇ: R, M, N: 'a Cent personnes Le boire et Le mangér des habits Maisons Licts et génerallémént toutes choses'
ᶜ…ᶜ: R, M: 'notre Curgre'; N: 'notre Europe'
ᵈ…ᵈ: R, M, N: 'suivant ces Calculs La Nouriture'
ᵉ…ᵉ: R, M, N: 'et autres Choses necessaires'
ᶠ…ᶠ: R, M: 'et pour travail'; missing in N.
ᵍ…ᵍ: R, M, N: 'et d'entrépréneurs de différentes éspéces'
ʰ…ʰ: R, M: 'rien'; N: 'en rien'
ⁱ…ⁱ: R, M, N: 'a la nouriture habilléménts et Commodités'
ʲ…ʲ: 'de Cent personnes'

ᵃ…ᵃ: R, M, N: 'des 25 personnnes restantes'
ᵇ…ᵇ: R, M, N: 'et des'
ᶜ…ᶜ: R, M, N: 'encore quil'
ᵈ…ᵈ: R, M, N: 'de nouritures habillemens et autres Choses Nécéssaires'

ᵃ…ᵃ: R, M, N: 'Un Couteau et une fourchette'
ᵇ…ᵇ: R, M: 'est' (N: 'sont')
ᶜ…ᶜ: R, M, N: 'Celles'
ᵈ…ᵈ: N: 'qui le sont'
ᵉ…ᵉ: T: 'Labor'
ᶠ…ᶠ: T: 'is'
ᵍ…ᵍ: T: 'takes'

D is found in the entry, 'Labour'. The correspondence starts from midway column 1, p. 6, vol. II, with the subheading reproduced in D183. Cf. C7i. **183**

i. Where E184 refers to the Supplement, D184 says 'it has been judged, by experience'. The most likely explanation for this difference may be that Postlethwayt removed references to a supplement. Cf. C66i. **184**

ii. In respect to V184b the French manuscript texts are closer to D184 than to the printed French version. Cf. C275.

iii. The odd spelling in R, copied in M (V184c), is doubtlessly rendered correctly in N and E. Other occurrences of the expression '*notre Europe*' are in E88 and E461. See Introduction p. 13.

iv. Harris (1757, I, i, 4 n): 'Some compute, that the labour of one-fourth of the people is sufficient to maintain the other three-fourth; that one-fourth, as infants, old people, &c. are quite helpless; that one-fourth live upon their lands; whence one-fourth are left for the learned professions, state offices, and for being merchants, shopkeepers, soldiers, &c.'

v. The young Alexander Hamilton copied the first sentence of D184 in his *Pay Book* p. 243.

E185, though not D185, appears to describe soldiers and domestic servants as 'unproductive' workers. This appears to contradict what is said of the same professions in E117. **185**

i. From here up to D200 there is a second version of D in Postlethwayt's 1757 publication. Cf. C64i and C78. The plagiarism in that publication starts near the bottom of p. 155, just after the text reproduced in D75 finishes. Variations are again designated with T. **186**
ii. Cf. V186b with V186f.
iii. For other uses of the *cæteris paribus* clause see C49ii.

187 |4| Il est vrai ᵃqu'il est assez indifférent dans un Etat, qu'on soit dans l'usage de porter de gros draps, ou des draps finsᵃ, si les uns & les autres sont également durables, ᵇ& qu'on y mange délicatement, ou grossierement, si l'on suppose qu'on en ait assez & qu'on se porte bien; attendu que le boire, le manger, l'habillement, &c. se consument également, soit qu'on les prépare proprement ou grossierement,ᵇ & qu'il ne reste rien dans l'Etat de ces espéces de richesses.

|| it is true, that, whether the inhabitants wear fine or coarse cloth, if equally lasting, and eat or drink, and are lodged nicely or coarsely, it is, in one respect, much the same thing, since coarse and fine food and cloathing are equally consumed;

188 |5| Mais il est toujours vrai de dire que les Etats, où l'on porte de beaux draps, de beau linge, &c., & où ᵃl'on mangeᵃ proprement & délicatement, sont plus [117] riches & plus estimés que ᵇceuxᵇ où tout cela est grossier; & même que les Etats où l'on voit plus d'Habitans, vivant de la façon des premiers, sont plus estimes que ceux où l'on en voit moins, à proportion.

but, in the general notion, the state that consumes fine cloathing is esteemed richer than that which consumes coarse, &c.

189 |6| Mais si l'on emploïoit les vingt-cinq personnes, en cent, dont nous avons parlé, à procurer des choses durables, comme à tirer des Mines ᵃle Fer, le Plomb, l'Etaim, le Cuivre, &c.ᵃ & à les travailler pour en faire des outils ᵇ& des instrumensᵇ pour la commodité des Hommes, des vases, ᶜde la vaisselle, & d'autres choses utilesᶜ, qui durent beaucoup plus que ceux qu'on peut faire de terre, l'Etat n'en paroîtra pas seulement plus riche, mais le sera réellement.

But when the additional labour of ᵈthe 25 persons, we mentionedᵈ, produces permanent wealth, as ᵉgold, silver, copperᵉ, &c. to serve for a ᶠcorps of reserveᶠ, whether by exchanging their ᵍlaboursᵍ with foreigners for ʰthoseʰ metals, or digging them out of the ground, the state is not only esteemed richer, but it is in every respect so;

190 |7| ᵃIl le sera sur-toutᵃ, si l'on emploie ces Habitans à tirer, du sein de la Terre, de l'Or & de l'Argent, qui sont des Métaux [118] non-seulement durables, mais ᵇpour ainsi direᵇ, permanens, que le feu même ne sauroit consumer, qui sont généralement reçus, comme la mesure des valeurs, & qu'on peut éternellement échanger pour tout ce qui est nécessaire dans la vie: & si ces Habitans travaillent à attirer l'or & l'argent dans l'Etat, en échange des Manufactures & des ouvrages qu'ils y font & qui sont envoïés dans les Païs étrangers, leur travail sera également utile, & ᶜameliorera réellement l'Etatᶜ.

and more particularly if ᵈsuch labour brings inᵈ gold and silver, for which, on any emergency, the state may have, even from ᵉit'sᵉ enemiesᵉ, any thing it ᶠmay stand in need ofᶠ.

It is true that it is of little difference in a State whether People are accustomed to wear coarse or fine clothes if both are equally lasting, and whether People eat nicely or coarsely if they have enough and are in good health, since Drink, Food, Clothing, etc. are equally consumed whether fine or coarse, and that nothing is left in the State of this sort of wealth.

^a...^a: R, M: 'que soit quon soit dans lusage de porter de gros draps ou des draps fins dans un état'; N: 'que soit que l'on porte de gros draps, ou des draps fins dans un etat'
^b...^b: R, M, N: 'sy on [N: si lon] y mange proprement dellicatémént ou [M: et] grossierémént, C'est toujours dans un sens asses indifferent attendu que le boire, Le Manger et lhabillement se Consume [N: consument] toujours egalement soit quil soit propre, soit quil soit grossier'

187

But it is always true to say that the States where fine Cloths, fine Linen, etc. are worn, and where the Feeding is dainty and delicate, are richer and more esteemed than those where these things are ruder, and even that the States where one sees more People living in the Manner of the first named are more highly esteemed than those where one sees fewer in Proportion.

^a...^a: R, M: 'lon boit et mange'; N: 'lon boit et lon mange'
^b...^b: R, M, N: 'Les etats'

188

But if the 25 persons in a hundred of whom we have spoken were employed to produce permanent commodities, to draw from the Mines Iron, Lead, Tin, Copper, etc. and work them up into Tools and Instruments for the use of Man, bowls, plates and other useful objects much more durable than earthenware, the State will not only appear to be richer for it but will be so in reality.

^a...^a: R, M, N: 'du fer, du plomb, de letain, du Cuivre'
^b...^b: R, M, N: 'et instrumens propres'
^c...^c: R, M, N: 'batteries et pots'
^d...^d: T: '25 persons we will suppose'
^e...^e: T: 'gold, copper'
^f...^f: T: '*Corps de Reserve*'
^g...^g: T: 'Labor'
^h...^h: T: 'these'

i There appears to be a difference between the argument in E189 and D189. The French text says that mining for metals by the 'idle' 25 out of a 100 will yield useful and durable tools and consumer goods by which the state is richer. The English version says that the state is richer when the 'idle' 25 out of a 100 work to obtain metals through mining or through foreign trade in order 'to serve for a corps of reserve' of durable wealth. The latter argument sounds more 'bullionist' and is more similar to what is said in E192. Also see D506, where the advantages of exporting products of mining and manufacturing are emphasised.
    ii. For V189f., see C192i.

189

It will be so especially if these people are employed in drawing from the Earth Gold and Silver which Metals are not only durable but so to speak permanent, which fire itself cannot destroy, which are generally accepted as the Measure of Value, and which can always be exchanged for any of the necessaries of Life: and if these Inhabitants work to draw Gold and Silver into a State in exchange for the Manufactures and Work which they produce and send abroad, their Labour will be equally useful and will in reality improve the State.

^a...^a: N joins last phrase of previous paragraph and first phrase of this paragraph: ', mais il le sera reellement et surtout' ^b...^b: 'on pourroit dire'
^c...^c: M: 'ameliorera letat reellement'
^d...^d: T: 'the Labouring in'; sic:'brings in'?
^e...^e: T: 'the Enemy'
^f...^f: T: 'wants'

i. Only D190 mentions national 'emergencies' and 'enemies' of the state. This appears to give a more warlike twist to the argument. However, note that similar phrases are found in E166–E167 and E192.
    ii. For the expression '*le feu … ne sauroit consumer*', see C209i.

190

191

‖ [a]Wherefore[a] the more [b]labour[b] there is in a state, the richer it is [II, 6, col. 2] esteemed; and, if that [b]labour[b] be well applied, [c]the richer in reality, and the more powerful, a state is.[c] For,

192 |8| [a]Car le point[a], qui semble déterminer la grandeur comparative des Etats, est le corps de réserve qu'ils ont, [b]au-delà de la consommation annuelle, comme les Magasins de draps, de linge, de blés, &c.[b] pour servir dans les [c]années stériles, en cas de besoin, ou de guerre[c]. Et d'autant que l'or & l'argent peuvent [119] toujours acheter tout cela des Ennemis même de l'Etat, le vrai Corps de réserve d'un Etat est l'or & l'argent, dont la plus grande ou [d]la plus[d] petite quantité actuelle détermine nécessairement la grandeur comparative des Roïaumes [e]& des Etats[e].

‖ The point, which seems to determine the comparative strength and riches of nations, is the corps de reserve [f]which they have[f]; as magazines of all things necessary for the use of man, exceeding the yearly consumption, to answer in bad years and wars; or, [g]forasmuch[g] as gold and silver answer all these things, the quantity of gold and silver seems to determine the comparative wealth and power of states; for those are permanent and lasting riches.

193 |9| [a]Si on[a] est dans l'habitude d'attirer l'or & l'argent de l'Etranger par l'exportation des denrées [b]& des produits[b] de l'Etat, [c]comme des blés, des vins, des laines, &c.[c] cela ne laissera pas d'enrichir l'Etat aux dépens du décroissement des Peuples; mais si on attire l'or & l'argent de l'Etranger, en échange du travail des Habitans, comme des Manufactures [d]& des ouvrages[d] où il entre peu de produit de terre, cela enrichira cet Etat utilement & essentiellement. Il est vrai [e]que dans un grand Etat on ne sauroit[e] emploïer les vingt-cinq personnes en cent, dont nous avons [120] [f]parlé, pour faire des Ouvrages[f] qui puissent être consommés chez l'Etranger. Un million d'Hommes [g]feront[g] plus de draps, par exemple, qu'il n'en [h]sera consommé annuellement dans toute la Terre commerçante[h]; parceque le gros des Habitans de chaque Païs est toujours habillé du crû du Païs: & rarement trouvera-t-on [i]en[i] aucun Etat cent mille personnes emploïées pour l'habillement des Etrangers; comme on [j]peut voir[j] au Supplément, par rapport à l'Angleterre, [k]qui de toutes les Nations de l'Europe, est celle qui fournit le plus d'étoffes aux Etrangers[k].

ᵃ…ᵃ: T: 'Thus'
ᵇ…ᵇ: T: 'Labor'
ᶜ…ᶜ: T: 'the richer will it be in Reality and the more powerful'

D191 repeats and expands upon the title of the chapter (see D183). **191**

The Point which seems to determine the comparative greatness of States is their reserve Stock above the yearly consumption, like Magazines of Cloth, Linen, Corn, etc. to answer in bad years, or war. And as Gold and Silver can always buy these things, even from the Enemies of the State, Gold and Silver are the true reserve Stock of a State, and the larger or smaller actual quantity of this Stock necessarily determines the comparative greatness of Kingdoms and States.

ᵃ…ᵃ: N: 'C'est le point' (R, M: 'Car le point')
ᵇ…ᵇ: R, M, N: 'Comme les magazins de draps linge bleds et generallémént de Toutes les Choses nécéssaires a la vie audela de la Consommation annuelle'
ᶜ…ᶜ: R, M, N: 'de sterilité, cas de besoin ou de guerres'
ᵈ…ᵈ: R, M, N: 'plus'
ᵉ…ᵉ: R, M, N: 'et etats'
ᶠ…ᶠ: T: 'they have'
ᵍ…ᵍ: 'for as much'

i. **D192** here retains the French term *corps de reserve* as also found in E192 (cf. V189f.) which therefore appears authentic. **192**

ii. For the use in E192 of the phrase '*Ennemis de l'Etat*', cf. C190i.

iii. The expression 'gold and silver answer all these things' in D192 is a quip on *Ecclesiastes* 10:19, just as is the title of Jacob Vanderlint's *Money Answers all Things* of 1734.

If it is the custom to draw Gold and Silver from abroad by exporting merchandises and produce of the State, such as Corn, Wine, Wool, etc. this will not fail to enrich the State at the cost of a decrease of the Population; but if Gold and Silver be attracted from abroad in exchange for the Labour of the People, such as Manufactures and articles which contain little of the produce of the soil, this will enrich the State in a useful and essential manner. In a great State, indeed, the 25 persons in a Hundred of whom we have spoken cannot be employed to make articles for foreign consumption. A million Men will make more Cloth, for example, than will be consumed annually in all the mercantile World, because the greater number of People in every country is always clothed from the raw material of the Country, and there will seldom be found in any State 100,000 persons employed upon Clothing for Foreigners. This is shown in the Supplement with regard to England, which of all the Nations of Europe supplies most cloth to Foreigners.

ᵃ…ᵃ: N: 'Si l'on' (R, M: 'Si on')
ᵇ…ᵇ: R, M, N: 'et produits'
ᶜ…ᶜ: R, M, N: 'comme bled, Vins fruits bœufs, Laines et autres Commodités pour Lusage des hommes'
ᵈ…ᵈ: R, M, N: 'et ouvrages'
ᵉ…ᵉ: R, M, N: 'qu'on ne sçauroit'
ᶠ…ᶠ: R, M, N: 'parlé dans un grand Royaume, ou [M: un] etat pour faire des ouvrages ou manufactures'
ᵍ…ᵍ: R, M, N: 'fera'
ʰ…ʰ: R, M, N: 'sera Consomme dans toute La terre Commerçante annuellement'
ⁱ…ⁱ: 1756b, 1769: 'dans'
ʲ…ʲ: 1756b, 1769: 'peut le voir'
ᵏ…ᵏ: R, M, N: 'qui est la nation qui fournit Le plus detoffe aux étrangérs de toutes Celles de LEuroppe'

i. The view that the export of manufactures is more advantageous than the export of agricultural produce is also expessed in D189, E505, D506 and E509. It was a widely held view by British and French authors and politicians of the time, although rarely supported with calculations as in E/D486–E/D504. Cf. C498ii. **193**

ii. Elsewhere in the *Universal Dictionary*, e.g. in the entry, 'Britain' (I, 349) Postlethwayt expresses a similar point of view, but this may not be due to the specific influence of Cantillon. The same may be true for Harris (1757, I, 24) and Steuart (1767, II, xxiv). Cf. C505.

iii. E193 suggests that there are absolute limits to the international market for textiles. D428 expresses the same view more explicitly and presents some calculations. Cf. C428.

iv. For other mentions of the Supplement see C33ii.

194 |10| ᵃAfin que la consommation des Manufactures d'un Etat devienneᵃ considérable chez l'Etranger, il faut les rendre bonnes & estimables par une grande consommation dans l'intérieur de l'Etat; ᵇil faut y décréditerᵇ [121] toutes les Manufactures Etrangeres, ᶜ& y donner beaucoup d'emploi aux Habitansᶜ.

195 |11| ᵃSi onᵃ ne trouvoit pas assez d'emploi pour occuper les vingt-cinq personnes, en cent, à des choses utiles & avantageuses à l'Etat, je ne trouverois pas d'inconvenient qu'on y encourageât le travail ᵇqui ne sert qu'à l'ornement ou à l'amusementᵇ. L'Etat n'est pas moins censé riche, par mille babioles qui regardent l'ajustement des Dames, & même des Hommes, & qui servent ᶜaux jeux & aux divertissemensᶜ qu'on y voit, que par les ouvrages qui sont utiles & commodes. Diogene, au siege de Corinthe, se mit, dit-on, à rouler son tonneau, afin de ne pas paroître oisif, pendant que tout le monde étoit occupé; & nous avons aujourd'hui des Sociétés entieres, tant d'Hommes que de Femmes, qui s'occupent ᵈde travaux [122] & d'exercicesᵈ aussi inutiles à l'Etat, que celui de Diogene. Pour peu que le travail d'un Homme apporte d'ornement ou même d'amusement dans un Etat, il vaut la peine d'être encouragé; à moins que cet Homme ne trouve moïen de s'emploïer utilement.

|| It is ᵉvery adviseableᵉ to encourage all sorts of work and ᶠlabourᶠ in a state, since a state is esteemed the richer for it; but the ᶠlabourᶠ which answers best, in case of war and ᵍdifficultyᵍ, is the most to be encouraged. Diogenes, at the siege of Corinth, ʰis said to have fellʰ a rolling in his tub, that he might not be idle, when all others were at work. ⁱWeⁱ would not recommend that sort of ᶠlabourᶠ; but rather than have a person idle in ʲtheʲ state, ⁱweⁱ would recommend the working of ᵏtoys andᵏ trinkets, that have a ˡshewˡ of ornament, ᵐthoughᵐ little of real ⁿuseⁿ.

196 |12| C'est toujours le génie des Propriétaires de terres qui ᵃencourageᵃ ou décourage les différentes occupations des Habitans & les différens genres de travail que ceux-ci imaginent.

[127] It is the Taste and Manner of Living, of the great Proprietors of Land, which either encourage or discourage the different Labour and Industry of the Inhabitants of the Community.

197 |13| L'exemple du Prince, qui est suivi de sa Cour, est ordinairement capable de déterminer le génie & ᵃles goûtsᵃ des autres Propriétaires de terres généralement; & l'exemple de ᵇceux-ci influe naturellementᵇ sur tous les ordres subalternes. Ainsi il n'est pas douteux qu'un Prince ne puisse par le seul exemple, & sans aucune contrainte, don-[123]ner ᶜtelleᶜ tournure qu'il voudra au travail de ses Sujets.

|| The Dress and Manner of Living at Court, are followed by its Dependants, and descend to all other Members of the Society; it is not [128] to be doubted, but that the Sovereign can by his own Example, prevent the Consumption of Foreign Commodities, and consequently their Importation, if he is pleased only to make use of that, which his own Country produces; it is therefore in the Power of the Court, and the great Proprietors of Land, to determine the Industry and Labour of the Inhabitants of a Kingdom.

In order that the consumption of the Manufactures of a State should become considerable in foreign parts, these Manufactures must be made good and valuable by a large consumption in the interior of the State. It is needful to discourage all foreign Manufactures and to give plenty of employment to the Inhabitants.

^a...^a: R, M, N: 'pour rendre la Consommation des manufactures d'un etat'
^b...^b: R, M, N: 'decouragér dans LEtat'
^c...^c: R, M, N: 'et donner Le plus d'employ quon Peut aux habitans de Letat'

There seems to be perhaps the germ of an 'infant industry' argument in E194. Cf. E328–E329, where the desirability of setting up manufactories in remote provinces is discussed. Also see E329, E356 and E398 where it is noted that it takes time for newly established manufactures to become competitive and E61 where it is argued that it would be advantageous 'to a State to teach its Subjects to produce the Manufactures which are customarily drawn from abroad'. **194**

If enough employment cannot be found to occupy the 25 persons in a hundred upon work useful and profitable to the State, I see no objection to encouraging employment which serves only for ornament or amusement. The State is not considered less rich for a thousand toys which serve to trick out the ladies or even men, or are used in games and diversions, than it is for useful and serviceable objects. Diogenes, at the Siege of Corinth, is said to have fell a rolling his tub that he might not seem idle while all others were at work; and we have today Societies of Men and Women occupied in work and exercise as useless to the State as that of Diogenes. How little soever the labour of a Man supplies ornament or even amusement in a State it is worth while to encourage it unless the Man can find a way to employ himself usefully.

^a...^a: N: 'Si l'on' (R, M: 'Si on')
^b...^b: R, M, N: 'qui sert [M: 'sort'] purement pour amuser et apporte quelque ornement'
^c...^c: R, M, N: 'a des jeux et divertissements'
^d...^d: R, M, N: 'd'exercises et de travaux'
^e...^e: T: 'adviseable'
^f...^f: T: 'Labor'
^g...^g: T: 'difficulties'
^h...^h: 'fell'
ⁱ...ⁱ: T: 'I'
^j...^j: T: 'a'
^k...^k: T: 'Toyes or'
^l...^l: T: 'Show'
^m...^m: T: 'tho' '
ⁿ...ⁿ: T: 'use, rather than Idleness.'

The story about Diogenes (412–323 BC) rolling (and doing various other things to) his tub at the siege of Corinth is told by François Rabelais in the Author's Prologue to the third book of *Gargantua et Pantagruel* (first published in 1546). **195**

It is always the inspiration of the Proprietors of Land which encourages or discourages the different occupations of the People and the different kinds of Labour which they invent.

^a...^a: R, M: 'encouragent'; (N: 'encourage')

A196 and A197 occur in chapter XXIII of the *Analysis* straight after the text reproduced in A123. Cf. C118iii. It is curious that exactly these two isolated paragraphs A196–A197 are missing from D. **196**

The example of the Prince, followed by his Court, is generally capable of determining the inspiration and tastes of the other Proprietors of Land, and the example of these last naturally influences all the lower ranks. A Prince, then, without doubt is able by his own example and without any constraint to give such a turn as he likes to the labour of his subjects.

^a...^a: R, M, N: 'le gout'; 1756b, 1769: 'le goût'
^b...^b: R, M:' ceux cy influent naturellement'; N: 'ceux qui naturellement influent'
^c...^c: M: 'cette' (R, N: 'telle')

The assumption of imitative behaviour in consumption by landowners and also farmers and artisans (see E143) was crucial for the analysis of the effects of *luxe de décoration* in the *Tablaux économiques*. See e.g. Mirabeau (1761: 68), Mirabeau (1763: 307–11). **197**

198 |14| Si chaque Propriétaire, dans un Etat, n'avoit qu'une petite portion de terre, semblable à celle qu'on laisse ordinairement à la conduite d'un seul Fermier, il n'y auroit presque point de Ville; ª& lesª Habitans seroient plus nombreux & l'Etat seroit bien riche, si chacun de ces Propriétaires occupoit ᵇà quelque travail utile les Habitans que sa terre nourritᵇ.

|| If all the proprietors of land had but just as much of it as they could oversee, and manage ᶜby themselvesᶜ, or as much as farmers commonly rent and oversee, without under officers to assist them; if the said proprietors became the undertakers of such their small estates, they would keep few or no idle servants, ᵈfew pleasure-horsesᵈ; they would live without luxury, and, consequently, the inhabitants of the state would be more numerous, and more laborious, ᵉcæteris paribus.ᵉ

199 |15| Mais lorsque les Seigneurs ont de grandes possessions de terres, ils entraînent nécessairement le luxe & l'oisiveté. Qu'un Abbé, à la tête de cinquante Moines, vive du produit de plusieurs belles Terres, ou qu'un Seigneur, qui a cinquante Domestiques, ª& des Chevaux, qu'il n'entretient que pour le servir, vive de ces terres,ª cela seroit indifférent à l'Etat, s'il pouvoit [124] demeurer dans une paix constante.

This makes it ᵇsensible,ᵇ that a great inequality in estates is prejudicial to a state, because of the luxury and idleness ᶜwhich greatᶜ estates commonly ᵈintroduceᵈ. And whether a convent of 50 monks ᵉliveᵉ on a large estate, or a lord with 50 servants and horses, who do nothing but attend him, it seems pretty much the same thing in times of peace;

200 |16| Mais un Seigneur avec sa suite & ses Chevaux est utile à l'Etat en tems de guerre; il peut toujours être utile dans la Magistrature & pour maintenir l'ordre ªdans l'Etat en tems de paixª; & en toute situation il y est d'un grand ornement: au lieu que les Moines ne sont, ᵇcomme on dit, d'aucune utilité ni d'aucun ornement en paix ni en guerre, en deçà du Paradisᵇ.

ᶜbut, in case of war, the lord, indeed, and his servants and horses, may be useful,ᶜ and is always an ornament; whereas the monks seem to be of no real use in peace or war, on this side of heaven.

If each Proprietor in a State had only a little piece of Land, like that which is usually leased to a single Farmer, there would be hardly any Cities. The People would be more numerous and the State very rich if every Proprietor employed on some useful work the inhabitants supported on his Land.

ᵃ…ᵃ: R, M, N: 'les'
ᵇ…ᵇ: R, M, N: 'les habitans que sa terre nourit a quelque occupation utile'
ᶜ…ᶜ: T: 'themselves'
ᵈ…ᵈ: T: 'and few pleasure-houses'
ᵉ…ᵉ: missing in T.

i. For other occurrences of the *cœteris paribus* clause, see C49ii.
ii. Since horses are mentioned in E/D199, V198d is probably a printing error.

198

But when the Nobles have great landed Possessions, they of necessity bring about Luxury and Idleness. Whether an Abbot at the head of a Hundred Monks live on the Produce of several fine Estates, or a Nobleman with 50 Domestic Servants, and Horses kept only for his service, live on these Estates, would be indifferent to the State if it could remain in constant peace.

ᵃ…ᵃ: R, M, N: 'et Chevaux quon n'entretient que pour le servir vivent [N: vive] de ses Terres' (in N this phrase was omitted and is inserted in the margin).
ᵇ…ᵇ: T: 'apparent'
ᶜ…ᶜ: T: 'great'
ᵈ…ᵈ: T: 'bring'
ᵉ…ᵉ: T: 'lives'

199

But a Nobleman with his Retinue and his Horses is useful to the State in time of War; he can always be useful in the Magistracy and the keeping of order in the State in peace time; and in every case he is a great ornament to the Country, while the Monks are, as People say, neither useful nor ornamental in peace or war on this side of heaven.

ᵃ…ᵃ: R, M, N: 'dans l'Etat'
ᵇ…ᵇ: R, M, N: 'daucune utilité ny ornement en paix ny en guerre en deça du paradis, comme Lon dit'
ᶜ…ᶜ: T: 'but the Lord, indeed, and his Servants and Horses, may be useful in Case of War,'

i. The different place where '*comme l'on dit*' ('as people say') occurs in the French manuscript texts (V200b) attaches the qualification to the phrase 'on this side of heaven' and not to the lack of usefulness of monks.
ii. In *L'Ami des hommes* (1756: 18–19) Mirabeau quotes the last part of the final sentence, from '*les Moines*', following V200b. Cf. C173ii.
iii. After this paragraph the correspondence between the *Universal Dictionary* and the 1757 text stops (p. 158). The 1757 text continues discussing the 'Competitorship against foreign states in the commercial Warfare', which sounds very much like Postlethwayt in anti-French, Seven-Years-War mode. The *Dictionary* version has one further paragraph that corresponds with the French version (D201).

200

201 |17| Les Couvens des Mandians sont bien plus pernicieux à un Etat, que ceux des Moines rentés. Les derniers ne font ᵃd'autre tortᵃ ordinairement, que d'occuper des terres, qui serviroient ᵇà fournir à l'Etatᵇ des Officiers & des Magistrats; au lieu que les Mandians, qui sont euxmêmes sans aucun travail utile, interrompent souvent & empêchent le travail des autres Habitans. Ils [125] tirent des pauvres gens en charités la subsistance qui doit les fortifier dans leur travail ᶜ. Ils leurᶜ font perdre beaucoup de tems ᵈen conversations inutilesᵈ; sans parler de ceux qui s'intriguent dans les Familles, & de ceux qui sont vicieux. L'expérience fait voir que les Etats qui ont embrassé le Protestantisme, & qui n'ont ni Moines ni Mandians, en sont devenus visiblement plus puissants. Ils jouissent aussi de l'avantage d'avoir supprimé un grand nombre de Fêtes qu'on ᵉchommeᵉ dans les païs Catholiques romains, & qui diminuent ᶠle travail des Habitansᶠ, de près d'une huitieme partie de l'année

|| But the convents of all Mendicants are baneful in a state; they are not only idle themselves, and live upon the industry of others, but are an hindrance to labour in many respects, by their holy devices: the number of holydays in Roman Catholic countries, and other institutions of devotion, seem to take off nearly one tenth part of the yearly labour of the state.

202 |18| ᵃSi l'on vouloit tirer parti de tout dans un Etat, on pourroit, ce me semble, y diminuer le nombre des Mandiansᵃ en les incorporant dans la Moinerie, à mesure qu'il y arriveroit des va-[126]cances ou des morts; sans interdire ces retraites à ceux qui ne pourroient pas donner des échantillons de leur habileté dans les Sciences spéculatives, qui sont capables d'avancer les Arts en pratique, c'est-à-dire, dans quelque partie ᵇdes Mathématiquesᵇ. ᶜLe célibat des Gens d'égliseᶜ n'est pas si désavantageux qu'on le croit vulgairement, suivant ce qu'on a établi dans le Chapitre précédent; mais leur fainéantise est ᵈtrès nuisibleᵈ.

The Convents of Mendicant Friars are much more pernicious to a State than those of the closed Orders. These last usually do no more harm than to occupy Estates which might serve to supply the State with Officers and Magistrates, while the Mendicants who are themselves without useful employment, often interrupt and hinder the Labour of other People. They take from poor people in charities the subsistence which ought to fortify them for their Labour. They cause them to lose much time in useless conversation, not to speak of those who intrigue themselves into Families and those who are vicious. Experience shews that the Countries which have embraced Protestantism and have neither Monks nor Mendicants have become visibly more powerful. They have also the advantage of having suppressed a great number of Holy Days when no work is done in Roman Catholic countries, and which diminish the labour of the People by about an eighth part of the year.

[a]...[a]: R: 'dautres torts' (M, N: 'd'autre tort')
[b]...[b]: R, M, N: 'a lEtat pour fournir'
[c]...[c]: R, M, N: 'et leur'
[d]...[d]: R: 'en exhortations pieuses, en Conversations seductrice'; M' en exhortations pieuses, et conversations seductrice'; N: 'en exhortations pieuses, en conservations seductrices'
[e]...[e]: R: 'Chommes' (M, N: 'chomme')
[f]..[f]: R, M, N: 'Le travail'

i. V201d makes the French **201** manuscript texts sound more anti-clerical than the printed text. Cf. C200i and C458.

ii. Amongst Petty's recommendations for the restoration of prosperity to Ireland in his *Political Anatomy of Ireland* (1691a: 130) are: '12. That the People be dissuaded from the observations of superfluous Holy-Days. 13. That the exorbitant Number of Popish-Priests and Fryars, may be reduced to a bare competency, as also the Number of Ale-houses.'

iii. E201 led Mirabeau to assume in *L'Ami des hommes* (1756: 18) that Cantillon had been a Protestant. He quotes the phrase about Protestant countries being more powerful and distances himself from this view (ibid: 19).

iv. Note that E201 and D201 have a different fraction in the last sentence, 1/8 and 1/10 respectively.

If it were desired to make use of everything in a State it might be possible, it seems, to diminish the number of Mendicants by incorporating them into the Monasteries as vacancies or deaths occur there, without forbidding these retreats to those who can give no evidence of their skill in speculative Sciences, who are capable of advancing the practical Arts, i.e. in some section of Mathematics. The celibacy of Churchmen is not so disadvantageous as is popularly supposed, as is shewn in the preceding Chapter, but their Idleness is very injurious.

[a]...[a]: R, N: 'on pouroit ce me semble diminuér Le nombre des mandians dans un état' M: 'on pouroit ce me semble diminuér Le nombre des mandians dans les états'
[b]...[b]: R, M, N: 'des Mathematiques si on vouloit que lEtat tirat partit de Tout.'
[c]...[c]: M: le celibat de leglise' (R, N: 'Le Celibat des gens dEglise'
[d]...[d]: R: 'tres nuisible?' (M, N: 'tres nuisible')

There is no corresponding **202** paragraph in D. Instead the entry 'Labour' continues with a discussion of the lowness of French wages compared to those of England.

203	**CHAPITRE ᵃXVIIᵃ.** *Des Métaux & des Monnoies, & particulierement de l'or & de l'argent*	*Mines* [II, 271, col.2] REMARKS	[25] **CHAP. XII.** *Of Mines and Barter.*	[86] **CHAP. XIX.** *Of Trade and Money, particularly Gold, Silver and Copper, their proportional Value and Variations, with respect to the Use made of them as Money.*

204 — |1| Comme la terre produit plus ou moins de blé, suivant ᵃsaᵃ fertilité & le travail qu'on y met; de même les Mines ᵇde fer, de plomb, d'étaim, d'or, d'ar-[127]gent, &c.,ᵇ produisent plus ou moins de ces Métaux, suivant ᶜla richesse de ces Minesᶜ & la quantité & la qualité du travail qu'on y met, soit pour creuser la terre, ᵈsoit pour faire écouler les eaux, pour fondre & affiner, &c.ᵈ Le travail des Mines d'argent est cher par rapport à la mortalité des Hommes qu'il cause, attendu qu'on ne passe guere cinq ou six ans dans ce travail.

|| As land produces more or less corn according to it's goodness or fertility, and the labour employed in manuring it; so the mines of iron, lead copper, coal, tin, silver, &c. produce more or less according to the richness of the veins, and of the labour of digging, drawing off the waters, melting, refining, &c. The labour of the silver miners is the dearest, by reason of the danger and mortality attending it; and the silver miners are esteemed to live, at a medium, but five or six years in that labour.

|| Land produces more or less according to the Goodness and Fertility of its Soil, or in Proportion to the Expence and Pains taken in its Culture and Improvement. So all Mines of Lead, Coals, Copper, Tin, [26] Silver, &c. produce more or less according to the Goodness and Richness of the Veins.

|| As Land produces more or less Corn and Grain, in proportion to its Fertility and the Labour had in cultivating and improving it; so Mines of Iron, Lead, Tin, Gold and Silver produce more or less Oar in proportion to the Richness of their Veins, and the Labour and Expence taken in draining, digging, melting refining, &c. The Labour attending Gold and Silver Mines is of a very expensive Nature; few People who work at them live more than six or seven Years, and consequently expect to be paid in proportion to the Risk they run.

205 — |2| La valeur réelle ou intrinseque ᵃdesᵃ Métaux, comme de ᵇtoutes chosesᵇ, est proportionnée à la terre & au travail nécessaires à leur production. La dépense de la terre, ᶜpour cette productionᶜ n'est considérable qu'autant que le Propriétaire de la Mine pourroit obtenir un profit par le travail des Mineurs, lorsque les veines s'en trouvent plus riches qu'à l'ordinaire. La terre nécessaire pour l'entretien des Mineurs & des Travailleurs, c'est-[128]à-dire, le travail de la Mine fait souvent l'article ᵈprincipalᵈ, & souvent ᵉla ruine, deᵉ l'Entrepreneur.

|| The value of metals is like everything else, proportionable to the land and labour that enters into their production, and the price of them varies according to the demand and consumption, which depends principally on the fancy and manner of living of the proprietors of land.

|| The Value of Metals taken from the Mines is proportioned to the Value of the Land and Labour made use of in their several Operations, and their Prices vary and change according to the Taste, Luxury, and Will of the Proprietors of Land.

|| The intrinsic and real Value of Metals, as also of all Things in general is proportioned to the Quantity of Land, Labour, and Skill necessarily had to produce them.

Chapter XVII

Of Metals and Money, and especially of Gold and Silver

^a...^a: R, N: '17^e'; M: '11'

i. D occurs in the *Universal Dictionary* entry 'Mines' (II, 270–74) in a subsection with the title 'Remarks'. This entry first appeared in issue 107, which was published in spring 1754.

ii. Curiously, in A we have two counterparts for the paragraphs reproduced in E/D203–D207. On the one hand, the passages on pp. 86–87 of *The Analysis*, including the chapter title, correspond more closely with E. Cf. C570ii. On the other hand pp. 25–28 of *The Analysis*, which follow directly after the text that ends at A100, show a closer correspondence with D203–D212. The title of that entry from the *Universal Dictionary* is also closer to that of chapter XII in A, especially since subsequently the correspondence continues in the entry, 'Barter' (D239ff). Perhaps Postlethwayt split up a chapter entitled 'Of Mines and Barter' in the manuscript at his disposal and included parts in the respective *Dictionary* entries 'Mines' and 'Barter'. Cf. C212iii and C239ii.

203

As Land produces more or less Corn according to its fertility and the Labour spent upon it, so the Mines of Iron, Lead, Tin, Gold, Silver, etc. produce more or less of these Metals according to the richness of the Mines and the quantity and quality of the Labour spent upon them, in digging, draining, smelting, refining, etc. Work in Silver Mines is dear on account of the mortality it causes, since rarely more than five or six years are spent in that labour.

^a...^a: R: 'la' (M, N: 'sa')
^b...^b: R, M, N: 'de fer, Cuivre etain, plomb, or et argent'
^c...^c: R, M, N: les richesses des mines'
^d...^d: R, M, N: 'écouler Les eaux, fondre, affiner &c.'

Of the English versions the wording of A p. 86 is closest to E. Note that A p. 25 and D both mention copper amongst the products of mines, like the French manuscript versions (V204b) and unlike the printed French version and A p. 86. Coal is mentioned only in D and A p. 25. Cf. A4 where, unlike the French counterpart, coal is mentioned. Also note that the final statements about the relation between the dearness of labour in mining and the mortality of miners correspond most closely between E and D.

204

The real or intrinsic Value of Metals is like everything else proportionable to the Land and Labour that enters into their production. The outlay on the Land for this production is considerable only so far as the Owner of the Mine can obtain a profit from the work of the Miners when the veins are unusually rich. The Land needed for the subsistence of the Miners and Workers, that is the Mining Labour, is often the principal expense and the Ruin of the Proprietor.

^a...^a: R, M, N: 'de Ces'
^b...^b: R, M, N: 'touttes autres Choses'
^c...^c: R, M, N: 'pour Leur simple production'
^d...^d: R, M, N: 'Capital'
^e...^e: R, M, N: 'ruine'

i. Only A p. 86 and E205 have the phrase 'intrinsic and real value'. On the other hand, only A p. 26 and D205 have the distinction between the 'value' of metals (their costs of production) and their market 'price'. Cf.C72iii.

ii. The French manuscript versions have the qualification 'simple' production (V205c). This adjective appears to indicate the direct land inputs, as opposed to the indirect land inputs, mentioned next, accounting for the labour of miners. Nowhere else in any of the versions is the word 'simple' used in the same manner, although the distinction between 'direct' and 'indirect' land inputs, without the use of those terms, is made in E97 and D/A101.

205

206

|| If all the tin that is drawn annually out of the mines of Cornwall, and which commonly sells at London for about 100,000l. has every year a constant consumption and vent, the land and labour that enters into it's production are equal to the land and labour that produce any other quantity of commodities which sell for 100,000l.

|| If the Tin found in the Mines of *Cornwall*, and which is sold in *London* for 100,000l. finds every Year the same Vent, the Value of the Labour attending its manufacturing to the Place of Sale, is equal to other Goods to the Amount of one hundred thousand Pounds.

207 |3| La valeur des métaux au Marché, de même ᵃque de toutes les marchandises ou denréesᵃ, est tantôt au-dessus, tantôt au-dessous, de la valeur intrinseque, & varie à proportion de leur abondance ᵇou de leur rareté, suivant la consommation qui s'en faitᵇ.

|| The Value of Metals at Market, as also that of all earthly Products, are at times more [87] or less than their intrinsic Worth; they change and vary in proportion to their more or less Quantity offered for Sale, or in proportion to the greater or less Demand for their Consumption and Uses.

208 |4| Si les Propriétaires de terres, & les autres Ordres subalternes d'un Etat qui les imitent, rejettoient l'usage de l'etaim & du cuivre, dans ᵃlaᵃ supposition, quoique fausse, que ces Métaux sont nuisibles à la santé, & ᵇs'ils se servoientᵇ universellement de vaisselle ᶜ& de batterie de terre, ces Métaux seroient à vil prix, dans les Marchésᶜ, & on discontinueroit le travail qu'on conduisoit pour les tirer de la Mine. [129] Mais ᵈcommeᵈ ces Métaux sont trouvés utiles, & qu'on s'en sert dans les usages de la vie, ils auront toujours ᵉau Marché, une valeurᵉ qui correspondra à leur abondance ᶠou raretéᶠ, & ᵍà la consommation qui s'en feraᵍ; & on en tirera toujours ʰde la Mineʰ, pour remplacer la quantité qui en périt dans l'usage journalier.

|| But if every body rejected the use of tin, and made use of earthen ware instead of it, it would cease to be in esteem, and to have a value, and the tin adventurers would discontinue the work of the tin mines.

|| But if the Use of Tin was discountenanc'd, and the Use of earthen Ware substituted in its Room, there would be no Demand for this Commodity; and consequently the Working of the Mines in *Cornwall* would cease, to the great Loss of the Proprietors.

i. There is no precise counterpart for **206** D/A206 in E. The intrinsic value of products is equated with the average market price that obtains at 'constant consumption and vent'. This phrase is reminiscent of '*débit constant*' in E213. Also the point made in E241 (and E207) about the relation between the intrinsic value of commodities and their average market price is similar.

ii. Cf. C129i for the tin mines of Cornwall

The Market Value of Metals, as of other Merchandise or Produce, is sometimes above, sometimes below, the intrinsic Value, and varies with their plenty or scarcity according to the demand.

^a..^a: R, M: que de Touttes autres marchandises en danrees'; N: 'que de toutes autres marchandises et denrées'; 1756b and 1769: 'que toutes les marchandises ou denrées'
^b...^b: R, M, N: 'ou rareté par raport a la demande ou Consommation'

i.   The   phrase   'demand   or **207** consumption' in V207b renders the French manuscript versions somewhat closer to the wording of A207 than the French print version.

ii. After A207 the rest of p. 87 up to p. 96 of the *Analysis* corresponds to E III, iv (see A572–A578, A584–A591). Thereafter, pp. 97–98 resume a brief correspondence to the current chapter (see A229 and A218–A219). Cf. C591ii.

If the Proprietors of Land and the lower orders in a State who imitate them, rejected the use of Tin and Copper, wrongly supposing that they are injurious to health, and if they all made use of dishes and utensils of earthenware, these Metals would be at a very low price in the Markets and the Work that was carried on to extract them from the Mine would be discontinued. But as these metals are found useful, and are employed in the service of life, they will always have a Market Value corresponding to their plenty or rarity and the demand for them; and they will always be mined to replace what is lost by daily use.

^a...^a: R, M, N: 'une'
^b...^b: R, M, N: 'quils se servent'
^c...^c: R, M, N: 'et batteries de Terres Le prix de Ces metaux au Marche ne seroit rien'
^d...^d: R, M, N: 'puis que'
^e...^e: R, M, N: 'une valeur au marché'
^f...^f: 1756b and 1769: 'ou à leur rareté'
^g...^g: R, M, N: 'a la Consommation'
^h...^h: R, M, N: 'des mines'

208

209

|| Let us suppose in a state without foreign trade, that a regular and uniform quantity of copper is annually dug out of the mines for the common uses of life, as pots, kettles, pans, and kitchen ware, to replace the quantity of copper which is yearly consumed by fire, or worn away, and then that copper is begun to be made use of as money; this additional demand of copper will make it dearer, and encourage the digging out of the mines more of it than usual, and there will be more copper yearly required to replace that which is consumed.

|| Let us suppose a small State or Community, without foreign Trade or Intercourse with its Neighbours, and that from Mines discovered a certain uniform Quantity of Cop-[27]per is drawn from them annually, to supply the necessary Use and Conveniences of each Individual, and to reimplace the Waste this Metal is subject to from its daily Use: And Suppose Part of this Metal is ordered to Pass for Money; it is clear that this new Use for it, would cause a greater Demand, and a greater Quantity would be taken from the Mines, than formerly, in order to supply this new Demand;

210 |5| Le Fer est non-seulement utile pour les usages de la vie commune, mais on pourroit dire qu'il est en quelque façon nécessaire; & si les ᵃAmériquainsᵃ, qui ne s'en servoient pas avant la découverte de leur Continent, en avoient découvert des Mines & en eussent connu les usages, il n'est pas douteux qu'ils n'eussent travaillé à la production de ce métal, quelques frais qu'il leur en eût couté.

211 |6| L'or & l'argent peuvent non-seulement servir aux mêmes usages que l'étaim & le cuivre, mais [130] encore à la plûpart des usages qu'on fait du plomb & du fer. Ils ont encore cet avantage pardessus les autres métaux, que le feu ne les consume pas, & ils sont si durables qu'on peut les regarder comme des corps permanens: ᵃil n'est donc pas étonantᵃ que les Hommes, qui ont trouvé les autres métaux utiles, aient ᵇestiméᵇ l'or & l'argent, avant même qu'on s'en servît dans le troc. Les Romains les éstimoient dès la fondation de Rome, & néanmoins ils ne s'en sont servis pour monnoie, que cinq cens ans après. Peut-être que toutes les autres Nations en faisoient de même, & qu'elles n'adopterent ces métaux pour monnoie que long-tems après qu'on s'en étoit servi pour les autres usages ordinaires. Cependant nous trouvons ᶜpar les plus anciens Historiens que de tems immémorial on se servoit d'or & [131] d'argent pour monnoie dans l'Egypte & dans l'Asie; & nous apprenons dans la Geneseᶜ qu'on fabriquoit des monnoies d'argent du tems d'Abraham.

|| All ordinary metals, as iron, lead, tin, copper, coals, &c. are consumed by fire, the computation of the land and labour that goes to their production. See the article LABOUR.
|| But silver and gold are not consumed by fire, and they wear out so slowly by friction and attrition, that they may be esteemed permanent metals in this regards, as well for their other qualities, as their volume, subdivision without waste, the impossibility of falsifying them , &c. They seem best fitted of any metals or commodities to serve for money.

but Gold and Silver which are not so easily consumed by Fire, is proper for Money, from their excellent Quality and Capacity of being wrought into such Variety of ornamental Things, and the Impossibility of falsifying or counterfeiting them without being discovered.

i. D/A209 have no direct counterpart in E, but the **209** observation that quantities of non-precious metals are yearly 'consumed by fire' also occurs in E190, E211, E225 and E226.

ii. Note the point that the use of copper as money increases the demand for copper. D209 explicitly states that this increased demand raises its price and that this leads to increased production. The view that the use of metal as money is an 'additional use' that raises its value is reminiscent of John Law *Money and trade considered* (1705: 10): '[from] the additional Use of Money Silver was apply'd to … it received an additional Value equal to the greater demand its Use as Money occasioned'.

iii. In A209 the word 'reimplace' may be too literal a translation of the French term '*remplacer*' ('replace'), while 'from Mines discovered' could be a rendering of '*des Mines découvert*' ('from mines opened up').

Iron is not merely serviceable for the daily use of common life but may be said to be in a certain sense necessary; and if the Americans, who did not make use of it before the discovery of their Continent, had found Mines of it and known how to use it, they would doubtless have laboured to produce it at any cost.

ᵃ…ᵃ: R: 'americains'; (M, N: 'ameriquains)

Cf. V210a with V153a. **210**

Gold and Silver are capable of serving not only the same purpose as Tin and Copper but most of the purposes of Lead and Iron. They have this further advantage over other metals that they are not consumed by fire and are so durable that they may be esteemed permanent bodies. It is not surprising, therefore, that Men who found the other metals useful should have esteemed Gold and Silver even before they are used in exchange. The Romans prized them from the foundation of Rome and yet only used them as money 500 years later. Perhaps all other Nations did the like and only adopted these Metals as Money long after using them for other purposes. However we find from the oldest historians that from time immemorial gold and silver were used as money in Egypt and Asia, and we learn in the Book of Genesis that silver monies were made in the time of Abraham.

ᵃ…ᵃ: R, M, N: 'il n'est pas étonnant'; 1756b and 1769: 'il n'est pas donc étonnant'
ᵇ…ᵇ: R, M, N: 'encore estimé'
ᶜ…ᶜ: R, M: 'par les plus anciens historiens'; N: 'dans les plus anciens historiens'

i. The biblical reference in the **211** last sentence of E211 is more specifically to Genesis 23:15–16 where Abraham pays Efron 400 silver shekels.

ii. The first sentence in D211 does not make sense. It seems that a word or words were omitted. Instead of 'the computation', one should perhaps read 'For the computation'. Also note the odd implication in the same sentence that 'coals' would be a kind of metal.

iii. The reference in D211 to the entry 'Labour' is more specifically to the passages reproduced in D64-D75.

212

‖ If there were constantly an equal demand and consumption in a state of corn and wool, there would also be a constant proportion of value between them, supposing also an equal quantity of each to be constantly produced.

‖ In this case, a measure of wheat would always bear a constant proportion of value to a pound of wool; and an accomptant might, by imagining aliquot parts, find out a common measure to know how much wool is worth so much wheat.

‖ But, in regard the consumption of these and all other commodities, as well as their quantities in a state, vary frequently, or rather constantly, no accomptant or algebraist can fix any proportion between them.

‖ Money alone (I do not here consider what is used for money) naturally finds out this proportion, and the quantity of money which is brought to market to barter for each kind of commodity, readily fixes the proportion of value that is between them all, Quæ eadem uni tertio sunt eadem inter se. Every body who brings his money to market knows what money he has to lay out, or, at least, what he intends to lay out for the expence of that day.

‖ If, for Instance, there was one constant uniform Want and Demand for Wheat and for Wool, and an equal Quantity in being to answer the Demand and the Consumption of those Sorts of Goods and Merchandize; there then would be a fixed Proportion between a Pound of Wool and a certain Measure of Wheat: but as the Demands of the Public for these different kinds of Goods, as also for all other Sorts of Goods and Merchandize, vary and fluctuate daily, it would be almost [28] impossible to fix this Proportion between any two Sorts of Merchandize, as the Humour and Luxury of the Great keep all Sorts of Goods, as to their Prices, in almost a perpetual Fluctuation backwards and forwards: but Gold and Silver, by its Quantity at Market, finds this Proportion, by passing there at a fixed Value in Exchange for the Land's Produce

213 |7| Supposons maintenant que le premier argent fut trouvé dans une Mine du Mont Niphates dans la Mésopotamie. Il est naturel de croire qu'un ou plusieurs Propriétaires de terres, trouvant ce ᵃmétalᵃ beau & utile, en ont d'abord fait usage, ᵇ& qu'ils ontᵇ encouragé volontiers ᶜle Mineur ou l'Entrepreneurᶜ, d'en tirer d'avantage de la Mine, en lui donnant, en échange de son travail & de celui de ses Assistans, autant de produit de terre qu'il en falloit pour leur entretien. Ce Métal devenant de plus en plus estimé dans la Mésopotamie, si les gros Propriétaires achetoient des aiguieres d'argent, les ordres subalternes, ᵈselon leurs moïens ou épargnes, [132] pouvoient acheterᵈ des gobelets d'argent; & l'Entrepreneur de la Mine, voyant un débit constant de sa ᵉmarchandiseᵉ, lui donna sans doute une valeur proportionnée ᶠà sa qualité ou à son poidsᶠ contre les autres denrées ou marchandises qu'il recevoit en échange. ᵍTandis queᵍ tous les Habitans regardoient ce métal comme une chose précieuse & durable, & s'efforçoient d'en posseder quelques pieces, l'Entrepreneur, qui seul en pouvoit distribuer, étoit en quelque façon maître d'exiger en échange ʰune quantité arbitraire des autres denrées & marchandisesʰ.

i. The argument at the beginning of D/A212 is **212** reminiscent of D/A206. The argument of the second paragraph of D212 bears some resemblance to E222, which also considers wheat as a common measure of value.

ii. The Latin phrase in D212, meaning 'What [are] identical with one third thing, are identical with one another', was a principle of equivalence used by various authorities, e.g. Aquinas 'On the Trinity', Descartes *Regulae* X, 17.

iii. The last sentence in D212 appears to allude to the argument in D240 (*Dictionary* entry, 'Barter'; see C239ii). One can imagine that the manuscript used by Postlethwayt carried on straight from D212 to D240. This suspicion is also based on the fact that, similarly, the text on p. 28 of the *Analysis* carries on from A212 to A241 without any break.

iv. After this passage in the *Dictionary* entry, 'Mines', the correspondence to E or A finishes. That entry continues with exerpts from another source, Sir John Pettus's *Fordinæ Regales* (1670).

Let us suppose that Silver was first found in a Mine of Mount Niphates in Mesopotamia. It is natural to think that one or more Proprietors of Land, finding this metal beautiful and useful, were the first to use it, and willingly encouraged the Miner or Undertaker to extract more of it from the Mine, giving him in return for his Work and that of his Assistants so much of the Produce of the Land as they needed for their Maintenance. This Metal becoming more and more esteemed in Mesopotamia, if the large Landowners bought ewers of silver, the lower classes, according to their means or savings, might buy silver cups; and the Undertaker of the Mine, seeing a constant demand for his Merchandise, gave it without doubt a Value proportionable to its quality or weight against the other products or merchandise which he took in exchange. While everybody looked on this Metal as a precious and durable object and strove to own a few pieces of it, the Undertaker, who alone could supply it, was in a manner master to demand in exchange an arbitrary quantity of other produce and Merchandise.

[a]...[a]: R, M, N: 'travail' [b]...[b]: R, M, N: 'et ont' [c]...[c]: R, M, N: 'les Mineurs ou entrepreneurs' [d]...[d]: R, N: 'suivant Leurs moyens et épargnes pourroient acheter'; M: 'suivant Leurs moyens et épargnes pouvoient acheter' [e]...[e]: R, M, N: 'marchandise ou metal' [f]...[f]: R, M, N: 'a la quantité ou au poids' [g]...[g]: R, M, N: 'pendant que' [h]...[h]: R, M, N: 'des autres danrées et marchandises presque arbitrairement dans Cet etat'

i. Classical authors **213** referred to Niphates as a mountain range in Armenia where the river Tigris originates. They do not appear to name it as a finding place of silver. In *Paradise Lost* (first published 1667) John Milton refers to it as an 'Assyrian Mount' (4: 126) and makes it the spot where Satan lands on earth and tempts Christ (3: 742). Could Cantillon's choice for Mount Niphates as the source of silver be meant as a witty reference to the place where temptation originates?

ii. Cf. V213a with V216c. In both cases manuscript version R appears incorrect. In the second case M and N have a correction.

214 |8| Supposons encore qu'on découvrit au-delà de la Riviere du Tigris, & par conséquent hors de la Mésopotamie, une nouvelle Mine d'argent, dont les veines se ᵃtrouverentᵃ incomparablement plus riches & plus abondantes que celles du Mont Ni-[133]phates, & que le travail de cette nouvelle Mine, ᵇd'oùᵇ les eaux s'écouloient facilement, ᶜétoitᶜ bien moindre que celui de la premiere.

215 |9| Il est bien naturel de croire que l'Entrepreneur de cette nouvelle Mine étoit en état de fournir de l'argent ᵃà bien plus bas prixᵃ, que celui du Mont Niphates; & que les Habitans de la Mésopotamie, ᵇqui désiroient de posséderᵇ des pieces ᶜ& des ouvragesᶜ d'argent, trouvoient mieux leur compte de transporter leurs marchandises hors du Païs, & de les donner à l'Entrepreneur de la nouvelle Mine en échange de ce métal, que d'en prendre de l'Entrepreneur ancien. Celuici, se trouvant moins de débit, diminuoit nécessairement son prix; mais le nouvel Entrepreneur baissant à proportion le sien, l'ancien Entrepreneur devoit nécessaire-[134]ment cesser son travail, & alors le prix de l'argent, contre les autres marchandises & denrées, se regloit nécessairement ᵈsur celuiᵈ qu'on y mettoit à la nouvelle Mine. L'argent coutoit donc ᵉmoins alors aux Habitans au-delà du Tigris, qu'àᵉ ceux de la Mésopotamie, puisque ceux-ci étoient obligés de faire les frais d'un long transport de leurs denrées & de leurs marchandises pour acquerir de l'argent.

216 |10| On peut aisément concevoir que lorsqu'on ᵃeutᵃ trouvé plusieurs Mines d'argent, & que les Propriétaires de terres ᵇeurentᵇ pris goût à ce ᶜmétalᶜ, ils ᵈfurentᵈ imités par les autres Ordres; & que les pieces & morceaux d'argent, lors même qu'ils n'étoient pas mis en œuvre, ᵉfurent recherchés avec empressementᵉ, parceque rien n'étoit plus facile que d'en faire ᶠtels ouvrages qu'on vouloitᶠ, à proportion de la [135] quantité & du poids qu'on en avoitᵍ. Commeᵍ ce métal étoit estimé au moins ʰsuivant la valeurʰ qu'il coutoit pour sa production, quelques gens qui en possedoient, se trouvant dans quelques nécessités, ⁱpouvoient le mettre en gageⁱ pour emprunter les choses dont ils avoient besoin, ʲ& même le vendre ensuite tout-à-faitʲ: delà est venue l'habitude d'en regler la valeur à proportion de sa quantité, c'est-à-dire de son poids, contre toutes les denrées & marchandises. ᵏMais comme on peut allier avec l'argentᵏ, le fer, le plomb, l'étaim, le cuivre, &c., qui sont des métaux moins rares, & qu'on tire des Mines avec moins de frais, le troc de l'argent étoit ˡsujet à beaucoupˡ de tromperie, & cela ᵐfitᵐ que plusieurs ⁿRoïaumesⁿ ont établi des Hôtels-de-Monnoie pour certifier, par une fabrication publique, la veritable quan-[136]tité d'argent que contient chaque piece, & pour ᵒrendreᵒ aux Particuliers qui y ᵖportentᵖ des barres ou lingots d'argent, la même quantité en pieces portant une empreinte ou certificat de la quantité ᵍvéritable d'argentᵍ qu'elles contiennent.

217 |11| Les frais de ces certificats ou fabrications sont païés quelquefois par le Public ou par le Prince, c'est la méthode qu'on suivoit anciennement à Rome, ᵃ& aujourd'huiᵃ en Angleterre; quelquefois les Porteurs ᵇdes matieres d'argentᵇ supportent les frais de la fabrication, comme c'est ᶜl'usage en Franceᶜ.

Suppose now that on the further side of the River Tigris, and therefore outside Mesopotamia, a new Silver Mine is discovered, of which the veins are incomparably richer and larger than those of Mount Niphates, and that the working of this new Mine which was easily drained was less laborious than that of the first.

The Undertaker of this new Mine was naturally in a position to supply silver much cheaper than the Undertaker of Mount Niphates, and the People of Mesopotamia who wished to have pieces and objects of silver would find it more advantageous to export their Merchandise and give it to the Undertaker of the new Mine in exchange for Silver than to take it from the original Undertaker. This last, finding a smaller demand, would of necessity reduce his price; but the new Undertaker lowering his price in proportion the first Adventurer would be obliged to stop his output, and then the price of Silver in exchange for other Merchandise and Produce would be necessarily fixed by that which was put upon it at the new Mine. Silver then cost less to the People beyond Tigris than to those of Mesopotamia who had to bear the cost of a long carriage of their Merchandise and produce to obtain Silver.

It is easy to perceive that when several Silver Mines were found and the Proprietors of Land had taken a fancy to this Metal, they were imitated by the other Classes, and that the pieces and fragments of silver, even when not worked up, were sought after eagerly, because nothing was easier than to make such articles from them as were desired, according to their quantity and weight. As this metal was esteemed at its cost value, at least, a few people who possessed some of it, finding themselves in need, could pawn it to borrow the things they wanted, and even to sell it later outright. Thence arose the custom of fixing its value in proportion to its quantity or weight as against all products and merchandise. But as silver can be combined with Iron, Lead, Tin, Copper, etc. which are not such scarce Metals and are mined at less expense, the exchange of Silver was subject to much fraud, and this caused several Kingdoms to establish Mints in order to certify by a public coinage the true quantity of silver that each coin contains and to return to individuals who bring bars or ingots of Silver to it the same quantity in coins bearing a stamp or certificate of the true quantity of Silver they contain.

The costs of these certificates or coinage are sometimes paid by the Public, or by the Prince,—the method followed in ancient times at Rome and today in England; sometimes those who take silver to be coined pay for minting as in the custom in France.

214
[a]...[a]: R, M, N: 'trouuassent'; 1756b, 1769: 'trouvassent'
[b]...[b]: M: 'dont' (R, N: d'ou)
[c]...[c]: 1756b: 'fût'; 1769: 'fnt'

215
[a]...[a]: R, M, N: 'bien a Meilleur Conte [M, N: Compte]'
[b]...[b]: R, M, N: 'qui souhaittoient posseder'
[c]...[c]: R, M, N: 'et ouvrages'
[d]...[d]: R, M, N: 'sur le Tau [M, N: taux]'
[e]...[e]: R: 'alors aux habitans audela du Tigris qua'; M, N: 'alors aux habitans au dela du tigris bien moins qu'a'

216
[a]...[a]: R, M, N: 'a'
[b]...[b]: R, M, N: 'ont'
[c]...[c]: M: 'travail' (R, N: 'Metal')
[d]...[d]: R, M, N: 'ont été'
[e]...[e]: R, M, N: 'ont été Recherchées'
[f]...[f]: R, M, N: 'tel usage que l'on vouloit'
[g]...[g]: R, M, N: ', et comme'
[h]...[h]: R, M, N: 'a la valeur'
[i]...[i]: R, M, N: 'le mettoient naturellement en gage'
[j]...[j]: R, M, N: 'et aussy naturellement Le vendoient ensuitte a fort fait'
[k]...[k]: R, M, N: 'mais attendu qu'on peut allier avec l'argent par la fonte'
[l]...[l]: 1756b: 'sujet beaucoup'
[m]...[m]: R, M, N: 'a fait'
[n]...[n]: R, M, N: 'Royaumes et etats'
[o]...[o]: R, M, N: 'vendre'
[p]...[p]: R, M, N: 'apportent'
[q]...[q]: R, M, N: 'd'argent veritable'

217
[a]...[a]: 1756b, 1769: '& qu'on suit aujourd'hui'
[b]...[b]: R, M, N: 'd'argent'
[c]...[c]: 1769: 'l'usage'

i. Cf. V216c with V213a.
ii. The convenience of stamped coins for guaranteeing silver content, was commonly recognised by authors following Aristotle's *Politics* I, 1372a.
iii. The expression '*à fort-fait*' (V216j) is used by Boizard (1692: 107–08) to indicate the inclusion of a charge for coinage. See C218i.

218 |12| [a]On ne trouve presque jamais l'argent pur dans les Mines[a]. Les Anciens ne savoient pas même l'art de l'affiner dans la derniere perfection. Ils fabriquoient toujours leurs Monnoies d'argent sur le fin; & cependant celles qui nous restent des Grecs [b], des[b] [137] Romains, des Juifs [c]& des[c] Asiatiques, ne se trouvent jamais de la derniere finesse. Aujourd'hui on est plus habile: on a le secret de rendre l'argent pur. Les différentes manieres de l'affiner ne sont point de mon sujet: plusieurs Auteurs en ont traité, [d]& entr'autres[d], M. Boizard. Je remarquerai seulement qu'il y a [e]beaucoup de frais à faire pour affiner l'argent[e], & que c'est la raison pour [f]laquelle on préfere une once[f] d'argent pur, par exemple, à deux onces d'argent qui contiennent une moitié de cuivre ou d'autre alloi. Il en coute pour détacher cet alloi & pour tirer [g]l'once d'argent réel qui est dans ces deux onces, au lieu que par une simple fonte on peut allier[g] tout autre métal avec l'argent, en telle proportion qu'on veut. [h]Si on allie quelquefois le cuivre avec l'argent pur, ce n'est que pour[h] le rendre plus malléable, [138] & plus propre pour les ouvrages qu'on en fait. Mais dans l'estimation [i]de tout argent[i], le cuivre ou l'alliage [j]n'est[j] compté pour rien, & on ne considere que la quantité d'argent réel & véritable. C'est pour cela qu'on fait toujours [j]un essai[j] pour connoître cette quantité d'argent véritable.

219 |13| Faire l'essai, n'est autre chose qu'affiner un petit morceau de la barre d'argent, par exemple, qu'on veut essaïer, pour savoir [a]combien elle contient[a] de véritable argent, & pour juger [b]de toute la barre par ce petit morceau[b]. On coupe donc un petit morceau de la barre, de douze grains par exemple, [c]& on le pese exactement dans des balances qui sont si justes qu'il ne faut quelquefois que[c] la millieme partie d un grain pour les faire trébucher [d]. Ensuite[d] on l'affine par l'eau-forte, [e]ou[e] par le feu, c'est-à-dire, [f]on[f] détache le cuivre [139] ou l'alliage [g]. Lorsque[g] l'argent est pur on le repese dans la même balance, & si le poids se trouve alors de onze grains, au lieu de douze [h]qu'il y avoit[h], l'Essaïeur dit que la barre est de onze *deniers de fin*, c'est-à-dire, qu'elle contient [i]onze parties[i] d'argent véritable, & [j]une douzieme partie[j] de cuivre ou d'alloi. [k]Ce qui se comprendra encore plus facilement[k] par ceux qui auront la curiosité de voir ces affinages. Il n'y a point d'autre mystere. [l]L'essai de l'or se fait de même[l], avec cette [m]seule différence[m], [n]que les dégrés de finesse de l'or se divisent[n] en vingt-quatre parties, qu'on appelle *Karats*, à cause que l'or est plus précieux; & ces Karats sont divisés en trente-deuxiemes, au lieu qu'on ne divise les dégrés de finesse de l'argent qu'en douze parties qu'on appelle deniers, & ces deniers en vingt-quatre grains chacun.

[97] Gold and Silver are seldom found pure, they are fined by Art, and when reduced to Purity are called fine Gold, and fine Silver; but when coined, there is a certain Quantity of Copper mixed with them, and this Mix-[98]ture is called Alloy, and it is according to the more or less Quantity of this Alloy, that these precious Metals are called of such and such a Fineness.

In *England* a Quantity of Silver, containing eleven Parts of pure Silver, and one Part of Copper, is called eleven twelfths sterling fine, or eleven Ounces fine, the Pound is here subdivided into twelve Ounces, and this Pound of Silver contains eleven Ounces, Two-penny Weight of fine Silver, and eighteen Penny Weight of Alloy, and is coined into sixty-two Shillings. The present Standard of our Gold is eleven Parts of fine Gold; and one Part of Alloy; and forty-four Guineas and a half are cut out of a Pound of Gold, a Guinea is equal to one forty-fourth Part and a half of eleven Ounces of fine Gold, the highest degree of pure Gold is called twenty-four Carrats; and it is necessary to remember, that by the Standard of Money, is understood the Quantity of pure Metal contained in any given Sum.

Pure Silver is hardly ever found in the Mines. The Ancients did not know the art of refining to perfection. They always made their silver coins of fine silver, and yet those which remain to us of the Greeks, Romans, Jews and Asiatics are never perfectly pure. Today there is more skill, the secret of making silver pure has been discovered. The different methods of refining it are not part of my subject. Many authors have treated of it, M. Boizard among others. I will only observe that there is a good deal of expense in refining silver and for this reason an ounce of fine silver is generally preferred to two ounces which contain one half of copper or other alloy. It is expensive to separate the alloy and extract the one ounce of pure silver which is in these two ounces, while by simple melting any other metal can be combined with silver in any proportion desired. If Copper is sometimes used as an alloy to fine silver it is only to render it more malleable and more suitable for the objects made of it. But in the valuation of all Silver the Copper or Alloy is reckoned at nothing and only the amount of fine pure silver is considered. For this reason an Assay is always made to ascertain the amount of pure silver.

Assaying is merely refining a little piece of a bar of silver, for example, to find how much pure silver it contains and to judge the whole bar by this small sample. A small portion of the bar, 12 grains for example, is cut off and nicely weighed in balances which are so accurate that a thousandth part of a grain will sometimes turn the scale. Then the sample is refined by aquafortis or by fire and the copper or alloy separated. When the Silver is pure it is weighed again in the same balance and if it then weighs 11 grains instead of 12 the Assayer says that the bar is 11 parts fine, i.e. it contains 11 parts of pure silver and 1 of copper or alloy. This will be more easily understood by those who have the curiosity to see assays carried out. There is nothing mysterious about it. Gold is assayed in the same way, with this difference only that the degrees of fineness of Gold are divided into 24 parts called Carats, since Gold is more precious; and these Carats are divided into 32 parts, while the degrees of fineness of silver are only divided into twelfths, called Deniers, and these are divided into 24 grains apiece.

ᵃ…ᵃ: R, N: 'On ne trouue presque jamais largent que dans les mines'; M: 'On ne trouve presque largent que dans les mines'
ᵇ…ᵇ: R, M, N: 'et des'
ᶜ…ᶜ: R, M, N: 'et'
ᵈ…ᵈ: R, M, N: 'et surtout'
ᵉ…ᵉ: R, M, N: 'asses de frais a affiner L'argent'
ᶠ…ᶠ: M: 'laquelle une once' (R, N: 'laquelle on préfere une once')
ᵍ…ᵍ: R, M, N: 'de Ces deux onces l'once d'argent Reel quil y a, aulieu qu'on peut par une simple fonte allier'
ʰ…ʰ: R, M, N: 'La Raison pour laquelle on allie le Cuiure quelque fois auec l'argent pur , C'est pour'
ⁱ…ⁱ: R, M, N: 'qu'on fait de Tout argent'
ⁱ…ⁱ: R, M, N: 'est'
ʲ…ʲ: 1756a: 'un essai essai'

ᵃ…ᵃ: R: 'Cequelle Contien Elle Contient'; M, N: 'ce qu elle contient'
ᵇ…ᵇ: R, M, N: 'par Ce petit Morceau de toutte La barre'
ᶜ…ᶜ: R, M, N: 'quon Peze dans une Balance exactement et Ces ballances sont si parfaites quelque fois quil ne faut que'
ᵈ…ᵈ: R, M, N: 'et apres Cette Pezeé'
ᵉ…ᵉ: R, M, N: 'et'
ᶠ…ᶠ: N: 'qu'on'; (R, M; 'on')
ᵍ…ᵍ: R, M, N: 'et lors que'
ʰ…ʰ: 1756b and 1769: 'qu'il y en avoit'
ⁱ…ⁱ: M: 'une partie' (R: 'Unze partye'; N: 'onze parties')
ʲ…ʲ: R, M, N: 'une partye en douze'
ᵏ…ᵏ: R, N: 'Cela se Comprendra encore mieux'; M: 'Cela se prendra encore mieux'
ˡ…ˡ: R, M, N: 'on peut dire de meme de l'or'
ᵐ…ᵐ: N: 'difference seulement' (R, M: 'seule difference')
ⁿ…ⁿ: R, M, N: 'quon divise Les degrés de finesse de l'or'

218

i. The reference in E218 to 'M. Boizard' is to Jean Boizard (or Boisard) *Traité des Monnoyes, de leurs circonstances et dépendances*. Paris: La Veuve de J.B. Coignard & J.B. Coignard 1692 (later prints and editions 1696, 1711, 1714 and 1723).

ii. In the *Analysis* A218 follows the passage reproduced in A229. After A219, chapter XIX in the *Analysis* continues with an exposition of how money traders benefit from differences in gold and silver contents of various coins (pp. 98–102). Cf. C207ii and C591ii.

219

220 [140] |14| L'usage a consacré ᵃà l'or & à l'argent le terme de valeur intrinseque, pour désigner & pour signifierᵃ la quantité d'or ou d'argent véritable que la barre de matiere contient ᵇ: cependant dans cet essai je me suis toujours serviᵇ du terme de valeur intrinseque, pour fixer ᶜla quantitéᶜ de terre & du travail qui entre dans la production des choses, n'aïant pas trouvé de terme plus propre pour exprimer ma pensée. ᵈAu reste je ne donne cet avertissement, qu'afin qu'onᵈ ne s'y trompe pas; & lorsqu'il ne sera pas question d'or & d'argent, le terme sera toujours bon, sans aucune équivoque.

221 |15| Nous avons vu que les métaux, ᵃtels que l'or, l'argent, le fer, &c.ᵃ servent à plusieurs usages, & qu'ils ont une valeur réelle, proportionnée à la terre & au travail qui ᵇentrentᵇ dans leur production ᶜ. Nousᶜ verrons dans la [141] seconde partie de cet essai, que les Hommes ont été obligés par nécessité, de se servir ᵈd'une mesure commune, pour trouver dans le troc la proportion & la valeurᵈ des denrées ᵉ& desᵉ marchandises ᶠdont ils vouloient faire échangeᶠ. Il n'est question que de voir quelle ᵍdoit êtreᵍ la denrée ʰou laʰ marchandise qui est la plus propre pour cette mesure commune; ⁱ& si ce n'a pas été la nécessité, & non le goût, qui a fait donner cette préférence, à l'or, à l'argent & au cuivre, dont on se sert généralement aujourd'hui pour cet usage.ⁱ

222 |16| Les denrées ordinaires, ᵃtelles que les grains, les vins, la viande, &c.,ᵃ ont bien une valeur réelle, & servent aux usages de la vie; mais elles sont toutes périssables, & même incommodes pour le transport, & par conséquent peu propres pour servir de ᵇmesure communeᵇ.

223 [142] |17| Les marchandises, ᵃc'est-à-dire, les draps, les linges, les cuirs, &c. sont périssables aussi,ᵃ & ne peuvent se subdiviser sans changer en quelque chose leur valeur pour les usages des Hommes; ᵇelles occasionnent, comme les denrées, beaucoup de frais pour le transport; elles demandent même de la dépense pour les garder: par conséquent elles sontᵇ peu propres pour servir de mesure commune.

Higgs Translation (H)	Variations and Errata (V)	Comments (C)

Usage has conferred upon Gold and Silver the title Intrinsic Value, to designate and signify the quantity of true gold or silver contained in a bar; but in this Essay I have always used the term Intrinsic Value to signify the amount of Land and Labour which enter into Production, not having found any term more suitable to express my meaning. I mention this only to avoid misunderstanding. When Gold and Silver are not in question the term will always hold good without any confusion.

ᵃ...ᵃ: R, M, N: 'Le terme de valleur intrinseque a lor et a largent pour designér et signiffiér'
ᵇ...ᵇ: R, M, N: 'aulieu que je me suis toujours serui dans cet essay'
ᶜ...ᶜ: R, M, N: 'la valeur'
ᵈ...ᵈ: R, M, N: 'en tout Cas jen donne cet auertissement pour qu'on'

220 The phrase 'amount of land' (*quantité de terre*) of the printed text appears as 'value of land' (*valeur de terre*) in the manuscript versions (V220c). For similar variations elsewhere between versions, see C65.

We have seen that the metals such as Gold, Silver, Iron, etc. serve several purposes and have a value proportionable to the Land and Labour which enter into their Production. We shall see in Part II of this essay that Men have been forced of necessity to employ a common measure to find in their dealings the proportion and the value of the Products and Merchandise they wished to exchange. The only question is what product or Merchandise would be most suitable for this common measure, and whether it has not been Necessity rather that Fancy which has given this preference to Gold, Silver and Copper which are generally in use today for this purpose.

ᵃ...ᵃ: R, M, N: 'de fer étain plomb, Cuivre, argent et or'
ᵇ...ᵇ: R, M, N: 'entre'
ᶜ...ᶜ: R, M, N: 'et nous'
ᵈ...ᵈ: R, M, N: 'dans Le troc d'une mesure Commune pour trouvér la proportion des valleurs'
ᵉ...ᵉ: R, M, N: 'et'
ᶠ...ᶠ: R, M, N: 'quils avoient besoin dEchangér'
ᵍ...ᵍ: R, M, N: 'est'
ʰ...ʰ: R, M, N: 'et'
ⁱ...ⁱ: R, M, N: 'et sy lor, L'argent ou le Cuiure dont on se sert aujourdhuy génerallement pour Cela nont pas par leur qualités merité de nécéssité et non par gouts Cette prefferance'

221 i. The argument here is somewhat reminiscent of D/A212.
ii. Cf. V221a and V204b, where the manuscripts also list more kinds of metal, especially copper.
iii. The reference to a further discussion in part II appears to be specifically to E235. However, that paragraph refers back to the discussion in part I. Cf. C235.

Ordinary products like Corn, Wine, Meat, etc. have a real value and serve the needs of life, but they are all perishable and difficult to be transported, and therefore hardly suitable to serve as a common measure.

ᵃ...ᵃ: R, M, N: 'Comme grains vins viande &c'
ᵇ...ᵇ: R, M, N: 'mesure Commune des valleurs'

222

Merchandise such as Cloth, Linen, Leather, etc. is perishable also and cannot be subdivided without in some sort changing their Value for the service of Man. Like raw produce they cost a good deal for carriage; they even cause expense for storage, and consequently are unsuitable for a common measure.

ᵃ...ᵃ: R, M, N: 'Comme draps linge Cuirs &c sont aussy perissables'
ᵇ...ᵇ: R, M, N: 'elles Causent aussi bien que Les Danreés des frais pour le transport et demandent deméme des frais pour Les garder et par consequént sont'

223

224 |18| ªLes diamans, & les autres pierres précieusesª, quand elles n'auroient pas une valeur intrinseque, ᵇ& qu'elles seroientᵇ estimées seulement par goût, seroient propres pour servir de mesure commune, si elles n'étoient pas reconnoissables, & si elles pouvoient se subdiviser sans déchet. Mais avec ces défauts & celui qu'elles ont de n'être pas propres pour l'utilité, elles ne peuvent servir de mesure commune.

225 [143] |19| Le fer, qui est toujours utile & assez durable, ne serviroit pas mal, si on n'en avoit pas d'autres plus propres. Il se consume par le feu; & par sa quantité ªil se trouveª de trop grand volume. ᵇOn s'en servoitᵇ depuis Lycurgue jusqu'à la Guerre du ᶜPelopponeseᶜ: mais comme ᵈsaᵈ valeur étoit nécessairement reglée sur l'intrinseque ou à proportion de la terre & du travail qui entroit dans sa production, il en falloit une grande quantité pour une petite valeur. Ce qu'il y avoit de bisare, c'est qu'on en gâtoit la qualité, par le vinaigre, pour le rendre incapable de servir aux usages de l'homme, & pour le conserver seulement ᵉpour le trocᵉ: ᶠainsiᶠ il ne pouvoit servir qu'au seul Peuple austere de Sparte, & n'a pû même continuer chez eux, dès qu'ils ont étendu leur communication avec les autres Païs. ᵍPour ruiner les Lacé-[144] démoniens, il ne falloit que trouver de riches Mines de fer, en faire de la monnoie semblable à le leur, & tirer en échange leurs denrées & leurs marchandises, tandis qu'ils ne pouvoient rien échanger avec l'Etranger, contre leur fer gâté.ᵍ Aussi ne s'attachoient-ils alors à aucun commerce avec l'Etranger, s'occupant uniquement à la Guerre.

226 |20| Le plomb & l'étaim ont le même désavantage de volume, que le fer, & ils sont périssables par le feu: mais dans un cas de nécessité, ils ne serviroient pas mal pour le troc, si le cuivre n'y étoit pas plus propre & plus durable.

227 |21| Le cuivre seul servoit de monnoie aux Romains, ªjusqu'àª l'an 484 de la Fondation de Rome; & en Suede, ᵇon s'en sertᵇ encore aujourd'hui même, dans ᶜlesᶜ gros paiemens: cependant il est de trop gros volume pour les paiemens [145] considérables, & les Suédois mêmes aiment mieux être païés en or & en argent, qu'en cuivre.

Diamonds and other precious stones, even if they had no intrinsic value and were esteemed only from fancy, would be suitable for a common measure if they were not susceptible of imitation and if they could be divided without loss. With these defects and that of being unserviceable in use they cannot serve as a common measure.

ᵃ…ᵃ: R, M, N: 'Les Diamants perles et autres pierreries Precieuses'
ᵇ…ᵇ: R, M, N: 'et seroient'

In E409 the same peculiar expression is **224** used that jewels and diamonds are less suited as means of payment because they are 'easily recognised' (*faciles à reconnoître*). Higgs here translates the expression with 'susceptible of imitation', but it is doubtful if that is what is meant.

Iron, which is always useful and fairly durable would not serve badly in default of a better. It is consumed by fire, and is too bulky owing to its quantity. It was used from the time of Lycurgus till the Peloponnesian War: but as its value was necessarily based intrinsically, or in proportion to the Land and Labour which entered into its production, a great quantity of it was needed for small value. It is curious that its quality was spoiled by Vinegar to make it useless for service and to keep it for exchange only. Thus it could serve the austere Spartans alone, and could not continue to do so even with them as soon as they extended their communication with other countries. To ruin the Spartans it needed only to find rich Iron Mines, to make Money like theirs, and to draw in exchange their products and Merchandise whilst they could get nothing from abroad for their spoiled iron. At that time they did not concern themselves with any foreign trade, but only with War.

ᵃ…ᵃ: R, M, N: 'se trouve'
ᵇ…ᵇ: R, M, N: 'on s'en servoit a lacedemone'
ᶜ…ᶜ: R, M, N: 'Pelopénoise [N: Péloponése] pour monnoye'
ᵈ…ᵈ: R, M, N: 'la'
ᵉ…ᵉ: 1756b and 1769: 'pour troc'
ᶠ…ᶠ: R, M, N: 'et par consequént'
ᵍ…ᵍ: R, M, N: 'il ne falloit pour Les perdres que trouvér de Riches mines de fer, en faire de la monnoye Comme la leur Et tirér touttes leurs Danreés et marchandises en Echanges, aulieu quils Ne pouvoient a Lacedemone Rien ~~livrer~~ tirér [N: a Lacedemone ils ne pouvoient rien tirer] de LEtrangér en Echange de leur fer gaté'

The probable source of information **225** about Sparta's experiment with iron money is Plutarch's *Lives* (late first century AD). The *Life of Lycurgus* has the following passage: '[Lycurgus, *c.* 700–630 BC] commanded that all gold and silver coin should be called in, and that only a sort of money made of iron should be current, a great weight and quantity of which was very little worth; so that to lay up twenty or thirty pounds there was required a pretty large closet, and, to remove it, nothing less than a yoke of oxen. With the diffusion of this money, at once a number of vices were banned from Lacedaemon; for who would rob another of such a coin? Who would unjustly detain or take by force, or accept as a bribe, a thing which it was not easy to hide, nor a credit to have, nor indeed of any use to cut in pieces? For when it was just red hot, they quenched it in vinegar, and by that means spoilt it, and made it almost incapable of being worked' (Dryden translation 1683). This Life of Plutarch was well known. Lycurgus is also referrred to in Hume's essay 'On the Balance of Trade' (1752); Steuart (1767, II. xiv); Smith (1776, IV, i, 13) also cf. Smith (1776, I, iv, 5).

For the phrase 'consumable by fire' see **226** C209i.

Lead and Tin have the same disadvantage of bulk as iron and are consumable by fire, but in case of need they would not do badly for exchange if copper were not more suitable and durable.

Copper alone served as money to the Romans until 484 A.U.C., and in Sweden it is still used even in large payments: but it is too bulky for very considerable payments, and the Swedes themselves prefer payment in gold or silver rather than in Copper.

ᵃ…ᵃ: M, N: 'jusqu'en' (R: Jusqua')
ᵇ…ᵇ: R, M, N: 'Le Cuivre sert'
ᶜ…ᶜ: R,M,N: 'de'

227

228 |22| Dans les Colonies d'Amérique, on s'est servi de Tabac, ᵃde Sucre & de Cacaoᵃ pour monnoie; mais ces marchandises, sont de trop grand volume, périssables & inégales dans leur bonté; par conséquent ᵇelles sont peu propresᵇ pour servir de monnoie ou de mesure commune des valeurs.

229 |23| L'or & l'argent seuls sont de ᵃpetit volumeᵃ, d'égale bonté, faciles à transporter, à subdiviser sans déchet, commodes à garder, beaux & brillans dans les ouvrages qu'on en fait, ᵇ& durables presque jusqu'à l'éternitéᵇ. Tous ceux, qui se sont servis d autre chose pour monnoie, en reviennent nécessairement à celle-ci, dès qu'ils en peuvent acquerir assez pour le troc. Il n'y [146] a que dans le plus bas troc, que l'or & l'argent sont incommodes: pour la valeur d'un liard ou d'un denier, ᶜles pieces d'or & même d'argent, seroientᶜ trop petites pour être maniables. ᵈOn dit que les Chinois dans les petits échanges coupoient avec des ciseaux, à de minces lames d'argent, de petites pieces qu'ils pesoient.ᵈ Mais depuis leur commerce avec l'Europe, ils commencent à se servir de cuivre ᵉdans ces occasionsᵉ.

[97] These Metals of Gold, Silver, and Copper are the fittest Materials for Money, they have all the Properties of a standard Measure, they ascertain and regulate the Value of all Thigns, not as Pledges to be redeemed, but as the equivalent in all Purchases, and as such pass from one Hand to another; their Value is permanent or unalterable, though their more or less Quantity in Exchange of other Things, are subject to daily Variations, according to the Circumstances of the Times, and the Manner of living of the Age; Gold and Silver are divisible into minute Parts, and may be again reunited together in a greater Mass, they are durable and susceptible of any Form, and convertible to Utensils of any Shape or Size, and from these into Money again, and when refined, are of equal Goodness, every where; I mean Gold and Silver, for as to Copper, properly speaking, it is only a Commodity reduced into Pieces for the Convenience of small Payments

230 |24| Il n'est donc pas étonnant que toutes les Nations soient ᵃparvenuesᵃ à se servir d'or & d'argent pour monnoie ou pour la mesure commune des valeurs, & de cuivre ᵇpour les petits échanges. L'utilité & le besoin les y ont déterminées, & non le goût ni le consentementᵇ. L'argent demande un grand travail, & un travail bien cher, pour sa produc-[147]tion. Ce qui cause la cherté des Mineurs d'argent, c'est qu'ils ne vivent guere plus de cinq à six ans dans ce travail qui cause une grande mortalité; de maniere qu'une petite piece d'argent correspond à autant de terre & de travail, qu'une grosse piece de cuivre.

Higgs Translation (H)	Variations and Errata (V)	Comments (C)

In the American Colonies Tobacco, Sugar, and Cocoa have been used as Money: but these commodities are too bulky, perishable, and of unequal quality: they are therefore hardly suitable to serve as money or a common measure of value.

ᵃ…ᵃ: R, M, N: 'et de sucre' ᵇ…ᵇ: R, M, N: 'moins propre'

Smith (1776, I, iv, 3) also names **228** tobacco and sugar as examples of commodities used as money in the American colonies.

Gold and Silver alone are of small volume, equal goodness, easily transported, divisible without loss, convenient to keep, beautiful and brilliant in the articles made of them and durable almost to eternity. All who have used other articles as Money return to these as soon as they can get enough of them for exchange. It is only in the smallest purchases that gold and silver are unsuitable. Gold or even silver coins of the value of a liard or a denier would be too small to be handled easily. It is said that the Chinese, in small transactions, cut off little pieces with scissors from their plates of silver, and weighed the pieces. But since their trade with Europe they have begun to use copper for such occasions.

ᵃ…ᵃ:R, M: 'petits volumes' ᵇ…ᵇ: R, M: 'durable quasi a lEtérnité'; N: 'durables presque a l'éternité'; 1769: 'durables presque jusqu'à l'éternité' ᶜ…ᶜ: R: 'Les pieces dor et méme d'argent seront'; M, N: 'les pieces d'or meme d'argent seront' ᵈ…ᵈ: R, N: 'Les Chinois avoient dit on, Coutume dans Les plus bas troc Coutume de Couper et pezér de petites pieces dargent quils Coupoient avec des Cizeaux a des lames d'argent minces'; M: 'Les Chinois avoient dit on, coutume dans les plus bas trocs de couper et pezér de petites pieces dargent quils coupoient avec des cizeaux a des lames d'argent minces' ᵉ…ᵉ: R, M, N: 'pour Le troc du menu'

i. A229 follows straight after **229** A591. It is reproduced here because E229 is the closest corresponding passage in terms of providing reasons, commonplace since Aristotle's *Politics* (I, ch. 6), why silver and gold are particularly suitable as money. Also, A229 occurs in chapter XIX of the *Analysis*, which contains various other fragments that correspond to E I, xvii. Cf. C203ii, C207ii and C591ii. In the *Analysis* A229 is followed by A218.

ii. Harris (1757: 43) has a very similar passage to A229. This is curious because Postlethwayt's *Dictionary*, on which Harris appears to rely elsewhere (see C67iv), does not appear to contain a corresponding passage.

It is then not surprising that all Countries have arrived at using gold and silver as money or a common measure of value and copper for small payments. Utility and Need have decided them, and not Fancy or Consent. Silver requires much Labour and dear Labour for its production. Silver Miners are highly paid because they rarely live more than five or six years at this work, which causes a high mortality: and so a little silver coin corresponds to as much Land and Labour as a large copper coin.

ᵃ…ᵃ: R, M: 'venûs'; N: 'venues' ᵇ…ᵇ: R: 'pour le bas troc. Ce na pas tant eté par gout et Conténtémént que par necessité et besoin'; M, N:'pour le bas troc. Ce n'a pas été tant par gout et contentement que par necessité et besoin'

230

231 |25| Il faut que la monnoie ou la mesure commune des valeurs corresponde, réellement & intrinsequement, en prix de terre & de travail, aux choses qu'on en donne en troc. Sans cela elle n'auroit qu'une valeur imaginaire. Par exemple, si un Prince ou une République ªdonnoientª cours dans l'Etat à quelque chose qui n'eût point une telle valeur réelle & intrinseque, non-seulement les autres Etats ne la recevroient pas sur ᵇce pié làᵇ, mais les Habitans mêmes la rejetteroient, lorsqu'ils s'apperce-[148] vroient ᶜdu peu de valeur réelleᶜ. Lorsque les Romains vers la fin de la premiere Guerre Punique, voulurent donner à des *as* de cuivre du poids de deux onces la même valeur qu'avoient auparavant les *as* du poids d'une livre ou de douze onces; cela ne put pas se soutenir long-tems dans le troc. Et l'on voit dans l'Histoire de tous les tems, que lorsque les Princes ont affoibli leurs monnoies en conservant ᵈla même valeur numeraireᵈ, toutes les marchandises ᵉ& lesᵉ denrées ont encheri dans la proportion de l'affoiblissement des monnoies.

232 |26| M. ªLockeª dit que le consentement des Hommes a donné ᵇune valeur à l'or & à l'argentᵇ. On n'en peut pas douter, puisque la nécessité absolue n'y a point ᶜeu de partᶜ. C'est le même consentement qui a donné, ᵈ& [149] qui donneᵈ tous les jours, une valeur à la dentelle, ᵉau linge, aux draps fins, au cuivre, & autres métauxᵉ. Les Hommes, ᶠà parler absolumentᶠ, pourroient subsister ᵍsans tout celaᵍ. Mais il n'en faut pas conclure que toutes ces choses n'aient qu'une valeur imaginaire. ʰElles en ont une, à proportionʰ de la terre & du travail qui ⁱentrentⁱ dans leur production. L'or & l'argent, comme les autres marchandises ʲ& comme les denréesʲ, ne peuvent être tirés qu'avec des frais proportionnés à la valeur qu'on leur donne à-peuprès; & quelque chose que les Hommes produisent par leur travail, il faut que ce travail fournisse leur entretien. C'est le grand principe qu'on entend tous les jours de la bouche même des petites Gens qui n'entrent point dans [150] nos spéculations, & qui vivent de leur travail ᵏouᵏ de leurs entreprises. ˡ*Il faut que tout le monde vive*ˡ.

233   ª*Fin de la premiere Partie.*ª

Money or the common measure of Value must correspond in fact and reality in terms of Land and Labour to the articles exchanged for it. Otherwise it would have only an imaginary Value. If for example a Prince or a Republic gave currency in the State to something which had not such a real and intrinsic value, not only would the other States refuse to accept it on that footing but the Inhabitants themselves would reject it when they perceived its lack of real value. When towards the end of the first Punic War the Romans wished to give the copper *as*, weighing two ozs., the same value as the *as* of 1 lb. or 12 oz. had before, it could not long be maintained in exchange. The History of all times shews that when Princes have debased their money, keeping it at the same nominal value, all raw produce and manufacturers have gone up in price in proportion to the debasement of the coinage.

^a...^a: R, M, N: 'donnoit'
^b...^b: R, M, N: 'ce pieds'
^c...^c: R, M, N: 'de sa moins valeur reelle'
^d...^d: R, M, N: 'Le méme Tau ou valeur Numeraire'
^e...^e: R, M, N: 'et'

231

Mr Locke says that the consent of Mankind has given its value to Gold and Silver. This cannot be doubted since absolute Necessity had no share in it. It is the same consent which has given and does give every day a value to Lace, Linen, fine Cloths, Copper, and other Metals. Man could subsist without any of these things, but it must not be concluded that they have but an imaginary value. They have a value proportionable to the Land and Labour which enter into their Production. Gold and Silver, like other merchandise and raw produce, can only be produced at costs roughly proportionable to the value set upon them, and whatever Man produces by Labour, this Labour must furnish his maintenance. It is the great principle that one hears every day from the mouths of the humble classes who have no part in our speculations, and who live by their Labour or their Undertakings. "Everybody must live."

End of the first Part

^a...^a: R, M, N: 'Lock'
^b...^b: R, M, N: 'a lor, et a largent une valeur'
^c...^c: 1756b and 1769: 'eu part'
^d...^d: R, M, N: 'et donne'
^e...^e: R, M, N: 'aux Linge draps fins, Cuivre et autre Metaux'
^f...^f: N: 'absolument parlant' (R, M: 'a parler absolument')
^g...^g: R, M, N: 'sans Cela'
^h...^h: R, M, N: 'elles en ont a proportion'
ⁱ...ⁱ: R, M, N: 'entre'
^j...^j: R, M, N: 'et danrees'
^k...^k: R, M, N: 'et'
^l...^l: underlined in R, M, N

i. On Locke, see C237i and C249i.
ii. Smith LJ (A) vi, 106: The value of gold and silver 'is not as Mr Locke imagines founded on an agreement of men to put it upon them; they have what we may call a naturall value and would bear a high <one> considered merely as a commodity, tho not used as an instrument of exchange'.

232

^a...^a: missing in R, M; present in N.

N finishes hereafter with a table of contents for part 1 of the *Essai*, which is not reproduced here.

233

234   ^a**DEUXIEME PARTIE.**

CHAPITRE PREMIER^a.

Du troc.

235 |1| ^aOn a essaïé de prouver,^a dans la Partie précédente, que la valeur réelle de toutes les choses à l'usage des Hommes, est leur proportion à la quantité de [152] terre ^bemploïée pour leur production & pour l'entretien de ceux qui leur ont donné la forme.^b Dans cette seconde Partie, après avoir fait une recapitulation des différens dégrés de bonté de la terre dans ^cplusieurs Contrées, &^c des diverses especes de denrées qu'elle peut produire ^davec plus d'abondance^d selon sa qualité intrinseque, ^e& après avoir supposé^e l'établissement des Bourgs ^f& de leurs Marchés^f pour la facilité de la vente ^gde ces^g denrées, ^hon démontrera^h, par la comparaison des échanges qui ⁱse pourroientⁱ faire, en vin contre du drap, en blé contre des souliers, des chapeaux ^j, &c., &^j par la difficulté que causeroit le transport ^kde ces^k différentes ^ldenrées ou marchandises, l'impossibilité^l qu'il y ^mavoit^m à statuer leur valeur intrinseque respectiveⁿ, & la nécessité absolue où les Hommes [153] se sont trouvés deⁿ chercher un être de facile transport, non corruptible, & qui ^oput^o avoir dans son poids une proportion, ou une valeur, égale aux différentes denrées ^p& aux^p marchandises, tant nécessaires que commodes. De-là est venu le choix de l'Or & de l'Argent pour le gros commerce, & ^qdu^q cuivre pour le bas trafic.

236 |2| Ces métaux sont non-seulement durables, de facile transport, mais ^aencore correspondent^a à un grand emploi de superficie de terre pour leur production; ce qui leur donne la valeur réelle qu'on cherchoit, pour avoir un équivalent.

Higgs Translation (H)	Variations and Errata (V)	Comments (C)	
Part II **Chapter I** *Of Barter*	[a]...[a]: R: 'Second Partie De L'Essay de la Nature du Commerce En général Chapitre I'; M: 'Section 4.e De l'Essai de la Nature du Commerce en général Chapitre I'	i. V234a repeats the title as it is found at the beginning of R (V1a.): note the word '*de*' instead of '*sur*', used in the print version (E1). The mention of 'section 4' in M is possibly due to Mirabeau's initial plan, later aborted, to publish a reworked version of Cantillon's work. See Introduction p. 7. ii. There are no counterparts for this chapter in D or A.	**234**
In Part I an attempt was made to prove that the real value of everything used by man is proportionate to the quantity of Land used for its production and for the upkeep of those who have fashioned it. In this second part, after summing up the different degrees of fertility of the Land in several countries and the different kinds of produce it can bring forth with greater abundance according to its intrinsic quality, and assuming the establishment of Towns and their Markets to facilitate the sale of these products, it will be shewn by comparing exchanges which may be made, wine for cloth, corn for shoes, hats, etc. and by the difficulty which the transport of these different products or merchandises would involve, that it was impossible to fix their respective intrinsic value, and there was absolute necessity for Man to find a substance easily transportable, not perishable, and having by weight a proportion or value equal to the different products and merchandises, necessary or convenient. Thence arose the choice of Gold and Silver for large business and of Copper for small traffic.	[a]…[a]: R, M: 'L'auteur a prouve' [b]…[b]: R, M: 'quil a fallu pour Les produire et pour faire subsister et entretenir Ceux qui y ont donne la forme' [c]…[c]: R, M: les differents endroits,' [d]…[d]: R, M: 'Le plus abondemment' [e]…[e]: R, M: 'suposant' [f]...[f]: R, M: 'avec foires et marchez' [g]...[g]: R, M: 'des' [h]...[h]: R, M: 'il demontre' [i]...[i]: R: 'pourroient'; M: 'se pourroient' [j]...[j]: R, M: 'en bois Contre du fer, de la batterie de Cuisine &c Il demontre dis je' [k]...[k]: R:'des' [l]...[l]: R, M: 'Choses, la difficulte' [m]...[m]: R, M: 'auroit' [n]...[n]: R, M: 'que Les hommes ont ete Moralement necessites a' [o]...[o]: 1756a: 'peut'; 1756b, 1769: 'pût' [p]...[p]: R, M: 'ou' [q]...[q]: R, M: 'le'	The reference to topics covered in part I is more specifically to chapters x and xi (E63–E105). The discussions promised in E235 for part II are more diffcult to locate. There appears to be no 'summing up [of] the different degrees of fertility of the land in several countries' anywhere in part II, and the discussion of how gold and silver came to be chosen as money is found in part I (E221–E232), rather than in part II. Perhaps the confusion attests to the unfinished nature of Cantillon's writings.	**235**
These metals are not only durable and easily transported but correspond to the employment of a large area of land for their production, which gives them the real value desirable in exchange.	[a]…[a]: R, M: 'correspondent encore'		**236**

237 |3| M. Locke, qui ne s'est attaché qu'aux prix des Marchés, ᵃcommeᵃ tous les autres Ecrivains Anglois qui ont ᵇtravaillé surᵇ cette matiere, établit que la valeur de toutes choses est proportionnée à leur abondance ᶜou à leur ra-[154]reté, & à l'abondance ou à la rareté de l'argent contre lequel on les échange.ᶜ On sait en général que ᵈle prix des denrées & des Marchandises a été augmentéᵈ en Europe, depuis qu'on ᵉy a apporté des Indes occidentales, une si grande quantité d'argentᵉ.

238 |4| Mais j'estime qu'il ne faut pas croire en général que le prix des choses au Marché doive être proportionné à ᵃleur quantité & à celle de l'argent qui circule actuellementᵃ dans le lieu, parceque les denrées ᵇ& lesᵇ marchandises, qu'on transporte pour ᶜêtre vendues ailleurs, n'influent pas sur le prix de celles qui restent.ᶜ Par exemple, si dans un Bourg où il y a deux fois plus de blé qu'on n'y en consume ᵈ, onᵈ comparoit cette quantité entiere à la quantité d'argent, le blé seroit plus abondant à proportion, que l'argent qu'on destine à l'acheter; cependant le prix du marché se [155] soutiendra, tout de même que s'il n'y avoit que la moitié de cette quantité de blé, parceque l'autre moitié peut, & même doit, être envoïée dans la Ville, & que les frais de voiture se trouveront dans le prix de la Ville, qui est toujours plus haut à proportion que celui du Bourg. Mais, hors le cas ᵉde l'esperance de vendreᵉ à un autre Marché, j'estime que l'idée de M. Locke est juste dans le sens du Chapitre suivant & non autrement.

Mr Locke who, like all the English writers on this subject, has looked only to Market Prices, lays down that the value of all things is proportionable to their abundance or scarcity, and the abundance or scarcity of the silver for which they are exchanged. It is generally known that the prices of Produce and Merchandise have been raised in Europe since so great a quantity of silver has been brought thither from the West Indies.

ᵃ…ᵃ: R, M: 'de meme que'
ᵇ…ᵇ: R, M: 'touche'
ᶜ…ᶜ: R, M: 'ou rarete Proportionnellement a labbondance ou rarete de L'argent, avec lequel on les achatte'
ᵈ…ᵈ: R, M: 'Les Denrees et marchandises ont hausse de Valeur'
ᵉ…ᵉ: R, M: a apporte tant dargent des indes occidentalles'

i. The reference to Locke is more particularly **237** to his *Some Considerations of the Consequences of the Lowering of Interest and Raising the Value of Money* (London, 1692). The passage in that work most reminiscent of the first sentence in E237 is (p. 45): 'I shall begin first with the Necessaries, or Conveniences of Life, and the consumable Commodities subsurvient thereunto; and shew, that the Value of Money, in respect to those, depends only on the Plenty, or Scarcity of Money, in proportion to the Plenty or Scarcity of those things.' Locke's statement appears in his discussion of the value and interest of money, and Cantillon's paraphrasing involves a switching around of money and commodities.

ii. Higgs translates 'abondance ou rareté' with 'abundance or scarcity'. However, in D, as in Locke, 'plenty', instead of 'abundance', is used as an antonym of 'scarcity' (see e.g. D119/248/261/286/421/610).

But I consider that we must not suppose as a general rule that the Market prices of things should be proportionable to their quantity and to that of the Silver actually circulating in one place, because the Products and Merchandise sent away to be sold elsewhere do not influence the Price of those which remain. If, for example, in a Market town where there is twice as much corn as is consumed there, we compared the whole quantity of corn to that of silver, the corn would be more abundant of corn to that of silver, the corn would be more abundant in proportion than the silver destined for its purchase; the Market-price, however, will be maintained just as if there were only half the quantity of corn, since the other half can be and even must be, sent into the City, and the cost of transport will be included in the City price which is always higher than that of the Town. But apart from the case of hoping to sell in another market, I consider that Mr Locke's idea is correct in the sense of the following chapter, and not otherwise.

ᵃ…ᵃ: R, M: 'la quantite de ces choses proportionnellement a la quantitte actuelle d'argent qui Circule'
ᵇ…ᵇ: R, M: 'et'
ᶜ…ᶜ: R, M: 'Les vendre ailleurs influe sur le prix de Celle qu'on vend actuellement.'
ᵈ…ᵈ: R and M: 'si on y'
ᵉ…ᵉ: R and M: 'des Nuees de vendues'

V238c argues the **238** opposite of E238: the act of sending quantities of goods away from a local market *does* influence the market prices of the goods remaining. This view is in keeping with what is argued in E247 and E343.

239   **CHAPITRE ^aII^a.**   [I, 222, col. 1] *Barter*
        ^b*Des*^b *prix des Marchés.*

240 |1| Supposons les Bouchers d'un côté & les ^aAcheteurs^a de l'autre. Le prix de la viande se déterminera après quelques altercations; & une livre de Bœuf sera ^bà-peu-près^b en valeur à une piece [156] d'argent, comme tout le Bœuf, qu'on expose en vente au Marché, est à tout l'argent qu'on y apporte pour acheter du Bœuf.

|| Let us suppose the butchers in their stalls at market, on one side, and the customers, or buyers, on the other; the price of the meat will be determined, and a pound of beef shall be to the price of silver, as all the beef at market to all the silver (if silver be made use of as money) that is intended to buy it.

Chapter II

Of Market Prices

ᵃ...ᵃ: R, M: '2ᵉ'

ᵇ...ᵇ: M: 'Du'

i. This chapter develops the brief argument of E/A26.

ii. The entry 'Barter' appeared in issue 19 of Postlethwayt's *Universal Dictionary* (I, 222–23), which was first published in Spring 1752. The entry starts with the following definition: 'BARTER, signifies the exchanging of one commodity for another, or the trucking wares for wares, among merchants. -So it is mentioned in the statute I Ric. III. cap. 9. And thus bartering was the original and natural way of commerce, precedent to buying; there being no buying till money was invented, though in exchanging both parties are buyers and sellers.' After this definition, under a new heading, '*Remarks*', the text as reproduced from D240 starts. Cantillon does not use the term 'barter' in a way that conforms to Postlethwayt's conventional definition. Curiously, the former also uses it, predominantly even, to denote exchanges of goods for money. Therefore it is perhaps curious that Postlethwayt chose to use this fragment here. One possible explanation is that he may have had access to a chapter with the title 'Of Mines and Barter', like A, chapter XII (see A203). He then proceeded to divide this chapter into two parts, the first to be used in the entry, 'Mines' (see D203) and the second in the entry, 'Barter'. In favour of this explanation is that the content of E213 to E238 is missing from both D and A, and chapter XII of the *Analysis* carries on from A241. Cf. C212iii.

239

Suppose the Butchers on one side and the Buyers on the other. The price of Meat will be settled after some altercations, and a pound of Beef will be in value to a piece of silver pretty nearly as the whole Beef offered for sale in the Market is to all the silver brought there to buy Beef.

ᵃ...ᵃ: R, M: 'Acheteurs et Consommateurs'

ᵇ...ᵇ: M: 'en peu pres'

i. The additional '*et Consommateurs*' in R and M (V240a) makes the phrase correspond more closely to 'customers or buyers' in D, although a closer French translation of 'customers' would be '*chalands*'. That term is used elsewhere in E (see E96, E124, E127, E128, E130, E636, E639 and E640). In a few places, the English counterpart in D is 'customers'. See D124, D127 and D128.

ii. It may be argued that D240, by referring to market stalls, makes it even clearer than E240 that the discussion is about a concrete market place.

240

241 |2| Cette ᵃproportionᵃ se regle par l'altercation. Le Boucher soutient son prix sur le nombre d'acheteurs qu'il voit; les Acheteurs, de leur côté, offrent moins selon qu'ils croient que le Boucher aura moins de débit; le prix reglé par quelques-uns est ordinairement suivi ᵇpar les autresᵇ. Les uns sont plus habiles à faire valoir leur marchandise, les autres plus adroits à la décréditer ᶜ. Quoiqueᶜ cette méthode de fixer les prix des choses au Marché n'ait aucun fondement juste ou géométrique, ᵈpuisqu'elleᵈ dépend souvent de l'empressement ou de la facilité ᵉd'un petitᵉ nombre d'Acheteurs, ou de Vendeurs; cependant il n'y a pas ᶠd'apparenceᶠ qu'on puisse y parvenir par aucune autre [157] voie plus convenable. Il est constant que la quantité des denrées ou des marchandises mises en vente, proportionnée à la demande ou à la quantité des Acheteurs, est la base sur laquelle on fixe, ᵍou sur laquelle on croit toujours fixerᵍ, les prix actuels des Marchés; & qu'en général, ces prix ne s'écartent pas beaucoup de la valeur intrinseque.

|| This proportion is come at by bargaining; the seller keeps up the price, according as he conceives there is a demand; the buyer stands out, according as he judges there is plenty of beef. And this altercation continues till either of them comes to the other's terms, and so determines the price. These altercations are, at first, carried on at an uncertainty, but gradually the quantity of commodities, and of the money there is to buy them, comes pretty nearly to an equilibrium, and the prices of the things are determined.

[28 continued] To explain how Money operates in bringing about this Proportion, I think the Words Haggling and Bargaining will shew it. He at Market who has any particular Species of Goods to dispose of, will set a Price on them, in order to answer the Questions proposed to him by such as appear Purchasers; and he who has Money will hold his Hand, and proportion his Terms of Buying to the Quantity of Goods he finds at Market, and the Demand he perceives there is for them: from this Sort of Inaction between Buyers and Sellers, a kind of Stagnation, for a Time, ensues; until the one or the other submit and open a public Price.

This proportion is come at by bargaining. The Butcher keeps up his Price according to the number of Buyers he sees; the Buyers, on their side, offer less according as they think the Butcher will have less sale: the Price set by some is usually followed by others. Some are more clever in puffing up their wares, other in running them down. Though this method of fixing Market prices has no exact or geometrical foundation, since it often depends upon the eagerness or easy temperament of a few Buyers or Sellers, it does not seem that it could be done in any more convenient way. It is clear that the quantity of Produce or of Merchandise offered for sale, in proportion to the demand or number of Buyers, is the basis on which is fixed or always supposed to be fixed the actual Market prices; and that in general these prices do not vary much from the intrinsic value.

[a]...[a]:1769: 'portion'
[b]...[b]: R, M: 'par tous les autres'
[c]...[c]: R, M: 'et quoique'
[d]...[d]: R, M: 'vu quelle'
[e]...[e]: R, M: 'd'un tres petit'
[f]...[f]: R, M: 'convenable'
[g]...[g]: R, but not M, has parentheses around these words.

i. In Philip Cantillon's book the text in A241 **241** follows on directly from A212. Hence the phrase, 'this Proportion', in A241 refers to the proportion mentioned in the last sentence of A212.

ii. There are some noteworthy variations between the descriptions of the market *process*, i.e. only E241 states that the market price is agreed by a few buyers and sellers first and then followed by (all) others (cf. E26); only A241 describes a kind of 'stand off' between parties before one of them gives in and announces a 'public price'; only D241 states that the 'altercations' are first 'carried on at an uncertainty', while subsequently an 'equilibrium' is established 'pretty nearly' (cf. C248i).

iii. Also note that only E241 makes the point that the current price that is established tends to coincide with the 'intrinsic value' of the goods traded. This is reminiscent of the point made in E74 and D206.

iv. The point in E241 that the bargaining process in the market does not have a 'geometrical' foundation is also made in E582.

v. The expression 'Haggling and Bargaining' in A241 is reminiscent of Adam Smith's famous phrase 'the higgling and bargaining of the market' (1776, I, v.4).

vi. Skinner (1966, I, 173 n2) sees a correspondence between E241 and the account of 'double competition' in Steuart (1767, II, vii); Groenewegen (2001: 184) suggests that the correspondence is with A241. The correspondence does not appear to be very close in either case.

242 |3| [a]Autre supposition. Plusieurs Maîtres d'hôtels ont reçu l'ordre, dans la premiere saison, d'acheter des Pois verds. Un Maître a ordonné l'achat de dix litrons pour 60 liv. un autre de dix litrons pour 50 liv. un troisieme en demande dix pour 40 1. & un quatrieme dix pour 30 1. Afin que ces ordres puissent être exécutés, il faudroit qu'il y eut au Marché quarante litrons de pois verds. Supposons qu'il ne s'y en trouve que vingt[a]: les Vendeurs voïant beaucoup d'Ache-[158] teurs soutiendront leur prix, & les Acheteurs monteront jusqu'à celui qui leur est prescrit; de sorte que ceux qui offrent 60 liv. pour dix litrons seront les premiers servis. Les Vendeurs, voïant ensuite que personne ne veut monter au-dessus de 50 liv. lâcheront les dix autres litrons à ce prix, mais ceux qui avoient ordre de ne pas excéder 40 & 30 livres s'en retourneront sans rien emporter.

|| If several maîtres d'hôtel at *Paris* have limited orders to buy green pease, and 10 measures of pease are limited by the said orders to 60 livres the measure, 10 to 50 livres, 10 to 40, and 10 to 30. On this supposition, the money corresponds to 40 measures of green pease: but, if there be but 20 measures at market, the sellers, seeing a great demand in proportion to the quantity of pease, will keep up the price. The altercations will begin by the maîtres d'hôtel, limited to 60 livres; and when they are supplied, the 10 measures there limited to 50 livres will be supplied, and the price of the pease will fall to 50 livres; and the *maîtres d'hôtel*, who are limited to 40 and 30, will go without pease; but, if 20 measures more are brought to market, those last will be also supplied, and the price of pease will fall to 30 livres the measure.

Suppose that four Corn-Factors have each of them Orders to purchase five hundred Quarters of Wheat, and that one is limited not to exceed 2 1. 10 s. the Quarter, another 2 1. 5 s. the other 2 1. and the fourth 1 1. 15 s. [29] there must in this Case be 2000 Quarters of Wheat at Market, to correspond to the Money which is to be offered in Exchange for this Wheat; but if it should happen, that there are but one thousand Quarters of Wheat at Market, the Sellers will quickly discover that there is a greater Demand for Wheat than the Market can on that Day supply, and consequently will keep up the Price; and the Factor, who has Orders to purchase at 2 1. 10 s. will begin his Offers, and finding, from the Result of his Enquiry, that he cannot beat down the Price, he opens the Market-Price of that Day at his Limit of 2 1. 10 s. and having purchased his Quantity, the Price must fall to 2 1. 5 s. or else the Wheat must be kept to next Market-Day, as the second Factor is limited to 2 1. 5 s. and so on to the other Purchasers.

Let us take another case. Several maîtres d'hôtels [at Paris] have been told to buy green Peas when they first come in. One Master has ordered the purchase of 10 quarts for 60 livres, another 10 quarts for 50 livres, a third 10 for 40 livres and a fourth 10 for 30 livres. If these orders are to be carried out there must be 40 quarts of green Peas in the Market. Suppose there are only 20. The Vendors, seeing many Buyers, will keep up their Prices, and the Buyers will come up to the Prices prescribed to them: so that those who offer 60 livres for 10 quarts will be the first served. The Sellers, seeing later that no one will go above 50, will let the other 10 quarts go at that price. Those who had orders not to exceed 40 and 30 livres will go away [b]empty[b].

[a]…[a]: R, M: 'Cas Different, si plusieurs Maitres dhotels dans la premiere saison ont ordre dacheter des poids verts, supposons que les maitres ayent ordonne lachat de dix Littrons jusqua 60[lb] Dix Litrons a 50[lb] Dix a 40[lb] et dix Litrons a trente Livres. P our remplir ces ordres il faut quil y ait quarante Litrons de poix Verds au marche Supposons quil ne sy [M: en] trouve'
[b]…[b]: *sic.* 'empty-handed'?

i. While the buyers in A242 are 'corn-factors' and in E/D242 *Maîtres d'hôtels*, they have in common that they work on orders to spend given budgets at specified prices. **242**

ii. Only D has the geographical specification 'at Paris' (adopted by Higgs). Cf. C10.

iii. The structure of the first sentence in the French manuscript texts (V242a) is closer to D242: not only is there an Anglicism, '*ont ordre*', also there are '*maitres*', instead of 'the first, second …'.

iv. Higgs's translation of '*litrons*' with 'quarts' is a reasonable approximation since 1 *litron* = 0.8310 litre and 1 dry quart = 1.1013 litres. Perhaps Higgs was influenced by the use of 'quarters' in A242. 'Measures' in D242 is less specific.

v. Skinner (1966, II, 349 n17) sees a parallel between Steuart (1767, II, xxviii) and E242. First Steuart notes Hume's view in 'Of Money' (1752) that '[i]t is the proportion between the circulating money, and the commodities in the market which determines the prices'. He then says that he 'almost' agrees and proceeds to give an extended example of the market for grain (in quarters). This appears rather closer to A242 than to E242.

243 |4| Si au lieu de quarante litrons, il s'en trouve ªquatre censª, non-seulement les Maîtres d'hôtel auront les pois verts beaucoup au dessous des sommes qui leur étoient prescrites, mais les Vendeurs ᵇ, pour être préférés les uns aux autres par le petit nombre d'acheteurs, baisseront leurs pois verts,ᵇ à-peu-près à leur valeur intrinseque, & dans ce cas plusieurs Maîtres d'hôtels qui n'avoient point d'ordre en acheteront.

|| But if, instead of 20 measures, 200 measures are brought to market, the price of green pease will fall considerably; and this fall of the price will be proportionable to the quantity of pease with regard to the quantity of money intended to be laid out; and it may so happen in the altercations, that the 200 measures shall sell for no more money than the 20 measures would have sold for. And, when the green pease fall so low [I, 223, col.1] as to answer the price of several others besides the *maîtres d'hôtel* we have mentioned, there will probably be buyers enough.

|| But suppose, that instead of 1000 Quarters, there were 10,000 Quarters of Wheat at Market, the Price would proportionably fall, and this Proportion would be regulated by the Quantity of Money at Market, compared to the Value of the Quantity of Wheat there to be sold; and things between Buyers and Sellers would come to a Proportion of Equality, so as to fix the Price of the Day between Mo-[30]ney and Wheat, according to the Quantity, Goodness, and Quality of the latter, and the Demand for it.

244   ª...ª

245 || Let us suppose another example: - That in a market-town, containing 500 inhabitants, the bakers expose to sale 1000 pounds weight of bread, for the buying of which the said inhabitants intend 10 ounces of silver, at 100 *d. per* ounce. - According to this supposition, the 500 inhabitants will have two pounds of bread each, at 1 *d. per* pound.

|| Now, if a detachment of 500 soldiers come to this town at the beginning of the market, and determine to buy bread, the bakers, seeing this increase of the demand, will raise the price of their bread. The inhabitants, who used to buy the bread at 1 *d. per* pound, and who know there is corn enough to make more, will buy no more than what is absolutely necessary, and they will be contented with roots, flour, or any thing they can meet with. But, if the soldiers must have bread, and the price of it comes out at three half-pence *per* pound in the altercations, and they buy 750 pounds of it, at 1 *d.* 1/2 *per* pound each, there will remain 250 pounds for the inhabitants; and, if they still refuse to give more than a penny a pound for it, the bakers will, at the close of the market, let them have it at that price, or else this 250 pounds of bread will remain unsold; and, perhaps, the next day, when the soldiers are gone, or when a greater quantity of bread is made, it will fall to a penny a pound.

If instead of 40 quarts there were 400, not only would the Maîtres d'hôtels get the new Peas much below the sums laid down for them, but the Sellers in order to be preferred one to the other by the few Buyers will lower their new Peas almost to their intrinsic value, and in that case many Maîtres d'hôtels who had no orders will buy some.

ᵃ...ᵃ: R: '100'; (M: '400')

ᵇ...ᵇ: R, M: 'seront obliges de laisser Leurs Pois [M; boids] Verds, par Le petit nombre dacheteurs'

In all versions, apart from R, **243** the quantity initially assumed in E/D/A242 is multiplied by 10. The occurrence in the Rouen manuscript of the expression '*100 Litrons*' is curious. It is clearly legible, but judging by the English counterparts the number is incorrect. If R is the source text of both M and E, then the producers of the latter two versions must have guessed correctly that the factor of muliplication was 10 and not 2.5.

ᵃ...ᵃ: R, M: ': Le Petit Nombre des Demandeurs oblige Les vendeurs a Baiser Le prix pour Etre preferez Les uns aux autres'

'The small number of demanders forces the sellers **244** to lower the price in order to be given the preference over one another.' This sentence occurs in the French manuscript texts only. One may argue that it does not follow exactly from E243: there, an increase in *supply* was discussed, while here a change in the number of *demanders* is mentioned. Note that D245 also discusses, at greater length, changes in the number of demanders, though not a decrease but an increase.

These paragraphs in D245 have no counterpart **245** in E or A (although there is a reference to the effect of passing armies on market prices in E146). The principal point is that a sudden increase in the number of additional demanders will lead sellers to raise their prices. Depending on the additional money available, sellers will receive more money than before, even if the original demanders do not wish to buy at the higher price (750 pounds weight of bread at 1.5d. equals 1,125d.). But, in order to sell the remaining 250 pounds, sellers may have to sell at the original, lower price of 1d. a pound. In total they will receive 1,375d., instead of 1,000d, for 1,000 pounds' weight of bread. Note that the analysis is the same with regard to the 'old' demanders as the buyers in E/D242: they refrain from buying at higher prices (cf. C242i) and some may be left empty-handed.

246 [159] |5| Il arrive souvent que les Vendeurs, en voulant trop soutenir leur prix au Marché, manquent l'occasion de vendre avantageusement leurs denrées, ou leurs marchandises, ᵃ& qu'ils y perdentᵃ, Il arrive aussi qu'en soutenant ces prix ils pourront souvent vendre plus avantageusement un autre jour.

|| It often happens that the sellers, in keeping up the price, miss the opportunity of selling. And it also happens that they may sell higher another day.

247 |6| Les Marchés éloignés peuvent toujours influer sur les prix du Marché où l'on est: si le blé est extrêmement cher en France, il haussera en Angleterre & dans les autres Païs voisins.

248 All that depends on the plenty or scarcity of money, or of the buyers, and of the plenty or scarcity of the commodity, and the knowledge which the buyers and sellers have of it. Though most of the undertakers buy and sell at an uncertainty, yet the altercations readily find out the proportion and equilibrium. And it commonly happens in commodities whereof the consumption is constant and uniform, as bread, that the magistrate is able to fix and determine the price for it, when there is no sudden plenty or scarcity of the said commodity, or of money.

|| I have dwelt upon this example, in order to make the reasons of the variations of the prices of the things at market more feeling and sensible. The plenty or scarcity of commodities, or of money, in every place, cause those variations immediately; and the mediate and remote causes of them are fancy, or fashion of living of the prince, and the landholders, &c.

249 || As to the Goodness and Quality of Money or Coin, it is fixed by public Authority and universal Consent, and does not vary as to its intrinsic Worth; and it is therefore very properly called the Measure of Barter and Trade.

|| From what is here said, may be perceived the Reasons why the Prices of Goods daily vary at Market, where the Quantity of Money, and the Necessity of exchanging it against a certain Quantity of Goods, bring about these Alterations. The Demand of the Public to supply the Taste, Luxury and Manner of living of the Rich is that which occasions these Alterations: The Variations in the Course of Price of Foreign Exchanges, are brought about in the same Manner at the Market or Exchange, where Merchants meet to exchange or barter so much *English* Coin against a certain Quantity of Money of other Countries, which they are to receive, by Orders given in a Piece of Paper, called Bills of Exchange; if there are more Bills of Exchange at Market one Day than Money, the Price of [31] Bills must fall lower than it was before; but if there is more Money than Bills, the Price will rise.

It often happens that Sellers who are too obstinate in keeping up their price in the Market, miss the opportunity of selling their Produce or Merchandise to advantage and are losers thereby. It also happens that by sticking to their prices they may be able to sell more profitably another day.

ᵃ...ᵃ: R, M: 'et perdent'

246

Distant Markets may always affect the prices of the Market where one is: if corn is extremely dear in France it will go up in England and in other neighbouring Countries.

The argument in E247 with respect to the influence of distant markets on local prices contradicts what is said in E238, but agrees with V238c. See C238.

247

i. Cf. D241 for the similar use of the terms 'altercations' and 'equilibrium'. The latter term also occurs in D650 and D652, but is not used anywhere in E or A. 'Altercations' on the other hand is a favoured term in both D and E (though not in A) for denoting the process of market bargaining (see E240/241 /348/386/387/435/465/481/582; D241/245/258/260/263/305/348/368/372/37 5/578/579/584). Its use is peculiar: the term was already used, in both English and French, to describe heated disputes or even conflicts, but there is no real indication that Cantillon sees market bargaining as a particularly discordant process. Perhaps he uses 'altercations' to stress instead that market prices are the oucome of an imprecise social process of 'Haggling and Bargaining' (A241), which requires skill and nerve on the part of the participants.

248

ii. The expression 'constant and uniform' is equivalent to '*constante & uniforme*' in E74. Also cf. E146 and D260.

i. Given the content of E232, the statement in A249 that the 'goodness and quality of money or coin is fixed by public authority and universal consent' is surprising. It appears to paraphrase Locke's *Several Papers Relating to Money, Interest and Trade* (1696: 31): 'For mankind, having consented to put an imaginary value upon gold and silver, by reason of their durableness, scarcity, and not being very liable to be counterfeited, have made them, by general consent, the common pledges.' Did Philip here substitute Locke's older views for those of his kinsman, or was the manuscript in his possession an earlier draft containing views closer to those of Locke? Cf. C463ii and see Introduction p. 33.

249

ii. Cf. the phrase 'The Demand of the Public to supply the Taste, Luxury and Manner of living of the Rich' with a similar phrase in A442. Perhaps there is also a connection with the mention at the end of D248 of the fancy of the prince and the landholders as the 'mediate and remote causes' of the variations in market prices. Perhaps both statements express the idea that market prices are affected immediately by the people who buy in the market place, but that these demands ultimately depend on the demands of the prince and landowners.

iii. The suggestion that the foreign exchange market, through the intermediation of bills of exchange, works according to the same general principles of supply and demand is not found in E or D. It appears to be referring to the discussion in A as reproduced from A530. Cf. C530iii.

250

|| *Further considerations upon* BARTER

|| If the money which carries on the barter of a city (which, at present, we will consider as if there was no other in the world) be 100,000 ounces of silver, that is to say, if all the proportions of the values of all goods and commodities in the said city, be measured by the 100,000 ounces; or, what still comes to the same thing, if these 100,000 ounces pass for pledges, and keep the accounts of the pretentions of all barters in the said city. And if, in these circumstances, the said city receives 100,000 ounces more, so distributed that every one who has had an ounce of silver, has now two ounces, and that the quantity of money in circulation becomes 200,000 ounces of silver; this city, considered in itself, is not in any respect richer or happier than before: it will only happen that all goods and commodities will grow twice as dear as they were.- Though this consequence seems mighty plain, yet I shall endeavour to set it in a clearer light under the article MONEY, when I come to consider particularly the effects of the increase and decrease of the real quantity of money in a state.

Let us suppose a Town, and the Lands about it, that has no Communication with its Neighbours, and that the Money necessary in Circulation, in such a Place is 100,000 l. to carry on all its Wants; and let it be supposed that this Sum by one Accident or other, increased to 200,000 l. so that such as had twenty Shillings, would by this increase have forty Shillings: this Town and its Districts about it, considered in itself, would not be richer, happier, or more powerful than it was before this Acquisition; but the Prices of every Thing would be double to what it was before: and this I shall attempt to make clear, by what I shall say of the consequential Effects of the Increase and Decrease of Money to a Community.

251

When *Augustus* returned to *Rome*, after the defeat of *Mark Anthony* and *Cleopatra*, he brought with him so great a quantity of money, that all goods and commodities sold immediately for double the value they sold for before, as *Dion Cassius* tells us. If all the money he brought to *Rome* had been laid up in the treasury, it would not have had this effect; for it would have entered but slowly into circulation and barter: but he distributed it among his soldiers, whom he was not able to pay after the battle of *Actium*, by which means it came quickly into circulation.

|| History informs us, that after the Defeat of *Anthony* and *Cleopatra*, by *Augustus Cæsar*, the immense Riches brought by him to *Rome*, and there dispersed in Circulation, raised the Price of Provisions and Merchandize to double what they were before;

i. The next five paragraphs, D/A250–D/A254, do not have a **250**
clear counterpart in E. The fact that in D this fragment starts
under a new heading may perhaps indicate that it was a separate
chapter in the manuscript available to Postlethwayt. However,
A250 follows on directly from A249, without a break.

ii. Note the clear statement of the quantity theory of money in
both D250 and A250. Crucial in this context is the simplifying
assumption that the additional money put in circulation is 'so
distributed that every one who has had an ounce of silver, has
now two ounces'. It would seem to preclude the 'Cantillon
effects' discussed at length from E338 and D345 onwards
(but only very sketchily in A349). Cf. E395 where the same
'proportional distribution case' figures less prominently.

iii. The reference in D250 to a later discussion in the entry
'Money' is more precisely to the fragments reproduced in
D345–D350 and D366–D384. The reference in A250 is to the
discussion in chapter XVI of the *Analysis* (A345–A355).

iv. The use of 'pretentions' in D250 to denote 'claims'
may be a Gallicism, although it was sometimes still used in
eighteenth-century English with that meaning. However, the
word *prétention(s)* is not used in E.

i. The battle of Actium took place in 31 BC and Octavian **251**
returned to Rome in 29 BC. The reference in D251 is to Cassius
Dio, *Roman History* (early third century AD) book 51, chapter
21. That text does not actually say anywhere that prices
doubled in Rome after Octavian's return. Instead it states:
'So vast an amount of money, in fact, circulated through all
parts of the city alike, that the price of goods rose and loans
for which the borrower had been glad to pay twelve per cent.
could now be had for one third that rate.' (E. Cary translation
vol. VI, p. 61.)

ii. Note that D251, but not A251, distinguishes between the
effects on prices of a sudden and of a gradual increase in the
money supply.

252

|| It is true that the 200,000 ounces of silver are intrinsically worth double the value of 100,000 ounces: that it will make double the quantity of plate, and that it corresponds to double the quantity of land and labour; but, if 200,000 ounces are applied precisely to circulate and barter, instead of 100,000 ounces, they will produce no real advantage or disadvantage to the city in question, considered in itself: whether one ounce of silver, or two ounces, be given in pledge, or barter, for any commodity, a small price, or a large one, it is all one.

and we have seen in modern Times, that the Quantity of Bullion annually brought to *Europe* from *America*, [32] and which by insensible degrees falls into Circulation and Trade, has by the same Progression augmented the Prices of all Necessaries and Goods, and though a Town or City with the Districts about it; considered in itself, as having no Trade or Communication with its Neighbours, does not become richer, happier, or more powerful, by an Increase of Money in Circulation;

253

|| But, if we compute the circulation of one city with another, or of one nation with another, it will appear hereafter that those nations which have most money in circulation, and, consequently, where commodities are dearest, have a great advantage over these which have less money, and where commodities are cheapest, all other circumstance being equal; and that the principal advantage of foreign commerce consists in bringing home a yearly *ballance of trade*. See MONEY, and it's circulation; SILVER, and it's value; and BALLANCE *of trade*.

yet in considering and comparing Barter and Trade which one Town has with another, and that of one Country with another, it appears that that Town, and consequently that Country which has most Money in Circulation, and where of course Goods and Necessaries are dearest, has great Advantages over those Towns and Countries where Money is less abundant, and the Necessaries of Life cheaper.
|| The principal Advantage of foreign Barter and Trade consists in our annually receiving of Bullion, by way of Ballance, in exchange of our Goods and Merchandize, and that is only saying, after having paid by our Goods the Value of the Foreign Goods and Merchandizes purchased from Abroad, there shall remain still a Sum of Money due to us from the Surplus Value or Amount of our [33] own native Labour, over and above that of the Value of the Goods purchased Abroad; which Surplus Value or Amount is called the Ballance of Trade, and which must always be paid in real and effectual Bullion of Gold or Silver.

254

|| It is this Ballance of Trade which enriches Nations in the present Situation of this World; as the Acquisition of this Bullion, of which Money is made, is that which acquires to one Nation, comparing it with another, a superiority of Power, Force, and Influence; for the Possession of these precious Metals purchases all the Means of acquiring this superior Force; supposing always that they are applied to the promoting Virtue, Religion, Morality and an elegant Luxury; but if applied to promote a vicious Luxury, Prodigality, Infidelity and Gaming, Effeminacy, Immorality and Debauchery is the Consequence, and they are the Instruments of procuring to a Kingdom both temporal and eternal Ruin and Perdition.

Only A252 refers to the money inflow to Europe from **252**
America and its effects on the general price level. The same
point is made in several places in the French text. See E237,
E341, E354, E405, E581. For references to 'Americans' as
suppliers of precious metals in the Postlethwayt text see
D263 and D346.

i. For similar statements in the French text to the observation **253**
in D/A253 that nations with more money in circulation, due
to positive balances of trade, have advantages over nations
with less money in circulation, see E406–E409.

ii. For other uses of the phrase 'all other circumstances
being equal', see C49ii.

iii. After D253 the *Dictionary* entry 'Barter' finishes. The
reference to 'Money' is to the fragment reproduced from
D338, and the reference to 'Ballance of trade' is to the
fragment reproduced from D486. The entry, 'Silver' does not
contain anything that may have been written by Cantillon.
For a possible explanation see C434.

i. For a statement similar to the end of A254 about the effect **254**
that the abundance of precious metals has on the establishment of
detrimental luxurious spending habits, see E400. But here the tone
is perhaps more moralistic.

ii. After A254 chapter XII of the *Analysis* finishes. The next
chapter, *Of Money and its Value*, (pp. 34–42) is not reproduced here.
Early on (p. 34) Philip Cantillon cites Hume's definition of money
from that author's essay 'Of Money' (1752). The chapter, which
contains a few more near-verbatim quotations from Hume's essay,
deals mostly with variations in the value of gold coins. However,
towards the end of the chapter, from the bottom of p. 39 to p. 42,
some conclusions are drawn that are reminiscent of E592–E593. Cf.
C593. From the beginning of chapter XIV the text of the *Analysis*
again starts to run parallel with D257ff.

255 [159] **CHAPITRE ᵃIIIᵃ.**   *Cash*   [42] **CHAP. XIV.**
       De la circulation de   [I, 463, col.1] *REMARKS, in a national*   *Of the Circulation of Money.*
            l'Argent.   *light*

256 || From the circulation of the cash of private
                                 traders, or gentlemen, we may, in some
                                 measure, judge of that of the nation, and what
                                 quantity is competent for the circulation of
                                 the commerce thereof. To trace things from
                                 their first principles.

257   Before the use of money, we may naturally || Before the Use of Money was found
                                 enough consider the proprietors of lands as   out, one may consider the Proprietors
                                 employing slaves, servants, or vassals, to   of Land obliged to employ Slaves,
                                 procure them the conveniencies of life. On   domestic Servants and Labourers, to
                                 this supposition, the proprietors must have   cultivate the Land; to all which they
                                 as much allowed them of the produce of the   must allot the Means of supporting
                                 land as was necessary to maintain them and   themselves and Families.
                                 their children.

258 || Since the use of money, it is further || In the Beginning, when the Use of
                                 natural to judge, that, when it's quantity, by   Money was discovered, and that its
                                 altercations, gradually found out a par, or   Quantity by degrees ascertained the
                                 proportion, to the other commodities, the   Value and Purchase of all Things,
                                 land-proprietors allowed those who worked   it is natural to imagine that a certain
                                 for them so much money per annum, or   Quantity thereof was allotted to the
                                 per diem, as answered to their subsistence,   Labourer, either by the Day or Year,
                                 and that of their children, according to the   to support himself, his Wife and
                                 manner of living to which they were used. If   Children, in pro-[43]portion to the
                                 the proprietors gave them less, they could not   Expence and Manner of living of the
                                 subsist; if they gave them more, others would   Times. If less Wages was given than
                                 [I, 463, col. 2] have offered themselves   what was necessary to purchase the
                                 to work for them cheaper: by which the   Means of living, they could not support
                                 proportion of men's wages in money was   it; if more was offered, Labourers and
                                 readily found out.   Artists would press in Emulation to
                                                                                  each other to be employed.

Chapter III   ª...ª: R, M: '3ᵉ'

*Of the Circulation
of Money*

i. The entry 'Cash' (I, 461–64) first appeared in issue 39 of **255** Postlethwayt's *Universal Dictionary*, which was published in late 1752. This entry starts with a discussion of cash in its meaning of the working capital that a merchant, trader or banker requires in his business and discusses various regulations relating to commercial credit in France. Under the subheading 'Remarks, in a national light' (I, 463–64) a 'macroeconomic' perspective is then introduced. The paragraphs from D256 up to D264 do not have a clear counterpart in E (but see C138). The parallels with A257–A259, before a correspondence with E is picked up in E/D265, suggest that these fragments from the *Dictionary* belong here.

ii. The entry, 'Cash' as a whole (as well as 'Circulation', see C118ii) was in turn plagiarised by Thomas Mortimer in the first edition of *A New and complete dictionary of trade and commerce* (London 1766).

iii. Chapter XIV, pp. 42–44, of the *Analysis* is not only very short compared to what we find in E and D, it also presents a far more rudimentary argument (see A257–A259 and A287–A288).

D256 serves as a kind of bridge between the preceding **256** discussion in the *Universal Dictionary* and what is to follow, taken from Cantillon. For this reason it is likely to be Postlethwayt's addition.

i. This starting point is strongly reminiscent of what we find **257** in E/D/A78, E139 and D437.

ii. D257 uses the term 'vassals'. It also occurs in D/A78, D/A82 and D98. The term suggests that the landed estates that Cantillon imagines are like the ones from feudal times. In E the equivalent French term, *vassaux*, is also used once (E82). The term 'slaves', on the other hand, carries connotations of colonial plantations. Perhaps the fact that the two terms, together with the more general term 'servants', are used side by side indicates that Cantillon does not intend to describe any specific historical kind of estate that preceded the establishment of commercial social relations and the money economy. Also see D437.

i. The argument in D/A258 is reminiscent of E387 and the **258** beginning of D437.

ii. For the term, 'altercations', see C248i.

259

In the like manner the uncertain wages of all undertakers have found out their proportion, according to the gain and manner of living wherewith those of that order contented themselves.

It is the same Thing with respect to Undertakers of Work and Improvements, Builders and Trades, who vye with each other for Employment: their Profits must be proportioned to the Expence of the Times, and their Expence must be proportioned to their Profits; for if this Proportion is broke in upon, the Consequence is Insolvency.

260

|| Suppose an equal quantity of cash, or money, to circulate constantly in a place, the proportion of money which every body brings to market, according to the means of subsisting which he hath, naturally keeps the altercations at market (cæteris paribus) in a uniform situation; and the variation of prices, in the ordinary commodities of constant consumption, proceed only from little inequalities, when some inhabitants spend more in one week than they do in another.

261

|| But the greater variations proceed from good or bad years of vent, and the plenty and scarcity of commodities.

262

|| To come to the nature of the circulation of money, let us consider the proprietors of a large landed estate, which he keeps in his own hands, and who has all sorts of labourers, servants, tradesmen, overseers, &c.

263

|| Let it be supposed, also, that several of these overseers and tradesmen, to whom the land-proprietor usually gave an allowance in commodities, for their maintenance, and the propagation of children [see the article BARTER] have, by their œconomy, from time to time, saved a good part of the said commodities, and then exchanged them with Americans for money, at such price as has been determined in the altercations between them. Let it be imagined, likewise, that all the inhabitants on the said estate are fond of silver, and willingly receive it as a pledge for any commodities they lend to, or barter with each other; and reciprocally take it and give it, in absolute barter, finding it so generally in request that they may have their commodities for it again, with little variation of price, whenever they want them.

i. For the uses in A259 of the term **259**
'Undertakers' see C119iii.

ii. Cf. the phrase 'uncertain wages' in D259
with D129 and with '*gages incertains*' in
E129.

i. See C49ii for other occurrences of the **260**
cæteris paribus clause.

ii. Cf. E146 for a similar combination of
the words 'natural' and 'uniform'. Also see
D248.

i. Cf. D261 with the statement in E146 **261**
that such causes of the variations in market
prices will not be considered, and with the
discussion in D245.

ii. For the term 'vent' see C25vi.

E262 is reminiscent of E139.   **262**

i. The reference to the entry, 'Barter' **263**
appears to be an error. It would have been
more appropriate to refer the readers of the
Universal Dictionary to the entry, 'Labour',
in particular the text corresponding to E I, xi,
3–5. See D79–81.

ii. Note this account of how money is
supposed to be introduced through the
agency of specific social groups. The money
stock can originate from a) savings in kind of
'overseers and tradesmen' that are exchanged
for precious metals offered by 'Americans'
(D263), or from b) the landowner doing the
same with savings in kind (D264), or from c)
a find of precious metal on the estate (D264).
For a further mention of the first possibility,
see D346; also cf. D437. For saving by
landowners, see C268.

264

|| Let us suppose a fixed quantity of this money circulating on this estate, as 2000 ounces of silver, and that subdivided into several small pieces, as is the current money in a state.

|| If the proprietor himself has purchased these 2000 ounces of silver from the Americans, or dug them out of his own ground, it will come to the same thing, provided he exchanges and barters them with the other inhabitants, his dependants, for the commodities which the land produces, and whereby they all subsist.

|| Let it be again conceived, that the proprietor, to avoid the trouble of keeping his estate in his own hands, and employing so many different overseers, labourers, tradesmen, &c. chusing to live out of his own landed estate, and lets in parcels, to several of his own overseers, on the ordinary foot that lands are let in England; and that he leaves the tradesmen to set up as undertakers for the supplying, as they can, the inhabitants, and himself and family. Suppose the quantity of money at which he lets his estate, be 1000 ounces of silver per annum.

265 |1| C'est une idée commune en Angleterre qu'un Fermier doit faire trois rentes. I°. la rente principale & veritable qu'il paie [160] au Propriétaire, & qu'on suppose égale en valeur au produit du tiers de sa Ferme; une seconde rente pour son entretien & celui des Hommes & des Chevaux dont il se sert pour cultiver sa Ferme, & enfin une troisieme rente qui doit lui demeurer, pour ᵃfaire profiterᵃ son entreprise.

|| It is the general opinion in England, that a farmer makes three rents; viz. the principal rent he pays to the proprietor; a second rent for the charge of his farm, and the wages of his servants; and a third rent for himself and family, whereon to subsist, and for the education of his children. This opinion is founded on experience, which shews, that, of a farm of 300 acres, of equal goodness, the produce of 100 acres sold at market is sufficient to pay the principal rent to the landlord, or proprietor.

264 i. The third paragraph in D264 has a partial counterpart in E140. However, here the emphasis is on the emergence of a money economy. The transition of waged overseers to independent farmers and from dependent tradesmen to undertakers working for their own account is closely related to this emergence. For other instances in D where the emergence of a money economy is associated with the appearance of undertakers, see D283, D437.

ii. The numerical example introduced in D264, of 2,000 ounces of silver being in circulation as money, is continued further down in this entry (see D270ff.) and in the entries 'Circulation' (D299ff.), and 'Money' (D345ff.). In E a similar example, using different absolute numbers but the same proportions, is introduced in E280.

265 i. In E an earlier statement of the 'three rents' theory is in E109–E117. That chapter in the French text has a counterpart in A, but not in D.

ii. Joseph Harris (1757, I, i, p. 3): 'It is commonly supposed that a farmer, to be enabled to live comfortably, must make three rents of his land.' While Harris probably borrowed this view from D265 (cf. C67iv), it is less clear which authors before Cantillon had expressed this 'general opinion'. James Steuart (1767, I, viii) arrives at a similar conclusion (a proportion of land rents in England to gross produce as 9:21) on the basis of calculations by William Petty and Charles Davenant, but this required an elaborate interpretation on Steuart's part of the calculations of the earlier authors.

iii. Adam Smith (1978, vi, 140): 'The rent of land in England can not be computed at above 1/3 of the produce; it is not in reality so much. In this country [i.e. Scotland] indeed, in all the low parts of it, where the rents are at the highest as they generally are at rack-rent, it will be in that proportion. But as England is a more opulent country the reward of the farmer must be higher.' Cf. LJ (B) 289; Smith 1776, I, xi, 20.

iv. There appears to be a difference between the descriptions of the third 'rent' in E265 and D265. While in both cases it is described as a farmers' income in excess of the contracted land rent and the direct costs of cultivation, in E265 it is characterised as '*profit*' and in D265 as generous subsistence income. Note, however, that the French words '*profit*' and '*profiter*' did not have the stricter meaning, of 'the return on capital advanced', but the more general meaning of 'benefit' or 'material advantage'. Cf. E/A109, E438 and D437. For the stricter use of 'profit' later in D see C437v.

It is the general opinion in England that a Farmer must make three Rents. (1) The principal and true Rent which he pays to the Proprietor, supposed equal in value to the produce of one third of his Farm, a second Rent for his maintenance and that of the Men and Horses he employs to cultivate the Farm, and a third which ought to remain with him to make his undertaking profitable.

ᵃ...ᵃ: R, M: 'le proffit de'

213

266 |2| On a généralement la même idée dans les autres États de l'Europe; quoique dans quelques États, comme dans le Milanez, le Fermier donne au Propriétaire la moitié du produit de sa terre au lieu du tiers; & que plusieurs Propriétaires dans tous les États, tâchent d'affermer leurs terres le plus haut qu'ils peuvent: mais lorsque cela se fait au-dessus du tiers du produit, les Fermiers sont ordinairement bien pauvres. Je ne doute pas que le Propriétaire Chinois ne retire de son Fermier plus des trois quarts du produit de sa terre.

But in France and Germany, and other countries, the proportion seems different; in several parts of France, the proprietors have two-thirds of the land free, which makes the farmers, and all dependent on them, live so much the worse.*

267 [161] |3| Cependant lorsqu'un Fermier a ^ades fonds^a pour conduire l'entreprise de sa Ferme, le Propriétaire, qui lui donne sa Ferme pour le tiers du produit, sera sur de son paiement, & se trouvera mieux d'un tel marché, que s'il donnoit sa Ferme à un plus haut prix à un Fermier gueux, au hasard de perdre toute sa rente. Plus la Ferme sera grande & plus le Fermier sera à son aise. C'est ce qui se voit en Angleterre, où les Fermiers sont ordinairement plus aisés que dans les autres Païs où les Fermes sont petites.

268 |4| La supposition donc que je suivrai dans cette recherche de la circulation de l'argent sera que les Fermiers font trois rentes, & même qu'ils dépensent la troisieme rente pour vivre plus commodement, au lieu de l'épargner. C'est en effet le cas du [162] plus grand nombre des Fermiers de tous les États.

269 |5| Toutes les denrées de l'État, sortent, directement ou indirectement, des mains des Fermiers, aussi-bien que tous les matériaux dont on fait de la marchandise. C'est la terre qui produit toutes choses excepté le Poisson; encore faut-il que les Pêcheurs qui prennent le poisson soient entretenus du produit de la terre.

The same idea obtains generally in the other Countries of Europe, though in some, like the Milanese State, the Farmer gives the Landlord half the produce instead of a third, and many Landlords in all Countries try to let their Farms at the highest Rent they can; but when this is above a third of the Produce the Farmers are generally very poor. I doubt not that the Chinese Landowner extracts from his Farmer more than three fourths of the Produce.

However when a Farmer has some capital to carry on the management of his Farm the Proprietor who lets him the Farm for a third of the Produce will be sure of payment and will be better off by such a bargain than if he let his Land at a higher rate to a beggarly Farmer at the risk of losing all his Rent. The larger the Farm the better off the Farmer will be. This is seen in England where the Farmers are generally more prosperous than in other Countries where the Farms are small.

The assumption I shall make in this enquiry as to the circulation of money is that Farmers earn three Rents and spend the third Rent on living more comfortably instead of saving it. It is in fact the case with the greatest number of Farmers in all Countries.

All the Produce of the Country comes directly or indirectly from the hands of the Farmers as well as all the materials from which commodities are made. It is the Land which produces everything but Fish, and even then the Fishermen who catch the Fish must be maintained on the Produce of the Land.

i. At * in D266 the *Dictionary* has a footnote, most probably inserted by Postlethwayt, which reads: 'This should give our farmers and country people, in general, a just notion of the difference, by living under a French government, and a true Old English one, according to the steady constitution of our kingdom; which, agreeably to the judgment of the wisest and best of men, can as little submit by absolute monarchy, as by republicanism or oligarchy.' **266**

ii. Note the different examples given: E266 has Milan and China, D266 has Germany and France as places where farmers retain a smaller proportion of incomes than in England. Cf. the example from Milan in D305.

iii. In his *Bilancio dello stato di Milano* of 1765, p. 23, Francesco Maria Carpani refers to Cantillon, '*autore dell' opera la piu profonda, e meditata in materia di economia politica*'. He notes that the '*principali Autori ... dividono in tre parti il prodotto della Terra, calcolandola a nove per cento, delle quali une per le spece della coltura, come istromenti rustici, une per l'alimento del Colono, e del conduttore, ed una al Padrone*'.

ᵃ...ᵃ: R, M: 'du fond'   **267**

The qualification that farmers are assumed not to save is also made in D272. More generally the implicit assumption of zero savings or 'leakages' is also made, for instance in D270–D272 and E278.   **268**

269

270 In this œconomy the tradesmen, who have set up for undertakers, buy of the farmers, &c. their materials; the clothier buys wool of the farmer, the tanner hides, the baker wheat, the butcher oxen, sheep, &c. the land-proprietor, for the use of his family, buys what he wants of all these, who are supposed to have each of them a portion of the 2000 ounces of silver to set up. - And, as the land-proprietor is paid 1000 ounces of silver by his farmer once a year, he pays the said quantity of money to them for that wherewith they supply him, by which they are reimbursed the sums they had advanced in their undertakings, and find also a maintenance for themselves and their children.

271 || The actors in regard to the second rent, viz. the tradesmen and undertakers, smiths, carpenters, &c. so far as they are assistant to the farmer; the labourers, servants, &c. belonging to the farmer; pay and receive of the farmer, and of one another, reciprocally, 1000 ounces per annum, according to the supposition.

272 || The farmers themselves, who are the actors in regard to the third rent, and have a third part of the produce of the estate [I, 464, col.1] free, supposing they save and lay up nothing, create also for extraordinary expences for the education of their children, or for the better conveniency of living, a circulation also of 1000 ounces of silver per annum, according to this supposition: and so, upon the whole, if the estate be let for 1000 ounces of silver per annum, it seems to require 3000 ounces of silver to carry on the circulation of the three rents, if the payments be made once a year.

273 |6| Il faut donc considerer les trois rentes du Fermier, comme les principales sources, ou pour ainsi dire le premier mobile de la circulation dans l'État. La premiere rente [a]doit être païée[a] au Propriétaire, en argent [b]comptant[b]; pour la seconde & la troisieme rente il faut de l'argent [b]comptant[b] pour le fer, l'étaim, le cuivre, le sel, le sucre, les draps, & généralement pour toutes les marchandises de la Ville qui sont con-[163]sumées à la Campagne; mais tout cela n'excede guere la sixieme partie du total, ou des trois Rentes. Pour ce qui est de la nourriture & de la boisson des Habitans de la Campagne, il ne faut pas nécessairement de l'argent [b]comptant[b] pour se la procurer.

But, as it frequently happens that the farmer pays the labourers in villages with corn and commodities for their work, that such part of their land as maintains the farmer's horses requires no circulation, or barter in money;

i. The numerical example in D270 and **270**
subsequent paragraphs is continued from
D264.

ii. The account of the circulation of goods
and money is reminiscent of E140, but the
description of the inter-class exchanges in D270
seems neater. Note the clear statement that in
the process of circulation the 'undertakers'
are 'reimbursed the sums they had advanced
in their undertakings', which hints at a notion
of a cycle of reproduction. The phrase is also
reminiscent of the last sentence of D437.

iii. For similar uses of the term 'œconomy',
see C79i.

Cf. the term 'actors' in regard to the **271**
second (D271) and third (D272) rents with
the statement in E143 that the proprietor
is 'l'Acteur principal' in spending his rent
income. Also see D280, D281, D293.

The assumption that farmers do not save is **272**
the same as in E268.

The three Rents of the Farmer | ᵃ...ᵃ: R, M: 'se | i. From this point the term 'argent sonnant', or **273**
must therefore be considered as | doit payer' | 'sounding money', i.e. metallic money, occurs
the principal sources or so to speak | ᵇ...ᵇ: R, M: | a number of times in the manuscript versions
the mainspring of circulation in the | 'sonnant' | (V273b). It appears to have been replaced in
State. The first Rent must be paid | | the print version with the more commonly used
to the Landowner in ready money: | | 'argent comptant', i.e. 'cash'. Only in one place
for the second and third Rents | | in the published text does 'argent sonnant' occur
ready money is needed for the Iron, | | (see E293).
Tin, Copper, Salt, Sugar, Cloth and | | ii. The view that the 'rents' of the farmer are 'the
generally all the merchandise of the | | mainspring' (le premier mobile) of circulation is
City consumed in the Country; but | | particularly reminiscent of Quesnay's descriptions
all that hardly exceeds the sixth part | | of circular flow from his encyclopédie article,
of the total or three Rents. As for | | 'Grains' (1757) onwards (see Quesnay 2005:
the Food and Drink of the Country | | 161–212). In a number of respects there are
folk ready money is not necessary to | | certainly clear differences between the analyses
obtain it. | | of circular flow that Quesnay went on to develop
in his Tableaux économiques and the patterns
of payments outlined by Cantillon from E268.
However, the latter do appear to have exercised a
clear formative influence on Quesnay's thinking.

274 |7| Le Fermier peut brasser sa biere, ou faire son vin sans dépenser d'argent [a]comptant[a], il peut faire son pain, tuer les Bœufs, les Moutons, les Cochons, &c. qu'on mange à la Campagne; il peut païer en blés, en viande & en boisson, la plûpart de ses Assistans, non-seulement Manœuvriers, mais encore Artisans de la Campagne, en évaluant ses denrées au prix du Marché le plus proche, & le travail au prix ordinaire du lieu.

that the subsistence of the farmer's servants and family requires no money, since they often kill their own meat, and brew their own drink, and bake their own bread; and since no more money seems requisite than for what the undertakers and tradesmen do, and there being little of that required in villages, but for clothing, carpenters work, smiths work, and the taylors, shoemakers, and the like: whereas all the proprietor's expence in his family, since he has no land in his own hands, is supplied by the undertakers; from which consideration it should seem, that the circulation of the last two rents does not require near so much money as the single rent of the proprietor, which is the principal source and cause of the circulation of money.

275 |8|Les choses nécessaires à la vie sont [a]la nourriture, le vêtement & le logement. On n'a pas be-[164]soin d'argent comptant pour se procurer la nourriture à la Campagne[a], comme [b]on vient[b] de l'expliquer[c]. Si[c] on y fait du gros linge & de gros draps [d], si on y bâtit des Maisons, comme cela se pratique souvent[d], le travail de tout cela [e]peut se païer[e] en troc par évaluation, sans que l'argent [f]comptant[f] y soit nécessaire.

276 |9| [a]Le seul argent comptant qui est nécessaire[a] à la Campagne, sera donc celui qu'il faut pour païer la rente principale du Propriétaire & les marchandises que la Campagne tire nécessairement de la Ville, [b]telles que[b] les couteaux, les cizeaux, les épingles, les aiguilles, les draps pour quelques Fermiers ou autres gens [c]aisés[c], la batterie de cuisine, la vaisselle & généralement tout ce qu'on tire de la Ville.

The Farmer may brew his Beer or make his Wine without spending cash, he can make his Bread, kill the Oxen, Sheep, Pigs, etc. that are eaten in the country: he can pay in Corn, Meat and Drink most of his Assistants—not only Labourers but country Artisans, valuing the Produce at the prices of the nearest Markets and Labour at the ordinary price of the Locality.

ᵃ...ᵃ: R, M: 'content'

i. The point in D274 that the rent of the landowner is paid exclusively in money is also made in E273. **274**

ii. The term '*content*' in the manuscripts (V274a) appears to be a misspelling of '*comptant*' (the same thing occurs below, see V275f and V279b, but thereafter '*comptant*' is written correctly on a number of occasions in the manuscript versions). This suggests that Cantillon himself used both '*sonnant*' and '*comptant*' (cf. C273i).

iii. The misspelling '*content*' might further indicate that the Rouen manuscript was dictated (since the words '*comptant*' and '*content*' *sound* identical in French), although it is a strange error to make for a scribe with a good knowledge of French. Other odd misspellings that may support this conjecture are the, admittedly, not exact homophones '*rangs*' for '*rentes*' (V282c), '*ordre*' for '*hors de*' (V311a), '*asiatiques*' for '*anséatiques*' (V403a), '*La part*' for '*l'appas*' (V436d), '*Les prix*' for '*l'esprit*' (V461f), '*l'aire*' for '*l'Ere*' (V574e) and see V339a.

The things necessary to Life are Food, Cloaths, and Lodging. There is no need of cash to obtain Food in the country, as I have just explained. If coarse Linen and Cloths are made there, if Houses are built there, as is often done, the Labour for all this may be paid in barter by valuation without cash being needed.

ᵃ...ᵃ: R, M: 'le manger, Le Boire lhabillement Les Maisons Lits &ᶜ. Pour Le Boire et le manger a la Campagne Largent sonnant ni est pas necessaire'
ᵇ...ᵇ: R, M: 'je viens'
ᶜ...ᶜ: R, M: 'et si'
ᵈ...ᵈ: R, M: 'a la Campagne comme cela se pratique souvent de méme que Les maisons', Lits &ᶜ.'
ᵉ...ᵉ: R , M: 'se peut payer'
ᶠ...ᶠ: R, M: 'contant'

The phrase '*le manger, le boire, l'habillement*' in the manuscript versions (V275a) is reminiscent of 'eating, drinking, cloathing', which occurs four times in D (see D134, D638, D639, D640). The editor of the print edition of the *Essai* may have found the French too literal a translation of the English and corrected it here and in other places (see V284e, V309a, V365e and also V184b/D184). In E672, however, the phrase occurs uncorrected. Cf. C672i. **275**

The only cash needed in the Country is that for the principal Rent of the Landlord and for the Manufactures which the Country necessarily draws from the City, such as Knives, Scissors, Pins, Needles, Cloaths for some Farmers or other well-to-do People, the kitchen utensils, plates, and generally all that is got from the City.

ᵃ...ᵃ: R, M: 'Largent sonnant qui est seul nécessaire '
ᵇ...ᵇ: R, M: missing
ᶜ...ᶜ: R, M: 'accomodés a la Campagne'

276

277 |10| J'ai déja remarqué qu'on estime que la moitié des Habitans d'un État demeure dans les [165] Villes, & par conséquent que ceux des Villes dépensent plus que la moitié du produit des terres. Il faut par conséquent de l'argent ᵃcomptantᵃ, non-seulement pour la rente du Propriétaire, qui correspond au tiers du produit, mais aussi pour les marchandises de Ville, consommées à la Campagne, qui peuvent correspondre à quelque chose de plus qu'au sixieme du produit de la terre. Or un tiers & un sixieme font la moitié du produit: par conséquent il faut ᵇque l'argent comptant, qui circule à la Campagne, soitᵇ égal au moins à la moitié du produit de la terre, au moïen de quoi l'autre moitié quelque chose moins, peut se consommer ᶜà la Campagne,ᶜ sans qu'il soit besoin d'argent comptant.

278 |11| La circulation de cet argent se fait en ce que les Propriétaires ᵃdépensent en détail, dans la [166] Ville,ᵃ les rentes que les Fermiers leur ont païées en gros articles, & que les Entrepreneurs ᵇdes Villes,ᵇ comme les Bouchers, les Boulangers, les Brasseurs, &c.ᶜ ramassent peu-à-peu ce même argent, pour acheter des Fermiers, en gros articles, les Bœufs, le blé, l'orge, &c. Ainsi toutes les grosses sommes d'argent sont distribuées par petites sommes, & toutes ᵈlesᵈ petites sommes sont ensuite ramassées pour faire des paiemens de grosses sommes aux Fermiers, directement ou indirectement, & cet argent passe toujours en gage tant en gros qu'en détail.

279 |12| Lorsque j'ai dit qu'il faut nécessairement pour la circulation de la Campagne, une quantité d'argent, souvent égale en valeur à la moitié du produit ᵃdes terresᵃ, c'est la moindre quantité; & pour que la circulation de la Campagne se fasse avec facilité, je [167] supposerai que l'argent ᵇcomptantᵇ qui doit conduire la circulation des trois rentes, est égal en valeur à deux de ces rentes, ou égal au produit des deux tiers de la terre. On verra par plusieurs circonstances dans la suite, que cette supposition n'est pas bien loin de la verité.

Yet I will suppose, that the circulation of the two last rents, together, are equal to that of the first rent.

I have already observed that it is reckoned that half the Inhabitants of a State live in the cities, and consequently the citizens spend more than half the Produce of the Land. Cash is therefore necessary, not only for the Rent of the Landlord, corresponding to one third of the Produce, but also for the City merchandise consumed in the Country, which may amount to something more than one sixth of the produce of the soil. But one third and one sixth amount to half the produce. The cash circulating in the Country must therefore be equal to at least one half the produce of the land, by which means the other half or somewhat less may be consumed in the Country without need of cash.

The circulation of this money takes place when the Landlords spend in detail in the City the rents which the Farmers have paid them in lump sums, and when the Undertakers of the Cities, Butchers, Bakers, Brewers, etc. collect little by little this same money to buy from the Farmers in lump sums Cattle, Wheat, Barley, etc. In this way all the large sums of money are distributed in small amounts, and all the small amounts are then collected to make payments in large amounts, directly or indirectly, to the Farmers, and this money large or small always passes in return for services.

When I stated that for the Country circulation there is needed a quantity of Money often equal in Value to half the Produce of the Land, this is the minimum; and in order that the Country circulation should be easily conducted I will suppose that the ready cash which conducts the circulation of the three rents, is equal in value to two of these rents, or two thirds of the Produce of the Land. It will be seen later that this supposition is not far from the truth.

ᵃ...ᵃ: R, M: 'sonnant'
ᵇ...ᵇ: R, M: 'quil Circule a la Campagne de Largent sonnant'
ᶜ...ᶜ: M: missing (present in R).

ᵃ...ᵃ: R, M: 'Rependent a la ville dans le troc du menu'
ᵇ...ᵇ: R, M: missing
ᶜ: R, M: 'dans la Ville'
ᵈ...ᵈ: R: 'Ces' (M: 'les')

ᵃ...ᵃ: R, M: 'de la terre'
ᵇ...ᵇ: R, M: 'content

---

i. For the assumption that half of the population lives in towns see C284v. **277**

ii. Condillac *Le commerce et le gouvernement*, 1776, I, ch. 16 has the following footnote: 'It is estimated that the money which circulates in the states of Europe is in general equal to at least half of the product of the land, and at most to two-thirds, *Essai sur la nature du Commerce*, Book 2 Chapter 3. I have drawn the basis of this chapter from this work, and several observations of which I have made use in other chapters. It is one of the best works I know on this subject: but I am far from knowing them all' (translation Eltis and Eltis 1997: 134).

i. The word '*rependent*' in the manuscript versions (V278a) appears to be a misspelling of '*repandent*', which would express the idea that the landowners 'spread' their money in the city through their small expenditures. The word is also used in the first sentence of E302 and V302d. Cf. C649. **278**

ii. For the expression '*le troc du menu*' in V278a, see C297ii.

Note that in E279 there is an attempt to reconcile the calculation of 1/3 + 1/2 x 2/3 = 2/3 with the fraction suggested in E277 (1/3 + 1/6 = 1/2). D279 also puts the fraction at 2/3 and does not need to reconcile it with the fraction 1/2 since D does not have a counterpart to E277. **279**

280 |13| Supposons maintenant que l'argent qui conduit toute la circulation d'un petit État, est égal à dix mille onces d'argent, & ᵃque tous les paiemensᵃ qu'on fait de cet argent, de la Campagne à la Ville, & de la Ville à la Campagne, se font une fois l'an; que ces dix mille onces d'argent sont égales en valeur, à deux rentes des Fermiers, ou aux deux tiers du produit des terres. Les rentes des Propriétaires correspondront à cinq mille onces, & toute la circulation ᵇd'argent, qui resteraᵇ entre les gens de la Campagne & ceux de la Ville, & qui [168] doit se faire par paiemens annuels, correspondra aussi à cinq mille onces.

|| So that, if the produce of all the land and labour in the estate in question is equal to 3000 ounces of silver, the exchange and barter of the said produce among the actors of the the three rents will require but 2000 ounces of silver to carry on the circulation of the whole, and make all the payment once a year.

281 |14| Mais si les Propriétaires de terres stipulent avec leurs Fermiers les paiemens par semestre au lieu de paiemens annuels, & si les Débiteurs des deux dernieres rentes font aussi leur paiemens tous les six mois, ce changement dans les paiemens changera le train de la circulation: & au lieu qu'il fallait auparavant dix mille onces pour faire les paiemens une fois l'an, il ne faudra maintenant que cinq mille onces, parceque cinq mille onces païées en deux fois auront le même effet que dix mille onces païées en une seule fois.

|| But, if the land-proprietor stipulates the payment of his rent with the farmer once in six months; and if all the payments, made by the actors in the three rents, are also made once in six months; 1000 ounces, in two payments, will answer 2000 ounces in one payment.

282 |15| De plus si les Propriétaires stipulent avec leurs Fermiers les paiemens par quartier, ou s'ils se contentent de recevoir de leurs Fermiers les Rentes à mesure que les quatre Saisons de l'année les [169] mettent en état de vendre leurs denrées, & si tous les autres paiemens se font par quartiers, il ne faudra que deux mille cinq cens onces pour la même circulation qui aurait conduite par dix mille onces en paiemens annuels. Par conséquent, supposant que tous les paiemens se fassent par quartiers dans le petit état en question, la proportion de la valeur de l'argent nécessaire pour la circulation est au produit annuel des terres, ᵃc'est-à-dire, aux trois rentes,ᵃ comme 2500 ᵇliv.ᵇ est à 15000 ᵇliv.ᵇ ᶜ ou comme 1 à 6, de telle sorte que l'argent correspondroit à la sixieme partie du produit annuel des terres.

|| And, if all the payments are made quarterly, 500 ounces will answer the whole circulation; and it often happens, that the farmers pay but a quarter's rent to the proprietors at a time, and 'tis observable in the country, that there is seldom any more money in the villages than what will answer a quarter's rent.

|| And, as the different kinds of the products of land seem to answer and correspond to the four seasons of the year, it seems natural to judge, that the wheels of cash-circulation and barter of commodities are set a going four times in a year, and in many countries the rents are stipulated to be paid quarterly.

Let us now imagine that the money which conducts the whole circulation of a little State is equal to 10,000 ounces of silver, and that all the payments made with this money, Country to City, and City to Country, are made once a year; and that these 10,000 ounces of silver are equal in value to two of the Rents of the Farmers or two thirds of the Produce of the Land. The Rents of the Landlords will correspond to 5000 ounces, and the whole circulation of the remaining silver between the Country people and the Citizens, made by annual payments, will correspond also to 5000 ounces.

But if the Landlords stipulate with their Farmers for half yearly instead of yearly payments, and if the Debtors of the two other Rents also make their payments every six months, this will alter the rapidity of circulation: and whereas 10,000 ounces were needed to make the annual payments, only 5000 will now be required, since 5000 ounces paid twice over will have the same effect as 10,000 ounces paid once.

Further if the Landlords stipulate with their Farmers for quarterly payments, or if they are satisfied to receive their Rents from the Farmers according as the four Seasons of the year enable them to sell their Produce, and if all other payments are made quarterly, only 2500 ounces will be needed for the same circulation which would have been conducted by 10,000 ounces paid once a year. Therefore, supposing all payments made quarterly in the little State in question, the proportion of the value of the money needed for the circulation is to the annual Produce of the soil (or the three Rents), as 2500 livres is to 15,000 livres, or as 1 to 6, so that the money would correspond to the sixth part of the annual produce.

[a]…[a]: R, M: 'que Les payéménts'
[b]…[b]: R , M: 'restante d'argent'

[a]…[a]: R, M: missing, but appearing at c
[b]…[b]: R, M:'[lb]'
[c]: R, M: '(c'est a dire aux trois Rangs)'

i. In E280 the numerical example **280** with annual incomes of 15,000 (money stock is 2/3 x 15,000; one 'rent' is 1/3 x 15,000) is introduced at this point. In D the numerical example with annual incomes of 3,000 (but using the same proportions, i.e. money stock is 2/3 x 3,000; one 'rent' is 1/3 x 3,000) is continued from D264 and D270–D272.

ii. The economy under consideration in E is said to be 'a small state', whilst in D it continues to be a single landed estate up to D287.

For the phrase 'actors in the three **281** rents' in D281, see C271.

i. Could the misspelling 'Rangs' **282** for 'rentes' in the manuscript versions (V282c) be due to a scribe mishearing the word? Cf. C274iii.

ii. The expression *par quartier* in E282 and subsequent paragraphs appears to be too literal a translation of the English 'quarterly'.

283 |16| Mais attendu que chaque branche de la circulation dans les Villes est conduite par des Entrepreneurs, que ªla consommation de la nourritureª se fait par des paiemens journaliers, ou [170] par semaines ou par mois, & que celle ᵇdu vêtementᵇ, quoique faite dans les Familles tous les ans, tous les six mois, ne laisse pas de se faire dans des tems différens par les uns & par les autres; que la circulation pour la boisson se fait journellement pour le plus ᶜgrandᶜ nombre; que celle de la petite biere, des charbons & de mille autres branches de consommation est fort prompte; il sembleroit que la proportion que nous avons établie dans les paiemens par quartiers seroit trop forte, & qu'on pourroit conduire la circulation d'un produit de terre de quinze mille onces ᵈd'argent avec beaucoup moins que deux mille cinq cens onces d'argent comptant.ᵈ

|| Now, if we suppose this land-proprietor and several others to live together in the common center of their lands, where they form a city, and draw thither most of the undertakers and tradesmen, who supply their families, and one another. As almost every thing is carried on and supplied in a city by undertakers, so almost all the barter requires money; but then, on this supposition, the circulation of money is very quick, all the undertakers and tradesmen commonly paying their workmen and journeymen once a week, and several families paying their expences daily at market.

284 |17| Cependant puisque les Fermiers sont dans la nécessité de faire de gros paiemens aux Propriétaires au moins tous les quartiers, & que les droits que ªle [171] Prince ou l'État perçoiventª sur la consommation ᵇsont accumulésᵇ par les Receveurs pour faire de gros paiemens ᶜaux Receveurs généraux;ᶜ il faut bien une quantité suffisante d'argent ᵈcomptantᵈ dans la circulation pour que ces gros paiemens puissent se faire avec facilité, sans empêcher la circulation du courant ᵉpour ce qui regarde la nourriture & le vêtement des habitans.ᵉ

|| But these small parcels of money, which go and come so frequently and quick in several small rivulets of barter, are gathered together again in lumps, by the undertakers, as bakers, butchers, brewers, &c. and paid to the farmer, from whom all commodities are bought; and then are again paid quarterly to the land-proprietors, out of whose hands they are again spread into the rivulets of barter: and, these payments made, the proprietors seem to be the principal object to judge by, of the quantity of money in circulation, there being no great sum required for the circulation of the other two rents. Cities are esteemed to contain half the inhabitants of a state, and to make more than half the consumption of the produce of the land.

But seeing that each branch of the circulation in the Cities is carried out by Undertakers, that the consumption of Food is met by daily, weekly or monthly payments, and that payment for the clothing purchased once or twice a year by Families is made at different times by different people; and whereas the expenditure on Drink is usually made daily, that on Small Beer, Coal, and a thousand other articles of consumption is very prompt, it would seem that the proportion we have established for quarterly payments would be too high and that the circulation of a land produce of 15,000 ounces of silver in value could be conducted with much less than 2500 ounces of silver in ready money.

^{a}...^{a}: R, M: 'La Consommation du Marché pour Le Manger'
^{b}...^{b}: R, M: 'de lhabillement'
^{c}...^{c}: missing in R, present in M.
^{d}...^{d}: R, M: 'bien moins D'argent sonnant que deux Mille Cinq Cens onces,'

283

i. In D283 the phrase about people living 'together in the common center of their lands' is reminiscent of the account in A30 about the formation of towns, which is based on Defoe (1728). Cf. C29 and C30.

ii. The close association in D283 of undertakers with people whose services are paid for in money is also found in D264 and D437.

As however the Farmers have to make large payments to the Landlords at least every quarter and the Taxes which the Prince or the State collects upon consumption are accumulated by the Collectors to make large payments to the Receivers-General, there must be enough ready cash in circulation to make these large payments without difficulty, without hindering the circulation of currency for the Food and Clothing of the people.

^{a}...^{a}: R, M: 'les revenus de l'estat qui se perçoivent'
^{b}...^{b}: R, M: 's'accumulent'
^{c}...^{c}: R, M: 'aux receveurs généréaux a peu pres de la Meme Maniere,'
^{d}...^{d}: 'sonnant'
^{e}...^{e}: R, M: 'qui Regarde toujours Le boire et Le manger et Lhabillement des habitans,'

284

i. The Prince and tax collectors who are introduced quite abruptly in E284 are missing from D284.

ii. The account in D284 of the quickening of circulation through small payments and its slowing into big payments of cash is reminiscent of E343 (also cf. E297, E309).

iii. E343/V343c also has a precise counterpart for the expression 'small rivulets of barter' in D284, namely 'les petits ruisseaux du troc' (translated by Higgs with 'the little rills of exchange'). Other occurrences of the expression 'rivulets of barter' are in D300 and D303. This hydrological metaphor is reminiscent of E389. Another occurrence of the term 'ruisseaux' is E151, but this is a literal use of the term. For other expressions, see C296 and C297ii.

iv. For the phrase 'le boire, le manger et l'habillement' (V284e), see C275i.

v. The last sentence in D284 about the proportion of the population living in towns is reminiscent of E111, which occurs in a chapter that is not found in Postlethwayt's *Dictionary*. A111 has the same assumption. Also cf. E120, E277 and E319, none of which has a counterpart in D. One wonders whether the inclusion of this assumption at this point in D is a conscious editing decision to make up for the information from omitted parts.

285 |18| On sentira bien par ce que je viens de dire, que la proportion de la quantité d'argent [a]comptant[a] nécessaire pour la circulation d'un État n'est pas une chose incompréhensible, & que cette quantité peut être plus grande ou plus petite dans les États, suivant le train qu'on y suit & la vîtesse des paiemens. Mais il est bien difficile de rien statuer de précis sur cette quantité en général, qui peut être différente à proportion dans différens Païs, [172] & ce n'est que par forme de conjecture que [b]je dis en général,[b] que [c]"l'argent comptant, nécessaire pour conduire la circulation & le troc dans un État, est à-peu-près égal en valeur au tiers des rentes annuelles des Propriétaires de terres."[c]

|| Though the detail of the circulation of money in a state be indefinite, yet it appears from what has been said, that it is not incomprehensible, and 'till some body has the curiosity to examine the said detail, and endeavours to come at better knowledge of the propositions of it, I shall lay it down as my opinion and conjecture of the matter in general, That the real cash or money, necessary to carry on the circulation and barter in any state, is nearly one third part of all the annual rents of the proprietors of the said state.

286 |19| Que l'argent soit rare, ou abondant, dans un État, cette proportion ne variera pas beaucoup, parceque dans les États où l'argent est abondant on afferme les terres plus haut, & plus bas dans ceux où l'argent est plus rare: c'est une regle qui se trouvera toujours véritable [a]dans tous les tems[a]. Mais il arrive ordinairement, dans les États où l'argent est plus rare, qu'il y a plus de troc par évaluation, que dans ceux où l'argent est plus abondant, & par conséquent la circulation est censée plus prompte & moins retardée que dans les États où l'argent est [b]moins [173] rare[b]. Ainsi pour juger de la quantité de l'argent qui circule, il faut toujours considerer la vîtesse de sa circulation.

|| Whether money be scarce or plenty in a state, this proportion will not change, because, if it be scarce, the proprietor will sell his land for less money; and, if it be plenty, he will sell it for more, and this will always hold good in the long-run. But, if the circulation of money be slower or quicker generally in a state, the proportion of money, required in circulation, will be more or less.

287 |20| Dans la supposition que l'argent qui circule est égal au tiers de toutes les rentes des propriétaires des terres, & que ces rentes sont égales au tiers du produit annuel des mêmes terres, il s'ensuit que [a]"l'argent qui circule dans un État est égal en valeur à la neuvieme partie de tout le produit annuel des terres."[a]

|| According to this supposition, if 2000 ounces of silver served to carry on all the circulation on the estate we considered, the proprietor's rents ought to have been 6000 ounces, and the three rents equal in value to 18,000 ounces, and consequently the money which carries on the circulation and barter in a state, may be esteemed equal in value to the ninth part of the annual product of the lands of the said state.

[43 continued] || The Payments made by Tenants to Landlords, Farmers to Labourers, and Tradesmen to Farmers for the Produce of the Land, Merchants to Manufacturers, the Proprietors of Lands to Tradesmen and Artists; and lastly, by the Prince to his Courtiers and Pensioners, is what is called Circulation of Money; the oftner these Payments are made, the quicker Money shifts Hands, and goes round; and it is calculated that the Coin which conducts the Circulation of a Kingdom, is about the ninth Part of the Value of the Produce of the Land, and the Value of [44] the Labour necessarily had to form it into Use.

It will be seen from this that the proportion of the amount of money needed for circulation in a State is not incomprehensible, and that this amount may be greater or less in a State according to the mode of living and the rapidity of payments. But it is very difficult to lay down anything definite as regards this quantity in general, as the proportion may differ in different countries, and it is only conjectural when I say that "the real cash or money necessary to carry on the circulation and exchange in a State is about equal in value to one third of all the annual Rents of the proprietors of the said State."

[a]...[a]: R, M: 'sonnant'
[b]...[b]: R, M: 'Je poseray'
[c]...[c]: R, M: quotation marks are missing

The assumption about the proportion between the amount of cash necessary for circulation and the amount of annual rents in E/D285 is repeated in E316 and D317. **285**

Whether money be scarce or plenty in a State this proportion will not change much because where money is abundant Land is let at higher Rents, and where money is scarce at lower Rents. This will be found to be the case at all times. But it usually happens in States where money is scarcer that there is more Barter than in those where Money is plentiful, and circulation is more prompt and less sluggish than in those where Money is not so scarce. Thus it is always necessary in estimating the amount of money in circulation to take into account the rapidity of its circulation.

[a]...[a]: R, M: ', a la longue,'
[b]...[b]: R, M: 'moins abondant'

i. The expression '*à la longue*' ('after a certain time', or 'eventually') in the French manuscript versions (V286a) is equivalent to 'in the long-run' in D286. Hence the alternative in the print version, '*dans tous les tems*' ('at all times'), which makes less sense, appears to be a later alteration. Very similar phrases occur in D370, ('at the long-run'), A641 ('at a long Run') and E513, E552 and E582 ('*à la longue*'). In all cases the phrase appears to indicate something like 'when all relevant factors have made their influence felt'. Cf. C370. **286**

ii. The expression '*moins abondant*' ('less abundant') (V286b) makes less sense than '*moins rare*' in the print version. For a case where R makes more sense instead, seeV388d and e and C388.

Supposing the money in circulation equal to the third of all the Rents of the Landowners and these Rents equal to the third of the annual Produce of the Land, it follows that "the money circulating in a State is equal in value to the ninth part of all the annual produce of the soil."

[a]...[a]: R, M: quotation marks are missing

i. In D287 a switch occurs from 'the estate' in the beginning of the paragraph to 'a state' at the end. Having lowered the estimate of the amount of money required for circulation in the 'estate' in D281 and D282 (following the same logic as in E281 and E282), D287 resumes the original example of a money stock of 2,000 ounces of silver (see D264). In order to make this equivalent to 1/9th of the total annual incomes of the 'state', the latter is set at six times the size of the incomes of the 'estate', i.e. instead of a total of 3,000 in D270–D271 it becomes 18,000 ounces in D287. **287**

ii. The text in A287 follows on directly from A259.

iii. In his *Pay Book*, dating from the late 1770s, on p. 234, the young Alexander Hamilton noted: 'Postlethwaite supposes the quantity of cash necessary to carry on the circulation in a state one third of the rents of the land proprietors or 1/9 the whole product of the land –See articles Cash and Circulation.'

288

|| In order to give a plain Instance of what Circulation is; suppose yourself at a Hazard-Table, where some have large Heaps of Money before them, others less; in short, all have something to venture. The Play begins, the Money flies about the Table from Hand to Hand; he that had large Sums is reduced to nothing and borrows of the Money-Lender; the quicker the Game goes on, the quicker the Money shifts Hands, and circulates from Hand to Hand: so fares it with a trading Country; all Commerce is carried on at Risk and Hazard, the Whole depends on the Landholders, to furnish their Taste, Luxury, and Expence. I am told that a Bank at *Faro* of ten thousand Pounds, will carry on Play for one hundred thousand Pounds in a Night; if so, it circulates this hundred thousand Pounds; and by the same Parity of Reason, about the tenth Part of Value in Money will circulate the Income of the Land's Produce, with the Value of the Labour necessarily had to manufacture it into Form for Use and Service to the Public.

289 |21| Le Chevalier Guillaume Petty, dans un Manuscrit de l'année ᵃ1685ᵃ, suppose souvent l'argent qui circule, égal en valeur au dixieme du produit des terres, sans dire pourquoi. Je crois que c'est un jugement qu'il forma sur l'expérience & sur la pratique qu'il avoit, tant de l'argent qui circuloit alors en Irlande, dont il avoit arpenté la plus grande par-[174]tie des terres, que des denrées dont il faisoit une estimation à vue ᵇd'œilᵇ. Je ne me suis pas beaucoup éloigné ᶜde son idée ᶜ; mais j'ai mieux aimé comparer la quantité d'argent qui circule, aux rentes des propriétaires, qui se paient ordinairement en argent, & dont on peut aisément savoir la valeur par une taxe égale sur les terres, que de comparer la quantité de l'argent aux denrées ᵈou auᵈ produit des terres, dont le prix varie journellement aux Marchés, ᵉ& dont même une grande partie se consomment sans passer par ces Marchésᵉ.

|| Sir William Petty, in a manuscript written in 1685, supposes frequently, that the circulating money in a state is equal to the tenth part of the annual product of the land; and, though he assigns no reason any-where for such a conjecture, it looks to me, as if his great experience and sagacity had let him into that proportion.

|| As his supposition differs from what has been suggested but 1/10, I should readily come into his notion, if it were able to lead me into any useful knowledge; whereas in fixing a proportion between the circulating money in a state and the rents of the proprietors, whereof the sum may be known by an exact land-tax, the knowledge of the actual sum of money requisite in circulation may be attained.

i. A288 has no clear counterpart in E or D. Together **288** with A287 it is all the *Analysis* has to offer as a counterpart for the discussion in E/D260–E/D298. Three things in A288 that are reminiscent of Richard Cantillon are a) the remark that 'all Commerce is carried on at Risk and Hazard', b) the statements that 'the Whole [circulation] depends on the Landholders' and c) the assumption that the money in circulation only has to be a tenth of the total product of a country (a proportion ascribed to William Petty in E/D289).

ii. After this paragraph, chapter XIV in A finishes. Of the next chapter XV (pp. 45–51) pp. 45 to 49 have a counterpart in D, but not E. These pages are reproduced in A416–A426. Cf. C416i and ii.

Sir Wm. Petty, in a Manuscript of 1685, supposes frequently that the money in circulation is equal to one tenth of the Produce of the Soil. He gives no reason. I suppose it is an opinion which he formed from experience and from his practical knowledge both of the money circulating in Ireland (a great part of the Land of which country he had measured as a Surveyor) and of the Produce which he estimated roughly from observation. I am not far removed from his conclusion to the Landlords' Rents (ordinarily paid in money and easily ascertainable by a uniform Land Tax) rather than to the Products of the Soil, the Prices of which vary daily in the Markets, and a large part of which is consumed without entering into the Market.

ᵃ...ᵃ: 1769: '1684'
ᵇ...ᵇ:R, M: 'de Payis'
ᶜ...ᶜ: R, M: 'de son idée au fond'
ᵈ...ᵈ: 'et'
ᵉ...ᵉ: missing in M, present in R

i. The work of Petty referred to is probably **289** *The political anatomy of Ireland*, written in 1672 but not published until 1691. On p. 83 Petty writes: 'The keeping or lessening of Money, is not of that consequence that many guess it to be of. For in most places, especially Ireland, nay England it self, the Money of the whole Nation is about 1/10 of the Expence of one Year.' Cantillon's remark that Petty does not explain his reasoning 'anywhere' is noteworthy. In 1691 *The political anatomy of Ireland* was printed together with *Verbum Sapienti* in which Petty went into some detail about how much money is required as a fraction of spending in a year (although his estimates differed). But Cantillon may not have known the latter work if he did indeed base himself on a manuscript of Petty's former work. Cf. C105i.

ii. Note that only E289 has the reflection on the abuse of inaccurate calculations.

iii. Locke, *Some Consideration* (1692: 32–41), also discussed the estimation of the quantity of the money in circulation taking into account the velocity of circulation.

290 Je donnerai, dans le Chapitre suivant, plusieurs ªraisons confirmées par des exemples,ª pour fortifier ma supposition. Cependant je la crois utile quand même elle ne se trouveroit pas physiquement vraie dans aucun ᵇEtatᵇ. Elle suffit si elle approche de la vérité, & si elle empêche les [175] Conducteurs des Etats de se former des idées extravagantes de la quantité d'argent qui y circule: car il n'est point de connoissance où l'on soit si sujet à s'abuser, que dans celle des calculs, lorsqu'on les laisse à la conduite de l'imagination; au lieu qu'il n'y a point de connoissance plus démonstrative, lorsqu'on les conduit par un détail de faits.

291 |22| Il y a des Villes & des Etats qui n'ont aucune terre qui leur appartiennent, & qui subsistent, en échangeant leur travail ªouª Manufacture contre le produit des terres d'autrui: telles sont Hambourg, Dantzick, plusieurs autres Villes impériales, & même une partie de la Hollande. Dans ces Etats il paroît plus difficile de former un jugement de la circulation. Mais si on pouvoit faire un jugement des terres Etrangeres qui fournissent leur subsistance, le calcul ᵇne différe-[176]roit pas probablementᵇ de celui que je fais pour les autres ᶜEtatsᶜ qui subsistent principalement de leurs propres fonds, & qui sont ᵈl'objetᵈ de cet Essai.

292 |23| A l'égard de l'argent ªcomptantª nécessaire pour conduire un commerce avec l'Etranger, il semble qu'il n'en faut pas d'autre que celui qui circule dans l'Etat, lorsque la balance du commerce avec l'Etranger est égale, c'est-à-dire, lorsque les ᵇdenrées & les marchandisesᵇ qu'on ᶜy envoieᶜ sont égales en valeur à celles qu'on en reçoit.

|| 'Tis easy to conceive, that foreign trade requires no great additional sum to carry on it's circulation in a state, when the ballance of trade is equal. [See BALANCE of Trade].

Higgs Translation (H)	Variations and Errata (V)	Comments (C)

In the next Chapter I shall give several reasons, supported by examples, to confirm my conclusion. I think it useful, even if not mathematically exact in each Country. It is enough if it is near the truth and if it prevents the governors of States from forming extravagant ideas of the amount of money in circulation. There is no branch of knowledge in which one is more subject to error than Statistics when they are left to imagination, and none more demonstrable when they are based upon detailed facts.

ª…ª: R, M: 'raisons et Circonstances'
ᵇ…ᵇ: R, M: 'Royaume ou Etat'

Cf. V290b with V291c. **290**

Some Cities and States which have no Land belonging to them subsist by exchanging their Labour or Manufactures for the Produce of the Land of others. Such are Hamburg, Dantzig, several other Cities of the Empire, and even part of Holland. In these States it seems more difficult to estimate the circulation. But if we could estimate the amount of foreign Land which furnishes their subsistence, the calculation would probably not differ from that I have made for the other States which live chiefly on their own produce and are the subject of this Essay.

ª…ª: R, M: 'et'
ᵇ…ᵇ: 1769: 'ne différoit probablement'
ᶜ…ᶜ: R, M: 'Etats et Royaumes'
ᵈ…ᵈ: 'principalement l'objet'

291

As to the cash needed to carry on Foreign Trade it seems that no more is required than what is in circulation in the State when the Balance of Foreign Trade is equal, that is when the Products and Merchandise sent abroad are equal in value to those imported.

ª…ª: R, M: 'sonnant'
ᵇ…ᵇ: R, M: 'marchandises et denrees'
ᶜ…ᶜ: 'y envoye chez Letranger'

The reference in D292 to the entry, 'Balance of trade' is to the fragment reproduced in D486–D569. **292**

293 |24| Si la France envoie des draps en Hollande, ᵃ& si elle en reçoit desᵃ épiceries, pour la même valeur, le propriétaire qui consomme ces épiceries en paie la valeur à l'Epicier, & l'Epicier paie cette même valeur au Manufacturier de draps, à qui la même valeur est due en Hollande pour le drap ᵇqu'il y aᵇ envoïé. [177] Cela se fait par Lettres de change dont j'expliquerai la nature dans la suite. Ces deux paiemens en argent se font en France hors la rente du propriétaire, & il ne sort pas pour cela aucun argent ᶜde Franceᶜ. Tous les autres ordres qui consomment les Epiceries d'Hollande les paient de même à l'Epicier; savoir, ceux qui subsistent ᵈdeᵈ la premiere rente ᵉ, c'est-à-dire, de celle duᵉ propriétaire, les paient de l'argent de la premiere rente, & ceux qui subsistent par les deux dernieres rentes, soit à la Campagne, soit à la Ville, paient l'Epicier directement ou indirectement de l'argent qui conduit la circulation des deux dernieres rentes. L'Epicier paie encore cet argent au Manufacturier ᶠpour sesᶠ Lettres de change sur Hollande; & il ne faut pas d'augmentation d'argent dans un État pour la circulation, par rapport au com-[178]merce avec l'Etranger, lorsque la balance de ce commerce est égale. Mais si cette balance n'est pas égale, c'est-à-dire, si on vend en Hollande plus de marchandise qu'on n'en tire, ou si l'on en tire plus qu'on n'y en envoie, il faut de l'argent pour l'excédent, & que la Hollande en envoie en France, ou que la France en envoie en Hollande: ce qui augmentera, ou diminuera, la quantité d'argent sonnant qui circule en France.

|| In this case, the goods and commodities exported pay the value of those that are imported; when the proprietors consume the foreign commodities, they pay the undertakers of the foreign trade what they had advanced for them; and these pay the same value to the undertakers of the exported goods, which compensate the imported ones; this is all paid out of the first rent: and, where the actors in the two other rents consume foreign commodities, the money, necessary for the circulation of the said rents also, is sufficient to answer it.

294 |25| Il peut même arriver ᵃque lorsque la balance est égale avec l'Etranger,ᵃ le commerce avec ce même Etranger retarde la circulation de l'argent ᵇcomptantᵇ, & par conséquent ᶜdemandeᶜ une plus grande quantité ᵈd'argentᵈ par rapport à ce commerce.

|| All the influence foreign trade seems to have upon the circulation of money in a state is, that it sometimes retards it, and makes it pass through the hands of more undertakers and brokers, than it otherwise would do.

If France sends Cloth to Holland and receives from her Spices, of equal value, the Landowner who consumes these Spices pays the value of them to the Grocer, who pays the same amount to the Clothmaker, to whom it is due in Holland for the Cloth he has sent there. This is done by Bills of Exchange which will be explained later. These two money payments take place in France apart from the Rent of the Landowner, and no money leaves France on that account. All other Classes of Society who consume Dutch spices, similarly pay the Grocer, viz. those who live on the first Rent, that is the Landowners, pay from this Rent, and those who live on the other two Rents in Country or in City pay the Grocer directly or indirectly out of the money which conducts the circulation of these Rents. The Grocer again pays this money to the Manufacturer for his Bill upon Holland, and no increase of money is needed for circulation in the State because of Foreign Trade when the balance is equal. But if it is not equal, if more merchandise is sold to Holland than is bought back, or vice versa, money is needed for the surplus which Holland must send to France or France to Holland. This will increase or diminish the amount of money circulating in France.

a…a: R, M: 'et en reçoit en'
b…b: R, M: 'quil Luy a'
c…c: R,M: 'en hollande'
d…d: R, M: 'par'
e…e: R, M: 'ou par Le'
f…f: R, M: 'Contre Ces'

i. The remark in E293 **293** that letters of exchange 'will be explained later' is a reference to E527ff.

ii. Only E293 mentions the spice trade between France and Holland. But see C541ii.

iii. For the phrase 'actors in the two other rents' in D293, see C143 and C271.

iv. The last sentence of E293 has the only occurrence of the term *argent sonnant* in the French print version. Cf. C273. This may be a case of 'editor's fatigue'. See Introduction p. 26, n. 19.

It may even occur that when the balance with the Foreigner is equal to the Trade with him may retard the circulation of ready money and therefore require a greater quantity of money by reason of this commerce.

a…a: R, M: 'lors que la balance est égale avec LEtranger que'
b…b: R, M: 'sonnant'
c…c: R, M: 'Rend'
d…d: R, M: 'dargent nécéssaire'

294

295 |26| Par exemple, si les Dames françoises, qui portent des étoffes de France, veulent porter des velours de Hollande, qui sont [179] compensés par les draps qu'on y envoie, ᵃelles paieront cesᵃ velours aux Marchands qui les ont tirés de Hollande, & ces Marchands les paieront aux Manufacturiers. Cela fait que l'argent passe par plus de mains, que si ces Dames portoient leur argent aux Manufacturiers, & se contentoient d'étoffes de France. Lorsque le même argent passe par les mains de plusieurs Entrepreneurs, la vîtesse de la circulation ᵇen est ralentieᵇ. Mais il est difficile de faire une estimation juste de ces sortes de retardemens, qui dépendent de plusieurs circonstances: car dans l'exemple présent, si les Dames ont paié aujourd'hui le velours au Marchand, & si demain le Marchand le paie au Manufacturier pour sa Lettre de change sur Hollande; si le Manufacturier le paie le lendemain au Marchand de laine, & celuici le jour d'après au Fer-[180]mier, il se peut faire que le Fermier le gardera en caisse plus de deux mois pour achever le paiement du quartier de rente qu'il doit faire au propriétaire; & par conséquent cet argent auroit pû circuler deux mois entre les mains de cent Entrepreneurs, sans retarder dans le fond la circulation nécessaire de l'État.

296 |27| Après tout, on doit considerer la rente principale du propriétaire, comme la branche la plus nécessaire & la plus considerable de l'argent par rapport à la circulation. Si le propriétaire demeure dans la Ville, & que le Fermier vende dans la même Ville toutes ses denrées, & y achete toutes les marchandises nécessaires pour la consommation de la Campagne, l'argent ᵃcomptantᵃ peut toujours rester dans la Ville. Le Fermier ᵇy vendra les denréesᵇ qui excéderont la moitié du produit de sa ferme; il paiera dans la même [181] Ville l'argent du tiers de ce produit à son propriétaire, & il paiera le surplus aux Marchands ou Entrepreneurs, pour les marchandises qui doivent être consommées à la Campagne. Cependant dans ce cas même, comme le Fermier vend ses denrées par gros articles, & que ces grosses sommes doivent être ensuite distribuées dans ᶜle détail, &ᶜ être de nouveau ramassées ᵈpourᵈ servir aux gros paiemens ᵉdes Fermiersᵉ, la circulation rend toujours le même effet (à la vîtesse près) que si le Fermier emportoit l'argent ᶠde ses denréesᶠ à la Campagne, pour le renvoïer ensuite à la Ville.

|| If the proprietors of land at Paris wear Genoa velvets to the value of 10,000 ounces of silver, and these velvets are compensated by 10,000 ounces value in French cloth, the proprietors out of their rents pay the velvet merchant, as undertaker, 10,000 ounces; he pays the sum to Genoa banker or remitter; he pays the same to the cloth merchant, who sends French cloth to Genoa on his bills of exchange. But, if the proprietors at Paris wore cloth instead of the velvets, they would pay directly the 10,000 ounces to the cloth merchant, and so that money would not go through so many hands; 'tis in this sense only, that foreign trade can affect the circulation of money. See more under the articles CIRCULATION, CREDIT, MONEY.

For example, if the French ladies who wear French stuffs wish to wear Dutch velvets, which are paid for by the Cloth sent to Holland, they will pay for these velvets to the Merchants who imported them from Holland, and these Merchants will pay the Manufacturers of Cloth. The money thus passes through more hands than if these Ladies took their money to the Manufacturers of Cloth and contented themselves with the fabrics of France. When the same money passes through the hands of several Undertakers the rapidity of circulation is slowed down. But it is difficult to make an exact estimate of this sort of delay which depends upon various circumstances. Thus, in our present example, if the Ladies pay the Merchant for the velvet today, and the Merchant pay the Manufacturer tomorrow for his Bill on Holland, if the Manufacturer pay the Wool Merchant the next day and this last pay the Farmer the day after, it is possible that the Farmer will keep the money in hand more than two months to make up the quarter's Rent which he must pay his Landlord. This money might in two months have circulated through the hands of a hundred Undertakers without locking up the circulating medium needed by the State.

After all, the principal Rent of the Landowner must be considered to be the most necessary and considerable branch of the Money in regard to circulation. If he lives in the City and the Farmer sells in the same City all his produce and buys there all the Merchandise necessary for Country use, the ready money may always remain in the City. The Farmer will sell there Produce exceeding half the output of his Farm; he will pay his Landlord in the same City the money value of one third of his Produce and the rest to Merchants or Undertakers for Merchandise to be consumed in the Country. Even here, however, as the Farmer sells his Produce for lump sums, which are subsequently distributed in retail purchases, and are again collected to serve for lump payments to the Farmers, the circulation has always the same effect (subject to its rapidity) as if the Farmer took to the Country the money received for his Produce and sent it back again to the City.

ᵃ...ᵃ: R: 'Ces dames payent les prix du'; M: 'ces dames payent le prix de'
ᵇ...ᵇ: R, M: 'se ralentit'

ᵃ...ᵃ: R, M: 'sonnant'
ᵇ...ᵇ: R, M: 'vendra dans la ville ses denrées'
ᶜ...ᶜ: R, M: 'la Racine du troc'
ᵈ...ᵈ: R, M: 'et'
ᵉ...ᵉ: R, M: 'pour Le fermier'
ᶠ...ᶠ: R, M: missing

295
i. Whilst in E295 the consumers of velvet are French ladies (cf. the 'Dames de Paris' in E490), and the velvet comes from Holland, in D295 the consumers are 'proprietors of land at Paris' and the velvet comes from Genoa. For other occurrences of Genoa see E/D465, E/D470 and E/A544.

ii. For the reference in D295 to the entry, 'Circulation', see D299ff. For the reference to 'Money', see D338ff. For the reference to 'Credit' see D671–D672 and D683–D689.

iii. After D295 the *Dictionary* entry, 'Cash' ends.

296
The odd phrase in V296c appears to convey an interesting image. In translation it says something like 'the large sums are subsequently distributed in *the root of barter*'. This may be a reference to the multifurcation that can be seen in a root system. Similar to the branching of a river into 'small rivulets of barter' (C284ii), the distribution of large payments into multiple small ones may be compared to the spreading out of a single trunk into a network of roots. Admittedly, the expression is obscure and this may have prompted the editor of the print version to drop it.

297 |28| La circulation consiste toujours en ce que les grosses sommes que le Fermier tire de la vente de ses denrées sont distribuées dans ᵃle détailᵃ, & ensuite ramassées pour faire de gros paiemens. Soit que cet argent ᵇsorteᵇ [182] en partie de la Ville ou qu'il y reste en entier, on peut le considerer comme faisant la circulation de la Ville & de la Campagne. Toute la circulation se fait entre les habitans de l'État, & tous ces habitans sont nourris & entretenus de toute façon du produit des terres & du crû de la campagne.

298 |29| Il est vrai que la laine, par exemple, qu'on tire de la Campagne, lorsqu'on en fait du drap dans la Ville, vaut quatre fois plus qu'elle ne valoit. Mais cette augmentation de valeur, qui est le prix du travail ᵃdes Ouvriers, & des Manufacturiers de la Ville,ᵃ se change encore contre les denrées de la Campagne qui servent à entretenir ᵇces Ouvriersᵇ.

The Circulation consists always of this, that the large sums which the Farmer receives on the sale of his produce are split up in detail and then brought together again to make large payments. Whether this money go partly out of the City or remain there entirely it may be regarded as the circulating medium between City and Country. All the circulation takes place between the inhabitants of the State, and they are all fed and maintained in every way from the Produce of the Soil and raw materials of the Country.

It is true that the Wool, for example, which is brought from the Country, when made up into Cloth in the City is worth four times its former value. But this increase of Value, which is the price of the Labour of the workmen and Manufactures in the City, is exchanged for the Country produce which serves for their maintenance.

ᵃ…ᵃ: R, M: 'Le Ménu'
ᵇ…ᵇ: M: 'soit'

ᵃ…ᵃ: R, M: 'de Ceux de la Ville, Comme ouvriers manufacturiers &c.'
ᵇ…ᵇ: R, M: 'Les ouvriers en question'

i. The argument of E297 is reminiscent of D284, D300, E309 and E343. **297**

ii. As in E278, the expression '*le detail*' here replaces '*le menu*' in the manuscript versions (V297a), and the same happens again in E303/V303d. However, the expression *le troc de menu* does occur in E308, E310, E313 and E575. One gets the impression that the editor of the print edition after a few occurrences gave up replacing the expression as found in the manuscript. '*Le detail*' is further used in E296, E301 and E343, but none of these occurrences has a counterpart in the manuscript versions. Even if this suggests that the editor introduced the expression *le detail*, it does not significantly affect the meaning of the argument: both expressions indicate the manifold small payments made in the economy for 'retail' purchases. Similar phrases occur in D; see D285, D376: 'the detail of barter', D284: 'small parcels of money', and D479: 'minute parts'. Also see C284iii and C296.

298

299   [183] **CHAPITRE** ᵃIVᵃ.
Autre reflexion sur la vitesse ᵇ*ou la lenteur*ᵇ *de la circulation de l'argent, dans le troc.*

[I, 498, col.2]
Of the CIRCULATION *of money.*

300 || In consequence of what has been said under the article CASH, we shall further add, in regard to the *circulation* of money; That we may consider the *money* which goes out of land-proprietor's pocket, and is spread into several rivulets of barter in circulation; out of which it is again gathered into the farmer's purse, to make another quarter's payment to the land-proprietor, according to what has been urged under the head of *cash*, as before intimated.

301 |1| Supposons que le Fermier paie 1300 onces d'argent par quartier au propriétaire, que celui-ci en distribue ᵃen détailᵃ toutes les semaines 100 onces ᵇau Boulanger, au Boucher,ᵇ &c., & que ces Entrepreneurs ᶜfassent retournerᶜ ces 100 onces toutes les semaines au Fermier, de maniere que le Fermier ramasse par semaine autant d'argent que le propriétaire en dépense. Dans ᵈcette suppositionᵈ il n'y aura que 100 onces d'argent en circulation perpétuelle, & les autres 1200 onces demeureront en caisse, partie entre les mains du propriétaire, ᵉ&ᵉ partie entre les mains du Fermier.

|| If, pursuant to our example, the farmer has paid 1500 ounces of silver to the proprietor, and he pays out 115 ounces a week, while, on the other hand, the farmer gathers together 115 ounces a week, there will be but 115 ounces, properly speaking, in motion; and at six weeks end, when the proprietor has but 750 ounces left, the farmer will have collected together the other 750 ounces: so that the whole 1500 ounces (with 115 ounces that are every week in circulation) are always kept up, and only paid and put in motion once a quarter.

302   [184] |2| Mais il arrive rarement que les propriétaires répandent leurs rentes dans une proportion constante & reglée. ᵃA Londres, sitôt qu'un propriétaire reçoit sa rente, il en metᵃ la plus grande partie entre les mains d'un Orfévre, ᵇou d'un Banquierᵇ, qui la prêtent à intérêt, ᶜparᶜ conséquent cette partie circule; ou bien ᵈce propriétaire en emploieᵈ une bonne partie ᵉdans l'achat deᵉ plusieurs choses nécessaires ᶠauᶠ ménage; & avant qu'il puisse recevoir ᵍun second quartier,ᵍ il empruntera peut-être de l'argentʰ. Ainsiʰ l'argent de ce premier quartier circulera en mille manieres avant qu'il puisse être ramassé & ⁱremisⁱ entre les mains du Fermier, ʲpour servir à faireʲ le paiement du second ᵏquartierᵏ.

|| But this seldom happens to be the case in a state; for money is spread out into the little channels of trade without rule or proportion, and likewise gathered together without any proportion. The same 1500 ounces are often paid away by several people to the land-proprietor, as soon as he has received them, and are not accumulated again together till near the end of the quarter, when the farmer receives them in a lump from the corn-chandler, woollen manufacturer, &c. in exchange for his commodities, which enables him to pay the landlord another quarter's rent.

Chapter IV

Further Reflection on the Rapidity or Slowness of the Circulation of Money in Exchange

ᵃ...ᵃ: R, M: '4ᵉ'
ᵇ...ᵇ: R, M: 'ou lenteur'

i. The entry 'Circulation' (I, 498–99), with its subsection 'Of the Circulation of money' first appeared in issue 42 of the *Universal Dictionary*, which was published in the last weeks of 1752 or the first weeks of 1753. In that entry the text reproduced in D299–D317 is immediately preceded by that of D118–D134. Cf. C118i.

ii. Mortimer (1766) plagiarised Postlethwayt's entry and hence included this chapter from Cantillon too. Cf. C118ii.

iii. There is no counterpart in A for this chapter.   **299**

i. D300 is reminscent of E297.

ii. The reference in D300 to the entry, 'Cash' is to the fragment reproduced immediately above (D256–D295).

iii. The phrase 'rivulets of barter' also occurs in D284 and D303. Cf. C284iii.   **300**

Let us suppose that the Farmer pays 1300 ounces of silver a quarter to his Landlord, who pays out of it every week 100 ounces to the Baker, Butcher, etc. and that these every week pay the Farmer these hundred ounces, so that the Farmer collects every week as much money as the Landlord spends. In this case there will be only 100 ounces in constant circulation, the other 1200 ounces will remain in hand partly with the Landlord and partly with the Farmer.

ᵃ...ᵃ: R, M: 'missing'
ᵇ...ᵇ: R, M: dans Le troc aux entrepreneurs Comme boulanger, Boucher'
ᶜ...ᶜ: R, M: 'Repayent'
ᵈ...ᵈ: R, M: 'ce Cas'
ᵉ...ᵉ: R, M: missing

i. Following the numerical example of E280, one would expect quarterly payments of rents in E301 to amount to 5000/4 = 1250. The use of the number 1,300, instead of 1,250, may be a way of simplifying this numerical example, since it allows 13 weekly payments of a round figure of 100 (instead of 96 2/13).

ii. The earlier example referred to in D301 is in D287, where yearly rents are assumed to be 6,000. Hence the sum of 1,500 for quarterly rents.

iii. There appears to be a basic numerical error in D301. One would think that the figure of 115 ounces should be 125 ounces, since 6 x 125 = 750. However, if a quarter of a year is assumed to comprise 13 weeks, as it is in E301, then the number 115 may be explained as follows. If a quarter rent is spent in 13 weeks, then the weekly expenditure of the proprietor, and money in circulation, is 1500/13 = 115 5/13. Thus the author (or editor) may simply be ignoring the fraction (cf. C301i). Halfway through the quarter, when the proprietor has 750 ounces left, would be after 6 1/2 weeks and not 'at six weeks end', but this may be another simplification rather than an error.   **301**

But it rarely happens that the Landlords spend their Rents in a fixed and regular proportion. In London as soon as a Landlord receives his Rent he puts most of it into the hands of a Goldsmith or Banker, who lends it at interest, so that this part is in circulation. Or else the Landlord spends a good part of it upon various things needful for his household, and before he gets his next quarter's Rent he will perhaps borrow money. Thus the money of the first quarter's Rent will circulate in a thousand ways before it can be brought together again and replaced in the hands of the Farmer to serve to pay his second quarter.

ᵃ...ᵃ: R, M: 'Le proprietaire a Londres sitost quil Reçoit sa rente en met'
ᵇ...ᵇ: R, M: 'ou Banquier'
ᶜ...ᶜ: R, M: 'et par'
ᵈ...ᵈ: R, M: 'Le propriétaire repend d'abord'
ᵉ...ᵉ: R, M: 'de sa rente a achetter'
ᶠ...ᶠ: M: 'en'
ᵍ...ᵍ: 'La Rente du second quartier'
ʰ...ʰ: R, M: ', et'
ⁱ...ⁱ: R, M: 'retourné'
ʲ...ʲ: R, M: 'pour faire'
ᵏ...ᵏ: R, M: 'quartier de rente'

i. In D302 should the phrase 'paid away by several people to the land-proprietor' not read instead 'paid away to several people by the land-proprietor'?

ii. E302 mentions the deposits of rents with goldsmiths and bankers; D302 does not. Cf. E/D628 and E/D631.   **302**

303 |3| Lorsque le ªtemsª du paiement de ce second quartier sera venu, le Fermier vendra ses denrées par gros articles; & ceux qui [185] achetent les bœufs, ᵇles blés, les foins, &c., en auront auparavant ramasséᵇ le prix, dans le détail: ainsi l'argent du premier quartier ᶜauraᶜ circulé ᵈdans les canaux du détailᵈ pendant près de trois mois, avant que d'être ramassé par les Entrepreneurs du détail, ᵉ& ceux-ci le donnerontᵉ au Fermier, ᶠqui en feraᶠ le paiement du second quartier. Il sembleroit par-là qu'une moindre quantité d'argent comptant, que celle que nous avons supposée, pourroit suffire à la circulation d'un État.

In this interval of time, these 1500 ounces may have gone to and fro in an hundred rivulets of barter, and helped on the circulation of the other two rents, as well as the principal rent they are understood to make the payment of.

‖ This would, methinks, make it probable, that a less proportion of money, even than that which we have supposed, might carry on the general circulation and barter necessary in a state: the following argument seems to strengthen the same notion.

304 |4| Tous les trocs qui se font par évaluation ne demandent guere d'argent comptant. Si un Brasseur fournit à un Drapier la bierre qu'il consomme dans sa Famille ª; & si le Drapier fournit réciproquement au Brasseur les draps dont il a besoin,ª le tout au prix courant du Marché reglé le jour de la livraison, il ne faut ᵇd'autre [186] argent comptant, entre ces deux Commerçans,ᵇ que la somme qui paiera la différence de ce que l'un a fourni ᶜde plusᶜ.

‖ All barters that are made by evaluation in a state, require no ready money. If the woollen-draper sells the baker 100 ounces of silver value of cloth, and the baker supplies the woollen-draper with the like value in bread, both at the market, or current price, it is so much bartered without money.

Higgs Translation (H)	Variations and Errata (V)	Comments (C)

When the time for paying this second quarter has come the Farmer will sell his produce in large amounts, and those who buy his Cattle, Corn, Hay, etc. will already have collected in detail the price of them. The money of the first quarter will thus have circulated in the rivulets of small traffick for nearly three months, before being collected by the retail dealers, and these will give it to the Farmer who will pay his second quarter therewith. It would seem from this that less ready money than we have supposed would suffice for the circulation of a State.

^a...^a: R, M: 'terme'
^b...^b: R: 'bled, ou saloire en auront ou pourront ramasser'; M: 'bled, en auront ou pouront ramasser'
^c...^c: R, M: 'aura pu'
^d...^d: R, M: 'parmy les Canaux du Menu troc'
^e...^e: R, M: 'qui Le payeront'
^f...^f: R, M: 'et autant quil puisse servir a faire'

303

i. The phrase 'rivulets of barter' in D303 also occurs in D284 and D300.

ii. Higgs translates the phrase '*les canaux du détail*' in E303 with 'rivulets of small traffic', which is most probably inspired by 'rivulets of barter' in D303. Cf. C284iii. However, D302 has a more precise equivalent in 'little channels of trade'.

Barters made by evaluation do not all call for much ready cash. If a Brewer supplies a Clothier with the Beer for his family, and if the Clothier in turn supplies the Brewer with the Cloaths he needs, both at the Market price current on the day of delivery, the only ready money needed between these two traders is the amount of the difference between the two transactions.

^a...^a: R, M: missing
^b...^b: R, M: 'aucun argent Comptant de part ny dautre'
^c...^c: R, M: missing

304

i. The missing phrase ^a...^a in the manuscript versions of E is curious, since the paragraph does not seem to make full sense without it. In the Rouen manuscript the preceding words '*sa Famille*' are at the bottom of a page and the following words, '*le tout*' at the top of the next page. This may mean that a copyist forgot the missing words as he moved from one page to the next. M simply copies the sentence as it appears in R. In contrast, the editor of E may have corrected the sentence by adding a missing phrase that can be inferred from the context.

ii. The second paragraph of D305 has a similar example of a 'wine-merchant' and a 'woollen-draper'.

305 |5| Si un ªMarchandª dans un Bourg, envoie à un ᵇcorrespondantᵇ dans la Ville des denrées de la Campagne pour vendre, & si celui-ci renvoie au premier les marchandises de la Ville dont on fait la consommation à la Campagne, ᶜla correspondance durant toute l'année entre ces deux Entrepreneurs, & la confiance mutuelle leur faisant porter en compte leurs denrées & leurs marchandisesᶜ au prix des Marchés respectifs, il ne faudra ᵈd'autre argent réelᵈ pour conduire ᵉce commerceᵉ, que la balance que ᶠl'unᶠ devra à l'autre à la fin de l'année; encore pourra-t-on porter cette balance à compte nouveau pour l'année suivante, sans débourser aucun argent effectif. ᵍTous les Entre-[187]preneurs d'une Ville, qui ont continuellement affaire les uns aux autres peuvent pratiquer cette méthode;ᵍ & ces trocs par évaluations semblent épargner beaucoup d'argent comptant dans la circulation, ou du moins en accélerer le mouvement, en le rendant inutile dans plusieurs mains où il devroit nécessairement passer sans cette confiance & cette maniere de troquer par évaluation. Aussi ce n'est pas sans raison, qu'on dit communément, la confiance dans le commerce rend l'argent moins rare.

|| Of these barters by evaluation there are several carried on in [I, 499, col.1] a state where trade, credit, and honesty flourish [see the article BARTER] there are many of them used in the country, as well as in the cities: but I am to observe they could not be carried on, if the barters against money at markets, and the altercations, which fix the par between money and commodities, did not first naturally find out the price of things: so that, when in a village a certain quantity of corn is bartered and exchanged for a certain quantity of iron, the evaluation is made of the corn and of the iron, according to the prices they bear at the nearest market.

|| The more barters are made by evaluation in a state, the less ready money generally seems requisite to carry on the circulation. If the woollen-draper supplies the wine-merchant with the cloth necessary for the consumption of his family, at the current price; and the wine-merchant supplies the woollen-draper with the wine his family consumes, also at the current price; and if they trust one another in accounts, when they come to settle their accounts, at the year's end; all the money required to carry on this trade will be the sum which pays the difference.

|| The barters by evaluation are most carried on by the undertakers and master tradesmen, and between the farmers and labourers, and others who assist them: so that they seem principally to help the circulation of the two last rents; whereas the circulation of the first rent must be always carried on by ready money, except when the land-proprietor consumes part of his farmer's commodities in kind, and allows it out of his rent, as is much practised in *Italy*. The *Milanese* nobility have a quantity of hay sent in by their farmers, in part of their rent, for the maintenance of their coach-horses, &c. and a quantity of wheat, which they exchange with the bakers for the bread they consume in their families, besides wine, &c. and these evaluations help out the circulation of the first rent.

|| From what has been said, it should seem to be inferred, that honesty and confidence in dealings in a state keep forward the barters by evaluation, and, consequently, make money go father in *circulation*; and experience tells us, that, when *credit* fails, the circulation is clogged, and money grows scarcer.

If a Merchant in a Market Town sends to a correspondent in the City country produce for sale, and if the latter sends back to the former the City merchandise consumed in the Country, the business lasting the whole year between these two dealers, and mutual confidence leading them to place to their accounts their produce and merchandise at their respective Market prices, the only real money needed for this commerce will be the balance which one owes to the other at the end of the year. Even then this balance may be carried forward to the next year, without the actual payment of any money. All the Undertakers of a City, who have continually business with each other, may practise this method. And these exchanges by valuation seem to economise much cash in circulation, or at least to accelerate its movement by making it unnecessary in several hands through which it would need to pass without this confidence and this method of exchange by valuation. It is not without reason that it is commonly said Commercial Credit makes Money less scarce.

ᵃ…ᵃ: R, M: 'Marchand ou Entrépreneur'
ᵇ…ᵇ: R, M: 'Commissionaire ou Correspondant'
ᶜ..ᶜ: R, M: 'pour Les y vendre, sy ces deux entrepreneurs sont en Correspondance Toute Lannée, se fiant l'un a lautre portant en Compte Les denrées et marchandises'
ᵈ…ᵈ: R, M: 'aucun argent effectif'
ᵉ…ᵉ: R, M: 'ce troc et Correspondance'
ᶠ.ᶠ: M: 'lon'
ᵍ…ᵍ: R, M: 'on peut pratiquer La méme Methode entre touts Les éntrépréneurs d'une Ville qui ont affaire Les une aux autres Continuéllémént,'

305

i. The four paragraphs in D305 present the argument of E304 and E305 in a different order and with additional elements.

ii. D305 puts particular emphasis on the idea that 'barters by evaluation' (credit on account) can flourish only when first market prices have been established through 'barters against money at markets'. This seems to express the idea that the economising effects of credit can only be obtained after the coordinating effects of money have been realised. The expression 'barter by evaluation' is equivalent to *'troquer par évaluation'* in E305 (also see E286 and E304). In D other mentions of 'evaluation' as a money substitute are in D317, D375, D419, D480.

iii. The reference to the entry, 'Barter' in D305 is to the text reproduced in D239–D253.

iv. The example in D305 of Milan, where part of the rent is paid in kind is missing in E305. But Milan is mentioned in E149 and especially E266. Cf. C266ii.

v. The final remark in D305 about the effects of a failure in credit on circulation seems to anticipate the further discussion in D375.

306 |6| Les Orfévres & les Banquiers publics, dont les billets passent couramment en paiement, comme l'argent comptant, contribuent aussi à la vîtesse de la circulation, qui seroit retardée s'il falloit de l'argent effectif dans tous les paiemens où l'on se contente de ces billets; & bien que ces Orfévres & Banquiers gar-188]dent toujours en caisse une bonne partie de l'argent effectif qu'ils ont reçu ªen faisantª leurs billets, ils ne laissent pas de répandre aussi dans la circulation une quantité considerable de cet argent effectif, comme je l'expliquerai ci-après, en traitant des Banques publiques.

|| Another circumstance, which helps circulation greatly, is goldsmiths and banks, as the *Bank of England*, that of *Amsterdam*, of *Venice*, of *Genoa*, &c. These prevent a great sum from being kept in private hands without motion, and accelerate circulation.

307 |7| Toutes ces réflexions semblent prouver qu'on pourroit conduire la circulation d'un Etat, avec bien moins d'argent effectif, que celui que j'ai supposé nécessaire pour cela; mais les inductions suivantes paroissent les contrebalancer, & contribuer au retardement de cette même circulation.

|| These reasons seem to confirm that the circulation in a state may be carried on with less money than what I have laid down under the article CASH: but the following reasons may, perhaps, seem to counterballance them in some measure.

308 |8| Je remarquerai d'abord que toutes les denrées sont produites à la Campagne par un travail qui peut se conduire, absolument parlant, avec peu ou point d'argent effectif, comme je l'ai déja souvent insinué: mais toutes les [189] marchandises ªse fontª dans les Villes ou dans les Bourgs par un travail d'Ouvriers qu'il faut païer en argent effectif. Si une Maison a couté cent mille onces d'argent à bâtir, toute cette somme, ou au moins la plus grande partie, doit avoir été païée toutes les semaines dans le ᵇmenu trocᵇ au Faiseur de briques, ᶜaux Maçons, aux Menuisiers, &c.ᶜ directement ou indirectement. La dépense des petites Familles, qui dans une Ville font toujours le plus grand nombre, ᵈne se fait nécessairement qu'avec deᵈ l'argent effectif; & dans ce bas troc le crédit, l'évaluation, & les billets ne peuvent avoir lieu. ᵉLes Marchands ou Entrepreneurs de détail demandentᵉ de l'argent comptant pour prix des choses qu'ils fournissent; ou s'ils se fient à quelque Famille pour quelques jours ou ᶠquelquesᶠ mois, ils ont besoin d'un bon paiement en [190] argent. Un Sellier qui vend un carosse quatre cens onces d'argent en billets, sera dans la nécessité de convertir ces billets en argent effectif, pour païer tous les matériaux & tous les Ouvriers qui ont travaillé à son carosse s'il en a eu le travail à crédit, ou, s'il en a fait les avances, pour en faire un nouveau. La vente du carosse lui laissera le profit de son entreprise, & il dépensera ce profit à l'entretien de sa famille. ᵍIl ne pourroit se contenter de billets, qu'en cas qu'il pût mettre quelques choses de côté ou à intérêts.ᵍ

The Goldsmiths and public Bankers, whose notes pass current in payment like ready money, contribute also to the speed of circulation, which would be retarded if money were needed in all the payments for which these Notes suffice: and although these Goldsmiths and Bankers always keep in hand a good part of the actual money they have received for their Notes, they also put into circulation a considerable amount of this actual money as I shall explain later in dealing with public Banks.

ᵃ...ᵃ: R, M: 'Lors quils ont fait'

The further discussion promised in E306 of the role of banks in circulation is in E III, vi (E627ff.). **306**

All these reflections seem to prove that the circulation of a State could be conducted with much less actual money than I have supposed necessary; but the following inductions appear to counterbalance them and to contribute to the slowing down of the circulation.

The reference to the entry 'Cash' is to the text reproduced in D255–D295. Note that, while Postlethwayt clearly altered the text in D307 by subsituting 'under the article CASH', perhaps for something like 'in the previous chapter', he did not bother to make changes to prevent the impression that the first person 'I', also used in E307, was a reference to himself. **307**

I will first observe that all Country produce is furnished by Labour which may possibly, as already often suggested, be carried on with little or no actual money. But all Merchandise is made in Cities or Market Towns by the Labour of Men who must be paid in actual money. If a House has cost 100,000 ounces of silver to build, all this sum or the greatest part of it, must have been paid every week in small amounts to the Brickmaker, Masons, Carpenters, etc. directly or indirectly. The expense of the humble Families, who are always the most in number in a City, is necessarily made with actual money. In these small exchanges Credit, Book debts, and Bills cannot have a place. The Merchants or Retailers demand cash for the things they supply: or if they give credit to a Family for a few days or months they require a substantial money payment. A Carriage builder who sells a carriage for 400 ounces of silver in Notes, will have to change them into actual money to pay for all the Materials and the Men who have worked on his carriage if they have worked on credit, or, if he has paid them already, to start a new one. The sale of the Carriage will leave his Profit and he will spend this to maintain his family. He could not be satisfied with Notes unless he can put something aside or lay it out at interest.

ᵃ...ᵃ: R, M: 'sont produittes'
ᵇ...ᵇ: R, M: 'meme troc'
ᶜ...ᶜ: R, M: 'massons Manoeuvres, menuisiers'
ᵈ...ᵈ: R, M: 'Correspond necessairement a'
ᵉ...ᵉ: R, M: 'il faut aux marchands et entrepreneurs du bas detail'
ᶠ...ᶠ: R, M: missing
ᵍ...ᵍ: R, M: 'Il ny a qu'En Cas quil eut pû mettre quelque chose a Costé ou a interest ou il puisse se Contenter du billet:'

i. E308 to E310 do not have a direct counterpart in D. They are in fact a deviation from what was said in E307 to be the next thing to be considered, i.e. factors that slow down circulation. These are addressed from E311 onwards, where the deviation is concluded with 'tout cela présupposé'. **308**

ii. V308b is difficult to read in R. While in M it is unthinkingly rendered as 'le meme troc', the editor of the print version has what is surely the intended meaning of 'small payments'. A very similar case is V575a. Cf. C297ii.

309 |9| La consommation des habitans d'un Etat ᵃn'est, dans un sens, uniquement que pour leur nourriture. Le logement, le vêtement, les meubles, &c. correspondent à la nourriture des Ouvriers qui y ont travaillé; & dans les Villes tout le boire & le manger ne se paie nécessaire-[191]ment qu'avec de l'argent effectif.ᵃ Dans les familles des propriétaires, en Ville, le manger se paie tous les jours ou toutes les semaines; le vin dans leurs familles se paie toutes les semaines ou tous les mois; ᵇles chapeaux, les bas, les souliers, &c.ᵇ se paient ordinairement avec de l'argent effectif, au moins ils correspondent à de l'argent comptant par rapport aux Ouvriers qui y ont travaillé. Toutes les sommes qui servent à faire de gros paiemens sont divisées, distribuées & répandues nécessairement en petits paiemens, pour correspondre à la subsistance des Ouvriers, des Valets, ᶜ&c.ᶜ, & toutes ces petites sommes sont aussi nécessairement ramassées & réunies par les bas Entrepreneurs & par les Détailleurs qui sont emploïés à la subsistance des habitans, pour faire de gros paiemens lorsqu'ils achetent les denrées des Fer-[192]miers. Un Cabaretier à bierre ramasse ᵈpar sols & par livres,ᵈ les sommes qu'il paie au Brasseur, & celui-ci ᵉs'en sert pour païerᵉ tous les grains & les matériaux qu'il tire de la Campagne. On ne sauroit rien imaginer de ce qu'on achete à prix d'argent dans un État, comme meubles, marchandises, &c. dont la valeur ne corresponde à la subsistance de ceux qui y ont travaillé.

310 |10| La circulation dans les Villes est conduite par des Entrepreneurs, & correspond toujours, directement ou indirectement, à la subsistance des Valets, des Ouvriers, ᵃ&cᵃ. Il n'est pas concevable qu'elle puisse se faire dans le bas détail sans argent effectif. Les billets peuvent servir de jettons dans les gros paiemens pour quelque intervalle de tems; mais lorsqu'il faut distribuer & répandre les grosses sommes dans le troc du menu, [193] comme ᵇil en fautᵇ toujours plutôt ou ᶜplûtardᶜ dans le courant de la circulation d'une Ville, les billets n'y peuvent pas servir, & il faut de l'argent effectif.

The consumption of the Inhabitants of a State is, in a sense, entirely for Food. Lodging, Clothing, Furniture, etc. correspond to the Food of the Men who have worked upon them; and in the Cities all Drink and Food are of necessity paid for in hard cash. In the Families of Landowners in the City food is paid for every day or every week: Wine in their families is paid for every week or every month; Hats, Stockings, Shoes, etc. are ordinarily paid for in actual money, at least the payments correspond to cash for the Men who have worked upon them. All the sums which serve to pay large amounts are divided, distributed, and spread in small payments corresponding to the maintenance of the Workmen, Menservants, etc. and all these sums are necessarily collected and reunited by the Undertakers and Retailers who are employed on the subsistence of the Inhabitants to make large payments when they buy the products of the Farmers. An Ale-house keeper collects by sols and livres the sums he pays to the Brewer, who uses them to pay for all the grain and materials he buys from the Country. One cannot imagine anything is bought for ready money in a State, like Furniture, Merchandise, etc. the value of which does not correspond to the maintenance of those who have worked upon it.

Circulation in the Cities is carried out by Undertakers and always corresponds directly or indirectly to the subsistence of the Menservants, Workmen, etc. It is not conceivable that it can be effected in small detail without cash. Notes may serve as counters in large payments for a certain time; but when the large sums come to be distributed and spread into small transactions, as is always the case sooner or later in the course of circulation in a City, Notes cannot serve the purpose and cash is needed.

[a]...[a]: R, M: 'N'est uniquement que pour le Boire et Le manger dans un Sens. Les Lits, maisons Habillements &c correspondent au boire et au manger des ouvriers qui y ont travaillez, et dans les villes le boire et le manger Correspondent Necessairement a de l'argent effectif'
[b]...[b]: R, M: 'Les Chapeaux bas, souliers, habits'
[c]...[c]: R, M: 'et entrepreneurs'
[d]...[d]: R, M: 'par liard sols et livre'
[e]...[e]: R, M: 'en paye'

[a]...[a]: R, M: 'et entrepreneurs'
[b]...[b]: R, M: 'il se fait'
[c]...[c]: R, M, 1756 a, b, 1769: 'plus tard'

309 i. The discussion in E309 is somewhat reminiscent of D284.
ii. For V309a see C275i.
iii. The *liard* (mentioned in V309d) was a small bronze coin introduced in 1654, worth three *deniers*. There were 12 *deniers* to a *sou* and 20 *sols* to a *livre*. While the *denier*, *sou* and *livre* were units of account, the *liard* was one of many units of payment, i.e. actual coins. For other occurrences of the *liard* see E229 and E478.

310 For the expression '*le troc de menu*' in E310 see C297ii.

311 |11| Tout cela présupposé: tous les ordres d'un Etat, qui ont de l'œconomie, épargnent, & tiennent ᵃhorsᵃ de la circulation, de petites sommes d'argent comptant, ᵇjusqu'à ce qu'ils en aient suffisamment pour les mettreᵇ à intérêts ou à profit.

|| Provident saving people, of all ranks and orders, lay up money, some to enable them to marry, some to give portions to their children, and all against an evil day; and this money they keep up till it makes a sum fit to bring them an interest.

312 |12| Plusieurs gens avares & craintifs enterrent & reserrent toujours de l'argent effectif pendant des intervalles de tems assez considérables

Several covetous and fearful people lay up and bury money:

313 |13| Plusieurs Propriétaires, Entrepreneurs, & autres, gardent toujours quelqu'argent comptant dans leurs poches ou dans leurs caisses, contre les cas imprévus, & pour n'être point à sec. Si un ᵃSeigneurᵃ a remarqué que pendant l'espace d'un an, il ne s'est [194] jamais vu moins de vingt louis dans sa poche, on peut dire que cette poche à tenu vingt louis hors de la circulation pendant l'année. On n'aime pas à dépenser jusqu'au dernier sou, on est bien aise de n'être pas dégarni tout-à-fait, & de recevoir un nouveau renfort ᵇavant que deᵇ païer, même une dette, de l'argent que l'on a.

314 |14| Le Bien des Mineurs & des Plaideurs est souvent déposé en argent comptant, & retenu hors de la circulation.

the money and estates of minors and pleading parties, deposited in the hands of the lawyers, make no small sum;

Higgs Translation (H)	Variations and Errata (V)	Comments (C)

All this being presupposed, all the classes in a State who practice some oeconomy, save and keep out of circulation small amounts of cash till they have enough to invest at interest or profit.

[a]...[a]: R, M: 'ordre'
[b]...[b]: R, M: 'Jusqua cequil y ayt de quoy le mettre'

D311, but not E311, mentions **311** providing for marriage as one of the motives for saving. This saving also figures in E85 (but not D85). The motive of saving 'against an evil day' is the same as '*contre les cas imprévus*' in E313.

Many miserly and timid people bury and hoard cash for considerable periods.

312

Many Landowners, Undertakers and others, always keep some cash in their pockets or safes against unforeseen emergencies and not to be run out of money. If a gentleman makes it his remark that he never had less than 20 louis in his pocket throughout the whole year, it may be said that this pocket has kept 20 louis out of circulation for a year. One does not like to spend up to the last sou, one is glad not be completely denuded, and to receive a new instalment before paying even a debt with the money one has.

[a]...[a]: R: '~~seigneur~~ proprietaire' (written above crossed out word)
[b]...[b]: R, M: 'auant de'

The example of the gentleman **313** keeping 20 *louis* also figures in D317.

The capital of Minors and of Suitors is often deposited in cash and kept out of circulation.

314

315 |15| Outre les gros paiemens qui passent par les mains des Fermiers dans les ᵃquatre termesᵃ de l'année, il s'en fait plusieurs autres, d'Entrepreneurs à Entrepreneurs dans les mêmes termes, aussi bien que dans des tems différens, des Emprunteurs aux ᵇPrêteursᵇ d'argent. Toutes ces sommes sont ramassées du troc du menu, y sont répandues de [195] nouveau, & reviennent tôt ou tard au Fermier; mais elles semblent demander un argent effectif plus considérable pour la circulation, que si ces gros paiemens se faisoient dans des tems différens de ceux auxquels les Fermiers sont païés de leurs denrées.

to which it may be added, that not only several proprietors, but also several undertakers, servants, and workmen, have always some money, more or less, in their hands, which are never so empty but that a part of the old money still remains, after they have received the new.

316 |16| ᵃAu reste il y aᵃ une si grande variété dans les différens ᵇOrdresᵇ des habitans de l'Etat, ᶜ&ᶜ dans la circulation d'argent effectif qui y correspond, qu'il semble impossible de rien statuer de précis ou d'exact dans la proportion de l'argent qui suffit pour la circulation; & je n'ai produit tant d'exemples & d'inductions que pour faire comprendre que ᵈje ne me suisᵈ pas bien éloigné de la vérité dans ma supposition, "que l'argent effectif nécessaire à la circulation de l'État correspond à-peu-près à la valeur du tiers de toutes [196] les rentes ᵉannuellesᵉ des propriétaires de terres." Lorsque les Propriétaires ont une rente ᶠqui fait laᶠ moitié du produit, ou plus que le tiers, il faut d'avantage d'argent effectif pour la circulation, ᵍtout autres choses étant d'ailleurs égalesᵍ. Lorsqu'il y a une grande confiance des Banques, & des trocs par évaluation, une moindre quantité d'argent pourroit suffire, de même que quand le train de la circulation peut être acceleré en quelqu'autre maniere. Mais je ferai voir dans la suite que les Banques publiques n'apportent pas tant d'avantages qu'on le croit communément.

317   It is very difficult to make an estimate of such articles, but they sufficiently prove, in general, that a considerable sum of the circulating money in a state may be esteemed to lie always without motion. If a gentleman makes it his remark that he never has less money in his hands than 20 *l.* at any time through the whole year, it is plain he might have kept the same individual 20 *l.* by him without motion at all that year; and that so much may be esteemed to have lain by without circulation. It also happens that several large payments are made between undertakers, as well as at the terms farmers pay their rents, though these may very well be made out of the money required for the circulation of the last two rents.

|| Upon the whole; I should think my conjecture, from what has been said under the article CASH and here, is not very wide; *viz. That the money which carries on the whole circulation of a state is near the quantity of one-third part of all the annual rents of the proprietors of the land; where the proprietors have one half or two thirds of the produce of the land, and where the circulation is not much helped by barters and by evaluation, the quantity of money must certainly be greater.*

Beside the large payments which pass through the hands of the Farmers in the quarterly terms of the year there are many others from one Undertaker to another in the same terms, and others at different times from Borrowers to Lenders of money. All these sums are collected in retail trade, are spread abroad anew and come back sooner or later to the Farmer: but they seem to require a more considerable amount of cash for circulation than if these large payments were made in different times from those when the Farmers are paid for their produce.

In fine there is so great a variety in the different orders of the Inhabitants of the State and in the corresponding circulation of actual money, that it seems impossible to lay down anything precise or exact as to the proportion of money sufficient for the circulation. I have adduced so many examples and inductions only to make it clear that I am not far out of the truth in my conclusion "that the actual money necessary for the circulation of the State corresponds nearly to the value of the third of all the annual Rents of the Landlords." When the Landlords have a Rent which amounts to half the produce or more than a third, a greater quantity of actual money is needed for circulation, other things being equal. When there is great confidence in the Banks and in book credits less money will suffice, as also when the rapidity of circulation is accelerated in any other way. But I shall shew later that public banks do not afford so many advantages as is usually supposed.

Variations and Errata (V)

a...a: R, M: 'quatres térmes et saisons'
b...b: R: 'porteurs'; (M: 'preteurs')

a...a: R, M: 'Il y a apres tout'
b...b: R, M: 'Rangs et Ordres'
c...c: missing in 1756b and 1769
d...d: R,M: 'je ne suis'
e...e: 1769: 'naturelles'
f...f: R, M: 'de la valleur de'
g...g: R, M: '(Touttes autres Choses etant egales) que'; 1756 a,b, 1769: 'toutes autres choses étant d'ailleurs égales'

Comments (C)

315 The arguments in E315 and D315 are not identical, but both appear to describe a 'transactions demand' for money that is due to a lack of synchronisation between payments and receipts. This argument is strongly reminiscent of Locke, *Some Considerations* (1692: 33–34).

316 i. The conclusion in D316 (and D317) that the amount of money in circulation is a third of annual rents is a repetition of the view expressed in E/D285.

ii. For other occurrences of the '*autres choses étant égale*' and equivalent expressions, see C49ii.

317 i. D317 combines (and perhaps gives a little development to) the arguments of E316 and E313.

ii. The reference to the *Dictionary* entry 'Cash' is to the fragment reproduced in D256 to D295.

iii. For the remark about places where farmers pay half or two thirds of their income to land owners, cf. E/D266.

iv. After D317 the *Dictionary* entry 'Circulation' ends.

318   [197] **CHAPITRE** ^aV^a.

De l'inégalité de la circulation de l'argent effectif, dans un Etat.

319 |1| La Ville fournit toujours à la Campagne plusieurs marchandises, & les propriétaires de terres qui ^arésident^a dans la Ville, y doivent toujours recevoir environ le tiers du produit de leurs terres: ainsi la Campagne ^bdoit^b à la Ville plus de la moitié du produit des terres. Cette dette passeroit toujours la moitié, si tous les propriétaires résidoient dans la Ville; mais comme plusieurs des moins considérables demeurent à la Campagne, je suppose que la balance ^c, ou la dette,^c qui revient continuellement de la Campagne à la Ville, est égale à la moitié du produit [198] des terres, & que cette balance se paie dans la Ville par la moitié des denrées de la Campagne, qu'on y transporte, ^d& dont le prix de la vente est emploïé à païer cette dette.^d

320 |2| Mais toutes les Campagnes d'un Etat ou d'un Roïaume doivent une balance constante à la Capitale, tant pour les rentes des propriétaires les plus considérables qui y font leur résidence, que pour les taxes de l'Etat même, ou de la Couronne, dont la plus grande partie se consomment dans la Capitale. Toutes les Villes provinciales doivent aussi à la Capitale une balance constante, soit pour l'Etat, sur les Maisons ou sur la consommation, soit pour les ^amarchandises différentes^a qu'elles tirent de la Capitale. Il arrive aussi que plusieurs particuliers & propriétaires, qui résident dans les Villes provinciales, vont passer quelques [199] tems dans la Capitale, soit pour leur plaisir, ou pour le jugement de leur Procès en dernier ressort, soit qu'ils y envoient leurs enfans pour ^bleur donner^b une éducation à la mode. ^cPar conséquent toutes ces dépenses,^c qui se font dans la Capitale, se tirent des Villes provinciales.

321 |3| On peut donc dire que toutes les Campagnes & toutes les Villes d'un Etat doivent ^aconstamment & annuellement^a une balance, ou dette, à la Capitale. Or comme tout cela se paie en argent, il est ^bcertain^b que les Provinces doivent toujours des sommes considérables à la Capitale; car les denrées & marchandises que les Provinces envoient à la Capitale s'y vendent pour de l'argent, & ^cde^c cet argent on paie la dette ou balance en question.

Chapter V

Of the inequality of the circulation of hard money in a State

ª...ª: R, M: '5'

There is no counterpart for this chapter in **318** D or A. Higgs (1931, Appendix) indicates that the entry 'Coin' of the *Universal Dictionary* contains fragments of *Essai* II, v (and iv), but this is a printing error and should have been *Essai* III, iv and v. (see below D570ff.). For speculation that Postlethwayt at some point intended to include a fragment corresponding to E II, v in the entry, 'Silver', see C434.

The City always supplies various merchandises to the Country, and the Landowners who reside in the City should always receive there about a third of the produce of their Land. The Country thus owes to the City more than half the produce of the Land. This debt would always exceed one half if all Landowners lived in the City, but as several of the least important live in the Country I suppose that the balance or debt which continually returns from the Country to the City is equal to half the produce of the Land and is paid in the City by half the products of the Country transported to it and sold to pay this debt.

ª...ª: R, M: 'demeurent'   **319**
ᵇ...ᵇ: R, M: 'doit toujours'
ᶜ...ᶜ: R, M: missing
ᵈ...ᵈ: R, M: pour y etre
Vendue et employee a payer
La dette'

But all the Countryside of a State or Kingdom owes a constant balance to the Capital, as well for the Rents of the more considerable Landowners who reside there as for the taxes of the State or Crown, most of which are spent in the Capital. All the provincial Cities owe a constant balance to the Capital, either for the State, upon houses or consumption, or for the different commodities which they draw from the Capital. It happens also that several individuals and Landowners who live in the provincial Cities go to spend some time in the Capital, for pleasure, or for the judgment of their Lawsuits in final appeal, or because they send their children thither for a fashionable education. Consequently all these expenses incurred in the Capital are drawn from the provincial Cities.

ª...ª: R: 'marchandises de marbres manufactures'; M: 'marchandises de marbre'
ᵇ...ᵇ: R, M: 'prendre'
ᶜ...ᶜ: 'Consequemment telle depence'

In R the **320** strange phrase '*marchandises de marbres*' ('marble commodities') is corrected with '*manufactures*' written above the crossed-out word. M copies the uncorrected expression and E makes the still awkward phrase less specific.

It may therefore be said that all the Countryside and all the Cities of a State owe regularly and annually a balance or debt to the Capital. But as it is all paid in money it is evident that the Provinces always owe considerable sums to the Capital; for the products and commodities which the Provinces send to the Capital are sold there for money, and with this money the debt or balance in question is paid.

ª...ª: R, M: 'constamment'   **321**
ᵇ...ᵇ: R, M: 'vrai'
ᶜ...ᶜ: R, M: 'avec'

322 |4| Supposons maintenant que la circulation de l'argent est égale dans les Provinces & dans la Ca-[200]pitale, tant par rapport à la quantité de l'argent, que par rapport à la vîtesse de ᵃsaᵃ circulation. La balance sera d'abord envoïée à la Capitale en espece, & cela diminuera la quantité de l'argent dans les Provinces & l'augmentera dans la Capitale, & par conséquent les denrées & marchandises seront plus cheres dans la Capitale que dans les Provinces, par rapport à la plus grande abondance de l'argent dans la Capitale. La différence des prix dans la Capitale & dans les Provinces doit païer les frais & les risques des voitures, ᵇautrement on continuera de transporter les especes à la Capitale pour le paiement de la balance, & cela durera jusqu'à ce que la différence des prix dans la Capitale & dans les Provinces vienne à niveau des frais & des risques des voitures.ᵇ Alors les Marchands ᶜouᶜ Entrepreneurs des Bourgs ache-[201]teront ᵈà bas prix les denrées des Villages, & ᵈ les feront voiturer à la Capitale pour les y vendre à un plus haut prix; & cette différence des prix paiera nécessairement l'entretien des ᵉchevaux & des Valetsᵉ, & le profit de l'Entrepreneur, sans quoi il cesseroit ses entreprises.

323 |5| Il résultera de-là que le prix des denrées d'égale bonté sera toujours plus haut dans les Campagnes qui sont plus près de la Capitale, que dans celles qui en sont loin, à proportion des frais & risques des voitures; &que les Campagnes adjaçentes aux Mers ᵃ& Rivieresᵃ qui communiquent avec la Capitale, ᵇtirerontᵇ un meilleur prix de leurs denrées, à proportion, ᶜque celles quiᶜ en sont éloignées (tout autres choses restant égales), parceque les frais des voitures ᵈd'eauᵈ sont moins considérables que ceux des voitures par terre. D'un autre côté [202] les denrées & les petites marchandises qu'on ne peut pas consommer dans la Capitale, soit qu'elles n'y soient pas propres, soit qu'on ne les y puisse transporter à cause de leur volume, ou ᵉparcequ'elles seᵉ gâteroient en chemin, seront infiniment à meilleur marché dans les Campagnes ᶠ& les Provincesᶠ éloignées, que dans la Capitale, par rapport à la quantité d'argent qui circule pour cela, qui est considérablement plus petite dans les Provinces éloignées.

Higgs Translation (H)	Variations and Errata (V)	Comments (C)

Suppose now that the circulation of money in the provinces and in the Capital is equal both in quantity of money and speed of circulation. The balance will be first sent to the Capital in cash and this will diminish the quantity of money in the Provinces and increase it in the Capital, and consequently the raw material and commodities will be dearer in the Capital than in the Provinces, on account of the greater abundance of money in the Capital. The difference of prices in the Capital and in the Provinces must pay for the costs and risks of transport, otherwise cash will be sent to the Capital to pay the balance and this will go on till the prices in the Capital and the Provinces come to the level of these costs and risks. Then the Merchants or Undertakers of the Market Towns will buy at a low price the products of the Villages and will have them carried to the Capital to be sold there at a higher price: and this difference of price will necessarily pay for the upkeep of the Horses and Menservants and the profit of the Undertaker, or else he would cease his enterprise.

[a]...[a]: R: 'la'
[b]...[b]: R, M: missing
[c]...[c]: R, M: 'et'
[d]...[d]: R, M: 'Les Denrées du Village a bas prix'
[e]...[e]: R, M: 'Chevaux voitures Vallets'

Arguably, the further explanation, which is missing from the manuscript versions (V322b), does not fit very well. According to Cantillon's reasoning, sending more cash to the capital would further increase the differences in prices already assumed to exist, rather than reducing them to margins necessary to cover risks and costs of transport.

322

It will follow from this that the price of raw Produce of equal quality will always be higher in the Country places which are nearest the Capital than in those more distant in proportion to the costs and risks of transport; and that the countries adjacent to Seas and Rivers flowing into the Capital will get a better price for their Produce in proportion than those which are distant (other things being equal) because water transport is less expensive than Land transport. On the other hand the Products and small wares which cannot be consumed in the Capital, because they are not suitable or cannot be sent thither on account of their bulk, or because they would be spoiled on the way, will be infinitely cheaper in the Country and distant Provinces than in the Capital, owing to the amount of money circulating for them which is much smaller in the distant Provinces.

[a]...[a]: 1756b, 1769: '& aux Riviéres'
[b]...[b]: R, M: 'tirera'
[c]...[c]: R, M: 'que celles qui'
[d]...[d]: R, M: 'par eau'
[e]...[e]: R, M: 'quelles se'
[f]...[f]: R, M: 'et Provinces'

323

324 |6| C'est ainsi que les œufs frais, [a]que le gibier, le beurre frais, le bois[a] à brûler, &c. seront ordinairement [b]beaucoup à meilleur marché[b] dans les Provinces de [c]Poitou, qu'à Paris[c]; au lieu que le [d]blés, les bœufs & les chevaux[d] ne seront plus chers à Paris, que de la différence des frais & des risques de l'envoi & des entrées de la Ville.

325 [203]|7| Il seroit aisé de faire une infinité d'inductions de même nature, pour justifier par l'expérience la nécessité d'une inégalité [a]de la circulation d'argent[a] dans les différentes Provinces d'un grand État ou Roïaume & démontrer que cette inégalité est toujours relative à la balance ou dette qui appartient à la Capitale.

326 |8| Si nous supposons que la balance due à la Capitale [a]aille au quart[a] du produit des terres de toutes les Provinces de l'Etat, la meilleure disposition qu'on puisse faire des terres, [b]ce[b] seroit d'emploïer les Campagnes voisines de la Capitale dans les especes de denrées qu'on ne sauroit tirer des Provinces éloignées sans beaucoup de frais ou de déchet. C'est en effet ce qui se pratique toujours. Le prix des Marchés de la Capitale servant de regle aux Fermiers pour l'emploi des terres [c]à tel ou tel usage, ils em[204]ploient les plus proches, lorsqu'elles s'y trouvent propres[c], en potagers, en prairies, &c.

327 |9| Mais on devroit ériger dans les Provinces éloignées, autant qu'il seroit possible, les Manufactures [a]de drap, de linge, de dentelles, &c.;[a] & dans le voisinage des Mines de Charbon, ou des Forêts, qui sont inutiles par leur éloignement, celles des outils [b]de fer, d'étaim, de cuivre[b], &c. Par ce moïen, on pourroit envoïer les marchandises toutes faites à la Capitale avec bien moins de frais de transport, [c]que si l'on envoïoit & les matériaux[c] pour les faire travailler dans la Capitale même, & la subsistance des ouvriers [d]qui les y travailleroient[d]. On épargneroit une infinité [e]de chevaux & valets de voiture,[e] qui seroient mieux emploïés pour le bien de l'État: les terres serviroient à maintenir sur les lieux des ouvriers [f]& des artisans[f] uti[205]les; & on retrancheroit [g]une multitude[g] de chevaux qui ne servent qu'à des voitures, sans nécessité [h]. Ainsi[h] les terres éloignées en rapporteroient des rentes plus considérables aux propriétaires, & l'inégalité de la circulation des Provinces & de la Capitale seroit mieux proportionnée & moins considérable.

So it is that new laid eggs, game, fresh butter, wood fuel, etc. will generally be much cheaper in the district of Poitou, whilst Corn, Cattle and Horses will be dearer at Paris only by the difference of the cost and risk of carriage and the dues for entering the City.	ᵃ...ᵃ: R, M: 'Gibier Beure frais bois' ᵇ...ᵇ: 1756b, 1769: 'à beaucoup meilleur marché' ᶜ...ᶜ: R, M: 'Poitou Limosin qua Paris' ᵈ...ᵈ: R, M: 'Les Boeufs et Chevaux'	**324**
It would be easy to make an infinite number of inductions of the same kind to justify by experience the necessity of an inequality in the circulation of money in the different Provinces of a great State or Kingdom, and to shew that this inequality is always relative to the balance or debt which belongs to the Capital.	ᵃ...ᵃ: R, M: 'd'argent'	**325**
If we suppose that the balance due to the Capital amounts to one fourth of the produce of the Land of all the Provinces of the State the best use that can be made of the Land would be to employ the Country bordering on the Capital to produce the kinds of produce which could not be drawn from distant Provinces without much expense or deterioration. This is in fact what always takes place. The market Prices of the Capital serving as a standard for the Farmers to employ the Land for such or such a purpose they use the nearest, when suitable, for market gardens, pasture, etc.	ᵃ...ᵃ: R, M: 'va a un quart' ᵇ...ᵇ: M: missing ᶜ...ᶜ: R, M: 'a tels ou tels usages on employe les terres Les plus proches qui se trouvent propres'	**326**
So far as possible Manufactures of Cloth, Linen, Lace, etc. ought to be set up in the remote Provinces; and, in the neighbourhood of Coal Mines or Forests, which are useless by their distance, Manufactures of tools of Iron, Tin, Copper, etc. In this way finished manufactures could be sent to the Capital with much less cost of carriage than the raw materials to be worked up in the Capital and the subsistence of the artisans who would work upon them there. This would save a quantity of horses and waggoners who would be better employed for the benefit of the State. The Land would serve to maintain on the spot workmen and useful mechanics; and a multitude of horses would be saved who serve only upon unnecessary transport. In this way the distant Lands would yield higher Rents to the Proprietors and the inequality of the Circulation of the Provinces and the Capital would be better proportioned and less considerable.	ᵃ...ᵃ: M, R: 'de drap Linge Dentelles' ᵇ...ᵇ: R, M: 'de fer Etain Cuivre' ᶜ...ᶜ: R, M: 'qu'on y pouroit envoyer des Materiaux' ᵈ...ᵈ: R, M: 'pour y travailler' ᵉ...ᵉ: R, M: 'de Chevaux de valets et de Voiture' ᶠ...ᶠ: R, M: 'et artisans' ᵍ...ᵍ: R, M: 'une Infinité' ʰ...ʰ: R, M: 'par ce moyen'	**327**

328 |10| Cependant, pour ériger ainsi des Manufactures, il faut non-seulement beaucoup d'encouragement & de fond, mais encore le moïen de s'assurer d'une consommation réguliere & constante, soit dans la Capitale même, soit dans quelques Païs étrangers, dont les retours ^apuissent servir à la Capitale, pour faire les paiemens des marchandises qu'elle tire de ces Païs étrangers, ou pour les retours d'argent en nature^a.

329 |11| Lorsqu'on érige ces Manufactures, ^aon n'arrive pas^a d'abord [206] à la perfection. Si quelque autre Province en a, qui soient plus belles, à meilleur marché, ou dont le voisinage de la Capitale, ou la commodité d'une Mer ou d'une Riviere qui y communiquent, en facilite considérablement le transport, les Manufactures en question n'auront pas de réussite. Il faut examiner ^btoutes ces circonstances dans l'érection^b des Manufactures. Je ne me suis pas proposé d'en traiter dans cet Essai, mais seulement d'insinuer qu'on devroit, autant qu'il se peut, ériger des Manufactures dans les Provinces éloignées de la Capitale, pour les rendre plus considérables & pour y produire une circulation d'argent moins inégale à proportion de celle de la Capitale.

330 |12| Car lorsqu'une Province éloignée n'a point de Manufacture, & ne produit que des denrées ordinaires ^asans avoir communi-[207]cation par eau avec la Capitale ou avec la Mer^a, il est étonnant combien l'argent y est rare, à proportion de celui qui circule dans la Capitale, & combien peu de revenus les plus belles terres produisent ^bau Prince, & aux Propriétaires qui résident dans la Capitale.^b

331 |13| Les vins de Provence & de Languedoc, envoïés ^aau tour^a du Détroit de Gibraltar dans le Nord, par une navigation longue & pénible, & après avoir passé par les mains de plusieurs Entrepreneurs, rendent bien peu aux Propriétaires de Paris.

332 |14| Cependant il faut nécessairement que ces Provinces éloignées envoient leurs denrées, malgré tous les désavantages des voitures & de l'éloignement, ou à la Capitale, ou ailleurs, soit dans l'État, soit dans les Païs étrangers, ^aafin que les retours fassent le paiement^a de la balance due à [208] la Capitale. Au lieu que ces denrées seroient en grande partie consommées sur les lieux, si on avoit des ouvrages ou Manufactures pour païer cette balance, & en ce cas le nombre des habitans seroit bien plus considérable.

Higgs Translation (H)	Variations and Errata (V)	Comments (C)

Nevertheless to set up Manufactures in this way would need not only much encouragement and capital but also some way to ensure a regular and constant demand, either in the Capital itself or in foreign Countries, whose exports in return may be of service to the Capital, to pay for the merchandise which it draws from these Foreign Countries or for the return of silver in kind.

ᵃ...ᵃ: R, M: 'puissent servir de payement dans la Capitalle, soit par les marchandises de Ce Pays etranger quelle Consomme soit par des retours d'argent en Nature'

For other places **328** where the desirability of setting up manufactories is discussed, see C194.

When these Manufactures are set up perfection is not at once attained. If some other Province have them better or cheaper or owing to the vicinity of the Capital or the convenience of a Sea or River communication have their transport considerably facilitated, the Manufactures in question will have no success. All these circumstances have to be considered in setting up a Manufactory. I have not proposed to treat of them in this Essay, but only to suggest that so far as practicable Manufactures should be set up in Provinces distant from the Capital, to render them more considerable and to bring about there a circulation of money less disproportionate to that of the Capital.

ᵃ...ᵃ: R: 'on arrive pas'; (M: 'on n'arrive pas')
ᵇ...ᵇ: R, M: 'toutes Les Circonstances d'une érection'

For the importance **329** of the availability of water transport, see also E39.

For when a distant Province has no Manufactory and produces only ordinary raw materials without water communication with the Capital or the ocean, it is astonishing how scarce money is there compared with that which circulates in the Capital and how little the best Lands produce to the Prince and to the Proprietors who reside in the Capital.

ᵃ...ᵃ: R, M: 'sans avoir aucune Comunication deau bien commode avec la Capitalle ou la mer'
ᵇ...ᵇ: R, M: 'aux proprietaires qui resident dans La Capitale et au Prince;'

330

The wines of Provence and of Languedoc sent to the North round the Straits of Gibraltar by long and difficult Navigation, after having passed through the hands of several Dealers yield very little to the Paris owners of the Land.

ᵃ...ᵃ: R, M: 'autour'

The high costs of **331** transporting wine by land are also mentioned in E165.

It is however necessary that these distant Provinces should send their produce, in spite of all the drawbacks of transport and distance to the Capital or elsewhere either in the State or in foreign Countries in order that the returns should provide for payment of the balance due to the Capital. But these products would be mostly consumed on the spot if there were works or Factories to pay this balance, in which case the number of inhabitants would be much larger.

ᵃ...ᵃ: R, M:'pour faire par les retours Le payement'

332

333 |15| Lorsque la Province ne paie la balance que de ses denrées, qui produisent si peu dans la Capitale par rapport aux frais de l'éloignement, il est visible que le Propriétaire, qui réside dans la Capitale, donne le produit de beaucoup de terre dans sa Province, ªpour recevoir peu dans la Capitale.ª Cela provient de l'inégalité de l'argent; & cette inégalité vient de la balance constante que la Province doit à la Capitale.

334 |16| Présentement, si un Etat ou un Roïaume, qui fournit ªd'ouvrages de ses Manufactures tousª les Païs étrangers, fait tellement ce [209] commerce, qu'il tire tous les ans une balance constante d'argent de l'Etranger, la circulation y deviendra plus considérable que dans les Païs étrangers, l'argent y sera plus abondant & par conséquent la terre & le travail y deviendront insensiblement à plus haut prix. Cela fera que dans toutes les branches du commerce l'Etat en question échangera ᵇune plusᵇ petite quantité de terre & de travail avec l'Etranger, pour une plus grande, tant que ᶜcesᶜ circonstances dureront.

335 |17| Que si quelque Etranger réside dans l'Etat en question, il sera à-peu-près dans la même ªsituation & la même circonstance où est à Paris le Propriétaireª qui a ses terres dans les Provinces éloignées.

336 |18| ªLa France, depuis l'érection en 1646 des Manufactures de draps, & des autres ouvragesª qu'on y a faits ensuite, paroissoit [210] faire le commerce dont je viens de parler, au moins en partie. Depuis la décadence de la France, l'Angleterre s'en est mise en possession; & tous les États ne paroissent fleurissans que ᵇpar la part plus ou moins qu'ils y ontᵇ. L'inégalité de la circulation d'argent dans les différens États en constitue l'inégalité de puissance comparativement, toutes choses étant égales; & cette inégalité de circulation est toujours respective à la balance du commerce qui revient de l'Etranger.

337 |19| Il est aisé de juger par ce qui a été dit dans ce Chapitre, que l'estimation par les Taxes de la Dixme roïale, comme M. de Vauban l'a faite, ne sauroit être avantageuse ni pratiquable. Si on faisoit la taxe sur les terres en argent, à proportion des rentes des Propriétaires, cela seroit plus juste. ªMais je ne dois pas m'écarter de mon sujetª, pour fai-[211]re voir les inconveniens & l'impossibilité du plan de M. de Vauban.

When the Province pays the balance only with its produce which yields so little in the Capital having regard to the expenses of distance, it is evident that the Proprietor living in the Capital pays the Produce of much Land in the Country to receive little in the Capital. This arises from the inequality of Money, and this inequality is owing to the constant balance due from the Province to the Capital.

ᵃ...ᵃ: R: 'pour Recevoir peu Le produit de terrre dans La Capitalle'; M: 'pour recevoir peu'

333

At present if a State or Kingdom which supplies all Foreign countries with work of its own Manufacture does so much of this commerce that it draws every year a constant balance of money from abroad, the circulation will become more considerable there than in foreign countries, money will be more plentiful there, and consequently Land and Labour will gradually become dearer there. It will follow that in all the branches of commerce the State in question will exchange a smaller amount of Land and Labour with the Foreigner for a larger amount, so long as these circumstances continue.

ᵃ...ᵃ: R, M: d'ouvrages ou manufacture a tous'
ᵇ...ᵇ: R, M: 'une bien plus'
ᶜ...ᶜ: M: 'les'; (R: 'Ces' but unclearly written)

334

But if some Foreigner reside in the State in question he will be in about the same situation and circumstances as the Proprietor at Paris who has his Land in distant Provinces.

ᵃ...ᵃ: R, M: 'scituation et circonstance que le proprietaire a paris'

335

France, since the erection in 1646 of Manufactories of cloth and other works since set up, appeared to trade, at least in part, in the way described. Since the decay of France England has taken possession of this trade; and all States appear flourishing only by the larger or smaller part they have in it. The inequality of the circulation of Money in the different States constitutes the inequality of their respective power, other things being equal; and this inequality of circulation is always respective to the balance of Foreign Trade.

ᵃ...ᵃ: R, M: 'La France depuis son erection des manufactures des draps en 1646, et Les autres ouvrages et manufactures'
ᵇ...ᵇ: 1756b, 1769: 'par la part qu'ils y ont plus ou moins'

i. In 1646 Nicolas Cadeau obtained a royal patent for the manufacture of fine woollen cloth, after which he started his famous manufactory in Sedan. Also see E403 and D424.

ii. For other occurrences of '*toutes choses étant égales*' and equivalent expressions see C49ii.

336

It is easy to judge from what has been said in this Chapter that the assessment by Taxes of the Royal Tithe, made by M. de Vauban, would be neither advantageous nor practicable. If the taxes on Land were levied in Money proportionable to the rents of the Proprietors, it would be fairer. But I must not wander from my subject to show the inconvenience and impossibility of M. de Vauban's proposal.

ᵃ...ᵃ: R, M: 'mais mon sujet ne me permet pas de mEcarter'

This is the only reference to the writings of Sébastien Le Prestre, Seigneur de Vauban (1633–1707), who in his *La Dixme royale* of 1707 proposed a national tax in kind on all agricultural produce.

337

Essai (E)	Dictionary (D)	Analysis (A)

338
CHAPITRE ᵃVIᵃ.
De l'augmentation ᵇ& de la dimunitionᵇ de la quantité d'argent effectif dans un Etat.

[II 283] Of the INCREASE and DECREASE of the ACTUAL QUANTITY OF REAL OR HARD MONEY in a STATE

[51] **CHAP. XVI.** *Of the consequential Effect, which the Increase and Decrease of the current Coin of a Country, has on the Community.*

339 |1| Si l'on découvre des Mines d'or ou d'argent dans un Etat, & si l'on en tire des ᵃquantitésᵃ considérables de matieres, le Propriétaire de ces Mines, les Entrepreneurs, & tous ceux qui y travaillent, ne manqueront pas d'augmenter leurs dépenses à proportion des richesses & des profits qu'ils ᵇferontᵇ: ils prêteront aussi à intérêt les sommes d'argent qu'ils ont au-delà de ce qu'il faut pour leur dépense.

340 |2| Tout cet argent, tant prêté que dépensé, entrera dans la cir-[212]culation, & ne manquera pas de rehausser ᵃle prix des denrées & des marchandises dans tous les canaux de circulationᵃ où il entrera. L'augmentation de l'argent entraînera une augmentation de dépense, & cette augmentation de dépense entraînera une augmentation des prix du Marché dans les plus hautes années du troc, & par degré dans les plus basses.

341 |3| Tout le monde est d'accord que l'abondance de l'argent ou son augmentation dans le troc, enchérit le prix de toutes choses. La quantité d'argent qu'on a apportée de l'Amérique en Europe depuis deux siecles, justifie par experience cette vérité.

342 |4| M. ᵃLockeᵃ pose comme une Maxime fondamentale que la quantité des denrées ᵇ& des marchandisesᵇ, proportionnée à la quantité de l'argent, sert de regle au prix du Marché. J'ai tâ-[213]ché d'éclaircir son idée dans les Chapitres précédens : il a bien senti que l'abondance de l'argent enchérit toute chose, mais il n'a pas recherché comment cela se fait. La grande difficulté de cette recherche consiste à savoir par ᶜquelle voieᶜ & dans quelle proportion l'augmentation de l'argent hausse le prix des choses.

Chapter VI

Of the increase and decrease in the quantity of hard money in a State

^a...^a: R, M: '6e'
^b...^b: R, M: 'et diminution'

i. D338 is the start of a subsection in the entry 'Money' (II, 282–84), which appeared in issue 108 of the *Universal Dictionary*, first published around April or May 1754. It was the last issue to carry fragments from Cantillon's work.

ii. A338 follows after chapter XV in the *Analysis*, part of which is presented out of sequence in A416–A426. Cf. C288ii and C416ii.

338

If Mines of gold or silver be found in a State and considerable quantities of minerals drawn from them, the Proprietors of these Mines, the Undertakers, and all those who work there, will not fail to increase their expenses in proportion to the wealth and profit they make: they will also lend at interest the sums of money which they have over and above what they need to spend.

^a...^a: R: 'Cantites' replaced with 'quantites'
^b...^b: R , M: 'font'

i. The same case is considered in D366.

ii. D374 discusses the consequences of the possibility that the additional money is lent at interest in some more detail.

iii. The original misspelling of '*quantités*' in V339a may indicate dictation. Cf. C274iii.

339

All this money, whether lent or spent, will enter into circulation and will not fail to raise the price of products and merchandise in all the channels of circulation which it enters. Increased money will bring about increased expenditure and this will cause an increase of Market prices in the highest years of exchange and gradually in the lowest.

^a...^a: R, M: 'le prix de touttes les denrées et marchandises dans le Cours de circulation'

D368 has a similar discussion to E340.

340

Everybody agrees that the abundance of money or its increase in exchange, raises the price of everything. The quantity of money brought from America to Europe for the last two centuries justifies this truth by experience.

For other references to the influx of money from America, see C252.

341

M. Locke lays it down as a fundamental maxim that the quantity of produce and merchandise in proportion to the quantity of money serves as the regulator of Market price. I have tried to elucidate his idea in the preceding Chapters: he has clearly seen that the abundance of money makes everything dear, but he has not considered how it does so. The great difficulty of this question consists in knowing in what way and in what proportion the increase of money raises prices.

^a...^a: R, M: 'Lock'
^b...^b: R, M: 'et marchandises'
^c...^c: R, M: 'quel degré'

Locke's monetary views are also mentioned in E232, E237, and E238. For an alternative qualification of Locke's views, see D376. Cf. C376i and C249i.

342

343 |5| J'ai déja ªremarquéª qu'une accélération, ou une plus grande vîtesse, dans la circulation de l'argent du troc, vaut autant qu'une augmentation d'argent effectif, jusqu'à un certain degré. J'ai aussi remarqué ᵇque l'augmentation ou la diminution des prix d'un Marché éloigné,ᵇ soit dans l'Etat, soit chez l'Etranger, influe sur les prix actuels du Marché. ᶜD'un autre côté l'argent circule dans le détail, par un si grand nombre de canaux, qu'il semble impossible de ne pas le perdre de vue, attendu qu'aiant été amassé pour [214] faire de grosses sommes, il est distribué dans les petits ruisseaux du troc, & qu'ensuite il se retrouve accumulé peu-à-peu pour faire de gros paiemens.ᶜ Pour ces opérations il faut constamment échanger les monnoies d'or, d'argent & de cuivre, suivant la diligence de ce troc.ᵈ Il arrive aussi d'ordinaire qu'on ne s'apperçoit pas de l'augmentation ou de la diminution de l'argent effectif dans un Etat, parcequ'il s'écoule chez l'Etranger, ou qu'il est introduit dans l'État, par des voies & des proportions si insensibles, qu'il est impossible de savoir au juste la quantité qui entre dans l'Etat, ni celle qui en sort.ᵈ

344 |6| Cependant toutes ces opérations se passent sous nos yeux, & tout le monde y a part ªdirectementª. Ainsi je crois pouvoir hasarder ᵇquelques réflexionsᵇ sur cette matiere, encore que je ne [215] puisse pas en rendre compte, d'une maniere exacte & précise.

345 || Let us familiarly consider the land estate of a country, where the general circulation is carried on by 2000 ounces of silver: this money passes through several hands, and always returns into those of the undertakers, whom we suppose the proprietors of it.

|| Suppose fifteen Millions of Specie sufficient to circulate the Trade of *England*; this Money would roll backwards and [52] forwards amongst the Individuals of Society, in Barter and Exchange of the Land's Produce, and in its several Windings and Turnings, it fixes the Rents of Land, as also the Hire of Labour and Artizans.

I have already remarked that an acceleration or greater rapidity in circulation of money in exchange, is equivalent to an increase of actual money up to a point. I have also observed that the increase or decrease of prices in a distant Market, home or Foreign, influences the actual Market prices. On the other hand money flows in detail through so many channels that it seems impossible not to lose sight of it seeing that having been amassed to make large sums it is distributed in little rills of exchange, and then gradually accumulated again to make large payments. For these operations it is constantly necessary to change coins of gold, silver and copper according to the activity of exchange. It is also usually the case that the increase or decrease of actual money in a State is not perceived because it flows abroad, or is brought into the State, by such imperceptible means and proportions that it is impossible to know exactly the quantity which enters or leaves the State.

However all these operations pass under our eyes and everybody takes part in them. I may therefore venture to offer a few observations on the subject, even though I may not be able to give an account which is exact and precise.

[a]...[a]: R, M: 'dit'

[b]...[b]: R, M: 'que la possibilité ou Vue des prix des marchés éloigneé'

[c]...[c]: R, M: 'dun autre Costé Largent Circule dans un si grand nombre de mains ou Canneaux du troc quil semble Impossible de ne pas perdre de Vue dans touts Les detours quil fait attendu que toutes Les grosses sommes* sont nécessairement distribuées dans les petite Ruisseaux du Troc, et qu'ensuitte de Ces Petits Ruisseaux on laccumule peu a peu pour faire des payements de grosses sommes'

[d]...[d]: R: ,'Ainsi que d'ordinaire que l'augmentation ou diminution de largent effectif dans un etat est Insensible, quil sEcoule Chez Letranger ou il est introduit par des degrés si insensible quil N'est pas absolument possible de scavoir au juste Les quantités, qui entrent dans LEtat ny Celles qui en sortent'

[a]...[a]: R: 'directement ou indirectement'

[b]...[b]: 'quelques reflexions a Remarquer'

i. About the influence of distant markets on prices, see E247 and V238c. Cf. C238. Note that V343b differs from E343 by saying that market prices are influenced by 'the *possibility or view* of prices in distant markets'. Thus the *expectations* of prices in other markets may already affect actual market prices.

ii. For a similar account to E343, see D284, which also has the English equivalent for '*les petits ruisseaux du troc*'.

iii. At *(in V343c) M780 breaks off and the righthand column of that manuscript, with Mirabeau's commentary, starts extending over the full page.

343

344

i. D345 again picks up the numerical example, first introduced in D264 and modified in D287, where 2,000 ounces of silver are assumed to be circulating and a total annual land rent paid of 6,000.

ii. The assumption in D345 that the undertakers are the 'proprietors' of the money in circulation is also found in D263.

345

346

|| Let us likewise suppose that these undertakers have received 2000 ounces more for a present from Americans, so that each undertaker has double the quantity of money he had before, and that the quantity of money in all becomes 4000 ounces of silver.

|| Let it be again supposed, that these fifteen Millions of Money, by some Accident or other, was all of a sudden doubled and put in the Channels of Trade; the Money then circulating in *England* would be thirty Millions;

347 |7| J'estime en général qu'une augmentation d'argent effectif cause dans un Etat une augmentation proportionnée de consommation, qui produit par degrés l'augmentation des prix.

348 |8| Si l'augmentation ªde l'argent effectif vient des Minesª d'or ou d'argent ᵇqui se trouvent dans un Etatᵇ, le Propriétaire de ces Mines, les Entrepreneurs, les Fondeurs, les Affineurs,ᶜ& généralement tous ceux qui y travaillentᶜ, ne manqueront pas d'augmenter leurs dépenses à proportion de leurs gains. Ils consommeront dans leurs ménages ᵈplus de viande & plus de vin ou de bierreᵈ, qu'ils ne faisoient, ils s'accoutumeront à porter de meilleurs habits, de plus beau linge, ᵉà avoir des Maisons plus ornées, & d'autres commodités plus recherchées.ᵉ Par conséquent ils [216] donneront de l'emploi à plusieurs Artisans qui n'avoient pas auparavant tant d'ouvrages, & qui par la même raison augmenteront ᶠaussi leur dépenseᶠ; toute cette augmentation de dépense ᵍen viande, en vin, en laine, &c. diminueᵍ nécessairement la part des autres habitans de l'Etat ʰqui ne participent pas d'abord auxʰ richesses des Mines en question. Les altercations du Marché, ou la demande ⁱpour la viande, le vin, la laine, &c. étantⁱ plus forte qu'à l'ordinaire, ne manquera pas d'en hausser les prix. Ces hauts prix détermineront les Fermiers à emploïer d'avantage de terre pour les produire en une autre année: ces mêmes Fermiers profiteront de cette augmentation de prix, & augmenteront la dépense de leur Famille, comme les autres.

|| Each undertaker will endeavour to enlarge and augment the quantity of his business: so the farmer's commodities will grow dearer in the altercations, by the greater demand made by the undertakers: but, perhaps, this will not immediately double the price of things, because some of the farmers wil at first be satisfied with a greater price than usual, but afterwards the price will double in the altercations; each undertaker will desire to live better than he did before, since he has got his additional sum, and, consequently, he will consume in his family more wine and meat than usual; therefore wine and meat will grow proportionably dearer than bread; and the farmers will endeavour to have more of these kinds the next season, since they yield in proportion a better price than corn, and, consequently, the corn will become scarcer, and grow dearer also.

this sudden Increase of Cash, would increase a proportional Demand for Merchandize, as also for Labour and Industry, and consequently enhance their Price, as also that of all Sorts of Goods and Merchandize; and whenever Things got up double in Price to what they formerly went at, properly speaking, no one would suffer, but the Landholders; the Farmers would be Gainers during the Term of their Leases; but when these expired, the Landholders would double their Rents, and justly, as the Land's Produce sold at double to what it formerly yielded.

i. The idea that 'Americans' supply the precious metals **346** is also found in D263, although there the money is paid for (by savings in kind).

ii. Note that, while E348 assumes the additional money to be owned by miners first (a case which is considered in D366–D368 too, though more briefly), in D346 'undertakers' are the initial receivers of the additional sum of money. For its part, A346 does not indicate any particular social group that receives the additional money first.

347

I consider in general that an increase of actual money causes in a State a corresponding increase of consumption which gradually brings about increased prices.

If the increase of actual money comes from Mines of gold or silver in the State the Owner of these Mines, the Adventurers, the Smelters, Refiners, and all the other workers will increase their expenses in proportion to their gains. They will consume in their households more Meat, Wine, or Beer than before, will accustom themselves to wear better cloaths, finer linen, to have better furnished Houses and other choicer commodities. They will consequently give employment to several Mechanicks who had not so much to do before and who for the same reason will increase their expenses: all this increase of expense in Meat, Wine, Wool, etc. diminishes of necessity the share of the other inhabitants of the State who do not participate at first in the wealth of the Mines in question. The altercations of the Market, or the demand for Meat, Wine, Wool, etc. being more intense than usual, will not fail to raise their prices. These high prices will determine the Farmers to employ more Land to produce them in another year: these same Farmers will profit by this rise of prices and will increase the expenditure of their Families like the others.

a...a: R: 'de l'argent vient de Riches Mines'
b...b: R: 'dans Letat'
c...c: R: 'mineurs travailleurs de Touttes especes'
d...d: 1769: 'plus de viande, plus de vin & de biére'
e...e: 'et avoir des maisons et autres Commodites dune plus grande propreté Et Convenance'
f...f: R: 'un peu Leur depence a leur Tour'
g...g: R: 'en viande vin Laine &c. diminura'
h...h: R: 'qui ne se sentent pas dabord des'; 1769: qui ne participent d'abord'
i...i: R: ' pour La vin la laine &c est'

i. The long eighth paragraph in **348** the French text is here reproduced in E348 and E349. There are a number of similarities and some significant differences with D348–D349 and A348–A349. A is the least clear about the sequence of increases in prices of different products that results from the increase in the supply of money (i.e. the 'Cantillon effect'). This appears to be related to the fact that A346 does not specify which social group first received the additional money or on what kinds of goods they spend it. Instead there is an emphasis on the eventual outcome that a doubling in the amount of money in circulation will lead to the doubling in prices (similar to A250). There is, however, some mention in A348 of the initial suffering of the landowners, like in E/D349 and the fact that relative prices will only be restored 'in the Course of Time'.

ii. The passage starting from the beginning of E348 up to '*mêmes Etrangers*' in E354 is quoted in Pluquet (1786, 2, 316–20).

349 Ceux donc, qui souffriront de ᵃcette cherté, & de l'augmentationᵃ de consom-[217]mation, seront d'abord les Propriétaires des terres, pendant le terme de leurs Baux,ᵇpuis leursᵇ domestiques, & tous les ouvriers ou gens à gages fixes qui en entretiennent leur famille. Il faut que tous ceux-là diminuent leur dépense à proportion de la nouvelle consommation; ce qui en obligera un grand nombre à sortir de l'État pour chercher fortune ailleurs. Les Propriétaires en congédieront plusieurs, & il arrivera que les autres demanderont une augmentation de gages pour pouvoir subsister à leur ordinaire. Voilà à-peu-près comment une augmentation considérable d'argent par des Mines augmente la consommation; & en diminuant le nombre des habitans, entraîne une plus grande dépense parmi ceux qui restent.

|| This increase of consumption of the produce of land, which, on the footing now introduced, cannot maintain all the inhabitants, will make it necessary for some of them to seek their livelihood elsewhere. These will be chiefly turned away by the proprietor of land, who, having but 6000 ounces per annum for his estate, cannot maintain his family as before, since all commodities are grown dearer. The labourers and journeymen, remaining, not being able to subsist upon their usual wages, must have an augmentation, as well as the remaining servants of the proprietor: and, in all the changes this new quantity of money produces, the farmers seem to be the only gainers, and the proprietors the only losers. The undertakers, who buy their commodities and materials dearer, will be for turning the loss upon the consumers: but, as they are themselves consumers with respect to one another, they will find the expences in their families increase beyond the additional consumption of meat, wine, &c. they intended; and, when the money introduced into barter shall gradually have doubled the price of everything, they will be obliged to retrench the said additional consumption, since their double quantity of money carries on but the same undertakings their single quantities carried on before; otherwise they will turn bankrupts, and be ruined, which is commonly the case, in regard people do not often care to retrench their expences; and then others, who saved money, will set up in their places.

|| This sudden Increase of Species would encourage Merchants and Manufacturers, to embark a-new in fresh Undertakings and Ad-[53]ventures, and from the Increase of their Money, they would naturally be induced to indulge themselves in better Living, to keep better Tables, and consequently a proportional Demand would arise both for the Necessaries of Life, and for Labourers and Artizans; and the Proprietors of Land would receive double Income to what they formerly received; and this Increase of Money being thus thrown into Circulation, and thereby the Prices of all Things becoming in proportion dearer, yet the Merchants not being able to get a proportional Profit on their new Undertakings and Adventures, they would in this Case, if guided by Prudence to themselves and Families, be necessitated to retrench their new Method of Living, and return to the Old; otherwise the Consequence must be Banktruptcy: and others, who lived with greater Oeconomy, and saved their Profits, would rise in their Place; all Things in the Course of Time, would return to their former Situation; for let who will suffer Money and Labour, by degrees, will at last find their due Proportion; because if it is certain that the Quantity of coined Money in the Channels of Trade, and the Credit there given, forms and [54] fixes from time to time the Prices of all Things at Market.

Those then who will suffer from this dearness and increased consumption will be first of all the Landowners, during the term of their Leases, then their Domestic Servants and all the Workmen or fixed Wage-earners who support their families on their wages. All these must diminish their expenditure in proportion to the new consumption, which will compel a large number of them to emigrate to seek a living elsewhere. The Landowners will dismiss many of them, and the rest will demand an increase of wages to enable them to live as before. It is thus, approximately, that a considerable increase of Money from the Mines increases consumption, and by diminishing the number of inhabitants entails a greater expense among those who remain.

ᵃ...ᵃ: R: 'Cette Charté et augmentation'

ᵇ...ᵇ: R: 'Leurs'

In addition to the differences indicated in C348i, A349 does not mention the emigration of wage labourers that is presumed to occur in E/D349.

349

350

‖ The proprietor, at the expiration of his lease, will demand 12000 ounces for his rent, instead of 6000: since the price of the farmers commodities is doubled; and, if he returns to his former manner of living, he will call back his servants, whom he had sent away, or have others in their place; and the new undertakers will live upon the same footing of consumption as the first, the farmers will have the same profits out of the lands that the farmers had at first, and all the dispositions of his estate will turn nearly to it's primitive state, with this difference only, that the farmers, who saved money are richer, and the undertakers, who ruined themselves, are forced to turn journeymen to others, who are set up in their room, and that 4000 ounces circulate instead of 2000.

‖ These changes, or something like them, commonly happen in a state, when a sudden quantity of money is introduced into the general barter; but, because money most commonly [II, 283, col.2] increases but slowly and gradually, commodities rise in their value insensibly.

351

Generally speaking, the coined Money of a trading Nation is in Circulation, it is not the Interest of the Possessors therof to keep it idle by them; for it is by its Windings and Turnings in the Channels of Commerce, that Interest and Gain is procured from it. These several Windings and Turnings, are traced by and from the several Degrees of People, whose Taste, Luxury, and Necessaries are to be supplied by the Produce of Land and Labour; this Produce is generally proportioned to the ready Money and Credit of the Market; and in considering the Use of Money in a Nation that has no Intercourse with its Neighbours, the Greatness or Smallness of its Quantity is indifferent;

352 |9| Si l'on continue de tirer l'argent des Mines, les prix de tou-[218]tes choses par cette abondance d'argent augmenteront à tel point, que non-seulement les Propriétaires des terres, à l'expiration de leurs Baux, augmenteront considérablement leurs Rentes, & se remettront dans leur ancien train de vivre, en augmentant à proportion les gages de ceux qui les servent; mais que les Artisans ᵃ& les Ouvriersᵃ tiendront si haut leurs ouvrages qu'il y aura un profit considérable ᵇà les tirerᵇ de l'Etranger, ᶜquiᶜ les fait à bien meilleur marché. Cela déterminera naturellement plusieurs à faire venir dans l'Etat quantité de Manufactures d'ouvrages travaillés dans les Païs étrangers, où on les trouvera à grand marché : ce qui ruinera insensiblement les Artisans & Manufacturiers de l'État qui ne sauroient y subsister en travaillant à si bas prix, attendu la chertée.

i. An important difference arises between the arguments as developed in **350**
D350, A351 and E352. D350 assumes that eventually the proportionality
principle will hold: prices will double too. In E352 this is not clear. The
main reason for the difference appears to be that in D350, unlike E352, the
possibility of foreign trade is not yet considered. The transition to an open
economy is postponed until D379, where it is stated explicitly that foreign
trade has been excluded up to that stage. Cf. C379.

ii. Note that, in D350, even though all prices will eventually undergo the
same proportional increase and economic activities be restored to previous
levels, it does not mean that the process of change has been 'neutral'. D350
emphasises that redistribution of wealth has taken place. Farmers who saved
while their profits were increased are richer, while entrepreneurs whose
families have problems with retrenching their consumption after expanding
it go bankrupt, giving way to new entrepreneurs. The latter view is also
expressed in A349.

iii. Harris (1757, I, chapter 2, sections xiv–xv, pp. 80–86) offers arguments
that are reminiscent of D345–D351. Especially noteworthy are i) a clear
statement that a state without foreign trade is considered (p. 80) and ii) an
emphasis on the differences between the effects of a sudden increase in the
money supply and a gradual one.

A351 differs from both D350 and E352 in the sense that it does not really **351**
discuss the effects of an increase in money on prices. The argument is
similar to D350 only with regard to the last statement that 'in considering
the Use of Money in *a Nation that has no Intercourse with its Neighbours*,
the Greatness or Smallness of its Quantity is indifferent'. In the very next
sentence (A355) the open economy is considered and the argument is similar
to that of E355 (Cf. C350i).

If more money continues to be drawn from the Mines all prices will owing   ᵃ...ᵃ: R: 'et ouvriers'   **352**
to this abundance rise to such a point that not only will the Landowners   ᵇ...ᵇ: R: 'a en tirer'
raise their Rents considerably when the leases expire and resume their old   ᶜ...ᶜ: R: 'ou on'
style of living, increasing proportionably the wages of their servants, but the
Mechanics and Workmen will raise the prices of their articles so high that
there will be a considerable profit in buying them from the foreigner who
makes them much more cheaply. This will naturally induce several people
to import many manufactured articles made in foreign countries, where
they will be found very cheap: this will gradually ruin the Mechanics and
Manufacturers of the State who will not be able to maintain themselves there
by working at such low prices owing to the dearness of living.

353 [219] |10| Lorsque la trop grande abondance de l'argent des Mines aura diminué les habitans ªd'un Etatª, accoutumé ceux qui ᵇrestentᵇ à une trop grande ᶜdépense, porté le produit de la terre & le travail des Ouvriersᶜ à des prix excessifs, ruiné ᵈles Manufacturesᵈ de l'État, ᵉpar l'usage que font de celles des païs étrangers les Propriétaires de terre & ceux qui travaillent aux Mines, l'argent du produit des Mines passera nécessairement chez l'Etranger pour païer ce qu'on en tire: ce qui appauvrira insensiblement cet État, & le rendraᵉ en quelque façon dépendant de l'Etranger auquel on est obligé d'envoïer annuellement l'argent, à mesure qu'on le tire des Mines. La grande circulation d'argent, qui au commencement étoit générale, cesse; la pauvreté & la misere suivent, ᶠ& le travail des Mines paroît n'êtreᶠ que [220] pour le seul avantage de ceux qui y sont emploïés, & pour les Etrangers qui en profitent.

354 |11| Voilà à-peu-près ce qui est arrivé à l'Espagne depuis la découverte des Indes. Pour ce qui est des Portugais, depuis la découverte des Mines d'or du Bresil, ils se sont ªpresqueª toujours servis des ouvrages ᵇ& desᵇ Manufactures des Etrangers; ᶜ& il semble qu'ils ne travaillentᶜ aux Mines, que pour le compte & l'avantage de ces mêmes Etrangers. Tout l'or & l'argent que ces deux États tirent des Mines, ne leur en fournit pas plus dans la circulation, qu'aux autres. L'Angleterre & la France en ont même ordinairement davantage.

355 |12| Maintenant si l'augmentation d'argent dans l'Etat provient d'une balance de commerce avec les Etrangers, ª(c'est-à-dire, en envoïant chez eux des ouvrages & des Manufactures en plus [221] grande valeur & quantité que ce qu'on en tire, & par conséquent en recevant le surplus en argent)ª cette augmentation annuelle d'argent enrichira un grand nombre ᵇde Marchands & d'entrepreneursᵇ dans l'État, & donnera de l'emploi à quantité d'artisans & d'Ouvriers qui fournissent ᶜles ouvragesᶜ qu'on envoie chez l'Etranger d'où l'on tire cet argent. Cela augmentera par degrés la consommation de ces habitans industrieux, & enchérira les prix de la terre & du travail. Mais les Gens industrieux qui sont attentifs à amasser du bien n'augmenteront pas d'abord leur dépense; ils attendront jusqu'à ce qu'ils aient amassé une bonne somme, dont ils puissent tirer un intérêt certain, indépendamment de leur commerce. ᵈLorsqu'unᵈ grand nombre d'habitans auront acquis des fortunes considérables, de [222] cet argent qui entre constamment & annuellement dans l'État, ils ne manqueront pas d'augmenter leurs consommations & d'encherir toutes choses. Quoique cette cherté les entraîne dans une plus grande dépense qu'ils ne s'étoient d'abord proposé de faire, ils ne laisseront pas pour la plûpart de continuer tant qu'il leur restera de capital; attendu que rien n'est plus aisé ni plus agréable que d'augmenter la dépense des familles, mais rien de plus difficile ni de plus désagréable que de ᵉlaᵉ retrancher.

[54 continued] but with respect to a Country, which carries on a foreign Commerce, and raises its Produce to exchange it with foreign Nations, the Question materially differs: the Evil lies in that, though the Increase of Money does by degrees increase the Price of Provisions and Labour, yet it never follows that the Merchant or Adventurer, gains a proportional Profit; but this Increase of the Price of Labour and Provisions brought about by [55] the Increase of Money acquired by the Consequence of a well regulated Trade, does not shew itself, but by insensible and slow Degrees, and is made amends for by the consequential Advantages we reap from the Possession of Gold and Silver , which gives Influence and Weight to all our foreign Negotiations; and though this great Quantity of Money is very disadvantageous to foreign Commerce, yet this Disadvantages does not produce its Effect, but by slow and insensible Degrees, and requires a Series of Time before it arrives at the Point of raising Labour and Provisions, to any great Inequality between us, and our Rivals in Trade; and before it arrives at this Point, great Advantages arise to the Public from the Encouragement given to Labour and Industry.

When the excessive abundance of money from the Mines has diminished the inhabitants of a State, accustomed those who remain to a too large expenditure, raised the produce of the land and the labour of workmen to excessive prices, ruined the manufactures of the State by the use of foreign productions on the part of Landlords and mine workers, the money produced by the Mines will necessarily go abroad to pay for the imports: this will gradually impoverish the State and render it in some sort dependent on the Foreigner to whom it is obliged to send money every year as it is drawn from the Mines. The great circulation of Money, which was general at the beginning, ceases: poverty and misery follow and the labour of the Mines appears to be only to the advantage of those employed upon them and the Foreigners who profit thereby.

a...a: R: 'de L'Etat'
b...b: R: 'reste'
c...c: R: 'depence et Consommation, porte La terre et Le travail'
d...d: R: 'Les ouvrages et Manufactures'
e...e: R: 'pendant que les proprietaires des Terres et Ceux qui Vivent par le travail des mines achettent les ouvrages a manufacture des étrangers, L'argent qu'on a tiré des mines passera necessairement Ches letranger pour payer Cequ'on en tire. Cela appauvrira Insensiblement LEtat et lhabitude oul'on sy trouve Le Rend'
f...f: R: 'on ne semble travailler aux mines'

353

This is approximately what has happened to Spain since the discovery of the Indies. As to the Portuguese, since the discovery of the gold mines of Brazil, they have nearly always made use of foreign articles and manufactures; and it seems that they work at the Mines only for the account and advantage of foreigners. All the gold and silver which these two States extract from the Mines does not supply them in circulation with more precious metal than others. England and France have even more as a rule.

a...a: R: 'quasy'
b...b: R: 'a'
c...c: R: 'et en semble travailler'

i. Cf. V354a with V572a.

ii. See C252 for other references to the influx of gold and silver from America.

354

Now if the increase of money in the State proceeds from a balance of foreign trade (i.e. from sending abroad articles and manufactures in greater value and quantity than is imported and consequently receiving the surplus in money) this annual increase of money will enrich a great number of Merchants and Undertakers in the State, and will give employment to numerous Mechanicks and workmen who furnish the commodities sent to the foreigner from whom the money is drawn. This will increase gradually the consumption of these industrial inhabitants and will raise the price of Land and Labour. But the industrious who are eager to acquire property will not at first increase their expense: they will wait till they have accumulated a good sum from which they can draw an assured interest, independently of their trade. When a large number of the inhabitants have acquired considerable fortunes from this money, which enters the State regularly and annually, they will, without fail, increase their consumption and raise the price of everything. Though this dearness involves them in a greater expense than they at first contemplated they will for the most part continue so long as their capital lasts; for nothing is easier or more agreeable than to increase the family expenses, nothing more difficult or disagreeable than to retrench them.

a...a: R: 'Cest a dire en envoyant des ouvrages des manufactures de chez Letranger en plus grande valeur et quantité que Cequ'on en retire, et par conséquent en en rétirant Lexcédent ou Le surplus en argent.'
b...b: R: 'de Marchands et Negocians ou entrepreneurs'
c...c: R: 'Les manufacturiers a ouvrages'
d...d: R: 'Mais Lors qu'un'
e...e: R: 'les'

i. Since a counterpart to E352–E354 is missing in A, there is less emphasis in the latter text on the effects of an influx of money on the competitiveness of the nation. Note, however, that A355, like E355, discusses the effects of an influx due to a trade surplus and not due to the mining of precious metals.

ii. The point about the positive aspects of an abundance of money in circulation is also made, less clearly, in D/A253.

iii. The remainder of chapter XVI in the *Analysis* is not reproduced here. On pp. 55–57 there are clear paraphrases of Hume's essay 'Of Money'. Pp. 57 to 62 argue against high indirect taxes in Britain and there is a pleading for Ireland to be treated on the same footing with the rest of Britain. The next chapter in the *Analysis* is reproduced from A433.

355

356 |13| Si une balance annuelle & constante a causé dans un État une augmentation ᵃconsidérable d'argentᵃ, elle ne manquera pas d'augmenter la consommation, d'encherir le prix ᵇde toutes choses, & mêmeᵇ de diminuer le nombre des habitans, à moins qu'on ne tire de l'Etranger une addi-[223]tion de denrées à proportion de l'augmentation de consommation. ᶜD'ailleursᶜ il est ordinaire dans les États qui ont acquis une abondance considérable d'argent de tirer beaucoup de choses des païs voisins où l'argent est rare, & où tout est par conséquent à grand marché: mais comme il faut envoïer de l'argent pour cela, la balance du commerce deviendra plus petite. Le bon marché de la terre & du travail dans les païs étrangers où l'argent est rare, y sera naturellement ériger des Manufactures & des ouvrages pareils à ᵈceuxᵈ de l'État, mais qui ne seront pas d'abord si parfaits ni si estimés.

357 |14| Dans cette situation, l'État peut subsister dans l'abondance d'argent, consommer tout son produit & même beaucoup du produit ᵃdes païs étrangersᵃ, & encore pardessus tout cela, [224] conserver une petite balance de commerce contre l'Etranger, ou au moins garder bien des années cette balance au pair; c'est-à-dire, ᵇtirer, en échange de ses ouvrages & de ses Manufactures, autant d'argent de ces païs étrangers, qu'il est obligé d'y en envoïer en échange des denrées ou des produits de terre qu'il en tire.ᵇ Si ᶜcet État est Étatᶜ maritime, la facilité & le bon marché de sa navigation pour le transport de ses ouvrages & de ses Manufactures dans les païs étrangers, pourront compenser en quelque façon la cherté du travail que la trop grande abondance d'argent y cause; de sorte que les ouvrages & les Manufactures de cet État, toutes cheres qu'elles y sont, ne laisseront pas de se vendre dans les païs étrangers éloignés, à meilleur marché quelquefois que les Manufactures [225] d'un autre État où le travail est à plus bas prix.

358 |15| Les frais de voiture augmentent beaucoup le prix des choses qu'on transporte dans les païs éloignés; mais ces frais sont assez modiques dans les États maritimes, où il y a une navigation reglée pour tous les Ports étrangers, au moïen de quoi on y trouve presque toujours des Bâtimens prêts à faire voile, qui se chargent de toutes les marchandises qu'on leur confie, pour un fret très raisonnable.

359 |16| Il n'en est pas de même dans ᵃles Étatsᵃ où la navigation n'est pas florissante; on est obligé d'y ᵇconstruireᵇ des navires exprès pour le transport des marchandises, ce qui emporte quelquefois tout le profit; ᶜ&ᶜ on y navigue toujours à grands frais, ᵈce qui décourage entierement le commerceᵈ.

If an annual and continuous balance has brought about in a State a considerable increase of money it will not fail to increase consumption, to raise the price of everything and even to diminish the number of inhabitants unless additional produce is drawn from abroad proportionable to the increased consumption. Moreover it is usual in States which have acquired a considerable abundance of money to draw many things from neighbouring countries where money is rare and consequently everything is cheap: but as money must be sent for this the balance of trade will become smaller. The cheapness of land and labour in the foreign countries where money is rare will naturally cause the erection of Manufactories and works similar to those of the State, but which will not at first be so perfect nor so highly valued.

ᵃ...ᵃ: R: 'dargent Considerable'
ᵇ...ᵇ: R: 'de toute Chose et autant'
ᶜ...ᶜ: R: 'en tout Cas'
ᵈ...ᵈ: R: 'Celles'

The point made in **356** the last sentence of E356, like the first sentence of E329, is related to the argument of E194. Cf. C194.

In this situation the State may subsist in abundance of money, consume all its own produce and also much foreign produce and over and above all this maintain a small balance of trade against the foreigner or at least keep the balance level for many years, that is import in exchange for its work and manufactures as much money from these foreign countries as it has to send them for the commodities or products of the land it takes from them. If the State is a maritime State the facility and cheapness of its shipping for the transport of its work and manufactures into foreign countries may compensate in some sort the high price of labour caused by the too great abundance of money; so that the work and Manufactures of this State, dear though they be, will sell in foreign countries cheaper sometimes than the Manufactures of another State where Labour is less highly paid.

ᵃ...ᵃ: R: 'du pays étranger'
ᵇ...ᵇ: R: 'en Echange de ses ouvrages a manuf.ʳᵉ autant d'argent quils ont tout Les ans, qu'on est obligé d'envoyer Ches Letranger en Echange de Denrées et produit de terre qu'on tire'
ᶜ...ᶜ: R: 'lEtat se trouve un etat'

357

The cost of transport increases a good deal the prices of things sent to distant countries; but these costs are very moderate in maritime States, where there is regular shipping to all foreign ports so that Ships are nearly always found there ready to sail which take on board all cargoes confided to them at a very reasonable freight.

D382 also discusses the **358** low costs of transport enjoyed by maritime states.

It is not so in States where navigation does not flourish. There it is necessary to build ships expressly for the carrying trade and this sometimes absorbs all the profit; and navigation there is always very expensive, which entirely discourages trade.

ᵃ...ᵃ: R: 'un état'
ᵇ...ᵇ: R: 'Construire ou équiper'
ᶜ...ᶜ: R: 'mais'
ᵈ...ᵈ: R: 'et cela en decourage'

359

360 |17| L'Angleterre consomme au-[226]jourd'hui non-seulement la plus grande partie de son peu de produit, mais encore beaucoup du produit des autres païs; comme soieries, vins, fruits, du linge ᵃen quantité, &c.,ᵃ au lieu qu'elle n'envoie chez l'Etranger que le produit de ses Mines, ᵇses Ouvrages & ses Manufacturesᵇ pour la plûpart, & quelque cher qu'y soit le travail, par l'abondance de l'argent, elle ne laisse pas de vendre ᶜsesᶜ ouvrages dans les ᵈpaïs éloignésᵈ, par l'avantage de sa navigation, à des prix aussi raisonnables ᵉqu'en Franceᵉ, où ces mêmes ᶠouvragesᶠ sont bien moins chers.

361 |18| L'augmentation de la quantité d'argent effectif dans un État peut encore ᵃêtre occasionnée,ᵃ sans balance de commerce, ᵇpar desᵇ subsides païés à ᶜcet Étatᶜ par des Puissances étrangeres; par les dépenses de plusieurs Ambassadeurs, ou de Voïageurs, que des [227] raisons de politique, ou la curiosité, ou les divertissemens, peuvent engager ᵈà y faireᵈ quelque ᵉséjourᵉ; par le transport des biens & des fortunes de quelques Familles qui, par des motifs de liberté de religion, ou ᶠpar d'autres causesᶠ, quittent ᵍleur patrieᵍ pour s'établir dans cet État. Dans tous ces cas, les sommes qui entrent dans l'État y causent toujours une augmentation de dépenses & de consommation, ʰ& par conséquent encherissentʰ toutes choses ⁱdans les canauxⁱ du troc où l'argent entre.

362 |19| Supposons qu'un quart des habitans de l'État consomment journellement de la viande, du vin, de ᵃla bierre, &c.ᵃ & se donnent ᵇfort fréquemment des habits, du linge, &c.,ᵇ avant l'introduction de l'augmentation de l'argent, mais qu'après cette introduction, un tiers ou une moitié des habitans consomment [228] ces mêmes choses, les prix de ces denrées & de ces marchandises ᶜne manqueront pasᶜ de hausser, & la cherté de la viande déterminera plusieurs des habitans qui faisoient ᵈle quartᵈ de l'État, à en consommer moins qu'à l'ordinaire. Un Homme qui mange trois livres de viande par jour ne laissera ᵉpas deᵉ subsister avec deux livres, mais ᶠil sent ce retranchement; au lieu que l'autre moitié des habitans qui n'en mangeoit presque point, ne s'en sentira pasᶠ. Le pain encherira à la vérité par degré, à cause de cette augmentation de consommation, comme je l'ai souvent insinué, mais il sera moins cher à proportion que la viande. L'augmentation du prix de la viande cause une diminution de la part d'une petite partie des habitans, ce qui la rend sensible; mais l'augmentation du prix du pain diminue la part de [229] tous les habitans, ce qui la rend ᵍmoinsᵍ sensible. Si cent mille personnes d'extraordinaire viennent demeurer dans un État qui contient dix millions d'habitans, leur consommation extraordinaire de pain ne montera qu'à une livre en cent livres, qu'il faudra retrancher aux anciens habitans; mais lorsqu'un homme au lieu de cent livres de pain en consomme quatre-vingt dix-neuf livres pour sa subsistance, il sent à peine ce retranchement.

England today consumes not only the greatest part of its own small produce but also much foreign produce, such as Silks, Wines, Fruit, Linen in great quantity, etc. while she sends abroad only the produce of her Mines, her work and Manufactures for the most part, and dear though Labour be owing to the abundance of money, she does not fail to sell her articles in distant countries, owing to the advantage of her shipping, at prices as reasonable as in France where these same articles are much cheaper.

^a...^a: R: 'et quantité de bois pour ses boissons immances'
^b...^b: R: 'ouvrages a manufacture'
^c...^c: R: Les'
^d...^d: R: 'paÿs étrangers éloignez'
^e...^e: R: 'que la france'
^f...^f: R: 'sortes d'ouvrages'; 1756b, 1769: 'avantages'

Cf. E180, which has a somewhat different account of England's success in foreign trade in spite of its relatively high labour costs.   **360**

The increased quantity of money in circulation in a State may also be caused, without balance of trade, by subsidies paid to this State by foreign powers, by the expenses of several Ambassadors, or of Travellers whom political reasons or curiosity or pleasure may induce to reside there for some time, by the transfer of the property and fortune of some Families who from motives of religious liberty or other causes quit their own country to settle down in this State. In all these cases the sums which come into the State always cause an increased expense and consumption there and consequently raise the prices of all things in the channels of exchange into which money enters.

^a...^a: R: 'provenir'
^b...^b: R: 'de'
^c...^c: R:'Letat'
^d...^d: R:'a faire'
^e...^e: R: 'sejours dans Letat'
^f...^f: R: 'ou autres'
^g...^g: R: 'Le Leur'
^h...^h: R: 'encherissent'
ⁱ...ⁱ: R: 'dans Caneaux'

361

Suppose a quarter of the inhabitants of the State consume daily Meat, Wine, Beer, etc. and supply themselves frequency with Cloaths, Linen, etc. before the increase in money, but that after the increase a third or half of the inhabitants consume these same things, the prices of them will not fail to rise, and the dearness of Meat will induce several of those who formed a quarter of the State to consume less of it than usual. A Man who eats three pounds of Meat a day will manage with two pounds, but he feels the reduction, while the other half of the inhabitants who ate hardly any meat will not feel the reduction. Bread will in truth go up gradually because of this increased consumption, as I have often suggested, but it will be less dear in proportion than Meat. The increased price of Meat causes diminished consumption on the part of a small section of the People, and so is felt; but the increased price of bread diminishes the share of all the inhabitants, and so is less felt. If 100,000 extra people come to live in a State of 10 millions of inhabitants, their extra consumption of bread will amount to only 1 pound in 100 which must be subtracted from the old inhabitants; but when a man instead of 100 pounds of bread consumes 99 for his subsistence he hardly feels this reduction.

^a...^a: R: 'la biere'
^b...^b: R: 'des habits fort fréquemment'
^c...^c: R: 'ne manqueront'
^d...^d: R: 'le tiers'
^e...^e: R: 'pas que de'
^f...^f: R: 'il s'en rétranchera une, aulieu que l'autre motié des habitans qui ne Mangé présque point de viande ne s'en sentira pas'
^g...^g: R:'plus'

i. D369 makes a similar distinction between markets for different consumables as E362, but the discussion there is more explicit.   **362**

ii. The effect of lower bread consumption per head also figures in D378.

iii. V362g implies a reversed meaning: the sentence in the manuscript states that an increase in the price of bread is felt *more* than an increase in the price of meat. Could the intended meaning in the manuscript be that the effect is felt more *widely*, whereas the meaning in the print version is that the effect is felt *less strongly*? The final sentence of E390 seems to support this interpretation.

363 |20| Lorsque la consommation de la viande augmente, ^ales Fermiers augmentent^a leurs prairies pour avoir plus de viande, ce qui diminue la quantité des terres labourables, par conséquent ^bla quantité du blé^b. Mais ce qui fait ordinairement que la viande encherit plus à proportion que le pain, c'est qu'on permet ordinairement dans l'État l'en-[230]trée du blé des païs étrangers librement, au lieu qu'on défend, absolument l'entrée des bœufs comme en Angleterre, ou qu'on en fait païer des droits d'entrée considérables, comme on fait dans d'autres États. C'est la raison pourquoi les rentes des prairies & des pâturages en Angleterre haussent, dans l'abondance d'argent au triple plus que les rentes des terres labourables.

364 |21| Il n'est pas douteux que les Ambassadeurs, ^ales Voïageurs^a, & les Familles qui viennent s'établir dans l'État n'y augmentent la consommation, & que le prix des choses n'y enchérisse dans tous les ^bcanaux du troc^b où l'argent est introduit.

365 |22| Pour ce qui est des subsides que l'État a reçus des Puissances étrangeres, ou on les resserre pour les besoins de l'État, ou on les répand dans la circulation. ^aSi on les suppose resserrés, [231] ils ne seront pas de mon sujet, car^a je ne considere que l'argent qui circule. L'argent resserré, la vaisselle, l'argent des Eglises, &c. sont des richesses dont l'État trouve à se servir dans ^bles grandes extrêmités^b, mais elles ne sont d'aucune utilité actuelle. Si l'État répand les subsides en question dans la circulation, ce ne peut être que par ^cla^c dépense, & cela augmentera ^dtrès sûrement^d la consommation & enchérira le prix des choses. Quiconque recevra cet argent, le mettra en mouvement dans l'affaire principale de la vie, qui est ^ela nourriture^e, ou de soi-même ou de quelqu'autre, puisque toutes choses y correspondent directement ou indirectement.

366 || Let us again suppose there are silver mines on this estate, that an undertaker farms them from the proprietor, or from the farmers, that the veins are so rich that he shall quickly get out of them the additional quantity of 2000 ounces on our hypothesis

367 || This new quantity of money will cause much the same variation in the price of all commodities, as we observed in the preceding example. The undertaker, or mine-adventurer, will increase his expence, and give great encouragement to the miners and others he employs. The facility wherewith he gets money will make him generous, and he will more chearfully than before bestow money on the poor. The douceurs he gives to those he employs will encourage them also to spend more than usual. All that are concerned under him feel the influence of his opulence, and consequently consume more commodities than usual.

When the consumption of Meat increases the Farmers add to their pastures to get more Meat, and this diminishes the arable Land and consequently the amount of corn. But what generally causes Meat to become dearer in proportion than Bread is that ordinarily the free import of foreign corn is permitted while the import of Cattle is absolutely forbidden, as in England, or heavy import duties are imposed as in other States. This is the reason why the Rents of meadows and pastures go up in England, in the abundance of money, to three times more than the Rents of arable Land.

There is no doubt that Ambassadors, Travellers, and Families who come to settle in the State, increase consumption there and that prices rise in all the channels of exchange where money is introduced.

As to subsidies which the State has received from foreign powers, either they are hoarded for State necessities or are put into circulation. If we suppose them hoarded they do not concern my argument for I am considering only money in circulation. Hoarded money, plate, Church treasures, etc. are wealth which the State turns to service in extremity, but are of no present utility. If the State puts into circulation the subsidies in question it can only be by spending them and this will very certainly increase consumption and send up all prices. Whoever receives this money will set it in motion in the principal affair of life, which is the food, either of himself or of some other, since to this everything corresponds directly or indirectly.

Variations and Errata (V)

[a]...[a]: R: missing

[b]...[b]: R: 'du bled'

[a]...[a]: R: 'Voyageurs'

[b]...[b]: R: 'Canaux ou allées du Troc'

[a]...[a]: R: 'tant quon les tiendra reservez il ne seront pas de nuls Sujets'

[b]...[b]: R: 'Les grands Cas de besoin et extremitées'

[c]...[c]: R:'sa'

[d]...[d]: R: 'tous seurement'

[e]...[e]: R: 'le boire et le Mangér'

Comments (C)

i. Cf. the first sentence of E363 with D372 and the second sentence of E363 with E391.

ii. The missing phrase in the manuscript (V363a) seems like a copying error because, without 'the farmers add', the sentence is unintelligible.

363

364

For similar phrases as found in V365e, see C275.

365

D366 follows directly from D350. It starts examining the case considered in the French text from E339 onwards, namely the situation in which the increase in the quantity of money is due to the mining of precious metals. Note that D366 still supposes an isolated estate.

i. The argument in D367 is reminiscent of E339.

ii. For other occurrences of the term 'mine-adventurer' see C129i.

366

367

368

They will enhance the price of them in the altercations; and which way soever these additional 2000 ounces of silver come into barter, they will raise the price of things. The circulating money will be 4000 ounces instead of 2000, and the price of commodities will be double.

369

|| It may be worth while to observe here, that we may distinguish several channels and walks of circulation at market. The corn, or bread-market, is proportioned to all the inhabitants in general, since the meanest workman must have bread, as well as the greatest lord. The wine-market corresponds to a smaller number of inhabitants, but yet is very considerable, since not only the proprietors of land and money, pensioners and officers, but likewise several middling undertakers, tradesmen, and workmen, drink more or less wine. The butchers, or meat-market, is much the same. The wild-fowl market, and that of rarities and delicacies, corresponds to a smaller number of inhabitants, as lords, wealthy proprietors, and others.

370

|| So that, if the additional money which is brought into a state is at first all in the hands of the wealthy sort, the price of wild fowl may very well rise, and continue high, without influencing the price of bread; and the price of wine and meat may rise long before bread grows dearer: but it will, at the long-run, affect the price of bread also.

371

|| Whenever the additional quantity of money ªdecreasesª, it will create an additional expence proportionable, mediately or immediately, and enhances, consequently, the price of commodities.

372

|| If we suppose that 10 persons increase the expences of their family on the estate we mentioned before, that they raise the price of wine, meat, &c. in the altercations, without much affecting that of bread: the farmer will have another year more cattle and wines, and, consequently less corn, and so corn will then grow also dearer.

Cf. D368 with E340. The quantity **368**
theory statement is much more explicit
here.

i. Cf. D369 with E362. The link **369**
between the markets for different
traded goods and the different income
groups that consume those goods is
more explicit here.

ii. The phrase 'middling undertakers,
tradesmen, and workmen' is reminiscent
of a few similar phrases in the *Analysis*.
See C25iv.

Note the interesting use of the phrase 'at the long-run' at the **370**
end of D370. It indicates the time by which the increase in
the money in circulation has had its effect on the prices of
all traded goods. The phrase 'at the long-run' was used in
English from the 1620s to indicate an 'ultimate outcome', or
'when events have run their course'. However, its use in an
economic-theoretical context appears to have been rare. For
another occurrence of the phrase see D286, and for its French
equivalent see V286a, E513, E552 and E582. Cf. C286i.

371

a...a: *sic*; 'increases'?

The argument of D372 is similar to the **372**
beginning of E363.

373

|| There is generally a stock of every commodity in a nation exceeding the yearly consumption, which answers the sudden and extraordinary consumption; and, as that wastes, the commodities grow dearer, and the dearness again, if it continues, makes several families diminish their consumption, till things return to their primitive state as to the consumption. But the dearness of the commodities continues, since the quantity of money in barter corresponds to it, and a double quantity of money in the hands of undertakers, when the price of things is doubled, has but the same effect the single quantity had before.

374

|| If the additional quantity of money belongs to money-lenders, it will diminish interest, and at the same increase the undertakings, which consequently will enhance the price of commodities, by an additional demand. The money-lenders will increase their expence and consumptions, and the additional undertakers will do the like; the demand for workmen in the several undertakings will raise the price of their wages; the price of things will keep up in barter, since the quantity of money continues to answer the advanced price, though several of the undertakers should break.

375

|| But, if an additional QUANTITY OF CREDIT* should, by the acceleration of circulation, and barters by evaluation, make the 2000 ounces answer the same circulation as 4000, it will have pretty much the same effect as 2000 ounces increase of money. It will occasion an additional number of undertakers, who will increase the price of commodities, which will grow dearer in the altercations. These will enhance the consumption, &c. but, when some of them come to break, their example will stagnate circulation, and the ready money only will carry it on as before; and consequently money will grow scarcer, and commodities will grow cheaper, and the difficulties in circulation will make the undertakers sell cheaper than they bought, and several of them will break and diminish their consumption, &c. So that a sudden augmentation of credit may for some time answer the same ends and purposes, as the sudden increase of the quantity of money, but will not continue to keep up the prices of commodities, as the real quantity of additional mo-[II, 284, col.1]ney does: but when a quickness of circulation is gradually introduced into barter, and continues naturally in the manner and methods of carrying on the undertakings, we don't see why it may not have constantly the same effect of keeping up the price of things.

373

There are similarities between the account **374** in D374 of the indirect effect on prices and production through the rate of interest and what is stated in E464, and to a lesser extent E410. Arguably, compared to those passages, the argument in D374 is clearer with regard to the presumed mechanism.

i. There is no counterpart in E for this **375** fascinating account of a 'credit crunch'. A further discussion of concerted attempts to extend credit in order to reduce interest rates is found in D683–D689. Both discussions appear to be inspired by Cantillon's experiences with the failure of John Law's system. Cf. C684i. Note however, that the final remarks in D375 make clear that the author does not object in principle to the extension of credit.

ii. At * Postlethwayt added the following note: 'This shews how injurious the effects of long personal credit are to trade in general. See the article, CREDIT [PRIVATE CREDIT].' In the subsection 'private credit', which does not appear to owe anything to Cantillon, Postlethwayt is so cautious about the extension of credit that his views appear to be at odds with the ending of D375. This can be seen as support for our suggestion that Cantillon originally wrote the passage reproduced in D375.

376 || I have enlarged upon these particulars and circumstances, to shew by what methods and steps in the detail of barter, an additional quantity of real money in a state increases the price of all commodities. As to the fact itself, it seems sufficiently proved by experience, and agreed upon by all hands. Mr. Locke lays it down as a principle, and frequently insinuates, that the price of all commodities is proportionable to the actual quantity of circulating money. But he seems to have clearly lost the view of this subject, when he supposes, nevertheless, that the profits and advantages made in a state increase without bounds, with the increase of the quantity of money: wheras it follows from his own principles, that, if the money is doubled, the price of commodities is also doubled, and consequently that a double quantity of money will buy but the same quantity of commodities, if they are doubled in value. [For what occasions the rise of labour and commodities, see the articles DUTIES, DEBTS [PUBLIC DEBTS], TAXES, LABOUR.]

377 || Let us now examine how things find their proportion in a state, when the price of commodities rises, either by an additional quantity of money introduced into barter, or by the scarcity of commodities ᵃandᵃ bad years.

378 || When there happens a great demand for any kind of commodities, several families will consume less of it than usual, by reason of it's dearness: a man who commonly eats three pounds of bread in a day, will subsist if he has but two pounds; and a state which maintains 1,000,000 of inhabitants, will, with little difficulty, and without any sensible hardship, maintain 1,100,000, and even 1,500,000 with difficulty and famine: but things will afterwards find their own proportion, and the inhabitants will proportion themselves in number to the means they find to subsist on, according to the manner of living of the place.

379 || Hitherto we have not any where considered foreign trade; but, by commerce with foreigners, a state may maintain a greater number of inhabitants than the land can maintain. For example:

i. The reference to John Locke's monetary views is **376** reminiscent of E342, although the commentary appears to be different. That is, in E342 it is stated that Locke did not investigate the mechanisms by which a proportional increase of all prices is eventually brought about. In D376 it is said that Locke did not recognise that profits made due to increased expenditure, brought about by increases in the money supply, are only of a transitory nature. It is not clear which precise passage in Locke's writings this is a comment on.

ii. Of the entries referred at the end of the paragraph, only 'Labour' contains fragments written by Richard Cantillon. However, Postlethwayt appears to be referring more specifically to a part of 'Labour' (II, 3–4) which he did not take from Cantillon (but from Sir Matthew Decker instead). Cf. C105iii.

ᵃ...ᵃ: *sic*; 'in'?   **377**

E362 has a similar argument to D378 about the ability for **378** a state to maintain a larger number of people without too much hardship.

The remark that foreign trade has so far not been considered may be significant. It is very **379** unlikely that Postlethwayt wrote this statement (occurring as it does 284 pages into the second volume of the *Universal Dictionary*) and it may explain various differences in this chapter between E and D. The French version considers the effects of the increases in prices on foreign trade early on (from E352 onwards). Also, in earlier chapters in the French text, e.g. in E I, xv and xvi, the effects of foreign trade are occasionally mentioned, despite a remark in E114 that foreign trade will not be taken into consideration (until later). Most of these occurrences do not have counterparts in the *Dictionary* fragments, and ones that do have counterparts play down the importance of foreign trade for the issues at hand (see e.g. E292/D292). Could the explanation for this be that in the manuscript version of Cantillon's work to which Postlethwayt had access, a greater attempt was made to separate the various effects of increases in the money supply more clearly, by first considering consequences inside the 'isolated' economy and only subsequently taking into account the effects with foreign trade? Cf. C350i.

380

|| The inhabitants of Provence may buy wool of the Spaniards, and pay the value of it with about a quarter part of the same wool manufactured; and export the other three quarters of it manufactured to Barbary, and bring home, in exchange for it, more corn than will answer the maintenance of all the workmen, undertakers, exporters, and importers, concerned in the whole commerce in question.

381

|| The little island of St. Dennis near Paris contains three parishes, the business of these inhabitants is mostly tanning of leather: the island produces nothing for their sustenance: they sell their labour in exchange for the produce of the lands of the continent, which maintains them; their tanned leather is mostly consumed at their doors [at Paris]. If it were to be transported, and consumed in Italy, it would scarce maintain them, because of the expence of the remote carriage.

382

|| But the Dutch find means, by the cheapness of their navigation, to exchange their labour with remoter parts, where the produce of their labour is not voluminous; their manufactures of linnen, their bleaching, their herring and whalefishery answer the charge, and so does their sawed timber and shipping to some places; for their saw-mills, one with another, save the labour of 25 persons. See the article LABOUR. That circumstance contributes to the cheapness of their shipping, as well as the timber of the countries adjacent to the Meuse, Moselle, and Rhine, which falls down these rivers to them with little expence of carriage. So it is not surprizing there are more inhabitants in Holland than their lands are able to maintain, but this cannot be increased in infinitum; but these latter considerations have insensibly carried me something from my subject.

383

|| The value of money, as well as of other commodities, arises from the quantity of, and demand for it. The quantity of silver, by the opening of the mines of Peru and Mexico being greater than gold, gave an extraordinary value to gold; and hence it was that in the 11th of king James I. the unity piece of gold was raised from 20 to 23s. On the contrary, a few years ago the demand for silver was so great, that we were obliged to lower the value of gold; and, in all probability, in a little time we shall think a farther dimunition absolutely necessary. But it is not alone the quantity of gold and silver that lessens the demand for them, but the circulation too; a great trade, making a greater demand for industry and commodities than money, lessen it's value, and consequently raises the price of the other two.

The argument in D380 may be compared to E179 and E180 **380**
where it is explained how foreign trade may support a larger
number of inhabitants in a country than would be possible
without it.

i. The island referred to is l'Île-Saint-Denis, about 10 km **381**
upstream from the centre of Paris in the Seine river.

ii. It seems most likely that the addition '[at Paris]' in the
penultimate sentence of D381 is a clarification deemed
necessary by Postlethwayt. It is not clear why on this occasion
he used parentheses.

iii. The final observation in D381 about the prohibitive costs
of transport is reminiscent of E359.

i. For the cheapness of Dutch navigation, cf. E180.   **382**

ii. The Dutch windmills are also mentioned in E520. It is one of very few
cases where Cantillon points to the importance of adoption of advanced
technology for success in foreign trade.

iii. The reference to the entry, 'Labour' is more precisely to a passage
where Postlethwayt considers one of his favourite themes, namely that
one of the means 'which will contribute to the keeping of the price of
labour low, and in proportion to that of other neighbouring commercial
states [is] by improvements in the mechanic arts and inventions'
('Labour', II, 4). He illustrates this by comparing the labour-intensive
way in which Russians make planks with the more technically advanced
use of water mills for sawing in Sweden (not, as in D382, the use of wind
mills in Holland for the same purpose). The Swedish example appears to
be paraphrased from Defoe (1728: 36).

i. Cf. E/D/A578 on the changed exchange rate between gold **383**
and silver due to discoveries of silver in Mexico and Peru.

ii. 'The 11th of king James I' in D383 is 1614.

iii. The gold/silver market price ratio tended to decline
during the first half of the eighteenth century, largely due to
the export of silver to Asia, which justifies the expectation
that 'in a little time we shall think a farther dimunition
absolutely necessary'. See E592–E593 for Cantillon's view
that the Mint overvalued gold relative to silver.

384

|| Trade and credit, as they are inseparable in themselves, so they are the parents of circulation: money, without these would be a dead treasure in few people's hands, and consequently the community little the better for it. France is to England as 8 to 3, their specie perhaps proportionable, yet there is a greater shew of money in England than in France; [II, 284, col.2] but, if the circulation of France were equal to that of England, then she would appear of course so much the richer. For more matter on this subject, see the articles BANKING, BARTER, CASH, CIRCULATION, COIN, GOLD, SILVER, BULLION, EXCHANGE.

i. With D384, the entry, 'Money' ends. It is perhaps **384**
more likely that this final paragraph was written by
Postlethwayt.

ii. The entries, 'Banking' (D627–D655), 'Barter'
(D239–D253), 'Cash' (D255–D295), 'Circulation'
(D118–D134, D299–D317) and 'Coin' (D578–D591,
D595–D622) all contain fragments plagiarised from
Cantillon. The entries 'Gold' (I, 901–12), 'Silver',
(II, 729–31), 'Bullion' (I, 388–99) and 'Exchange'
(I, 741–50) do not appear to contain such fragments.
With regard to 'Silver', see C434.

385   [232] **CHAPITRE VII.**

ᵃ*Continuation du même sujet de l'augmentation* ᵇ*& de la diminution*ᵇ *de la quantité d'argent effectif dans un Etat.*ᵃ

386 |1| Comme l'or, l'argent & le cuivre ont une valeur intrinseque, proportionnée à la terre & au travail qui entrent dans leurs productions, sur les lieux où l'on les tire des Mines, & encore aux frais de leur importation ou introduction dans les États qui ᵃn'ontᵃ pas de Mines, la quantité de l'argent, comme celle de toutes les autres marchandises, détermine sa valeur dans les altercations des Marchés contre tout autres choses.

387 |2| Si l'Angleterre commence pour la premiere fois à se servir d'or, d'argent & de cuivre dans [233] les trocs absolus, l'argent sera estimé, suivant la quantité qu'il y en a dans la circulation, proportionnellement à sa valeur contre toutes les autres marchandises ᵃ&ᵃ denrées, & on parviendra à cette estimation grossierement par les altercations des Marchés. ᵇSur le pié de ces estimationsᵇ, les Propriétaires de terres & les Entrepreneurs fixeront ᶜles gagesᶜ des Domestiques & des Ouvriers qu'ils emploient, à tant par jour ou par année, de telle ᵈfaçonᵈ qu'ils puissent eux & leur famille s'entretenir des gages qu'on leur donne.

388 |3| Supposons maintenant que par la résidence des Ambassadeurs & Voïageurs étrangers en Angleterre, on y ait introduit autant d'argent dans la circulation qu'il y en avoit au commencement; cet argent passera d'abord entre les mains de plusieurs Artisans, Domestiques, [234] Entrepreneurs, & autres qui auront eu part au travail ᵃdes équipages, des divertissemens, &c.,ᵃ de ces Etrangers: ᵇles Manufacturiers, les Fermiers & les autres Entrepreneursᵇ se sentiront de cette augmentation d'argent qui mettra un grand nombre de personnes dans l'habitude d'une plus grande dépense que par le passé, ce qui conséquemment encherira les prix des Marchés. Les Enfans même de ces Entrepreneurs ᶜ& de ces Artisansᶜ entreront dans une nouvelle dépense: leurs Peres leur donneront dans cette abondance quelque argent pour leurs menus plaisirs, dont ils acheteront des échaudés, des petits patés, &c. & cette nouvelle quantité d'argent se distribuera de façon que plusieurs personnes qui subsistoient sans manier aucun argent, ne laisseront pas d'en avoir dans le cas présent. Beaucoup de trocs [235] qui se faisoient auparavant par évaluation, se seront maintenant l'argent à la main, & par conséquent il y aura ᵈplusᵈ de vitesse dans la circulation de l'argent, ᵉqu'il n'y en avoitᵉ au commencement en Angleterre.

Chapter VII

Continuation of the same subject

^a…^a: 1756b, 1769: 'Continuation du même sujet'
^b…^b: Missing in R

i. There are no counterparts for this chapter in D or A.

ii. This chapter does not discuss decreases in the money supply, which seems the reason for V385b.

iii. H385 follows the Mauvillon edition by having a shortened chapter title (V385a).

385

As Gold, Silver, and Copper have an intrinsic value proportionable to the Land and Labour which enter into their production at the Mines added to the cost of their importation or introduction into States which have no Mines, the quantity of money, as of all other commodities, determines its value in the bargaining of the Market against other things.

^a…^a: R: 'n'en ont'

The intrinsic value of metals is also discussed in E/D/A205.

386

If England begins for the first time to make use of Gold, Silver, and Copper in exchanges money will be valued according to the quantity of it in circulation proportionably to its power of exchange against all other merchandise and produce, and their value will be arrived at roughly by the altercations of the Markets. On the footing of this estimation the Landowners and Undertakers will fix the wages of their Domestic Servants and Workmen at so much a day or a year, so that they and their families may be able to live on the wages they receive.

^a…^a: R: 'ou'
^b…^b: R: 'sur Le pied de Ces altercations'
^c…^c: R: 'Les prix et gages'
^d…^d: R: 'maniere'

The argument and wording in E387 is reminiscent of D258/A258 and the start of D437.

387

Suppose now that the residence of Ambassadors and foreign travellers in England have introduced as much money into the circulation there as there was before; this money will at first pass into the hands of various Mechanicks, Domestic Servants, Undertakers and others who have had a share in providing the equipages, amusements, etc. of these Foreigners; the Manufacturers, Farmers, and other Undertakers will feel the effect of this increase of money which will habituate a great number of people to a larger expense than before, and this will in consequence send up Market prices. Even the children of these Undertakers and Mechanicks will embark upon new expense: in this abundance of money their Fathers will give them a little money for their petty pleasures, and with this they will buy cakes and patties, and this new quantity of money will spread itself in such a way that many who lived without handling money will now have some. Many purchases which used to be made on credit will now be made for cash, and there will therefore be greater rapidity in the circulation of money in England than there was before.

^a…^a: R: 'des équipages tables et divertissements'
^b…^b: R: 'Les Manufacturiers fermiers et autres entrepreneurs'
^c…^c: R: 'et artisans'
^d…^d: R: 'moins'
^e…^e: R: 'qu'en avoit'

Contrary to the last sentence of E388, the Rouen manuscript (V388d and e) states that, when the use of metallic money is extended to transactions that were previously concluded '*par évaluation*', i.e. by credit, this occasions a *reduction* in the velocity of money circulation. This is in keeping with the view that, when the opposite happens, i.e. when credit is used as a money substitute, the velocity of circulation *increases*. See E305, D375 and also E295.

388

389 |4| Je conclus de tout cela que par l'introduction d'une double quantité d'argent dans un État, on ne double pas toujours les prix des denrées & des marchandises. Une Riviere qui coule & serpente dans son lit, ne coulera pas avec le double de rapidité, en doublant la quantité de ses eaux.

390 |5| La proportion de la cherté, ªque l'augmentation & la quantité d'argent introduisentª dans l'État, dépendra du tour que cet argent donnera à la consommation & à la circulation. Par quelques mains que l'argent qui est introduit passe, il augmentera naturellement la consomma-[236]tion; mais cette consommation sera plus ou moins grande suivant les cas; elle tombera plus ou moins sur certaines especes de denrées ou de marchandises, suivant le génie de ceux qui ᵇacquerentᵇ l'argent. Les prix des Marchés enchériront plus pour certaines especes que pour d'autres, quelque abondant que soit l'argent. En Angleterre, le prix de la viande pourroit encherir du triple, sans que le prix du blé enchérît de plus d'un quart.

391 |6| Il est toujours permis en Angleterre d'introduire des blés des païs étrangers, mais il n'est pas permis d'y introduire des bœufs. Cela fait que quelque considérable que puisse devenir l'augmentation de ªl'argent effectifª en Angleterre, le prix du blé ᵇn'y peut être portéᵇ plus haut que dans les autres païs où l'argent est rare, que de la valeur des frais & des risques qu'il y a à y [237] introduire le blé de ces mêmes païs étrangers.

392 |7| Il n'en est pas de même du prix des bœufs, qui sera nécessairement proportionné à la quantité d'argent qu'on offre pour la viande, proportionnellement à la quantité de cette viande & au nombre des bœufs qu'on y nourrit.

393 |8| Un bœuf pesant huit cens livres se vend aujourd'hui en Pologne & en Hongrie deux ou trois onces d'argent, au lieu qu'on le vend communément au Marché de Londres plus de quarante onces d'argent. Cependant le septier de froment ne se vend pas à Londres au double de ce qu'il se vend en Pologne & en Hongrie.

394 |9| L'augmentation de l'argent n'augmente le prix des denrées & des marchandises, que de la différence des frais du transport, lorsque ce transport est permis. [238] Mais dans beaucoup de cas ce transport couteroit plus que la valeur de la chose, ce qui ªfait queª les bois sont inutiles dans beaucoup d'endroits. Ce même transport est cause que le lait, le beurre frais, la salade, le gibier, &c. sont pour rien dans les Provinces éloignées de la Capitale.

From all this I conclude that by doubling the quantity of money in a State the prices of products and merchandise are not always doubled. A River which runs and winds about in its bed will not flow with double the speed when the amount of its water is doubled.

For other comparisons of **389** the circular flow of money to the flowing of water, see C284iii and C303ii.

The proportion of the dearness which the increased quantity of money brings about in the State will depend on the turn which this money will impart to consumption and circulation. Through whatever hands the money which is introduced may pass it will naturally increase the consumption; but this consumption will be more or less great according to circumstances. It will be directed more or less to certain kinds of products or merchandise according to the idea of those who acquire the money. Market prices will rise more for certain things than for others however abundant the money may be. In England the price of meat might be tripled while the price of corn went up only one fourth.

^a...^a: R: 'que l'augmentation de la quantité d'argent a introduitte'
^b...^b: R: 'attrapent'; 1756b, 1769: 'acquiérent'

390

In England it is always permitted to bring in corn from foreign countries, but not cattle. For this reason however great the increase of hard money may be in England the price of corn can only be raised above the price in other countries where money is scarce by the cost and risks of importing corn from these foreign countries.

^a...^a: R: 'l'argent Comptant et effectif'
^b...^b: R: 'ny seroit étre porté'

The English import **391** ban on cattle is also mentioned in E363.

It is not the same with the price of Cattle, which will necessarily be proportioned to the quantity of money offered for Meat in proportion to the quantity of Meat and the number of Cattle bred there.

392

An ox weighing 800 pounds sells in Poland and Hungary for two or three ounces of silver, but commonly sells in the London Market for more than 40. Yet the bushel of flour does not sell in London for double the price in Poland and Hungary.

393

Increase of money only increases the price of products and merchandise by the difference of the cost of transport, when this transport is allowed. But in many cases the carriage would cost more than the thing is worth, and so timber is useless in many places. This cost of carriage is the reason why Milk, Fresh Butter, Salads, Game, etc. are almost given away in the provinces distant from the Capital.

^a...^a: R: 'est Cause que'

394

395 |10| Je conclus qu'une augmentation d'argent effectif dans un État y introduit toujours une augmentation de consommation & l'habitude d'une plus grande dépense. Mais la cherté que cet argent cause, ᵃne se répand pas également sur toutes les especes de denrées & de marchandises, proportionnément à la quantité de cet argent;ᵃ à moins que ᵇceluiᵇ qui est introduit ne soit continué dans les mêmes ᶜcanauxᶜ de circulation que l'argent primitif; c'est-à-dire, à moins que ceux qui offroient aux Marchés [239] une once d'argent, ne soient les mêmes & les seuls qui y offrent maintenant deux onces, depuis que l'argent est augmenté du double de poids dans la circulation, ᵈce quiᵈ n'arrive guere. Je conçois que lorsqu'on introduit dans un État une bonne quantité d'argent de surplus, ᵉleᵉ nouvel argent donne un tour nouveau à la consommation, & même ᶠune vitesse à la circulationᶠ; mais il n'est pas possible d'en marquer le degré véritable.

I conclude that an increase of money circulating in a State always causes there an increase of consumption and a higher standard of expense. But the dearness caused by this money does not affect equally all the kinds of products and merchandise, proportionably to the quantity of money, unless what is added continues in the same circulation as the money before, that is to say unless those who offer in the Market one ounce of silver be the same and only ones who now offer two ounces when the amount of money in circulation is doubled in quantity, and that is hardly ever the case. I conceive that when a large surplus of money is brought into a State the new money gives a new turn to consumption and even a new speed to circulation. But it is not possible to say exactly to what extent.

[a]...[a]: R: 'n'est pas toujours proportionnée a la quantité dargent dans une méme proportion a toutes Les especes de Denrees et marchandises'
[b]...[b]: R: 'Cet argent'
[c]...[c]: R: 'allées'
[d]...[d]: R: 'Cas, qui'
[e]...[e]: R: 'Ce'
[f]...[f]: R: 'une Vitesse de Circulation'

395 What is said in E395 to be a rare case, i.e. that the additional money is distributed exactly proportionally to earlier money holdings, is precisely what is assumed at the outset in D250 and A250. Following that assumption the conclusion is reached there that 'this [additional] money *does* affect equally all the kinds of products and merchandise, proportionably to the [additional] quantity of money'. In D in particular the assumption is next relaxed from D345 onwards and conclusions are reached similar to E about the importance of the entry point of additional money into circulation and the sequential effects on spending patterns (or the 'Cantillon effect'). In A the discussion of these effects is far less developed. Cf. C250ii and C348i.

396   [239] **CHAPITRE** ªVIIIª.

Autre Reflexion sur l'augmentation ᵇ& *sur la diminution*ᵇ *de la quantité d'argent effectif dans un Etat.*

397 |1| Nous avons vû qu'on pouvoit augmenter la quantité d'argent ªeffectif dans un État, par [240] le travail des Minesª qui s'y trouvent, par les subsides des Puissances étrangeres, par le transport des Familles ᵇétrangeresᵇ, par la résidence d'Ambassadeurs & de Voïageurs, mais principalement par une balance constante & annuelle de commerce, en fournissant des ᶜouvragesᶜ à l'Etranger, pour en tirer au moins une partie du prix en especes d'or & d'argent. C'est par cette derniere voie qu'un Etat s'agrandit le plus solidement, surtout lorsque le commerce est ᵈaccompagné & soutenuᵈ par une grande navigation, & par un produit considérable dans l'intérieur de l'Etat, qui ᵉpuisse fournirᵉ les materiaux nécessaires pour les ouvrages & les Manufactures qu'on envoie au-dehors.

398 |2| Cependant, comme la continuation de ce commerce introduit par degré une grande abondance d'argent, & augmente [241] peu-à-peu la consommation, ª& comme pour y suppléer, il faut tirer beaucoup de denrées de l'Etrangerª, il sort une partie de la balance annuelle pour les acheter. D'un autre côté, l'habitude de la dépense enchérissant le travail des Ouvriers, les prix des ouvrages des Manufactures haussent toujours; & il ne manque pas d'arriver que quelques-uns des païs étrangers tâchent d'eriger chez eux les mêmes especes d'ouvrages & de Manufactures, au moïen de quoi ils cessent d'acheter ceux de l'Etat en question: & quoique ᵇcesᵇ nouveaux établissemens d'ouvrages ᶜ& deᶜ Manufactures ne soient pas d'abord parfaits, ᵈils retardent cependant & empêchent même l'exportation de ceux de l'État voisinᵈ dans leur propre païs, où l'on se fournit à meilleur marché.

399 |3| C'est ainsi que l'Etat commence à perdre quelques bran-[242]ches de son commerce lucratif; & plusieurs de ses Ouvriers & Artisans qui voient le travail rallenti, sortent de l'Etat pour trouver plus d'emploi dans les païs de la nouvelle Manufacture. Malgré cette diminution de la balance du commerce de l'Etat, on ne laisse pas d'y continuer dans les usages où l'on étoit de tirer plusieurs denrées de l'Etranger. Les ouvrages ª& lesª Manufactures de l'Etat aïant une grande réputation, & la facilité de la navigation donnant les moïens de les envoïer à peu de frais ᵇdans les païs éloignésᵇ, l'Etat l'emportera ᶜpendant bienᶜ des années sur les nouvelles Manufactures dont nous avons parlé, & maintiendra encore une petite balance de commerce, ou du moins le maintiendra au pair. Cependant ᵈsi quelqu'autre Etat maritime tâcheᵈ de perfectionner les mêmes ouvrages & [243] en même-tems sa navigation, il ᵉenleveraᵉ par le bon marché de ses Manufactures plusieurs branches du commerce ᶠà l'Etatᶠ en question. Par conséquent cet Etat commencera à perdre la balance, & sera obligé d'envoïer tous les ans une partie de son argent chez l'Etranger, pour le paiement des denrées qu'il en tire.

Chapter VIII
Further Reflection on the same subject

^a...^a: R: '8.e'
^b...^b: R: 'et diminution'

An alternative to part **396** of this chapter occurs in D and A. See D/A416ff. Cf. C416i.

We have seen that the quantity of money circulating in a State may be increased by working the Mines which are found in it, by subsidies from foreign powers, by the immigration of Families of foreigners, by the residence of Ambassadors and Travellers, but above all by a regular and annual balance of trade from supplying merchandise to Foreigners and drawing from them at least part of the price in gold and silver. It is by this last means that a State grows most substantially, especially when its trade is accompanied and supported by ample navigation and by a considerable raw produce at home supplying the material necessary for the goods and manufactures sent abroad.

^a...^a: R: '~~dans un état~~ effectis en Le Tirant des mines'
^b...^b: R: 'étrangeres dans L'Etat'
^c...^c: R: 'ouvrages et manufactures'
^d...^d: R: 'soutenu et accompagné'
^e...^e: R: 'fournissent'

397

As however the continuation of this Commerce gradually introduces a great abundance of money and little by little increases consumption, and as to meet this much foreign produce must be brought in, part of the annual balance goes out to pay for it. On the other hand the habit of spending increasing the employment of labourers the prices of Manufactured goods always go up. Without fail some foreign countries endeavour to set up for themselves the same kinds of Manufactures, and so cease to buy those of the State in question; and though these new Establishments of crafts and Manufactures be not at first perfect they slacken and even prevent the exportation of those of the neighbouring State into their own country where they can be got cheaper.

^a...^a: R: 'quil faut tirer beaucoup de Denrées de L'etragér pour y supléér'
^b...^b: R: 'les'
^c...^c: R: 'a'
^d...^d: R: 'ils ne laisse pas de Retarder ou méme d'empecher Lexploittation de Celle de Letat voisin''

The argument of **398** E398 and E399 is reminiscent of D422.

Thus it is that the State begins to lose some branches of its profitable Trade: and many of its Workmen and Mechanicks who see labour fallen off leave the State to find more work in the countries with the new Manufacture. In spite of this diminution in the balance of trade the custom of importing various products will continue. The articles and Manufactures of the State having a great reputation, and the facility of navigation affording the means of sending them at little cost into distant countries, the State will for many years keep the upper hand over the new Manufactures of which we have spoken and will still maintain a small Balance of Trade, or at least will keep it even. If however some other maritime State tries to perfect the same articles and its navigation at the same time it will owing to the cheapness of its manufactures take away several branches of trade from the State in question. In consequence this State will begin to lose its balance of trade and will be forced to send every year a part of its money abroad to pay for its importations.

^a...^a: R: 'et'
^b...^b: R: 'dans Les ports et payis éloignées'
^c...^c: R: 'encore bien'
^d...^d: R: 'si quelques autres états maritimes tachent'
^e...^e: R: 'exclura'
^f...^f: R: 'de Letat'

Pluquet (1786, 2, **399** 308–11) quotes E from the last sentence of E399 up to '*leurs puissances*' in the penultimate sentence of E402.

400 |4| Bien plus, quand même l'Etat en question pourroit conserver une balance de commerce dans sa plus grande abondance d'argent, on peut raisonnablement supposer que cette abondance n'arrive pas sans qu'il n'y ait beaucoup de Particuliers opulens qui se jettent dans le luxe. Ils acheteront des Tableaux, des Pierreries de l'Etranger, ils voudront avoir de leurs soieries ᵃ& plusieurs raretésᵃ, mettront l'Etat dans une telle habitude de luxe, que malgré les avantages de son [244] commerce ordinaire, son argent s'écoulera annuellement chez l'Etranger pour le paiement de ce même luxe: cela ne manquera pas d'appauvrir l'Etat par degré, & de le faire passer d'une grande puissance dans une grande foiblesse.

401 |5| Lorsqu'un Etat est parvenu au plus haut point de richesse, Je suppose toujours que la richesse comparative des Etats consiste dans les quantités respectives d'argent qu'ils possedent principalement, il ne manquera pas de retomber dans la pauvreté par le cours ordinaire des choses. La trop grande abondance d'argent, qui fait, tandis qu'elle dure, la puissance des Etats, les rejette insensiblement, mais naturellement, dans l'indigence. ᵃAussiᵃ il sembleroit que lorsqu'un Etat ᵇs'étendᵇ par le commerce, & que l'abondance de l'argent enchérit trop les prix de la terre [245] & du travail, le Prince, ou la Législature devroit ᶜretirerᶜ de l'argent, le garder pour des cas imprevus, & tâcher de retarder sa circulation par toutes les voies, hors celles de la contrainte & de la mauvaise foi, ᵈafinᵈ de prévenir la trop grande cherté de ses ouvrages, & d'empêcher les inconveniens du luxe.

402 |6| Mais comme il n'est pas facile de s'appercevoir du tems propre pour cela, ni de savoir quand l'argent est devenu ᵃplus abondant qu'il ne doit l'êtreᵃ pour le bien & la conservation des avantages de l'Etat, les Princes, & les Chefs des Républiques, qui ne s'embarrassent guere de ces sortes de connoissances, ne s'attachent qu'à se servir de la facilité qu'ils trouvent, par l'abondance des revenus de l'Etat, à étendre leurs puissances, & à insulter d'autres Etats sur les prétextes les plus frivoles. Et toutes [246] choses bien considerées, ils ne font peut-être pas si mal de travailler à perpétuer la gloire de leurs Regnes & de leur administration, & de laisser des monumens de leur puissance & de leur opulence; car puisque, selon le cours naturel des choses humaines, l'Etat doit retomber de lui-même, ils ne font qu'accélerer un peu sa chûte. Il semble néanmoins qu'ils devroient tâcher de faire durer leurs puissances pendant tout le tems de leur propre administration.

Moreover, even if the State in question could keep a balance of trade in its greater abundance of money it is reasonable to suppose that this abundance will not arrive without many wealthy individuals springing up who will plunge into luxury. They will buy Pictures and Gems from the Foreigner, will procure their Silks and rare objects, and set such an example of luxury in the State that in spite of the advantage of its ordinary trade its money will flow abroad annually to pay for this luxury. This will gradually impoverish the State and cause it to pass from great power into great weakness.

When a State has arrived at the highest point of wealth (I assume always that the comparative wealth of States consists principally in the respective quantities of money which they possess) it will inevitably fall into poverty by the ordinary course of things. The too great abundance of money, which so long as it lasts forms the power of States, throws them back imperceptibly but naturally into poverty. Thus it would seem that when a State expands by trade and the abundance of money raises the price of Land and Labour, the Prince or the Legislator ought to withdraw money from circulation, keep it for emergencies, and try to retard its circulation by every means except compulsion and bad faith, so as to forestall the too great dearness of its articles and prevent the drawbacks of luxury.

But as it is not easy to discover the time opportune for this, nor to know when money has become more abundant than it ought to be for the good and preservation of the advantages of the State, the Princes and Heads of Republics, who do not concern themselves much with this sort of knowledge, attach themselves only to make use of the facility which they find through the abundance of their State revenues, to extend their power and to insult other countries on the most frivolous pretexts. And all things considered they do not perhaps so badly in working to perpetuate the glory of their reigns and administrations, and to leave monuments of their power and wealth; for since, according to the natural course of humanity, the State must collapse of itself they do but accelerate its fall a little. Nevertheless it seems that they ought to endeavour to make their power last all time of their own administration.

a...a: R: 'a rareté'

a...a: R: 'Ainsy'
b...b: R: 'sEleve'
c...c: R: 'résserrer'
d...d: R: 'Cela a fin'

a...a: R: 'trop abondant'

400 i. In D426 the purchase of pictures and jewels from abroad is also mentioned, but in connection to the *favourable* effect of reducing the amount of money in circulation.

ii. The behaviour of the *Particuliers opulens* in E400 is the same as that of the French undertakers and proprietors in D422.

401 i. In D426 the same point is made about the need for the authorities to reduce the quantity of money in circulation. Also see D423/A423.

ii. Cf. the phrase 'highest point of wealth' in E401 with similar phrases in D/A423 and see C423i.

iii. The final sentence of this paragraph from '*il sembleroit*' is quoted in Mably's *Entretiens de Phocion* (1763, 241).

402 Skinner (1966, I, 205 n1) sees a similarity between the argument in E402 with Steuart's (1767, II, xii) complaint about the indifference of statesmen: 'and when a statesman looks coolly on, with his arms across, or takes it into his head, that it is not his business to interpose, the prices of the dextrous workman will rise, ... trade will decay where it flourished most, and take root in a new soil'.

403 |7| Il ne faut pas un grand nombre d'années pour porter dans un Etat l'abondance au plus haut degré, & il en faut encore moins pour le faire entrer dans l'indigence, faute de commerce & de Manufactures. Sans parler de la puissance & de la chûte de la République de Venise, des Villes ᵃanséatiquesᵃ, de la Flandre & du Brabant, de la République [247] de Hollande, &c. qui se sont succedées dans les branches lucratives du commerce, on peut dire que la puissance de la France n'est allée en augmentant que depuis 1646, qu'on y érigea des Manufactures de draps, au lieu qu'auparavant on les tiroit de l'Etranger, jusqu'en 1684, qu'on en chassa nombre d'entrepreneurs & d'artisans Protestans, & que ce Roïaume n'a fait que baisser depuis cette derniere époque.

404 |8| Pour juger de l'abondance & de la rareté de l'argent dans la circulation, je ne connois pas de meilleure régie que celle des baux & des rentes des Propriétaires de terres. Lorsqu'on afferme des terres ᵃà haut prixᵃ c'est une marque que l'argent abonde dans l'Etat; mais lorsqu'on est obligé de les affermer bien plus bas, cela fait voir, tout autres choses étant égales, que l'argent [248] est rare. J'ai lu ᵇdans un étatᵇ de la France, que l'arpent de vigne qu'on avoit affermé en 1660, en argent fort, auprès de Mante, & par conséquent pas bien loin de la Capitale de France, pour 200 liv. tournois, ne s'affermoit en 1700, en argent plus foible, ᶜqu'àᶜ 100 liv. tournois : quoique l'argent ᵈapportéᵈ des Indes occidentales dans cet intervalle dût naturellement rehausser le prix des terres, dans l'Europe.

405 |9| L'Auteur ᵃattribueᵃ cette diminution de la rente à un défaut de consommation. Et il paroît qu'il avoit remarqué en effet que la consommation de vin étoit diminuée. Mais j'estime ᵇqu'il a pris l'effet pour la causeᵇ. La cause étoit une plus grande rareté d'argent en France, dont l'effet étoit naturellement une diminution de consommation. Tout au contraire j'ai toujours insinué dans ᶜcet Essaiᶜ, que l'abondance de [249] l'argent augmente naturellement la consommation, & contribue sur toutes choses à mettre les terres en valeur. Lorsque l'abondance de l'argent éleve les denrées à un prix honnête, les habitans s'empressent de travailler pour en acquerir; mais ils n'ont pas le même empressement de posséder aucunes denrées ou marchandises au-delà de ce qu'il faut pour leur entretien.

406 |10| Il est apparent que tout Etat, qui a plus d'argent en circulation que ᵃsesᵃ voisins, a un avantage sur eux, tant qu'il conserve cette abondance d'argent.

It does not need a great many years to raise abundance to the highest point in a State, still fewer are needed to bring it to poverty for lack of Commerce and Manufactures. Not to speak of the power and fall of the Republic of Venice, the Hanseatic Towns, Flanders and Brabant, the Dutch Republic, etc. who have succeeded each other in the profitable branches of trade, one may say that the power of France has been on the increase only from 1646 (when Manufactures of Cloths were set up there, which were until then imported) to 1684 when a number of Protestant Undertakers and Artisans were driven out of it, and that Kingdom has done nothing but recede since this last date.

To judge of the abundance and scarcity of money in circulation, I know no better measure than the Leases and Rents of Landowners. When Land is let at high Rents it is a sign that there is plenty of Money in the State; but when Land has to be let much lower it shows, other things being equal, that Money is scarce. I have read in an État de la France that the acre of vineyard which was let in 1660 near Mantes, and therefore not far from the Capital of France, for 200 livres tournois in money of full weight, only let in 1700 for 100 livres tournois in lighter money, though the silver brought from the West Indies in the interval should naturally have sent up the price of Land in Europe.

The author [of the *État*] attributes this fall in Rent to defective consumption. And it seems that he had in fact observed that the consumption of Wine had diminished. But I think he has mistaken the effect for the cause. The cause was a greater rarity of money in France, and the effect of this was naturally a falling off in consumption. In this Essay I have always suggested, on the contrary, that abundant money naturally increases consumption and contributes above everything to the cultivation of Land. When abundant money raises produce to respectable prices the inhabitants make haste to work to acquire it; but they are not in the same hurry to acquire produce or merchandise beyond what is needed for their maintenance.

It is clear that every State which has more money in circulation than its neighbours has an advantage over them so long as it maintains this abundance of money.

Variations and Errata (V)

ᵃ…ᵃ: R: 'asiatiques'

ᵃ…ᵃ: R: 'bien hautes'
ᵇ…ᵇ: R: 'dans quelqetat
ᶜ…ᶜ: R: 'que'
ᵈ…ᵈ: R: 'qu'on apportast'

ᵃ…ᵃ: R: 'Raporte'
ᵇ…ᵇ: R: 'quil a prise La Cause pour L'effet'
ᶜ…ᶜ: R: 'Ces Essays'

ᵃ…ᵃ: R: 'les'

Comments (C)

i. V403a seems a curious spelling mistake. Might it be due to a mishearing in dictation? See C274iii.
ii. For the dating of France's economic upturn, see C336i. In 1685 Louis XIV revoked the Edict of Nantes causing the mass emigration of Huguenots. Cf. D424–D425.   **403**

The most likely work referred to in E404 is Boisguilbert's *Le détail de la France*. In the later, enlarged editions of this work, e.g. the 1712 Brussels edition, p. 149, Boisguilbert writes that in 1660 there were in the region of Mantes 15,000 *arpens* of vineyard that each yielded at least 200 *livres* of rent and that due to taxation this had since halved.   **404**

Instead of 'this Essay', the Rouen manuscript has 'these Essays' (V405c). For a possible significance of this, see C561ii.   **405**

406

407 |11| En premier lieu, dans toutes les branches du commerce il donne moins de terre & de travail qu'il n'en retire : le prix de la terre & du travail étant par tout estimé en argent, ce prix est plus fort dans l'État où l'argent abonde le plus. Ainsi l'État en question retire quelquefois le [250] produit de deux arpens de terre en échange de celui d'un arpent, & le travail de deux hommes pour celui d'un seul. C'est par rapport à cette abondance d'argent dans la circulation à Londres, que le travail d'un seul Brodeur Anglois, couse plus que celui de dix Brodeurs Chinois; quoique les Chinois brodent bien mieux & fassent plus d'ouvrages dans la journée. On s'étonne en Europe comment ces Indiens peuvent subsister en travaillant à si grand marché, & comment les étoffes admirables qu'ils nous envoient, coutent si peu.

408 |12| En second lieu, les revenus de l'Etat où l'argent abonde, se levent avec bien plus de facilité & en plus grande somme comparativement; ce qui donne les moïens à l'Etat, en cas de guerre ou de contestation, de gagner toutes sortes d'avantages sur ses [251] Adversaires chez qui l'argent est plus rare.

409 |13| Si de deux Princes qui se font la guerre pour la Souveraineté ᵃou la Conquête d'un Etat, l'un a beaucoup d'argent, & l'autre peu, mais plusieurs domaines qui puissent valoirᵃ deux fois plus que tout l'argent de son Ennemi; le premier sera plus en état de s'attacher des Généraux & des Officiers par ᵇdesᵇ largesses en argent, que le second ne le sera en donnant aux siens le double de la valeur en terres ᶜ& en domainesᶜ. Les cessions des terres sont sujettes à des contestations & à des rescisions, & on n'y compte pas si bien que sur l'argent qu'on reçoit. On achete avec de l'argent les munitions de guerre & de bouche, ᵈmême des Ennemis de l'État. On peut donner de l'argent pour des services secrets & sans témoins:ᵈ les terres, les denrées, & les mar-[252]chandises ne sauroient servir dans ces occasions, ni même les bijoux ni les diamans, ᵉparcequ'ilsᵉ sont faciles à reconnoître. Après tout, il me semble que la puissance & la richesse comparatives des États consistent, tout autres choses étant égales, dans la plus ou moins grande abondance d'argent qui y circule, *hic et nunc*.

In the first place in all branches of trade it gives less Land and Labour than it receives: the price of Land and Labour being everywhere reckoned in money is higher in the State where money is most abundant. Thus the State in question receives sometimes the produce of two acres of Land in exchange for that of one acre, and the work of two men for that of only one. It is because of this abundance of money in circulation in London that the work of one English embroiderer costs more than that of 10 Chinese embroiderers, though the Chinese embroider much better and turn out more work in a day. In Europe one is astonished how these Indians can live, working so cheap, and how the admirable stuffs which they send us cost so little.

In the second place, the revenues of the State where money abounds, are raised more easily and in comparatively much larger amount. This gives the State, in case of war or dispute, the means to gain all sorts of advantages over its adversaries with whom money is scarce.

If of two Princes who war upon each other for the Sovereignty or Conquest of a State one have much money and the other little money but many estates which may be worth twice as much as all the money of his enemy, the first will be better able to attach to himself Generals and Officers by gifts of money than the second will be by giving twice the value in lands and estates. Grants of Land are subject to challenge and revocation and cannot be relied upon so well as the money which is received. With money munitions of war and food are bought even from the enemies of the State. Money can be given without witnesses for secret service. Lands, Produce, Merchandise would not serve for these purposes, not even jewels or diamonds, because they are easily recognised. After all it seems to me that the comparative Power and Wealth of States consist, other things being equal, in the greater or less abundance of money circulating in them *hic et nunc*.

[a]...[a]: R: 'ou Conquéste dun état; que lun ayt beaucoup d'argent, mais L'autre n'ayt guerre dargent a Cependant des états et domaines qui peuvent valoir'
[b]...[b]: 1756b, 1769: 'ses'
[c]...[c]: R: 'et domaines'
[d]...[d]: R: des ennemis méme de LEtat'
[e]...[e]: R: 'qui'

The advantages of having 'an abundance of money in circulation' due to a positive balance of trade discussed in E407–E409 are mentioned more briefly in D/A253 and A254. **407**

408

i. William Petty in *Political Arithmetick* (1691b: 36) uses the same Latin expression as at the end of E409 (meaning 'here and now') in a similar context, although not precisely to make the same point. Petty argues that silver and gold are the best stores of value and hence the most desirable in foreign trade, '[w]hereas other Commodities which are perishable, or whose value depends upon the Fashion; or which are contingently scarce and plentiful, are wealth, but *pro hic & nunc*'. **409**

ii. For the curious expression in E409 that jewels are '*faciles à reconnoître*' see C224.

410 |14| Il me reste encore à parler de deux autres ᵃmoïensᵃ d'augmenter la quantité d'argent effectif dans la circulation d'un Etat. ᵇLe premierᵇ est lorsque les Entrepreneurs ᶜ& lesᶜ Particuliers empruntent de l'argent de leurs Correspondans étrangers, pour leur en païer l'intérêt, ou que les Particuliers étrangers envoient leur argent dans l'Etat, pour y acheter des actions ou fonds publics. Cela fait souvent des sommes très considérables dont l'État doit païer annuellement à ces Etrangers un intérêt, ᵈ& cesᵈ fa-[253]çons d'augmenter l'argent dans ᵉl'Etatᵉ y rendent ᶠréellementᶠ l'argent plus abondant, & diminuent le prix de l'intérêt. Par le moïen de cet argent, les Entrepreneurs de l'Etat trouvent moïen d'emprunter plus facilement, de faire faire ᵍdes ouvrages & d'établir des Manufacturesᵍ, dans l'esperance d'y gagner; les Artisans, ʰ& tous ceuxʰ par les mains ⁱde quiⁱ cet argent passe, ne manquent pas de consommer plus qu'ils n'eussent fait, s'ils n'avoient été emploïés au moïen de cet argent, qui hausse par conséquent les prix de toutes choses, ʲcommeʲ s'il appartenoit à l'Etat; & au moïen de l'augmentation de dépense ᵏou de la consommationᵏ qu'il cause, les revenus que le Public perçoit sur la consommation en sont augmentés. Les sommes prêtées à l'État en cette maniere y causent bien des avantages présens, mais [254] la suite en est toujours onéreuse & désavantageuse. Il faut que l'Etat en paie l'intérêt aux Etrangers annuellement, & outre cette perte l'Etat se trouve à la merci des Etrangers, qui peuvent toujours le mettre dans l'indigence lorsqu'il leur prendra fantaisie de retirer leurs fonds; & il arrivera certainement ˡqu'ils voudront les retirer, dans l'instant queˡ l'Etat en aura le plus de besoin; comme lorsqu'on se prépare à avoir une guerre & qu'on y craint quelque ᵐéchetᵐ. L'intérêt qu'on paie à l'Etranger est toujours bien plus considerable que l'augmentation du revenu public que cet argent cause. On voit souvent ⁿpasserⁿ ces prêts d'argent d'un Païs à un autre, suivant la confiance des Prêteurs pour les Etats où ils les envoient. Mais à dire le vrai, il arrive le plus souvent que les Etats qui sont chargés de ces emprunts & qui en ont païé plu-[255]sieurs années de gros intérêts, tombent ᵒà la longue dans l'impuissanceᵒ de païer les capitaux, par une banqueroute. Pour peu que la méfiance s'en mêle, les fonds ou actions publiques tombent, les Actionnaires étrangers n'aiment pas à les ᵖrappellerᵖ avec perte, & aiment mieux se contenter de leurs intérêts, en attendant que la confiance puisse revenir; mais elle ne revient quelquefois plus. Dans les Etats qui tombent en décadence, le principal objet des Ministres est ordinairement de ranimer la confiance, & par ce moïen d'attirer l'argent des Etrangers par ces sortes de prêts: car à moins que le Ministere ne manque à la bonne foi & à ses engagemens, l'argent des Sujets circulera sans interruption. C'est celui des Etrangers qui peut augmenter la quantité de l'argent effectif dans l'Etat.

It remains to mention two other methods of increasing the amount of money in active circulation in a State. The first is when Undertakers and private individuals borrow money from their foreign correspondents at interest, or individuals abroad send their money into the State to buy shares or Government stocks there. This often amounts to very considerable sums upon which the State must annually pay interest to these foreigners. These methods of increasing the money in the State make it more abundant there and diminish the rate of interest. By means of this money the Undertakers in the State find it possible to borrow more cheaply to set people on work and to establish Manufactories in the hope of profit. The Artisans and all those through whose hands this money passes, consume more than they would have done if they had not been employed by means of this money, which consequently increases prices just as if it belonged to the State, and through the increased consumption or expense thus caused the public revenues derived from taxes on consumption are augmented. Sums lent to the State in this way bring with them many present advantages, but the end of them is always burdensome and harmful. The State must pay the interest to the Foreigners every year, and besides this is at the mercy of the Foreigners who can always put it into difficulty when they take it into their heads to withdraw their capital. It will certainly arrive that they will want to withdraw it at the moment when the State has most need of it, as when preparations for war are in hand and a hitch is feared. The interest paid to the Foreigner is always much more considerable than the increase of public revenue which his money occasions. These loans of money are often seen to pass from one Country to another according to the confidence of investors in the States to which they are sent. But to tell the truth it most commonly happens that States loaded with these loans, who have paid heavy interest on them for many years, fall at length by bankruptcy into inability to pay the Capital. As soon as distrust is awakened the shares or Public stocks fall, the Foreign shareholders do not like to realise them at a loss and prefer to content themselves with the interest, hoping that confidence will revive. But sometimes it never revives. In States which decline into decay the principal object of Ministers is usually to restore confidence and so attract foreign money by loans of this kind. For unless the Ministry fails to keep faith and to observe its engagements the money of the subjects will circulate without interruption. It is the money of the foreigners which has the power of increasing the circulating currency in the State.

^a...^a: R: 'façons'
^b...^b: R: 'La premiere'
^c...^c: R: 'et'
^d...^d: R: 'et'
^e...^e: R: 'un Etat'
^f...^f: R: 'a la vérité'
^g...^g: R: 'des ouvrages a Manufactures'
^h...^h: R: 'et autres'
ⁱ...ⁱ: R: 'desquels'
^j...^j: R: 'tant comme'
^k...^k: R: 'ou consommation'
^l...^l: R: 'quils viendront Justémént Les retirér quand'
^m...^m: R: 'Échec'; 1769: 'echec'
ⁿ...ⁿ: R: 'rouler'
^o...^o: R: 'dans limpuissance a la longue'
^p...^p: R: 'repetter'

i. The effect of **410** interest payments to foreigners on the balance of the 'current account' is more clearly spelled out in D558.

ii. The effect of increased sources of lending (though not foreign ones) on the rate of interest is also discussed in E464 and D374.

iii. Like the 1769 edition of the *Essai*, Higgs assumed the intended spelling of the word '*échet*' to be '*échec*' translating it with 'hitch'. The same spelling in the Rouen manuscript suggests that this is right (V410m).

411 [256] |15| Mais la voie de ces emprunts, ªqui donneª un avantage
présent, conduit à une mauvaise fin, & c'est un feu de paille. Il faut
pour ᵇreleverᵇ un Etat, s'attacher à y faire rentrer annuellement &
constamment une balance réelle de commerce, faire fleurir par la
Navigation les Ouvrages & les Manufactures qu'on est toujours
en état d'envoïer chez les Etrangers à un meilleur marché,
lorsqu'on est tombé en décadence & dans une rareté d'especes ᶜ.
Lesᶜ Négocians commencent à faire les premieres fortunes,
les Gens de robbe pourront ensuite s'en approprier une partie,
le Prince & les Traitans pourront en acquerir aux dépens des
uns & des autres, & distribuer les graces ᵈselon leurs volontésᵈ.
Lorsque l'argent deviendra trop abondant dans l'Etat, le luxe s'y
mettra, & il tombera en décadence.

412 [257] |16| Voilà à-peu-près ªle cercleª que pourra faire un Etat
considérable qui a du fond & des habitans industrieux. Un
habile Ministre est toujours en état de lui faire recommencer ce
cercle, il ne faut pas un grand nombre d'années pour en voir
l'expérience & le succès, au moins des commencemens qui en
est la situation la plus intéressante. On connoîtra l'augmentation
de la quantité de l'argent effectif, par plusieurs voles que mon
sujet ne me permet pas d'examiner présentement.

413 |17| Pour ce qui est des Etats qui n'ont pas un bon fond, &
qui ne ªpeuventª s'agrandir que par des accidens ᵇ& selon lesᵇ
circonstances des tems, ᶜil est difficile de trouver lesᶜ moïens
de les faire fleurir par les voies du commerce. Il n'y a pas de
Ministres qui puissent remettre les Républiques de Venise &
de Hollan-[258]de ᵈdans la situation brillante dont elles sont
tombéesᵈ. Mais pour l'Italie, l'Espagne, la France, & l'Angleterre,
en quelque état de décadence qu'elles poissent être, elles sont
capables d'être toujours portées, par une bonne administration, à
un haut degré de puissance, par le seul fait du commerce; pourvu
qu'on l'entreprenne séparement : car si tous ces États étoient
ᵉégalement bien administrésᵉ, ils ne ᶠseroient considérablesᶠ que
ᵍproportionnellementᵍ à leurs fonds respectifs & à la plus ou
moins grande industrie de leurs habitans.

But the resource of these borrowings which gives a present ease comes to a bad end and is a fire of straw. To revive a State it is needful to have a care to bring about the influx of an annual, a constant and a real balance of Trade, to make flourishing by Navigation the articles and manufactures which can always be sent abroad cheaper when the State is in a low condition and has a shortage of money. Merchants are first to begin to make their fortunes, then the lawyers may get part of it, the Prince and the Farmers of the Revenue get a share at the expense of these, and distribute their graces as they please. When money becomes too plentiful in the State, Luxury will instal itself and the State will fall into decay.

Such is approximately the circle which may be run by a considerable State which has both capital and industrious inhabitants. An able Minister is always able to make it recommence this round. Not many years are needed to see it tried and succeed, at least at the beginning which is its most interesting position. The increased quantity of money in circulation will be perceived in several ways which my argument does not allow me to examine now.

As for States which have not much capital and can only increase by accidents and conjuncture it is difficult to find means to make them flourish by trade. No ministers can restore the Republics of Venice and Holland to the brilliant situation from which they have fallen. But as to Italy, Spain, France, and England, however low they may be fallen, they are always capable of being raised by good administration to a high degree of power by trade alone, provided it be undertaken separately, for if all these States were equally well administered they would be great only in proportion to their respective capital and to the greater or less industry of their People.

[a]…[a]: R: 'pour donner'
[b]…[b]: R: 'élévér'
[c]…[c]: R: ', que les' [d]…[d]: R: 'a leurs volontés'

[a]…[a]: R: 'Le Coule'

[a]…[a]: R: 'sçavroient'
[b]…[b]: R: 'et les'
[c]…[c]: R: 'Il ni a pas de plaisir a sattacher aux'
[d]…[d]: R: 'dans la passe ou on Les a vue'
[e]…[e]: R: 'en aucuns temps administrés aux mieux'
[f]…[f]: R: 'seroient dans Ce Cas Considerables'
[g]…[g]: 1756b: 'portionnellement'

i. Mably in *Entretiens de Phocion* (1763: 243) quotes E411 from the second sentence onwards. He misquotes the beginning: '*Pour réparer, dit M. Cantillon, les malheurs causés par l'abondance de l'argent, & relever l'Etat, il faut s'attacher d'y faire rentrer annuellement & constamment une balance réelle de commerce.*'

ii. Graslin (1767), *Essai analytique* pp. 365–75, in turn quotes Mably's discussion of Cantillon at length. On pp. 375–79 Graslin exposes his own views: instead of the republican virtue of Mably, he proposes protectionism to protect the wealth of rich nations.

Perhaps '*le coule*' (V412a) means something like 'the course of events', since *la coulée* can be used to indicate a slow flow, like a slide of mud, or a slow river. Elsewhere Cantillon uses the verbs *couler*, in a literal sense (E389) and *s'écouler*, in a figurative sense (E343 and E400).

411

412

413

414 |18| ᵃLe dernier moïenᵃ que je puisse imaginer ᵇpour augmenter dans un Etat la quantité d'argent effectif dans la circulationᵇ, est la voie de la violence & des armes, & elle se mêle souvent avec les autres, attendu que dans tous les Traités de paix on pourvoit ordinairement à se conserver les [259] droits de commerce & les avantages ᶜqu'on a pu en tirerᶜ. Lorsqu'un Etat se fait païer des contributions, ou se rend ᵈplusieurs autresᵈ Etats tributaires, c'est un moïen bien certain d'attirer leur argent. Je n'entreprendrai pas de rechercher les moïens de mettre cette voie en usage, je me contenterai de dire que toutes les Nations qui ont fleuri par cette voie, n'ont pas laissé de ᵉtomberᵉ dans la décadence, comme les Etats qui ont fleuri par leur commerce. Les anciens Romains ont été plus puissans par cette voie que tous les autres Peuples dont nous avons connoissance; cependant ces mêmes Romains avant que de perdre ᶠun pouce du terreinᶠ de leurs vastes Etats, tomberent en décadence par le luxe, & s'appauvrirent par la diminution de l'argent effectif qui avoit circulé chez eux, & que leur luxe fit [260] passer de leur grand Empire chez les Nations orientales.

415 |19| Tandis que le luxe des Romains, qui ne commença qu'après la défaite d'Antiochus, Roi d'Asie, vers ᵃl'an de Rome 564ᵃ, se contentoit du produit & du travail de tous les vastes États de leur domination, la circulation de l'argent ne faisoit qu'augmenter au lieu de diminuer. Le Public étoit en possession de toutes les Mines d'or, d'argent & de cuivre qui étoient dans l'Empire. Ils avoient les Mines d'or d'Asie, de Macedoine, d'Aquilée, & les riches Mines, tant d'or que d'argent, d'Espagne & de plusieurs autres endroits. Ils avoient plusieurs Monnoies où ils faisoient battre des especes d'or, d'argent & de cuivre. La consommation qu'ils faisoient à Rome de ᵇtous les ouvrages & de toutes les marchandisesᵇ qu'ils tiroient de leurs vastes [261] Provinces, ne diminuoit pas la circulation de l'argent effectif; non plus que les Tableaux, les Statues & les Bijoux qu'ils en tiroient. ᶜQuoique les Seigneurs y fissent des dépenses excessives pour leurs tables, & païassentᶜ des quinze mille onces d'argent pour un seul poisson, tout cela ne diminuoit pas la quantité d'argent qui circuloit dans Rome, attendu que les tributs des Provinces l'y faisoient incessamment rentrer, sans parler de celui que les Préteurs & les Gouverneurs y apportoient par leurs extorsions. ᵈLes sommesᵈ qu'on tiroit annuellement des Mines, ne faisoient qu'augmenter à Rome la circulation pendant tout le regne d'Auguste. ᵉCependant, le luxe étoit déja fort grand, & on avoit beaucoup d'avidité, non-seulement pour tout ce que l'Empire produisoit de curieux, mais encore pour les bijoux des [262] Indes, pour le poivre & les épiceries, & pour toutes les raretés de l'Arabie; & les soieries qui n'étoient pas du crû de l'Empire, commençoient à y être recherchées.ᵉ Mais l'argent qu'on tiroit des Mines surpassoit encore les sommes qu'on envoïoit hors de l'Empire pour acheter tout cela. On sentit néanmoins sous Tibere une rareté d'argent : cet Empereur avoit resserré dans son Fisc deux milliards & sept cent millions de sesterces. Pour rétablir l'abondance & la circulation, il n'eut besoin d'emprunter que trois cens millions sur les hypotheques ᶠdes terresᶠ. Caligula dépensa en moins d'un an tout ce trésor de Tibere après sa mort, & ce fut alors que l'abondance d'argent dans la circulation fut au plus haut point à Rome. La fureur du luxe augmenta toujours; & du tems de Pline l'Historien, il sortoit de [263] l'Empire tous les ans au moins cent millions de sesterces, suivant son calcul. On n'en tiroit pas tant des Mines. Sous Trajan le prix des terres étoit tombé d'un tiers & au-delà, au rapport de Pline le jeune; & l'argent diminua toujours ᵍjusqu'au tems de l'Empereur Septime Severeᵍ. L'argent fut alors si rare à Rome, que cet Empereur fit des magasins étonnans de blé, ne pouvant pas ramasser des trésors assez considérables pour ses entreprises. Ainsi l'Empire Romain tomba en décadence par la perte de son argent, avant que d'avoir rien perdu de ses États. Voilà ce que le luxe causa, & ce qu'il causera toujours en pareil cas.

The last method I can think of to increase the quantity of money actually circulating in a State is by Violence and Arms and this is often blended with the others, since in all Treaties of Peace it is generally provided to retain the trading rights and privileges which it has been possible to derive from them. When a State exacts contributions or makes several other States tributary to it, this is a very sure method of obtaining their money. I will not undertake to examine the methods of putting this device into practice, but will content myself with saying that all the Nations who have flourished in this way have not failed to decline, like States who have flourished through their trade. The ancient Romans were more powerful in this wise than all the other Peoples we know of. Yet these same Romans before losing an inch of the Land of their vast Estates fell into decline by Luxury and brought themselves low by the diminution of the money which had circulated among them, but which Luxury caused to pass from their great Empire into oriental countries.

So long as the luxury of the Romans (which did not begin till after the defeat of Antiochus, King of Asia about A.U.C. 564) was confined to the produce of the Land and Labour of all the vast Estates of their dominion, the circulation of money increased instead of diminishing. The Public was in possession of all the Mines of Gold, Silver, and Copper in the Empire. They had the gold Mines of Asia, Macedonia, Aquilaea and the rich mines both of gold and silver of Spain and other countries. They had several Mints where gold, silver and copper coins were struck. The consumption at Rome of all the articles and merchandise which they drew from their vast Provinces did not diminish the circulation of the currency, any more than Pictures, Statues and Jewels which they drew from them. Though the patricians laid out excessive amounts for their feasts and paid 15,000 ounces of silver for a single fish, all that did not diminish the quantity of money circulating in Rome, seeing that the tribute of the Provinces regularly brought it back, to say nothing of what Praetors and Governors brought thither by their extortions. The amounts annually extracted from the Mines merely increased the circulation at Rome during the whole reign of Augustus. Luxury was however already on a very great scale, and there was much eagerness not only for curiosities produced in the Empire but also for jewels from India, pepper and spices, and all the rarities of Arabia, and the silks which were not made with raw materials of the Empire began to be in demand there. The Money drawn from the Mines still exceeded however the sums sent out of the Empire to buy all these things. Nevertheless under Tiberius a scarcity of money was felt. That Emperor had shut up in his Treasury 2 milliards and 700 millions of sesterces. To restore abundance of circulation he had only to borrow 300 millions on the mortgage of his Estates. Caligula in less than one year spent all this treasure of Tiberius after his death, and it was then that the abundance of money in circulation was at its highest in Rome. The fury of Luxury kept on increasing. In the time of Pliny, the historian, there was exported from the Empire, as he estimated, at least 100 millions of sesterces annually. This was more than was drawn from the Mines. Under Trajan the price of Land had fallen by one-third or more, according to the younger Pliny, and money continued to decrease until the time of the Emperor Septimus Severus. It was then so scarce at Rome that the Emperor made enormous granaries, being unable to collect large treasure for his enterprises. Thus the Roman Empire fell into decline through the loss of its money before losing any of its estates. Behold what Luxury brought about and what it always will bring about in similar circumstances.

a...a: R: 'La Derniere façon'   **414**

b...b: R: 'pour y augmenter La quantité dargent effectif dans la Circulation dargent dans un état'

c...c: R: 'qu'on en a pu tirér'

d...d: R: 'Les autres'

e...e: R: 'Touchér'

f...f: R: 'une partye de Terrain'

a...a: R: 'lan 564'   **415**

b...b: R: 'Tous Les ouvrages et Marchandises'

c...c: R: 'Les Seigneurs avoient beau y faire des depences énormes pour leurs tables et payér'

d...d: R: 'Les fonds'

e...e: R: 'on ne laissoit pas deja d'avoir beaucoup de luxe non seulement pour toutes Les Rarétés que l'empire produisoit mais encore pour Les bijoux des Indes, Le Poivre, Le poivre les épices et Les Rarétés de l'arabie Les soyeries qui N'estoient pas du Cru de l'empire Commançoient a Etre Recherchées'

f...f: R: 'de Touts'

g...g: R: 'Jusquau temps septiéme sévére'

Essai (E)	Dictionary (D)	Analysis (A)

416

[II, 5, col.1] Of the natural causes of the rise and decay of nations in wealth and power, with regard to the price of labour.

[45] **CHAP. XV.**

Of the Ways and Means by which real Species Increase and Decrease in a Kingdom.

417

In all trading States where there are not Mines of Gold, or Silver, the only natural Way of acquiring these precious Metals, is by foreign Commerce; and this by a very few Words is explained, by the Acquisition of the surplus Value of our Exports, more than that of our Imports; this surplus Value must be paid us in Bullion, which brings what is called the general Ballance of Trade on our Side; and it is this Ballance which increases our real Specie, and consequently if this Ballance is against us, that is to say, if the Amount of what we import, exceeds that of what we export, the Excess must be paid in Bullion, and consequently will decrease our real Specie.

418

Let us suppose France in a middling state, the land pretty well cultivated, and the proprietors rents pretty well paid; if in these circumstances there happens a civil war, the proprietors will take party, some on one side and some on the other; they will engage and mortgage their estates, to lend money to the chief of their faction to support his quarrel, since, if the opposite chief prevails, their lands and estates will be confiscated, the undertakers will be disheartened, the country rifled, the magazines and warehouses plundered, and labour will be discouraged; so the land will not produce wherewithal to maintain the inhabitants, and to supply necessaries for the armies. The chiefs of the parties will be obliged to get stores and other necessaries from the neighbouring states which are in peace, and consequently they will send money out of France to pay for them.

In order to illustrate this Matter, let us suppose, *France* in the State in which it was in the Year 1740, the Land tollerably well tilled, Rents well paid, but that the Calamity of a civil War broke out: the great Proprietors of Land would take some one Side, some [46] the other; all Ways and Means to raise Money by Mortgage and Credit would be practised, in order to support their respective Parties; the Land in general would be uncultivated; Manufacturers and Undertakers in Trade would be disconcerted and at a loss what to do, consequently very cautious how they engaged in Business; Countries, Towns, Cities, and Villages, would be pillaged and plundered. The Farmer could not bring to Market the Produce of his Land; in this unhappy Situation of Affairs, a Necessity must arise to import from foreign Countries the Materials necessary to support this domestic Contention; Money must be had for this Purpose, which would carry away the current Coin of the Country,

i. The many correspondences between the following fragments from **416** D and A suggest that they derive from Richard Cantillon's manuscripts. They are included in this place because they deal with the same subject matter as E II, viii [E396–E415]. Although the wording is very different, some of the arguments correspond to those in the French version.

ii. A is presented out of sequence. In Philip Cantillon's book it follows directly after A288. However, note the similarities between the chapter titles in A416 and in E338, E385 and E396.

iii. The different title of the subsection in D is probably due to Postlethwayt who decided to include this fragment in the entry 'Labour'. This entry was included in issue 85 of the *Universal Dictionary*, first published in September 1753. Cf. C7i.

iv. Harris (1757: 88–95) has a section, entitled *The quantity of money every where, will naturally find a certain level or proportion*, which may be indebted to this account in D. Cf. C67iv and C426v. This does not exclude the possibility that Harris may have been indebted to Hume as well.

A417 is reminiscent of the beginning of E355.   **417**

i. There is no counterpart anywhere in E to this discussion of the **418** economic consequences of a civil war in France. Although the argument in D418 and A418 is similar, the wording is quite different. Note that A mentions the year 1740 and presents the case as a hypothetical one. Even though D too initially presents the civil war as a hypothetical case, in D424 he reveals that it is also the historical case of France in the 1640s. This suggests that Philip may simply have changed the date by a century.

ii. Perhaps the significance of the starting point of this discussion is that the initial outflows of money, and the decline in production and population are caused not by the increase in prices (as in E353), but by the 'external shock' of a civil war. Only thereafter the sequence of events is ruled by economic factors.

419

[II, 5, col.2] || This will gradually create a scarcity of money in France; besides that great sums will be buried, and that all barters in evaluation and credit will be diminished, the uncertainty of the event of war will hinder marriages and multiplication, and the mortality in the war will diminish the inhabitants.

and consequently occasion a great Scarcity; many of the Inhabitants would quit the Country, the general Face of all Things would wear the Complexion of Blood, Confusion, Poverty, and Want;

420

|| In this situation France will be in a deplorable condition, and in danger of being oppressed by a foreign power. A general plague in France will occasion much the same mischiefs.

and the Country would be in Danger of being invaded by some of its ambitious Neighbours.

421

|| Now let us suppose the civil war ended, the proprietors who received little or no rent during the troubles, and whose lands lay waste and uncultivated, will now farm them out at a small rent, as well because of the scarcity of money, which makes all commodities cheap, as because they must encourage the farmers, in regard to the decrease of the inhabitants. As the rents are small, they will live without luxury, and consume little or no foreign commodities which will be dear, since more money circulates on this hypothesis in the neighbouring states, than in France. The labourers and peasants, by reason of the thinness of the inhabitants, will be encouraged, and, as they will consequently find it easy to subsist, they will breed up a great number of children, and so France will become again very populous. The scarcity of money in France will make their commodities so cheap, that they will export great quantities of them, particularly if valuable manufactures are set up in France. So that France will in this case get a yearly ballance, and fall naturally into the channels of trade. This will gradually bring great sums of money into France, where it's plenty will begin to raise the price of all things, and where several undertakers will have amassed good sums of money.

|| Now let us suppose this Plague of civil Contention happily composed; the Consequence would naturally be, that the Landholders receiving little or no Money from [47] their Lands, would be necessitated to lett them at low Rents; and Money being scarce, the Land's Produce would be cheap, the Landlords would be obliged to live in a proportionable Compass; few or no foreign Goods would be imported, being too dear, with respect to the Poverty of the Country, where its own native Produce would be so cheap as to encourage foreign Nations, to come and purchase them: this would bring in a Flow of Money; the Cheapness of Rents to the Farmers would produce Plenty; the Country People finding easy Means of subsisting would be induced to marry, and bring up a Stock of Children; valuable Manufactures would be established; the Cheapness of Merchandize would introduce a large Demand for foreign Exportation, all Things being in Peace and Tranquillity, Money would insensibly increase in Circulation, and get into the Channels of Trade; the Inhabitants would become numerous, the Prices of all Things would, in proportion to the Increase of Money, insensibly augment;

The expression 'barters in evaluation' in **419**
D419 corresponds to the French '*troc par*
évaluation'. See C305ii.

420

421

422

‖ Now, since the prices of all things are risen insensibly, the proprietors will raise the price of their estates, the increase of the inhabitants will make them offer to work for less sustenance than at first; and, as there is plenty of money in circulation, foreign commodities will come at a cheap price, the exportation of commodities will slacken because of their dearness, and the neighbouring nations will be able to set up cheaper manufactures; and, as the business decreases in France, several French tradesmen will go into foreign parts, where there is work for them, and improve the manufactures there. The quantities of money amassed by the French undertakers in the course of their business, while France gained the ballance of trade, will encourage to spend more money, and consume more foreign commodities, than usual, as they are now cheaper; and the proprietors, with their additional rent, will do the same, and so luxury will come into fashion.

Merchants and Tradesmen would by their Savings grow rich; the Landholders would increase their Rents, Luxury and Profusion would soon take the Place of Oeconomy and Industry; the landed Gentry, [48] who before lived with great Care and Parsimony, would now keep great Tables well covered with Delicacies; Merchants and Traders becoming rich, would launch out into Expence, and would consume more of the Land's Produce than before.

423

‖ In the beginning of this turn of affairs, the balance of trade will be pretty equal, France being not yet quite beaten out of the channels of trade, but only beginning to lose some branches of it. In this situation France is in it's acmé, or highest state of power, having more ready money than the neighbouring states, and consequently the king can raise greater sums from his subjects than at any time. But, as the increase of expence and luxury has taken root, 'tis remarkable those who begin it seldom lay it aside till they are undone; this will cause a continuance of the expence of foreign commodities, and, the exportation slackening and decreasing in proportion, the ballance of trade will turn against France, and their money will be sent out annually in payment of the surplus of those foreign commodities they consume: and thus France will decline in it's wealth and power, by the decrease of the quantity of actual money, and the thinning of it's inhabitants, which it's luxury and decay of trade and manufactures will necessarily occasion.

And in this Situation of Luxury and Expence, *France* would be looked upon by its Neighbours in the highest Point of Power and Riches; and the Country possessing more Money than its Neighbours, every thing would proportionably be dearer; Foreigners would cease buying, and would attempt supplying themselves by their own Manufactures; the Channels of Commerce would be turned into different Courses; the Increase of Coin would increase a Demand for more than the Land could produce; and consequently this Demand must be supplied by foreign Produce, which would carry the Ballance of Trade against *France*; Manufacturers, Artizans and Merchants would quit the Kingdom, and in a Course of Years the Nation would be drained of all its Coin. Luxury is seldom introduced into a Country or Community, but when it is believed that it can always be supported; but once begun, People generally ruin themselves before they are prevailed upon to quit it.

Cf. D422 with E398–E400. The parallels between **422**
E and A are less strong. See e.g. the argument in
E399 and D422 that French tradesmen will move
abroad, but which does not figure in A. For a similar
difference, see C349. Also, the final remarks in D422
about the spending of French undertakers who have
grown rich on foreign luxuries are reminiscent of the
'*Particuliers opulens*' in E400 who do the same.

i. The phrases 'acmé, or highest state of power' in **423**
D423 and 'the highest Point of Power and Riches' in
A423 correspond to '*le plus haut point de richesse*'
in E401. The term 'acmé' used to carry the medical
connotation of the culmination of a condition that
carries within it the seeds of a downturn. The 'disease'
here can be diagnosed as being luxury consumption
about which the author observes that 'tis remarkable
those who begin it seldom lay 'it aside till they are
undone'. A similar point about the persistence of
changed spending habits is made at the end of D349.
ii. The observation in A423 that the increase in
money supply could lead to a 'Demand for more than
the Land could produce' appears to assume some
definite limits to the productive potential of a country.
iii. Groenewegen (2001: 184) suggests a
correspondence of A423 with Steuart (1767, II, x);
Skinner (1966, I, 196 n3) suggests instead that the
correspondence is with E, II, viii, but also notes the
more widespread views among authors of the period
about the cyclical nature of the opulence of trading
nations.

424

‖ This example of France is historical. After the composing of the civil war there about 1652, the prime minister of the finances, Mr Colbert, set up and encouraged fine manufactures there, and France lived several years without luxury, and few coaches were seen at Paris.

425

‖ They gained greatly in the ballance of trade, and Lewis the XIVth grew very powerful: money grew very plenty, and about 1680, the ballance of trade grew pretty equal, and luxury began; and then it would have naturally turned against France, which must have necessarily declined in process of time, if that operation had not been hastened by the expulsion of the ªHugonotsª, which, by the money and inhabitants sent out of the kingdom, hastened the decline of France; which nevertheless did not happen visibly, till about the year 1715, when she was in peace.

426

‖ The rise and decline of all other kingdoms, naturally and abstractedly from wars and conquests, are owing to causes of the like nature; and, when a nation gets a great plenty of money, and increases exorbitantly in it's paper circulation, it naturally tends to decline, by the dearness that happens of land, labour, and commodities; and the greatest prudence of a legislator seems to be, when money and paper circulation are rising to that plenty, to take methods to clog their circulation, and, if possible, to lock up great sums of money gradually and insensibly, to encourage the use of plate, and take any other methods than those that naturally and commonly happen, which is to send it again to foreign parts, in payment of jewels, pictures and other ornaments of luxury.

[49] ‖ By these Explanations, the Causes which enrich and impoverish trading Nations are easily traced. Kingdoms after public Calamities, provided they are but tolerably well governed and protected, grow rapidly wealthy; those who survive the Calamities of their Country become wise sober and industrious. Had the Calamities introduced by the Schemes of the Year 1720 been wisely applied, and Labour and Industry eased of its oppressive Taxes, the Community in general had long since been restored to its Senses, from the Madness and Folly which the Schemes of that Year possessed us with, and still seem to govern us by; and it had not been verified what was then introduced (to our Scandal and Reproach) as a Maxim, that every Man in Great Britain was to be purchased for his Price. The learned Mr. *Hume* observes, that Mankind are such Dupes, that notwithstanding any violent Shock to the Community, yet it would not be long before Credit would again revive; and though Men are commonly governed by what they have seen more than by what they foresee; yet Promises, fair Appearances with the Allurements of Gain, are powerful Temptations which few are able to resist.

The revival of the manufactures of France is also mentioned **424**
in E336 and E403, but the year mentioned there is 1646.
Cf. C336i. The 'civil war' referred to here was the Fronde,
which according to some datings lasted from 1649 until 1652.
Colbert was controller-general from 1665. This makes the
presumed starting-point of the revival of the French economy
later than in the French version.

ᵃ...ᵃ: *sic.*

The expulsion of the Huguenots is also mentioned in E403. **425**
In both E403 and D425 the turning point in France's fortunes
is in the early 1680s. These versions also agree about the
subsequent decline, although only D425 states that the decline
was not clearly visible until 1715. This latter date coincides
with the beginning of John Law's System.

i. E400 also makes the point that expenditures on jewels and pictures from abroad **426**
are a drain on money. But there it is seen as a negative effect.

ii. E401 offers similar advice to D426, namely that '*le Prince ou la Legislature*'
should withdraw money from circulation. This advice is not found in A.

iii. Note the emphasis in D426 on the 'natural' course of things. Cf. the phrase '*le
cours naturel des choses humaines*' in E402. Political decisions can only slow down
or speed up this natural course (i.e. France would have revived without Colbert; she
would have become uncompetitive without the expulsion of the Huguenots).

iv. A426 starts to diverge substantially from D. After a few sentences the former
moves away from the main topic (the increase and decrease of money in a state) and
embarks on a discussion of public debt. This shift happens from the quote of Hume
onwards, which is taken from his essay 'Of Public Credit', first published in 1752. The
remainder of chapter XV of the *Analysis*, pp. 49–51, equally appears to be inspired
by Hume. Only the final paragraph, on p. 51, is perhaps more likely to be due to
Richard Cantillon. It reads: 'Luxury, which requires to be supported by foreign Aids,
inevitably brings Ruin to a Nation, unless timely prevented by our great and opulent
Rulers; not by Prohibitions, but by Example, encouraging thereby the Consumption
of our own Manufactures, which in my humble Opinion, would have more effectual
good Consequences, than all the Prohibitions which Law can contrive.'

v. The following passage in Harris (1757: 99–100, section 'Hoarding the precious
metals, beneficial'), especially the reference to plate at the end, suggests a reliance
on D426: 'In the days of prosperity therefore, it would be prudent to lay up a kind
of dead stock of the precious metals, against any emergencies that might happen.
This stock must be kept out from the circulating cash; for an increase there, would
not answer the end; and indeed an overflow of money in circulation, would spend
itself, by draining up the sources that produced it. But people generally will not
hoard up cash; all like to display their wealth, and lay out their superfluities in some
costly things. There seems then no method so effectual for the securing of a dead
stock of treasure, in any country, as the encouraging the use of plate; by making it
fashionable, preferable to more brittle or more perishable commodities.' For other
places where Harris relies on D, see C67iv.

427
The next [II, 6, col.1] essential thing to be done, also, is the gradual annihilation of their paper debts, and the taxes thereby occasioned. If this could be effected, a state would continue, by a reasonable price of it's commodities, to keep up the channels of trade and exportation; but, where things go on in their natural course, the too great plenty of money, or paper credit, by enhancing the price of things, gives other rival nations an opportunity to take the trade into their hands, and to get the money along with it.

428
|| There seems to be but a limited quantity of trade in Europe: suppose that in the trade of the woollen manufacture the quantity of foreign cloth consumed in Italy, Spain, Portugal, Germany, Turkey, and the North, may amount to 30,000,000 ounces of silver, and that the cloth is chiefly supplied by England, France, Flanders, Holland, &c. That England is in the channel of exporting and supplying to the value of 15 millions; if it should in any year supply 20 millions, it must be at the expence and diminution of the sales of others: and, if France should get into the channel of supplying large quantities of woollen manufactures more than usual, it would be probably so much taken away from the English trade.

429
|| Sir William Petty seems not to have had any thought of this limitation of consumption, when he insinuated, that it would be best for England to abandon the manure of the land, and make all the inhabitants turn tradesmen, weavers, &c.

430
|| If we suppose there are 90 millions of inhabitants in Europe, it will not, perhaps, be found that one in 50 of the whole number consumes yearly foreign manufactures: France and England principally consume their own; and even the greatest number of inhabitants of all other countries are cloathed at home.

431
|| Let us suppose the circulating money of England to have been four millions sterling, and the lands to be farmed out at 12 millions, the yearly produce of the land, according to the method we have followed, will be 36 millions; if, in process of time, the circulating money of England comes to seven or eight millions, the rents of the land will naturally come to exceed 20 millions, without any other alteration than the increase of the quantity of circulating money; and whereas the lands of England may have been worth, at 20 years purchase, 240 millions, in the first supposition, they will, in the second, be computed at 400 millions, for no other reason than because from three to four million additional money was introduced into barter, though the said sum should be due to foreigners, and pays them a yearly interest, to the great disadvantage of the English ballance of trade.

432
|| Now if the said sum, from three to four millions, should be sent back to the foreigners, the rents of the lands would fall to 12 millions, as before; and here would appear, on computation, a vast decrease of wealth of England, without any real decrease in the intrinsic value of land and labour, and the annual produce of the land.

For the phrase, 'natural course' see C426iii. **427**

In E193 Cantillon states that in the (now missing) Supplement he **428**
has made calculations about the size of the international market
for textiles. Perhaps the figures mentioned in D428 derive from
the same calculations.

The reference in D429 to Petty is probably to that author's view **429**
in *Political Arithmetick* (1691b: 12) that '[t]here is much more to
be gained by Manufacture than Husbandry and by Merchandise
than Manufacture', and, p. 33, that: 'if all the Husbandmen of
England who now earn but 8*d*. a day, or thereabouts, become
tradesmen and earn 16*d*. a day ... that then it would be the
advantage of *England* to throw up their Husbandry, and to make
no use of their lands but for Grass Horses, Milch Cows, Gardens
and Orchards, &c.' In E193 Cantillon also objects to similar
schemes that depend on the assumption that any additional
production can be absorbed by foreign markets. For other
mentions of Petty, see E/D105, E175, E/D290 and D508.

430

i. The phrase 'according to the method of calculation we have **431**
followed' in D431 is a reference to the earlier assumption that
the amount of money is circulation is one-third the size of rents
paid and one-ninth of total annual produce. See D287 and D317.
ii. E404 also discusses the relation between the amount of
money in circulation, the value of rents and the price of land.
iii. At the end of this paragraph it is stated, rather suddenly,
that the increase in the amount of money in circulation is due to
borrowing from foreigners. This is reminiscent of E410.

i. For other occurrences in D of the term 'intrinsic' see D70, 75, **432**
76, 77, 107, 137, 210 and 254.
ii. Here the fragment in the *Dictionary* entry 'Labour'
corresponding to E II, viii ends. That entry continues immediately
with a fragment corresponding to E I, xvi (reproduced in D183–
D201).

Essai (E)	Dictionary (D)	Analysis (A)

433 [264] **CHAPITRE** ᵃ**IX**ᵃ.

De l'intérêt de l'argent, & de ses causes.

[I, 995, col.2]
Of the INTEREST of MONEY, considered in a national and political view.

[62] **CHAP. XVII.**
Of the Interest of Money.

434

|| Under the article BARTER we have, from the plainest principles of reason, shewed the nature of money and commodities, considered by way of exchange for each other; also under the articles CASH and CIRCULATION of MONEY, as well as the article SILVER, we have pursued this point, upon one consistent plan of reasoning, we apprehend. And, [I, 996, col.1] Agreeably to the same principles, we shall now inquire into the interest of money.

435 |1| Comme les prix des choses se fixent dans les altercations des marchés par les quantités des choses exposées en vente proportionnellement à la quantité d'argent qu'on en offre, ou ce qui est la même chose, par la proportion numerique des Vendeurs & des Acheteurs; ᵃde mêmeᵃ l'intérêt de l'argent dans un Etat se fixe par la proportion numérique des Prêteurs & des Emprunteurs.

|| Under the preceding articles, we have supposed a fixed quantity of money, and considered the nature of it's circulation, as it is given and received in pledge and barter for all other commodities, between which it fixes a par and proportion of value.

Chapter IX
*Of the Interest of Money and its
Causes*

^a...^a: R:' 9^e'

D is part of the entry 'Interest' (I, 988–99) which appeared **433**
in issue 83 of the *Universal Dictionary*, first published
around August/September 1753. The addition to the
title, in comparison to those of E and A, of 'considered
in a national and political view' is surely Postlethwayt's
addition to distinguish it from his preceding arithmetical
exposition of the calculation of interest rates.

The 'consistent plan of reasoning' mentioned in **434**
D434 appears to reveal something about the order of
the manuscript Postlethwayt plagiarised: 'Barter' (see
D239–D253) corresponds to E II, ii; 'Cash' (see D255–
D295) to E II, iii; and 'Circulation of Money' (see
D299–D317) to E II, iv. One would therefore perhaps
expect the entry, 'Silver' (also mentioned in D253,
D384) to contain fragments corresponding to E II, v.
However, this entry (*Universal Dictionary* II, 729–31)
contains nothing that may have been written by Richard
Cantillon. One may speculate that in the autumn of
1753 it was Postlethwayt's intention to include such a
fragment but by the time he came to the letter S, in 1755,
decided not to do so. A possible reason for this was that
by this time Postlethwayt was aiming to finish his work
quickly and no longer resorted to padding out his entries
with materials that did not relate directly to the topics at
hand. See Introduction p. 20.

Just as the Prices of things are fixed
in the altercations of the Market by
the quantity of things offered for
sale in proportion to the quantity of
money offered for them, or, what
comes to the same thing, by the
proportionate number of Sellers
and Buyers, so in the same way
the Interest of Money in a State is
settled by the proportionate number
of Lenders and Borrowers.

^a...^a: R: 'Tout
deméme'

i. The remark in D435 that a 'fixed quantity of **435**
money' had been supposed previously probably
relates to the fragments corresponding to E II, ii–v
(cf. C434). Only from E/D/A338 onwards is the
'increase and decrease' of the amount of money in
circulation considered.

ii. E435 is reminiscent of Turgot's statement in
section 72 of his *Reflections* that interest 'like
the price of every commodity, is determined by the
chaffering of seller and buyer; by the balance of the
offer and the demand' (Turgot [1766] 1977: 77). But
cf. C436ii.

436 |2| ᵃQuoique l'argent passe pour gages dans le troc, cependant il ne se multiplie point, & ne produit point un interêt dans la simple circulationᵃ. Les nécessités des Hommes semblent ᵇavoirᵇ [265] introduit l'usage de l'interêt. Un Homme qui prête son argent sur de bons gages ou sur l'hypotheque des terres, court au moins le hazard de l'inimitié de l'Emprunteur, ᶜou celui des frais, des procès & des pertesᶜ; mais lorsqu'il prête sans sureté, il court risque de tout perdre. Par rapport à ces raisons, les Hommes nécessiteux doivent avoir dans les commencemens tenté les Prêteurs par ᵈl'appasᵈ d'un profit; & ce profit doit avoir été proportionné aux nécessités des Emprunteurs ᵉ& àᵉ la crainte & à l'avarice des Prêteurs. Voilà ce me semble la premiere source de l'intérêt. Mais son usage constant dans les Etats paroît fondé sur les profits que les Entrepreneurs en peuvent faire.

|| Of the INTEREST of MONEY.

|| It does not appear that money begets an interest by passing for a pledge in barter, nor that it's exchange for other commodities produces a great quantity of it in a state.

437

|| If we consider a proprietor, who keeps his land in his own hands, and employs slaves to procure him the necessaries and conveniences of life, and sets overseers to inspect them, it does not appear, in that œconomy, that money is necessary to carry it on, since he can attribute so much meat, drink and cloaths, to maintain them and their children, as he thinks fit, out of the produce of the land and their own labour; as also what he pleases to the overseers, to maintain them on a better foot than the slaves.

|| But, if the business be carried out by undertakers, money seems absolutely necessary to fix the par and proportion of values; since, in that case, they must barter absolutely their commodities one with another: and it appears, from the inductions made under the foregoing articles, that money, and it's circulation, is only necessary for barters with undertakers.

|| Now it is plain that the undertakers get a subsistence and profit by the business they undertake (whereby they correspond to the overseers of slaves) and that the said profit is naturally proportionable to the quantity of the business that is carried on under their inspection, and the number of workmen and journeymen they employ; and, since they carry on their business by advances of money for the materials they purchase to work upon, and for the maintenance of their servants, their profits are naturally proportionable to the quantities of money they advance in their business.

Though money passes for a pledge in exchange it does not multiply itself or beget an interest in simple circulation. The needs of man seem to have introduced the usage of Interest. A man who lends his money on good security or on mortgage runs at least the risk of the ill will of the Borrower, or of expenses, lawsuits and losses. But when he lends without security he runs the risk of losing everything. For this reason needy men must in the beginning have tempted Lenders by the bait of a profit. And this profit must have been proportionate to the needs of the Borrowers and the fear and avarice of the Lenders. This seems to me the origin of Interest. But its constant usage in States seems based upon the Profits which the Undertakers can make out of it.

[a]...[a]: R: 'Largent pour avoir passé pour gage dans Le troc, ne se multiplie pas, et ne produit pas un interest dans La simple Circulation'

[b]...[b]: R: 'd'avoir'

[c]...[c]: R: 'de frais de procés et pérte'

[d]...[d]: R: 'La part'

[e]...[e]: R: 'et'

436

i. Might V436d be due to an error in dictation? See C274iii.

ii. It appears that Turgot in paragraph 72 of his *Reflexions*, paraphrases and contradicts the last sentence of E436: '*Le prix du prêt n'est point du tout fondé, comme on pourrait l'imaginer, sur le profit que l'emprunteur espère qu'il pourra faire.*' 'The price of the loan is by no means founded, as might be imagined, on the profit the Borrower hopes to make with the capital of which he purchases the use' (Turgot [1766] 1977: 77). Cf. C435ii.

437

i. D437 appears to be an alternative for E438–E440.

ii. Unlike E438, which reinvokes the 'three rents theory', here the initial supposition of a money-less economy of a single estate is briefly resumed as a starting point (cf. D262–D264 and D345).

iii. Cf. the statement in D437 'that money, and its circulation, is only necesarry for barters with undertakers' with D264, D283 and also D638–D639.

iv. For the term 'œconomy' see C79i.

v. Note the remarkable statement about profit in the final sentence of D437 as being 'proportionable to the quantities of money [undertakers] advance in their business'. It is arguably the clearest statement in any of the versions of Cantillon's work akin to later classical conceptions of profit as a return on capital advanced. Also see E440, E/D/A442 and C442iv.

438 |3| La terre produit naturellement, ᵃaidée du travail de l'Homme, quatre, dix, vingt, cinquante, cent, cent-cinquante [266] foisᵃ, la quantité de blé qu'on y seme, suivant la bonté du terroir ᵇ& l'industrie des Habitansᵇ. Elle multiplie ᶜles fruits & les bestiauxᶜ. Le Fermier qui en conduit le travail a ordinairement les deux tiers du produit, dont un tiers paie ses frais & son entretien, ᵈl'autreᵈ lui reste pour profit de son entreprise.

439 |4| Si le Fermier a assez de fond pour conduire son entreprise, s'il a tous les outils & les instrumens nécessaires, les chevaux pour labourer, les bestiaux qu'il faut pour mettre la terre en valeur, &c., il prendra pour lui, tous frais faits, le tiers du produit de sa Ferme. Mais si un Laboureur entendu, qui vit de son travail à gages au jour la journée, & qui n'a aucun fond, peut trouver quelqu'un qui veuille bien lui prêter un fond ou de l'argent pour en acheter, il sera en état de donner à ce Prêteur toute la [267] troisieme rente, ou le tiers du produit d'une Ferme dont il deviendra le Fermier ou l'Entrepreneur. Cependant, il croira sa condition meilleure qu'auparavant, attendu qu'il trouvera son entretien dans la seconde rente, & deviendra Maître, de Valet qu'il étoit : que si ᵃpar sa grande œconomie, & en se fraudant quelque chose du nécessaireᵃ, il peut ᵇpar degrésᵇ amasser quelques petits fonds, il aura tous les ans moins à emprunter, & parviendra ᶜdans la suiteᶜ à s'approprier toute la troisieme rente.

440 |5| Si cet Entrepreneur nouveau trouve à acheter à crédit du blé ou des bestiaux, pour les païer à long terme & lorsqu'il sera en état de faire de l'argent par la vente du produit de sa Ferme, il en donnera volontiers un plus grand prix que celui du marché contre argent comptant: & cette façon sera la même chose que s'il em-[268]pruntoit de l'argent comptant pour acheter le blé au comptant, en donnant pour l'interêt la différence du prix du comptant & de celui à terme : mais de quelque façon qu'il emprunte soit au comptant, soit en marchandises, il faut qu'il lui reste dequoi s'entretenir par son entreprise, sans quoi il fera banquerouteᵃ. Ceᵃ hazard fera ᵇqu'on exigera de luiᵇ vingt à trente pour cent ᶜde profit ou d'interêtᶜ sur la quantité de l'argent ou sur la valeur des denrées ou des marchandises qu'on lui prêtera.

The Land naturally produces, aided by human Labour, 4, 10, 20, 50, 100, 150 times the amount of corn sown upon it, according to the fertility of the soil and the industry of the inhabitants. It multiplies Fruits and Cattle. The Farmer who conducts the working of it has generally two thirds of the produce, one third pays his expenses and upkeep, the other remains for the profit of his enterprise.

ᵃ...ᵃ: R: 'aidée du travail 4.10..20..100...150 fois'
ᵇ...ᵇ: et Lindustrie'
ᶜ...ᶜ: R: 'Les Bestiaux qui paissent et Les fruits'
ᵈ...ᵈ: R: 'Lautre tiers'

For other occurrences **438** in E of the 'three rents theory', see E109– E113 and E265ff.

If the Farmer have enough capital to carry on his enterprise, if he have the needful tools and instruments, horses for ploughing, cattle to make the Land pay, etc. he will take for himself after paying all expense a third of the produce of his Farm. But if a competent Labourer who lives from day to day on his wages and has no capital, can find some one willing to lend him land or money to buy some, he will be able to give the Lender all the third rent, or third part of the produce of a Farm of which he will become the Farmer or Undertaker. However he will think his position improved since he will find his upkeep in the second rent and will become Master instead of Man. If by great oeconomy and pinching himself somewhat of his necessities he can gradually accumulate some little capital, he will have every year less to borrow, and will at last arrive at keeping the whole of his third rent.

ᵃ...ᵃ: R: 'par la grande Economie et Contentent du nécéssaire'
ᵇ...ᵇ: R: 'par la suitte'
ᶜ...ᶜ: R: 'par la Suitte'

439

If this new Undertaker finds means to buy corn or cattle on credit, to be paid off at a long date when he can make money by the sale of his farm produce, he will gladly pay more than the market price for ready money. The result will be the same as if he borrowed cash to buy corn for ready money, paying as interest the difference between the cash price and the price payable at a future date. But whether he borrow cash or goods there must be enough left to him for upkeep or he will become bankrupt. The risk of this is the reason why he will be required to pay 20 or 30 per cent. profit or interest on the amount of money or value of the produce or merchandise lent to him.

ᵃ...ᵃ: R: ', et Ce'
ᵇ...ᵇ: R: 'que l'on éxigéra de luy'
ᶜ...ᶜ: R: 'd'Interets et de proffit'

Cf. the phrase '*païer* **440** *à long terme*' with 'payable at a long term' in D445.

441

[62 continued] ‖ The far greatest Number of Labourers, Husbandmen, and Artizans in the Community live from Hand to Mouth, treasuring little or nothing of their Earnings; and Money with them is only an Hire to enable them to purchase the Necessaries of Life, without appearing to carry any other Interest.

442 |6| D'un autre côté, un maître Chapelier, ᵃqui a du fond pour conduire sa Manufacture de chapeaux soit pour louer une maison, acheter des castors, des laines, de la teinture, &c., soit pour païer toutes les semaines, la subsistance de ses Ouvriers,ᵃ doit non-seulement trouver son entretien dans ᵇcetteᵇ en-[269]treprise, mais encore un profit ᶜsemblable àᶜ celui du Fermier, qui a la troisieme partie pour lui. Cet entretien, de même que ᵈceᵈ profit, doit se trouver dans la vente des chapeaux, dont le prix doit païer non-seulement les matériaux, mais aussi l'entretien du Chapelier ᵉ& de ses Ouvriers, & encoreᵉ le profit en question.

‖ A master hatter, who sets up for an undertaker, hires a workhouse of a proprietor for his work, buys wool, poil de castor, &c. buys utensils and instruments fit for the work, hires several journeymen for daily wages, and makes all advances of money necessary in that business: as he corresponds to the overseer of slaves, and is the master and inspector of his journeymen; as he lays out his money at an uncertainty, and runs the hazard of losing it; he must get, in the price of his hats, a profit proportionable to his risque, expence, and situation; and so he commonly does, lives pretty well, and maintains a family, and breeds up children; and, if he computes what his advances of money amount to, and what money he has by his profits, which he spends in his family, he will find that he has made 30 or 40 per cent. of his money; he will have sold 10,000 hats, or more, in a year, to a haberdasher of hats, who has paid him money for them, which reimburses his advance, and leaves the said profit, and enables him to go on with his employment, and advance for the ensuing year.

[63] ‖ But Merchants and Undertakers in Manufacture, whom I consider in my Supposition as the Proprietors of Money, acquire Subsistence from its Income, by employing it to the Use of the Labourer and Artizan: this Profit is proportioned to the Demand the Public has to support or supply the Taste and Luxury of the Proprietors of Land, and the Quantity of Money in several Hands to be advanced. A young Tradesman who has not wherewith to establish himself, is obliged to act as a Journeyman for Wages with some Master, Artist, or Manufacturer, the more Money the Master has to buy his Materials to supply the Calls of the Public, the more Men he is enabled to employ; by which he has the better Chance of enriching himself and Family, by his Care and Industry.

With A441 starts the body of chapter XVII of the **441** *Analysis*.

Again, a master Hatter who has capital to carry on his manufacture of Hats, either to rent a house, buy beaver, wool, dye, etc. or to pay for the subsistence of his workmen every week, ought not only to find his upkeep in this enterprise, but also a profit like that of the Farmer who has his third part for himself. This upkeep and the profit should come from the sale of the Hats whose price ought to cover not only the materials but also the upkeep of the Hatter and his Workmen and also the profit in question.

ᵃ...ᵃ: R: ' (qui a du fond pour Conduire sa manufacture de Chapeaux, Soit pour Louer une maison achetér ustancilles, teintures, laines, outils &c Soit pour payér toutes Les semaines Les nouritures de ses ouvriérs et Compagnons)'
ᵇ...ᵇ: R: 'son'
ᶜ...ᶜ: R: 'semble a'
ᵈ...ᵈ: R: 'Le'
ᵉ...ᵉ: R: 'et de ses assistans et ouvriers &c mais encore'

i. D442 uses the French term '*poil de castor*' ('beaver **442** skin'), where E442 only has 'castor' ('beaver'); but see E515, where the full term *peaux de castor* is used.

ii. In the French manuscript version (see V442a and also V444b) beaver is not mentioned (although it does occur in the manuscript counterpoint to E515). The significance of this is that it is one of the few instances to throw some doubt on the hypothesis that the Rouen manuscript was the actual source text for the print edition of the *Essai* of 1755: if that manuscript was the source, could the editor have guessed the word 'castor' (the presence of which in D442 suggests it belongs in E442)? See Introduction p. 15.

iii. Note, on the other hand, that the manuscript version, but not the published text, has the term '*ustancilles*' ('*ustensiles*', that is 'utensils') and that this is also present in D442.

iv. Note that each version offers a different explanation of profit. E442 argues that the hatter's profit should be comparable to the third of the revenues made by the farmer, as assumed in E438. D442 refers to profit as 'proportionable' compensation for 'risque, expence, and situation'. This is along the lines of the argument of D437. A442 states that profit is 'proportioned' to the demand for goods and the ('supply' or) 'Quantity of Money in several Hands to be advanced'. This formulation is reminiscent of A249. In A448 and A449 it is also applied to an explanation of interest. These formulations perhaps owe something to Locke. See C463ii.

443

‖ The haberdasher of hats hires a shop from the proprietor of land, advances to the hatter, at one or different times, the value of 10,000 hats, hires servants to attend the sale by retail, and sells his hats gradually to 10,000 different persons: he is also an undertaker, who advances his money at an uncertainty, depends on his customers, pays his servants, and maintains his family, by selling his hats at an advanced price, which also may answer from 10 to 20 per cent. advantage on the money he advances in his undertaking: so that the profits of the hatter, as well as of the haberdasher, are found in the price the consumers give for the hats. Other petty undertakers make ᵃcent. per cent.ᵃ of their money, otherwise they cannot subsist; and, if customers, will employ them, they must give them such advanced prices as will enable them to subsist.

‖ A Shopkeeper who sells by Retail, and purchases from the Manufacturer or Wholesale Dealer, is intitled to make a Profit proportional to the Time, Credit, and Risk attending his Business; the several Profits made from Hand to Hand, down to the Consumer, must be paid by the Landed Gentry, who are the great Consumers of rich Manufactures, and consequently they are those who keep [64] Labour and Industry in almost perpetual Motion.

444

|7| Mais un Compagnon Chapelier entendu, mais sans fond, peut entreprendre la même Manufacture, en empruntant de l'argent & des matériaux, ᵃ& en abandonnant l'article du profit à quiconqueᵃ voudra lui prêter de l'argent, ou à quiconque voudra lui confier ᵇdu castor, de la laine, &c., qu'il ne paiera qu'à long terme &ᵇ lorsqu'il aura vendu ses chapeaux. Si à l'expiration du terme de ses billets le Prêteur d'argent redemande son capital, ou si le Marchand de laine & les autres Prê-[270]teurs ne veulent plus s'y fier, il faut qu'il quitte son entreprise; auquel cas il aimera peut-être mieux faire banqueroute. ᶜMaisᶜ s'il est sage & industrieux, il pourra faire voir à ses créanciers qu'il a en argent ou en chapeaux la valeur du fond qu'il a emprunté à-peu-près, & ils aimeront mieux probablement continuer à s'y fier & se contenter, pour le présent, de leur interêt ou du profit. Au moïen dequoi il continuera, & peut-être ᵈamassera-t'ilᵈ par degrés quelque fond en se frustrant un peu de son nécessaire. Avec ce secours il aura tous les ans moins à emprunter, & lorsqu'il aura amassé un fond suffisant pour conduire sa Manufacture qui sera toujours proportionnée au débit qu'il en a, l'article du profit lui demeurera en entier, & il s'enrichira s'il n'augmente pas sa dépense.

‖ Now, if any one who has saved a sum of money, offers to lend it to a journeyman hatter, who earns but his small daily wages, by which the said journeyman may be enabled to set up for a master hatter, and turn undertaker, he would gladly promise him a share of his profits; for, though he would not to clear so much as the master hatter abovementioned, who had money of his own to set up with, yet it would mend his condition to be an undertaker; and a little experience would determine how much this journeyman, now master hatter, might well allow out of his profits to the person who lends the money, and enables him to set up; and his share of profit would be proportionable to the sum lent, and be called INTEREST of the money.

If a Wholesale Dealer finds himself in good Circumstances, he naturally will be inclined to Ease and Retirement; and in order to make an Interest of the Money which he has acquired, he will be induced to lend to a young Undertaker in his Business a Sum to enable him to set up; this young Man, to promote himself in the World, will very naturally agree to divide a certain Part of his Gains with his Wholesale Friend; and this Profit thus allotted to be divided, is proportioned to the Sum lent, and may be called the Interest of that Money.

Higgs Translation (H)	Variations and Errata (V)	Comments (C)

ᵃ...ᵃ: *sic.*

The argument in D443 **443** somewhat resembles that of E450, with this difference that in D443 the borrowing of capital has not yet been introduced.

But a capable Journeyman Hatter with no capital may undertake the same Manufacture by borrowing money and materials and abandoning the profit to anybody who is willing to lend him the money or entrust him with the beaver, wool, etc. for which he will pay only some time later when he has sold his hats. If when his bills are due the Lender requires his capital back, or if the Wool-Merchant and other Lenders will not grant him further credit he must give up his business, in which case he may prefer to go bankrupt. But if he is prudent and industrious he may be able to prove to his creditors that he has in cash or in hats about the value of what he has borrowed and they will probably choose to continue to give him credit and be satisfied for the present with their interest or profit. In this way he will carry on and will perhaps gradually save some capital by retrenching a little upon his necessities. With the aid of this he will have every year less to borrow, and when he has collected a capital sufficient to conduct his manufacture, which will always be proportionable to his sales, the profit will remain to him entirely and he will grow rich if he does not increase his expenditure.

ᵃ...ᵃ: R: 'pour payér a Long termes et en abbandonnant ce Tiers du proffit a quiconque'
ᵇ...ᵇ: R: 'de la laine et autres matereaux don't il a besoin pour Les payer a long Termes'
ᶜ...ᶜ: R: 'Cépéndant'
ᵈ...ᵈ: R: 'amasséra'

i. In D444 the phrase 'he would **444** not to clear so much as' means something like 'he would earn as high an income net of the costs of materials and wages'.

ii. A444 and D444 are more similar to each other than to E444 in wording and structure. But only A444 identifies the lender as 'a Wholesale Dealer ... inclined to Ease and Retirement'. This is reminiscent of Hume in 'Of Interest' who describes lenders as 'merchants [who] possess great stocks [and who] become tired of business' (Hume [1752] 1955: 54).

iii. Note the definition of interest at the end of D/A444. It is somewhat reminiscent of the 'origin of interest' mentioned at the end of E436. Also cf. D/ A446.

iv. There is no mention of '*castor*' in the French manscript version (V444b), but neither is there in D444. Cf. C442ii.

445

|| If this new master hatter, by his skill, industry, and assiduity, works himself into good business, and has many customers, he will be able to increase and augment his undertakings; he will borrow more money to carry them on, out of which he will give a share of profit, or an interest; or, if he can buy wool and other materials, payable at a long term, he will give a higher price for them than the current, which is, in effect, to give a share of his profit, or an interest.

|| If this young Adventurer by his Assiduity and Industry can find a quick Sale for his Goods, he will be encouraged to increase his Undertakings; and for the Purchase of Materials he will apply to borrow more Money, which if he cannot find Lenders at Market to supply him with, he will be obliged to purchase the Materials of his Business at Time and Credit, and give an advanced Price for Want of Money to pay down.

446

|| This seems to be the source and original cause of interest in a state. The wool merchant, or undertaker, gets an interest [I, 996, col. 2] for the price of his wool from the hatter, in the term he gives him for payment; he himself borrows money, at a smaller interest, from some richer undertaker, and takes also time for payment; and this undertaker again gives a smaller interest to the monied-man, who commonly lends it to the most solvable and considerable undertakers.

|| This is, I apprehend, the Source of the Interest of Money, and is determined, as to [65] its Quantum *per Cent.* by the several Adventurers in Commerce, who, from the Nature of their Business, judge how much of their Profits they can afford to divide with the Proprietors of these precious Metals.

447

|| The monied-man, who has no hire to pay for workhouses, nor shops, nor no care of the labour, which originally produces interest or profit, gets less for lending, or advancing his money.

|| As the proprietor of land sets and farms out his land, so the proprietor of money farms out his money, to avoid the trouble of managing it himself, and turning undertaker.

448

|| From these considerations it may be inferred, that all commodities which have gone through the hands of undertakers, include in their price an INTEREST of money. That all bills, bonds, and notes, payable at a remote term, suppose an interest, and the proportion of interest is grounded upon the state of profit given by undertakers, and that all interest falls ultimately upon the consumers.

|| From this Reasoning I conceive it is clearly implied, that in all Contracts, either by Wholesale or Retail, where Time is given, the Interest of Money is comprehended, and its Rate is governed by the Demand of the Public to supply their Luxury and Taste, from the Produce of Land and Labour, and the Exigence of the State for this Produce of Land and Labour.

i. Cf. the phrase 'payable at a long term' **445**
in D445 with '*païer à long terme*' in E440.

ii The new '*sage & industrieux*' hatter
in E444 will try to pay off his debt. In
contrast the new master hatter in D445
and the young Adventurer in A445, when
successful through 'skill, industry and
assiduity', will expand their business by
borrowing more.

Cf. the phrases 'the source and original **446**
cause of interest' in D446 and 'the Source
of the Interest of Money' in A446 with
'*la premiere source de l'intérêt*' in E436.
The notion that interest is paid for the time
during which credit in the form of money
or goods is enjoyed in D445, D446 and
D448, as well as in A445, is similar to what
is said in E440.

This passage appears to suggests a more **447**
or less clear-cut distinction between that
part of profit that is due to the advancing
of money and that which is due to 'the
trouble of managing' a business. This and
the comparison between rent as the income
from farming out one's land, and interest
as the income from farming out one's
money, is also found in somewhat different
wording in A449.

i. The observation in D448 that 'the **448**
proportion of interest is grounded upon
the state of profit given by undertakers' is
similar to the statement at the end of E436.

ii. For the explanation of interest in A448,
see C449ii.

iii. After D448, the entry 'Interest' in
Postlethwayt's *Dictionary* continues with
the text reproduced in D465.

449

|| Land is lett to Farmers, to spare the Proprietors thereof the Trouble of cultivating it; and the Proprietor of Money disposes thereof at Interest, to avoid the Risk and Trouble annexed to Trade; and its Income fixes itself, by the Demand the public has for Labour and Industry, and is proportioned by the Quantity of Specie in Circulation: In a Nation where there is no Trade or Industry, the greater or lesser Quantity of Money is of no Use; it is the hard Hand of Labour and Industry which gives it a Value, and the Agreement [66] and Convention of the Society has fixed its Standard as a Measure in Exchange and Barter for the Produce of Land and Labour.

450 |8| Il est bon de remarquer que [271] l'entretien d'un tel Manufacturier est d'une petite valeur ᵃà proportion de celle des sommesᵃ qu'il emprunte dans son commerce, ᵇouᵇ des matériaux qu'on lui confie; & par conséquent les Prêteurs ne courent pas un grand risque de perdre leur capital, s'il est honnête homme & industrieux : mais comme il est très possible qu'il ne le soit pas, les Prêteurs exigeront toujours de lui un profit ou interêt de vingt à trente pour cent de la valeur du prêt : encore n'y aura-s'il que ceux qui en ont bonne opinion ᶜqui s'y fierontᶜ. On peut faire les mêmes inductions par rapport à tous les Maîtres, Artisans, Manufacturiers & autres Entrepreneurs dans l'Etat, qui conduisent des entreprises dont le fond ᵈexcede considérablement la valeurᵈ de leur entretien annuel.

451 |9| Mais si un Porteur d'eau à [272] Paris s'érige en Entrepreneur de son propre travail, tout le fond dont il aura besoin sera le prix de deux seaux, qu'il pourra acheter pour une once d'argent, après quoi tout ce qu'il gagne devient profit. S'il gagne par son travail cinquante onces d'argent par an, la somme de son ᵃfond, ou empruntᵃ, sera à celle de son profit, comme un à cinquante. C'est-à-dire, qu'il gagnera cinq mille pour cent, au lieu que le Chapelier ne gagnera pas cinquante pour cent, & qu'il sera même obligé d'en païer vingt à trente pour cent au Prêteur.

i. The first two points in A449 **449**
resemble the argument in D447. The
comparison between letting out land
and 'letting' money is reminiscent of
Locke, *Some Considerations* (1692:
54–55).

ii. The subsequent views in A449 about
what determines the rate of interest are
reminiscent of the explanation of profit
in A442, which differs from E442 and
D442 (cf. C442iv). Also note that the
view that interest is 'proportioned by
the Quantity of Specie in Circulation'
appears to be directly contradicted
in E463, E465 and D465. Cf. C463ii
for similarities with Locke's views on
interest.

It is well to observe that the upkeep of such   ª...ª: R: 'a   The argument in E450 somewhat **450**
a Manufacturer is small compared with the   proportion des   resembles that of D443.
sums he borrows in his trade or with the   sommes'
materials entrusted to him, and therefore   ᵇ...ᵇ: R: 'et'
the Lenders run no great risk of losing their   ᶜ...ᶜ: R: 'qui si fient'
capital if he is respectable and hard working: ᵈ...ᵈ: R: 'éxcéde La
but as it is quite possible that he is not so the   valeur'
Lenders always require from him a profit or
interest of 20 to 30 per cent. of the value of
their loan. Even then only those who have
a good opinion of him will trust him. The
same inductions may be made with regard to
all the Masters, Artisans, Manufacturers and
other Undertakers in the State who carry on
enterprises in which the Capital considerably
exceeds the value of their annual upkeep.

But if a water-carrier in Paris sets up as the   ª...ª: R: 'fond en   **451**
Undertaker of his own work, all the capital   emprunt'
he needs will be the price of two buckets
which he can buy for an ounce of silver and
then all his gains are profit. If by his labour he
gains 50 ounces of silver a year, the amount
of his capital or borrowing will be to that
of his profit as 1 to 50. That is he will gain
5000 per cent. while the Hatter will gain only
50 per cent. and will also have to pay 20 or
30 per cent. to the lender.

452 |10| Cependant un Prêteur d'argent aimera mieux prêter mille onces d'argent à un Chapelier à vingt pour cent d'interêt, que de prêter mille onces ªà mille Porteursª d'eau à cinq cent pour cent d'interêt. Les Porteurs d'eau dépenseront bien vîte à leur entretien non-seulement [273] l'argent qu'ils gagnent par leur travail journalier, mais tout celui qu'on leur ᵇa prêtéᵇ. ᶜCes capitauxᶜ qu'on leur prête, sont petits à ᵈproporrionᵈ de la somme qu'il leur faut pour leur entretien: soit qu'ils soient beaucoup ou peu emploïés, ils ᵉpeuvent facilementᵉ dépenser tout ce qu'ils gagnent. Ainsi on ne peut guere déterminer les gains de ces bas Entrepreneurs. On diroit bien qu'un Porteur d'eau gagne cinq mille pour cent de la valeur des seaux qui servent de fond à son entreprise, & même dix mille pour cent, si par un rude travail il gagnoit cent onces d'argent par an. Mais comme il peut dépenser pour son entretien les cent onces aussi-bien que les cinquante, ce n'est que par la connoissance de ce qu'il met à son entretien qu'on peut savoir combien il a de profit clair.

453 [274] |11| Il faut toujours défalquer la subsistance & l'entretien des Entrepreneurs avant que de statuer sur leur profit. C'est ce que nous avons fait dans l'exemple du ªFermierª & dans celui du Chapelier: & c'est ce qu'on ne peut guere déterminer pour les bas Entrepreneurs; aussi font-ils pour la plûpart banqueroute, s'ils doivent.

454 |12| Il est ordinaire aux Brasseurs de Londres, de prêter quelques barils de biere aux Entrepreneurs de Cabarets à biere, & lorsque ceux-ci paient les premiers barils, on continue à leur en prêter d'autres. Si la consommation de ces Cabarets à biere devient forte, ces Brasseurs font quelquefois un profit de cinq cent pour cent par an; & j'ai oui dire que les gros Brasseurs ªne laissoient pas de s'enrichirª lorsqu'il n'y a que la moitié des Cabarets à biere qui leur font [275] banqueroute dans le courant de l'année.

455 |13| Tous ªles Marchandsª dans l'Etat, sont dans une habitude constante ᵇde prêter à termes des marchandises ou des denrées à des Détailleursᵇ, & proportionnent la mesure de leur profit, ᶜou leur interêtᶜ, à celle de leur risque. Ce risque est toujours grand par la grande proportion de l'entretien de l'emprunteur à la valeur prêtée. Car si l'emprunteur ou détailleur n'a pas un prompt débit dans le bas troc, il se ruinera bien vîte & dépensera tout ce qu'il a emprunté pour ᵈsaᵈ subsistance, & par conséquent sera obligé de faire banqueroute.

Nevertheless a Money Lender will prefer to lend 1000 ounces of silver to a Hatmaker at 20 per cent. interest rather than to lend 1000 ounces to 1000 water-carriers at 500 per cent. interest. The Water-carriers will quickly spend on their maintenance not only the money they gain by their daily labour but all that which is lent to them. These capitals lent to them are small compared with what they need for their maintenance: whether they be much or little employed they can easily spend all they earn. Therefore it is hardly possible to arrive at the profits of these little undertakers. It might well be that a Water-carrier gains 5000 per cent. of the value of the buckets which serve as his capital, even 10,000 per cent. if by hard work he gains 100 ounces of silver a year. But as he may spend on his living 100 ounces just as well as 50, it is only by knowing what he devotes to his upkeep that we can find how much he has of clear profit.

[a]...[a]: R: 'a un porteur'
[b]...[b]: R: 'aura pretté'
[c]...[c]: R: 'Les Capitaux des somme'
[d]...[d]: R, 1756a, 1756b, 1769: 'proportion'
[e]...[e]: R: 'peuvent parfaitemént bien facilément'

Due to V452a the Rouen manuscript does not contrast the lending of money to a single hatmaker with lending it to many water-carriers, but with lending it to a single water-carrier. Hence the author is perhaps less concerned with disintinguishing between large loans and multiple small loans, than with distinguishing between loans that are used mostly for the purchase of materials and loans that are mostly used for living expenses.

452

The subsistence and upkeep of Undertakers must always be deducted before arriving at their profit. We have done this in the example of the Farmer and of the Hatmaker, but it can hardly be determined in the case of the petty Undertakers, who are for the most part insolvent when they are in debt.

[a]...[a]: R: 'premiér'

453

It is customary for the London Brewers to lend a few barrels of Beer to the keepers of Ale-houses, and when these pay for the first barrels to continue to lend them more. If these Ale-houses do a brisk business the Brewers sometimes make a profit of 500 per cent. per annum; and I have heard that the big Brewers grow rich when no more than half the Ale-houses go bankrupt upon them in the course of the year.

[a]...[a]: R: 'ne Laissent pas que de senrichir'

454

All the Merchants in a State are in the habit of lending merchandise or produce for a time to Retailers, and proportion the rate of their profit or interest to that of their risk. This risk is always great because of the high proportion of the Borrower's upkeep to the loan. For if the borrower or retailer have not a quick turnover in small business he will quickly go to ruin and will spend all he has borrowed on his own subsistence and will therefore be forced into bankruptcy.

[a]...[a]: R: 'Les gros Marchands'
[b]...[b]: R: 'de préttér des Marchandises et dénrées a termes a des detaillans'
[c]...[c]: R: 'ou intérést'
[d]...[d]: R: 'La'

455

456 |14| Les Revendeuses de poisson, qui l'achetant à Billingaste, à Londres, pour le revendre dans les autres quartiers de la Ville, paient ordinairement par contrat passé par un Ecrivain ex-[276]pert, ªun schelling par guinée, ou par vingt-un schellingsª, d'interêts par semaine; ce qui fait deux cens soixante pour cent par année. Les Revendeuses des Halles à Paris dont les entreprises sont moins considérables paient cinq sols par semaine d'interêts d'un écu de trois livres, ce qui passe quatre cents trente pour cent par an : cependant il y a peu de Prêteurs qui fassent fortune avec de si grands interêts.

457 |15| Ces gros interêts sont non-seulement tolérés, mais encore en quelque façon utiles & nécessaires dans ªun Etatª. Ceux qui achetent le poisson dans les rues paient ces gros interêts par l'augmentation de prix qu'ils en donnent; cela leur est commode, & ils n'en ressentent pas la perte. De même un Artisan qui ᵇboitᵇ un pot de biere, & en paie un prix qui fait trouver au Bras-[277]seur cinq cents pour cent de profit, se trouve bien de cette commodité & n'en sent point la perte dans un si bas détail.

458 |16| Les Casuistes, ªqui ne paroissent guere propres à juger de la nature de l'interêt & des matieres de commerceª, ont imaginé un terme (*damnum emergens*) au moïen duquel ils veulent bien tolerer ces hauts prix d'interêt : & plutôt que de renverser l'usage & la convenance des Sociétés, ils ont consenti & permis à ceux qui prêtent avec un grand risque, de tirer proportionnellement un grand interêt; & cela sans bornes: car ils seroient bien embarassés à en trouver de certaines, puisque la chose dépend réellement des craintes des Prêteurs & des nécessités des emprunteurs.

459 |17| On loue les Négocians sur Mer, lorsqu'ils peuvent faire profiter ªleur fond dans leur en-[278]trepriseª, ᵇfusseᵇ à dix mille pour cent; & quelque profit que les Marchands en gros fassent ou stipulent en vendant à long terme les denrées ᶜouᶜ les marchandises à des Marchands-détailleurs inférieurs, je n'ai pas oui dire que les Casuistes leur en fissent un crime. Ils sont ou paroissent un peu plus scrupuleux au sujet des prêts en argent sec, quoique ce soit dans le fond la même chose. Cependant ils tolerent encore ces prêts au moïen d'une distinction (ᵈ*lucrum cessans*ᵈ) qu'ils ont imaginée; je crois que cela veut dire, qu'un Homme qui a été dans l'habitude de faire valoir son argent à cinq cens pour cent dans son commerce, peut stipuler ce profit en le prêtant à un autre. Rien n'est plus divertissant que la multitude des Loix & des Canons qui ont été faits dans tous les siécles au sujet de l'interêt de l'argent, tou-[279]jours par des Sages qui n'étoient guere au fait du commerce, & toujours inutilement.

The Fishwives, who buy Fish at Billingsgate in London to sell again in the other quarters of the City, generally pay under a contract made by an expert scrivener, one shilling per guinea, or twenty-one shillings, interest per week, which amounts to 260 per cent. per annum. The Market-women at Paris, whose business is smaller, pay 5 sols for the week's interest on an écu of 3 livres, which exceeds 430 per cent. per annum. And yet there are few Lenders who make a fortune from such high interest.

These high rates of interest are not only permitted but are in a way useful and necessary in a State. Those who buy Fish in the streets pay these high interest charges in the increased price. It suits them and they do not feel it. In like manner an Artisan who drinks a pot of Beer and pays for it a price which enables the Brewer to get his 500 per cent. profit, is satisfied with this convenience and does not feel the loss in so small a detail.

The Casuists, who seem hardly suitable people to judge the nature of Interest and of matters of Trade, have invented a term, *damnum emergens*, by whose aid they consent to tolerate these high rates of interest; and rather than upset the custom and convenience of Society, they have agreed and allowed to those who lend at great risk to exact in proportion a high rate of interest: and this without limit, for they would be hard put to it to find any certain limit since the business depends in reality on the fears of the Lenders and the needs of the Borrowers.

Maritime Merchants are praised when they can make a profit on their Adventures, even though it be 10,000 per cent.; and whatever Profit wholesale Merchants may make or stipulate for in selling on long credit produce or Merchandise to smaller retail Merchants, I have not heard that the Casuists make it a crime. They are or seem to be a little more scrupulous about loans in hard cash though it is essentially the same thing. Yet they tolerate even these loans by a distinction, *lucrum cessans*, which they have invented. I understand this to mean that a Man who has been in the habit of making his money bring in 500 per cent. in his trade may demand this profit when he lends it to another. Nothing is more amusing than the multitude of Laws and Canons made in every age on the subject of the Interest of Money, always by Wiseacres who were hardly acquainted with Trade and always without effect.

Variations and Errata (V)

ᵃ...ᵃ: R: 'un Chelim par guine, ou Vingt un Schellings'

ᵃ...ᵃ: R: 'un etat ou Ville'
ᵇ...ᵇ: R: 'voy'

ᵃ...ᵃ: R: 'qui de touts Les hommes paroissent Les moins propres a juger de La Nature de linterest'

ᵃ...ᵃ: 'leurs fonds dans leurs éntréprisés'
ᵇ...ᵇ: 1756b: 'fût-ce'; 1769: 'fût ce'
ᶜ...ᶜ: R: 'et'
ᵈ...ᵈ: R: 'Lucrum Censens'

Comments (C)

i. The fish-women of Billingsgate market also figure in D689.

ii. Somewhat curiously, Cantillon appears to assume that there are 20 shillings to the guinea, since $1/20 \times 52 \times 100 = 260$. But he also states that there were 21 shillings to the guinea, which was indeed the case after 1717.

iii. With regard to the French money, there were 20 *sous* to the *livre* and hence the calulation is $5/60 \times 52 \times 100 = 433\ 1/3$.

456

457

The Rouen manuscript (V458a) is even more critical of the casuists. They 'of all men appear the least suitable to judge the nature of interest'. Cf. C201i.

458

459

460 |18| Il paroît par ces exemples & par ces inductions, qu'il y a dans un Etat plusieurs classes ᵃ&ᵃ allées d'interêts ou de profit; que dans les plus basses classes, l'interêt est toujours le plus fort à proportion du plus grand risque; & qu'il diminue de classe en classe jusqu'à la plus haute qui est celle des Négocians riches & réputés solvables. L'intérêt qu'on stipule dans cette classe, est celui qu'on appelle le prix courant de l'intérêt dans l'Etat, ᵃ&ᵃ il ne differe guere de l'interêt qu'on stipule sur l'hypotheque des terres. On aime autant le billet d'un Négociant solvable & solide, au moins pour un court terme, qu'une action sur une terre; parceque la possibilité d'un procès ᵇou d'une contestationᵇ au sujet de celle-ci, com-[280]pense la possibilité de la banqueroute du Négociant.

461 |19| ᵃSi dans un Etat il n'y avoit pas d'entrepreneursᵃ qui pussent faire du profit ᵇsur l'argent ou sur les marchandisesᵇ qu'ils empruntent, l'usage de l'intérêt ne seroit pas probablement si fréquent qu'on le voit. Il n'y auroit que les Gens extravagans & prodigues qui feroient des emprunts. Mais dans l'habitude où tout le monde est de se servir d'entrepreneurs, il y a une source constante pour les emprunts & par conséquent pour l'intérêt. ᶜCe sontᶜ les Entrepreneurs qui cultivent les terres, les Entrepreneurs qui fournissent le pain, la viande, les habillemens, &c. à tous les Habitans d'une ville. Ceux qui travaillent aux gages de ces Entrepreneurs, cherchent ᵈaussiᵈ à s'ériger eux-mêmes en Entrepreneurs, à l'envie ᵉlesᵉ uns des autres. La multi-[281]tude des Entrepreneurs est encore bien plus grande parmi les Chinois; & comme ils ont tous ᶠl'espritᶠ vif, le génie propre pour les entreprises, & une grande constance à les conduire, il y a ᵍparmi eux des Entrepreneursᵍ qui parmi nous sont fournis par des gens gagés : ils fournissent les repas des Laboureurs, même dans les champs. Et c'est peut-être cette multitude de bas Entrepreneurs, & des autres, ʰde classe en classeʰ, qui, trouvant le moïen de gagner beaucoup par la consommation sans que cela soit sensible aux consommateurs, soutiennent le prix de l'intérêt dans la plus haute classe à trente pour cent; au lieu qu'il ne passe guere cinq pour cent dans notre Europe. L'intérêt a été à Athênes, du tems de Solon, à dix-huit pour cent. Dans la République romaine il a été le plus souvent à douze pour cent, [282] on l'y a vu à quarante huit pour cent, à vingt pour cent, à huit pour cent, à six pour cent, ⁱau plus basⁱ à quatre pour cent : il n'a jamais été si bas librement que vers la fin de la République & sous Auguste après la conquête de l'Egypte. L'Empereur Antonin & Alexandre Severe, ne réduisirent l'intérêt à quatre pour cent, qu'en prêtant l'argent public sur l'hypotheque des terres.

From these examples and inductions it seems that there are in a State many classes and channels of Interest or Profit, that in the lowest classes Interest is always highest in proportion to the greater risk, and that it diminishes from class to class up to the highest which is that of Merchants who are rich and reputed solvent. The Interest demanded in this class is called the current rate of Interest in the State and differs little from interest on the Mortgage of Land. The Bill of a solvent and solid Merchant is as much esteemed, at least for a short date, as a lien upon Land, because the possibility of a Lawsuit or a Dispute on this last makes up for the possibility of the Bankruptcy of the Merchant.

ᵃ...ᵃ: R: 'ou'
ᵇ...ᵇ: R: 'ou contestation'

460

i. The ideas about different 'classes' of interest in E460 are very similar to those in D479.

ii. E460 refers to the 'highest class' as those loans where repayment is most assured and hence the interest rate is lowest. Cf. E461, E470, E474 and E481. D479 does not use the same terminology.

iii. The phrase *le prix courant de l'interêt* in E460 is also used in E481 and E483. The notion that it expresses is the same as what is called 'common interest' in D479, i.e. the interest paid in cases 'where payment is certain'.

If there were in a State no Undertakers who could make a Profit on the Money or Goods which they borrow, the use of Interest would probably be less frequent than it is. Only extravagant and prodigal people would contract loans. But accustomed as every one is to make use of Undertakers there is a constant source for Loans and therefore for Interest. They are the Undertakers who cultivate the Land and supply Bread, Meat, Clothes, etc. to all the Inhabitants of a City. Those who work on wages for these Undertakers seek also to set themselves up as Undertakers, in emulation of each other. The multitude of Undertakers is much greater among the Chinese, and as they all have lively intelligence, a genius for enterprise, and great perseverance in carrying it out, there are among them many Undertakers who are among us people on fixed wages. They supply Labourers with meals, even in the Fields. It is perhaps this multitude of small Undertakers and others, from class to class, who finding the means to gain a good deal by ministering to consumption without its being felt by the consumers, keep up the rate of Interest in the highest class at 30 per cent. while it hardly exceeds 5 per cent. in our Europe. At Athens in the time of Solon interest was at 18 per cent. In the Roman Republic it was most commonly 12 per cent., but has been known to be 48, 20, 8, 6, and at the lowest 4 per cent. It was never so low in the free market as towards the end of the Republic and under Augustus after the conquest of Egypt. The Emperor Antoninus and Alexander Severus only reduced Interest to 4 per cent. by lending public money on the mortgage of Land.

ᵃ...ᵃ: R: 'Sil Ni avoit des entrepreneurs dans un Etat'
ᵇ...ᵇ: R: 'de largent ou des denrées'
ᶜ...ᶜ: R: 'Cest'
ᵈ...ᵈ: R: 'a leurs Tours'
ᵉ...ᵉ: R: 'des'
ᶠ...ᶠ: R: 'Les prix'
ᵍ...ᵍ: R: 'des entrepreneurs parmis eux'
ʰ...ʰ: R: 'de Classes en classes'
ⁱ...ⁱ: R: 'et au plus bas'

461

i. Cf. the discussion of China in E461 with D472.

ii. Could V461f be due to an error in dictation? See C274iii.

462   CHAPITRE ªDIXIEMEª ET DERNIER.

Des causes de l'augmentation ᵇ& de la diminutionᵇ de
l'interêt de l'argent, dans un Etat.

463 |1| C'est une idée commune & reçûe de tous ceux qui ont écrit sur le commerce, que l'augmen-[283]tation de la quantité de l'argent effectif dans un État y diminue le prix de l'interêt, parceque lorsque l'argent abonde, il est plus facile d'en trouver à emprunter. Cette idée n'est pas toujours vraie ni juste. Pour s'en convaincre, il ne faut que se souvenir qu'en l'année 1720, presque tout l'argent d'Angleterre fut apporté à Londres, & que par-dessus cela, le nombre des billets qu'on mit sur la place accélera le mouvement de l'argent d'une maniere extraordinaire. Cependant cette abondance d'argent & de circulation au lieu de diminuer l'interêt courant qui étoit auparavant à cinq pour cent, & au-dessous, ne servit qu'à en augmenter le prix, qui fut porté à cinquante & soixante pour cent. Il est facile de rendre raison de cette augmentation du prix de l'interêt, par les principes & les causes de l'in-[284]terêt, que j'ai établies dans le chapitre précédent. ªLa voiciª, tout le monde ᵇétoit devenuᵇ Entrepreneur dans le systeme de la Mer du Sud, & demandoit à emprunter de l'argent pour acheter des Actions, comptant de faire un profit immense au moïen duquel il pourroit aisément païer ce haut prix d'intérêt.

464 |2| Si l'abondance d'argent dans l'Etat vient par les mains de ªgens qui prêtent, elle diminueraª sans doute l'interêt courant en augmentant le nombre des prêteurs: mais ᵇsi elleᵇ vient par l'entremise de personnes qui dépensent ᶜelle aura l'effetᶜ tout contraire, & ᵈelleᵈ haussera le prix de l'interêt en augmentant le nombre des Entrepreneurs qui auront à travailler au moïen de cette augmentation de dépense, & qui auront besoin d'emprunter pour fournir à leur entreprise, dans toutes les classes d'interêts.

465 [285] |3| L'abondance ou la disette d'argent dans un Etat, hausse toujours ou baisse les prix de toutes choses dans les altercations du troc, sans avoir aucune liaison nécessaire avec le prix de l'intérêt, qui peut très bien être haut dans les Etats où il y a abondance d'argent, & bas dans ceux ou l'argent ªest plus rareª: haut où tout est cher, & bas où tout est à grand marché: haut à Londres, & bas à ᵇGênesᵇ.

[I, 996, col.2 continued] || The quantity of money which circulates in a state (regard being always had to the quickness of it's circulation) fixes the price of commodities; and, where there is most money in circulation, or paper that answers the end of money, commodities are dearest, and vice versa; but the quantity of money does not fix the price of interest, which is often higher in countries where commodities are dear, and lower in others where they are cheap: higher in London, and lower in Genoa.

Chapter X and last
Of the Causes of the Increase and Decrease of the
Interest of Money in a State

It is a common idea, received of all those who have written on Trade, that the increased quantity of currency in a State brings down the price of Interest there, because when Money is plentiful it is more easy to find some to borrow. This idea is not always true or accurate. For proof it needs only to be recalled that in 1720, nearly all the money in England was brought to London and over and above this the number of notes put out accelerated the movement of money extraordinarily. Yet this abundance of money and currency instead of lowering the current rate of interest which was before at 5 per cent. and under, served only to increase the rate which was carried up to 50 and 60 per cent. It is easy to account for this increased rate of interest by the principles and the causes of Interest laid down in the previous Chapter. The reason is that everybody had become an Undertaker in the South Sea scheme and wanted to borrow money to buy Shares, expecting to make an immense profit out which it would be easy to pay this high rate of Interest.

If the abundance of money in the State comes from the hands of money-lenders it will doubtless bring down the current rate of interest by increasing the number of money-lenders: but if it comes from the intervention of spenders it will have just the opposite effect and will raise the rate of interest by increasing the number of Undertakers who will have employment from this increased expense, and will need to borrow to equip their business in all classes of interest.

Plenty or Scarcity of Money in a State always raises or lowers the price of everything in bargaining without any necessary connection with the rate of interest, which may very well be high in States where there is plenty of money and low in those where money is scarcer: high where everything is dear, and low where everything is cheap: high in London, low in Genoa.

462
a...a: R: '10e'
b...b: R: 'et diminution'

463
a...a: R: 'Le Voicy'
b...b: R: 'etoit deméme'

i. The argument in E463 with regard to the South Sea Bubble is the same as in D466.

ii. One of the authors who Cantillon may have had in mind at the beginning of E463 is John Locke. In *Several Papers Relating to Money, Interest and Trade* (1696: 72) Locke wrote: 'The Natural Value of Money, as it is apt to yield such an yearly Income by Interest, depends on the whole quantity of the then passing Money of the Kingdom, in proportion to the whole Trade of the Kingdom.' This is reminiscent of a similar statement in A449. Cf. C449 and C442iv.

iii. Graslin, *Essai analytique* (1767: 148) refers to Cantillon's discussion that it is not the scarcity or abundance of money in circulation that determines the interest rate.

464
a...a: R: 'gens a prétér, il dimunera'
b...b: R: 'sil'
c...c: R: 'il en a leffet'
d...d: 'il'

The argument about the effect of an abundance of money in the hands of money-lenders is similar to that in D374. Cf C374.

465
a...a: R: 'n'est pas abbondant'
b...b: R: 'Genne'; 1756b, 1769: 'Gennes'

In the *Universal Dictionary* the text in D465 follows on directly from that in D448.

466

In the South-Sea time, all the ready money almost in England was brought to London, and the paper credit vastly accelerated in motion and circulation. Commodities were indeed grown dearer, so far as money was brought into that channel of barter; yet the interest of money arose to 50 per cent. per annum, instead of falling; the reason was, that almost every body turned undertaker in the South-Sea stock and bubbles; there were more borrowers than lenders. Those undertakers offered a share of the profits they expected to make to the lenders, just as the journeyman hatter to him who sets him up. This shews that the greater or lesser quantity of money is not the essential cause of the fall or rise of interest, according to the notion commonly received.

467 |4| Le prix de l'interêt hausse & baisse tous les jours sur de simples bruits, qui tendent à diminuer ou à augmenter la sureté des Préteurs, sans que le prix des choses dans le troc soit alteré pour cela.

468 |5| La source la plus constante d'un interêt haut dans un Etat, est la grande dépense des Seigneurs & des Propriétaires de terres, ou des autres Gens riches. Les Entrepreneurs & maîtres Ar-[286]tisans, sont dans l'habitude de fournir de grosses Maisons dans toutes les branches de leur dépense. Ces Entrepreneurs ont presque toujours besoin d'emprunter de l'argent pour les fournir: & lorsque les Seigneurs consomment leurs revenus par avance & empruntent de l'argent, ils contribuent doublement à hausser le prix de l'interêt.

|| There are two circumstances which seem mostly to contribute to the keeping interest high in a state: the first and principal one is, where noblemen and wealthy proprietors spend their incomes upon tick, and pay the butcher, baker, wine-merchant, &c. slowly. In this circumstance, these undertakers and tradesmen sell their commodities at an advanced price, and get commonly 20 per cent. more than if they sold for ready money: so they not only can afford to pay a good interest, but they want also to borrow money to go on with their undertakings, till they are paid by the proprietors. The second circumstance is, when the proprietors run out, and pay a great interest to supply their extravagancies; this is the source of mortgages; but the price they give undertakers for what they consume upon credit, is the source of higher interest;

[66 continued] || There are two Circumstances which principally contribute to raise the Interest of Money; the first and most essential is, the Consumption and Luxury of Gentlemen of Estates whose Tastes and Appetites are furnished and indulged by Shopkeepers, Tradesmen, and Artizans; these People finding Employment from the great Men of the Community, to furnish them with more than their Stock in Trade will yield, are thereby encouraged to apply to the monied Men and to pay them an Interest, that they may be enabled to purchase the Materials to supply the Demand of their Customers.
|| The second Circumstance is the Dissipation and extravagant Expence of the great Proprietors of Land, who generally in all Countries live above their Incomes, and consequently are forced to borrow Money at Interest to support this immoderate Expence, and also their paying an exorbitant Price for every thing they purchase at Time and Credit, from the Wine-Merchant down to the [67] Chandler's Shop, by which forty to fifty *per Cent.* is gained. This Credit, thus given, obliges the several Undertakers in Trade, who benefit thereby, to apply to the monied Men for Assistance; which is a constant Source to procure Interest;

i. For the account of the **466**
South Sea time, cf. E463.

ii. The mention of the journeyman hatter is a reference to D444.

The rate of interest rises and falls every day upon mere rumours which tend to diminish or increase the security of Lenders, without the prices of things in exchange being affected thereby.

467

The most regular cause of a high rate of interest in a State is the great expense of Nobles and Landowners or other rich people. Undertakers and Master-Craftsmen are in the custom of supplying the great Houses in all their branches of expenditure. These Undertakers have nearly always need to borrow money in order to supply them: and when the Nobility consume their revenues in advance and borrow money they contribute doubly to raise the rate of interest.

A468 follows on directly **468**
from A449.

469

but, where the state itself anticipates it's revenues, as in cases of war, then interest will naturally rise still higher: and this is the source of public debts.

as also when the State is obliged to raise Money by anticipating its Revenue:

470 |6| Au contraire, lorsque les Seigneurs de l'Etat vivent d'œconomie, ᵃ& achetent de la premiere main autant qu'ils le peuvent, ils se fontᵃ procurer par leurs Valets beaucoup de choses ᵇsans qu'elles passentᵇ par les mains des Entre preneurs, ils diminuent les profits & le nombre des Entrepreneurs dans l'État, & par conséquent le nombre des Emprunteurs, & encore le prix de l'interêt, parceque ces sortes d'entrepreneurs travaillant sur leurs propre fonds n'em-[287]pruntent que le moins qu'ils peuvent, & en se contentant d'un petit gain empêchent ceux qui n'ont point de fonds de s'ingérer dans les entreprises en empruntant. Voilà aujourd'hui la situation des Républiques de ᶜGênesᶜ & de Hollande, où l'interêt est quelquefois à deux pour cent, & au-dessous dans la plus haute classe; au lieu qu'en Allemagne, en Pologne, ᵈen France, en Espagne,ᵈ en Angleterre & en d'autres Etats, la facilité & la dépense ᵉdes Seigneurs & des Propriétairesᵉ de terres entretiennent toujours les Entrepreneurs & ᶠmaîtres Artisansᶠ de l'Etat dans l'habitude de ᵍces gros gainsᵍ, au moïen desquels ils ont dequoi païer un interêt haut, & encore plus lorsqu'ils tirent tout de l'Etranger avec risque pour les entreprises.

|| The contrary reasons fall interest; as when a state is small and frugal, and has but few proprietors in it who are expensive, and where every undertaker has money enough of his own to carry on his business, as in Genoa, Holland, &c.

471

And to conclude this Subject of Interest, it is evident to me that an Increase of Labour and Industry is an Increase of Real Riches; foreign Trade increases Labour and Industry, and consequently acquires Money to a Kingdom, and this brings a great many Lenders thereof into the public Channels of Commerce, and consequently creates a Lowness of Interest: In short, an Increase of Labour and Industry is ~~an Increase~~ Decrease to the Rate and Hire of Money.

On the contrary when the Nobility of the State live oeconomically and buy at first hand so far as they can, they get through their servants many things without their passing through the hands of Dealers, they diminish the profits and numbers of the Undertakers in the State and therefore of Borrowers as well as the rate of interest, because this class of Undertakers working on their own capital borrow the least they can, and contenting themselves with small profits prevent those who have no capital from embarking in these enterprises on borrowed money. Such is today the position of the Republics of Genoa and Holland, where interest is sometimes at 2 per cent. or under in the highest class, whilst in Germany, Poland, France, Spain, England and other countries the easiness and expense of Noblemen and Landowners always keep the Undertakers and Master Craftsmen of the country accustomed to large profits enabling them to pay a high rate of interest, which is higher still when they import everything from abroad with attendant risk.

[a]...[a]: R: 'achettent tant quils peuvent de la premiére main et se font'
[b]...[b]: R: 'sans passér'
[c]...[c]: R: 'Gennes'; 1756b, 1769: 'Gennes'
[d]...[d]: R: 'et en France'
[e]...[e]: R: 'des seigneurs proprietaire'
[f]...[f]: R: 'autres artisans'
[g]...[g]: R: 'ses gross guains'

While in E the borrowing of the nobility (E468, E470) and that of the state (E473–E474) are discussed separately, in D468–D470 and A468–A469 they are discussed together.

470

i. The change of 'increase' to 'decrease' (by hand in the copy in the Goldsmith Library) in A471 is according to the instruction on the Errata page.

ii. The parallels of chapter XVII of A with E and D stop with A471, although that chapter continues for a little over a page (bottom third of p. 67 and most of p. 68). Most of this is taken up with a quote from John Locke's *Some Considerations of the Consequences of the Lowering of Interest* (1696: 78).

471

472

‖ It seems pretty extraordinary that the interest of money is commonly in China at 30 per cent. It is allowed, that the workmen and labourers in China are satisfied to work for what barely subsists them, at the lowest expence. It is probable that the farmer in China gives the landlord, or proprietor there, five parts in six of the produce of his land: the Chinese are so hardy and skilful naturally, that the learning of trades is little or no expence, and the undertakers and tradesmen, if they get but little more than common labourers, are contented; so that they probably allow the proprietors of the land, and the proprietors of money the most part of their gains; and, as they are all very industrious and intelligent, they are all able and ready to turn undertakers, and the number of borrowers to lenders is probably so great, as to keep up that high interest. It is allowed that almost every thing in China is carried on by undertakers; the very labourers dinners are carried to them by undertakers, into the streets and the fields where they work.

473 |7| Lorsque le Prince ou l'Etat fait une grosse dépense comme [288] en faisant la guerre, cela hausse le prix de l'interêt par deux raisons: la premiere est que cela multiplie le nombre des Entrepreneurs par plusieurs nouvelles entreprises considérables de fournitures pour la guerre, & par conséquent les emprunts. La seconde est par rapport ªau plus grand risqueª que la guerre entraîne toujours.

474 |8| Au contraire, la guerre ªfinieª, les risques diminuent, le nombre des Entrepreneurs diminue, & les Entrepreneurs même de la guerre cessant ᵇde l'êtreᵇ, diminuent leurs dépenses, & deviennent prêteurs de l'argent qu'ils ont gagné. Dans cette situation, si le Prince ou l'Etat offre de rembourser une partie de ses dettes, il diminuera considérablement le prix de l'interêt; & cela aura un effet plus certain, s'il est en état de païer réellement une partie de la dette [289] sans emprunter d'un autre côté, parceque les remboursemens augmentent le nombre des prêteurs dans la plus haute classe de l'interêt, & que cela pourra influer ᶜsur les autres classesᶜ.

| | | Cf. the arguments with regard to China with E461. | **472** |

When the Prince or the State incurs heavy expense, such as making war, the rate of interest is raised for two reasons: the first is that this multiplies the number of Undertakers by several new large enterprises for war supplies, and so increases borrowing. The second is because of the greater risk which war always involves.

ᵃ...ᵃ: R: 'aux grands Risques'

Briefer remarks about government borrowing are found in D/A469.

473

On the contrary when the War is over risk diminishes, the number of Undertakers is lessened and War-contractors ceasing to be so retrench their expenses and become Lenders of the money they have gained. If now the Prince or State offer to repay part of the debt it will considerably reduce the rate of interest, and this will have a more assured result if part of the debt can be really paid off without borrowing elsewhere, because the repayments increase the number of lenders in the highest class of interest which will affect all the other classes.

ᵃ...ᵃ: R: 'Cessée'
ᵇ...ᵇ: R: 'a letre'
ᶜ...ᶜ: R: 'sur autres choses'

i. D470 also mentions the relation between low interest rates and 'frugal' states.
ii. For the phrase 'lenders in the highest class of interest', see C460ii.

474

475 |9| Lorsque l'abondance d'argent dans l'Etat est introduite par une balance constante de commerce, cet argent passe d'abord par les mains des Entrepreneurs; & encore ªqu'il augmenteª la consommation, ᵇil ne laisse pasᵇ de diminuer le prix de l'interêt, à cause que la plûpart des Entrepreneurs ᶜacquerentᶜ alors assez de fond pour conduire leur commerce ᵈsans argentᵈ, & même deviennent prêteurs des sommes qu'ils ont gagnées au-delà de celles qu'il faut pour conduire leur commerce. S'il n'y a pas dans l'Etat un grand nombre de Seigneurs ᵉ& de Gensᵉ riches qui fassent une grosse dépense, dans [290] ces circonstances l'abondance de l'argent ne manquera pas de diminuer le prix de l'interêt, autant qu'elle augmentera ᶠle prixᶠ des denrées & des marchandises dans le troc. Voilà ce qui arrive d'ordinaire dans les Républiques qui n'ont guere de fond ni de terres considérables, & qui ne s'enrichissent que par le commerce étranger. Mais dans les Etats qui ont ᵍun grand fondᵍ & des Propriétaires de terres considérables, l'argent qui s'introduit ʰparʰ le commerce avec l'Etranger augmente leur rente, & leur donne moïen de faire une grande dépense qui entretient ⁱplusieurs Entrepreneurs & plusieurs Artisansⁱ, outre ceux qui maintiennent le commerce avec l'Etranger: cela soutient toujours un haut interêt, malgré l'abondance de l'argent.

476   But to return to the Europeans. When the wealthy expensive proprietors of land do not buy every thing of the butcher, baker, &c. for ready money, though they be punctual in paying them afterwards, yet it is easy to conceive they lose 20 per cent. more or less, of their revenues, by that method of living upon credit; and this sum naturally goes to the undertakers and money-lenders, who have each their share of it

477 |10| Lorsque ªles Seigneurs & les [291] Propriétairesª de terres se ruinent par leurs dépenses extravagantes, les prêteurs d'argent qui ont des hypotheques sur ᵇleursᵇ terres, en attrapent souvent la propriété absolue; & il peut bien arriver dans l'État que les prêteurs soient créanciers de beaucoup plus d'argent qu'il n'y en circule: auquel cas on peut les regarder comme Propriétaires subalternes des terres ᶜ& desᶜ denrées qu'on hypotheque pour leur sureté. Que si cela n'a pas lieu, leurs capitaux se perdront par les banqueroutes.

     || But, when the proprietors exceed their income, they spend their estates, and the money-lenders, or undertakers, get them.

|| From whence it is apparent, that, though there be a fixed quantity of money in a state, yet the interest of it, which is accumulated constantly, will be found real by mortgages on the said estates, or the absolute possession or property of them. [I, 997, col.1] And so it may happen that particular people may be proprietors of more money than there is actually in the state; but, in that case, they may be considered as subaltern proprietors of a proportionable quantity of the LAND, or of the GOODS and COMMODITIES that are in the state; otherwise their pretensions wil end in bankruptcies.

When the plentifulness of money in the State is due to a continuous Balance of Trade, this money first passes through the hands of Undertakers, and although it increases consumption it does not fail to bring down the rate of interest, because most of the Undertakers then acquire enough Capital to carry on their business without money, and even become lenders of the sums they have gained beyond what they need to carry on their trade. If there are not in the State a great number of Noblemen and rich people who spend heavily then the abundance of money will certainly bring down the rate of interest, while increasing the price of goods and merchandise in exchange. This is what usually happens in Republics which have neither much Capital nor considerable landed property and grow rich merely by foreign trade. But in States which have a large Capital and great Landowners the money brought in by foreign trade increases their Rents, and enables them to incur heavy expenditure which maintains several Undertakers and Mechanicks besides those who trade with the foreigner. This always keeps interest at a high rate in spite of the abundance of money.

a...a: R: 'quils augmentent'
b...b: R: 'Ils ne Laissent pas'
c...c: R: 'attrapent' ; 1756b, 1769: 'acquiérent'
d...d: R: 'sans emprunt'
e...e: R: 'et gens'
f...f: R: 'au prix'
g...g: R: 'des grands fonds'
h...h: R: 'dans'
i...i: R: 'plusieurs artisans et entrepreneurs pour y fournir'

475 The view that the 'plentifulness of money' causes the rate of interest in a nation to fall seems to contradict the argument of E463 and D466. But the further point that it is more precisely the increase of sums of money in the possession of 'savers' rather than 'spenders' which reduces the rate of interest, is consistent with the argument of E464 and D374.

476

When the Nobility and Landowners ruin themselves by extravagances, the Money lenders who have mortgages on their lands often acquire the absolute ownership of them, and it may well arrive in the State that the lenders are creditors for much more money than there is circulating there, in which case one may consider them as subaltern Owners of the land and goods mortgaged for their security. If not their capital will be lost by bankruptcies.

a...a: R: 'les seigneurs proprietaires'
b...b: R: 'Les'
c...c: R: 'et'

477 A related discussion of the dependence of landowners on money lenders is also found in E135–E137.

478 |11| De même on peut considérer les Propriétaires des Actions & des fonds publics, comme Propriétaires subalternes des revenus de l'Etat qu'on emploie à païer leurs interêts. Mais si la législature étoit obligée par les besoins de l'Etat d'emploïer ses revenus à d'autres usages, les [292] Actionnaires ou Propriétaires de fonds publics perdroient tout, sans que l'argent qui circule dans l'Etat fût diminué pour cela d'un seul liard.

The proprietors also of the public debts may be esteemed subaltern proprietors of such part of the public revenues as are appropriated for the payment of their interest; and if these revenues were, through any exigencies of that state, to be applied to other uses, they would find that their money was lost, though, in reality, the money of the nation was not diminished one farthing.

479

|| It may be further observed, that the highest price of interest is offered by the lowest undertakers and tradesmen, whose business and payment is most uncertain; and this high interest commonly comes out of the extravagant price they gave for commodities, payable at time; but, where the undertakers are men of substance, the lenders let them have money at less interest, in regard to the greater confidence in the payment; and where the payment is certain, by mortgages in land, or security in goods and effects, the interest is lowest; and it is this interest is called common interest, and it rises and falls in some proportion with that of money lent upon uncertainty; and, in these several channels of loans upon interest the price always rises and falls in proportion to the number of lenders and borrowers.

480

|| The undertakings in a state which are concerned in supplying meat, drink, and cloaths, and other conveniencies of life, are the principal channels of the circulation of hard money; as they are all branched into as many minute parts of consumption as there are inhabitants to maintain, they require hard money to circulate them.

|| There seems no more hard money necessary for the circulation of the sales and purchases of funds, than what pays the interest of them, which commonly goes to the subsistence of the proprietors of them; the rest may be carried on by evaluation and paper credit. See the articles CREDIT [PAPER CREDIT] CURRENCY [PAPER CURRENCY;] see also the article MONEY, and those others to which we have before referred.

In the same way one may consider the owners of shares and public funds as subaltern Owners of the revenues of the State devoted to payment of their interest. But if the Legislature were compelled by the necessities of the State to employ these revenues for other purposes, the shareholders or Owners of public funds would lose everything without the money circulating in the State being diminished on that account by a single liard.

478

The discussion in D479 is similar to that in E460.

479

i. For phrases similar to 'meat, drink, and cloaths, and other conveniencies of life', see C275. E275 specifies that the circulation of hard money is required for the provision of these goods in towns, rather than in the countryside, and D134 emphasises the link with money and the provision by 'undertakers'. Also see D638–D640 and E672.

480

ii. For phrases similar to money 'branched into … minute parts', see C284iii and C297ii.

iii. For other uses of the term 'evaluation', see C305ii.

iv. After D480 the subsection 'Of the Interest of Money' of the *Dictionary* entry 'Interest' ends. That entry continues with sections, 'Of Legal Interest' (I, 997, col.1) and 'Of the Reduction of the Interest of Money in the Public Funds' (I, 997, col. 2 to I, 999). Neither is likely to be based on anything that Cantillon wrote, but at the end of that latter section Postlethwayt does make a reference to the notion of creditors of the public debt as 'subaltern owners' of public revenue and paraphrases part of D478.

v. Of the entries referred to at the end of D480, the long entry, 'Credit' (I, 574–81) contains a short fragment that may be ascribed to Cantillon (reproduced in D683–D689 and D671–D672) and the entry, 'Money' (II, 282–84) a longer one (reproduced in D338–D384). However, the entry, 'Currency' [Paper Currency]' (I, 581–82) does not appear to contain anything that Cantillon may have written.

481 |12| Si le Prince ou les Administrateurs de l'Etat veulent regler le prix de l'interêt courant par des loix, il faut en faire le réglement sur ᵃle pié du prix courantᵃ du Marché dans la plus haute classe, ou approchant: autrement la loi sera inutile, parceque les Contractans, qui suivront la regle des altercations, ou le prix courant reglé par la proportion des Prêteurs aux Emprunteurs, feront des marchés clandestins; & cette contrainte de la loi ne servira qu'à géner le commerce & à hausser le prix de l'interêt, au lieu de le fixer. ᵇAutrefois les Romainsᵇ, après plusieurs loix ᶜpour restreindre l'interêt, en firent une autreᶜ pour défendre [293] absolument de prêter de l'argent. Cette loi n'est pas plus de succès que les précédentes. La loi que fit Justinien pour restreindre les Gens de qualité à ne prendre que quatre pour cent, ceux d'un ordre inférieur six pour cent, & les Gens de commerce huit pour cent, étoit également plaisante & injuste, ᵈtandisᵈ qu'il n'étoit pas défendu de faire cinquante & cent pour cent de profit par toutes sortes d'entreprises.

482 |13| S'il est permis & honnête à un Propriétaire de terre de donner une Ferme à haut prix à un Fermier indigent, au hasard d'en perdre toute la rente d'une année, il semble qu'il devroit être permis au Prêteur de prêter son argent à un Emprunteur nécessiteux, au hasard de perdre non-seulement son interêt ou profit, mais encore son capital, & stipuler tel interêt que l'autre con-[294]sentira volontairement de lui accorder; il est vrai que les prêts de cette nature font plus de malheureux ᵃqui en emportantᵃ les capitaux aussi-bien que l'interêt, sont plus dans l'impuissance de se relever, que le Fermier ᵇqui n'emporte pas la terreᵇ: mais les loix pour les banqueroutes étant assez favorables aux Débiteurs pour les mettre en état de se relever, il semble qu'on devroit toujours accommoder les loix de l'interêt au prix du marché, comme on fait en Hollande.

If the Prince or Administrators of the State wish to regulate the current rate of interest by law, the regulation must be fixed on the basis of the current market rate in the highest class, or thereabout. Otherwise the law will be futile, because the Contracting parties, obedient to the force of competition or the current price settled by the proportion of Lenders to Borrowers, will make secret bargains, and this legal constraint will only embarrass trade and raise the rate of interest instead of settling it. The Romans of old after several laws to restrict interest passed one to forbid altogether the lending of money. This law had no more success than its predecessors. The law of Justinian to restrain patricians from taking more than 4 per cent., those of a lower order 6 per cent., and traders 8 per cent. was equally amusing and unjust, whilst it was not forbidden to make 50 and 100 per cent. profit in all sorts of business.

[a]...[a]; R: 'le pied Courant'
[b]...[b]: R: 'Les Romains autre fois'
[c]...[c]: R: 'pour fixér et Réstraindre linterest en Vinrent a faire'
[d]...[d]: R: 'pendant'

481

If it is allowable and respectable for a Landlord to let a Farm to a poor Farmer at a high Rental, risking the loss of the Rent of a whole year, it seems that it should be permissible to a Lender to advance his money to a needy Borrower, at the risk of losing not only his Interest or Profit but also his Capital, and to stipulate for so much interest as the Borrower will freely consent to pay him. It is true that Loans of this character make more people wretched. Making away with both capital and interest they are more impotent to recover themselves than the Farmer who does not carry off the Land. But the Bankruptcy laws being favourable enough to Debtors to allow them to start again it seems that Usury laws should always be adjusted to market rates, as in Holland.

[a]...[a]: R: 'qui emportent'
[b]...[b]: R: 'qui manquera de terre'

482

483 |14| Les prix courans de l'interêt dans un Etat, semblent servir de base & de regle pour les prix de l'achat des terres. Si l'interêt courant est à cinq pour cent, qui répond au denier vingt, le prix des terres devroit être de même : mais comme la propriété des terres donne ªun rang & une [295] certaine Jurisdictionª dans l'Etat, il arrive que lorsque l'interêt est au denier vingt, le prix des terres est au denier vingt-quatre ou vingt-cinq, quoique les hypotheques sur les mêmes terres ne passent gueres le prix courant de l'interêt.

484 |15| Après tout, le prix des terres, comme tous les autres prix, se regle naturellement par la proportion des Vendeurs ªaux Acheteurs, &c.;ª & comme il se trouvera beaucoup plus d'Acquereurs à Londres, par exemple, que dans les Provinces, & que ces Acquereurs qui résident dans la Capitale, aimeront mieux acheter des terres dans leur voisinage que dans les Provinces éloignées, il arrivera qu'ils aimeront mieux acheter des terres voisines au denier trente ou trente-cinq, que celles qui sont éloignées au denier vingt-cinq ou [296] vingt-deux. Il y a souvent d'autres raisons de convenances qui influent sur le prix des terres, & qu'il n'est pas nécessaire de marquer ici, parcequ'elles ne détruisent pas les éclaircissemens que nous avons donnés sur la nature de l'interêt.

485 ª*Fin de la seconde Partie.*ª

The current rate of Interest in a State seems to serve as a basis and measure for the purchase price of Land. If the current interest is 5 per cent. or one-twentieth part the price of Land should be the same. But as the ownership of Land gives a standing and a certain jurisdiction in the State it happens that when interest is one-twentieth part, the price of Land is at 1/24 or 1/25, though mortgages on the same Land hardly pass the current rate of interest.

^a...^a: R: 'un certain Rang et Jurisdiction'

483

After all, the price of Land, like all other prices, naturally settles itself by the proportion of Sellers to Buyers, etc.; and as there will be many more Buyers in London, for example, than in the Provinces, and as these Buyers who live in the Capital will prefer to buy land in their locality rather than in distant Provinces, they will rather buy land in the vicinity at 1/30 or 1/35 than land at a distance at 1/25 or 1/22. There are often other reasons of expediency affecting the price of Land, unnecessary to mention here, since they do not invalidate our explanations of the nature of Interest.

^a...^a: R: 'aux acheteurs'

484

End of the second Part.

^a...^a: Missing in R

485

486

TROISIÈME PARTIE.ᵃ

CHAPITRE PREMIER.

Du Commerce avec l'Etranger.   [I, 184, col.1] BALLANCE *of trade*

487 |1| Lorsqu'un Etat échange un petit produit de terre contre un plus grand dans ᵃleᵃ commerce avec l'Etranger, il paroît avoir l'avantage dans ce commerce: [298] & si l'argent y circule en plus grande abondance que chez l'Etranger, il échangera toujours un plus petit produit de terre contre un plus grand.

488 |2| Lorsque l'Etat échange son travail contre le produit de terre de l'Etranger, il paroît avoir l'avantage dans ce commerce; attendu que ᵃsesᵃ habitans sont entretenus aux dépens de l'Etranger.

489 |3| Lorsqu'un Etat échange son produit ᵃconjointement avec son travailᵃ, contre un plus grand produit de l'Etranger conjointement avec un travail égal ou plus grand, il paroît encore avoir l'avantage dans ce commerce.

490 |4| Si les Dames de Paris ᵃconsommentᵃ, année commune, des dentelles de Bruxelles pour la valeur de cent mille onces d'argent, le quart d'un arpent de terre en Brabant, qui produira [299] cent cinquante livres pesant de lin, qu'on travaillera en dentelles fines à Bruxelles, correspondra à cette somme. Il faudra le travail d'environ deux mille personnes en Brabant pendant une année pour toutes les parties de cette Manufacture, depuis la semence du lin jusqu'à la derniere perfection de la dentelle. Le Marchand de dentelle ou Entrepreneur à Bruxelles en fera les avances; il paiera directement ou indirectement toutes les fileuses & faiseuses de dentelles, & la proportion ᵇdu travail de ceuxᵇ qui font leurs outils; tous ceux qui ont part ᶜau travailᶜ, acheteront leur entretien directement ou indirectement du Fermier en Brabant, qui paie en partie la rente de son Propriétaire. Si on met le produit de terre qu'on attribue dans cette œconomie à ces deux mille personnes, à trois arpens [300] par tête, tant pour l'entretien de ᵈleurs personnesᵈ que pour celui de leurs familles qui en subsistent en partie, il y aura six mille arpens ᵉde terreᵉ en Brabant emploïés à l'entretien de ceux qui ont part au travail de la dentelle, & cela aux dépens des Dames de Paris qui paieront & porteront cette dentelle.

|| [I, 184, col.2] If the ladies of quality of *Paris*, for instance, are fond of ᶠ*Brussels*ᶠ lace, and consume of it yearly to the value of 100,000 oz. of silver, about 150 ᵍpounds weight of flaxᵍ, which grew upon a quarter of an acre of land, will answer this value: this will require the yearly labour ʰof 2000ʰ women, for the several parts of the work. The undertaker, or ⁱprincipal lace-manufacturerⁱ at ᶠ*Brussels*ᶠ, will set ʲtheseʲ women to work, and pay them their daily wages. They will buy of the butcher, baker, brewer, &c. their necessaries, and these will pay the value to the farmer, and he will pay his rent to the land proprietor in *Brabant*, whose land is applied to produce the necessary maintenance for these women: and, if they consume in their maintenance the produce of ᵏthreeᵏ acres per head, here will be 6000 acres in *Brabant*, employed for the use and maintenance of ˡtheˡ lace-women.

Part III,
Chapter I

Of Foreign Trade

ᵃ...ᵃ: R: 'Second Troisieme Partye De LEssay de La Nature Du Commérce en general'

i. Note the odd phrase, 'second third part' in the Rouen manuscript (V486a). It is hard to know if there is any significance to this apparent error. The beginning of the actual second part is clearly indicated in R (see V234a).

ii. Also note the phrase '*de la nature*' instead of '*sur la nature*'. This does not appear to be a mistake. Cf. C1i.

486

When a State exchanges a small product of Land for a larger in Foreign Trade, it seems to have the advantage; and if current money is more abundant there than abroad it will always exchange a smaller product of Land for a greater.

ᵃ...ᵃ: R: 'un'

487

When the State exchanges its Labour for the produce of foreign land it seems to have the advantage, since its inhabitants are fed at the Foreigner's expense.

ᵃ...ᵃ: R: 'Ces'

488

When a State exchanges its Produce conjointly with its Labour, for a larger Produce of the Foreigner conjointly with equal or greater labour, it seems again to have the advantage.

ᵃ...ᵃ: R: 'avec son travail'

489

If the ladies of quality of Paris consume yearly Brussels lace to the value of 100,000 ounces of silver, a quarter of an acre of land in Brabant, which will grow 150 pounds weight of flax, to be made into fine lace in Brussels, will answer this value. This will require the yearly labour of about 2000 people in Brabant for the several parts of the work from the sowing of the flax to the final perfection of the lace. The lace merchant or undertaker at Brussels will advance the capital. He will directly or indirectly pay all the spinners and lace-women and the proportion of the labour of those who make their tools. All those who have taken part in the work will buy, directly or indirectly, their maintenance from the Farmer in Brabant who pays in part the Rent of his Landlord. If in this oeconomy the produce of the Land attributed to these 2000 persons be put at 3 acres per head as well for the maintenance of themselves as for that of their families who subsist in part upon it, there will be 6000 acres of land in Brabant employed for the support of those who have worked on the lace, at the expense of the ladies of Paris who will pay for and wear the lace.

ᵃ...ᵃ: R: 'consomme'
ᵇ...ᵇ: R: 'de ceux'
ᶜ...ᶜ: R: 'a Ce travail'
ᵈ...ᵈ: R: 'de leur personne'
ᵉ...ᵉ: R: 'de terres'
ᶠ...ᶠ: P: 'Bruxells'
ᵍ...ᵍ: P: 'pounds of flax'
ʰ...ʰ: P: 'of about 2000'
ⁱ...ⁱ: P: 'lace merchant'
ʲ...ʲ: P: 'those'
ᵏ...ᵏ: P: '3'
ˡ...ˡ: P: 'these'

i. D490–D569 occur in the entry, 'BALLANCE of trade', part of issue 16 of the *Universal Dictionary* (I, 184–89), which first appeared in February or March 1752. However, another version of this and the next two chapters had already been published in 1749 in Postlethwayt's *A Dissertation on the Plan, Use and Importance of The Universal Dictionary of Trade and Commerce*, pp. 41–49. Variations in the 1749 text are denoted with P.

ii. Higgs (1931: 382) attached special importance to the phrase 'the ladies of quality of Paris' in D490. In his opinion it showed that the text in the *Universal Dictionary* was *not* a translation from the French, because 'an English translator would have needed an exceptional talent for the fine shades of language' not to translate '*les Dames de Paris*' simply with 'the Paris ladies'. This does not seem a wholly convincing argument.

iii. Note how '*Bruxells*' in the 1749 text (V490f) is changed to 'Brussels' in the *Universal Dictionary* (although not consistently: see D492). The word '*Bruxels*' also appears once in Postlethwayt's 1757 publication (see V66a).

iv. For the phrase '*dans cette œconomie*' in E490 cf. C79i.

490

491 |5| Les Dames de Paris y paieront les cent mille onces d'argent, chacune suivant la quantité qu'elles en prennent; il faudra envoïer tout cet argent en ªespecesª à Bruxelles, en déduisant les frais seulement de l'envoi, & il faut que l'Entrepreneur à Bruxelles y trouve non-seulement le paiement de toutes ses avances, & l'intérêt de l'argent qu'il aura peut-être emprunté, mais encore un profit de son entreprise pour l'entretien de sa famille. Si le prix que les Dames donnent de la dentelle ne rem-[301]plit pas tous les frais & profits en géneral, il n'y aura pas d'encouragement pour cette Manufacture, & les Entrepreneurs cesseront de la conduire ou seront banqueroute; ᵇmais comme nous avonsᵇ supposé qu'on continue cette Manufacture, il est de nécessité que tous les frais se trouvent dans les prix que les Dames de Paris en donnent, & qu'on envoie les cent mille onces d'argent à Bruxelles, si les Brabançons ne tirent rien de France pour en faire la compensation.

|| The families at *Paris*, where the lace is ᶜwornᶜ, must pay their money at ᵈ*Brussels*ᵈ, to answer this expence; and also enough to answer the ᵉlace-merchant'sᵉ maintenance, with his family and servants, and the interest and risque of the advance of his money; all which will be found in the price they give for the lace: and this money must be sent in specie from *Paris* to ᵈ*Brussels*ᵈ, if *France* sends no commodity to *Brabant* to answer and compensate this debt.

492 |6| Mais si ªlesª habitans du Brabant ᵇaimentᵇ les vins de Champagne, & en consomment, année commune, la valeur de cent mille onces d'argent, l'article des vins pourra compenser celui de la dentelle, & la balance du commerce, par rapport à ces deux branches, sera égale. La compensation & la circulation se fera [302] par l'entremise des Entrepreneurs ᶜ& desᶜ Banquiers en mêleront de part & d'autre.

|| But, if on the other hand, the land-proprietors and nobility in *Brabant*, and others, are fond of *Champagne* wine, and consume thereof annually the value of 100,000 ᵈouncesᵈ of silver; if the ᵉmuidᵉ of *Champagne* wine, ᶠbeing transportedᶠ to ᵍ*Brussels*ᵍ, costs there 60 oz. of silver; if an acre of vineland produces in *Champagne* four muids, this quantity of wines, which sells for 100,000 oz. will require 4166 2/3 acres for ʰit'sʰ production; besides, about 1000 carriage horses for the transportation to ᵍ*Brussels*ᵍ, which at two acres of land for the maintenance of each horse, makes 2000 acres more. And so there will be 6166 2/3 acres of land in *Champagne*, applied to the production of these wines, and the transport horses; and consequently, so much taken from the maintenance of the *French* inhabitants.

|| These wines will pay and compensate the value of the lace, by bills of exchange between the wine-merchants in *Champagne*, and the lace-merchants at *Bruxells*; or between the bankers, who are the brokers and mediators of payments of this kind.

The ladies of Paris will pay the 100,000 ounces of silver, each according to the amount she has bought. All this silver must be sent to Brussels in specie, less only the cost of remittance, and the Undertaker at Brussels must find in it not only payment of all his advances and the interest of the money which he has perhaps borrowed, but also a profit on his undertaking for the maintenance of his family. If the price which the ladies pay for the lace does not cover all the costs and profits there will be no encouragement for this Manufacture, and the Undertakers will cease to carry it on or become bankrupt; but as we have supposed this Manufacture is continued, it is necessary that all costs be covered by the prices paid by the Ladies of Paris, and the 100,000 ounces of silver sent to Brussels if the people of Brabant take no commodity from France to compensate this debt.

[a]...[a]: R: 'Expece'
[b]...[b]: R: 'mais nous avons'
[c]...[c]: P: 'wore'
[d]...[d]: P: *Bruxells*
[e]...[e]: P: 'undertaker or lace-merchant's'

491 Cf. E/D66 and E168 which offer shorter discussions of the same case. In both earlier paragraphs in the French version there are references to the missing Supplement. Therefore presumably the figures used in E/D491–E/D502 derive from this same elusive source. Cf. C66i.

But if the inhabitants of Brabant are fond of Champagne wine and consume thereof annually the value of 100,000 ounces of silver, the heading under Wine will answer that under Lace, and the Balance of Trade with regard to these two branches will be level. The compensation and circulation will be effected through the agency of Dealers and Bankers taking a hand in it on each side.

[a]...[a]: R: 'Ces'
[b]...[b]: R: 'aime'
[c]...[c]: R: 'et'
[d]...[d]: P: 'oz'
[e]...[e]: P: 'muid, or barrel,'
[f]...[f]: P: 'transported'
[g]...[g]: P: *Bruxells*
[h]...[h]: P: 'its'

492 i. The calculation in D492 of the amount of land required to produce 100,000 ounces of silver's worth of wine corresponds to the calculation in E498. Note that the result there is 4166 1/2, instead of 4166 2/3. Given that the calculation is 100,000 / (60 x 4) the result in D492 is the correct one, apart from the fact that it should be a tenth of the figure stated (416.667). This peculiar error occurs in both versions.

ii. Note that in D492 'oz.' is not consistently replaced with 'ounces'; neither is *Bruxells* with *Brussels* (see last sentence). This is probably due to 'editor's fatigue'.

iii. V492h, like V70d, shows that the rogue apostrophe, which occurs in many places in the *Dictionary*, is due to Postlethwayt. Cf. C70ii.

iv. The term *muid* ('or barrel' V492e) of wine occurs also in E498.

493

|| Those wines which are drank in *Brabant*, will save the produce of about 4000 acres of land in *Brabant*, which other-[I, 185, col.1]wise would have been employed to produce beer [a], &c.[a] and so *France* not only loses the produce of 6166 2/3 acres of land, in this [b]commerce or exchange[b], but saves to *Brabant* 4000 acres; and, upon the whole, the loss is no less to France than 10,166 2/3 acres; for which it receives the produce of no more than one quarter of an acre.

494 |7| Les Dames de Paris paieront cent mille onces d'argent à celui qui leur vend & livre la dentelle; [a]celui-ci les paiera[a] au Banquier qui lui donnera une ou plusieurs lettres de change sur son correspondant à Bruxelles. Ce Banquier remettra l'argent aux [b]Marchands[b] de vin de Champagne qui ont [c]100000[c] onces d'argent à Bruxelles, & qui lui donneront leurs lettres de change de même valeur [d]tirées sur lui par son Correspondant[d] à Bruxelles. Ainsi les [c]100000[c] onces païées pour le vin de Champagne à Bruxelles, compenseront les [c]100000[c] onces païées pour la dentelle à Paris; au moïen de quoi on épargnera la peine de voiturer l'argent reçu à Paris jusqu'à Bruxelles, & la peine de voiturer l'argent reçu à Bruxelles jusqu'à [303] Paris. Cette compensation se fait par lettres de change, dont je tacherai de faire connoître la nature dans le chapitre suivant.

495 |8| Cependant on voit dans cet exemple que les cent mille [a]onces[a] que les Dames de Paris paient pour la dentelle, viennent entre les mains des Marchands qui envoient le vin de Champagne à Bruxelles : & que les cent mille onces que les consommateurs du vin de Champagne paient pour ce vin à Bruxelles, tombent entre les mains des Entrepreneurs ou Marchands de dentelles. Les Entrepreneurs de part & d'autre, distribuent cet argent à ceux qu'ils font travailler, soit pour ce qui regarde les vins, soit pour ce qui regarde les dentelles.

	ᵃ...ᵃ: P: ';' ᵇ...ᵇ: P: 'exchange, or commerce'	Similar calculations to those in D493 are found in E498. The reasoning seems questionable: why not include in the costs of lace the 6,000 acres necessary to maintain lace makers in Brabant? See D490.	**493**

The ladies of Paris will pay 100,000 ounces to him who sells and delivers to them the lace; he will pay them to the Banker who will give him one or more Bills of Exchange on his Brussels correspondent. The Banker will remit the money to the Wine merchants in Champagne who have 100,000 ounces of silver at Brussels and who will give him their Bills of Exchange of the same value drawn upon him by his Brussels correspondent. Thus the 100,000 ounces paid for the Champagne wine at Brussels will balance the 100,000 ounces paid for the lace at Paris, and in this way the trouble of sending to Brussels the money received at Brussels will be avoided. This balance is effected by Bills of Exchange, the nature of which I will try to explain in the next chapter.

ᵃ...ᵃ: R: 'celuy cy payera'
ᵇ...ᵇ: R: 'Marchand'
ᶜ...ᶜ: R: 'cent mille'
ᵈ...ᵈ: R: 'sur leur coréspondant'

In E494 and E495 the expressions, *'cent mille'* and '100000' are both used, where R consistently has *'cent mille'*. However, in E498 all figures are put in words where R has numbers. **494**

Meanwhile this example shews that the 100,000 ounces which the Ladies of Paris pay for the lace, come into the hands of the Merchants who send Champagne wine to Brussels; and that the 100,000 ounces which the consumers of the Champagne pay for this wine at Brussels fall into the hands of the Undertakers or Lace merchants. The Undertakers on each side distribute this money to those whose Labour they employ, either on the wines or on the lace.

ᵃ...ᵃ: R: 'onces d'argent'

495

496 |9| Il est clair par cet exemple que les Dames de Paris soutiennent & entretiennent tous ceux qui [304] travaillent à la dentelle en Brabant, ᵃ& qu'elles y causentᵃ une circulation d'argent. Il est également clair que les consommateurs du vin de Champagne à Bruxelles soutiennent & entretiennent en Champagne, non-seulement tous les Vignerons & autres qui ont part à la production du vin, tous les Charons, Maréchaux, Voituriers, &c. qui ont part à la voiture, aussi-bien que ᵇlesᵇ chevaux qu'on y ᶜemploieᶜ, mais qu'ils paient aussi la valeur du produit de la terre pour le vin, & causent une circulation d'argent en Champagne.

497 |10| Cependant cette circulation ᵃouᵃ ce commerce en Champagne, qui fait tant de fracas, qui fait vivre le Vigneron, le Fermier, le Charon, le Maréchal, le Voiturier, & qui fait païer exactement, tant la rente du Propriétaire de la vigne, que celle du Propriétaire des prairies [305] qui servent à entretenir les chevaux de ᵇvoitureᵇ, est dans le cas présent, un commerce onéreux & désavantageux à la France, à l'envisager par les effets qu'il produit.

498 |11| Si le Muid de vin se vend à Bruxelles pour ᵃsoixanteᵃ onces d'argent, & si on suppose qu'un arpent ᵇproduiseᵇ quatre muids de vin, il faut envoïer à Bruxelles le produit de ᶜquatre mille cent soixante-six arpens & demi de terreᶜ, pour correspondre à cent mille onces d'argent, & il faut emploïer autour de ᵈdeux milleᵈ arpens de prairies ᵉ& de terres, pour avoir le foin & l'avoine que consommentᵉ les chevaux de transport, & ne les emploïer ᶠdurant toute l'annéeᶠ à aucun autre usage. ᵍAinsi on ôteraᵍ à la subsistance des François environ ʰsix milleʰ arpens de terres, ⁱ& on augmentera celleⁱ des Brabançons de plus de ʲquatre milleʲ ar-[306]pens de produit, puisque le vin de Champagne qu'ils boivent épargne plus de ʲquatre milleʲ arpens ᵏqu'ils emploieroientᵏ vraisemblablement à produire de la biere pour leur boisson, s'ils ne ˡbuvoientˡ pas de vin. Cependant la dentelle avec laquelle on paie tout cela, ne ᵐcouteᵐ aux Brabançons que le quart d'un arpent de lin. Ainsi avec un arpent de produit, conjointement à leur travail, les Brabançons paient plus de ⁿseize milleⁿ arpens aux François conjointement à un moindre travail. Ils retirent une augmentation de subsistance, & ne donnent qu'un instrument de luxe qui n'apporte aucun avantage réel à la France, parceque la dentelle s'y use & s'y détruit, & qu'on ne peut l'échanger pour quelque chose d'utile après cela.

It is clear from this that the Ladies of Paris support and maintain all those who work on the lace in Brabant and cause money to circulate there, and equally that the consumers of Champagne wine at Brussels support and maintain in Champagne not only the Vineyard keepers and others who take part in the production of the Wine, the Cartwrights, Farriers, Carters, etc. who take part in the transport, and the Horses engaged in it, but that they also pay the value of the produce of the Land for the Wine, and cause a circulation of money in Champagne.

a...a: R: 'et y Causent' **496**
b...b: R: 'Ces'
c...c: R: 'employent'

Nevertheless this circulation or trade in Champagne, which makes so great a stir, which maintains the Keeper of the Vineyard, the Farmer, the Cartwright, the Farrier, the Carter, etc. and which pays precisely as well the Rent of the owner of the Vineyard as that of the Owner of the pastures which serve to feed the Carthorses, is in the present case a burdensome and unprofitable trade to France in its results.

a...a: R: 'et'   Part of the **497**
b...b: R: argument of E497
'voitures'   corresponds to
       D502.

If the muid of wine sells at Brussels for 60 ounces of silver and if we suppose one acre of vine-land produces 4 muids there must be sent to Brussels the produce of 4166½ acres of land to correspond to 100,000 ounces of silver, and about 2000 acres of pasture and arable for the hay and oats consumed by the cart horses if they are solely employed on this work all the year round. And so there will be about 6000 acres of land abstracted from the maintenance of Frenchmen, and that of the people of Brabant increased by over 4000 acres of produce, since the Champagne wine which they drink saves more than 4000 acres which they would probably use to produce beer for their drink if they did not drink wine. However the lace with which all that is paid for costs the people of Brabant only one quarter of an acre of flax. Thus with one acre of produce allied to their Labour, the people of Brabant pay for more than 16,000 acres to the French, their conjoined labour being less. They obtain an increase of subsistence and give only an article of luxury which brings no real advantage to France, since the lace is worn and consumed there and cannot then be exchanged for anything useful.

a...a: R: '60'
b...b: R: 'produit'
c...c: R: '4166 1/2 arpends de terres'
d...d: R: '2000'
e...e: R: 'et terres qui produit Lavoine pour L'entretient'
f...f: R: 'touttes Lannée'
g...g: R: 'il faut ostér'
h...h: '6000'
i...i: R: 'pour augmenter La subsistance'
j...j: R: '4000'
k...k: R: 'quil faudroit employér'
l...l: R: 'Boivent'
m...m: R: 'coutent'
n...n: R: '16000'

i. The arguments in E498 are very similar to those in D492 and D493. **498**

ii. For several decades after the publication of the *Essai* the calculations in E498 were quoted in support of arguments that the production of high-quality textiles should be promoted. Thus the *Corps d'observations 1757–8* of the *Société d'Agriculture de Commerce & des Arts de Bretagne* (1760: 196) noted that Cantillon had observed 'C'est la filature qui tire d'un arpent de terre des environs de Bruxelles, des valeurs égales au revenu de toute la Province de Champagne.' Other authors who quoted Cantillon's precise calculations are Bellepierre de Neuve-Eglise, *L'agronomie et l'industrie* (1761–63, vol. 8, p. 91 n); the Copenhagen edition of Savary's *Dictionnaire* (1759–65, vol. 3, p. 585, entry '*Lin*'); Bilistein, *Essai sur les duchés de Lorraine et de Bar* (1762: 240); Bertholon, *Du commerce et des manufactures distinctives de la ville de Lyon* (1787: 217–18); and Beausobre, *Introduction générale a l'étude, des finances et du commerce*, (1791 vol. 1, p. 202).

499 Suivant la regle intrinseque des valeurs, la terre qu'on emploie en Champagne pour la produc-[307]tion du vin, celle pour l'entretien des Vignerons, ᵃdes Tonneliers, des Charons, des Maréchaux, des Voituriersᵃ, des chevaux pour le transport, &c. devroit être égale à ᵇla terre qu'on emploieᵇ en Brabant à la production du lin, & à celle qu'il faut pour l'entretien ᶜdes fileuses, des faiseusesᶜ de dentelles ᵈ& de tous ceux quiᵈ ont ᵉquelque partᵉ à la fabrication de cette Manufacture de dentelle.

‖ If the circulation of money in *Brabant* be equal to that in *France*, the land and the labour employed about the lace will be equal to the land and labour employed about the wine; and the produce of the land given in payment to the undertaker, or lace-merchant in ᶠ*Brussels*ᶠ, and to the lace-women, &c. will be equal to the land given in payment to the wine-merchants in *Champagne*, to the labourers employed in the production of the wine, to the carriers, &c. and to the land that goes to the production of the wines, the maintenance of horses, &c.

500 |12| Mais si l'argent est plus abondant dans la circulation en Brabant qu'en Champagne, la terre & le travail y ᵃserontᵃ à plus haut prix, & par conséquent dans l'évaluation qui se fait de part & d'autre en argent, les François perdront encore considérablement.

‖ But, if the quantity of money circulating in *Brabant* be ᵇtrebleᵇ to that circulating in *France*, as the exchange is made ᶜby the evaluationᶜ in money, one third part of the land and labour in *Brabant* will answer, and correspond in value to the whole land and labour in *France*; and the product of one acre in *Brabant* will exchange for that of three acres in *France* of equal goodness. ᵈBesidesᵈ this disadvantage in the present example, the 1/3 part of the land in *Brabant* will be applied to the maintenance of the inhabitants of that country; whereas the 4166 2/3 acres, which produced the wine in *Champagne*, are also applied ᵉto the maintenance of the *French* inhabitantsᵉ.

501 |13| On voit dans cet exemple une branche de commerce qui fortifie l'Etranger, qui diminue les habitans de l'Etat, & qui, sans [308] en faire sortir aucun argent effectif, affoiblit ce même Etat. J'ai choisi ᵃcetᵃ exemple pour mieux faire sentir comment un Etat peut être la dupe d'un autre par ᵇle faitᵇ du commerce, & pour faire comprendre la maniere de connoître les avantages ᶜ& les desavantagesᶜ du commerce avec l'Etranger.

Higgs Translation (H)	Variations and Errata (V)	Comments (C)

Following the rule of intrinsic values, the land used in Champagne for the production of the wine, the maintenance of the Vineyard-keepers, the Coopers, the Cartwrights, Farriers, Carters, Carthorses, etc., ought to be equal to the Land used in Brabant for the production of the Flax, the support of the spinners and lace makers, and all those who have taken part in the manufacture of this lace.

^a...^a: R: des Charpentiers ou faiseurs de tonneaux, des Charons, Mareschaux, voituriers'
^b...^b: R: 'la Terre (bien Petit) qu'on Employe'
^c...^c: R: 'de touttes Les filleuses faiseuses'
^d...^d: R: 'et autres qui'
^e...^e: R: 'quelques parts'
^f...^f: P: 'Bruxells'

E499 is actually part of the eleventh paragraph of E III, i. The paragraph is here divided between E498 and E499 for convenience of presentation. **499**

But if money is more abundant in circulation in Brabant than in Champagne, Land and Labour will be dearer there and consequently, valuing in silver both sides, the French will lose still more considerably.

^a...^a: R: 'sera'
^b...^b: P: 'triple'
^c...^c: P: 'by evaluation'
^d...^d: P: 'And beside'
^e...^e: P: 'to the maintenance of the inhabitants in Brabant, and taken from the maintenance of the French inhabitants'

The additional phrase in the last sentence in Postlethwayt's 1749 publication (V500e) changes its meaning, making it much closer to the argument in E498. The missing words in the *Dictionary* version may simply be an error in copying the text. **500**

This is an example of a branch of trade which strengthens the Foreigner, lessens the number of inhabitants of the State, and without causing any circulating money to leave it weakens the same State. I have chosen it to shew more strikingly how one State may be the dupe of another in Trade, and the method of judging the advantages and disadvantages of Foreign trade.

^a...^a: R: 'un'
^b...^b: R: 'Leffet'
^c...^c: R: 'et desavantages'

501

502

‖ By this example we see a branch of luxury carried on in *France*, which indeed supports a commerce, maintains vintners, wine-merchants, horses for carriages, wheelwrights, &c. circulates the farmer's rent in *Champagne*, with that of the proprietor in *Paris*: and yet, upon the whole, this trade is disadvantageous to *France*, diminishes ᵃit'sᵃ inhabitants to the number of at least 1500 souls, and is of no use or emolument to that kingdom. But, on the other hand, it turns to very good account to *Brabant*, where the land is by this means applied to the maintenance of ᵃit'sᵃ own inhabitants; and where they have the produce of 4000 acres of ground in *France*, brought to them without any charge or disadvantage.

503 |14| C'est en examinant les effets de chaque branche de commerce en particulier, qu'on peut regler utilement le commerce avec les Etrangers : ᵃon ne sauroit le connoîtreᵃ distinctement par des raisonnemens généraux.

‖ ᵇFromᵇ the method of enquiry followed in this example, we ᶜmayᶜ examine the advantages, or disadvantages of every particular branch of trade with any foreign country, when the ballance appears equal.

504

‖ ᵃWhen contests arise concerning the national advantage or disadvantageᵃ of any branch of foreign trade, it would be easy to put the truth in a clear light, by examining the series of facts ᵇaccording toᵇ the method herein suggested.

505 |15| On trouvera toujours par l'examen des particularités, que l'exportation de toute Manufacture est avantageuse à l'Etat, parce qu'en ce cas l'Etranger paie & entretient toujours des Ouvriers utiles à l'Etat; que les meilleurs retours ou paiemens qu'on retire sont les especes, [309] & au défaut des especes, ᵃle produitᵃ des terres de l'Etranger où il entre le moins de travail. Par ces moïens de commercer on voit souvent des Etats qui n'ont presque point de ᵇproduits de terreᵇ, entretenir des habitans en grand nombre aux dépens de l'Etranger: & de grands Etats maintenir leurs habitans avec plus d'aisance & d'abondance.

| | ᵃ...ᵃ: P: 'its' | Part of the argument in D502 has a counterpart in E501. | **502** |

| It is by examining the results of each branch of commerce singly that Foreign trade can be usefully regulated. It cannot be distinctly apprehended by abstract reasons. | ᵃ...ᵃ: R: 'quon Ne sçauroit Connoistre'
ᵇ...ᵇ: P: 'By'
ᶜ...ᶜ: P: 'ought to' | | **503** |

| | ᵃ...ᵃ: P: 'And when several corporations and merchants dispute about the advantage'
ᵇ...ᵇ: P: 'by' | | **504** |

| It will always be found by examining particular cases that the exportation of all Manufactured articles is advantageous to the State, because in this case the Foreigner always pays and supports Workmen useful to the State: that the best returns or payments imported are specie, and in default of specie the produce of Foreign land into which there enters the least labour. By these methods of trading States which have very little raw produce are often seen to support inhabitants in great numbers at the expense of Foreigners, and large States maintain their inhabitants in greater ease and abundance. | ᵃ...ᵃ: R: 'les produits'
ᵇ...ᵇ: R: 'produit' | Skinner (1966, I, 291 n1) sees a correspondence with Steuart's statement (1767, II, xxiv): 'It is therefore a general maxim, to discourage the importation of work, and to encourage the exportation of it.' This maxim occurs in a chapter devoted to the question: 'What is the proper Method to put a Stop to a foreign Trade in Manufactures; when the Balance of it turns against a Nation?' However, many eighteenth-century authors put forward maxims about the encouragement of the export of manufactures and discouragement of the import of foreign manufactures. Few authors supported their arguments with such precise reasoning as Cantillon, although some borrowed his calculations. See C498ii. Mirabeau's change of mind on this issue is instructive, because it concerns one of the principal points of disagreement between Cantillon and Quesnay. Initially Mirabeau was clearly influenced by Cantillon on the importance of encouraging manufactures (see *L'Ami des hommes* 1756, part 3, chap. 2). However, that same author in *Philosophie rurale* (Amsterdam 1763: 141–42) explained that such encouragements could not be reconciled with Quesnay's ideas: '*Lorsque, dans un Royaume agricole, on s'occupe de favoriser un commerce de main d'oeuvre, au préjudice de celui des denrées du crû, ce faux calcul émane d'une erreur dont je dois parler avec ménagement. ... dans l'ouvrage de Cantillon, vaste & forte tête, mais qui avoit manqué les principes,* [one can read] *que l'objet des manufactures devoit être d'attirer les produit de l'Etranger, en échange de nos marchandises ouvrées, pour que ce produit servît à la consommation d'un excédent de population au-delà de ce que le territoire en auroit nourri. Mon homme* [probably Mirabeau himself], *qui étoit alors grand populateur, faisit cette idée, & eût volontiers gressé les manufactures sur tous les sauvageons de son canton. Heureusement il trouva sur son chemin un autre prophete* [i.e. Quesnay] *qui le redressa, & le mit sur la bonne voie, qu'il n'a plus quitté depuis.*' | **505** |

506

|| It will always appear by such enquiries, that the exportation of ᵃmineralsᵃ and manufactures, &c. are advantageous; since the land and labour which produce them ᵇareᵇ applied to the support of the inhabitants at home; but that the ᶜexportsᶜ of the fruits and products of the earth ᵇareᵇ disadvantageous for the contrary reasons, except where a good year has produced a great surplusage of them, beyond the yearly consumption of the inhabitants: ᵈand,ᵈ when the returns for mines and manufactures exported, consist in other mines and manufactures imported, by examining which maintain more inhabitants, or more useful ones to the state, there will be no difficulty in determining on which side the advantage lies.

507

|| ᵃIn general, wheneverᵃ there arises a doubt or difficulty about trade, the method to decide the controversy effectually, will be to compute the land and labour, as in ᵇthe precedingᵇ example, instead of being hurried away with general maxims and received notions of trade.

508

ᵃ...ᵃ

^a...^a: P: 'mines'
^b...^b: P: 'is'
^c...^c: P: 'export'
^d...^d: P: 'wheras'

D506 appears to be a counterpart **506**
to E505. But it also resembles the
content of E193 and D189.

^a...^a: P: 'And in general, wherever'   **507**
^b...^b: P: 'this'

i. The passage V508a only appears in Postlethwayt's 1749 **508**
publication, on p. 44. There are several reasons to believe that
Cantillon rather than Postlethwayt wrote it. First, Postlethwayt is
on the whole respectful of the views of the authors concerned. For
example, in various places Charles Davenant's views on foreign
trade are quoted as authoritative (see especially the entries
'Britain', I, 356–57; 'Labour' II, 4; 'People' II, 439). Similarly,
Gregory King's estimates are cited without qualifications
(entries 'Annuity' I, 73 and 'People' II, 438). John Locke is
cited throughout the *Dictionary*, almost invariably in a positive
manner. A similar thing is true for William Petty (although in
one place in the entry 'Political Arithmetic', II, 487, the latter
is criticised for underestimating the strength of France). Hence
the passage in V508a is at odds with what Postlethwayt says
about these authors in other places in his *Dictionary* and this
would appear to be the reason for him to omit it from that work.
Cantillon, on the other hand, is elsewhere ready to blame some
of the authors concerned for faulty or imprecise reasoning; see
E105, E175, E232, E237, E238, E289 and E342. Thus the critical
tone in V508a is in keeping with statements in E. In addition,
even though Josiah Child and John Law are not mentioned
anywhere in E, they both, like the other authors, wrote well
before the early 1730s and Cantillon is likely to have known
their works. Other paragraphs missing from the *Dictionary* but
present in the 1749 publication are reproduced in V550a, V551d,
D564, D567 and D569.

^a...^a: P: ' || *Sir William Petty, Mr Davenant, Mr Locke, Sir Josiah Child, Mr Law, Mr King*, and others, seem to borrow their general notions one from another, and rather to puzzle the nature of trade instead of making it clearer.'

ii. Especially the reference to Law is interesting. Law who
was at different times a friend and adversary of Cantillon is also
named in A610 and A684.

iii. Cf. the term 'general notions' in V508a to '*raisonnemens
généraux*' in E503.

iv. Both the *Universal Dictionary* and the 1749 publication
continue hereafter with the text reproduced in D528ff.

509 |16| Mais attendu que les grands Etats n'ont pas besoin d'augmenter le nombre de leurs habitans, il suffit ᵃd'y faireᵃ vivre ceux qui y sont, du crû de l'Etat, avec plus d'agrément ᵇ& d'aisanceᵇ, & de rendre les forces de l'Etat plus grandes pour sa défense & sa sureté. Pour y parvenir par le commerce avec l'Etranger, il faut encourager, tant qu'on peut, l'exportation des ouvrages ᶜ& des Manufacturesᶜ de l'Etat, pour en retirer, autant qu'il est possible, de l'or & de [310] l'argent en nature. S'il arrivoit par des récoltes abondantes qu'il y eût ᵈenᵈ l'Etat beaucoup de produits au-delà de la consommation ordinaire & annuelle, il seroit avantageux d'en encourager ᵉl'exportationᵉ chez l'Etranger pour en faire entrer la valeur en or & en argent: ces métaux ne périssent ᶠpasᶠ & ne se dissipent pas comme les produits de la terre, & on peut toujours avec l'or & l'argent faire entrer dans l'Etat tout ce qui y manque.

510 |17| Cependant il ne seroit pas avantageux de mettre l'Etat dans l'habitude annuelle d'envoïer chez l'Etranger de grandes quantités du produit de son crû, pour en tirer le paiement en Manufactures étrangeres. Ce seroit affoiblir & diminuer les habitans & les forces de l'Etat par les deux bouts.

511 |18| Mais je n'ai point ᵃdesseinᵃ [311] d'entrer dans le détail des branches du commerce qu'il faudroit encourager pour le bien de l'Etat. Il me suffit de remarquer qu'il faut toujours tâcher d'y faire entrer le plus d'argent qu'il se peut.

512 |19| L'augmentation de la quantité d'argent qui circule dans un Etat, lui donne de grands avantages dans le commerce avec l'Etranger, tant que cette abondance d'argent y continue. L'Etat échange toujours ᵃpar là une petiteᵃ quantité de produit & de travail, contre ᵇune plus grandeᵇ. Il leve les taxes avec facilité, & ne trouve pas de difficulté à faire de l'argent dans les cas de besoins publics.

513 |20| Il est vrai que la continuation de l'augmentation de l'argent causera dans la suite par son abondance une cherté de ᵃterreᵃ & de travail dans l'Etat. Les ouvrages ᵇ& lesᵇ Manufactures cou-[312]teront tant, à la longue, que l'Etranger cessera peu-à-peu de les acheter, & s'accoutumera à les prendre ailleurs à meilleur marché; ce qui ruinera insensiblement les ouvrages ᵇ& lesᵇ Manufactures de l'Etat. La même cause qui augmentera les rentes ᶜdes Propriétaires des terresᶜ de l'Etat (qui est l'abondance de l'argent) les mettra dans l'habitude de tirer quantité d'ouvrages ᵈdes païs étrangersᵈ où ils les auront à grand marché: ce sont là des conséquences naturelles. La richesse qu'un Etat ᵉacquertᵉ par le commerce, le travail & l'œconomie le jettera insensiblement dans le luxe. Les Etats qui haussent par le commerce ne manquent pas de baisser ensuite: il y a des regles ᶠque l'on pourroit mettre en usage, ce qu'on ne fait guereᶠ pour empêcher ce déclin. Toujours est-il vrai que tandis ᵍque l'Etatᵍ est en possession actuelle ʰde [313] la balance du commerce, & de l'abondance de l'argentʰ il paroît puissant, & il l'est en effet tant que cette abondance y subsiste.

But as great States have no need to increase the number of their inhabitants it is enough to make those who are in it live there on the raw produce of the State with more comfort and ease and to increase the strength of the State for its defence and security. To do so by foreign trade it is needful to encourage as much as possible the export of goods and manufactures of the State in exchange so far as may be for gold and silver in kind. If by abundant harvests it happened that there was in the State much produce over and above the ordinary annual consumption it would be profitable to encourage the exportation of it in return for its value in gold and silver. These metals do not corrupt and disappear like the produce of the Land, and with gold and silver one can always import into the State what is lacking there.

It would not however be profitable to put the State into the annual custom of sending abroad large quantities of its raw produce in return for foreign manufactures. It would be to weaken and diminish the inhabitants and the strength of the State at both ends.

But I have no intention of entering into detail as to the branches of trade which should be encouraged for the good of the State. Enough to say that it should always be endeavoured to import as much silver as possible.

The increase in the quantity of silver circulating in a State gives it great advantages in foreign trade so long as this abundance of money lasts. The State then exchanges a small quantity of produce and labour for a greater. It raises its taxes more easily and finds no difficulty in obtaining money in case of public need.

It is true that the continued increase of money will at length by its abundance cause a dearness of Land and Labour in the State. The goods and manufactures will in the long run cost so much that the Foreigner will gradually cease to buy them, and will accustom himself to get them cheaper elsewhere, and this will by imperceptible degrees ruin the work and manufactures of the State. The same cause which will raise the rents of Landlords (which is the abundance of money) will draw them into the habit of importing many articles from foreign countries where they can be had cheap. Such are the natural consequences. The Wealth acquired by a State through Trade, Labour and Oeconomy will plunge it gradually into luxury. States who rise by trade do not fail to sink afterwards. There are steps which might be, but are not, taken to arrest this decline. But it is always true that when the State is in actual possession of a Balance of Trade and abundant money it seems powerful, and it is so in reality so long as this abundance continues.

514 |21| On pourroit tirer des inductions à l'infini pour justifier ces idées du commerce avec l'Etranger, & les avantages de l'abondance de l'argent. Il est étonnant de voir la disproportion de la circulation de l'argent en Angleterre & à la Chine. Les Manufactures des Indes, comme ªles Soieries, les Toiles peintes, les Mousselines, &c. nonobstantª les frais d'une navigation de dix-huit mois, reviennent à un très bas prix en Angleterre, qui les paieroit avec la trentieme partie de ses ouvrages & de ses Manufactures si les Indiens les vouloient acheter. Mais ils ne sont pas si foux de païer des prix extravagans pour nos ouvrages, pendant qu'on travaille mieux chez eux & infiniment à meil-[314]leur marché. ᵇAussi ne nousᵇ vendent-ils leurs Manufactures que contre argent comptant, que nous leur portons annuellement pour augmenter leurs richesses & diminuer les nôtres. Les Manufactures des Indes qu'on consomme en Europe ne font que diminuer notre argent & le travail de nos propres Manufactures.

515 |22| Un Amériquain, qui vend à un Européen des peaux de ªCastorª, est surpris avec raison d'apprendre que les chapeaux qu'on fait de laine sont aussi bons pour l'usage, que ceux qu'on fait de poil de castor, & que toute la différence, qui cause une si longue navigation, ne consiste que dans la fantaisie de ceux qui ᵇtrouventᵇ les chapeaux de poil de castor plus legers & plus agréables à la vûe ᶜ& au toucherᶜ. Cependant comme on paie ordinairement les peaux de Castor [315] à ces Amériquains en ouvrages ᵈde fer, d'acier, &c.ᵈ & non en argent, c'est un commerce qui n'est pas nuisible à l'Europe, d'autant plus qu'il ᵉentretientᵉ des Ouvriers & particulierement des Matelots, qui dans les besoins de l'Etat sont très utiles, au lieu que le commerce des Manufactures des Indes orientales, ᶠemporte l'argent & diminueᶠ les Ouvriers de l'Europe.

516 |23| Il faut convenir que le commerce des Indes orientales est avantageux à la République de Hollande, & qu'elle en fait tomber la perte sur le reste de l'Europe en vendant les épices & Manufactures, en Allemagne, en Italie, ªenª Espagne & dans le Nouveau Monde, qui lui rendent tout l'argent qu'elle envoie aux Indes & bien au-delà: il est même ᵇutile à la Hollande d'habillerᵇ ses femmes & plusieurs autres habitans, des Manufactu-[316]res des Indes, plutôt que d'étoffe d'Angleterre & de France. Il vaut mieux pour les Hollandois enrichir les Indiens que leurs voisins, qui pourroient en profiter pour les opprimer ᶜ: d'ailleurs ilsᶜ vendent aux autres habitans de l'Europe ᵈles toiles & les petites Manufacturesᵈ de leur crû, beaucoup plus cher qu'ils ne vendent ᵉchez eux lesᵉ Manufactures des Indes, qui s'y consomment.

Infinite inductions might be added to justify these ideas of Foreign Trade and the advantages of abundant money. It is astonishing to observe the disproportion in the circulation of money in England and in China. The Manufactures of the Indies, like silks and printed calicoes, muslins, etc. in spite of a sea voyage of 18 months, are at a very low price in England, which would pay for them with the thirtieth part of her articles and manufactures if the Indians would buy them. But they are not so foolish as to pay extravagant prices for our work while work is done better and infinitely cheaper in their own country. So they sell us their Manufactures only for ready cash, which we carry to them annually to increase their wealth and diminish our own. The Indian manufactures consumed in Europe only diminish our money and the work of our own Manufactures.

An American who sells beaver skins to a European is rightly astonished to learn that woollen hats are as serviceable as those made of beaver, and that all the difference, which causes so long a sea journey, is in the fancy of those who think beaver hats lighter and more agreeable to the eye and the touch. However as these beaver skins are ordinarily paid for to the American in articles of iron, steel, etc. and not in silver, it is a trade which is not injurious to Europe, especially since it supports workmen and particularly Sailors, who in the needs of the State are very useful, whilst the trade with the Manufactures of the East Indies carries off the money and diminishes the workmen of Europe.

It must be admitted that the East India trade is profitable to the Dutch Republic and that she makes the loss of it fall on the rest of Europe by selling the spices and manufactures in Germany, Italy, Spain and the New World, which return to her all the money which she sends to the Indies and much more. It is even useful to Holland to clothe her women and other folk with the Manufactures of India rather than with English or French fabrics. It suits the Dutch better to enrich the Indians than their neighbours who might profit by it to oppress them. Moreover they sell to the other peoples of Europe the cloths and small Manufactures of their own raw produce much dearer than they sell the Indian manufactures at home where they are consumed.

Variations and Errata (V)

[a]...[a]: R: 'soyries Toilles peintres et autres nonobstant'
[b]...[b]: R: 'aussy nous'

[a]...[a]: R: 'Castors'
[b]...[b]: R: 'trouve'
[c]...[c]: 'et a lattouchémént'
[d]...[d]: R: 'de fer acier et autres'
[e]...[e]: R: 'maintient'
[f]...[f]: 'emportent l'argent et diminuent'

[a]...[a]: R: 'et en'
[b]...[b]: R: 'utile dhabiller'
[c]...[c]: R: 'ils'
[d]...[d]: R; 'leurs Toilles et petites manufactures'
[e]...[e]: R: 'ches eux les eux les'

Comments (C)

514

For the phrase '*poil* **515** *de castor*' see C442ii.

The Dutch spice trade **516** is also mentioned in E293, E611 and perhaps in D541. See C541ii.

517 |24| L'Angleterre & la France auroient tort d'imiter en cela les Hollandois. Ces Roïaumes ont chez eux les moïens d'habiller leurs femmes, de leur crû; & quoique leurs étoffes reviennent à un plus haut prix que celles des Manufactures des Indes, ils doivent obliger leurs habitans ᵃdeᵃ n'en point porter d'étrangeres; ils ne doivent pas permettre la diminution de leurs ouvrages ᵇ& de leursᵇ Manufactures, ni se mettre dans la dépendance des [317] Etrangers, ils doivent encore moins laisser enlever leur argent pour cela.

518 |25| Mais puisque les Hollandois trouvent moïen de débiter dans les autres Etats de l'Europe les marchandises des Indes, les Anglois & les François en devroient faire autant, soit pour diminuer les forces navales de la Hollande, soit pour augmenter les leurs, & sur-tout afin de se passer du secours des Hollandois dans les branches de consommation, qu'une mauvaise habitude a rendues nécessaires dans ces Roïaumes: c'est un désavantage visible de permettre qu'on porte des Indiennes dans les Roïaumes d'Europe qui ont de leur crû dequoi habiller leurs habitans.

519 |26| De même qu'il est désavantageux à un Etat d'encourager des Manufactures étrangeres, il est aussi désavantageux d'encourager la navigation des étrangers. [318] Lorsqu'un Etat envoie chez l'Etranger ses ouvrages ᵃ& sesᵃ Manufactures, il en ᵇtireᵇ l'avantage en entier s'il les envoie par ses propres Vaisseaux: par-là il entretient un bon nombre de Matelots, qui sont aussi utiles à l'Etat que ᶜlesᶜ Ouvriers. Mais ᵈs'il en abandonneᵈ le transport à des Bâtimens étrangers, il fortifie la Marine étrangere & diminue la sienne.

520 |27| C'est un point essentiel du commerce avec l'Etranger que celui de la navigation. ᵃDe toute l'Europe, les Hollandois sontᵃ ceux qui construisent des Vaisseaux à ᵇmeilleurᵇ marché. Outre les rivieres qui leur ᶜapportentᶜ du bois flotté, le voisinage du Nord leur fournit à moins de frais ᵈles mâts, le bois, le goudron, les cordages, &c.ᵈ Leurs Moulins à scier le bois en ᵉfacilitentᵉ le travail. ᶠDe plusᶠ ils naviguent avec moins d'équipage, & leurs Ma-[319]telots vivent à très peu de frais. Un de leurs Moulins à scier le bois épargne journellement le travail de quatre-vingts hommes.

521 |28| Par ces avantages ils seroient ᵃdans l'Europe les seuls voituriers par Merᵃ, si l'on suivoit toujours le meilleur marché: & s'ils avoient de leur propre crû dequoi faire un commerce étendu, ils auroient sans doute la plus florissante Marine de l'Europe. Mais le grand nombre de leurs Matelots ne suffit pas, sans les forces intérieures de l'Etat, pour la superiorité de leurs forces navales : ils ᵇn'armeroientᵇ jamais de Vaisseaux de ᶜguerreᶜ, ni de Matelots si l'Etat avoit de ᵈgrandsᵈ revenus pour les construire ᵉ& les solderᵉ: ils profiteroient en tout du grand marché.

England and France would be mistaken to imitate the Dutch in this respect. These kingdoms have at home the means of clothing their women with their own raw material, and though their fabrics are dearer than those of Indian manufacture they should prevent their people from wearing the foreign material. They ought not to permit the falling off of their own articles and manufactures nor become dependent on the foreigner, still less allow their money to be taken away for that purpose.

[a]...[a]: R: 'a'
[b]...[b]: R: 'et'

517

But as the Dutch find means to sell Indian merchandise in the other States of Europe, the English and French should do the same, whether to diminish the naval power of Holland or to increase their own, and above all to do without the aid of Holland in the branches of consumption which a bad habit has rendered necessary in these kingdoms. It is an evident disadvantage to allow the wearing of Indian fabrics in the kingdoms of Europe which have wherewith to clothe their people with their own products.

The argument in E518–E522 provides implicit support for policies like the Navigation Acts. In this context see the praise for the Navigation Acts in A6.

518

Just as it is disadvantageous to a State to encourage foreign manufactures so it is to encourage foreign navigation. When a State sends abroad its articles and manufactures it derives the full advantage if it sends them in its own ships. It then maintains a good number of sailors who are as useful to the State as workmen. But if it leaves the carriage of them to foreign vessels it strengthens the foreign shipping and weakens its own.

[a]...[a]: R: 'et'
[b]...[b]: R: 'retire'
[c]...[c]: R: 'des'
[d]...[d]: R: 'sils abbandonnent'

519

Navigation is an essential point in foreign trade. In the whole of Europe the Dutch are those who build ships the cheapest. Timber is floated down to them by river, and the proximity of the North supplies them at less expense with masts, wood, pitch, rope, etc. Their Windmills for sawing wood facilitate the working of it. Also they navigate with smaller crews and their sailors live very cheaply. One of their Windmills for sawing wood saves the labour of 80 men a day.

[a]...[a]: R: 'Les hollandois sont de toute L'europe'
[b]...[b]: R: 'meilleurs'
[c]...[c]: R: 'apporte'
[d]...[d]: R: 'les Mats, Bois godrons chanvres et cordage et'
[e]...[e]: R: 'facilite'
[f]...[f]: R: 'pardessus Cela'

The Dutch windmills are also mentioned in D382. Note that there it is estimated that a sawmill saves the labour of 25 persons per day, while here the estimate is 80 persons. Cf. C382ii.

520

Owing to these advantages they would be the only sea-carriers in Europe if cheapness only were followed. And if they had enough of their own raw material to form an extensive commerce they would doubtless have the most flourishing maritime service in Europe. But the greater number of their seamen does not suffice without the interior strength of the State, for the superiority of their naval power. They would never arm warships nor sailors if the State had large revenues to build the ships and pay the men: they would profit in everything from extended markets.

[a]...[a]: R: 'les seuls voituriers de Mers de lEurope'
[b]...[b]: R: 'manqueroient'
[c]...[c]: R: 'guerres'
[d]...[d]: R: 'grand'
[e]...[e]: R: 'et solder'

521

522 |29| L'Angleterre pour les empêcher d'augmenter à ses dépens leur avantage sur Mer par ce bon marché, a défendu à ªtou-[320]te Nationª d'apporter ᵇchez elleᵇ d'autres marchandises que celles de leur crû; au moïen dequoi les Hollandois n'aïant pû servir de voituriers pour l'Angleterre, les Anglois même ont fortifié par-là leur Marine : & bien qu'ils naviguent à plus de frais que les Hollandois, les richesses de leurs charges au dehors rendent ces frais moins considérables.

523 |30| La France & l'Espagne sont bien des Etats maritimes, qui ont un riche produit qu'on envoie dans le Nord, d'où on leur porte chez eux les denrées & marchandises. Il n'est pas étonnant que leur marine ne soit pas considérable à proportion de leur produit & de l'étendue de ªleurs Côtesª maritimes, puisqu'ils laissent à des Vaisseaux étrangers le soin de leur apporter du Nord tout ce qu'ils en reçoivent, & de leur venir enlever les denrées que les Etats [321] du Nord tirent de chez eux.

524 |31| Ces Etats, je dis la France & l'Espagne, ne font pas entrer dans les vues de leur politique la considération du Commerce au point qu'elle y seroit ªavantageuseª; la plûpart des Commerçans en France & en Espagne qui ont relation avec l'Etranger, sont plutôt des Facteurs ou des Commis de Négocians étrangers que des Entrepreneurs, pour conduire ce commerce de leur fond.

525 |32| Il est vrai que les Etats du Nord sont, par leur situation ª& par leª voisinage des ᵇpaïs qui produisentᵇ tout ce qui est nécessaire à la construction des Navires, en état de voiturer tout à meilleur marché, que ne seroit la France & l'Espagne: mais si ces deux Roïaumes prenoient des ᶜmesuresᶜ pour fortifier leur marine, cet obstacle ne les en empêcheroit pas. L'Angleterre leur en a mon-[322]tré il y a déja long-tems l'exemple en partie : ils ont chez eux & dans leurs Colonies tout ce qu'il faut pour la construction des Bâtimens, ou du moins il ne seroit pas difficile de les y faire produire : & il y a une infinité de voies qu'on pourroit prendre pour faire réussir un tel dessein, si ᵈla legislatureᵈ ou le ministere y vouloit concourir. Mon sujet ne me permet pas d'examiner dans ᵉcet Essaiᵉ, le détail de ces voies: je me bornerai à dire, que dans les païs où le commerce n'entretient pas constamment un nombre considérable de Bâtimens & de Matelots, il est presque impossible que le Prince puisse entretenir une Marine florissante, sans des frais qui seroient seuls capables de ruiner les trésors de son Etat.

526 |33| Je conclurai donc, en remarquant que le commerce qui est le plus essentiel à un Etat pour [323] l'augmentation ou la diminution de ses forces est le commerce avec l'Etranger, que celui de l'intérieur d'un Etat n'est pas d'une si grande considération dans la politique; qu'on ne soutient qu'à demi le commerce avec l'Etranger, lorsqu'on n'a pas l'œil à augmenter ª& maintenirª de gros Négocians naturels du païs, des Bâtimens & des Matelots, des Ouvriers & des Manufactures, & surtout qu'il faut toujours s'attacher à maintenir la balance contre les Etrangers.

England, in order to prevent the Dutch from increasing at her expense their advantage on the Sea by this cheapness, has forbidden any nation from bringing into England other merchandise than that of their own growth. In this way, the Dutch being unable to serve as Carriers for England, the English have strengthened their own shipping. And though they sail at greater costs than the Dutch the wealth of their overseas cargoes renders these costs less considerable.

France and Spain are maritime States which have rich produce sent to the North, whence goods and merchandise are brought to them. It is not surprising that their shipping is inconsiderable in proportion to their produce and the extent of their seaboard, since they leave it to foreign vessels to bring them all they receive from the North and to take away from them the goods which the States of the North receive from them.

These States, France and Spain, do not take into account in their policy the consideration of Trade in the way in which it would be advantageous. Most Merchants in France and Spain who have to do with the foreigner are rather Agents or Clerks of foreign merchants than Adventurers carrying on the trade on their own account.

It is true that the States of the North are, by their situation and the vicinity of countries which produce all that is needed for building ships, in a position to carry everything cheaper than France and Spain could do. But if these two kingdoms took steps to strengthen their shipping, this obstacle would not prevent them. England has long since partly shewn them the example. They have at home and in their Colonies all that is needed for the construction of ships, or at least it would not be difficult to get them produced there, and there is an infinity of methods that might be used to make such a policy successful if the legislature or the ministry would concur in it. My subject does not allow me in this Essay to examine these methods in detail. I will limit myself to saying that in countries where trade does not regularly support a considerable number of ships and sailors it is almost impossible for the Prince to maintain a flourishing navy without such expense as would be capable by itself of ruining the treasure of his State.

I will conclude then by observing that the trade most essential to a State for the increase or decrease of its power is foreign trade, that the home trade is not of equally great importance politically, that foreign trade is only half supported when no care is taken to increase and maintain large merchants who are natives of the country, ships, sailors, workmen and manufacturers, and above all that care must always be taken to maintain the balance against the foreigner.

ᵃ…ᵃ: R: 'toutes nations'   522
ᵇ…ᵇ: R: 'ches eux'

ᵃ…ᵃ: R: 'leur cote'   523

ᵃ…ᵃ: R: 'avantageux'   524

ᵃ…ᵃ: R: 'et'   525
ᵇ…ᵇ: R: 'paÿs propre a produire'
ᶜ…ᶜ: R: 'Vues'
ᵈ…ᵈ: R: 'le Legislateur'
ᵉ…ᵉ: R, 1756 a, b: 'ce Essai'

ᵃ…ᵃ: 1756b, 1769: '& à maintenir'   526

527　　**CHAPITRE ªIIª.**　　　　　　　　　　　　　　　　　　[68] **CHAP. XVII.**
　　　　　Des Changes & de leur　　　　　　　　　　　　　　*Of Inland and Foreign*
　　　　　　　　nature.　　　　　　　　　　　　　　　　　　　　*Exchange.*

528
　　　　　　　　　　　　　　‖ To know when the nation really prospers
　　　　　　　　　　　　　　by ªit'sª general commerce, ᵇbeingᵇ a matter
　　　　　　　　　　　　　　of ᶜgreatᶜ concernment to ᵈthe community,ᵈ
　　　　　　　　　　　　　　ᵉit may be useful to pursue this point a step
　　　　　　　　　　　　　　furtherᵉ
　　　　　　　　　　　　　　‖ Various characteristics hereof may be
　　　　　　　　　　　　　　assigned; but there are but two, perhaps,
　　　　　　　　　　　　　　which can be depended on; and ᶠthoseᶠ are the
　　　　　　　　　　　　　　courses of exchange and the price of bullion.

529　|1| Dans la Ville même de Paris, il coute ordinairement
　　　　　cinq sols par sac de mille livres, pour porter de l'argent
　　　　　d'une maison à [324] une autre; s'il falloit toujours
　　　　　le porter du Fauxbourg Saint Antoine, aux Invalides,
　　　　　il en couteroit plus du double, & s'il n'y avoit pas
　　　　　communément de porteurs d'argent de confiance, il en
　　　　　couteroit encore davantage : que s'il y avoit souvent
　　　　　des Voleurs en chemin on l'enverroit par grosses
　　　　　sommes, escorté, & avec plus de frais; & si quelqu'un
　　　　　se chargeoit du transport, à ªsesª frais & risques, il se
　　　　　feroit païer de ce transport, à proportion des frais ᵇ& des
　　　　　risquesᵇ. C'est ainsi, que les frais du transport, de Rouen
　　　　　à Paris, & de Paris à Rouen coutent ordinairement
　　　　　cinquante sols par sac de mille livres, ce qu'on appelle
　　　　　dans le langage des Banquiers, un quart pour cent; les
　　　　　Banquiers envoient l'argent ordinairement en doubles
　　　　　barils, que les Voleurs ne peuvent gueres emporter, à
　　　　　cause du fer & de la pesanteur, [325] & comme il y
　　　　　a toujours des Messagers sur cette route, les frais sont
　　　　　peu considérables, sur les grosses parties qu'on envoie
　　　　　de part & d'autre.

530　|2| Si la Ville de Châlons ªsur Marneª　‖ ᵇTo the end that our meaning　[74] let it be supposed that
　　　　　paie tous les ans au Receveur des　may　be　conveyedᵇ　with　the Receiver-General of the
　　　　　Fermes du Roi, dix mille onces　perspicuity, let it be supposed that　County of *Somerset* collects
　　　　　d'argent d'un côté, & si de l'autre　the city of *Chalons sur Marne*　yearly for his Majesty's
　　　　　côté les Marchands de vin de Châlons　in *Champagne* pays yearly, to　Revenue 100,000 l. and
　　　　　ou des environs vendent à Paris, par　the king's receiver there, 10,000　suppose the Traders at [75]
　　　　　l'entremise de leurs correspondans,　ᶜouncesᶜ of silver, and that the　*Bristol* sell yearly to the
　　　　　des vins de Champagne pour la　*Chalons* wine-merchants sell at　Merchants of *London* to the
　　　　　valeur de dix mille onces d'argent;　*Paris*, by their correspondents,　Value 100,000 l.
　　　　　si l'once d'argent en France passe　wines to the value of 10,000
　　　　　dans le commerce pour cinq livres, la　ᶜouncesᶜ of silver, supposing the
　　　　　somme des dix mille onces en question　ounce of silver ᵈof the same value
　　　　　s'appellera cinquante mille livres, tant　in livresᵈ at *Chalons* as at *Paris*.
　　　　　à Paris qu'à Chalons.

Chapter II　　　　ᵃ…ᵃ: R: '2ᵉ'　　　　**527**

Of the Exchanges and their Nature

ᵃ…ᵃ: P: 'its'　　　　　　　　　　　　　　　　　　　D occurs in the entry, **528**
ᵇ…ᵇ: P:'is'　　　　　　　　　　　　　　　　　　　　'BALLANCE　　of
ᶜ…ᶜ: P: 'highest'　　　　　　　　　　　　　　　　　trade'. D528 follows
ᵈ…ᵈ: P: 'these kingdoms;'　　　　　　　　　　　　immediately after D507
ᵉ…ᵉ: P: 'and therefore if I dwell a little longer upon a topic of　and the first paragraph
this nature, it will not perhaps be disagreeable to such who　looks like something
have delighted in those useful and important studies; and　written by Postlethwayt
who have the true interest and happiness of these kingdoms　to link what goes before
really at heart.'　　　　　　　　　　　　　　　　　and what follows.
ᶠ…ᶠ: P: 'these, as before observed,'

Inside the City of Paris the carriage of money from one house　ᵃ…ᵃ: R: 'Ces'　**529**
to another usually costs 5 sols per bag of 1000 livres. If it were　ᵇ…ᵇ: R: 'et Risques'
necessary to carry it from the Fauxbourg St Antoine to the
Invalides it would cost more than twice as much, and if there
were not generally trustworthy porters of money it would cost
still more. If there were often robbers on the road the money
would be sent in large amounts, with an escort, at greater cost,
and if some one charged himself with the transport at his own
cost and risks he would require payment for it in proportion to
these costs and risks. So it is that the expense of transport from
Rouen to Paris and from Paris to Rouen amounts generally to 50
sols per bag of 1000 livres which in Bank language is ¼ percent.
The Bankers generally send the money in strong kegs which
robbers can hardly carry off because of the iron and the weight,
and as there are always mail coaches on this route the Costs are
not considerable on the large sums sent between these two places.

If the City of Châlons sur　ᵃ…ᵃ: R: 'en　i. Variation V530a is not material. Both texts refer to　**530**
Marne every year pays the　Champagne'　the town Châlons-en-Champagne (until 1998 officially
Receiver of the King's taxes,　ᵇ…ᵇ: P: 'In　named Châlons-sur-Marne).
10,000 ounces of silver on the　order to convey
one hand, and on the other the　our meaning'　ii. Note that in the *Universal Dictionary* the rate of
wine Merchants of Châlons　　　　　　　5 *livres* to the ounce of silver is omitted. In the subsequent
and its neighbourhood sell to　ᶜ…ᶜ: P: 'oz.'　paragraphs (D531–D533) the numerical example of
Paris, through their agents,　ᵈ…ᵈ: P: 'worth　50,000 livres is omitted, too. In contrast, the 1749 text
Champagne wine of the value　5 livres as　includes these figures, just like the French text.
of 10,000 ounces of silver, if　well'
the ounce of silver in France　　　　　　iii. A530 occurs some pages into chapter XVIII, *Of
passes in trade for 5 livres,　　　　　　*Inland and Foreign Exchange* (pp. 68–85). Until near the
the total of the 10,000 ounces　　　　　end of p. 74 there is no clear correspondence with either
in question will be 50,000　　　　　　　E or D.
livres both in Paris and in
Châlons.　　　　　　　　　　　　　　　iv. In this chapter A consistently uses London and
Bristol as example of places between which payments
are made. It may be significant that the distance between
Châlons-en-Champagne and Paris and between Bristol
and London is very similar, approximately 160km.
Moreover, in E London and Bristol also appear once; see
C540ii.

531 |3| Le Receveur des Fermes dans cet exemple a ᵃcinquante mille livresᵃ à envoïer à Paris, & les correspondans des Marchands de vin de Châlons ont ᵃcinquan-[326]te mille livresᵃ à envoïer à Châlons; on pourra épargner ce double emploi ou transport par une compensation ou comme on dit par lettres de ᵇchangeᵇ, si les parties s'abouchent & s'accommodent pour cela.

|| The ᶜlivresᶜ at *Paris* are to be sent in specie to *Chalons*, and the ᵈlivresᵈ at *Chalons* are to be sent to *Paris*; but the trouble may be saved on both sides, ᵉby exchangeᵉ. ᶠThe wine-merchantsᶠ correspondents will carry their ᵈlivresᵈ to the custom-house, and take there in exchange a rescription, order, bill, or bills of exchange, upon the receiver at *Chalons*; which bills they will endorse to the wine-merchants, and they will receive upon them ᵈthe like quantity of livresᵈ.

there will in these Suppositions be due to the King at *Bristol* 100,000 l. and there will be due in *London* to the *Bristol* Merchants 100,000 l. the King's Exchequer will require to receive from the Agent at *Bristol* the 100,000 l. due to his Majesty, and the *Bristol* Merchants will want to receive from the Correspondents in *London* an equal Sum due to them, for the Value of the Goods and Merchandize sent up to *London*: this Matter thus stated, may be adjusted by Bills of Exchange, without the immediate Intervention, Expence, and Risk of sending Money backwards and forwards; for if the *Bristol* Merchants apply to the Receiver-General of the County, he may take their Bills on their Correspondents in *London*, and transmit them to the *Exchequer*; or else the several Merchants in *London* may apply to the *Treasury*, and there pay in their Money in Exchange for Bills, or Orders on his Majesty's Receiver at *Bristol*, which Bills or Orders these Gentlemen of *London* may transmit to *Bristol*;

532 |4| Que les correspondans des Marchands de vin de Châlons portent ᵃ(chacun sa part)ᵃ les cinquante mille livres chez le Caissier du Bureau des Fermes à Paris; qu'il leur donne une ou plusieurs rescriptions, ou lettres de change sur le Receveur des Fermes à Châlons, païables à leur ordre; qu'ils endossent ᵇouᵇ passent ᶜleur ordreᶜ aux Marchands de vin de Châlons, ceux-ci recevront du Receveur à Châlons les cinquante mille livres. De cette maniere, les cinquante mille livres à Paris seront païées au Caissier des Fermes à Paris, & les ᵈcinquante mille livresᵈ à Châlons seront païées aux Mar-[327]chands de vin de cette Ville, & par cet échange ou compensation, on épargnera la peine de voiturer cet argent d'une ville à l'autre. Ou bien que les Marchands de vin à Châlons, qui ont ᵈcinquante mille livresᵈ à Paris, aillent offrir leurs lettres de change au Receveur qui les endossera au Caissier des Fermes à Paris, ᵉlequel yᵉ touchera le montant, & que le Receveur à Châlons leur paie contre ᶠleurs lettres de changeᶠ les ᵈcinquante mille livresᵈ qu'il a à Châlons : de quelque côte qu'on fasse cette compensation, soit qu'on tire les lettres de change de Paris sur Châlons, soit de Châlons sur Paris, comme dans cet exemple on paie once pour once, & ᵈcinquante mille livresᵈ pour ᵈcinquante mille livresᵈ, on dira que le change est au pair.

|| ᵍOrᵍ, the receiver of *Chalons* will pay his ʰlivresʰ to the wine-merchants, and take their bills of exchange, on their correspondent at *Paris*, which he will endorse to the ⁱtreasurer of the customsⁱ, who will receive the ʰsum of livresʰ on the said bills.

and by means of these Bills of Exchange the 100,000 l. Due to the King at *Bristol* will be paid into his Teasury at *London*, and the 100,000 l. due in *London* to [76] *Bristol* will be there paid: And these equal Payments are what is properly called the Par of the Exchange between *Bristol* and *London*, or between *London* and *Bristol*.

The Receiver of Taxes in this example has 50,000 livres to send to Paris, and the agents of the Châlons Wine-merchants have 50,000 livres to send to Châlons. This double transaction or transport may be avoided by a set-off or as they are called bills of exchange, if the parties get together and arrange it.

ᵃ…ᵃ: R: 'Cinquante Mille'

ᵇ…ᵇ: R: 'changes'

ᶜ…ᶜ: P: 'livres 50,000'

ᵈ…ᵈ: '50,000 livres'

ᵉ…ᵉ: P: 'by a compensation in exchange'

ᶠ…ᶠ: P: 'To this end The wine-merchants'

In addition to the repeated occurrence of the sum of 50,000 *livres*, the term 'compensation' in V531e also occurs in E531. This suggests that the wording of Postlethwayt's 1749 publication is in places more faithful to the (unknown) source from which he borrowed.

531

Let the agents of the Châlons wine-merchants take (each his own part) the 50,000 livres to the cashier of the Tax Office at Paris. Let him give them one or more cheques or bills of exchange on the Receiver of Taxes at Châlons, payable to their order. Let them endorse or transfer their order to the Châlons wine-merchants and these will obtain from the Receiver at Châlons the 50,000 livres. In this way the 50,000 livres at Paris will be paid to the Cashier of the Tax department at Paris and the 50,000 livres at Châlons will be paid to the wine-merchants of that City, and by exchange or set-off there will be saved the trouble of sending this money from one city to the other. Or else let the wine-merchants at Châlons, who have 50,000 livres at Paris, go and offer their bills of exchange to the Receiver of Taxes, who will endorse them to the Cashier of the Tax Office at Paris who will collect the amount there, and let the Receiver at Châlons pay the merchants for their bills of exchange the 50,000 livres which he has at Châlons. Whichever way this set-off is effected, whether the bills of exchange be drawn from Paris on Châlons or from Châlons on Paris, as in this example ounce for ounce is paid, and 50,000 livres for 50,000 livres, the exchange is said to be at par.

ᵃ…ᵃ: R: parentheses are missing

ᵇ…ᵇ: R: 'et'

ᶜ…ᶜ: R: 'leurs ordres'

ᵈ…ᵈ: R: '50000ˡᵇ'

ᵉ…ᵉ: R: 'qui en'

ᶠ…ᶠ: R: 'Ces Lettres'

ᵍ…ᵍ: P: 'Or else'

ʰ…ʰ: P: '50,000 livres'

ⁱ…ⁱ: P: 'Custom-house treasurer there'

532

533 |5| La même methode se pourra pratiquer, entre ces Marchands [328] de vin à Châlons, & les Receveurs des Seigneurs de Paris qui ont des terres ou des rentes aux environs de Châlons, & encore entre les Marchands de vin, ou tout autres ᵃMarchands à Châlonsᵃ, qui ont envoïé des denrées ou des marchandises à Paris, & qui y ont de l'argent, & tous Marchands qui ont tiré des marchandises de Paris & les ont vendues à Châlons. Que s'il y a un grand commerce entre ces deux Villes, il s'érigera des Banquiers à Paris & à Châlons, qui s'aboucheront avec les interressés de part & d'autre, & seront les agens ou entremeteurs des paiemens qu'on auroit à envoïer d'une de ces Villes à l'autre. Maintenant si tous les vins, & autres denrées & marchandises qu'on a envoïées de Châlons à Paris, & qu'on y a effectivement ᵇvenduesᵇ pour argent comptant, ᶜexcedentᶜ en valeur la somme de la [329] recette des Fermes à Châlons, celles des rentes que les Seigneurs de Paris ont aux environs de Châlons, & encore la valeur de toutes les denrées ᵈ& de toutes les marchandisesᵈ qui ont été envoïées de Paris à Châlons & qu'on y a vendues pour argent comptant, de la somme de cinq mille onces d'argent ou de vingt-cinq mille liv. il faudra nécessairement que le Banquier à Paris envoie cette somme en argent à Châlons. Cette somme sera l'excédent ou la balance du commerce entre ces deux Villes; on l'enverra dis-je nécessairement en especes à Châlons, & cette opération se trouvera conduite de la maniere suivante ou de quelqu'autre maniere approchante.

|| The same method may be practised between ᵉthe wine-merchantsᵉ at *Chalons*; and the stewards of the *Paris* ᶠland-pro-[I, 185, col.2] prietorsᶠ, who have estates near *Chalons*; and, if the returns be considerable, bankers will set up at *Paris* and at *Chalons*, to make the remittances, and supply the necessary bills of exchange between those two cities: and as, on this supposition, the ᵍsame sum of livresᵍ at *Chalons* ʰisʰ exchanged by ⁱthe like sumⁱ at *Paris*, the exchange of money will be said to be at *par*.

The same Method of Negotiation may be practised by the Stewards of Gentlemen who have Estates in or about *Bristol*, but who reside in *London*; yet suppose it happens that the Value of all the Goods and Merchandize which *London* supplies *Bristol* with, the King's Revenue in *Somersetshire*, and that of the Income of Gentlemens Estates, is less in Amount than the Value of the Goods and Merchandize furnished by *Bristol* to *London*; then and in this Case, this Excess must be paid by *London* to *Bristol* in Money, and this Excess or Difference may be paid in the following, or such like Manner, and is called the Ballance of Trade.

The same method might be adopted between these wine-merchants at Châlons and the Agents of the Nobility in Paris who have land in the Châlons district, and the Wine Merchants or other Merchants at Châlons who have sent goods or merchandise to Paris and have money there and other merchants who have drawn merchandise from Paris and sold it at Châlons. If there is a large trade between these two cities Bankers will set up at Paris and Châlons who will enter into relations with the interested parties on both sides and will be the agents or intermediaries for the payments which would have to be sent from one of these cities to the other. Now if all the wine and other goods and merchandise which have been sent from Châlons to Paris and have actually been sold there for ready money exceed in value the total receipts of the taxes at Châlons, and the Rents which the nobility of Paris have in the Châlons district as well as the value of the goods and merchandise sent from Paris to Châlons and sold there for ready money, by 5000 ounces of silver or 25,000 livres it will be necessary for the Banker in Paris to send this amount to Châlons in money. This will be the excess or balance of trade between these two cities. It will, I say, be of necessity sent to Châlons in specie, and this operation will be carried out in the following way or in some similar fashion.

[a]...[a]: R: 'Marchands'
[b]...[b]: R: 'Vendu'
[c]...[c]: R: 'excede'
[d]...[d]: R: 'et marchandises'
[e]...[e]: P: 'said wine-merchants'
[f]...[f]: P: 'proprietors'
[g]...[g]: R: '50,000 livres'
[h]...[h]: P: 'are'
[i]...[i]: P: 'bills for 50,000 livres'

533

534 |6| Les Agens, ou Correspondans des Marchands de vin de Châlons & des autres qui ont envoïé des denrées ou ᵃdes Marchandisesᵃ de Châlons à Paris, [330] ont l'argent de ᵇcesᵇ ventes en caisse à Paris: ils ont ordre de le remettre à Châlons; ils ne sont pas dans l'habitude de le risquer par les voitures, ils s'adresseront au Caissier des Fermes qui leur donnera des rescriptions ou lettres de change sur le Receveur des Fermes à Châlons, jusqu'à la concurrence des fonds qu'il a à Châlons, & cela ordinairement au pair; mais comme ils ont besoin de remettre ᶜencore d'autres sommes à Châlonsᶜ, ils s'adresseront pour cela au Banquier ᵈqui aura à sa dispositionᵈ les rentes des Seigneurs à Paris qui ont des terres aux environs de Châlons. Ce Banquier leur fournira, de même que le Caissier des Fermes, des lettres de change sur son correspondant à Châlons jusqu'à la concurrence des fonds qu'il a à sa disposition à Châlons, & qu'il avoit ordre de faire revenir à Paris: cette com-[331]pensation se fera aussi au pair, si ce n'est que le Banquier cherche à y trouver quelque petit profit pour sa peine, tant de la part de ces Agens qui s'adressent à lui pour remettre leur argent à Châlons, que de celle des Seigneurs qui l'ont chargé de faire revenir leur argent de Châlons, à Paris. Si le Banquier a de même à sa disposition à Châlons, la valeur des Marchandises qui y ont été envoïées de Paris, & qui y ont été vendues pour argent comptant; il fournira encore de même des lettres de change pour cette valeur.

|| The several Correpondents of the *Bristol* Merchants in *London*, must, at the limited Time of Payment, be in Cash for the Produce of the Goods and Merchandize, sent to them from *Bristol*, and must transmit this Ballance to *Bristol*, to compass which they may apply to the Treasury, and know there, [77] if any Money is wanting in Exchange of Bills, which Bills to the Amount of what the Receiver General is in Cash for, may be sent to *Bristol*, and the Exchange between these two Places, will be at Par; that is to say, by the Payment of any supposed Sum in Cash at *Bristol*, in Compensation of an equal Sum paid at *London*; and the same Method may be taken with Gentlemen who have Cash in their Receiver's Hands from the Income of their *Somersetshire* Estates.

The Agents or correspondents of the Wine merchants of Châlons and of others who have sent goods or merchandise from Châlons to Paris have the money for these sales in hand at Paris. They are ordered to remit it to Châlons. They are not accustomed to risk it by carriage, they will apply to the Cashier of the Tax Office who will give them cheques or bills of exchange on the Receiver of Taxes at Châlons up to the amount which he has at Châlons, and generally at par. But as they need to send further sums to Châlons they will apply to the Banker who will have at his disposal the Rents of the Paris nobility who have lands in that district. This Banker will furnish them, like the Cashier of the Tax Office, with bills of exchange on his correspondent at Châlons up to the amount of the funds which he has at his disposal at Châlons and had been ordered to bring to Paris. This set-off will also be made at par, unless the Banker tries to make some little profit out of it for his trouble, as well from the Agents who apply to him to send their money to Châlons as from the nobility who have charged him with the transmission of their money from Châlons to Paris. If the Banker has also at his disposal at Châlons the value of the merchandise sent thither from Paris and sold there for ready money he will also furnish letters of exchange for this value.

ᵃ…ᵃ: R: 'Marchandises'
ᵇ…ᵇ: R: 'ses'
ᶜ…ᶜ: R: 'encore a Chalons'
ᵈ…ᵈ: R: 'qui a ordinairement a sa disposition'

534

535 |7| Mais dans notre supposition les Agens des Marchands de Châlons, ont encore en caisse à Paris vingt-cinq mille livres qu'ils ont ordre de remettre à Châlons, au-delà de toutes les sommes ci-dessus mentionnées. S'ils offrent cet argent au Caissier des Fermes, il répondra qu'il [332] n'a plus de fonds à Châlons, & qu'il ne sauroit leur fournir de lettres de change ou des rescriptions sur cette Ville. S'ils offrent l'argent au Banquier il leur répondra, qu'il n'a pas non plus de fonds à Châlons, & qu'il n'a pas occasion de tirer, mais que si l'on veut lui païer trois pour cent de ᵃchangeᵃ, il fournira des lettres: ils offriront un ou deux pour cent, & enfin deux & demi, ne pouvant faire mieux. A ce prix le Banquier se déterminera à leur donner des lettres, c'est-à-dire, qu'en lui païant à Paris deux livres dix sols, il fournira une lettre de change de cent livres, sur son correspondant de Châlons, païable à dix ou ᵇquinjoursᵇ, afin de mettre ce correspondant en état de faire ce paiement des ᶜvingt-cinq milleᶜ livres qu'il tire sur lui : à ce prix de change, il les lui enverra ᵈpar le Messagerᵈ ou Carrosse en espece [333] d'or, ou au défaut ᵉde l'or, en argent. Il paieraᵉ dix livres pour chaque sac de mille livres, ou suivant le langage des Banquiers un pour cent; il paiera à son Correspondant de Châlons pour commission cinq livres-par sac de mille livres, ou demi pour cent, & il gardera pour son profit un pour cent. Sur ce pied le change est à Paris pour Châlons à deux & demi pour cent au-dessus du pair, parcequ'on paie ᶠdeux livres dix solsᶠ sur chaque cent livres pour le prix du change.

‖ ᵍBut, ifᵍ the quantity of wines, and other commodities sent from *Chalons* to *Paris*, and sold there, exceed ʰin their valueʰ the king's revenue at *Chalons*, and the commodities sent from *Paris* to *Chalons*, which are consumed and sold there, by the sum of 5000 ⁱouncesⁱ of ʲsilver,ʲ the *Paris* bankers will send this sum to *Chalons* in specie; and the expence of the carriage of this money will fall upon the *wine-merchants*, and others, at *Chalons*, who have this sum in cash in the hands of their correspondents at *Paris*, and want to have it at *Chalons*: they, therefore, will order their correspondents to remit it to them; but the banker at *Paris*, who has no money at *Chalons*, will refuse to give his bills on his correspondent banker there *at par*, ᵏandᵏ demand 102 livres for his bill on *Chalons* for 100 livres: if they will give him that price, he will draw for it upon his correspondent, and send him the money in specie, to answer the payment; and as he ˡmustˡ pay a livre for the carriage of every 100 livres, or 1 *per cent*, he will still have 1 *per cent* for his own and his corresponding banker's commission: and, in this case, the exchange at *Paris* for *Chalons* will be 2 *per cent* above par, as the exchange of *Chalons* for *Paris* will be 2 *per cent* under par: and, if *Chalons* be indebted to *Paris*, the exchange will be ᵐthe reverseᵐ.

‖ But in my Supposition, there is a considerable Sum due from *London* to *Bristol* more than the King's Revenue, and the Income of Gentlemens Estates, as also that of the Value of the Goods furnished by *London* to *Bristol*; suppose this surplus Sum to be 400,000 l. and offered to the Treasury, and there refused, as the Receiver General is not in Cash for the King's Account; if Application is made to Gentlemen of Estates, they ought to say, that their Stewards are not in Cash for them; the *London* Merchants will the apply to their Neighbours, who will answer that the Ballance of Trade being against *London*, they have no Money at *Bristol*, but yet if three *per Cent.* is given them, they consent to furnish [78] Bills for the Sum demanded; that is to say, for the Consideration of 103 l. they will give a Bill for 100 l. to be paid at *Bristol*. The *London* Merchants not being willing to run the Risk of sending Money to *Bristol*, will be forced, in order to pay their Debts at *Bristol*, to accept of these Conditions, and the Drawer of such Bill will be obliged to send down to *Bristol* this 100 l. in order to put his Friend there in Cash to pay the Bill drawn upon him, the Expence of which may be ten Shillings, and his Friend's Commission ten Shillings more, in all one Pound; so that this Drawer will have two Pounds clear Profit, which he calls the Consideration payed him for the Risk and Hazard of sending Money to *Bristol*; in this Case, the Exchange between *London* and *Bristol* is stiled three *per Cent.* above Par; because at *London* there is given 103 l. to receive at *Bristol* only 100 l. and at the latter Place the Exchange will be called at three Pounds *per Cent.* under Par, because to receive in *London* 100 l. there will be paid for it at *Bristol* but 97 l.

Higgs Translation (H)	Variations and Errata (V)	Comments (C)

But in our case supposed the Agents of the Châlons merchants have still in hand at Paris 25,000 livres which they are ordered to remit to Châlons above all the sums mentioned above. If they offer this money to the Cashier of the Tax Office he will reply that he has no more funds at Châlons, and cannot supply them with bills of exchange or cheques on that city. If they offer the money to the Banker he will tell them that he has no more funds at Châlons and has no need to draw, but if they will pay him 3 per cent. for exchange he will provide cheques. They will offer one or two per cent. and at last 2½, not being able to do better. At this price the Banker will decide to give them bills of exchange, that is if they pay to him at Paris 2 livres 10 sols he will supply a bill of exchange for 100 livres on his Châlons correspondent, payable at 10 or 15 days, so as to put his correspondent in a position to make the payment of the 25,000 livres for which he draws upon him. At this rate of exchange he will send him the money by mail or carriage in specie, gold or, in default of gold, silver. He will pay 10 livres for each bag of 1000 livres, or in Bank parlance 1 per cent. He will pay his Châlons correspondent as commission 5 livres per bag of 1000 livres or ½ per cent., and will keep one per cent. for his own profit. On this footing the exchange at Paris for Châlons is at 2½ per cent. above par, because one pays 2 livres 10 sols for each 100 livres as the commission on exchange.

[a]...[a]: R: 'sange'
[b]...[b]: R: 'quinze jours'; 1756 a, b: 'quinze jours' 1769?
[c]...[c]: R: '25000[fb]'
[d]...[d]: R: 'par messager'
[e]...[e]: R: 'dor de largent et payera'
[f]...[f]: R: 'deux Livres et demie'
[g]...[g]: P: 'If'
[h]...[h]: P: 'in value'
[i]...[i]: P: 'oz.'
[j]...[j]: P: 'silver, or 25,000 livres'
[k]...[k]: P: 'but will'
[l]...[l]: P: 'may perhaps'
[m]...[m]: P: 'quite the reverse'

With regard to **535** V535f, since the *livre* was subdivided into 20 *sous* or *sols*, 'two and a half livres' is the same as '2 livres 10 sols'.

536 |8| C'est ainsi à peu-près que la balance du commerce se transporte d'une ville à l'autre, par l'entremise des Banquiers, & en gros articles ordinairement. Tous ceux qui portent le titre de Banquiers ne sont pas dans cette habitude; & il y en a plusieurs qui ne se mêlent que de commissions ᵃ& deᵃ spéculation de banque. Je ne mettrai au nombre des [334] Banquiers que ceux qui font voiturer l'argent. C'est à eux à régler toujours les changes, dont les prix suivent les frais ᵃ& lesᵃ risques du transport des especes, dans les cas différens.

537 |9| On fixe rarement le prix du change entre Paris & Châlons à plus de deux & demi ou trois pour cent, au dessus ou au dessous du pair. Mais de Paris à Amsterdam le prix du change montera à cinq ou six pour cent ᵃlors qu'il faudraᵃ voiturer ᵇlesᵇ especes. Le chemin est plus long le risque est plus grand; il faut plus de Correspondans & de Commissionnaires. Des Indes en Angleterre, le prix du transport sera de dix à douze pour cent. De Londres à Amsterdam, le prix du change ne passera guere deux pour cent en tems de paix.

538 |10| Dans notre exemple présent, on dira que le change à Paris pour Châlons sera à deux & demi [335] pour cent, au dessus du pair; & on dira à Châlons que le change ᵃpourᵃ Paris est à deux & demi pour cent, au dessous du pair: parceque dans ces circonstances celui qui donnera de l'argent à Châlons pour une lettre de change pour Paris ne donnera que ᵇquatre-vingt-dix-sept livres dix solsᵇ, pour recevoir cent livres à Paris: & il est visible que la Ville ou Place où le change est au dessus du pair doit à celle où il est au dessous, tant que le prix du change subsiste sur ce pied. Le change ᶜn'estᶜ à Paris à deux & demi pour cent, au dessus du pair pour Châlons, que parceque Paris doit à Châlons, ᵈ& qu'on a besoin de voiturer l'argent de cette dette de Paris à Châlons:ᵈ c'est pourquoi lorsqu'on voit que le change est communement ᵉau dessousᵉ du pair dans une ville, par rapport à une autre, on pourra conclure que cette premiere ville [336] doit la balance du commerce à l'autre, & lorsque le change est à Madrid ou à Lisbonne ᶠau dessusᶠ du pair pour tous les autres païs, cela fait voir que ces deux Capitales doivent toujours envoier des especes à ces autres païs.

It is somewhat in this way that the balance of trade is transported from one city to the other through Bankers, and generally on a large scale. All those who bear the name of Bankers are not accustomed to these transactions and many of them deal only in commissions and bank speculations. I will include among Bankers only those who remit money. It is they who always fix the exchange, the charge for which follows the cost and risks of the carriage of specie in the different cases.

ᵃ...ᵃ: R: 'et'

536

The charge of exchange between Paris and Châlons is rarely fixed at more than 2½ or 3 per cent. over or under par. But from Paris to Amsterdam the charge will amount to 5 or 6 per cent. when specie has to be sent. The journey is longer, the risk is greater, more Correspondents and Commission agents are involved. From India to England the charge for carriage will be 10 to 12 per cent. From London to Amsterdam it will hardly exceed 2 per cent. in peace time.

ᵃ...ᵃ: R: 'Lors quil faut'
ᵇ...ᵇ: R: 'des'

537

In our present example it will be said that the exchange at Paris for Châlons will be 2½ per cent. above par, and at Châlons it will be said that the exchange for Paris is 2½ per cent. below par, because in these circumstances he who will give money at Châlons for a letter of exchange for Paris will give only 97 livres 10 sols to receive 100 livres at Paris. And it is evident that the City or Place where exchange is above par is in debt to that where it is below par so long as the exchange continues on this basis. Exchange at Paris is 2½ per cent. above par for Châlons only because Paris is indebted to Châlons and that the money for this debt must be carried from Paris to Châlons. This is why when exchange is commonly seen to be below par in one city as compared with another it may be concluded that this first city owes a balance of trade to the other, and that when the exchange at Madrid or Lisbon is above par for all other countries it shows that these two Capitals must send specie to other countries.

ᵃ...ᵃ: R: 'sur'
ᵇ...ᵇ: R: '97ᵗᵇ 10s'
ᶜ...ᶜ: R: 'est'
ᵈ...ᵈ: R: missing in R
ᵉ...ᵉ: R: 'audessus'
ᶠ...ᶠ: R: 'audessous'

V538e and V538f turn the meaning of the last sentence in E538 around: the place where the exchange is *above* (*au dessus*) par is indebted to the place where it is *below* (*au dessous*) par. H538 translates the printed version faithfully, even though the reasoning appears faulty. The double alteration from the manuscript version suggests a deliberate, if misconceived, editorial decision. Note that A539 and D540 also have the correct reasoning.

538

539

From this Reasoning it appears to me very clear, that that Town or Place where the Exchange is above Par, must be indebted by [79] Ballance of Trade, to that Place where the Exchange is under Par, it therefore seems to me very extraordinary, what is asserted by many People, to wit, that the Price or Course of the Exchange is not a sure Sign to judge the Ballance of Trade to be for, or against a Nation. If the Price of the Exchange at *Lisbon, Madrid,* and *Cadiz* on *London,* is generally above Par, that is to say, if more *Spanish* and *Portugal* Money is paid for sterling Coin, than it is really and intrinsically worth, it is to me a Demonstration, that *Spain* and *Portugal* are obliged to transmit Bullion to *England* to pay their Debts, and it is also very clear to me, that when the Exchange between *London* and *Paris* is above Par, that is to say in other Words, when we pay in the Price of the Exchange, more Money for their Crown of three Livres, than it is really worth; or that the *French* pay us for our sterling Coin, less than it is really and intrinsically worth, as is now (and has been for these many Years) the Case, we are obliged to send Money or Bullion to *France,* notwithstanding all our heavy Duties and Prohibitions on their Trade.

540 |11| Dans toutes les Places & Villes qui se servent de la même monnoie & des mêmes especes d'or & d'argent, comme Paris & Châlons sur Marne, Londres & Bristol, l'on connoît & l'on exprime le prix du change en donnant ª& en prenantª tant pour cent, de plus ou de moins que le pair. ᵇQuand on paie quatre-vingt-dix-huit livres dans une place, pour recevoir cent livres dans une autre, on dit que le change est à deux pour cent au dessous du pair à-peu-près: lorsqu'on paie cent deux livres dans une place, pour ne recevoir que cent livres dans une autre, on dit que le change [337] est à deux pour cent exactement au-dessus du pair:ᵇ quand on donne cent livres dans une place, pour en recevoir ᶜcent livresᶜ dans une autre, on dit que le change est au pair. En tout cela il n'y a aucune difficulté, ᵈni aucun mystereᵈ.

|| From this example, which may be applied to any two cities in the same state, it appears that the variation of exchanges between two places, where the same coin is used, is known by so much *per cent.* over, or under *par*; ᵉthatᵉ the place where the exchange is above *par* has the ballance of trade against it, and that the place where the exchange is under *par* has the ballance in ᶠit'sᶠ favour, or due to it. In this there is no mystery.

In all Places where the same Denomination of Coin passes current, as in *London* and [80] *Bristol,* the Exchange is expressed and known by so much *per Cent.* be the same more or less, either above or under Par; and when 97 l. is only paid at *Bristol* for the Consideration of receiving 100 l. in *London,* it is said that the Exchange at *Bristol* on *London* is three *per Cen*t. under Par, and when 100 l. is paid at *London* to receive 100 l. at *Bristol,* the Exchange is said to be at Par; and in all this there does not appear any great Difficulty or Mystery.

539

i. A539 does not have a clear counterpart in E or D, although there are some similarities with E/D553. The observation that a 'Town or Place where the Exchange is above Par, must be indebted by Ballance of Trade' agrees with V538e, f, and D540; cf. C538. However, compared to E/D553 there is an absence here of the cautionary note that, when the exchange is above or under par between any two countries, this does not allow one to say whether the general balance is against or in favour of a country.

ii. The 'Crown of three Livres' in A539 is equivalent to the '*écu ou trois livres tournois*' mentioned in E542.

540

In all Places and Cities which use the same money and the same gold and silver specie like Paris and Châlons sur Marne, London and Bristol, the charge for exchange is known and expressed by giving and taking so much per cent. above or below par. When 98 livres are paid in one place to receive 100 livres in another it is said that exchange is about 2 per cent. below par; when 102 livres are paid in one place to receive only 100 livres in another it is said that the exchange is exactly 2 per cent. above par, when 100 livres are given in one place for 100 livres in another it is said that the exchange is at par. There is no difficulty or mystery in all this.

a...a: R: 'et prenant'
b...b: R: 'quand on paye 98ᵗᵇ dans une place pour Récévoir 100ᵗᵇ dans une autre, on dit que Le Change est a deux pour Cent exactement audessus du Change du payé'
c...c: R: 'Cent'
d...d: R: 'ny mistere'
e...e: P: 'and that'
f...f: P: 'its'

i. The penultimate sentence in the Rouen manuscript (V540b) corresponds more closely to A540 than the more extended one in E540. It translates as: 'when 98 livres are paid in one place to receive 100 livres in another, it is said that the Exchange [where it is received] is exactly two per cent above the Exchange of where it was paid'. This is not different from saying, as in A, that the exchange of the place where the money was paid is below par. Cf. C538.

ii. E540 mentions, beside Paris and Châlons-sur-Marne, also '*Londres & Bristol*'. It is the only mention of Bristol in E. Given the consistent use in A of place names, London and Bristol, could the one occurrence of '*Londres & Bristol*' in E be a case of 'editor's fatigue' on the part of the editor or author of the French manuscript text? That is to say, could an earlier draft have been using the English place names, found in A, which were subsequently replaced with the French names, apart from the occurrence in E540? If so, then this would in this case be 'editor's fatigue' on the part of Cantillon, (since R and E agree) and not on the part of the editor of the print edition E (see Introduction p. 26 n. 19).

541

|| If the city of *Bourdeaux* owes [a]100,000 ounces of silver at *Paris*,[a] and sends wines and brandies to *Holland* for [b]100,000[b]: and, if *Holland* sends [c]specie[c] to *Paris* for 100,000 [d]ounces[d], [e]the bankers at *Bourdeaux* send their bills on *Holland* to *Paris*, for 100,000 ounces due to *Bourdeaux*[e]; and with these the [f]specie-merchants[f] at *Paris* remit and pay the 100,000 [g]ounces[g] they owe to *Holland* [h]: in these cases,[h] the exchange between *Bourdeaux* and *Paris*, *Bourdeaux* and *Holland*, and *Paris* and *Holland*, will be [i]all at *par*[i]; there will be no variation but what proceeds, from the commission of the negociators concerned in the returns.

[a]...[a]: P: '100,000 oz. of silver at *Paris*, or 500,000 livres'

[b]...[b]: P: '100,000 oz.'; DI92: '100,000 ounces'

[c]...[c]: P: 'specie, &c.'

[d]...[d]: P: 'oz.'

[e]...[e]: DI92: 'due to the bankers at *Bourdeaux*' ; P: 'the bankers at Bourdeaux send their bills on Holland to Paris, for 100,000 oz. due to *Bourdeaux*'

[f]...[f]: P: 'spice-merchants'

[g]...[g]: P:'oz.'

[h]...[h]: P: '. In this case'

[i]...[i]: P: 'at *Par*'; DI92: 'at *par*'

i. From D541 up D549 we have three **541** versions in Postlethwayt's works. In addition to the *Plan* of 1749 and the *Dictionary* entry 'Ballance of trade', the entry 'Arbitration, in matters of foreign exchange' (vol. I, 92, col. 1 from near the top to two-thirds down) also plagiarises the same manuscript. It was first published in issue 8 of the *Dictionary*, which appeared in January 1752. Variations are indicated with DI92.

ii. The fact that the 1749 version has 'spice-merchants' instead of 'specie-merchants' (V541f) suggests that the original manuscript mentioned the sending of spices, rather than specie, from Holland. This makes more sense, because the discussion is about letters of exchange, which avoid the need to send specie. Cf. E293 and E611, which also refer to the spice trade of Holland.

542 |12| Mais lorsqu'on regle le change entre ᵃdeux Villes ou Placesᵃ, où la monnoïe est toute différente, où les especes sont de différentes grandeurs, finesses, tailles, & même de différens noms, la nature du change paroît d'abord plus difficile à expliquer; mais dans le fond ce change étranger ne differe de celui entre Paris & Châlons que par la différence du jargon dont les Banquiers se servent. On parle à Paris du change avec la Hollande en reglant l'écu de trois livres contre tant de deniers de gros de Hollande, mais le pair du change entre Paris & Amsterdam est toujours cent on-[338]ces d'or ou d'argent contre cent onces d'or ou d'argent ᵇdeᵇ même poids & titre: cent deux onces païées à Paris pour recevoir seulement cent onces à Amsterdam, ᶜreviennentᶜ toujours à deux pour cent au dessus du pair. Le Banquier qui fait ᵈles transportsᵈ de la balance du commerce, doit toujours savoir calculer le pair; mais dans le langage des changes avec l'Etranger, on dira le prix du change à Londres avec Amsterdam se fait en donnant une livre sterling à Londres pour recevoir trente-cinq escalins d'Hollande en banque: avec Paris, en donnant à Londres trente deniers ou peniques sterling, pour recevoir à Paris un écu ou trois livres tournois. Ces façons de parler ᵉn'expriment pas siᵉ le change est au-dessus ou au dessous du pair; mais le Banquier qui transporte la balance du commerce en sait bien le compte, ᶠ& combien il rece-[339]vra d'especes étrangeres pour celles de son païs qu'il fait voiturerᶠ.

|| But, in regard that the coin in *France* is reckoned by livres, sols, and deniers, and in *Holland* by florins, stivers, and groots; that the coin in use in *Holland* differs in the standard, bulk, and mark, from that used in *France*, the computation of the exchange is made by the exchanging so many *Dutch* groots for ᵍa *French* exchange crownᵍ; ʰwhich,ʰ at first view, does not seem to denote that the exchange is so much *per cent.* over or under par, ⁱbutⁱ in reality it is so; and the banker concerned in the *Dutch* exchange knows how to ʲevaluateʲ this par in the sale of *French* crowns and *Dutch* groots.

|| But, when the Exchange is to be regulated between two Cities or Places where there is a great Difference between their Coins, and where the Coins are of a different Bulk, Fineness, Size and Denomination, the Mystery of this Species of Commerce appears to be more difficult to explain; yet, in fact, this foreign Exchange differs only from that of the inland, in the Jargon made use of by the Traders, who carry on this Business. When these People talk of the Exchange between *London* and *Paris*, they say, so many Sterling Pence for one Crown of three Livres *French* Money; but the Par of the Exchange in Fact is only one hundred Ounces of Gold or Silver, to be paid in Exchange of one hun-[81]dred Ounces of Gold or Silver, of equal Weight and Fineness; therefore, one hundred and two Ounces of Gold and Silver, paid in *Paris*, in order to be intitled by Bill of Exchange to receive one hundred Ounces of Gold or Silver in *London*, will always be two *per Cent.* above Par. Those who follow this Business ought to know how to calculate the Pars of all Exchanges; but in their Language they say, that between *London* and *Amsterdam* one Pound Sterling for thirty-five Shillings *Dutch*, and between *London* and *Paris* thirty-one Pence Sterling for one Crown of three Livres *Tournois*; this manner of Expression, does not shew whether the Exchange is either under or above Par; but the Merchants who carry on this Trade, and are the Agents made use of to pay the Ballance of the Debts contracted by Nations in their Dealings with each other, know how to calculate, and find their Profit in discovering how much foreign Coin they will receive in Exchange for that of the current Coin of the Country, where they reside, and which must be exported Abroad to pay this Ballance; and it is upon this Basis they regulate the several Courses of the Exchange.

But when exchange is regulated between two Cities or Places where the money is quite different, where the coins are of different size, fineness, make, and names, the nature of exchange seems at first more difficult to explain, though at bottom this exchange differs from that between Paris and Châlons only in the jargon of Bankers. At Paris one speaks of the Dutch exchange by reckoning the écu of three livres against so many deniers de gros of Holland, but the parity of exchange between Paris and Amsterdam is always 100 ounces of gold or silver against 100 ounces of gold or silver of the same weight and fineness. 102 ounces paid at Paris to receive 100 ounces at Amsterdam always comes to 2 per cent. above par. The Banker who effects the remittance of the balance of trade must always know how to calculate parity. But in the language of Foreign exchange the price of exchange at London with Amsterdam is made by giving a pound sterling in London to receive 35 Dutch escalins at the bank: with Paris in giving at London 30 deniers or pence sterling to receive at Paris one écu or three livres tournois. These methods of speech do not say whether exchange is above or below par, but the Banker who remits the balance of trade reckons it up well and knows how much foreign money he will receive for the money of his own Country which he despatches.

ᵃ…ᵃ: R: 'deux places ou Villes'
ᵇ…ᵇ: R: 'du'
ᶜ…ᶜ: R: 'revient'
ᵈ…ᵈ: R: 'Le transport'
ᵉ…ᵉ: R: 'n'Expriment si'
ᶠ…ᶠ: R: 'et Combien des especes etrangeres Il aura des especes de son paÿs quil fait voiturer'
ᵍ…ᵍ: P: 'three French livres'
ʰ…ʰ: P: 'and this'; DI92: 'and, although this'
ⁱ…ⁱ: DI92: 'yet'
ʲ…ʲ: DI92: 'calculate'

i. D542 is a pared-down version compared to E542 and A542, which correspond very closely.

ii. The expression 'a *French* exchange crown' in D542, which occurs as 'three French livres' in P, is equivalent to '*un écu ou trois livres tournois*' in E542 and 'one Crown of three Livres *Tournois*' in A542. Cf. C539ii. The term '*exchange* crown' was used to distinguish the French money of account from the circulating currency. As explained by T.H. Croker in *The Complete Dictionary of Arts and Sciences* (London 1765): 'the kings of France often raise the species of the kingdom, to rates considerably higher than those for which they were at first coined, and consequently far above their intrinsic value: so that a crown in specie will pass at four, five, or six livres. And three such livres are still named an ecu, or crown, though of a far less value than the ecu blanc, or white crown, that is, a crown in specie.'

542

543

|| So that the exchange ᵃbetween *Paris* and *Amsterdam*ᵃ is, in effect, carried on just as it is ᵇbetween *Paris* and *Chalons*ᵇ; only with this difference, that the accounts are kept in another gibberish, and that the charge and risque of sending money ᶜfrom *Paris* to *Amsterdam*ᶜ, is greater than that of sending money ᵈfrom *Paris* to *Chalons*. Whenᵈ the ballance of trade with *Amsterdam* is against *Paris*, the exchange at *Paris* will be from 5 to 6 *per cent.* above par by bills on *Amsterdam*; whereas it will seldom exceed ᵉ2 *per cent* above par for *Chalons*ᵉ.

544 |13| Qu'on fixe le change à Londres pour argent d'Angleterre en Roubles de Moscovie, en Marcs Lubs de Hambourg, en Richedales d'Allemagne, en Livres de gros de Flandres, en Ducats de Venise, en Piastres de ᵃGènesᵃ ou de Livourne, en ᵇMilleraysᵇ ou Crusades de Portugal, en Pieces de huit d'Espagne, ou Pistoles &c. le pair du change pour tous ces païs, sera toujours ᶜcent oncesᶜ d'or ou d'argent contre cent onces: & si dans le langage des changes il se trouve qu'on donne plus ou moins que ce pair, cela ᵈvientᵈ au même dans le fond que si l'on disoit le change est de tant au dessus ou au dessous du pair, & on connoîtra toujours si l'Angleterre doit la balance ou ᵉnonᵉ à la place avec laquelle ᶠon regleᶠ le change, ni plus ni moins [340] qu'on le sait dans notre exemple de Paris & de Châlons.

|| Whether *France* pays livres, sols, and deniers, for ᵍrialsᵍ of plate and marvadees, new or old, ʰof *Spain*ʰ; for *crusades* or *millrees* of *Portugal*; for *guilders*, *rixdollars*, or *mark-lubs*, in the north; for *pounds*, *shillings*, and *pence* sterling; for *marks*, *piasters*, and *ducats* of *Italy*; the *par* of the exchange is always ⁱounce for ounceⁱ of silver, or rather of gold, that being of easier carriage, and most ʲcommonly transportedʲ in the payment of the ballance of trade; and the computations and evaluations of the exchange will square every where with our first example.

[82] || If the Par of sterling Coin is calculated with the Rubles of *Russia*, the Marc Lubs of *Hamburgh*, the *German* Rix Dollars, the Pounds Flemish of *Flanders*, the *Venetian* Ducat, the Dollars of *Genoa* and *Leghorn*, the Mill-Rea and Crusado of *Portugal*, the Piece of Eight and Pistole of *Spain*, &c. this Par with all Countries must ever be 100 Ounces of Gold or Silver, against an equal Number of Ounces of Gold or Silver, of equal Fineness and Weight; and if by the Language made Use of by Merchants who carry on this Business, it is found, that more or less than this Par is given, in fact and reality it is the same Thing, as if they said the Exchange is so much more *per Cent.* higher or so much *per Cent.* lower than Par, which Par of more or less *per Cent.* always follows the Ballance of Trade, in the same Manner, as in the Instance I have given between *London* and *Bristol*, and the Ballance must be paid in Coin, indeed Goods and Merchandizes may do it, but if these Goods and Merchandize are not wanted, or are so dear, as not to afford a Profit, they will not be received, and Cash or Bullion must supply their Place.

| | ᵃ…ᵃ: DI92: 'between *London* and *Paris*, and *Paris* and *Amsterdam*, &c.'
 ᵇ…ᵇ: DI92: 'between *London* and *Wiltshire*, or *London* and *Norwich*'
 ᶜ…ᶜ: DI92: 'from *London* to *Paris*, or from *Paris* to *Amsterdam*'
 ᵈ…ᵈ: P: 'from *Paris* to *Chalons*; when'; DI92: 'from *London* to *Wiltshire*, or *Norwich*; and, when'
 ᵉ…ᵉ: DI92: 'an half per cent. above par between London and Norwich' | The explanation **543** for the additional place names in 'Arbitration' (V543 a to e) is probably that Postlethwayt in that entry proceeds to discuss price arbitration between multiple European cities. |

Whether we fix the exchange at London for English silver in Muscovy roubles, in Mark Lubs of Hamburg, in Rixdollars of Germany, in Livres of Flanders, in Ducats of Venice, in Piastres of Genoa or Leghorn, in Millreis or Crusadoes of Portugal, in Pieces of Eight of Spain, or Pistoles, etc. the parity of exchange for all these countries will be always 100 ounces of gold or silver against 100 ounces; and if in the language of exchange it happens that one gives more or less than this parity, it comes to the same in effect as if exchange is said to be so much above or below par, and we shall always know whether or not England owes a balance to the place with which the exchange is settled just as in our example of Paris and Châlons.

ᵃ…ᵃ: 1756b, 1769: 'Gennes'; R: 'Génnes'
ᵇ…ᵇ: R: 'millerets'
ᶜ…ᶜ: R: 'de cent onces'
ᵈ…ᵈ: R: 'revient'
ᵉ…ᵉ: R: 'Nom'
ᶠ…ᶠ: R: 'on a Regle'
ᵍ…ᵍ: P, DI92: 'ryals'
ʰ…ʰ: P: 'in *Spain*'
ⁱ…ⁱ: P: 'oz. for oz.'
ʲ…ʲ: P, DI92: 'commonly is transported'

A544 is followed by **544** A554.

545   **CHAPITRE ᵃIIIᵃ.**

Autres eclaircissemens pour la connoissance de la nature des changes.

546 |1| On a vu que les changes sont reglés sur la valeur intrinseque des especes, c'est-à-dire, sur le pair, & que leur variation provient des frais ᵃ& desᵃ risques des ᵇtransportsᵇ d'une place à ᶜl'autreᶜ, lorsqu'il faut envoïer en especes la balance du commerce. On n'a pas besoin de raisonnement pour une chose qu'on voit dans le fait & dans la pratique. Les Banquiers apportent quelquefois ᵈdes raffinemensᵈ dans cette pratique.

547 |2| Si l'Angleterre doit à la France cent mille onces d'argent pour [341] la balance du commerce, si la France en doit cent mille onces à la Hollande, & la Hollande cent mille onces à l'Angleterre, toutes ces trois sommes se pourront compenser par lettres de change entre les Banquiers respectifs de ces trois Etats, sans qu'il soit besoin d'envoïer aucun argent d'aucun côté.

|| If *France* owes a ballance in trade to *Flanders* of 100,000 ᵃouncesᵃ; *Flanders* to *Holland* of 100,000 ᵃouncesᵃ; *Holland* to *England* of 100,000 ᵃouncesᵃ; *England* to *Spain* of 100,000 ᵃouncesᵃ; *Spain* to *Italy* of 100,000 ᵃouncesᵃ; *Italy* to *Germany* of 100,000 ᵃouncesᵃ; *Germany* to *France* of 100,000 ᵃouncesᵃ; the exchange may be carried on at *par* between all these countries, without any transportation of gold and silver.

548

|| But, as the ballance of trade grows due gradually from one country to ᵃanotherᵃ, by an importation of commodities, the variation of exchanges follows the same proportion.

Higgs Translation (H)	Variations and Errata (V)	Comments (C)	

Chapter III

Further explanations of the nature of the Exchanges

^a...^a: R: '3^e'　　545

We have seen that the exchanges are regulated by the intrinsic value of specie, that is at par, and their variation arises from the costs and risks of transport from one place to another when the balance of trade has to be sent in specie. Argument is unnecessary in a matter which we see in fact and practice. Bankers sometimes introduce refinements into this practice.

^a...^a: R: 'et'
^b...^b: R: 'transports ou voitures'
^c...^c: R: 'une autre'
^d...^d: R:'du Rafinement'

546

If England owes France 100,000 ounces of silver for the balance of trade, if France owes 100,000 ounces to Holland, and Holland 100,000 to England, all these three amounts may be set off by bills of exchange between the respective Bankers of these three States without any need of sending silver on either side.

^a...^a: P: 'oz.'

D547 continues from D544 without a new section heading.

547

^a...^a: P, DI92: 'any other'

Ater D548 the correspondence in the *Dictionary* entry 'Arbitration' finishes. Postlethwayt continues this entry with: 'And it is the business of the judicious general merchant, and the sagacious remitter, to speculate where the ballance of trade lies, among the *European* nations at all points of time; for by that means he may embrace his opportunities of advantage, and these almost daily between some nation or other, provided his credit and correspondence are duly established to admit thereof.' This is followed by a detailed account of arbitration practice in foreign exchanges.

548

549 |3| Si la Hollande envoie en Angleterre ᵃpendant le mois de Janvierᵃ des marchandises pour la valeur de cent mille onces d'argent, & l'Angleterre n'en envoie en Hollande dans le même mois que pour la valeur de cinquante mille onces, (je suppose la vente & le paiement faits dans le même mois de ᵇJanvier de part & d'autreᵇ) il reviendra à la Hollande dans ce mois une balance de commerce de ᶜcinquante mille oncesᶜ, & le change d'Amsterdam sera à Londres au mois de Janvier à deux ou trois pour cent [342] au dessus du pair, c'est-à-dire dans le langage des changes, que le change de Hollande qui étoit en Décembre au pair ou à trente cinq escalins ᵈparᵈ livre sterling à Londres, y montera en Janvier à trente six escalins ou environ; mais lorsque les Banquiers auront envoïé cette dette de cinquante mille onces en Hollande, le change pour Amsterdam retombera naturellement au pair à Londres, ou à trente-cinq escalins.

|| For example: if *Holland* sends into *England*, in *January*, the value of 100,000 ᶜouncesᶜ in merchandize, and receives from *England*, in that month, but the value of 50,000 ᶜouncesᶜ, the merchants of *London*, who owe this sum to *Amsterdam*, will offer the negociator money for his bills on *Amsterdam*; [I, 186, col.1] ᶠand heᶠ having no money due to him there, and refusing to draw, the merchant will offer him 1, 2, to 3 *per cent.* above par, in the language of exchange: then the negociator will draw on his correspondents on ᵍthoseᵍ terms, and send over the money to him to answer the payment, and get the 3 *per cent.* for the charge of sending the money, the risque, and for his commission: and when this ballance is paid, by sending the money, the exchange will fall again to par.

550

ᵃ...ᵃ

551 |4| Mais si ᵃun Banquier Angloisᵃ prévoit en Janvier, par l'envoi qu'on y fait en Hollande d'une quantité extraordinaire de marchandises, que la Hollande lors des paiemens & ventes en Mars recevra considerablement ᵇàᵇ l'Angleterre, il pourra dès le mois de Janvier, au lieu d'envoïer les cinquante mille écus ou onces qu'on y doit ce mois-là à la Hollande, fournir ses lettres de chan-[343]ge sur son Correspondant à Amsterdam, païables à deux usances ou deux mois pour en païer la valeur à l'échéance: & par ce moïen profiter du change qui ᶜétoitᶜ en Janvier au dessus du pair, & qui sera en Mars au dessous du pair : & par ce moïen gagner doublement sans envoïer un sol en Hollande.

ᵈ...ᵈ

549

If Holland sends to England in January merchandise of the value of 100,000 ounces of silver and England only sends to Holland in the same month merchandise to the value of 50,000 ounces (I suppose the sale and payment made in January on both sides) there will be due to Holland in this month a balance of trade of 50,000 ounces, and the exchange on Amsterdam will be in London in January 2 or 3 per cent. above par, or in the language of exchange, the exchange on Holland which was in December at par or at 35 escalins to the pound sterling in London will rise there in January to about 36 escalins. But when the Bankers have sent this balance of 50,000 ounces to Holland the exchange on Amsterdam will naturally fall back to par or 35 escalins in London.

^a...^a: R: 'en Janvier'

^b...^b: R: 'Janvier'

^c...^c: R: 'Cinquante onces'

^d...^d: R: 'pour'

^e...^e: P: 'oz.'

^f...^f: P: 'he'

^g...^g: P: 'these'

550

^a...^a: P: '‖ Now if England sends in April to Holland 100,000 oz. value of goods and receives but 50,000 oz. value, the contrary variation will happen in the Dutch exchange, and the 50,000 oz. exported for London in January, will, by the like methods, come back in April. Thus it may happen the exchange with Holland may be against England in January, and for England in April.'

This paragraph (V550a) and the next (V551d) only appear in Postlethwayt's 1749 publication, on p. 47, and are omitted from his *Dictionary* entry 'Ballance of Trade'. For other omissions from the *Dictionary* version, see V508a, D564, D567 and D569.

551

But if an English Banker foresees in January, owing to the sending into Holland of an unusual quantity of merchandise, that at the time of payments and sales in March Holland will be indebted considerably to England, he may instead of sending the 50,000 écus or ounces due in January to Holland, furnish in that month bills of exchange on his Amsterdam correspondent payable at double usance or two months, the amount of the value to be paid on maturity, and by this method profit on the exchange which in January was above par and in March will be below par, and so gain doubly without sending a sol to Holland.

^a...^a: R: 'le Banquier'

^b...^b: R: 'en'

^c...^c: R: 'etait'

^d...^d: P: '‖ Could the London negociator foresee this in January, by the quantity of goods preparing to be sent in April, he may draw in January, at 4 usances or months, get 3 per cent. and repay the value of his bills at par in April.'

552 |5| Voilà ce que les Banquiers appellent des spéculations qui causent souvent des variations dans les changes pour un peu de tems, independamment de la balance du commerce: mais il en faut toujours à la longue revenir à cette balance qui fait la regle constante & uniforme des changes; & quoique les spéculations & crédits des Banquiers puissent quelquefois retarder le transport des sommes qu'un Ville ou Etat doit a un autre, il faut toujours a la fin païer la dette & envoïer la balance du commerce en espe-[344]ces, à la Place où elle est due.

553 |6| Si l'Angleterre gagne constamment une balance de commerce avec le Portugal, & perd toujours une balance avec la Hollande, les prix du change avec la Hollande & avec le Portugal ᵃle feront ᵃ bien connoître; on verra bien qu'à Londres le change pour Lisbonne est au dessous du pair, & que le Portugal doit à l'Angleterre; on verra aussi que le change pour Amsterdam est au dessus du pair, & que l'Angleterre doit à la Hollande: mais on ne pourra pas voir par les changes la quantité de la dette. On ne verra pas si la balance d'argent qu'on tire de Portugal sera plus grande ou plus petite que celle qu'on est obligé d'envoïer en Hollande.

|| From these examples and reflections it is plain, that the *course of exchange* ᵇindicatesᵇ where the ballance of trade lies, since ᶜthierᶜ variation is proportionable to the ᵈballanceᵈ with any country distinctly. But as the *Spanish* exchange may be in favour of *France*, and the *Dutch* exchange at the same time against *France*, the course of exchange will not shew whether *France* receives more money from *Spain* than it sends to *Holland*; and consequently it will be but conjecture to judge, from the course of exchange, whether *France* gains or loses in the *general ballance* of trade.

554

[83] || Coin is in Reason and Fact no more than a Commodity, or a Species of Merchandize, which ascertain the Value of every Sort of Purchase, and ought simply to be considered as such, the Prohibition of Exporting it Abroad, will always prove ineffectual, nothing that can be invented will preserve Money in a Country carrying on a foreign Trade, but that of preserving a Ballance in general against foreign Nations.

552

This is what Bankers call speculation, which often causes variations in the exchanges for a short period independently of the balance of trade; but in the long run we must get back to this balance which fixes the constant and uniform rule of exchange. And though the speculations and credits of Bankers may sometimes delay the transport of the sums which one City or State owes to another, in the end it is always necessary to pay the debt and send the balance of trade in specie to the place where it is due.

553

If England gains regularly a balance of trade with Portugal and always loses a balance with Holland the rates of exchange with Holland and Portugal will make this evident: it will be seen that at London the exchange on Lisbon is below par and that Portugal is indebted to England. It will be seen also that the exchange on Amsterdam is above par and that England is indebted to Holland. But the quantity of the debt cannot be seen from the exchanges. It will not be seen whether the balance of silver drawn from Portugal will be greater or less than what has to be sent to Holland.

^a...^a: R: 'se feront'
^b...^b: P: 'shews'
^c...^c: *sic.*; P: 'their'
^d...^d: P: 'said ballance of trade'

i. There are similarities between E553, D553 and A539. Curiously, in A539 Portugal and Spain, England, France and Holland are all mentioned, whereas E553 has one of the pairs (Portugal and England) and D553 the other pair (Spain and France).

ii. Vivant de Mezague, *A general view of England* (1766: 89), refers to the discussion in p. 344ff. of the *Essai*. The former work was a translation of *Bilan général et raisonné de l'Angleterre* (1762).

554

A554 continues from A544 without a section break. The view that prohibitions on the exportation of species 'will always be ineffectual' is also found in E565.

555 |7| Cependant il y a une chose qui fera toujours bien connoître à Londres, si l'Angleterre gagne ou perd la balance générale de [345] son commerce (on entend par la balance générale, la différence des balances particulieres avec tous les Etats étrangers ᵃqui commercent avecᵃ l'Angleterre), c'est le prix des matieres d'or & d'argent, mais particulierement de l'or, ᵇ(aujourd'hui que la proportion du prix de l'or & de l'argent en especes monnoïées differe de la proportion du prix du marché, comme on l'expliquera dans le Chapitre suivant)ᵇ. Si le prix des matieres d'or au marché de Londres, qui est le centre du commerce d'Angleterre, est plus bas que le prix de la Tour ou l'on fabrique les guinées ou especes d'or, ou au même prix que ces especes intrinséquement; & si on porte à la Tour des matieres d'or pour en recevoir la valeur en guinées ou especes fabriquées, c'est une preuve certaine que l'Angleterre gagne dans la balance générale de son commer-[346]ce; c'est une preuve que l'or qu'on tire du Portugal suffit non-seulement pour païer la balance que l'Angleterre envoie en Hollande, en Suede, en Moscovie, & dans les autres Etats où elle doit, mais qu'il reste encore de l'or pour envoïer fabriquer à la Tour, & la quantité ou somme de cette balance générale ᶜse connoît par celleᶜ des especes fabriquées à la Tour de Londres.

|| But, as *France* keeps up the current *specie* at a higher price in the mint than *bullion*, if the negotiators of money are forced to send out the current specie in payments to foreigners, this will shew most of the bullion is already gone, and that the *general ballance* is against *France*: and in *England*, if bullion wich is allowed to be exported, grows dearer than the standard, it is also a plain ᵈsign thatᵈ the *general ballance* is against *England*. ᵉSo thatᵉ the only rule, whereby we can make a judgment of the ballance of *general trade* ᶠseems to be from the course ofᶠ the exchange and the price of bullion.

|| When the Market Price of Bullion is greater than the standard Price at the Mint, it is to me a sure Sign, no Money can be coined, and that the heavy Money of the Kingdom is melted down, or sent Abroad in real Specie, and that the general Ballance of Trade is against such a Country.

556 |8| Mais si les matieres d'or se vendent à Londres au marché, plus haut que le prix de la Tour, qui est ordinairement de ᵃtrois livres dix-huit schelingsᵃ par once, on ne ᵇporteraᵇ plus de ces matieres à la Tour pour les fabriquer, & c'est une marque certaine qu'on ne tire pas de l'Etranger, par exemple du Portugal, autant d'or qu'on est obligé d'en envoïer dans les autres païs où l'Angleterre doit: c'est une preuve que la balance générale du com-[347] merce est contre l'Angleterre. Ceci ne se connoîtroit pas s'il n'y avoit pas une défense en Angleterre d'envoïer des especes d'or hors du Roïaume: mais cette défense est cause que les Banquiers timides à Londres aiment mieux acheter les matieres d'or, ᶜ(qu'il leur est permis de transporter dans les païs étrangers) ᶜ à ᵈtrois livres dix-huit schelingsᵈ jusqu'à quatre livres sterling l'once, pour les envoïer chez l'Etranger, que d'y envoïer les guinées ᵉouᵉ especes d'or monoïées à ᶠtrois livres dix-huit schelingsᶠ, contre les loix, & ᵍau hasardᵍ de confiscation. Il y en a pourtant qui s'y hasardent, ʰd'autres fondent les especesʰ d'or, pour les envoïer en guise de matieres, & il n'est pas possible de juger de la quantité d'or que l'Angleterre perd, lorsque la balance générale du commerce est contre elle.

There is however one thing which will always shew at London whether England gains or loses the general balance of her trade (by general balance is understood the difference of the individual balances with all the foreign states which trade with England), and that is the price of gold and silver metal but especially of gold (now that the proportion between gold and silver in coined money differs from the market rate, as will be explained in the next Chapter). If the price of gold metal in the London market, which is the centre of English trade, is lower than the price at the Tower where guineas or gold coins are minted, or at the same price as these coins intrinsically, and if gold metal is taken to the Tower in exchange for their value in guineas or minted coins, it is a certain proof that England is a gainer in the general balance of her trade. It proves that the gold taken from Portugal suffices not only to pay the balance which England sends into Holland, Sweden, Muscovy, and the other States where she is indebted, but that there remains some of the gold to be sent to the Mint, and the quantity or sum of this general balance of trade is known from that of the specie coined at the Tower of London.

But if the gold metal is sold in the London market above the Tower price, which is usually £3.18.0 an ounce, the metal will no longer be taken to the Mint, and this is a certain sign that so much gold is not drawn from abroad (from Portugal for instance) as must be sent into the other countries where England is indebted. It is a proof that the general balance of trade is against England. This would not be known but for the prohibition in England to send gold coin out of the country. But this prohibition is the reason why the timid London bankers prefer to buy gold metal (which they are allowed to send abroad) at £3.18.0 up to £4 an ounce for export rather than send out guineas or gold coins at £3.18.0 against the law and at the risk of confiscation. Some of them take this risk, others melt the gold coins to send them out as bullion, and it is impossible to judge how much gold England loses when the general balance of trade is against her.

$^a...^a$: R: 'qui ont Commerce auec'
$^b...^b$: R: parentheses missing
$^c...^c$: 'ne Connoist pas Celles'
$^d...^d$: P: 'sign'
$^e...^e$: P: 'But if it could be so managed, that all the sums of money exported as well as imported into a state, might be registered, a nation might easily keep an account of the ballance of its trade, and know the increase and the decrease of its money. As that however seems impracticable,'
$^f...^f$: P: 'is'

$^a...^a$: R:' 3^{lb} 18 schelling'
$^b...^b$: R: 'parlera'
$^c...^c$: R: parentheses missing
$^d...^d$: R: ' 3^{lb} 18^e 67'
$^e...^e$: R: 'en'
$^f...^f$: R: 3^{lb} 18^e sterling'
$^g...^g$: R: 'aux hazards'
$^h...^h$: R: 'dautres fonde Leurs especes'

555

i. The expression in V555a '*avoir commerce avec*' is best translated by 'having intercourse with' (as in A560). Already in eighteenth-century French it had sexual connotations. This may explain its replacement in the print version with '*commercer avec*'. The occurrence in the manuscript version of V555a may reflect the author's less than perfect command of French.

ii. V555c is curious because it implies quite a different position. However, given the fact that D555 agrees with the French print version, V555c is perhaps more likely to be due to transcription error.

iii. Note the fascinating suggestion of keeping national trade accounts as an alternative way of determining the general balance of trade in V555e.

556

557 |9| En France on déduit les frais [348] de la fabrication des especes, qui va d'ordinaire à un & demi pour cent, c'est-à-dire, qu'on y regle toujours le prix des especes au dessus de celui des matieres. Pour connoître si la France perd dans la balance générale de son commerce, il suffira de savoir si les Banquiers envoient chez l'Etranger les especes de France; car s'ils le font c'est une preuve qu'ils ne trouvent pas de matieres à acheter pour ce transport, attendu que ces matieres quoiqu'à plus bas prix en France que les especes, sont de plus grande valeur que ᵃcesᵃespeces dans les païs étrangers, au moins de un & demi pour cent.

558 |10| Quoique les prix des changes ne varient guere que par rapport a la balance du commerce, entre l'Etat & les autres Païs, & que naturellement cette balance n'est que la différence de la valeur des denrés ᵃ& desᵃ marchan-[349]dises que l'Etat envoie dans les autres païs, & de celles que les autres païs envoient dans l'Etat; cependant il arrive souvent des circonstances & causes accidentelles qui font transporter des sommes considerables d'un Etat ᵇaᵇ un autre, sans qu'il soit question de marchandises & de commerce, & ces causes influent sur les changes tout de même que feroient la balance & l'excédent de commerce.

|| Though the courses of exchange generally follow the proportion of goods exported and imported, which form the ballance of trade; yet, if particular people send their money from one country to another to lay out at interest, it will have the same effect in exchange as a ballance of trade; ᶜwith this difference onlyᶜ, that it brings home an annual interest, ᵈandᵈ the principal may be called back: whereas the money ᵉacquiredᵉ in the ballance of trade ᶠis clear gain to the nation.ᶠ The sums also sent for the payment of armies and alliances, ᵍand forᵍ the maintenance of foreign ambassadors and travellers, ʰhaveʰ also the same effect upon exchanges as a ballance of trade; but the natural and constant course of the valuation of exchanges is the ballance of trade.

|| From these Explanations it is not difficult to discover, that the Variations in the Course of Exchange are influenced by the Ballance of Trade; indeed, the sending large Sums of Money from one Country to another will have the same Influence on the Exchange, as this Ballance, but this is a Circumstance which only happens when People chuse to employ [84] their spare Money in the public Funds of a Country, or where large Sums are to be paid for foreign Subsidies, but these and the like Cases being a Species of Trade between Nations, do not destroy my Assertion, that the natural and constant Rule, which governs the daily Variations of the Course of Exchange, arises from the Ballance of Commerce.

559 |11| De cette nature sont les sommes d'argent qu'un Etat envoie dans un autre pour des services secrets & des ᵃvuesᵃ de politique d'Etat, pour des subsides d'allliance, pour l'entretien de troupes, ᵇd'Ambassadeurs, de Seigneursᵇ qui voïagent, &c. les capitaux que les Habitans d'un Etat envoient dans un autre, pour s'y interesser dans les fonds publics ou particuliers, ᶜl'intérêtᶜ que ces Habitans tirent annuel-[350]lement de pareils ᵈfonds &c.ᵈ Les changes ne manquent pas de varier avec toutes ces causes accidentelles, & de suivre la regle du transport d'argent dont on a besoin; & dans la considération de la balance du commerce, on ne sépare pas, & même on auroit de la peine à en séparer ᵉcesᵉ sortes d'articles; ils influent bien sûrement sur l'augmentation & la diminution de l'argent effectif d'un Etat, & de ses forces & puissances comparatives.

In France the cost of minting is deducted, usually 1½ per cent., i.e. the price for coin is always higher than for uncoined metal. To know whether France loses in the general balance of her trade, it will suffice to know whether the Bankers send French coins abroad. If they do so it is a proof that they do not find bullion to buy for export, since the bullion though at a lower price than coined money in France, is of greater value than these coins in foreign countries by at least 1½ per cent.

ᵃ...ᵃ: R: 'les'

557

i. D558 combines much of the argument of E558 and E559 but is much briefer.

ii. Where E558 mentions 'accidental circumstances and causes', D558 is clearer in identifying incomes from investments as items on the 'current account'. Cf. E410.

iii. The explanation of the reasons for sudden capital outflows and their effects on the course of foreign exchanges formed the crux of Cantillon's defence in a criminal case in the French courts in 1730 and the reasoning presented here is reminiscent of a memoire of his lawyer Cochin (see Cochin 1822, vi, 242–67 and Murphy 1986: 246–47).

iv. Cf. the mention of ambassadors and travellers in D558 with E364 and E559.

v. Note the similarity in the phrase 'natural and constant' rule/course in both D and A, but not in E. But cf. E552.

vi. The correspondence in the *Dictionary* entry 'Ballance of Trade' ends after D558. In that entry the next paragraph, presumably written by Postlethwayt, reads: 'Exchange, at some times, may rise and fall every week, and, at particular times of the year, run high against a nation, and, at other times, run as high on the contrary: as against a vintage, a great mart, or public sale; the exchange may run higher to Bourdeaux, Frankfort, or Holland, upon an East-India sale; at other times, the exchange may have run to the same places as much on the contrary: and no exchange can run high constantly against a nation; for then merchants who trade to that country must always be losers; and it cannot be supposed that persons will always trade to a country where they must always lose.' The next paragraph (not reproduced here) has a reference to the 'late' Sir Matthew Decker, who died in 1749, and is for this reason certainly written by Postlethwayt.

vii. The correspondence in the *Plan* of 1749 with the *Essai* continues a little longer, see C564ii.

558

Though the exchanges rarely vary apart from the balance of trade between one country and others, and though this balance is naturally the mere difference in value of the goods and merchandise which the State sends to other countries and receives from them, yet there are often circumstances and accidental causes which cause considerable sums to be conveyed from one State to another without any question of merchandise or trade, and these causes affect the exchanges just as the balance of trade would do.

ᵃ...ᵃ: R: 'et'
ᵇ...ᵇ: R: 'dans'
ᶜ...ᶜ: P: 'but with this difference indeed'
ᵈ...ᵈ: P: 'and that'
ᵉ...ᵉ: P: 'gained'
ᶠ...ᶠ: P: 'is clearly got.-'
ᵍ...ᵍ: P: 'for'
ʰ...ʰ: P: 'has'

Such are the sums of money which one State sends into another for its secret services and political aims, for subsidies to allies, for the upkeep of troops, Ambassadors, noblemen who travel, etc., Capital which the inhabitants of one State send to another to invest in public or private funds, the interest which these inhabitants receive annually from such investments, etc. The exchanges vary with all these accidental causes and follow the rule of the transport of silver required. In considering the balance of trade matters of this kind are not separated, and indeed it would be very difficult to separate them. They have very certainly an influence on the increase and decrease of circulating money in a State and on its comparative strength and power.

ᵃ...ᵃ: R: 'vuées'
ᵇ...ᵇ: R: 'Ambassadeurs, seigneurs'
ᶜ...ᶜ: 1756b: 'l'y intérêt', R: Lintéréts'
ᵈ...ᵈ: R: 'fonds'
ᵉ...ᵉ: R: 'les'

559

560

|| By what I have here said, it does I think clearly appear, that though the chief Object of Intercourse betwixt Nations, is the mutual Exchange of the Goods and Merchandize of one Nation, with that of another, and that this is carried to a very great Extent, yet from the Consequence of these mutual Dealings, a Necessity arises between Countries of keeping strict Accounts with each other, and that to avoid the Expence, Hazard, and Trouble of sending Money and Bullion backwards and forwards, this Invention of Bills of Exchange, is of excellent Use.

561

|| The Wisdom of all civilized Countries has formed Laws and Customs for the good Government of this Business, the Knowledge (as I have before observed) of the executive Part of this Branch of Trade, is to be acquired by [85] Practice, all that can be expected from me, is to lay down its true Principles and Theory, as briefly as I can, in which I hope to have succeeded. But if these Essays have the good Fortune to merit the Approbation of the Public, I propose from a Number of Calculations by me, collected from a Course of many Years Experience, to publish a small Treatise of Arithmetic, wherein this useful Science shall be fully but briefly explained, also its speculative and practical Utility in the Occurrences of common Life, and vulgarly, and decimally applied, to the several Operations of foreign Exchanges, their Par and Arbitration, all divested from the unintelligible Jargon of Authors, who have hitherto treated this Subject, and as far as I can conceive, did not themselves understand what they meant in their Calculations; or at least if they did, their Intention must be, that they themselves should be applied to for explaining what never could be attained but by Guess-work, from their Writings.

562 |12| Mon sujet ne me permet pas de m'étendre sur les effets de ces causes accidentelles, je me bornerai toujours aux vues simples de commerce, de peur d'embarrasser mon sujet, qui ne l'est que trop par la multiplicité des faits qui s'y présentent.

560

i. This paragraph has been included because there seems to be a possibility that **561** the treatise of [Political] Arithmetic referred to in A561 has a connection with the famous missing Supplement. As was noted in C33ii, none of the paragraphs where in E the Supplement is mentioned has a counterpart in A (apart from E33/A33). The allusions to a supplement in the French text all occur in the context of precise arithmetical examples that are invariably missing from A. In contrast, most of these examples are present in D, even though that text nowhere mentions a supplement. While in the case of D this may simply be explained by assuming that Postlethwayt removed such references (cf. C66i), A561 suggests a different explanation for their absence from the *Analysis*. The first person 'I' in this passage may be Richard Cantillon and the remark that he proposes to write a 'small Treatise of Arithmetic' may imply that at the time he wrote the manuscript version on which Philip Cantillon was to base his *Analysis*, the former had not yet written the additional work that he would later refer to as his Supplement.

ii. Here the text as a whole is referred to as 'these Essays'. The only other place in the *Analysis* where this term is used, again in the plural, is in the preface, p. xvi: 'The weak Attempt I make in the following Essays, is to convey a general Idea of Trade, and its Influence upon and Consequence to the Society. This I attempt by tracing it to its original Source, and stripping it of that Mystery in which most People, who have wrote on this Subject have disguised it.' Note that the description of the work as 'Essays to convey the general Idea of Trade' appears to echo the title of the French text, not otherwise used by Philip Cantillon. In the body of the text of the French print edition the work is referred to in a number of places as '*cet Essai*', in the singular (see E115, E220, E221, E291, E329, E405, E525). The singular is also used in the manuscript versions (where the spelling is '*cet essay*'), apart from one place where, like in A561, the plural '*ces Essays*' occurs (see V405c).

iii. With A561, chapter XVIII of the *Analysis* finishes. Chapter XIX starts at A570.

My subject does not allow me to enlarge **562** on the effects of these accidental causes: I confine myself always to the simple views of commerce lest I should complicate my subject, which is too much encumbered by the multiplicity of the facts which relate to it.

563 |13| Les changes haussent plus ou moins au dessus du pair à proportion des grands ou petits frais, & risques du transport d'argent, [351] & cela supposé, les changes haussent bien plus naturellement au dessus du pair dans les Villes ou Etats où il y a des défenses de transporter de l'argent hors de l'Etat, que dans celles où le transport en est libre.

564 |14| Supposons que le Portugal consomme annuellement & constamment des quantités considerables de Manufactures de laine & autres d'Angleterre, tant pour ses propres habitans que pour ceux du Bresil; [a]qu'il en paie[a] une partie en vin, huiles, &c. [b]mais que pour le surplus du paiement il y ait[b] une balance constante de commerce qu'on envoie de Lisbonne à Londres. Si le Roi de Portugal fait de rigoureuses défenses, & sous peine non-seulement de confiscation, mais même de la vie, de transporter [c]aucune matiere[c] d'or [d]ou[d] d'argent hors de ses Etats, la terreur de ces [e]défenses[e] empêchera [f]d'abord les Ban-[352] quiers[f] de se mêler d'envoïer la balance. Le prix des Manufactures Angloises restera en [g]caisse[g] à Lisbonne. Les Marchands Anglois ne pouvant avoir de Lisbonne leurs fonds, n'y enverront plus de draps. Il arrivera que les draps deviendront d'une cherté extraordinaire; cependant les draps ne sont pas encheris en Angleterre, on s'abstient seulement de les envoïer à Lisbonne à cause qu'on n'en peut pas retirer la valeur. Pour avoir de ces draps la Noblesse Portugaise & autres qui ne sauroient s'en passer, en offriront jusqu'au double du prix ordinaire; mais comme on n'en sauroit avoir assez qu'en envoïant de l'argent hors de Portugal, l'augmentation du prix du drap deviendra le profit de quiconque enverra [h]l'or ou l'argent[h], contre les défenses, hors du Roïaume; cela encouragera plusieurs Juifs, & autres de porter l'or & l'argent [353] aux Vaisseaux Anglois qui sont dans la Rade de Lisbonne, même au hasard de la vie. Ils gagneront d'abord cent ou cinquante pour cent à faire ce métier, & ce profit est païé par les habitans Portugais, dans le haut prix qu'ils donnent pour le drap. Ils se familiariseront peu-à-peu à ce manége, après l'avoir pratiqué souvent avec succès, & dans la suite on verra porter l'argent à bord des Vaisseaux Anglois pour le prix de deux ou un pour cent.

The ballance of trade with *Portugal* is commonly in favour of *England*. *Lisbon* commonly consumes a great quantity of English goods, and sends large quantities also to *Brazil*; the Lisbon wines and commodities sent to England answer but part of the value, and the ballance is constantly sent to England in gold.

|| Let it be supposed that the king of *Portugal* should absolutely prohibit the exportation of gold and silver out of his dominions, what will be the consequence of this?

|| If this prohibition be so strict as to deter every body from sending any money out of *Portugal*, the English will send no more woollen goods to *Lisbon*, than what may be repaid and compensated by the wines and other commodities of Portuguese growth, which are consumed in *England*. If they should send the usual quantities, the money they receive for them would remain deposited at *Lisbon*; and so, in little time, there would not be woollen goods enough at *Lisbon* for the wear of those who use them: wherefore the price of such goods at *Lisbon* will grow extravagantly dear; the consumers will offer 20 to 50 per cent. more for them rather than go without, but no more can be had unless money be exported to pay for them.

|| This additional price of 20 to 50 per cent. will go to those who will venture to export money to answer it, while the English do not raise their price. This great profit will determine some of the *Portuguese* to export money, even at the hazard of their lives; and its plain this hazard is paid by the Portuguese consumers, in the advanced price they give for their cloth.

|| If the exportation be made by *England*, the profit centers there; and is consequently lost to *Portugal*: if the Jews and other Portuguese make the gains, they will not only export the money required, but also their profits, and probably send out their whole fortune, and follow it to escape the rigor of the law: thus the prohibition to export money, will occasion a greater export of it than usual, and consequently the law will not only prove ineffectual but prejudicial.

563

Exchanges rise more or less above par in proportion to the great or small costs and risks of the transport of money and this being granted they naturally rise much more above par in the cities or States where it is forbidden to export money than in those where its export is free.

Suppose that Portugal consumes regularly every year considerable quantities of woollen and other Manufactures of England, as well for its own people as for those of Brazil, that it pays for them partly in wine, oils, etc., but for the surplus payment there is a regular balance of trade remitted from Lisbon to London. If the King of Portugal rigorously prohibits under penalty not only of confiscation but of life the transport of any gold or silver metal out of his States, the terror of this prohibition will in the first place stop the Bankers from meddling about sending the balance. The price of the English manufactures will be kept in hand at Lisbon. The English merchants unable to receive their funds from Lisbon will send no more cloth thither. The result will be that cloth will become extraordinarily dear. Though their price has not gone up in England they cease to be sent to Lisbon because their value cannot be recovered. To have these cloths the Portuguese nobility and others who cannot do without them will offer twice the usual price, but as they cannot get enough of them without sending money out of Portugal, the increased price of cloth will become the profit of any one who in spite of the prohibition will export gold or silver. This will encourage various Jews and others to take gold and silver to English vessels in the port of Lisbon, even at the risk of their lives. They will gain at first 100 or 50 per cent. in this traffic and this profit is paid by the Portuguese in the high price they give for the cloth. They will gradually familiarise themselves with this manœuvre after having often practised it successfully, and at length money will be seen to be put on board English ships for a payment of 2 or 1 per cent.

ᵃ...ᵃ: R: 'quils en payent'
ᵇ...ᵇ: 1756b, 1769: 'mais pour le surplus du paiement qu'il ait'; R: 'mais que pour Le surplus du payément il y a'
ᶜ...ᶜ: R: 'aucunes matiéres'
ᵈ...ᵈ: R: 'et'
ᵉ...ᵉ: R: 'etats'
ᶠ...ᶠ: R: 'lés banquiérs dabord'
ᵍ...ᵍ: R: 'laisse'
ʰ...ʰ: R: 'Lors Et L'argent'

i. The argument of E564 **564** and E565 was discussed at some length in the *Journal de Commerce et d'Agriculture*, January 1760, pp. 69–73, with the concluding comment that '[*l*]es observations du célèbre Cantillon ne laissent aucune objection à faire en faveur des prohibitions'.

ii. D564, D567 and D569 do not actually occur in the *Universal Dictionary*. Postlethwayt only adopted them in his *Plan* of 1749, on pp. 48–49. For convenience of presentation these paragraphs have been put in column D. For other paragraphs missing from the *Dictionary*, see V508a, V550a and V551d.

565 |15| Le Roi de Portugal fait la loi ou la défense: ᵃsesᵃ Sujets, même ses Courtisans, paient les frais du risque qu'on court pour rendre la défense inutile, & pour l'éluder. On ne ᵇtireᵇ donc aucun avantage d'une pareille loi, au contraire elle cause un désavantage réel au Portugal parcequ'elle est cause qu'il sort plus d'argent de l'Etat qu'il n'en sortiroit s'il n'y avoit pas une telle loi.

566 [354] |16| Car ceux qui gagnent à ce manége, soit Juifs ou autres, ne manquent pas d'envoïer leurs profits ᵃen païs étrangers, & lorsqu'ilsᵃ en ont assez ou lorsque la peur les prend ils suivent souvent ᵇeux-même leur argentᵇ.

567 |17| Que si l'on prenoit quelques-uns de ces contrevenans sur le fait, qu'on ᵃconfisquâtᵃ leurs biens & qu'on les ᵇfîtᵇ mourir, cette circonstance ᶜ& cette exécutionᶜ au lieu d'empêcher la sortie de l'argent ne ᵈferontᵈ que l'augmenter, parceque ceux qui se contentoient auparavant de un ou deux pour cent pour sortir ᵉde l'argentᵉ, voudront avoir vingt ou cinquante pour cent, ᶠainsi il est nécessaireᶠ qu'il en sorte toujours ᵍde quoiᵍ païer la balance.

|| Provided any money exported should be seized in the fact, and his fortune conficated, the sum seized would seldom or never amount to the profits the exporter had already made; nor would the example only enhance the price of exporting money, but always turn, in the consequences, to the loss and disadvantage of *Portugal*.

568 |18| ᵃJe ne saisᵃ si j'ai bien réussi à rendre ces raisons sensibles à ceux qui n'ont point d'idée de commerce. ᵇje saisᵇ que pour ceux qui ont quelque connoissance de la [355] pratique, rien n'est plus aisé à comprendre, & qu'ils s'étonnent avec raison que ceux qui conduisent les Etats & administrent les Finances des grands Roïaumes, aient si peu de connoissance de la nature des changes, que de défendre la sortie des matieres & des especes d'or & d'argent, en même tems.

569 |19| Le moïen unique de les ᵃconserver dans un Etatᵃ, c'est de conduire si bien le commerce avec l'Etranger que la balance ne soit pas contraire à l'Etat.

The most effectual way therefore to prevent the exportation of money, is from what has already been suggested; and to maintain the general ballance of trade against foreigners.

The King of Portugal lays down the law or prohibition. His subjects, even his courtiers, pay the cost of the risk run to circumvent and elude it. No advantage then is gained by such a law, on the contrary it causes a real loss to Portugal since it causes more money of the State to go abroad than if there were no such law.

ᵃ…ᵃ: R: 'Ces'
ᵇ…ᵇ: R: 'tirent'

The view that prohibitions **565** of the exportation of specie are ineffectual is also found in A554.

For those who gain by this manœuvre, whether Jews or others, send their profits abroad, and when they have enough of them or when they take fright they often themselves follow their money.

ᵃ…ᵃ: 1756b, 1769: 'en païs étrangers, lorsqu'ils'; R: 'en pays étrangér, Et lors quils'
ᵇ…ᵇ: R: 'Leur argent éux memes'

566

If some of these lawbreakers were taken in the act, their goods confiscated and their lives forfeited, this circumstance and execution instead of stopping the export of money would only increase it, because those who formerly were satisfied with 1 or 2 per cent. for exporting money will ask 20 or 50 per cent., and so the export must always go on to pay the balance.

ᵃ…ᵃ: R: 'confisque'
ᵇ…ᵇ: R: 'fasse'
ᶜ…ᶜ: R: 'et execution'
ᵈ…ᵈ: R: 'fera'
ᵉ…ᵉ: R: 'L'argent'
ᶠ…ᶠ: R: 'et quil est de nécéssité'
ᵍ…ᵍ: R: 'pour'

The expression 'seized **567** in the fact' (D567) is too literal a translation of '*prenoit sur le fait*' ('caught red-handed').

I do not know whether I have succeeded in making these reasons clear to those who have no idea of trade. I know that for those who have practical knowledge of it nothing is easier to understand, and that they are rightly astonished that those who govern States and administer the Finances of great kingdoms have so little knowledge of the nature of exchanges as to forbid the export of bullion and specie of gold and silver.

ᵃ…ᵃ: 1756b, 1769: 'Je ne sai'; R: 'Je Ne sçay'
ᵇ…ᵇ: 1756b, 1769: 'Je sai'; R: 'je sçay'

568

The only way to keep them in a State is so to conduct foreign trade that the balance is not adverse to the State.

ᵃ…ᵃ: R: 'Conservér'

After D569 the borrowed **569** passages in Postlethwayt's 1749 *Plan* finish (at the top of p. 49).

570

Des variations de la proportion des valeurs, par raport aux Métaux qui servent de monnoie.

[I, 527, col.2] *Of the augmentation or diminution of the* COIN *in denomination, to fix a par between* GOLD *and* SILVER.

[86] **CHAP. XIX.**
Of Trade and Money, particulary Gold, Silver and Copper, their proportional Value and Variations with respect to the Use made of them as Money.

571

|| The proportion of the value between gold and silver, has varied in different ages and countries, according to the quantity of these metals.

572

|1| Si les Métaux étoient aussi faciles à trouver, que l'eau l'est communément, chacun en pren-[356]droit pour ses besoins, & ces métaux n'auroient ᵃpresqueᵃ point de valeur. Les métaux qui se trouvent les plus abondans & qui coutent le moins ᵇde peine à produireᵇ, sont aussi ceux qui sont à meilleur marché. Le fer paroît le plus nécessaire; mais comme on le trouve ᶜcommunément en Europeᶜ, avec moins de peine & de travail que le cuivre, il est à bien meilleur marché.

[87] || If Metals were as easily found as Water they would be of little or no Value; Water is of the greatest Use, but as it flows spontaneously, and not be witheld within the Limits of private Property, and is common to all at the Expence of bringing and conducting; therefore its intrinsic Value is but small.

|| Metals which are discovered in greatest Abundance and Quantity, and which are cheapest brought to light, are also cheapest at Market: Iron is one of the Metals of the greatest Use, but as its Mines are in great Numbers found in *Europe*, and their Produce brought to light, and wrought into Use at less Expence, Trouble, and Labour than Copper, it is therefore much cheaper.

573

|2| Le cuivre, l'argent & l'or, sont les trois métaux dont on se sert communément pour monnoie. Les Mines de cuivre sont les plus abondantes & coutent le moins de ᵃterreᵃ & de travail à produire. Les plus abondantes Mines de cuivre sont aujourd'hui en Suede: il y faut plus de quatre-vingts onces de cuivre au Marché pour païer une once d'argent. Il est aussi à remarquer que le cuivre qu'on tire de certaines Mines est plus parfait & [357] plus beau que celui qu'on tire d'autres Mines. Celui du Japon & de Suede est plus beau que celui d'Angleterre. Celui d'Espagne étoit du tems des Romains, plus beau que celui de l'Ile de Chypre. Au lieu que l'or & l'argent, de quelque ᵇMineᵇ qu'on ᶜlesᶜ tire, sont toujours de la même perfection, lorsqu'on les a rafinés.

|| Copper, Gold, and Silver are the three Metals which are generally made use of as Coin, or Money; the working Copper-Mines costs less Expence, Risk, and Labour in producing their Oar to light than Gold or Silver; [88] the greater Number of Copper-Mines in proportion to other Countries are now a-days found in *Sweden*; in that Country eighty Ounces of this Metal passes in Exchange for one Ounce of Silver. It must be observed, that the Oar of some Mines is of a better Nature and Quality than the Oar which is produced from others; the *Swedish* and *Japan* Copper is in Nature and Colour of a better Quality than *English*; but Gold and Silver from whatever Mines they are produced, are the same as to Quality and Perfection when fined down.

Chapter IV

Of the variations in the proportion of values with regard to the Metals which serve as Money

ᵃ…ᵃ: R: '4ᵉ'

i. D occurs in the long *Dictionary* entry 'Coin' (I, 521–532). This entry first appeared in issue 44 of the *Universal Dictionary*, which was published in the first weeks of 1753. The section reproduced in D570–D591 is directly preceded by a section that is reproduced in D595–D621.

ii. The title of *Analysis* chapter XIX is also reproduced in A203. It appears to combine the titles of E I, xvii and E III, iv. Cf. C203ii. The first paragraphs of this chapter correspond quite closely with E I, xvii, 1–3, and hence are reproduced in A204–A207.

570

571

If Metals were as easily found as water commonly is everybody would take what he wanted of them and they would have hardly any value. The Metals which are most plentiful and cost the least trouble to produce are also the cheapest. Iron seems the most necessary, but as it is commonly found in Europe with less trouble and labour than copper it is much cheaper.

ᵃ…ᵃ: R: 'quasy'
ᵇ…ᵇ: R: 'a produire'
ᶜ…ᶜ: R: 'Communémént'

i. A572 follows directly on from the paragraph reproduced in A207.

ii. An earlier discussion of the intrinsic value of water is in E/D69 and an earlier discussion of the intrinsic value of metals in E/D204–E/D207. This latter discussion has a counterpart on pp. 86–87 of the *Analysis*, which are reproduced in A204–A207.

iii. Cf. V572a with V354a.

572

Copper, Silver, and Gold are the three metals in general use for money. Copper mines are the most abundant and cost less in Land and Labour to work. The richest copper Mines today are in Sweden. 80 ounces of copper are needed there to pay for an ounce of silver. It is also to be observed that the copper extracted from some mines is more perfect and lustrous than what is obtained from others. The copper of Japan and Sweden is brighter than that of England. That of Spain was, in the time of the Romans, better than that of Cyprus. But gold and silver, from whatever Mine extracted, are always of the same perfection when refined.

ᵃ…ᵃ: R: 'Terres'
ᵇ…ᵇ: R: 'mines'
ᶜ…ᶜ: 1756 a,b, 1769: 'le'

573

574 |3| La valeur du cuivre, comme de tout autres choses, est proportionnée à la terre & au travail qui ᵃentrentᵃ dans sa production. Outre les usages ordinaires ᵇauxquels on l'emploie, comme pour des pots, des vases, de la batterie de cuisine, des serrures, &c.,ᵇ on s'en sert presque dans tous les Etats pour monnoie, dans le troc du menu. En Suede on s'en sert ᶜsouvent mêmeᶜ dans les gros paiemens lorsque l'argent y est rare. ᵈPendant les cinq premiers siecles de Ro-[358]me, on ne se servoit pas d'autre monnoie.ᵈ On ne commença à se servir d'argent dans le troc, que dans l'année quatre cent quatre-vingt-quatre. La proportion du cuivre à l'argent fut alors réglée dans les monnoies, comme 72 à 1; dans la fabrication de cinq cent douze, comme 80 à 1; dans l'évaluation de cinq cent trente-sept, comme 64 à 1; dans la fabrication de cinq cent quatre-vingt-six, comme 48 à 1; dans celle de six cent soixante-trois de Drusus, & celle de Sylla de six cent soixante & douze, comme 53 1/3 à 1; dans celle de Marc Antoine de sept cent douze, & d'Auguste de sept cent vingt-quatre, comme 56 à 1; dans celle de Neron l'an de Jesus-Christ cinquante-quatre, comme 60 à 1; dans ᶜcelle d'Antonin l'an de l'Ereᶜ présente cent soixante, comme 64 à 1; dans le tems de Constantin trois cent [359] trente, style présent, comme 120 & 125 à 1; dans le siecle de Justinien environ cinq cent cinquante, comme 100 à 1; & cela a toujours varié depuis au-dessous de la proportion de 100 dans les monnoies en Europe.

|| The Value of Copper as also that of all other earthly Things, is proportioned to the Value of the Land, Labour, Expence, Risk and Time had in producing them to light. || Copper (besides the many other Uses it is put to) is made Use of in almost every State, as Money to pass in Exchange for small Payments, in *Sweden* it happens at times when Gold and Silver are scarce, that large Payments must be made in Copper; in the first five Ages of the *Romans*, Copper was the only Money made Use of, Silver came into Fashion about the Year of *Rome* 484, the Proportion [89] about this Time settled between these two Metals, as 72 is to 1; that is to say, 72 Ounces of Copper was paid for one Ounce of Silver, in 512 of *Rome* as 80 is to 1, in 537 as 64 is to 1, in 586 as 48 to 1, in that of 672 the Time of *Sylla* as 53 is to 1, in the Time of *Mark Anthony*, 712, as 56 is to 1, and in the Time of *Augustus*, 784, as 75 is to 1, in that of *Nero* the 54th, of our Redemption, as 60 is to 1, that of *Constantine* in 330 according to our present Stile, as 120 is to 1, and in the Time of *Justinian* as 100 is to 1, and ever since this Time this Proportion of Copper to Silver has kept under 100 to 1.

The value of copper, as of everything else, is proportionable to the Land and Labour which enter into its production. Beside the ordinary uses to which it is put, like pots and pans, kitchen utensils, locks, etc. it is in nearly all States used as money in small purchases. In Sweden it is used even in large payments when silver is scarce there. During the first five centuries of Rome it was the only money. Silver only began to be employed in exchange in the year 484. The ratio of copper to silver was then rated in the mints at 72 to 1: in the coinage of 512 at 80 to 1: in 537, 64 to 1: in 586 at 48 to 1; in 663 by Drusus and 672 by Sulla at 53 1/3 to 1: in 712 by Marcus Antonius and 724 by Augustus 56 to 1: in A.D. 54 under Nero 60 to 1: in 160 A.D. under Antoninus 64 to 1; in the time of Constantine A.D. 330, 120 and 125 to 1: in the age of Justinian about A.D. 550 at 100 to 1. Since then it has always varied below the ratio of 100 to 1 in the European mints.

ᵃ...ᵃ: R: 'entre'

ᵇ...ᵇ: R: 'quon en fait pour pots vases sérrures portes &c.'

ᶜ...ᶜ: R: 'souvent'

ᵈ...ᵈ: R: 'dans lancienne Rome, on ne se servoit pas d'autre Monnoye pendant Les Cinq premiers siecles'

ᵉ...ᵉ: R: 'Cette Dantonin Lan de laire'

574

i. There are some small differences between E574 and A574 in the detailed historical series. A does not mention Drusus (year 663) and distinguishes the ratio under Marcus Antonius (year 712) from that of Augustus (in the year 784, instead of 724 in E): E has 56 to 1 for both; A has 56 to 1 and 75 to 1, respectively. A also does not mention Antonius (in AD160).

ii. There also appear to be some small historical inaccuracies. E574 has the year 724 as a year under Augustus. This equates with 29 BC (see C577ii), but Augustus only reigned from 27 BC . A574 has 784 as a year in the reign of Augustus, which equates with AD 31. But, as also noted in E577, Augustus died in AD 14.

575 |4| Aujourd'hui qu'on ne se sert guere de cuivre pour monnoie, que dans le troc du ᵃmenuᵃ, soit qu'on l'allie avec la calamine, pour faire du cuivre jaune, comme en Angleterre, soit qu'on l'allie avec une petite partie d'argent, comme en France & en Allemagne, on le fait valoir communément dans la proportion de 40 à 1; quoique le cuivre au Marché soit ordinairement à l'argent comme 80 & 100 à 1. ᵇLa raison estᵇ, qu'on diminue ordinairement sur le poids du cuivre les frais de la fabrication; & lorsqu'il n'y a pas trop de cette petite monnoie pour la circulation du bas [360] troc dans l'Etat, les monnoies de ᶜcuivre seulᶜ, ou de cuivre allié, ᵈpassentᵈ sans difficulté malgré le défaut de leur valeur intrinseque. Mais lorsqu'on les veut faire passer dans le troc dans un païs étranger, on ne les veut recevoir qu'au poids du cuivre & de l'argent qui est allié avec le cuivre; & même dans les Etats où, par l'avarice ou l'ignorance de ceux qui gouvernent, on donne cours à une trop grande quantité de cette petite monnoie pour la circulation du bas troc, & où ᵉl'onᵉ ordonne qu'on en reçoive une certaine partie dans le gros paiemens, on ne la reçoit pas volontiers, & la petite monnoie perd un agiot contre l'argent blanc, c'est ce qui arrive à la monnoie de Billon & aux Ardites en Espagne pour les gros paiemens; cependant la petite monnoie passe toujours sans difficulté dans le bas troc, [361] la valeur dans ces paiemens étant ordinairement petite en elle-même, par conséquent la perte l'est encore davantage: c'est ce qui fait qu'on s'en accommode sans peine, & qu'on change le cuivre contre de petites pieces d'argent au-dessus du poids & valeur intrinseque du cuivre dans l'Etat même, mais non dans les autres Etats; chaque Etat en aïant de sa propre fabrication de quoi conduire son troc du menu.

‖ In these our present Times, Copper with respect to Money is of little Use, but in small Payments, in this respect it is very serviceable, but in coining this Metal into Money, great Care ought to be taken that its proportional Price at Market, with respect to Silver, may as near as possible be observed, if a base Metal is suffered to pass, and this just Proportion broke in upon, the Consequence would be that Foreigners would counterfeit your base Coin, and pour it in upon you in Exchange of your real Specie of Gold and Silver, as was like to have happened by a scandalous Imposition on [90] the late King *George* the First, to grant a Patent to one *Wood*, for coining Copper for the Use of a neighbouring Kingdom.

576 |5| L'or & l'argent ont, comme le cuivre, une valeur proportionnée à la terre & au travail nécessaires à leur production; & si le public se charge des frais de la fabrication de ces métaux, leur valeur en lingots & en especes est la même, leur valeur au Marché & à la Monnoie est la même chose, leur valeur dans l'Etat & dans les païs étrangers est constamment la même, tou-[362]jours reglée sur le poids ᵃ& sur le titreᵃ; c'est-à-dire, sur le poids seul, si ces métaux sont purs & sans alliage.

‖ Gold and Silver, like Copper, have a Value in Proportion to the Value of the Land, the Expence, Time, Risk, and Labour had for producing them, and forming them into Use; in *England* the Public pay the Expence of Coining these Pieces of precious Metals into Money, and as this is the Case, their Value will be the same in Ingots, as if they were coined into Species, and they will bear the same Price at Market.

Today when copper money is only used in small dealings, whether alloyed with calamine to make yellow copper as in England, or with a small portion of silver as in France and Germany, it is generally rated in the, proportion of 40 to 1, though the market price of copper is ordinarily to that of silver as 80 or 100 to 1. The reason is that the cost of coining is generally deducted from the weight of the copper. When there is not too much of this small money for effecting the petty exchanges in the State, coins of copper or copper and alloy pass without difficulty in spite of their defect in intrinsic value. But when it is attempted to pass them in a foreign country they will only be taken at the weight of the copper and the silver alloy. Even in States where through the avarice or ignorance of the governors, currency is given to too great a quantity of this small cash for the transaction of small dealings, and it is ordered that it should be received up to a certain limit in large payments it is unwillingly accepted and small cash is at a discount in silver coin, as in the token money and Ardites in Spain in large payments. Yet small coins always pass without difficulty in small purchases, the value of the payments being usually small in themselves the loss is still less. This is why they are accepted without difficulty, and that copper is exchanged for small silver coins above the weight and intrinsic value of copper in the State itself, but not in other States, each State having wherewith to carry on its small dealings with its own copper coins.

[a]...[a]: R: 'méme'
[b]...[b]: 1756b, 1769: 'La raison en est'
[c]...[c]: R: 'Cuivre'
[d]...[d]: R: 'passe'
[e]...[e]: R: 'on'

i. The reference in A575 **575** to 'one *Wood*' is to the granting of letters patent in 1722 to William Wood for producing copper coins up to a value of £108,000 for use in Ireland. In his *Drapier's Letters*, published in the form of seven pamphlets in 1724 and 1725, Jonathan Swift succesfully agitated for the abolition of this patent for the private minting of what he believed to be inferior coin.

ii. The reference in A575 to George I, who died in 1727, as '*the late* King George the First' may indicate that the passage was written not too long after 1727, because it is perhaps unlikely that one should still refer to such a famous person as 'the late' more than 30 years after his death (i.e. 1759).

Gold and silver, like copper, have a value proportionable to the Land and Labour necessary for their production; and if the public assumes the cost of minting these metals their value in bars and in coin is identical, their market value and their Mint value is the same, their Value in the State and in foreign countries is always alike, depending on the weight and fineness, that is on weight alone if the metals are pure and without alloy.

[a]...[a]: R: 'et Titre'

576

577 |6| Les Mines d'argent se sont toujours trouvées plus abondantes que celles de l'or, mais non pas également dans tous les païs, ni dans tous les tems : il a toujours fallu plusieurs onces d'argent pour païer une once d'or; mais tantôt plus tantôt moins, suivant l'abondance de ces métaux & la demande. L'an de Rome trois cent dix, il falloit en Grece treize onces d'argent pour païer une once d'or, c'est-à-dire, que l'or étoit à l'argent comme 1 à 13; l'an quatre cent ou environ, comme 1 à 12; l'an quatre cent soixante, comme 1 à 10, tant en Grece qu'en Italie, & par toute l'Europe. Cette proportion d'1 à 10 paroît avoir continué constamment pendant trois siecles jusqu'à la [363] mort d'Auguste, l'an de Rome sept cent soixante-sept, ᵃou l'an de graceᵃ quatorze. Sous Tibere, l'or devint plus rare, ou l'argent plus abondant, la proportion a monté peu-à-peu à celle de 1 à 12, 12 1/2 & 13. Sous Constantin l'an de grace trois cent trente, & sous Justinien cinq cent cinquante, elle s'est trouvée comme 1 à 14 2/5. L'histoire est plus obscure depuis; quelques-uns croient avoir trouvé cette proportion comme 1 à 18, sous quelques Rois de France. L'an de grace huit cent quarante, sous le regne de Charles le Chauve, on fabriqua les monnoies d'or & d'argent sur le fond, & la proportion se trouva comme 1 à 12. Sous le regne de Saint Louis, qui mourut en mil deux cent soixante & dix, la proportion étoit comme 1 à 10; en mil trois cent soixante-un, comme 1 à 12; en mil quatre [364] cent vingt-un, au-dessus de 1 à 11; en mil cinq cent au-dessous de 1 à 12; en mil six cent environ, comme 1 à 12; en mil six cent quarante-un, comme 1 à 14; en mil sept cent, comme 1 à 15; en mil sept cent trente, comme 1 à 14 1/2.

|| Mines of Silver are found in greater Numbers than Mines of Gold, and there has been in all Places, and in all Times a Number of Ounces of Silver given in Exchange of one Ounce of Gold, according to the Circumstances of the Times; in *Greece*, the Age of *Rome* 310, the Proportion between Gold and Silver was as 1 is to 13; that is to say, one Ounce of Gold would purchase thirteen Ounces of Silver; in 460 as 1 is to 10, and this Proportion of 1 to 10 seems to have continued to the Time of *Augustus Cæsar*; under *Constantine* [91] the Year 330, this Proportion was as 1 is to 13, and in 550 the Age of *Justinian* as 1 is to 14 two fifths. From this Æra History is very obscure as to this Proportion, yet some curious Writers say, that under the *French* Kings, this Proportion was a 1 is to 18, and that in the Reign of *Charles* the Bald, 840, Gold was to Silver as 1 is to 12, and in 1270, it was as 1 is to 10, and in 1361, as 1 is to 12, in 1421, as 1 is to 11, in 1500 as 1 is to 12, in 1600, as 1 is to 12, in 1640, as 1 is to 14, in 1700, as 1 is to 15, in 1730, as 1 is to 14 and an half.

Silver mines have always been found more abundant than those of gold, but not equally in all countries or at all times. Several ounces of silver have always been needed to buy one ounce of gold, sometimes more sometimes less according to the abundance of these metals and the demand for them. In the year A.U.C. 310, 13 ounces of silver were needed in Greece to buy an ounce of gold, i.e. gold was to silver as 1 to 13: A.U.C. 400 or thereabouts 1 to 12, A.U.C. 460 1 to 10 in Greece, Italy and the whole of Europe. This ratio of 1 to 10 seems to have persisted for 3 centuries to the death of Augustus, A.U.C. 767 or A.D. 14. Under Tiberius gold became scarce or silver more plentiful, and the ratio gradually rose to 1 to 12, 12½, and 13. Under Constantine A.D. 330 and Justinian A.D. 550 it was 1 to 14 2/3. Later history is more obscure. Some authors think it was 1 to 18 under certain French kings. In A.D. 840 under Charles the Bald gold and silver coins were struck at 1 to 12. Under St Louis, who died in 1270 the ratio was 1 to 10: in 1361, 1 to 12: in 1421 over 1 to 11: in 1500 under 1 to 12: about 1600, 1 to 12: in 1641, 1 to 14: in 1700, 1 to 15: in 1730, 1 to 14½.

[a]...[a]: R: 'ou de grace'

i. The latest date in this **577** historical series in both E577 and A577 is 1730. Murphy (1986: 246) pointed out that the occurrence of this date in the French text implies that the manuscript on which the print edition of 1755 was based was written after 1730. For the same reason, one may argue the same for the manuscript on which the *Analysis* was based, or at least this passage of it.

ii. In the Higgs translation A.U.C. stands for *anno urbis conditae*, or *ab urbe condita*, meaning in the year from the building of Rome. Cantillon used the building of Rome as the basis for the dates quoted in this paragraph and in E/A574. The building of Rome was dated as 753 BC. This means that A.U.C. 310 translates into the year 440 BC. Later in the paragraph there is the date 'A.U.C. 767 or AD 14'. This is obtained by subtracting 753 from 767 to give AD 14.

578 |7|ᵃLa quantité d'or & d'argent qu'on avoit apportée du Mexique & du Pérou dans le siecle passéᵃ, a rendu non-seulement ces métaux plus abondans, mais même ᵇa hausséᵇ la valeur de l'or contre l'argent qui s'est trouvé plus abondant, de maniere qu'on en fixe la proportion ᶜdans les monnoies d'Espagneᶜ, suivant les prix du Marché, comme 1 à 16; les autres Etats de l'Europe ont suivi d'assez près le prix de l'Espagne dans leurs monnoies, les uns les mirent comme 1 à 15 7/8, les autres comme 1 à 15 3/4, à ᵈ15 5/8ᵈ, &c. suivant le génie & les vues des Directeurs [365] des Monnoies. Mais depuis que le Portugal tire des quantités considérables d'or du Bresil, la proportion a commencé à baisser de nouveau, sinon dans les Monnoies, au moins dans les prix du Marché, qui donne une plus grande valeur à l'argent, que par le passé; outre qu'on apporte assez souvent des Indes orientales beaucoup d'or, en échange de l'argent qu'on y ᵉporteᵉ d'Europe, parceque la proportion est bien plus basse dans les Indes.

[I, 527, col. 2 continued] || Before the discovery of the plate mines in the *West-Indies*, an ounce of gold in *Europe*, was equal in value to ten ounces of silver; but, since silver has been brought in great quantities out of *New Spain*, it was found in the altercations at market in *Spain*, that an ounce of gold was equal to 16 ounces of silver, and the value of gold and silver was fixed by law in that proportion; and the same rule was kept too nearly in the other countries of *Europe*, allowing for some small differences for the conveniencies of barter, and the management of some directors of mints. The *East-India* trade brought in gradually some little variation in this par, by exporting silver and bringing home gold; and, since that, the discovery of the *Brazil* gold mines has influenced it still more.

|| The large Quantities of Gold and Silver imported into *Europe*, in the last Age, from *Mexico* and *Peru*, have not only greatly increased the Quantities of these precious Metals, but also altered their Proportions; the *Spaniards* fixed it as 1 is to 16, several other States in *Europe* have within a Trifle followed the *Spaniards* Rule.

579 |8| Dans le Japon où il y a des Mines d'argent assez abondantes, la proportion de l'or à l'argent est aujourd'hui comme 1 à 8; à la Chine, comme 1 à 10; dans les autres païs des Indes en-deçà, comme 1 à 11, comme 1 à 12, comme 1 à 13, & comme 1 à 14, à mesure qu'on approche de l'Occident & de l'Europe: mais si les Mines du [366] Bresil continuent à fournir tant d'or, la proportion pourra bien baisser à la longue, comme 1 à 10, même en Europe, qui me paroît la plus naturelle, si on pouvoit dire qu'il y eut autre chose que le hasard qui guide cette proportion : il est bien certain que dans le tems que toutes les Mines d'or & d'argent en Europe, ᵃen Asie & en Afriqueᵃ, étoient le plus cultivées pour le compte de la République Romaine, la proportion dixieme a été la plus constante.

|| In *Japan*, the proportion of gold to silver is 1 to 8, in *China* 1 to 10, in the *Mogul* empire 1 to 12, and so westward as you come nearer to the silver mines, as 1 to 13, to 14, &c. But, as the quantities of gold began to increase in *Europe* beyond the proportion of those of silver, this last metal grew again in request, and sold in the altercations at an agio or profit against gold (upon the foot of the par of 1 to 16) of 2, 3, 5, 8 *per cent.*

The quantity of gold and silver brought from Mexico and Peru in the last century has not only made these metals more plentiful but has increased the value of gold compared with silver which has been more abundant, so that in the Spanish mints, following the market prices, the ratio is fixed at 1 to 16. The other States of Europe have followed pretty closely the Spanish price in their Mints, some at 1 to 15 7/8, others at 15¾, 15 5/8, etc. following the ideas and views of the Directors of the Mints. But since Portugal has drawn great quantities of gold from Brazil the ratio has commenced to fall again if not in the Mints at least in the Markets, and this gives a greater value to silver than in the past. Moreover a good deal of gold is often brought from the East Indies in exchange for the silver taken thither from Europe, because the ratio is much lower in India.

ᵃ...ᵃ: R: 'La quantité quon avoit apporté dans le siecle Passé dor et dargent du mexique et du Perou'

ᵇ...ᵇ: R: 'haussé'

ᶜ...ᶜ: R: 'en espagne dans les Monnois'

ᵈ...ᵈ: R: '15 7/8'

ᵉ...ᵉ: 1756a, b, 1769: 'apporte'

D578 follows directly after D570. **578**

In Japan where there are a good many silver mines the ratio of gold to silver is today 1 to 8: in China 1 to 10: in the other countries of the Indies on this side 1 to 11, 1 to 12, 1 to 13, and 1 to 14 as we get nearer to the West and to Europe. But if the mines of Brazil continue to supply so much gold the ratio may probably fall eventually to 1 to 10 even in Europe which seems to me the most natural if anything but chance is the guide to the ratio. It is quite certain that when all the gold and silver mines in Europe, Asia and Africa were the most exploited for the Roman republic the ratio of 1 to 10 was the most constant.

ᵃ...ᵃ: R: 'asie et affrique'

i. D579 does not have the (historically correct) **579** remark about abundant silver mines in Japan. On the other hand, E579 gives no explanation why the proportion of silver to gold is not higher in Japan if silver (but not gold) is mined there.

ii. Also missing from D579 is the view in E579 that a proportion of 1 to 10 would be the most 'natural'.

iii. The proportions in E/D579 agree more or less with Newton's report of 1717 (see C584iii and iv): 'In China and Japan, one pound weight of fine gold is worth but 9 or 10 pounds weight of fine silver; and in the East-Indies, it may be worth 12. And this low price of gold, in proportion to silver, carries away the silver from all Europe. So then, by the course of trade and exchange between nation and nation in all Europe, fine gold is to fine silver as $14\,^4/_5$ or 15 to one.'

iv. It is difficult to say whether later eighteenth-century authors based themselves on Cantillon or Newton, or yet other sources, when presenting similar proportions. Perhaps Smith (1776, I, xi, g, 28) is closer to Newton's statement, while Raynal *Histoire philosophique* (1775, iii, 381) appears to paraphrase Cantillon.

580　|9| Si toutes les Mines d'or rapportoient constamment la dixieme partie de ce que les Mines d'argent rapportent, on ne pourroit pas encore pour cela déterminer que la proportion entre ces deux métaux seroit la dixieme. Cette proportion dépendroit toujours de la demande & du prix du Marché: il se pourroit faire, que des personnes ri-[367]ches aimeroient mieux porter dans leurs poches de la monnoie d'or que celle d'argent, & qu'ils ᵃse mettroientᵃ dans le goût des dorures & ouvrages d'or préferablement à ceux d'argent, pour hausser le prix de l'or au Marché.

581　|10| On ne pourroit pas non plus déterminer la proportion de ces métaux, en considérant ᵃla quantitéᵃ qui s'en trouve dans un Etat. Supposons la proportion dixieme en Angleterre, & que la quantité de l'or & de l'argent qui y circule se trouve ᵇde vingtᵇ millions d'onces d'argent & ᶜde deuxᶜ millions d'onces d'or, cela seroit équivalent à quarante millions d'onces d'argent; qu'on envoie hors d'Angleterre, un million d'onces d'or des deux millions d'onces qu'il y a, & ᵈqu'on apporteᵈ en échange dix millions d'onces d'argent, il y aura alors trente millions d'onces d'argent [368] & seulement un million d'onces d'or, c'est-à-dire, toujours l'équivalent de quarante millions d'onces d'argent : si l'on considere la quantité d'onces, ᵉil y en a trente millions d'argentᵉ & un million d'onces d'or; & par conséquent si la quantité de l'un & de l'autre métal en décidoit, la proportion de l'or à l'argent seroit trentieme, c'est-à-dire, comme 1 à 30, mais cela est impossible. La proportion dans les païs voisins étrangers est dixieme, il ne coutera donc que dix millions ᶠd'onces d'argentᶠ, avec quelques bagatelles pour les frais du transport, pour faire rapporter dans l'Etat un million d'onces d'or en échange de dix millions d'onces d'argent.

If all the gold mines regularly produced a tenth part of what the Silver mines produce, it could not be determined that for that reason the ratio between these two metals would be as 1 to 10. The ratio would always depend on the demand and on the market price. Possibly rich people might prefer to carry gold money in their pockets rather than silver and might develope a taste for gildings and gold ornaments rather than silver, thus increasing the market price of gold.

ᵃ...ᵃ: R: 'se mettent'

580

Neither could the ratio between these metals be arrived at by considering the quantity of them found in a State. Suppose the ratio 1 to 10 in England and that the quantity of gold and silver in circulation there were 20 million ounces of silver and 2 million ounces of gold, that would be equal to 40 million ounces of silver, and suppose that 1 million ounces of gold be exported from England out of the 2 millions, and 10 million ounces of silver brought in in exchange, there would then be 30 million ounces of silver and only 1 million ounces of gold, still equivalent in all to 40 million ounces of silver. If the quantity of ounces be considered there are 30 millions of silver and 1 million of gold, and therefore if the quantity of the two metals decided the ratio it would be as 1 to 30, but that is impossible. The ratio in the neighbouring countries is 1 to 10, and it would therefore cost only 10 million ounces of silver with a trifle for the cost of carriage to bring back to the State 1 million ounces of gold in exchange for 10 million ounces of silver.

ᵃ...ᵃ: R: 'Les qualités'
ᵇ...ᵇ: R: 'vingt'
ᶜ...ᶜ: R: 'deux'
ᵈ...ᵈ: R: 'qu'on én Raporte'
ᵉ...ᵉ: R: 'il y aura trente millions donces dargent'
ᶠ...ᶠ: R: 'donces'

581

582 |11| Pour juger donc de la proportion de l'or à l'argent,
il n'y a que le prix du Marché qui puisse décider : le
nombre de ceux qui ont besoin d'un métal [369] en
échange de l'autre, & de ceux qui veulent faire cet
échange, en détermine le prix. La proportion dépend
souvent de la fantaisie des Hommes: les altercations se
font grossierement & non géometriquement. Cependant
je ne crois pas qu' on puisse imaginer aucune regle pour
y parvenir, que celle-là : au moins nous savons dans
la pratique, que c'est celle-là qui décide, ᵃde même
queᵃ dans le prix & la valeur de toute autre chose. Les
Marchés étrangers influent sur le prix de l'or & de
l'argent plus que sur le prix d'aucune autre denrée ou
marchandise, parceque rien ne se transporte avec plus
de facilité & moins de déchet. S'il y avoit un commerce
ouvert & courant entre l'Angleterre & le Japon, si on
emploïoit constamment un nombre de Vaisseaux pour
faire ce commerce, & que la balance du [370] commerce
fût en tous points égale, c'est-à-dire, qu'on envoïât
constamment d'Angleterre autant de marchandises au
Japon, eu égard au prix & valeur, qu'on y tireroit des
marchandises du Japon, il arriveroit qu'on tireroit ᵇà
la longue tout l'or du Japon en échange d'argentᵇ, &
qu'on rendroit la proportion au Japon pareille entre l'or
& l'argent, ᶜà celleᶜ qui regne en Angleterre; à la seule
différence près des risques de la navigation: car les frais
du voïage, dans notre supposition, seroient supportés
par le commerce des marchandises.

583 |12| A compter la proportion quinzieme en Angleterre,
ᵃ& huitiemeᵃ au Japon, il y auroit plus de 87 pour cent
à gagner, en portant l'argent d'Angleterre au Japon, ᵇ&
en rapportantᵇ l'or : mais cette différence ne suffit pas
dans le train ordinaire, pour païer [371] les frais d'un
si penible & long voïage, il vaut mieux rapporter ᶜdesᶜ
marchandises du Japon, contre l'argent que de rapporter
l'or. Il n'y a que les frais & risques du transport de l'or
& de l'argent qui puissent laisser une différence de
proportion entre ces métaux dans des Etats différens;
dans l'Etat le plus prochain ᵈcette proportionᵈ ne
différera guere, il y aura de différence, d'un Etat à
l'autre, un, deux ou trois ᵉpour centᵉ, & d'Angleterre au
Japon la somme de toutes ces différences de proportion
se montera au-delà de quatre-vingt-sept pour cent.

To judge then of the ratio between gold and silver the Market price is alone decisive: the number of those who need one metal in exchange for the other, and of those who are willing to make such an exchange, determines the ratio. It often depends on the humour of men: the bargaining is done roughly and not geometrically. Still I do not think that one can imagine any rule but this to arrive at it. At least we know that in practice it is the one which decides, as in the price and value of everything else. Foreign markets affect the price of gold and silver more than they do the price of any other goods or merchandise because nothing is transported with greater ease and less injury. If there were a free and regular trade between England and Japan, if a number of ships were regularly employed in this trade and the balance of trade were in all respects equal, i.e. if as much merchandise were always sent from England to Japan, having regard to price and value, as was imported from Japan, it would end in drawing at last all the gold from Japan in exchange for silver, and the ratio between gold and silver in Japan would be made the same as it is in England, subject only to the risks of navigation; for in our hypothesis the costs of the voyage would be supported by the trade in merchandise.

Taking the ratio at 1 to 15 in England and 1 to 8 in Japan there would be more than 87 per cent. to gain by carrying silver from England to Japan and bringing back gold. But this difference is not enough in the ordinary course to pay the costs of so long and difficult a voyage. It pays better to bring back merchandise from Japan rather than gold in exchange for silver. It is only the costs and risks of the transport of gold and silver which can leave a difference in the ratio between these metals in different States: in the nearest State the ratio will differ very little, there will be a difference from one State to another of 1, 2 or 3 per cent. and from England to Japan the total of all these differences of ratio will amount to more than 87 per cent.

a...a: R: 'tout Comme'

b...b: R: ' tout l'or du jappon en Echange d'argent a la longue'

c...c: R: 'que Celle'

a...a: 1756b, 1769: '& la huitiéme'

b...b: R: 'et Raportant'

c...c: R: 'Les'

d...d: R: 'Cette difference'

e...e: R: 'pour dix'

582

i. For the expression *à la longue* in E582 cf. C286i and C370.

ii. The point that the outcome of bargaining processes can only be described 'roughly and not geometrically' is also made in E241.

583

584 |13| C'est le prix du Marché qui décide la proportion de la valeur de l'or à celle de l'argent : le prix du Marché est la base de cette proportion dans la valeur qu'on donne aux especes d'or & d'argent monnoïées. Si le prix du Marché varie considérable-[372]ment, il faut réformer celui des especes monnoïées pour suivre la regle du Marché ; si on néglige de le faire, la confusion & le desordre ᵃse mettentᵃ dans la circulation, on prendra les pieces de l'un ou ᵇde l'autreᵇ métal à plus haut prix que celui qui est fixé à la Monnoie. On en a une infinité d'exemples dans l'antiquité ; on en a un tout récent en Angleterre par les loix faites à la Tour de Londres. L'once d'argent blanc, du titre d'onze deniers de fin, y vaut cinq schellings & deux deniers ou peniques sterling : depuis que la proportion de l'or à l'argent ᶜ(qu'on avoit fixée à l'imitation de l'Espagne ᵈcomme 1 à 16ᵈ)ᶜ est tombée comme 1 à 15 & 1 à 14 1/2, l'once d'argent se vendoit à cinq schellings & six deniers sterling, pendant que la guinée d'or continuoit d'avoir toujours cours à vingt-un ᵉschelingsᵉ & six [373] deniers sterling, cela fit qu'on emporta d'Angleterre tous les écus d'un écu blanc, schellings & demi-ᵉschellinsᵉ blancs qui n'étoient pas usés dans la circulation : l'argent blanc devint si rare en ᶠmil sept cent vingt-huitᶠ ᶜ(quoiqu'il n'en restât que les pieces les plus usées)ᶜ, qu'on étoit obligé de changer une guinée à près de cinq pour cent de perte. L'embarras & la confusion que cela produisit dans le commerce & la circulation, ᵍobligerentᵍ la Trésorerie de prier ʰle célebre le Chevalier Isaac Newtonʰ, Directeur des Monnoies de la Tour, de faire ⁱun rapportⁱ des moïens qu'il croïoit les plus convenables pour remedier à ce désordre.

The *French*, in order to have a larger quantity of silver in circulation, as it is fitter in barter than gold, fixed the proportion of their gold coin to their silver coin in 1700, as 1 to 15 : but the *English* let the old par remain, and the coins to find their own proportions in the altercations at market : but then, finding the inconveniencies of this in barter, where silver passed in coin for less than it did at the market ; and consequently, observing that no silver remained in circulation but such as was worn, in order to preserve some for the common circulation and barter, they set themselves to consider of fixing a new par between gold and silver.

|| But the only true Method of judging this Proportion between these precious Metals, is, the Market Prices taken at a Medium of thirty or forty Years ; for it is impossible to fix it at a Certainty, as these Prices daily vary, and [92] depend on the Circumstances of the Times, the Taste and Expence of the State, and the Luxury of the great Proprietors of Land ; but yet notwithstanding these Variations, a Medium is still to be found, which ought to be the only Guide to the Directors of all Mints, to govern this Proportion in their standing Prices : if this Rule is not followed, great Confusion in the Public will be the Consequence, of which there are many Instances in former Times, and a very recent one in our own Country, where the Pound of Silver of eleven Ounces two Grains fine, sells at the Mint at five Shillings and Two-pence the Ounce, but where from the Increase of the Quality of Gold imported from *Portugal*, this Proportion was reduced by the Market, as 1 is to 15, or rather 1 is to 14 and an half, the Price for Silver at Market got up to five Shillings and Sixpence the Ounce, the Guinea passed at twenty-one Shillings and Sixpence ; this Inequality of Proportion gave an Opportunity to many Dealers (an Opportunity which these Sort of People will never let slip when it offers) of buying up all the heavy Silver Coin in the Country, so that Silver became so scarce in 1728, that People gave a Premium for changing Guineas, though this Change was paid them in wore [93] out Crowns, half Crowns, Shillings, and Six-pences. The Trouble and Confusion which this introduced into public Circulation, induced the Lords of the Treasury to desire the celebrated Sir *Isaac Newton*, who was then Master of the Mint, to look into this Matter, and report his Opinion, how this Confusion and Disorder was to be remedied.

It is the market price which decides the ratio of the value of gold to that of silver. The Market price is the base of this proportion in the value assigned to coins of gold and silver. If the market price varies considerably, that of the coinage must be reformed to follow the market rate. If this be not done confusion and disorder set in in the circulation, and coins of one or the other metal will be taken above the Mint value. There are an infinity of examples of this in antiquity. There is a quite recent one in England under the regulations made at the London Mint. The ounce of silver, eleven twelfths fine, is worth there 5s. 2d. sterling. Since the ratio of gold to silver (which had been fixed at 1 to 16 in imitation of Spain) has fallen to 1 to 15 and 1 to 14½, the ounce of silver sold at 5s. 6d. sterling, while the gold guinea continued to circulate at 21s. 6d. sterling, which caused the export from England of all the silver crowns, shillings and sixpences which were not worn by circulation, silver money became so scarce in 1728 (though only the most worn pieces remained) that people had to change a guinea at a loss of nearly 5 per cent. The trouble and confusion thus produced in trade and circulation obliged the Treasury to request the celebrated Sir Isaac Newton, Master, of the Tower Mint, to make a Report on the measures he thought most suitable to remedy this disorder.

a...a: R: 'se met'
b...b: R: 'lautre'
c...c: R: parentheses missing
d...d: 1756b: 'comme à 16'; R: 'Comme un a seize'
e...e: R: 'chelings'
f...f: R: '1728'
g...g: R: 'obligea'
h...h: R: 'Le Cellebre Monsieur Le Chevalier Izaac Neuton';1756b, 1769: 'le célébre Chevalier Isaac Newton'
i...i: 1769: 'un transport'

i. The correspondence between E584 and A584 is very close. D584 is a pared-down version (apart from the mention of the French situation in the first sentence, which is missing in E and A).

ii. A584 states that the official ratio of gold to silver should reflect the market rate 'taken at a Medium of thirty or forty Years' something not found in E584; A584 also has a very Cantillonian mention of 'the Luxury of the great Proprietors of Land'; and it refers to the purity of silver as 'two grains fine' where the French text has 'eleven twelfths fine'.

iii. The incorrect reference in E584 to the year 1728 also occurs in A584. Commentators since Jevons (1881 [1931: 358]) have puzzled about this date: Sir Isaac Newton's presumed subsequent involvement is impossible due to the fact that the famous man had died in March 1727 (old style 1726). This confusion of dates is hard to explain. Some commentators (Hayek [1931] 1985: n61; Brian and Théré 1997: 155 n 1) have ascribed importance to the fact that '1728' is written out in the printed text. However, the date occurs in numerals in the Rouen manuscript (V584f).

iv. Sir James Steuart (1767 III, 7, 3 p. 47) copied the incorrect date 1728 from A584. In contrast, the Prussian master of the mint Johann Philipp Graumann in his *Gesammelte Briefe von dem Gelde* (Berlin 1762) quotes E584 to E594 in German translation on pp. 114–18. On p. 115 Graumann changed 1728 to the, almost correct, year 1718. In Postlethwayt's *Dictionary* Newton's involvement is noted a little later (D586), without the controversial date. Postlethwayt also includes the full text of Newton's report (dated 21 Sept 1717) in the same entry, 'Coin', after the borrowed pages from Cantillon come to an end.

v. The odd sequence of words in the 1755 text '*le célebre le Chevalier*', changed in later editions to '*le célebre Chevalier*', may be explained by the occurrence in the manuscript '*Le Cellebre Monsieur Le Chevalier*' (V584h). The editor of the printed text may have wanted to alter the formulation "Mr Sir" by removing '*Monsieur*', but forgetting to omit the redundant second '*le*'.

584

585 |14| Il n'y avoit rien de si aisé à faire; il n'y avoit qu'à suivre dans la fabrication des especes d'argent à la Tour le prix de l'argent au Marché; & au lieu [374] que la proportion de l'or à l'argent étoit depuis long-tems par les loix & regles de la Monnoie de la Tour, comme 1 à 15 3/4, il n'y avoit qu'à fabriquer les especes d'argent plus foibles dans la proportion du Marché qui étoit tombée au-dessous de celle de 1 à 15, & pour aller au-devant de la variation que l'or du Bresil apporte annuellement dans la proportion de ces deux métaux, on auroit même pû l'établir sur le pié de 1 à 14 1/2, comme on a fait en mil sept cent vingt-cinq en France, & comme il faudra bien qu'on fasse dans la suite en Angleterre même.

‖ This might have been easily done, perhaps, if they had agreed to give silver coin that value by law, which it found at market by the agio given for it in exchange for gold; and if the ounce of standard silver, which sold for 5, 5 1/2, had been coined to pass at a proportionable price by law, having regard to avoid fractions.

‖ And in regard the same causes, which raised an agio upon silver, long subsisted, they might reasonably, for that time, have put the coin at 5 s. 6 d. by law, since it was nearly worth that at the market.

‖ In order to compass this, all that was necessary to be done, was to compare the Price of coined Silver at the Tower with that of the Market which had reduced this Proportion between Gold and Silver, as 1 is to 15, or rather as 1 is to 14 and an half. This Proportion of 1 to 14 and an half, was fixed in *France* in 1726 between Gold and Silver, and continues to this Day, and ought to be followed in *England*.

586 |15| Il est vrai qu'on pouvoit également ajuster les especes monnoïées d'Angleterre, au prix & proportion du marché, en diminuant la valeur numéraire des especes d'or, c'est le parti ᵃqui fut pris parᵃ le Chevalier New-[375]ton dans son rapport, & par le Parlement en conséquence de ce rapport. Mais c'étoit le parti le moins naturel & le plus désavantageux, comme je vais le faire comprendre. Il étoit d'abord plus naturel de hausser le prix des especes d'argent, puisque le public les avoit déja haussées au Marché, puisque l'once d'argent qui ne valoit que soixante deux deniers sterling au prix de la Tour, en valoit au-delà de soixante-cinq au Marché, & qu'on portoit hors de l'Angleterre toutes les especes blanches que la circulation n'avoit pas considérablement diminuées de poids: d'un autre côté, il étoit moins désavantageux à la Nation Angloise de hausser les especes d'argent que de baisser celles d'or, par rapport aux sommes que l'Angleterre doit à l'Etranger.

‖ But, instead of that, it was determined by Sir *Isaac Newton*'s representation to the treasury to lower gold, and in consequence guineas were reduced from 21 s. 6 d. to 21 s. This reduction did not bring the proportion near enough, and the mischief was only a little eased but not cured; and no silver for a long time was coined at the *Tower*, but some *South Sea* shillings under the old standard, which was, 'tis conceived, very necessary, and ought to have been done at first.

‖ Though the reduction of gold was not so natural, perhaps, as the raising the value of silver (or rather giving silver in coin the value it had at market) yet it would have equally answered the end of fixing the par necessary between these metals, if the reduction had been great enough. But still it would have been, as in effect it was, a disadvantage to *England*, with regard to foreigners.

‖ It is very true, that this Proportion between Gold and Silver, may be regulated in a different Manner to that which I have mentioned, that is by lowering the Denomination of Gold Coin; it is this Method which Sir *Isaac Newton* chose in his Report to the Lords of the Treasury; but I apprehend this Remedy was not so effectual, and was more disadvantageous to the Public, than that of rais-[94]ing the Denomination of Silver; it would have been more natural to have done this, as the Market Price had already done, than to have lowered that of Gold Coin, with respect to the Public's Connections with foreign Nations.

There was nothing easier. It was only necessary to follow the market price of silver in coining silver at the Tower. And whereas the ratio of gold to silver was of old time by the laws and regulations of the Tower Mint 1 to 15¾, it was only necessary to make the silver coins lighter in the proportion of the market price which had fallen below 1 to 15; and, to anticipate the variation which the gold of Brazil brings about annually in the ratio between these two metals, it might even have been possible to fix it on the footing of 1 to 14½, as was done in 1725 in France and as they will be forced later to do in England itself.

i. The correspondence **585** between E585 and A585 is very close, although E is more detailed and has the date 1725 in the last sentence, while A has 1726.
ii. The view in D585 that silver coins should have been put at 5s. 6d. is also found in E/A584.

It is true that the coinage in England might equally have been adjusted to the market price and ratio by diminishing the nominal value of gold coins. This was the policy adopted by Sir Isaac Newton in his Report, and by Parliament in consequence of this Report. But, as I shall explain, it was the least natural and the most disadvantageous policy. Firstly it was more natural to raise the price of silver coins, because the public had already done so in the market, the ounce of silver which was worth only 62d. sterling at the Mint being worth more than 65d. in the market, and all the silver money being exported except what the circulation had considerably reduced in weight. On the other hand it was less disadvantageous to the English nation to raise the silver money than to lower the gold money considering the sums which England owes the foreigner.

ᵃ...ᵃ: R: 'que prit'

The observation in D586 **586** that the reduction was from 21s. 6d. to 21s. is also made in E/A588.

587 |16| Si l'on suppose que l'Angle-[376]terre doit à l'Etranger cinq millions sterlings de capital, qui y est placé dans les fonds publics, on peut également supposer que l'Etranger a païé ce capital en or à raison de vingt-un schellings six deniers la guinée, ou bien en argent blanc à raison de soixante-cinq deniers sterlings l'once, suivant le prix du Marché.

|| Let it be supposed that *England* owed to Foreigners five Millions employed in the Funds, and it may be equally supposed that this five Millions was paid in Gold, in Proportion to the Guineas passing at twenty-one Shillings and Sixpence, or else in Silver at the Rate of five Shillings and Sixpence the Ounce.

588 |17| ᵃCesᵃ cinq millions ont par conséquent couté à l'Etranger à ᵇvingt-un schellings six deniersᵇ la guinée, quatre millions six cents cinquante & un mille cent soixante-trois guinées; mais présentement que la guinée est réduite à vingt-un schellings, il faudra païer pour ces capitaux, quatre millions sept cents soixante-un mille neuf cents quatre guinées, ce qui fera de perte pour l'Angleterre ᶜcent dix mille sept cents quarante-une guinéesᶜ, ᵈsans compterᵈ ce qu'il y aura à perdre sur les intérêts annuels qu'on paie.

|| The foreigners remitted all their money in the *English funds*, in gold or guineas at 21*s*. 6*d*. If they sent any part in silver, they had the market-price for it, 5*s*. 4*d*. to 5*d*. 1/2; and, if we suppose their capitals in the *English* funds to amount to no more, at that time, than only 5 millions sterling, they paid for them in guineas at 21*s*. 6*d*. or something equivalent, 4,651,163 guineas; and they received for them at 21*s*. 4,761,904 guineas, which was a clear loss of 110741 guineas.

|| These five Millions must consequently have stood to Foreigners at the Rate of twenty-one Shillings, and Sixpence the Guinea, four Millions, six Hundred, fifty-one Thousand, one Hundred and sixty-three Guineas; but now that the Guinea is reduced in Denomination to twenty-one Shillings, this foreign Capital of five Millions must be paid by four Millions seven Hundred, and sixty-one Thousand, nine Hundred and four Guineas, which leaves a Loss to *England* of one Hundred and ten Thousand, seven Hundred and forty-one Guineas, and that exclusive of the annual Interest of this Fund of five Millions.

589

|| If it should be objected that foreigners remitted their *funds* by *bills of exchange*, it might be answered, that would have [I, 528, col.1] been the same thing as remitting them in guineas of 21 *s*. 6*d*. since that operation would have hindered the exportation of so many guineas at 21 *s*. 6*d*. or so much silver at 5 *s*. 5 *d*. 1/2 *per* ounce: and I have taken notice of this frivolous objection, because some grave writers have used it on the like occasions.

If it is supposed that England owes the foreigner 5 millions sterling of capital, invested in the public funds, it may be equally supposed that the Foreigner paid this amount in gold at the rate of 21s. 6d. a guinea or in silver at 65d. sterling the ounce, according to the market price.

There is a slight difference **587** with regard to money value of the ounce of silver. Where A has 5s. and 6d., E has 65d. Since a shilling was 12 pence (d.), E converts to 5s. and 5d., so there is one penny difference.

These 5 millions have therefore cost the Foreigner at 21s. 6d. the guinea 4,651,163 guineas; but now that the guinea is reduced to 21s. the capital to be repaid is 4,761,904 guineas, a loss to England of 110,741 guineas, without counting the loss on the interest annually paid.

ᵃ...ᵃ: R: 'Les'
ᵇ...ᵇ: R: '21 : 6"
ᶜ...ᶜ: R: '11741'
ᵈ...ᵈ: R: 'La sans Contér'

i. D588 combines the **588** content of E587 and E588. A588 and E588 are very similar including in regard to the writing out of numbers.

ii. V588c is clearly an error: a zero is missing as the third digit. Arguably, it could easily arise if the number was dictated. It would not have been difficult for the editor of the print edition to correct the error, because he would only have had to calculate the difference between the two preceding amounts.

589

590 |18| [377] Monsieur Newton ᵃm'aᵃ dit pour réponse à cette objection, que suivant les loix fondamentales du Roïaume, l'argent blanc étoit la vraie & seule monnoie, & que comme telle, il ne la falloit pas altérer.*

|| If it should be objected, that silver is the true old money of *England* by law, and as such ought not to be altered,

[95] || This Objection was laid before Sir *Isaac Newton*, and all that he could say to it, was, that by the established Laws of this Kingdom, Silver was the only fixed Coin of the Country, and as such could not be altered.

591 |19| Il est aisé de répondre que le public aïant altéré cette loi par l'usage & le prix du Marché, elle avoit cessé d'être une loi; qu'il ne falloit pas dans ces circonstances s'y attacher scrupuleusement, au désavantage de la Nation, ᵃ& païerᵃ aux Etrangers plus qu'on ne leur devoit. Si l'on n'avoit pas regardé les especes d'or comme une monnoie véritable, l'or auroit supporté la variation, comme cela arrive en Hollande & à la Chine, où l'or est plutôt regardé comme marchandise que comme monnoie. Si l'on avoit augmenté les [378] especes d'argent au prix du Marché, sans toucher à l'or, on n'auroit pas perdu avec l'Etranger, & on auroit eu abondamment des especes d'argent dans la circulation; on en auroit fabriqué à la Tour, au lieu qu'on n'en fabriquera plus jusqu'à ce qu'on fasse un arrangement nouveau.

I answer in that case, that gold ought to have been merchandize as in *China*, and not money by law: if that had been the case in *England*, guineas would not have passed at market for above 20*s*. 8*d*. and there would have been no need of fixing any par between these metals; but, as the case stood, guineas were money at 21*s*. 6*d*. and nobody could refuse them at that price: and, as silver grew in request above the value or proportion given it by law, it is humbly submitted, whether or no a law ought not to have been made to give it that value, which the market gave it. And all laws for fixing the proportion of *gold* and *silver* were made in consequence to the market-price in all ages, for there was no other rule but the market-price whereby to find their proportion.

|| But the great Man did not, or more likely would not enter into the Consideration that this established Law was already broke in upon by the Market Price of Silver, and that therefore this Law was really of no Effect, and the Observance thereof ought not to extend its Force to the manifest Prejudice of the Public, by obliging them to pay to Foreigners more than they were really indebted to them; and if Silver had been raised in Denomination equal to the Market Price, and Gold to have remained on its old Footing, the Public would have sustained no Loss, and there would have remained great Abundance of Silver in Circulation. Until some Reformation of this Sort takes Place, Silver will not be coined, but for some temporary Parade or Shew; for, can it be expected, where the Market Price affords Five Shillings and Six-pence for the Ounce of Silver, People will carry it to the Tower, and receive but [96] five Shillings and Two-Pence for the same Ounce. Therefore, I submit it, that the Market-Price for Gold and Silver, is the only true and natural Way of settling the Proportion between these valuable Metals: this I am certain, that Experience in Commerce shews it is so; but if this is not thought proper to be done, the Guinea must be lowered to twenty Shillings, though it will be attended with this bad Consequence of doubling the Loss above-mentioned to the Public when Foreigners take their Money out of the Funds; for this Reason I cannot help thinking, that as the Market-Price for Gold and Silver is the true Rule of ascertaining its proportional Value, as also the proportional Value of all earthly Products, I say, I cannot help but being of Opinion, that if Sir *Isaac Newton* had reported that the Guinea was to remain at 21s. and 6d. and that Silver ought to have been raised in Denomination in order to bring its Proportion to Gold as one is to fourteen and a half, it had been less disadvantageous to the Public than the Method he was pleased to take, and would have prevented the Inconvenience which now actually subsists in the Public, of the Scarcity of Silver.

Newton told me in answer to this objection that according to the fundamental laws of the Kingdom silver was the true and only monetary standard and that as such it could not be altered.

ᵃ...ᵃ: illegible in the Rouen manuscript due to a small rectangular hole in the paper, that appears to have been made with the tip of an inkpen. See Figure 2.7 on p. 26.

* [in footnote:] 'Ici M. Newton sacrifia le fond & la forme' ('Here Mr. Newton sacrificed essence to form'). This note is missing in R. It is therefore possibly an addition by the editor of the print edition.

The phrase '*Monsieur Newton m'a dit*' in the printed French text suggests a personal acquaintance of Cantillon with the famous natural philosopher. Different opinions have been expressed as to the likelihood of this acquaintance (see Murphy 1986: 191). The English versions do not suggest a personal contact between Newton and the author. D590 does not even mention Newton. Of course this could be explained by efforts of Postlethwayt and Philip Cantillon to hide their plagiarism. But in addition the Rouen manuscript raises some doubt (V590a): instead of *m'a* the text may simply have read *a* (and hence the statement would be 'Newton has said...'). Who disfigured the manuscript, when and why is not clear. Cf. V593b. **590**

It is easy to answer that the public having altered this Law by custom and the price of the market it had ceased to be a law, that in these circumstances there was no need to adhere scrupulously to it to the detriment of the nation and to pay to Foreigners more than their due. If the gold coins were not considered true money, gold would have supported the variation, as in Holland and China where gold is looked upon rather as merchandise than money. If the silver coins had been raised to their market price without touching gold there would have been no loss to the Foreigner, and there would have been plenty of silver coins in circulation. They would have been coined at the Mint, whereas now no more will be coined until some new arrangement is made.

ᵃ...ᵃ: R: 'et de payer'

i. In D/A591, like in E590, the first person singular is used, which may possibly suggest a personal disagreement with someone else (Newton?). In contrast this is not the case in E591. Cf. C590. **591**

ii. After A591 the *Analysis* has a paragraph that corresponds to an extent with E229 and hence is reproduced in A229. For the same reason the subsequent paragraph is reproduced in A218 and A219. Cf. C207ii. Thereafter, from the bottom of p. 98 until the end of the chapter on p. 102, the *Analysis* still reads like something Richard Cantillon could have written but there is no direct correspondence with passages in E or D. These pages have been omitted here. The next chapter picks up a correspondence to E III, v and the *Dictionary* entry, 'Coin' and is reproduced from A595 onwards.

iii. Steuart (1767, II, 17) quotes a passage from the omitted p. 99 of the *Analysis*, citing his source.

592 |20| Par la diminution de la valeur de l'or, que le rapport de M. Newton a produit de vingt-un schellings six deniers à vingt-un schellings, l'once d'argent qui se vendoit au Marché de Londres ᵃauparavant à 65 & 65 peniques 1/2ᵃ ne se vendoit plus à la vérité qu'à soixante-quatre deniers: mais le moïen qu'il s'en fabriquât à la Tour, l'once valoit au Marché soixante-quatre, & si on ᵇle portoitᵇ à la Tour pour monnoïer, elle ne devoit plus valoir que soixante-deux; aussi n'en porte-t'on plus. On a véritablement fabriqué aux dépens [379] de la Compagnie de la Mer du Sud, quelques schellings, ou cinquiemes d'écu, en y perdant la différence du prix du Marché; mais on les a enlevés aussi-tôt qu'on les a mis en circulation; on ne verroit aujourd'hui aucune espece d'argent dans la circulation si elles étoient du poids legitime de la Tour, on ne voit dans le troc que des especes d'argent usées, & qui n'excedent point le prix du Marché dans ᶜleurᶜ poids.

593 |21| Cependant la valeur de l'argent blanc au Marché hausse ᵃtoujours insensiblementᵃ; l'once qui ne valoit que soixante-quatre après la réduction dont nous avons parlé, est encore remontée au Marché à ᵇ65ᵇ 1/2 & 66; & pour qu'on puisse avoir des especes d'argent pour la circulation & en faire fabriquer à la Tour, il faudra bien encore réduire la valeur de la guinée d'or [380] à vingt schellins au lieu de vingt-un schellins, & perdre avec l'Etranger le double de ce qu'on y a déja perdu, si on n'aime mieux suivre la voie naturelle, ᶜmettreᶜ les especes d'argent au prix du Marché. Il n'y a que le prix du Marché qui puisse trouver la proportion de la valeur de l'or à l'argent, de même que toutes les proportions des valeurs. La réduction de M. Newton de la guinée à vingt-un schellings n'a été calculée que pour empêcher qu'on n'enlevât les especes d'argent ᵈfoibles & uséesᵈ qui restent dans la circulation: elle n'étoit pas calculée pour fixer dans les monnoies d'or & d'argent la véritable proportion de leur prix, je veux dire par leur véritable proportion, celle qui est fixée par les prix du Marché. Ce prix est toujours la pierre de touche dans ces matieres; les variations en sont assez lentes, pour donner [381] le tems de regler les monnoies & empêcher les desordres dans la circulation.

594 |22| Dans certains siecles la valeur de l'argent hausse lentement contre l'or, dans d'autres, la valeur de l'or hausse contre l'argent; c'étoit le cas dans le siecle de Constantin, qui rapporta toutes les valeurs à celle de l'or comme la plus permanente; mais le plus souvent la valeur de l'argent est la plus permanente, & l'or est le plus sujet à variation.

By reducing the value of gold (brought about by Newton's Report from 21s. 6d. to 21s.) the ounce of silver which was sold in the London market before at 65 pence and 65½ pence no longer sold in truth but at 64d. But as it was coined at the Tower the ounce was valued in the market at 64d. and if it was taken to the Tower to be coined it would be worth no more than 62d. So no more is taken. A few shillings or fifths of crowns have been struck at the expense of the South Sea Company, losing the difference of the market price; but they disappeared as soon as they were put into circulation. Today no silver coins can be seen in circulation if they are of full mint weight, only coins which are worn and do not exceed in weight the market price.

a...a: 1769: 'auparavant à 65 peniques 1/2'; R: 'auparavant a 65 et 65 1/2 Peniques'
b...b: R: 'laportoit'
c...c: R: 'le'

The minting of silver **592** coins for the South Sea Company is also referred to in D586.

However the value of silver continues to rise imperceptibly in the market. The ounce which was worth only 64 after the reduction of which we have spoken has risen again to 65½ and 66 in the market; and in order to have silver coin in circulation and coined at the Tower, it will be necessary again to reduce the value of the gold guinea from 21s. to 20s. and to lose to the Foreigner double of what is lost already unless it is preferred to follow the natural course and to adjust silver coin to the market price. Only the market price can find the ratio of the value of gold and silver as of all other values. Newton's reduction of the guinea to 21s. was devised only to prevent the disappearance of the light and worn coins which remain in circulation, and not to fix in gold and silver coins the true ratio of their price, I mean by their true ratio that which is fixed by Market prices. This price is always the touchstone in these matters. Its variations are slow enough to allow time to regulate the mints and prevent disorders in the circulation.

a...a: R: 'toujours'
b...b: R: this number is illegible in the Rouen manuscript due to the damage noted in V590a which went right through the page
c...c: R: et mettre'
d...d: R:'usées et foibles'

On pp. 39 to 42 of the **593** *Analysis*, at the end of chapter XIII, a number of points are made that are reminiscent of the arguments of E592–E593. The central point of the discussion in the *Analysis* is to show 'the absolute Necessity we lie under, of lowering the Proportion between our coined Gold and Silver'. For reasons explained in C254ii, none of chapter XIII in A is reproduced here.

In some centuries the value of silver rises slowly against gold, in others the value of gold rises against silver. This was the case in the age of Constantine who reduced all values to that of gold as the more permanent; but the value of silver is generally the more permanent and gold is more subject to variation.

594

595

CHAPITRE [a]V[a].

De l'augmentation [b]*& de la diminution*[b] *de la valeur des especes monnoïées en denomination.*

[I, 526, col. 1] *Of the augmentation and diminution of* COIN *in denomination.*

[102] **CHAP. XX.**

Of the Increase and Decrease of Coin in Denomination.

596

|1| Suivant les principes que nous avons établis, les quantités d'argent qui circulent dans le [382] troc, fixent & déterminent les prix de toutes choses dans un Etat, eu égard à la vîtesse [a]ou lenteur[a] de la circulation.

‖ Under the article *Money*, I shall endeavour to shew the effects of the increase and decrease of the actual quantity of circulating money in a state; what I propose to consider, at present, is the *nominal* increase and decrease of *money*, as it hath been commonly practised in *France*.

‖ In Chapter the Sixteenth I have explained the Effect which the Increase and Decrease of Bullion produces in a trading Country, here I shall consider, that of the Increase and Decrease of Coin in Denomination, as it [103] has happened in *France*.

597

|2| Cependant nous voïons si souvent, à l'occasion des augmentations & diminutions qu'on pratique en France, des changemens & diminutions qu'on pratique en France, des changemens si étranges, qu'on pourroit s'imaginer que les prix du Marché correspondent plutôt à la valeur nominale des especes qu'a leur quantité dans le troc; a la quantité des livres tournois monnoie de compte, plutôt qu'à la quantité des marcs & des onces, & cela paroît directement opposé à nos principes.

598

‖ Let the ounce or crown of silver in *France* be at 4 livres, and then let a recoinage be made with a new stamp; let an edict be issued, ordering the new stamped ounce to pass for 5 livres in payments, while the old stamped ounce shall continue to pass but for 4 livres, and in a month or two to be [I, 526, col.2] decried and made bullion, to be received only at the mint, like other bullion, at 4 livres the ounce.

Suppose the *French* King by public Edict, commands a new Coinage, and orders that the Ounce of Silver to be coined, shall pass in Currency of Payments for a Crown of five Livres, and commands that the old Money or Ounce of Silver, shall not be received at his Mint, but at the Rate of four Livres, and that the Prices of all other Bullion shall be regulated by the same Proportion.

Higgs Translation (H)	Variations and Errata (V)	Comments (C)

Chapter V

Of the augmentation and diminution of coin in denomination

^a...^a; R: '5.^e'
^b...^b: R: 'et diminution'

D595-D621 occurs in the entry 'Coin' of the *Universal Dictionary*. This entry also contains the text reproduced in D570–D591. See C570i. **595**

According to the principles we have established the quantity of money circulating in exchange fixes and determines the price of everything in a State taking into account the rapidity or sluggishness of circulation.

^a...^a: 1756b, 1769: 'ou à la lenteur'

The earlier discussion referred to in all three texts is in the chapter that starts at E/D/A338. The reason why D596 refers to this discussion in the future tense is that Postlethwayt decided to put it in the *Dictionary* entry 'Money', which, being later in the alphabet, was published about a year and a half later than 'Coin'. Cf. C338i. **596**

597

We often see however in the increases and decreases practised in France such strange variations that it might be supposed that market prices correspond rather to the nominal value of coin than to its quantity in exchange, the quantity of livres tournois in money of account rather than the quantity of marks and ounces, which seems directly opposed to our principles.

D598–D601 and A598–D601 show clear similarities in argument and are for this reason included here. **598**

599

|| If the general ballance of trade be at this time against *France*, this disposition of the coin will prove soon ineffectual; for, as in this case there is money due to foreigners, the money-exporters will at first give 4 livres 5 sols in new money for an old crown, or for an ounce of bullion; and then 4 liv. 10, 4 liv.15, 4 liv. 17, 6, because the old coin is as good in foreign countries as the new, and so the intention of the edict for the recoinage will be null and eluded: for, although the ignorant people may at first keep to the tenor of the edict, yet, as the money-exporters offer them more for their old coin than the mint, they will sell it under the rose, or make evasive bargains against the law.

|| If the Ballance of Trade happens at this Time to be against *France*, this new Regulation will not have the Effect expected from it, because the old Crown or Ounce of Silver will intrinsically be of as much worth in the Payment of this Ballance as the new Crown; and foreign Nations where *France* is indebted, will be satisfied to receive the old Crown at the same Rate with the new Crown; an Ounce of Silver of the same Weight and Fineness being equal to another Ounce of Silver.

|| But it may happen that at the Commencement of this new Regulation some Profit will arise to the Mint from the Necessity of inland and domestic Payments, which will oblige the [104] ignorant and middling Rank of People to carry their old Money and Bullion to be coined into a new Specie: But the Merchants and Exchangers, being the Persons employed for the Payment of this Ballance due from *France*, they will give a Premium from ten to eighteen Sols in new Money, for the old; that is, they will give four Livres ten Sols to four Livres eighteen Sols, in new coined Money, for the old Coin or Bullion which is received at the Mint, but at the Rate of four Livres the Ounce; and when by these Purchases, the old Money is exhausted, and none of it to be found, these Exchangers will be obliged to export the new Coin, supposing the Ballance of Trade is and continues against *France*.

|| Therefore, in this Case, the new Regulation between new and old Money will not answer the proposed Profits of the Mint, any longer than the immediate Barter of the middling People, and their Fear of disobeying the King's Ordonnance, oblige them to it, which seldom exceeds eight or ten Months; and then the Mint (the Ballance of Trade being against *France*) hears no more of its projected Profits.

600

|| This will be the case, if the general ballance of trade be against *France* at the time of the recoinage; but, if the ballance be in favour of *France*, a good part of the old coin will be carried to the mint, according to the intention of the edict, to be recoined; for, though several money-proprietors will lock up the old species, and chuse to keep it by them without interest for a year or two, rather than lose 20 *per cent.* of their weight, yet, as there is no demand for the old species for exportation, those who do not lock it up, have no way to employ it but to carry it to the mint: all undertakers and consumers must do so for the necessary exigences of barter, and the foreigners who have money payable in *France*, having none of the new stamp, must send their bullion to the mints in *France* by their correspondents, to pay their debts.

[105] || But if *France* has his Ballance of Trade in its Favour, not only the ignorant and middling People but also the Merchant and Bankers, who carry on the Trade of Money, will carry Bullion into the Mint, there to be coined into new Specie; and the old Specie will have no Currency in Barter of Exchange, as foreign Nations are, upon this Supposition, indebted to *France*; but it must by the Nature of Things happen, that rich People will lock up their Money of old Specie, rather than lose twenty *per Cent.* by exchanging it for new Specie; that is, by selling their old Coin at four Livres the Ounce, to be paid in an Ounce of Silver which passes in Denomination for five Livres; whereas this new Coin is intrinsically and really worth no more than four Livres.

599

i. Part of the argument in D/A599 is also made in E632.

ii. The expression 'under the rose' in D599 is a translation from the Latin phrase *sub rosa* and means 'in secret'.

iii. Note the expression 'ignorant and middling Rank of People' in A599, also occurring in A600. Other references to the 'middling class' are in A25, A32 and D369. There does not seem to be an equivalent expression in E.

600

601

|| Let us suppose 10,000,000 ounces of silver of 4 livres, or 40,000,000 of livres, carried on the circulation in *Paris* before the recoinage; that 2,000,000 ounces are locked up, and that 8,000,000 ounces are gradually recoined at the mint; these 8 million, new stamped at 5 livres, will make 40,000,000 of livres in circulation, and consequently a livre will go as far now as before, though it be one fith part lighter:

|| Suppose the circulating Cash at *Paris*, before this new Regulation, was ten Millions of Ounces in Silver, and that two Millions of these ten were locked up or buried; the ten Millions, at four Livres the Ounce, will be worth forty Millions in Denomination, but two Millions of this forty is locked up; and consequently there will be a Fifth less in Cir-[106]culation, and the eight Millions remaining consists partly of old and new coined Money: yet by degrees the old Money will be coined (except the two Millions locked up) into new Specie of five Livres in Denomination, which will make forty Millions in Denomination.

|| Upon my Supposition there were forty Millions of Livres in Circulation before the new Coinage, and by this new Regulation there are forty Millions in Denomination also circulating, and as the Ballance of Trade is in Favour of *France*, the Prices of Labour, Provisions and Goods will be on the same Footing, as to Denomination, as they were before; consequently forty Millions in Denomination of Coin circulated the Trade of *Paris*, before the Augmentation, as forty Millions in Denomination carried it on afterwards; and it follows (all Things being equal) that the Livre will purchase or pass for as much in Barter as it did before this Alteration. Nevertheless, this new Coin is in real and intrinsic Value one Fifth less than the old, and there is one Fifth less or real and intrinsic Specie in Circulation, as there was two Millions of the old Coin locked up; therefore as the Ballance of Trade is in Favour of *France*, one answers the other.

602

but, if about a year after the old coin is also raised to 5 livres the ounce, and the money locked up comes into circulation, there will be then 50,000,000 of livres in circulation, though still no more than 10,000,000 of ounces of silver, and consequently commodities will be dearer in denomination, or in livres, though still of the same price as before, in weight of money.

[107] || But let it be supposed that in about a Year after this new Coinage, when it appears that no Bullion is carried to the Mint, that the old Crown is received and ordered to pass for five Livres, equal with the new, and that Bullion shall be received for Coinage at the Mint at a proportional Rate; consequently the two Millions of old Money, which was locked up, will be brought into Circulation, and will equal ten Millions of Livres in Denomination, there will then be Fifty Millions of Livres circulating, instead of forty, and the real and intrinsic Quantity of Silver in the Channels of Commerce, will equal what it was before this Alteration: It follows that the Prices of Goods and Merchandize will equal what they were at before, with regard to real and intrinsic Specie; but yet they will be one Fifth dearer in Denomination of Coin.

|| Ten Millions in Ounces of Silver conducted the Channels of Commerce, before the new Coinage, and they passed for forty Millions in Denomination, but were afterwards ordered to pass for fifty; though these fifty Millions in new Coin were really and intrinsically twenty *per Cent*. less in Value than the old Specie.

For other occurrences **601**
of the phrase 'all Things
being equal', in A601, see
C49ii.

602

603 |3| Supposons ce qui est arrivé en mil sept cent quatorze, que l'once d'argent ou l'écu ait cours pour cinq livres, & que le Roi publie un Arrêt, qui ordonne la diminution des écus tous les mois pendant vingt mois, c'est-à-dire, d'un pour cent par mois, [383] pour réduire la valeur numéraire à quatre livres au lieu de cinq livres; voïons quelles en seront naturellement les conséquences, eu égard au génie de la Nation.

|| Let us again suppose the coin to be diminished by an edict 1 sol, or 1 *per cent*. monthly for 20 months, when the ounce, or coin of 5 livres, shall be reduced to 4 livres, these will be, and commonly are, the consequences.

[108] || By these Explanations, the Effects produced in *France* by raising the Denomination of Coin are easily seen, when that Country has the Ballance of Trade in its Favour, and consequently when Money or Bullion is not sent to foreign Parts. I shall now consider the Effect produced in the Public by raising the Denomination of Coin, in consequence of several preceding Diminutions, as they have happened in *France* in these our latter Days.

604 |4| Tous ceux qui doivent de l'argent s'empresseront de le païer, pendant les diminutions, afin de n'y pas perdre : les Entrepreneurs & Marchands trouvent une grande facilité à emprunter de l'argent, cela determine les moins habiles, & les moins accrédités à augmenter leurs entreprises: ils empruntent de l'argent, à ce qu'ils croient, sans intérêt, & se chargent de marchandises au prix courant; ils en haussent même les prix par la violence de la demande qu'ils en font; les vendeurs ont de la peine à se défaire de leurs marchandises contre un argent qui doit diminuer entre leurs mains dans sa valeur numeraire: on se tourne du côté des marchandises des [384] païs étrangers, on en fait venir des quantités considérables pour la consommation de plusieurs années: tout cela fait circuler l'argent avec plus de vîtesse, tout cela hausse les prix de toutes choses, ces hauts prix empêchent l'Etranger de tirer les marchandises de France à l'ordinaire: la France garde ses propres marchandises, & en même tems ᵃtireᵃ de grandes quantités de marchandises de l'Etranger. Cette double opération est cause qu'on est obligé d'envoïer des sommes considerables d'especes dans les païs étrangers, pour païer la balance.

|| The undertakers of the foreign trade will, from the facility they find of borrowing, as they fancy, without interest, bring in large quantities of foreign commodities for the consumption of two or three years sometimes, and at high prices, so raised and enhanced by the greatness of the demand: on the other hand, the undertakers of the *French* commodities will raise the price of them, and chuse to keep their goods by them, rather than sell them for a species that diminishes monthly, unless they can raise the price in proportion to the fall of money. Thus not only the foreign commodities, but also the home commodities in *France*, rise extravagantly in their price, during the dimunitions; and this dearness of the *French* commodities makes the foreigners buy as little of them as possible.

|| When by the *French* King's Edict the circulating Coin was to receive several monthly Diminutions, Merchants and foreign Traders increased their Undertakings, and stored themselves with a superabundant Quantity of Goods, rather than, as they imagined, to suffer the Loss in the Fall of their Money in Denomination, and kept up the Prices of these Goods at a very high Rate, equal, or above the several Diminutions the Coin was ordered to bear; so that Foreigners were discouraged from dealing with them, from the high Price the Produce of *France* was raised to;

Suppose, as happened in 1714, the ounce of silver or écu is current for 5 livres and the King publishes an Arrêt which orders the lowering of the écu every month for 20 months, viz. 1 per cent. per month to reduce its nominal value to 4 livres instead of 5. Let us see will be naturally the consequences of this having regard to the spirit of the Nation.

i. While E603 names 1714 as the date when **603** diminutions happened in France, A603 refers more vaguely to 'these our latter Days'. D603 does not specify any particular historical moment.

ii. The start of the first sentence of A603 hints at a possible explanation for the different exposition in this chapter in D and A, compared to E: 'By these Explanations' suggests that first the general effects of the raising and diminution of the denominations of coins were explained (in A601–602). Next these effects are illustrated by the historical case of France, where first diminutions were ordered and subsequently an augmentation. E only has the exposition of the historical case of the diminutions in France and only discusses the effects of an augmentation in passing in E625.

All those who owe money will make haste to pay it during the diminutions so as not to lose by them. Undertakers and Merchants find it easy to borrow money, which decides the least able and the least accredited to increase their enterprise. They borrow money, as they fancy, without interest and load themselves with merchandise at current prices. They even raise prices by the violence of their demands. Vendors have difficulty in getting rid of their merchandise for money which must diminish in their hands in nominal value. They turn towards foreign merchandise and import considerable quantities of it for the consumption of several years. All this causes money to circulate more rapidly and raises the price of everything. Then high prices prevent the foreigner from taking merchandise from France as usual. France keeps her own merchandise and at the same time imports great quantities. This double operation is the reason why considerable amounts of specie must be sent abroad to pay the balance.

ᵃ...ᵃ: R: 'tire̶n̶t̶'

i. In the Rouen manuscript (V604a) the last **604** two letters are crossed out. This corrects the verb from plural to singular and this is also found in the printed text.

ii. Most of the argument of the first sentences of E604 has no counterpart in D or A; the correspondence only starts where the French text starts to consider the differences between foreign traders and home traders.

605 |5| Le prix des changes ne manque jamais d'indiquer ce désavantage. On voit communement les changes à six & dix pour cent contre la France, dans le courant des diminutions. Les personnes éclairées en France resserrent leur argent dans ces mêmes [385] tems; le Roi trouve moïen d'emprunter beaucoup d'argent sur lequel il perd volontiers les diminutions: il propose de se dédommager par une augmentation à la fin des diminutions.

|| From these two operations it is plain, that the ballance of trade ought to turn against *France*, during the time of the diminution, and 'tis remarkable, that the *exchange* with foreign places, in these circumstances, is 8 to 12 *per cent*. to the disadvantage of *France*: so violent is the demand for the exportation of money. In the mean time the *French public funds* rise in value, and the king is enabled, by the fear people have of losing by the diminution, to borrow good sums upon which he is content to lose the diminution himself; but, in order to retrieve part of that loss, he commonly makes a recoinage and augmentation, about the end of the time fixed for the diminution.

and in this Case the Ballance of Trade gradually turned against *France*, and its Money and Bullion would be exported to foreign [109] Nations; the Exchange would be by eight to twelve *per Cent*. higher than Par, from the violent Demand raised in the Public to transmit their Money Abroad, rather than suffer these projected Diminutions; and besides this Loss to *France* from the Exportation of its Specie, many of its rich Inhabitants would run the Risk of disobeying their King's ªOrdonnonceª by Locking up their Money:

606 |6| Pour cet effet on commence, après plusieurs diminutions, à resserrer l'argent dans les coffres du Roi, à reculer les paiemens, pensions & la paie des armées; dans ces circonstances, l'argent devient extrêmement rare à la fin des diminutions, tant par rapport aux sommes resserrées par le Roi & par plusieurs particuliers, que par rapport à la valeur numéraire des especes, laquelle valeur est diminuée. Les sommes envoïées chez l'Etranger contribuent ªaussi beaucoupª à la rareté de l'argent, & peu-à-peu cette rareté est cause qu'on offre les magasins de marchandises dont tous les Entrepreneurs sont chargés à cinquante & soixante pour [386] cent à meilleur marché qu'elles n'étoient du tems des premieres diminutions. La circulation tombe dans des convulsions; l'on trouve à peine assez d'argent pour envoïer au marché; plusieurs Entrepreneurs & Marchands font banqueroute, & leurs marchandises se vendent à vil prix.

|| At this juncture, the money in the king's coffers is locked up, till it can be issued in the new augmented coin. Several money-proprietors not only keep up their sums at this time, but also long after the augmentation, rather than exhange them for new money at 20 *per cent*. loss in the weight. Great sums, as we observed, have been exported in the payment of the ballance of trade, and consequently the scarcity of money in *France* at the close of the diminution, and beginning of the augmentation, is so great, that barter and trade are in perfect convulsions.

Higgs Translation (H)	Variations and Errata (V)	Comments (C)

The rate of exchange never fails to shew this disadvantage. Exchange is commonly seen at 6 and 10 per cent. against France during these diminutions. Enlightened people in France hoard their money in these times. The King finds means to borrow much money on which he willingly loses the diminution, proposing to compensate himself by an augmentation at the end of the diminution.

^a...^a: *sic*.

605

i. The remark in D605 about the balance being against France has a counterpart in E604.

ii. Note the difference in the percentage by which the exchange is said to be against France: E605 has 6 to 10 per cent and D605 and A605 have 8 to 12 per cent.

iii. Note the differences in elements of the argument: only E605 mentions the hoarding by 'enlightened people'; only D605 explains why it is easy for the king to borrow money. A605 makes no mention of the consequences for the king's finances.

With this object after several diminutions they begin to hoard money in the King's Treasury, to postpone the payments, pensions, and army pay. In these circumstances money becomes extremely rare at the end of the diminutions both by reason of the sums hoarded by the King and various individuals and by reason of the nominal value of the coin, which value is diminished. The amounts sent abroad also contribute greatly to the scarcity of money, and this scarcity gradually brings it about that the merchandise with which the Undertakers are loaded up is offered at 50 or 60 per cent. below the prices prevailing at the time of the first diminutions. Circulation falls into convulsions. Hardly enough money can be found to send to market. Many Undertakers and Merchants go bankrupt and their merchandise is sold at bargain prices.

^a...^a: R: 'aussi de beaucoup'

606

607 |7| Alors le Roi augmente ᵃderechefᵃ les especes, met ᵇl'écu neufᵇ, ou l'once d'argent de la nouvelle fabrique, à cinq livres, il commence à païer ᶜavecᶜ ces nouvelles especes les troupes & les pensions : les vieilles especes sont mises hors de la circulation, & ne sont reçues ᵈqu'à la Monnoie àᵈ plus bas prix numéraire; ᵉle Roiᵉ profite de la différence.

608 |8| Mais toutes les sommes de nouvelles especes qui sortent de la Monnoie ne rétablissent pas l'abondance d'argent dans la circulation: les sommes resserrées toujours par des particuliers, & [387] celles qu'on a envoïées dans le païs étranger, excedent de beaucoup la quantité de l'augmentation numéraire sur l'argent qui sort de la Monnoie.

609 |9| Le grand marché des marchandises en France commence à y attirer l'argent de l'Etranger, qui ᵃles trouvantᵃ à cinquante & soixante pour cent, ᵇ& àᵇ plus bas prix, envoie des matieres d'or & d'argent en France pour les acheter: par ce moïen l'Etranger qui les fait porter à la Monnoie se dédommage bien de la taxe qu'il y paie sur ces matieres: il trouve le double d'avantage sur le vil prix des marchandises qu'il achete; & la perte de la taxe de la monnoie tombe réellement sur les François dans la vente des marchandises qu'ils font à l'Etranger. Ils ont des marchandises pour la consommation de plusieurs années: ils revendent aux Hollandois, par exemple, [388] les épiceries qu'ils avoient tirées d'eux-mêmes, pour les deux tiers de ce qu'ils en avoient païé. Tout ceci se fait lentement l'Etranger ne se détermine à acheter ces marchandises de France que par rapport au grand marché; la balance du commerce qui étoit contre la France, au tems des diminutions, ᶜse tourneᶜ en sa faveur dans le tems de l'augmentation, & le Roi peut profiter de vingt pour cent ou plus sur toutes les matieres qui entrent en France, ᵈ& qui se portentᵈ à la Monnoie. Comme les Etrangers doivent à présent la balance du commerce à la France, & qu'ils n'ont point chez eux des especes de la nouvelle fabrique, il faut qu'ils fassent porter leurs matieres ᵉ&ᵉ vieilles especes à la Monnoie, pour avoir des nouvelles especes pour païer; mais cette balance de commerce que les Etrangers doivent à la France, ne provient [389] que des marchandises qu'ils en tirent à vil prix.

||'Tis not surprizing, that, in these circumstances, all commodities grow vastly cheap in *France*; they have foreign commodities for the consumption of several years, and their own commodities unexported by foreigners, and lying on their hands, are in great plenty. On the other hand, money, though lighter since the augmentation, is excessively scarce, and the king issues it out of the mint for the payment of his troops, officers, &c. barely for their sustenance. So that the increase of the money in denomination does not answer, even nominally, the diminution of it's quantity by exportation and hoarding. [I, 527, col.1] || Now the foreigners, finding the *French* commodities cheaper by 50 or 60 *per cent.* than before, will buy large quantities of them, while the *French*, on the other hand, want to buy nothing from the foreigners, and so the ballance of trade which was against *France* during the diminution, turns in it's favour about the time of the augmentation.

Then the King augments anew the coinage, settles the new écu or ounce of silver of the new issue at 5 livres, begins with this new coinage to pay the troops and the pensions. The old coinage is demonetised and received at the Mint at a lower nominal value. The King profits by the difference.

ᵃ...ᵃ: R: 'de Rechef'
ᵇ...ᵇ: R: 'Les Neuves'
ᶜ...ᶜ: R: 'dans'
ᵈ...ᵈ: R: 'a la Monnoye qua'
ᵉ...ᵉ: R: 'il'

607

But all the sums of new coinage which come from the Mint do not restore the abundance of money in circulation. The amounts kept hoarded by individuals and those sent abroad greatly exceed the nominal increase on the coinage which comes from the Mint.

608

The cheapness of merchandise in France begins to draw thither the money of the foreigner, who finding it 50 or 60 or more per cent. cheaper sends gold and silver metal to France to buy it. In this way the foreigner who sends his bullion to the Mint recoups himself easily from the tax paid there on this bullion. He finds the double advantage of the low price of the merchandise he buys, and the loss of the Mint charge falls really on the French in the sale of their merchandise to the foreigner. They have merchandise enough for several years' consumption. They resell to the Dutch, for example, the spices which they bought of them for two thirds of what they paid. All this takes place gradually, the foreigner decides to buy these merchandises from France only because of their cheapness. The balance of trade, which was against France at the time of the diminutions turns in her favour at the time of augmentation, and the King is able to profit by 20 per cent. or more on all the bullion brought into France and taken to the Mint. As Foreigners now owe a trade balance to France and have not in their country coins of the new issue they must take their bullion and coins of the old issue to the Mint to obtain new coins for payment. But this trade balance which Foreigners owe to France arises only from the merchandise which they import from it at low prices.

ᵃ...ᵃ: R: 'trouvant'
ᵇ...ᵇ: R: 'a'
ᶜ...ᶜ: R: 'a Tourné'
ᵈ...ᵈ: R: 'et se porte'
ᵉ...ᵉ: R: 'en'

609

610 |10| La France est partout la duppe de ces operations, elle paie des prix bien hauts pour les marchandises étrangeres lors des diminutions, elle les revend à vil prix lors de l'augmentation aux mêmes Etrangers: elle vend à vil prix ses propres marchandises, qu'elle avoit tenues si haut lors des diminutions, ainsi il seroit difficile que toutes les especes qui sont sorties de France lors des diminutions y puissent rentrer lors de l'augmentation.

|| And this turn, it should seem, ought to bring back into *France* the money exported, but it is to be considered, that the *French* bought the foreign goods at high prices, and now sell their goods at very low prices; and so, upon the whole of these operations, the *French* are great losers. On the contrary, the *French* undertakers bought foreign commodities for the consumption of several years, and the foreigners who fear to lose by the diminutions in their own country, do not go so far, and their undertakers and merchants only buy reasonable large quantities, without over-trading themselves by borrowing money. And thus it happens the ballance of trade against *France* is strong and violent at the time of the diminution, but the ballance, which turns in favour of *France* at the time of the augmentations, is slower and more regular. Though the new species after the augmentation is current at 20 *per cent.* above the price of the old species, and bullion at the mints in *France*; yet the foreigners will send bullion to be recoined in the *French* mints at 20 *per cent.* loss in the weight, because they have no new coin to send, and that they find the *French* commodities from 50 to 60 *per cent.* cheaper than before, out of which they can afford to lose the 20 *per cent.* tax at the mint.

From all these Effects the Coin of the Country would become very scarce, and Merchants loaded with foreign Products, as also with those of their own native Produce, consequently a gradual Decrease in their Price must follow, and many Bankruptcies among Merchants must ensue, by the Consequence of the Fall in the Price of Goods and Merchandize, with which they had superabundantly stored themselves, to avoid the Loss upon the Diminution of Coin, as was the Case in *France* in 1716, when Mr. *Law* there established his Bank. But *France* being thus overstocked with Goods, she would not require to be furnished from Abroad; but Foreigners being from this Superabundance of Merchandize enabled to purchase its Produce at very cheap Rates, they consequently would employ their Funds of Money to this Purpose, and the [110] Ballance of Trade would take its Turn again in Favour of *France.* But as this Ballance never produces its Effects but by slow and gradual Degrees (except in War-time, when by some sudden Acquisition of Wealth, always destructive to the Good of Society in general) and Money increasing by the same Progression, the Price of Goods would hold their natural Proportion therewith; and if under the Circumstances of *France*'s having the Ballance of Trade in its Favour, the Mint receiving Bullion at twenty *per Cent.* less than its real and intrinsic Value; yet the Cheapness of the Prices of Goods will force People to bring their Money to the Mint to be there coined, though at a Loss of twenty *per Cent.* which Loss is repaired to Foreigners by the Cheapness of the Prices of Merchandize;

France is all round the dupe of these operations. She pays very high prices for foreign goods during the diminutions, sells them back at very low prices at the time of the augmentation to the same foreigners, sells her own merchandise at low prices which she had kept so high during the diminutions and so it would be difficult for all the money which left France during the diminutions to come back during the augmentation.

In A610 John Law is mentioned **610** by name. Nowhere in E does this happen, even though one of the motivations for the writing of the *Essai* has been thought to be the refutation of Law's 'system'. For another mention of Law see A684 (and A624 for a reference to his policies). In Postlethwayt's 1749 publication John Law is also mentioned once. See V508a.

611

|| It has been often observed, that the *Hollanders*, who, in the time of the diminutions, sold the *French* merchants tea and spices, have had the same commodities sent back to them after the augmentation for about 2/3 of the original cost in *Holland*, and that the tax of the mint has come out of the said 2/3 sent in specie to *Paris* from *Holland*.

and even these Foreigners are enabled to purchase the Produce of their own Country (which the *French* preceding the Diminution of their Coin, overloaded themselves with) at forty to fifty *per Cent.* cheaper than what they can purchase at home.

612

|| From what has been said, it seems pretty apparent, that the king may levy a tax of 20 *per cent.* or more upon all the money carried to the mint, and that a great part is carried in at that disadvantage, when the ballance of trade is in favour of *France*. -That, if an augmentation on recoining is made after diminutions, the ballance of trade will be naturally in favour of *France*. - And that the said tax at the mint is levied at the expense of the *French* subjects only, and not of foreigners, who find the cheapness of *French* commodities an advantage, not only proportionable to the said tax, but considerably exceeding it. And experience shews, that foreigners who travel in *France*, find their account better to spend their money there, while the tax of 20 *per cent.* is levied at the mint, than when the old and the new coin are at the same price, and the ballance of trade is equal or in favour of *France*. For, in this case, all the money in *France* enters into circulation, and *enhances the price of commodities*.

|| The Affairs of *France* being thus situated, the Mint from these several Circumstances will avail itself of his Profit of twenty *per Cent.* [111] on Coinage; and the Foreigners who are indebted to *France* must pay their several Ballances in real Value of Gold and Silver, which will not be received but at the Mint Prices, and by the Courses of Exchange will be regulated by the Prices at the Mint, and not by the intrinsic Worth of Gold and Silver:

613 |11| Si on falsifie les especes de la nouvelle fabrique chez l'Etranger, comme cela arrive presque toujours, la France perd les vingt pour cent que le Roi etablit pour la taxe de la monnoie c'est autant de gagne pour l'Etranger, qui profite en outre du bas prix des Marchandises en France.

|| Nor does the tax at the mint only fall upon the *French* subjects, but it hurst them in the ballance of trade, when the new coin is counterfeited in foreign parts, and sent into *France*. For, in this case, the foreigners get 20 *per cent.* from the *French* subjects for nothing, and yet have their commodities at low and cheap prices. And so much as they get by falsifying the *French* new coin, diminishes the sum due to the *French* nation in the ballance of trade.

But this Profit of twenty *per Cent.* gained by the Mint would be attended with this very fatal Consequence, of tempting Foreigners to counterfeit the Coin of *France*, which they would certainly do to gain twenty *per Cent.* And besides, the Prices of Goods and Merchandize continuing cheap, they would avail themselves of this Advantage, as also of the Profit of twenty *per Cent.* imposed on the Public; consequently this Tax thus imposed is ruinous to the Society, tho' at first View it carries the Appearance of a Gain of twenty *per Cent.* to the Kingdom.

611

612

If coins of the new issue are
counterfeited abroad, as is
nearly always the case, France
loses the 20 per cent. which
the King has established as
the Mint charge. This is so
much gained for the Foreigner
who profits further by the
low prices of merchandise in
France.

613

614 [390] |12| Le Roi fait un profit considérable par la taxe de la monnoie, mais il en coute le triple à la France pour lui faire trouver ce profit.

615

‖ From this Reasoning it is clear to me, that when the Denomination of Coins are once well and proportionally fixed, all Rises and Falls are ruinous Schemes to the State; and though the King may at times profit thereby, yet it is a Profit gained at the Expence of his Kingdoms, and that of his Subjects, it is a Gain beneath his Dignity and that of the Reputa-[112]tion of his State; Experience shewing such Alterations productive of infinite Confusion to the Individuals of the Society, and is accompanied with the Dishonour of impressing a Prince's Effigy on a counterfeit Coin, besides a Breach of Faith, in calling a Thing what it is not.

616

‖ 'Tis easy to conceive, that while the ballance is due to *France*, and the tax of 20 *per cent.* levied at the mint, the rule of *foreign exchange* with *France*, must be taken from the par of the price of bullion at the mints in France, ounce for ounce, and not ounce for ounce of new coin; this tax, being a force and restraint on trade for the time it is practicable , makes an exception to the *rule of exchanges* we have laid down elsewhere in one respect; though, as an ounce of silver in bullion or old specie is worth in *France* so much at that time, an ounce, sent from a foreign country thither, will be just worth the same, and the exchange will be fixed upon that par, and consequently the *rule of exchanges*, laid down in this work, will stand universally true. See the articles BALLANCE *of Trade*, CASH, CIRCULATION, EXCHANGE, MONEY.

The King makes a considerable profit by the Mint tax, but it costs France three times as much to enable him to make this profit.

614

The next two pages after A615 in the **615** *Analysis* (most of 112 up to the top of 114) do not have counterparts in E or D. There are references to the opinions of Sir Robert Cotton (1570–1631) and Pope Innocent II (1130–43) against altering the denomination of coin. On p. 114 chapter XX concludes. The next chapter (bottom half of p. 114 to p. 118) corresponds to E I, xii, 1–10 and is reproduced in A106–A117.

All entries referred to at the end of **616** D616, apart from 'Exchange' contain fragments taken from Cantillon. For 'Ballance of Trade' (I, 184–89) see D490–D558; for 'Cash' (I, 461–64) see D255–D295; for 'Circulation' (I, 498–99) see D118–D134 and D299–D317; for 'Money' (II, 282–84) see D338–D384. The long entry 'Exchange' (I, 741–50) is a typical patchwork of acknowledged and unacknowledged extracts from British and French authorities. The passages that read most like Cantillon are in a subsection with the title 'Of Exchange in a Political Light' (I, 741 col, 2 to 743 col. 1.), but since no passages have been found that closely correspond to ones in E or A, none of this is included here.

617 || However, the mischief of this restraint of trade, as we have observed, falls wholly upon *France*; it is must surprize every one, who maturely considers the matter, to hear, that even a minister of the finances in *France* should alledge, that this tax was a mighty advantage *France* maintained against foreigners, who were forced to pay 120 ounces for every 100 ounces they owed in *France*: and suppose it might be continued as long as the *French* government thought fit.

618 || But, if the inductions we have made were not sufficient to prove the mistake of these notions, it would be sufficient to prove the error in the first of them, from this single fact; That *France* is always lower and in greater distress at the times it makes that seeming advantage by foreign trade, than at any other time, all other circumstances being equal.

619 || Now it seems to be a matter of surprize, that whereas the augmentations and diminutions in *France* were so constantly practised for above 30 years, and that *France* lost considerably in all these operations, as has been explained; and that many other ways of levying money for the king would be less prejudicial to the subject; I say, it seems surprizing, [I, 527, col.2] that the effects of these operations have not proved more fatal to *France* than they have appeared to be.

620 || But it is to be observed, that the bankruptcies in *France* occasioned by the diminutions, whereby foreigners have often lost greatly, have frequently saved *France* very large sums: nothing clears a ballance due to foreign nations faster, than the bankruptcy of the undertakers and dealers concerned in it. In the year 1715, there were 19 foreign dealers in 20 broke in *France*. Of 27 dealers for foreign parts in the little city of *Rochelle*, 24 were broke in that year. And, of about 200 bankers at *Paris*, not above three or four stood it. After the *South Sea* frenzy in *England*, the bankruptcies saved the nation above four million of ounces, which otherwise must have been made good to foreigners.

621 || But this is a very sorry way of clearing the ballance of trade, and 'tis apparent upon the whole, that the diminutions and augmentations in *France*, not only contribute to the impoverishing the kingdom, but keep it commonly under great uneasinesses, difficulties, and distractions.

It is unclear who the 'minister of **617** the finances in France' mentioned in D617 was. It may be a reference to John Law who was *contrôleur général des finances* for some months in 1720, but it may also be one of his predecessors or successors.

For other occurrences of the **618** phrase 'all other circumstances being equal' and similar phrases, see C49ii.

619

620

In the entry 'Coin' D621 is **621** immediately followed by the fragment reproduced in D570–D591. Cf. C570i.

622 |13| On comprend bien que dans les tems qu'il y a une balance courante de commerce en faveur de la France contre les Etrangers, le Roi est en état de tirer une taxe de vingt pour cent ou plus, par une nouvelle fabrication d'especes & par une augmentation de leur valeur numéraire. Mais si la balance du commerce étoit contre la France, lors de cette nouvelle fabrication, & augmentation, elle n'auroit pas ᵃdeᵃ succès, & le Roi n'en tireroit pas un grand profit: ᵇla raisonᵇ est que dans ces circonstances, on est obligé d'envoïer constamment de l'argent chez l'Etranger. Or l'écu vieux est aussi bon dans les païs étrangers que ᶜl'écu de la nouvelle fabriqueᶜ: cela étant les [391] Juifs ᵈ&ᵈ Banquiers donneront une prime ou bénéfice entre quatre yeux pour les vieilles especes, & le particulier qui les peut vendre au dessus du prix de la Monnoie ᵉne les y portera pasᵉ. On ne lui donne à la Monnoie qu'environ quatre livres de son écu, mais le Banquier lui en donnera d'abord quatre livres cinq sols & puis quatre livres dix, & finalement quatre livres quinze: voila comment il peut arriver qu'une augmentation des especes manque de succès; cela ne peut guere arriver lorsqu'on fait l'augmentation après des diminutions indiquées, parcequ'alors la balance se tourne naturellement en faveur de la France, de la maniere que nous l'avons expliqué.

623 |14| L'expérience de l'augmentation de l'année 1726, peut servir à confirmer tout ceci, les diminutions qui avoient précédé cette augmentation furent faites [392] tout-d'un-coup sans avoir été indiquées, cela empêcha les opérations ordinaires des diminutions, cela empêcha que la balance du commerce ne se tournât fortement en faveur de la France lors de l'augmentation de l'année 1726, aussi peu de personnes porterent leurs vieilles especes à la Monnoie, & on fut obligé d'abandonner le profit de la taxe qu'on avoit en vue.

624 |15| Il n'est pas de mon sujet d'expliquer les raisons des Ministres pour diminuer les especes tout-d'un-coup, ni celles qui les tromperent dans le projet de l'augmentation de l'année 1726; je n'ai voulu parler des augmentations & diminutions en France que parceque les effets qui en résultent quelquefois ᵃsemblentᵃ combattre les principes que j'ai établis, que l'abondance ou la rareté de l'argent dans un Etat, hausse ᵇouᵇ baisse les prix de toutes choses à proportion.

It is well understood that when there is a current balance of trade in favour of France against the foreigner the King is able to raise a tax of 20 per cent. or more by a new coinage and an increase in the nominal value of coins. But if the trade balance was against France at the time of this new coinage and augmentation the operation would have no success and the King would not derive a great profit from it. The reason is that in this case it is necessary to send money continually abroad. But the old écu is as good in foreign countries as the new. That being so the Jews and Bankers will give a premium or bonus in secret for the old coins and the individual who can sell them above the Mint price will not take them thither. At the Mint they give him only about 4 livres for his écu, but the Banker will give him at first 4 livres 5 sols, and then 4 livres 10, and at last 4 livres 15. And this is how it may happen that an augmentation of the coinage may lack success. It can hardly happen when the raising is made after the lowerings indicated, because then the balance naturally turns in favour of France, as we have explained.

The experience of the augmentation of 1726 may serve to confirm all this. The diminutions which had preceded this augmentation were made suddenly without warning, which prevented the ordinary operations of diminutions. This prevented the trade balance from turning strongly in favour of France at the augmentation of 1726, few people took their old coin to the Mint, and the profit of the Mint tax which was in view had to be abandoned.

It is not within my subject to explain the reasons of Ministers for lowering the coinage suddenly nor the reasons which deceived them in their project of the augmentation of 1726. I have mentioned the increases and decreases in France only because their results seem sometimes to clash with the principles I have established that abundance or scarcity of money in a State raises or lowers all prices proportionably.

[a]...[a]: R: 'le'
[b]...[b]: 1756b, 1769: 'la raison en est'
[c]...[c]: R: 'Lecu Neuf de la Nouvelle fabrique'
[d]...[d]: R: 'ou'
[e]...[e]: R: 'ne les portera pas a Cette monnoye'

[a]...[a]: R: 'semble'
[b]...[b]: R: 'Et'

Cf. the remark about a 'tax of 20 per cent' with a similar statement in D617.   **622**

623

The criticism of French ministers in E624 is more muted than the more explicit discussion of the harm done by the lowering and raising of denominations of coin in D617–D621.   **624**

459

625   [393] |16| Après avoir expliqué les effets des diminutions & augmentations des especes, pratiquées en France, Je soutiens qu'elles ne détruisent ni n'affoiblissent mes principes car si l'on me dit que ce qui coutoit vingt livres ou cinq onces d'argent avant les diminutions indiquées, ne coute pas même quatre onces ou vingt livres de la nouvelle fabrique lors de l'augmentation; ᵃj'enᵃ conviendrai sans m'écarter de mes principes, parcequ'il y a moins d'argent dans la circulation qu'il n'y en avoit avant les diminutions, comme je l'ai expliqué. L'embarras du troc dans les tems & opérations dont nous parlons, cause des variations dans les prix des choses, & dans celui de l'intérêt de l'argent qu'on ne sauroit prendre pour regle dans les principes ordinaires de la circulation ᵇ& duᵇ troc.

626 |17| Le changement de la valeur [394] numéraire des especes a été dans tous les tems l'effet de quelque misere ou disette dans l'Etat, ou bien celui de l'ambition de quelque Prince ou Particulier. L'an de Rome 157, Solon augmenta la valeur numéraire des drachmes d'Athênes, après une sédition, & abolition des dettes. Entre l'an 490 & 512 de Rome, la République Romaine augmenta par plusieurs fois la valeur numéraire de ses monnoies de cuivre, de façon que leur as est venu à en valoir six. Le pretexte étoit de subvenir aux besoins de l'Etat, & d'en païer les dettes, accrues par la premiere guerre Punique: cela ne laissa pas de causer bien de la confusion. L'an 663, Livius Drusus, Tribun du peuple, augmenta la valeur numéraire des especes d'argent d'un huitieme, en affoiblissant leur titre d'autant: ce qui donna lieu aux Faux-monnoïeurs de mettre la confu-[395]sion dans le troc. L'an 712, Marc Antoine dans son Triumvirat, augmenta la valeur numéraire de l'argent, de cinq pour cent, pour subvenir aux besoins du Triumvirat, en ᵃmettantᵃ du fer avec l'argent. Plusieurs Empereurs dans la suite ont affoibli ou augmenté la valeur numéraire des especes: les Rois de France en ont fait autant en différens tems; & ᵇc'est ce qui est causeᵇ que la livre tournois, qui valoit ᶜordinairementᶜ une livre pesant d'argent, est venue à si peu de valeur. Cela n'a jamais manqué de causer du désordre dans les Etats: il importe peu ᵈou point du toutᵈ quelle soit la valeur numéraire des especes, pourvû qu'elle soit permanente: la pistole d'Espagne vaut neuf livres ou florins en Hollande, environ dix-huit livres en France, trente-sept livres dix sols à Venise, cinquante livres à Parme: on [396] échange dans la même proportion les valeurs entre ces différens païs. Le prix de toutes choses augmente insensiblement lorsque ᵉla valeur numéraire des especes augmenteᵉ, & la quantité actuelle en poids & titre des especes, eu égard à la vîtesse de la circulation, est la base & la regle des valeurs. Un Etat ne gagne ni ne perd par l'augmentation ou diminution de ces especes, pendant ᶠqu'ilᶠ en conserve la même quantité, quoique les particuliers puissent gagner ou perdre par la variation, suivant leurs engagemens. Tous les peuples sont remplis de faux préjugés & de fausses idées sur la valeur numéraire de leurs especes. Nous avons fait voir dans le chapitre des changes que la regle constante en est ᵍle prix & le titreᵍ des especes courantes des différens païs, marc pour marc, & once pour once: si une aug-[397]mentation ou diminution de la valeur numéraire change pour quelque tems cette regle en France, ce n'est que ʰpendantʰ un état de crise & de gêne dans le commerce : on revient toujours peu-à-peu à l'intrinseque; on y vient nécessairement dans les prix du marché autant que dans les changes avec l'Etranger.

After explaining the effects of lowering and raising the coinage, as practised in France, I maintain that they neither destroy nor weaken my principles, for if I am told that what cost 20 livres or 5 ounces of silver before the lowering referred to does not even cost 4 ounces or 20 livres of the new money after the augmentation, I will assent to this without departing from my principles, because there is less money in circulation than there was before the diminutions, as I have explained. The difficulties of exchange in the times and operations of which we speak cause variations in the prices of things and in that of the interest of money which cannot be taken as a rule in the ordinary principles of circulation and dealing.

The change in the nominal value of money has at all times been the effect of some disaster or scarcity in the State, or of the ambition of some Prince or individual. In the year A.U.C. 157 Solon increased the nominal value of the drachma of Athens after a sedition and abolition of debt. Between A.U.C. 490 and 512 the Roman Republic several times increased the nominal value of its copper coins, so that their as came to be worth six. The pretext was to provide for the needs of the State and to pay the debts incurred in the first Punic War. This did not fail to cause great confusion. In 663 Livius Drusus, Tribune of the people, increased the nominal value of silver coins by one eighth, lowering their fineness by that amount, and this gave occasion to introduce confusion into exchange. In A.U.C. 712 Mark Antony in his Triumvirate increased the nominal value of silver by 5 per cent., mixing iron with the silver, to meet the needs of the Triumvirate. Many Emperors subsequently debased or increased the nominal value of the coinage. The Kings of France at different times have done likewise. This is why the livre tournois, which was worth a pound weight of silver has sunk to so little value. These proceedings have never failed to cause disorder in States. It matters little or nothing what is the nominal value of coins provided it be permanent. The pistole of Spain is worth 9 livres or florins in Holland, about 18 livres in France, 37 livres 10 sols at Venice, 50 livres at Parma. In the same proportion values are exchanged between these different countries. The price of everything increases gradually when the nominal valne of coins increases, and the actual quantity in weight and fineness of the coins, taking into account the rapidity of circulation, is the base and regulator of values. A State neither gains nor loses by the raising or lowering of these coins so long as it keeps the same quantity of them, though individuals may gain or lose by the variation according to their engagements. All people are full of false prejudice and false ideas as to the nominal value of their coinage. We have shewn in the Chapter on Exchanges that the invariable rule of them is the price and fineness of the current coins of different countries, marc for marc and ounce for ounce. If a raising or lowering of the nominal value changes this rule for a time in France it is only during a crisis and difficulty in trade. A return is always made little by little to intrinsic value, to which prices are necessarily brought both in the market and in the foreign exchanges.

ᵃ...ᵃ: R: 'J'y'
ᵇ...ᵇ: R: 'du'

625

ᵃ...ᵃ: R: 'meslant'
ᵇ...ᵇ: R: 'Cest Ce qui Cause'
ᶜ...ᶜ: R: 'originairement'
ᵈ...ᵈ: R: 'ou il nimporte point'
ᵉ...ᵉ: R: 'la valeur numeraire augmente'
ᶠ...ᶠ: R: 'quelle'
ᵍ...ᵍ: R: 'Le prix et titre'
ʰ...ʰ: R: 'durant'

626

627

CHAPITRE ^aVI^a.

Des Banques, & de leur crédit.

[I, 195, col. 2] *Further REMARKS on BANKING*

[169] **CHAP. XXIV.**

Of Bankers and Banks.

628 |1| Si cent Seigneurs ou Propriétaires de terre, œconomes, qui amassent annuellement de l'argent par leurs épargnes pour en acheter des terres dans les occasions, déposent chacun ^adix mille^a onces d'argent entre les mains d'un Orfévre ou Banquier de Londres, pour n'avoir pas l'embarras de garder cet argent [398] chez eux, ^b&^b pour prévenir les vols qu'on leur en pourroit faire, ils en tireront des billets païables à volonté, souvent ils le laisseront là long-tems, & lors même qu'ils auront fait quelque achat, ils avertiront ^cbeaucoup de tems d'avance le Banquier^c de leur tenir leur argent prêt ^ddans l'intervalle des délais^d des consultations & écritures de Justice.

|| Let us suppose a goldsmith, or a banker, sets up for keeping people's cash for them upon notes, payable on demand; if an hundred gentlemen, or land-proprietors, who keep a provision by them of money, lodge it in such banker's hands, and take out such part of it as they occasionally require, but replace it when their rents come in:

|| If one hundred Gentlemen, whose Property lies in Land, deposit 2500 l. each in a Goldsmith's Hands, and take each of them Credit in his Books, or else take his Cash-Notes payable, or accountable on Demand, in order that their Money may be ready at a Call to answer their Purpose, of laying it out on a Mortgage, or in the Purchase of Land; the Consequence would generally be, that this Money would remain with the Banker for Months, nay, sometimes for Years, waiting the Opportunity for such Purchases, &c. and even when this Money was wanted, many of these Gentlemen would give Notice to the Banker to have their Money ready by such and such a Time, as it must be paid away for the Purchase of a Landed Estate, or laid out upon a Mortgage, as soon as the Title is approved of by Counsel, and the Conveyance properly prepared.

Chapter VI

Of Banks and their Credit

^a...^a: R: '6^e'

i. D occurs as part of the entry 'Banking', **627**
Universal Dictionary (I, 193–197), first
published in issue 17, which appeared in
February or March 1752.

ii. Chapter XXIV in A, pp. 169–94,
contains various passages that correspond
to parts of the last three chapters of E. Pp.
169–76 largely correspond to E, III, vi
(reproduced in A627–A641). Thereafter the
order is jumbled: pp. 176–82 correspond to
parts of E III, viii (A675–A684); and pp.
182–86 correspond to parts of E III, vii,
but in a changed order within the chapter
(A656, A664–A671, A643, A651–A653).
See also C653.

If a hundred economical
gentlemen or Proprietors of Land,
who put by every year money
from their savings to buy Land on
occasion, deposit each one 10,000
ounces of silver with a Goldsmith
or Banker in London, to avoid the
trouble of keeping this money in
their houses and the thefts which
might be made of it, they will
take from them notes payable on
demand. Often they will leave
their money there a long time, and
even when they have made some
purchase they will give notice to
the Banker some time in advance
to have their money ready when the
formalities and legal documents
are complete.

^a...^a: R: 'Mille'
^b...^b: R: 'ou'
^c...^c: R: 'le Banquiér
Longtemp d'avance'
^d...^d: R: 'pendant les
delais'

i. There appears to be a basic error in **628**
E628 with regard to the amount that each
gentleman deposits: in the first sentence of
E629 the total deposits with the bank are
assumed to be 100,000 (a figure also found
in D629 and D631). To obtain this figure
one hundred individuals would have to
deposit only 1,000 each. This is the amount
found in R (V630a), which suggests that
the editor of the 1755 print edition made
this alteration.

ii. The correspondence between E628
and A628 is the greatest, with A providing
most detail. D628 is more pared down.
Only E628 (and E629) mentions London
as the place where the banker is supposed
to reside.

629 |2| Dans ces circonstances le Banquier pourra prêter souvent ᵃquatre vingt-dixᵃ mille onces d'argent ᵇ(des cent mille qu'il doit)ᵇ pendant toute l'année, & n'aura pas besoin de garder en caisse plus de dix mille onces ᶜpour faire face à tout ce qu'on pourra lui redemander: il a affaire à des personnes opulentes & œconomes, à mesure qu'on lui demande mille oncesᶜ d'un côté, on lui apporte ordinairement mille onces d'un autre côté: il lui suffit pour l'ordinaire de [399] garder en caisse la dixieme partie de ce qu'on lui a confié. On en a eu quelques exemples & experiences dans Londres, & cela fait qu'au lieu que les particuliers en question garderoient en caisse pendant toute l'année la plus grande partie des cent mille onces, l'usage de ᵈleᵈ déposer entre les mains d'un Banquier fait que quatre vingt-dix mille onces des cent mille sont d'abord mises en circulation. Voilà ᵉpremierementᵉ l'idée qu'on peut former de l'utilité de ces sortes de banques; les Banquiers ou Orfévres contribuent à accélérer la circulation de l'argent, ils le mettent à interêt à leurs risques & périls, & cependant ils sont ou doivent être toujours prêts à païer leurs billets à volonté & à la présentation.

630 |3| Si un particulier a mille onces à païer à un autre, il lui donnera en paiement le billet du Banquier [400] pour cette somme: cet autre n'ira pas peut-être demander l'argent au Banquier; il gardera le billet & le donnera dans l'occasion à un troisieme en paiement, & ce billet pourra passer dans plusieurs mains dans les gros paiemens, sans qu'on en aille de long-tems demander l'argent au Banquier: il n'y aura que quelqu'un qui n'y a pas une parfaite confiance, ou quelqu'un qui a plusieurs petites sommes à païer qui en demandera le montant. Dans ce premier exemple la caisse d'un Banquier ne fait que la dixieme partie de son commerce.

if these sums amount to 100,000 ounces of silver, it may happen that not above 10,000 ounces of the whole money shall be wanted, or called for out of the goldsmith's hands during the whole year; and, if he has credit enough to raise money upon exigencies, he may commonly venture to lend out at interest 90,000 ounces all the year round, and not keep above one tenth part of the sums he gave his notes for, in his hands, to answer the calls upon him: by which means 90,000 ounces, which would otherwise have been kept up during the year, will circulate in traffic.

|| In this Instance, this Goldsmith or Banker may employ at his own Risk and for his own Account, two hundred and twenty-five thou-[170]sand Pounds (of the two hundred and fifty thousand Pounds deposited with him) and not keep by him in Cash more than twenty-five thousand Pounds; by which, with his own Credit, he could answer the Calls of his Customers. It generally happens, if one thousand Pounds are called for, an equal Sum is brought into him: Experience therefore shews, that the tenth Part of the Money deposited, and the well-established Credit of such a Banker, will circulate the total Amount of all his Deposits.

|| If these hundred Gentlemen were their own Cashiers, and locked up their Money, these two hundred and fifty-thousand Pounds would be dead to the Society: But this Method of employing Bankers brings Money into the Channels of Circulation, and is one of the first striking Ideas of the supposed Advantage the Public reaps from Banks or Bankers, who contribute to the Circulation of Money; yet they must, or at least to be always prepared to discharge their Notes on Demand.

|| If a Gentleman has one thousand Pounds to pay, he often discharges this Debt by his Banker's Note or Notes; it frequently hap-[171]pens, that the Person who received this thousand Pounds, being well acquainted with the Credit of the Shop, from whence it was issued, is satisfied to keep these Notes by him till he pays them away to other Persons; and these Notes may circulate from Hand to Hand for many Months, without their Cash's being demanded. It is remarked in *Paris*, by the Bankers, who have large Sums of Money to pay, and where Paper does not circulate to do the Offices of Money, that one and the same Bag of Money has been brought into them four or five Times in the Course of one Day: Bags containing one thousand Livres, pass from Hand to Hand with a Label fixed to them, without telling, upon the Faith and Credit of the Shop or Compting-House, from whence they were first issued.

Higgs Translation (H)	Variations and Errata (V)	Comments (C)

In these circumstances the Banker will often be able to lend 90,000 ounces of the 100,000 he owes throughout the year and will only need to keep in hand 10,000 ounces to meet all the withdrawals. He has to do with wealthy and economical persons; as fast as one thousand ounces are demanded of him in one direction, a thousand are brought to him from another. It is enough as a rule for him to keep in hand the tenth part of his deposits. There have been examples and experiences of this in London. Instead of the individuals in question keeping in hand all the year round the greatest part of 100,000 ounces the custom of depositing it with a Banker causes 90,000 ounces of the 100,000 to be put into circulation. This is primarily the idea one can form of the utility of banks of this sort. The Bankers or Goldsmiths contribute to accelerate the circulation of money. They lend it out at interest at their own risk and peril, and yet they are or ought to be always ready to cash their notes when desired on demand.

ᵃ…ᵃ: R: 'neuf' replaced with 'quatre vingt dix'
ᵇ…ᵇ: R: parentheses missing
ᶜ…ᶜ: missing in R
ᵈ…ᵈ: R: 'les'
ᵉ…ᵉ: R: 'dabord'

629
i. Despite the correspondence between E629 and D629 with regard to the figures used, the correspondence between E629 and A629 is much stronger. The only substantial point missing from A629, present in E629 and D629, is the observation that the bankers lend out the deposits at an interest.

ii. Note that E629 and A629 have parentheses in corresponding places, while these are missing from R (V629c). Also the missing phrase from R (V629d) appears to have a counterpart in A629. Both cases throw some doubt on the hypothesis that R was source text for E. For a similar case, see C114 and see Introduction p. 14.

If an individual has 1000 ounces to pay to another he will give him in payment the Banker's note for that amount. This other will perhaps not go and demand the money of the Banker. He will keep the note and give it on occasion to a third person in payment, and this note may pass through several hands in large payments without any one going for a long time to demand the money from the Banker. It will be only some one who has not complete confidence or has several small sums to pay who will demand the amount of it. In this first example the cash of a Banker is only the tenth part of his trade.

630
The observation in A630 that bags of money circulate amongst bankers in Paris is also made in E529 and in E659.

631 |4| Si cent Particuliers, ou Propriétaires de terres, déposent chez un Banquier leur revenu tous les six mois, à mesure qu'ils en sont païés, & ensuite redemandent leur argent à mesure qu'ils ont besoin de le dépenser, le Banquier sera en état de prê-[401]ter beaucoup plus de l'argent qu'il doit & reçoit au commencement des semestres, pour un court terme de quelques mois, qu'il ne le sera vers la fin de ᵃces semestresᵃ: & son experience de la conduite de ses Chalans lui apprendra qu'il ne peut guere prêter pendant toute l'année, sur les sommes qu'il doit, qu'environ la moitié. Ces sortes de Banquiers seront ruinés de crédit s'ils ᵇmanquentᵇ d'un instant à païer leurs billets à là premiere présentation; & lorsqu'il leur manque des fonds en caisse, ils donneroient toutes choses pour avoir promptement de l'argent, c'est-à-dire beaucoup plus d'interêt qu'ils ne tirent des sommes qu'ils ont prêtées. Cela fait qu'ils se reglent sur leur expérience pour garder en caisse de quoi faire ᶜtoujours faceᶜ, & plutôt plus que moins; ainsi plusieurs Banquiers de cette espece, (& [402] c'est le plus grand nombre) gardent toujours en caisse la moitié des sommes qu'on dépose chez eux, & prêtent l'autre moitié à ᵈinterêtᵈ & le mettent en circulation. Dans ce second exemple, le Banquier fait circuler ᵉsesᵉ billets de cent mille onces ou écus avec cinquante mille écus.

|| If an hundred gentlemen put all their rents, as they receive them, into a goldsmith's hand, and only draw weekly for the common expences of their families; and if the sums amount to 100,000 ounces of silver *per* quarter; the goldsmith will be able to lend out more money for a short time in the beginning of the quarter, than towards the end of it; and he can only afford to lend out for the whole year so much as he finds by experience is left in his hands at the end of every quarter.

|| If one hundred Persons, Gentlemen of Estates, order their half-yearly Rents to be paid as they become due to their Banker, and call for Money as their Calls for spending it require; this Banker, at the Beginning of these half-yearly Payments, will be able to lend for a short Term of three or four Months, more than he would at the Expiration of six Months; his Experience, from the Manner [172] of Living of his Customers, teaches him for what Time, in Prudence to his Credit, and upon what Security, he ought to lend his Money, so as he may be always ready to discharge his Notes on Demand. In this Instance, where Money is deposited, to be called for as People's Expences require; I think, a prudent Banker ought not to make use of more than one half of the Amount of all the Cash deposited with him. A Put-off for Money in a Banker's Hours of Payment would destroy his Credit, and bring a Run upon him from all Quarters; their Prudence and Experience must be their Guide, to employ their Money in that Way, as to have it convertable into Cash, in order to answer all Calls payable on Demand. This Experience also has shewn, that Bankers, with whom Money is deposited, in this Instance of being liable to be called for, as People's Occasion for spending it requires, ought always to have in Cash, half the Amount of what is deposited with them, to answer the daily Calls of their Employers; and in this Case, if two hundred and fifty thousand Pounds is the Amount of their Deposits, one hundred and twenty-five thousand Pounds in Cash, and the Credit of their Notes, will circulate the total Amount of their [173] Deposit of two hundred and fifty thousand Pounds.

Higgs Translation (H)	Variations and Errata (V)	Comments (C)

If 100 individuals or Landowners deposit with a Banker their income every six months as it is received, and then demand their money back as and when they have need to spend it, the Banker will be in a position to lend much more of the money which he owes and receives at the beginning of the half years, for a short term of some months, than he will be towards the end of these periods. And his experience of the conduct of his clients will teach him that he can hardly lend during the whole year more than about one half of the sums which he owes. Bankers of this kind will be ruined in credit if they fail for one instant to pay their notes on their first presentation, and when they are short of cash in hand they will give anything to have money at once, that is to say a much higher interest than they receive on the sums they have lent. Hence they make it a rule based on their experience to keep always in hand enough to meet demands, and rather more than less. Many Bankers of this kind (and they are the greatest number) always keep in hand half the amount deposited with them and lend the other half at interest and put it into circulation. In this second example the Banker causes his notes of 100,000 ounces or écus to circulate with 50,000 écus.

ᵃ...ᵃ: 1769: 'ses semestres'
ᵇ...ᵇ: R: 'manque'
ᶜ...ᶜ: R: 'face Toujours'
ᵈ...ᵈ: R: 'in˜ts'
ᵉ...ᵉ: R: 'Ces'

i. E631 and A631 mention twice-yearly payments of rent, while D631 has quarterly payments. In other details, too, the correspondence between E631 and A631 is greater.

ii. Note the description in A631 of a run on a bank. Cf. the discussion in E/A679–E/A681.

631

632 |5| S'il a un grand courant de dépôts & un grand crédit, cela augmente la confiance qu'on a en ses billets, & fait qu'on s'empresse moins à en demander le paiement; mais cela ne retarde ses paiemens que de quelques jours ou semaines, lorsqu'ils tombent entre les mains de personnes qui n'ont pas coutume de se servir de lui, & il doit toujours se regler sur ceux qui sont dans l'habitude de lui confier leur argent: si ses billets tombent entre les mains de ceux de son métier, ils n'auront rien de plus pressé que d'en retirer l'argent.

|| The Cash for Bankers Notes of undoubted Capitals and Credit, such as a *Child*, a *Hoare*, and a *Colebrook*, is but rarely called for; but if these Notes happen to fall into People's Hands who are not their Customers, their Payment is immediately demanded. The prudent Banker regulates his Conduct by the Practice of such who make use of his Shop: If his Notes fall into his Brethren's, or into the Hands of a Bank, such as that of *England*, nothing will be more pressing than they will be for their Cash.

633 [403] |6| Si les personnes qui déposent ᵃde l'argentᵃ chez le Banquier sont des Entrepreneurs & Négocians, qui y mettent journellement de grosses sommes, & bientôt après les redemandent, il arrivera souvent que si le Banquier détourne plus du tiers de sa caisse il se trouvera embarrassé à faire face.

|| If the persons who keep money in the goldsmith's hands are undertakers, or dealers in business, who commonly put in large sums, and as commonly draw them soon out of his hands, to answer the demands of their business; such goldsmith will often find, that, if he lends two-thirds of his cash, the demands upon him will exceed the one-third he has in his hands; and so he must hastily re-borrow money at disadvantage, to answer those calls; and, therefore, experience will shew him that he cannot prudently venture to lend out above one half of the cash, for which he has given his notes.

|| That Banker or Goldsmith who carries on his Trade or Business with the Cash of Merchants or other Persons, Adventurers in Trade and Business, and where Money is daily paid in and taken out, will find himself under Difficulties, if he makes use of more than one Third of the whole Amount of his Deposits.

634 |7| Il est aisé de comprendre par ces inductions, que les sommes d'argent qu'un Orfévre ou Banquier ᵃpeutᵃ prêter à interêt, ou détourner de sa caisse, sont naturellement proportionnées à la pratique ᵇ& conduiteᵇ de ses Chalans: que pendant qu'il s'est vu des Banquiers qui faisoient face avec une caisse de la dixieme partie, d'autres ne peuvent guere moins garder que la moitié ou les deux tiers, encore que leur crédit ᶜsoit aussi estiméᶜ que celui du premier.

[I, 196, col.1] || From these examples it is apparent, that the quantity of money a goldsmith may be able to lend out of his cash, is proportionable to the method of acting of those who deposit their money in his hands. Whence it follows, that one goldsmith may be able to lend out 9/10, when another cannot afford to lend out 1/2; and this may be the case, though we suppose the credit of both equally good.

|| From what is here explained, it is not very difficult to conceive, that the different Sums of Money which Bankers, from their [174] Deposits, are enabled to put out, or employ at Interest, is proportioned to the Nature of the Trade, Conduct, and Manner of Living of their Customers; and that some Bankers are enabled to carry on their Trade with the tenth Part of the Amount of their Deposits, some with the Half, and some with ᵈone Thirdᵈ.

If he has a great flow of deposits and great credit this increases confidence in his notes, and makes people less eager to cash them, but only delays, his payments a few days or weeks when the notes fall into the hands of persons who are not accustomed to deal with him, and he ought always to guide himself by those who are accustomed to entrust their money to him. If his notes come into the hands of those of his own business they will have nothing more pressing than to withdraw the money from him.

The bankers referred to in A632 were prominent City names. 'Child' refers to (the banking house of) Sir Francis Child (1642–1713), the first London banker who gave up the goldsmith's business and who was established at the Marygold in Fleet Street from 1671. From 1713 the firm was called Child & Co. Subsequently many other Childs were involved (initially his sons Robert, Francis junior and Samuel). 'Hoare' refers to (the banking house of) Sir Richard Hoare (1648–1719) who from 1672 ran a bank at Cheapside and from 1690 at the Golden Bottle, 37 Fleet Street. In 1702 his son Henry Hoare joined him and subsequently other Hoares joined the bank. 'Colebrook' refers to (the banking house of) James Colebrook (1681–1752), who ran James Colebrook & Co. at 62 Threadneedle Street from 1706 until 1743. His son Sir James Colebrook ran the firm between 1743 and 1773. In short, the names of these three banking houses were established by the time Richard Cantillon wrote and were still well known when Philip wrote. Hence these facts by themselves do not allow a clear attribution of this paragraph to either Cantillon. **632**

If those who deposit money with the Banker are Undertakers and Merchants who pay in large sums daily and soon after draw them out it will often happen that if the Banker divert more than one third of his cash he will find himself in difficulty to meet the demands.

ᵃ...ᵃ: R: 'largent'

D633 concludes that bankers who take deposits from 'undertakers, or dealers in business' cannot lend more than *half* of deposits (similar to the bankers in E/A631 who, however, take deposits from landowners). In contrast, E/A633 state that bankers who take deposits from Merchants or Adventurers/*Entrepreneurs* should not lend out more than *one third*. **633**

It is easy to understand by these examples that the sums of money which a Goldsmith or a Banker can lend at interest or divert from his cash are naturally proportionable to the practice and conduct of his clients; that while we have seen Bankers who were safe with a cash reserve of one-tenth, others can hardly keep less than one half or two-thirds, though their credit be as high as that of the first.

ᵃ...ᵃ: R: 'peuvent'
ᵇ...ᵇ: 1756b, 1769: '& à la conduite'
ᶜ...ᶜ: R: 'fut plus estimé'
ᵈ...ᵈ: in the copy of Goldsmith's Library someone has corrected this by hand to '2 Thirds'. This correction, while agreeing with E634, is not given on the errata page.

634

635 |8| Les uns se fient à un Banquier, les autres à un autre, le plus [404] heureux est le Banquier qui a pour Chalans des Seigneurs riches qui cherchent toujours des emplois solides pour leur argent sans vouloir, en attendant, le mettre à intérêt.

|| There are many Bankers, and they have many Customers; fortunate is the Banker whose Customers are great Proprietors of Land, and who by their Oeconomy, save yearly Sums of Money, in order for new Purchases, or to be laid out on Mortgages.

636 |9| Une banque générale & nationale a cet avantage sur la banque d'un Orfévre particulier, qu'on y a toujours plus de confiance; qu'on y porte plus volontiers les plus gros dépôts, même des quartiers de la ville les plus éloignés, & qu'elle ne laisse d'ordinaire aux petits Banquiers que les dépôts de petites sommes, dans leurs quartiers: on y porte même les revenus de l'Etat, dans les païs où le Prince n'est pas absolu; & cela bien loin d'en altérer le crédit & la confiance, ne sert qu'à l'augmenter.

|| A well-constituted national bank having a better reputation than a private goldsmith, the largest sums, and such as are not soon called for, are commonly lodged there.

|| A national Bank has great Advantages over private Bankers, its Establishment is upon public Authority, and its Capital is publicly known, all which acquire great Credit and Confidence; People, who have great Deposits to make, carry them to the Bank; the Money of the Exchequer is there paid in, all which strengthen their Credit and Reputation; but this must be understood in a Country, whose supreme Magistrate is not arbitrary.

637 |10| Si les paiemens dans une banque nationale se font en écritures ou ªvirementª de Parties, il y aura cet avantage, qu'on n'y [405] sera pas sujet aux falsifications, au lieu que si la Banque donne des billets on en pourra faire de faux & causer du désordre : il y aura aussi ce désavantage, que ceux qui sont dans les quartiers de la ville, éloignés de la Banque, aimeront mieux païer & recevoir en argent que d'y aller, & surtout ceux de la campagne; au lieu que si l'on répand des billets de Banque. On s'en pourra servir de près & de loin. On paie dans les Banques nationales de Venise & d'Amsterdam en écriture seulement; ᵇmais à celleᵇ de Londres on paie en écritures, en billets & en argent, au choix des particuliers: aussi c'est aujourd'hui la Banque la plus forte.

If the national bank makes payments, and keeps money upon transfers, as that of *Amsterdam*, *Venice*, &c. it is safer than bank-bills, because these may be falsified; but it is not so generally convenient, because the attendance on the transfer-books is troublesome, and many will take bank-bills in payment who would not be at the trouble of going to the bank for a transfer: besides, payments in bank-notes may be made in the country, but the transfers require being on the spot.

|| If the Payments made by a National Bank, are by Transfers of Credit, it will have the [175] Advantage of not being liable to Robbery and Forgery, to both which Banks who issue out their Notes are subject; but the Banks who pay by Credit, have this Disadvantage, that such who live at a great Distance from them, pariculary in the Country, will not chuse to make use of them; whereas Banks who issue out their Notes, are made Use of both at Home and Abroad; the Banks of *Holland* and *Venice*, pay by Transfers of Credit, that of *England* pays not only by Transfers of Credit, but also by Cash, and Cash Notes payable to Bearer on Demand, at the Option of the Demanders.

Some trust one Banker, some another. The most fortunate is the Banker who has for clients rich gentlemen who are always looking out for safe employment for their money without wishing to invest it at interest while they wait.

635

A general national bank has this advantage over the bank of a single Goldsmith that there is always more confidence in it. The largest deposits are willingly brought to it, even from the most remote quarters of the city, and it leaves generally to small Bankers only the deposit of petty sums in their neighbourhood. Even the revenues of the State are paid in to it in countries where the Prince is not absolute. And this, far from injuring credit and confidence in it, serves only to increase them.

The references to the 'absolute' power of 'the Prince' in E636 and to the 'arbitrary' power of the 'supreme Magistrate' in A636 appear to be veiled criticism of France.

636

If payments in a national bank are made by transfers or clearings there will be this advantage, that they are not subject to forgeries, but if the Bank gives notes false notes may be made and cause disorder. There will be also this disadvantage that those who are in the quarters of the city at a distance from the Bank will rather pay and receive in money than go thither, especially those in the country. But if the bank notes are dispersed they can be used far and near. In the national Banks of Venice and Amsterdam payment is made only in book credit, but in that of London it is made in credit, in notes, and in money at the choice of the individuals, and it is today the strongest Bank.

ᵃ...ᵃ: R: 'viremens'; 1756b, 1769: 'viremens'

ᵇ...ᵇ: 1756b, 1769: 'mais celle'

D637 and A637 do not have the final observation in E637 about the Bank of England being the strongest, but for the rest the correspondence between E and A is much closer.

637

638
|| Money is only necessary in barter, where men of business are so concerned that payments by evaluation may answer, in most cases, and in those of minute payments, as for eating, drinking, cloathing &c. The building of a house also requires ready money for the weekly payment of workmen employed in it.

639
|| Let us suppose that 10,000 ounces of silver have been laid out in building of the said house: if the undertaker who built it, and laid out that money, letts it for 500 ounces a year, he shall, in 20 years, get in his original money, in small payments, which he laid out for the common sustenance of his familiy; but if he sells the house for 10,000 ounces, he may be paid in bank-bills, and in bank-transfers, but need not be paid any part in money, till it is wanted for eating, drinking, cloathing, &c. for himself and family, or for those to whom he assigns it. If he lays it out in a mortgage, the payment may be made in bank-bills, or transfers, and no part is required in money till it is turned somewhere to minute payments, for family necessaries.

640
|| The gentleman who borrows money on his estate, if it be to pay great debts, will also make payment in bank-bills; but if he applies it to building, the money must be taken out gradually for the maintenance of his workmen; as, if he owes it to undertakers of any branches of business, they will apply the money to their employments: and, let this inquiry be carried on never so far, it will be found, that no money in specie is absolutely required till you come to eating, drinking, cloathing &c. or to minute payments, and therein specie must be applied.

641

|11| On comprendra donc que tout l'avantage des Banques publiques ou particulieres dans une ville, c'est d'accélérer la circulation de l'argent, & d'empêcher qu'il n'y en ait autant de [406] resserré qu'il y en auroit naturellement dans plusieurs intervalles de tems.

And the use of banks is to keep hand-money circulating in the channels of minute payments, and to hinder it from stagnating, or being kept up in larger parcels, for any considerable time.

|| From what I have said, it is easy to conceive, that all the supposed national Advantage, the Trade of Banking consists of, is only the accelerating and facilitating the circulating Cash of the Kingdom, and preventing but a small Matter thereof to lie dead and useless in the Channels of Commerce; and if this facilitating the Circulation of Money, was confined only to the real Species of Gold and Silver in a Nation, I should have no doubt, but this Business of Banking, would be of real national Advantage; but if this Trade is made Use of, to introduce a fictitious and sudden Overflow of [176] artificial Wealth to do the Offices of Money, it must, I doubt, have very fatal Effects at a long Run, in the same Manner as the like Scheme had in *France*.

i. For other places where the **638**
argument is made that money
is only necessary for 'minute
payments', see C297ii.

ii. For the phrase 'eating, drinking
and cloathing' in this and the next
two paragraphs, see C275.

639

640

It will then be understood that all the   i. The reservations at the end of A641 about **641**
advantage of Banks, public or private
in a city, is to accelerate the circulation
of money and to prevent so much of
it from being hoarded as it would
naturally be for several intervals.

i. The reservations at the end of A641 about
the benefits of paper money, which recall the
experiences in France during the financial
experiments of John Law, are reminiscent of
E656. In particular, the phrase 'a fictitious
and sudden Overflow of artificial Wealth' in
A641 is similar to '*une abondance d'argent
fictive & imaginaire*' in E656.

ii. For other occurrences of the phrase 'at a
long Run' see C286i and C370.

iii. Directly after A641 the *Analysis*
continues with the text reproduced A675–
A684. See C627ii.

642   **CHAPITRE ªVIIª.**
Autres éclaircissemens & recherches sur l'utilité d'une
Banque nationale.

643 |1| Il est peu important d'examiner pourquoi la Banque
de Venise & celle d'Amsterdam, tiennent leurs écritures
dans des monnoies de compte différentes de la courante &
pourquoi il y a toujours un agiot à convertir ces écritures
en argent courant, ce n'est pas ªun point qui soit d'aucune
utilitéª pour la circulation. La Banque de Londres ne l'a
pas suivie en cela; ses écritures, ses billets & ses paiemens,
se font & se tiennent en especes courantes: cela me paroît
ᵇplus [407] uniforme & plus naturelᵇ & non moins utile.

644 |2| ªJe n'ai pû avoirª des informations exactes de la quantité
des sommes qu'on porte ordinairement à ces Banques,
ni le montant de leurs billets & écritures, non plus que
celui des prêts qu'ils font, & des sommes qu'ils gardent
ordinairement en Caisse pour faire ᵇfaceᵇ: quelqu'autre
qui sera plus à portée de ces connoissances en pourra
mieux raisonner.

645 |3| Cependant, comme ªje saisª assez bien que ces sommes
ne sont pas si immenses qu'on le croit communément, je
ne laisserai pas d'en donner une idée.

646 |4| Si les ªbillets & écrituresª de la Banque de Londres, qui
me paroît la plus considérable, se montent ᵇune semaineᵇ
portant l'autre à quatre millions d'onces d'argent ou
environ un million sterling; & si on se contente d'y [408]
ᶜgarder communément en Caisse le quartᶜ ou deux cents
cinquante mille livres sterling, ou un million d'onces
d'argent en especes, l'utilité de cette Banque pour la
circulation correspond à une augmentation de l'argent de
l'Etat de trois millions d'onces, ou sept cents cinquante
mille livres sterling, qui est sans doute une somme bien
forte & d'une utilité très grande pour la circulation dans
les circonstances que cette circulation a besoin d'être
accélérée : car j'ai remarqué ailleurs qu'il y a des cas
où il vaut mieux pour le bien de ᵈl'Etat de retarderᵈ la
circulation que de l'accélérer. J'ai bien oui dire, que les
billets & écritures de la Banque de Londres ont monté
dans certains cas, à deux millions sterling; mais cela ne
me paroît avoir été que par un accident extraordinaire; &
je crois que l'utilité de cette Ban-[409]que ne correspond
en général qu'à environ la dixieme partie de tout l'argent
qui circule en Angleterre.

[185] || The Bank of
Amsterdam has the
Reputation of immense
Treasure; their Paymenst
are not made in Money,
but by Transfers of
Credit.

Chapter VII
Further explanations and enquiries as to the utility of a National Bank

It is of little importance to examine why the Bank of Venice and that of Amsterdam keep their books in moneys of account different from current money, and why there is always an agio on converting these book credits into currency. It is not a point of any service for circulation. The Bank of England has not followed it in this. Its accounts, its notes and its payments are made and are kept in current coin, which seems to me more uniform and more natural and no less useful.

I have not been able to obtain exact information of the quantity of sums ordinarily brought to these Banks, nor the amount of their notes and accounts, loans, and sums kept as reserve. Some one who is better informed on these points will be better able to discuss them.

As, however, I know fairly well that these sums are not so huge as commonly supposed I will not omit to give an idea of them.

If the bills and notes of the Bank of England which seems to me the most considerable, amount weekly on an average to 4,000,000 ounces of silver or about 1 million sterling, and if they are content to keep regularly in reserve a quarter or £250,000 sterling or 1 million ounces of silver in coin, the utility of this Bank to circulation corresponds to an increase of the money of the State by 3 million ounces or £750,000 sterling which is without doubt a very large sum and of very great utility for the circulation when it has need to be speeded up: for I have remarked elsewhere that there are cases where it is better for the welfare of the State to retard the circulation than to accelerate it. I have heard that the notes and bills of the Bank of England have risen in some cases to 2 millions sterling, but it seems to me this can only have been by extraordinary accident. And I think the utility of this Bank corresponds in general only to about one tenth part of all the money in circulation in England.

[a...a]: R: '7e'   **642**

[a...a]: R: 'un point d'aucune utilité'   **643**
[b...b]: 1756b, 1769: 'plus uniforme plus naturel'

A643 follows directly on from the fragment finishing in A671. See C627ii.

[a...a]: R: 'Je nait pas pu avoir'   **644**
[b...b]: R: 'fasse'

[a...a]: 1756a, 1756b: 'je sai';   **645**
R: 'je scait'

[a...a]: R: 'billets, dettes et Ecritures'   **646**
[b...b]: R: 'en semaines'
[c...c]: R: 'garder Communement Le quart
[d...d]: 1756a, 1756b, 1769: 'l'Etat, retarder'.

647 |5| Si les éclaircissemens qu'on m'a donnés en gros sur les revenus de la Banque de Venise en mil sept cent dix-neuf sont véritables, on pourroit dire en général des Banques nationales que leur utilité ne correspond jamais à la dixieme partie de l'argent courant qui circule dans un Etat : voici à-peu-près ce que j'y ai appris.

||'Tis pretty difficult to judge what proportion of celerity in circulation a national bank, or banks, may give the money of a state: but, if I have been rightly informed in regard to the circumstances of the bank of *Venise*, it may give some useful light into this matter.

648 |6| Les revenus de l'Etat de Venise peuvent monter annuellement à quatre millions d'onces d'argent qu'il faut païer en écritures à la Banque, & les ᵃCollecteurs établisᵃ pour cet effet, qui reçoivent à Bergame & dans les païs les plus éloignés les taxes en argent, sont obligés de les convertir en ᵇécritures de Banqueᵇ lors des paiemens qu'ils en font à la République.

|| The revenues of the state of *Venice*, which amount to about 4,000,000 ounces of silver *per annum*, are payable in bank-money, or in transfers, at the bank of *Venice*; and the state-revenue, collected even at *Bergamo*, remote from *Venice*, when it is brought into that capital, is to answer in bank.

649 [410] |7| Tous les paiemens à Venise pour négociations, achats, & ventes, au-dessus d'une certaine somme modique, doivent par la loi se faire en écritures de Banque: tous les Détailleurs, qui ont amassé de l'argent courant dans le troc, se trouvent obligés d'en acheter des écritures pour faire leurs paiemens des gros articles; & ceux qui ont besoin, pour leur dépense ou pour le détail de la basse circulation, de ᵃreprendreᵃ de l'argent, sont dans le cas de vendre leurs écritures contre de l'argent courant.

All bargains and negociations between dealers above a certain sum are invalid, if not paid in bank:

650 |8| On a trouvé que les vendeurs & acheteurs de ces écritures, sont communément de niveau, lorsque la somme de tous les crédits ᵃouᵃ écritures sur les Livres de la Banque, n'excedent pas la valeur de huit cent mille onces d'argent ou environ.

and the money constantly paid and repaid, in these transfers, keeps up naturally a circulation of transfers of 800,000 ounces of silver. If a man, who has credit on the transfer-books, wants specie for minute payments, he will find another who has gathered specie from minute payments, and wants a transfer, wherewith to make a large payment: and, so far as that sum of 800,000, the money and transfers are found to keep up an equilibrium. Time and experience brought this to light.

If the explanations given to me in round figures in 1719 on the receipts of the Bank of Venice are correct it may be said of national banks generally that their utility never corresponds to the tenth part of the current money circulating in a State. This is approximately what I ascertained there.

D647 follows directly on from D641 in the entry 'Banking' (I, 196, midway first column).

647

The revenues of the State of Venice may amount annually to 4 million ounces of silver, which must be paid in Bank money, and the Collectors set up for that purpose who receive at Bergamo and in the most distant places taxes in money, are obliged to change them into bank money when they make payment of them to the Republic.

[a]...[a]: R: 'Collecteurs'
[b]...[b]: R; 'ecritures en banque'

648

All payments at Venice for negociations, purchases and sales above a certain modest sum must by law be made in Bank money. All the retailers who have collected current money in their dealings are compelled to buy Bank money with it to make their payments for large amounts. And those who need for their expenses or for the detail of small circulation to get back current money have to sell their Bank money to obtain it.

[a]...[a]: 1756b, 1769: 'répandre'

The correction in the later print editions from '*reprendre*' to '*répandre*' (V649a) changes the meaning of the sentence. Instead of consumers needing to 'get back' cash, they 'spread' cash around by spending it in small amounts. This is similar to the meaning of V278a, discussed in C278i. However, here, R agrees with E.

649

It is found that the sellers and buyers of the Bank money are regularly equal when the total of all the credits or inscriptions on the books of the Bank do not exceed the value of 800,000 ounces of silver or thereabout.

[a]...[a]: R: 'et'

For other occurrences of the term 'equilibrium' see C248i.

650

651 |9| C'est le tems & l'expérience [411] ᵃqui ont donné (suivant mon Auteur) cette connoissance à ces Venitiensᵃ. A la premiere erection de la Banque, les particuliers apportoient leur argent à la Banque, pour y avoir des crédits en écritures, pour ᵇla même valeurᵇ: dans la suite cet argent déposé à la Banque, fut dépensé pour les besoins de la République, & cependant les écritures conservoient encore leur valeur primordiale, parcequ'il se trouvoit autant de particuliers qui avoient besoin d'en acheter, que de ceux qui avoient besoin d'en vendre : ensuite l'Etat se trouvant pressé donna aux Entrepreneurs de la guerre des crédits en écritures de Banque, au défaut d'argent, & doubla la somme de ces crédits.

|| The money was first lodged in the bank of *Venice*, for the credit given in the transfer-books; the government, in their wars, spent the money deposited, and their further necessities obliged them to give new transfers in the bank, for the service of the war, without any money being deposited. These transfers were enlarged to about 1,600,000 ounces of silver;

[185] || The Bank of *Venice* pursues the same Method with that of *Amsterdam*, and this Transfer-Money finds Buyers and Sellers of it daily at Market; but I am informed that it happened, when this *Venetian* Republic was obliged to run in Debt, to pay the Expences of a War, that they raised new Credits in their Bank-Books, with which they paid their Creditors:

652 |10| Alors le nombre des Vendeurs d'écritures étant devenu bien supérieur à celui des Acheteurs, ces écritures commencerent à [412] perdre contre l'argent, & tomberent à vingt pour cent de perte : par ce discrédit le revenu de la République diminua d'un cinquieme, & le seul remede qu'on trouva à ce désordre, fut d'engager une partie des fonds de l'Etat, pour emprunter à intérêt de l'argent en écritures. Par ces emprunts en écritures on en éteignit une moitié, & alors les Vendeurs ᵃ& Acheteursᵃ d'écritures se trouvant à-peu-près de niveau, la Banque à recouvré son crédit primitif, & la somme des écritures se trouve réduite à huit cent mille onces d'argent.

and then it proved that there were more transfers than money, and the price of *transfers* against *money* fell above 20 per cent. of the original value, and, consequently, the yearly revenues of the state diminished in proportion as they were payable in bank.
|| To remedy this disorder, the state borrowed money on the revenue, and contracted the transfers gradually, by paying them off, till they came to answer the original price at market; and this equilibrium was not discovered till the transfers were reduced to about 800,000 ounces.

But this fictitious Creation of Wealth brought a greater number of its Sellers to Market, for current Money, than were Buyers; which reduced the Price of this transfer Money, to a Discount of Twenty *per Cent.* to remedy which the State was [186] obliged to mortgage a Part of its Revenue, in order to raise a Fund of real Current Specie, to purchase these transfer Credits, and this brought the Buyers and Sellers thereof, to near an Equality; and thereby restored the Credit of their Bank.

653

|| This Method of Payment, by way of Transfers of Credit, seems to me to be less detrimental to the real Interest of a commercial Nation, than that of issuing out Bank Notes payable on Demand: Assignments of Credit keep Circulation within proper Bounds, with respect to the real Quantity of Cash in being, to flow the Channels of Trade and Commerce.

Time and experience (according to my informant) have given this knowledge to the Venetians. When the Bank was first set up individuals brought their money to the Bank to have credit at the Bank of the same value. This money deposited at the Bank was later spent for the needs of the Republic and yet the Bank money preserved its original value because there were as many people who had need to buy it as those who had need to sell it. Finally the State being pressed for money gave to the War Contractors credits in Bank money instead of silver and doubled the amount of its credits.

[a]...[a]: R: 'qui a appris cette Connoissance a Ces Venitiens suivant mon auteur'

[b]...[b]: R: 'La valeur'

The identity of Cantillon's **651** informant, mentioned in E651, is unknown.

Then the number of sellers of Bank money being much greater than the buyers Bank money began to be at a discount against silver and fell 20 per cent. below. By this discredit the revenue of the Republic fell off one fifth and the only remedy found for this disorder was to pledge part of the State revenue to borrow Bank money at interest. By these borrowings of Bank money half of them were cancelled and then the sellers and buyers being about equal the Bank regained its original credit and the total of Bank money was brought back to 800,000 ounces of silver.

[a]...[a]: 1756b, 1769: '& les Acheteurs'

For other occurrences of the **652** term 'equilibrium' see C248i.

A653 may have been written by Philip Cantillon. Hereafter **653** the text in the *Analysis* continues with a very long quotation, running from the bottom of p. 186 to the bottom of p. 193, from David Hume's essay 'Of Money', which was first published in 1752. The chapter ends on p. 194 with a short conclusion. The next and final chapter of the *Analysis* is chapter XXV, 'The Subject of Exchanges continued', pp. 194 to 215. It deals with the financial 'Art and Knowledge' of foreign traders 'conveyed to them from Father to Son, without ever entering into, or seeking the Means of acquiring the Knowledge of the Nature of general Commerce' (p. 215). The latter phrase is reminiscent of the title of E (cf. C561ii) and it is not impossible that some of this chapter is due to Richard Cantillon. However, despite some similarities with passages in the *Dictionary* entry 'Exchange' (see C616), this is perhaps too speculative a conclusion and therefore none of this final chapter has been reproduced here.

654 |11| C'est par cette voie qu'on a reconnu que l'utilité de la Banque de Venise, par rapport à la circulation, correspond à environ huit cent mille onces d'argent: & si l'on suppose que tout l'argent courant qui circule dans les Etats de cette République [413] peut monter à huit millions d'onces d'argent, l'utilité de la Banque correspond au dixieme de cet argent.

|| If we suppose the proprietors rents in the state of *Venice* to amount to 21 millions of ounces of silver *per annum*, and the circulating money from 7 to 8 millions, the advantage of circulation gained by the bank of *Venice* will not exceed the eighth part of the circulating money in the state; and the service they receive by the bank is reduced to this, that from 7 to 8 millions of money, with the help of the bank, [I, 196, col.2] answer as well as 7 to 8 millions, added to the 800,000 ounces in money, without any bank; and that benefit which the government have obtained by the bank of *Venice* has been this, that they have borrowed 800,000 ounces, for which they never pay any interest.

655 || From this example it appears, that the advantage gained in the circulation of the money of a nation by banks, and goldsmiths or bankers, is not so great in proportion as is commonly believed; and the proportion of such advantage seems to be less in a great kingdom than in so small a state as that of *Venice*. For, as banks and goldsmiths give a circulation to a small part only of the real money of the nation, which would otherwise be locked up in particular people's hands, the quickness they give to circulation cannot bear a great proportion to the whole circulating money of a nation. To judge farther to what greater degree banks may be useful for the support of the public and private credit of a nation, and to the reduction of the interest of public finds, and the national rate of interest, see the articles CREDIT, MONEY, INTEREST, FUNDS.

656 |12| Une Banque nationale dans la Capitale d'un grand Roïaume ou Etat, semble devoir moins contribuer à l'utilité de la circulation, à cause de l'éloignement de ses Provinces, que dans un petit Etat; & lorsque l'argent y circule en plus grande abondance que chez ses Voisins, une Banque nationale y fait plus de mal que de bien. Une abondance d'argent fictif & imaginaire cause les mêmes désavantages, qu'une augmentation d'argent réel en circulation, pour y hausser le prix de la terre & du travail, soit pour encherir les ouvrages & Manufactures au hasard de les perdre dans la suite: mais cette abondance furtive s'évanouit à la premiere bouffée de discrédit, & précipite le désordre.

[182] || A National Bank, established in the Capital of a great and extended State, seems to me to contribute less to the Advantage of Circulation, from the Distance of its Towns and Provinces from the Capital, than in small States, where, if Money is scarce, with respect to its Neighbours, this Bank is of great Use.

|| A small State where where Money, of real Gold and Silver, is in greater Abundance, in Proportion to its neighbouring Kingdoms, there a National Bank is more prejudicial than advantageous to its commercial Interest. An Increase of ficticious and imaginary Wealth, occasions and brings about in Circulation the same Inconvenience, of a more than necessary Increase in Circulation of real Specie; it raises the Prices of every Thing beyond their Proportion at Foreign Markets, and occasions the Risk of losing our Trade, by heightening the Price of our Labour, and adding a fictious Value to our Manufactures, which prevents their Sale, and thereby turns the Course of our Trade into other Channels, from whence [183] it will be very hard, if ever possible, to get it back.

It is thus that it has been ascertained that the utility of the Bank of Venice as regards circulation corresponds to about 800,000 ounces of silver: and if it is supposed that all the current money in the States of that Republic amount to 8 million ounces of silver the utility of the Bank corresponds to one tenth of that silver.

i. The assumption in D654 that the amount of money in circulation is about 1/3 of annual rent incomes is the same as is found in E/D/A287. **654**

ii. E654, like E647, states that the 'uitility' of bank money consists in adding 1/10 to the money supply. This fraction is obviously found by dividing 800,000 by 8 million. Analogously, the statement in D654 that the 'advantage' of bank money does not exceed 1/8 of circulating money, may be based on the calculation 800,000/7 million which is 1/8.75, the denominator being rounded down.

i. The conclusion that public banks are more useful in small states than in large ones is similar to E660. **655**

ii. The first three entries referred to at the end of D655 all contain fragments taken from Cantillon's work. For 'Credit' (I, 575–81) see D671–D672 and D683–D689; for 'Money' (II, 283–84) see D338–D384; and for 'Interest' (I, 995–96) see D433–D480). The entry 'Funds' (I, 876–83) is made up mostly of excerpts from proposals by authors like Sir John Barnard and Sir Matthew Decker to reduce the state debt. It is unlikely that amongst this there is anything written by Cantillon.

iii. After D655 the plagiarism from Cantillon's work appears to come to an end, as far as the *Dictionary* entry 'Banking' is concerned. The next two paragraphs in that entry may possibly still be due to Cantillon, but are more likely Postlethwayt's summing up. The entry then continues (p. I, 196 top of column 2 until halfway through p. 197) with an interesting argument in favour of banks providing 'venture capital' for the introduction of new inventions. This, however, is unlike anything Cantillon wrote.

A national Bank in the Capital of a great Kingdom or State must, it seems, contribute less to the utility of circulation because of the distance of its Provinces, than in a small State. And when money circulates there in greater abundance than among its neighbours a national Bank does more harm than good. An abundance of fictitious and imaginary money causes the same disadvantages as an increase of real money in circulation, by raising the price of Land and Labour, or by making works and manufactures more expensive at the risk of subsequent loss. But this furtive abundance vanishes at the first gust of discredit and precipitates disorder.

A656 follows directly after the fragment reproduced in A684. Cf. C672ii. **656**

657 [414] |13| Vers le milieu du Regne de ᵃLouis XIVᵃ en France, on y voïoit plus d'argent en circulation que chez les Voisins, & on y levoit les revenus du Prince sans le secours d'une Banque, avec autant d'aisance & de facilité qu'on leve ᵇaujourd'hui ceux d'Angleterreᵇ, avec le secours de la Banque de Londres.

658 |14| Si les viremens de partie à Lyon montent dans une de ses quatre Foires à quatre-vingt millions de livres, si on les commence, & si on les finit avec un seul million d'argent ᵃcomptantᵃ, ils sont sans doute d'une grande commodité pour épargner la peine d'une infinité de transports d'argent ᵇd'une maison à une autreᵇ; mais à cela près, on conçoit bien qu'avec ce même million de ᶜcomptantᶜ qui a commencé & conclu ces viremens, il seroit très possible de conduire dans trois mois tous [415] les paiemens de quatre-vingt millions.

659 |15| Les Banquiers, à Paris, ont souvent remarqué que le même sac d'argent leur est rentré quatre à cinq fois dans les paiemens d'un seul jour, lorsqu'ils avoient beaucoup à païer & à recevoir.

660 |16| Je crois les Banques publiques ᵃd'une très grande utilitéᵃ dans les petits Etats, & dans ceux ou l'argent est un peu rare; mais je les crois ᵇpeu utilesᵇ pour l'avantage solide d'un grand Roïaume.

661 |17| L'Empereur Tibere, Prince severe & œconome, avoit amassé dans le Trésor de l'Empire deux milliards sept cents millions de Sesterces, ce qui correspond à vingt-cinq millions sterlings, ou cent millions d'onces d'argent: somme immense en especes pour ces tems-là, & même pour aujourd'hui: il est vrai qu'en resserrant tant d'ar-[416]gent, il gêna la circulation, & que l'argent devint bien plus rare à Rome qu'il n'avoit été.

662 |18| Tibere, qui attribuoit cette rareté aux monopoles des Gens d'affaires & Financiers qui affermoient les revenus de l'Empire, ordonna par un Edit qu'ils achetassent des terres pour les deux tiers au moins de leurs fonds. Cet Edit, au lieu d'animer la circulation, la mit entierement en désordre: tous les Financiers resserroient & rappelloient leurs fonds, ᵃsous, prétexteᵃ de se mettre en état d'obéir à l'Edit, en ᵇachetantᵇ des terres, qui au lieu d'encherir devenoient à beaucoup plus vil prix par la rareté de l'argent en circulation. Tibere remedia à cette rareté d'argent, en prêtant aux particuliers ᶜsousᶜ bonnes cautions, seulement trois cents millions de Sesterces: c'est-à-dire, la neuvieme partie des especes qu'il avoit dans son trésor.

Towards the middle of the reign of Louis XIV there was more money in circulation in France than in neighbouring countries, and the King's revenue was collected there without the help of a Bank, as easily and conveniently as it is collected today in England with the help of the Bank of England.

ᵃ...ᵃ: R: 'Louis IIII'
ᵇ...ᵇ: R: 'ceux dangletére aujourdhui'

657

If the clearings at Lyons in one of its four Fairs amount to 80 millions of livres, if they are begun and finished with a single million of ready money, they are doubtless of great convenience in saving the trouble of an infinity of transports of silver from one house to another. But with that exception it seems that with this same million of cash which began and ended these clearings it would be quite feasible to conduct in three months all the payments of 80 millions.

ᵃ...ᵃ: R: 'Content'
ᵇ...ᵇ: R: 'dune nation a une autre'
ᶜ...ᶜ: R: 'Content'

For the misspellings **658** V658a and c, see C274iii.

The Paris bankers have often observed that the same bag of money has come back to them 4 or 5 times in the same day when they had a good deal to pay out and receive.

For other mentions of the **659** bags of money circulating amongst Paris bankers, see C630.

I think pubic banks of very great utility in small States and those where silver is rather scarce, but of little service for the solid advantage of a great State.

ᵃ...ᵃ: R: 'dun grand avantage et utilité'
ᵇ...ᵇ: R: 'plus utiles'

The conclusion of E660 is **660** similar to what is found in D655.

The Emperor Tiberius, a Prince strict and economical, had saved up in the Imperial Treasury 2700 millions of sesterces, equal to 25 millions sterling or 100 million ounces of silver, an enormous sum in coin for those times and even for today. It is true that in tying up so much money he embarrassed the circulation and that silver became scarcer at Rome than it had been.

661

Tiberius, who attributed this scarcity to the monopoly of Contractors and Financiers who farmed the Imperial revenues, ordered by an edict that they should buy land up to at least two thirds of their capital. This Edict, instead of animating the circulation threw it completely into disorder. All the Financiers hoarded and called in their capital under the pretext of putting themselves into a position to obey the Edict by buying land, which instead of rising in value sunk to a much lower price owing to the scarcity of silver in circulation. Tiberius remedied this scarcity by lending to individuals on good security only 300 million sesterces, a ninth part of the money which he had in his Treasury.

ᵃ...ᵃ: R, 1756a,b, 1769: 'sous prétexte'
ᵇ...ᵇ: R: 'achétérent'
ᶜ...ᶜ: R: 'sur'

662

663 [417] |19| Si la neuvieme partie du trésor suffisoit à Rome pour rétablir la circulation, il sembleroit que l'établissement d'une Banque générale dans un grand Roïaume, où son utilité ne corresponderoit jamais à la dixieme partie de l'argent qui circule, lorsqu'on n'en ªresserreª point, ne seroit ᵇd'aucunᵇ avantage réel & permanent, & qu'à le considerer dans sa valeur intrinseque, ᶜon ne peut le regarderᶜ que comme un expédient pour gagner du tems.

664

[183 continued] || An unbounded Circulation of Paper-Credit, to do or answer the Offices of real Species of Gold and Silver, is very hurtful to the Interest of a commercial Kingdom, or that of any other State; it introduces Luxury, which is the Abuse of Riches, it effeminates the Spirit of a Nation, and unbraces the Strength and Sinews of its Inhabitants.

665 |20| Mais ªuneª augmentation réelle de la quantité d'argent qui circule est d'une nature différente. Nous en avons déja parlé, & le Trésor de Tibere nous donne encore occasion d'en toucher un mot ici. Ce Tresor de deux milliards sept cents millions de Sesterces, laissé à la mort de Tibere, fut dissipé par l'Empereur Caligula son Successeur ᵇdansᵇ [418] moins d'un an. Aussi ne vit-on jamais à Rome l'argent si abondant. Quel en fut l'effet? Cette quantité d'argent plongea les Romains dans le luxe, & dans toutes sortes de crimes pour y subvenir. Il sortoit tous les ans plus de six cents mille livres sterlings hors de l'Empire pour les marchandises des Indes; & en moins de trente ans l'Empire s'appauvrit ᶜ, & l'argentᶜ y devint très rare sans aucun démembrement ni perte de Province.

|| This Abuse of Riches effaces all Generosity from the Soul of Man, in turning all its Views and Ambition towards Acquisition of Money, in order to support this Luxury; many are the Instances of the fatal Consequences, to be given, from the Abuse of Riches; a remarkable one happened at *Rome* in the Time of *Caligula*, whose Predecessor *Tiberius* amassed together an immense Sum in Specie, equal to the Value of twenty-five Millions Sterling; but his Successor *Caligula*, spent and squandered away this immense Sum, and Money was never seen in greater Plenty than at that Time; but what was the Consequence? These great Sums of Money plunged the *Romans* into Luxury, and all Sorts of [184] Crimes to support this Abuse of Riches. There was annually exported to *Asia*, more than the Value of six hundred thousand Pounds to pay for *India* Goods; and in less than thirty Years the *Roman* Empire was impoverished, without suffering the Loss of either Town or Province.

If the ninth part of the Treasury sufficed at Rome to re-establish the circulation it would seem that the establishment of a general Bank in a great Kingdom where its utility would never correspond to the tenth part of the money in circulation when it is not hoarded, would be of no real and permanent advantage, and that considered in its intrinsic value it can only be regarded as an expedient for gaining time.

[a]...[a]: R:'Resserrera'
[b]...[b]: R: 'Jamais daucun'
[c]...[c]: 'on ne le peut Considérér'

663

A664 follows directly from A656.   **664**

But a real increase in the quantity of circulating money is of a different nature. We have already spoken of it and the Treasure of Tiberius gives us again occasion to say a word of it here. This treasure of 2700 millions of sesterces, left at the death of Tiberius, was squandered by the Emperor Caligula his successor in less than a year. Money was never seen so abundant at Rome. What was the result? This mass of money plunged the Romans into luxury and into all sorts of crimes to pay for it. More than 600,000 pounds sterling left the Empire every year for the merchandise of the Indies, and in less than 30 years the Empire grew poor and silver became very scarce there without any dismemberment or loss of a Province.

[a]...[a]: 1769: 'cette'
[b]...[b]: 1756b, 1769: 'en'
[c]...[c]: R: ' . Largent'

i. There is perhaps a greater **665** emphasis in A665 on the detrimental effects of luxury. However, the discussion of the effects of luxury in ancient Rome is quite in keeping with similar views found in E414 and E415, including the observation that due to luxury consumption Rome lost substantial amounts of money to oriental countries (see E414). This is reminiscent of the end of A665.

ii. In E661 it is stated that 2,700 million Sesterces (E665) is equivalent to 25 million Sterling (A665).

666 |21| Quoique j'estime qu'une Banque générale ᵃestᵃ dans le fond de très peu d'utilité solide dans un grand Etat, je ne laisse pas de convenir qu'il y a des circonstances où une Banque peut avoir des effets qui paroissent étonnans.

667 |22| Dans une Ville où il y a des dettes publiques pour des sommes considérables, la facilité d'une Banque fait qu'on peut vendre & acheter ses fonds ca-[419]pitaux dans un ᵃinstantᵃ, pour des sommes immenses, sans causer aucun dérangement dans la circulation. Qu'à Londres un particulier vende son capital de la Mer du Sud, pour acheter un autre capital dans la Banque ou dans la Compagnie des Indes, ou bien dans l'esperance que dans quelques-tems il pourra acheter à plus bas prix un capital dans la même Compagnie de la Mer du Sud, il s'accommode toujours de Billets de banque, & on ne demande ordinairement l'argent de ces Billets que pour la valeur des intérêts. Comme on ne dépense guere son capital, on n'a pas besoin de le convertir en especes, mais on est toujours obligé de demander à la Banque l'argent nécessaire pour la subsistance, car il faut des especes dans le bas troc.

|| In a Country greatly indebted, a National Bank is of great Use, in circulating and facilitating the Purchase and Sale of these Debts for immense Sums; People who deal in this Way, furnish themselves with large Sums in Bank Notes without calling for the Money, except for Expences, or to exchange large Sums for small ones, in order to accommodate their Payments and Dealing.

668 |23| Qu'un Propriétaire de terres [420] qui a mille onces d'argent, ᵃen paieᵃ deux cents pour les intérêts des fonds publics, & en dépense lui-même huit cents onces, les mille onces demanderont toujours des especes: ᵇceᵇ Propriétaire en dépensera ᶜhuit centsᶜ, & les Propriétaires des fonds en dépenseront ᵈ200ᵈ. Mais lorsque ces Propriétaires sont dans l'habitude de l'agiot, de vendre & d'acheter des fonds publics, il ne faut point d'argent ᵉcomptantᵉ pour ces opérations, il suffit d'avoir des billets de banque. S'il falloit retirer de la circulation, des especes pour servir dans ces achats & ventes, cela monteroit à une somme considérable, & gêneroit souvent la circulation, ou plutôt il arriveroit dans ce cas, qu'on ne pourroit pas vendre & acheter ᶠsesᶠ capitaux si fréquemment.

Though I consider a general Bank is in reality of very little solid service in a great State I allow that there are circumstances in which a Bank may have effects which seem astonishing.

^a...^a: 1756b, 1769: 'soit'

666

In a city where there are public debts for considerable amounts the facility of a Bank enables one to buy and sell capital stock in a moment for enormous sums without causing any disturbance in the circulation. If at London a person sells his South Sea stock to buy stock in the Bank or in the East India Company, or hoping that in a short time he will be able to buy at a lower price stock in the same South Sea Company, he always takes Banknotes, and generally money is not asked for in respect of these Notes but only for the interest on them. As one hardly spends one's capital there is no need to change it into coin, but one is always forced to ask the Bank for money for subsistence since cash is needed for small dealings.

^a...^a: R: 'intéréts'

667

If a Landowner who has 1000 ounces of silver pays 200 of them for the interest of public stock and spends 800 ounces of them himself, the thousand ounces will always require coinage. This proprietor will spend 800 and the Owners of the funds will spend 200 of them. But when these Proprietors are in the habit of speculation, selling and buying public stock, no ready silver is needed for these operations, bank notes suffice. If it were necessary to draw hard cash out of circulation to serve in these purchases and sales it would amount to a great sum and would often impede the circulation, or rather it would happen in that case that the stocks could not be sold and bought so often.

^a...^a: R: 'quil en paye'
^b...^b: R: 'Le'
^c...^c: R: 'luy méme huit Cens onces'
^d...^d: R: 'les deux Cens onces'
^e..^e: R: 'Content'
^f...^f: R: 'Cés'

668

669 |24| C'est sans doute l'origine de ces capitaux, ou l'argent qu'on [421] a déposé à la Banque & qu'on ne retire que rarement, comme lorsqu'un Propriétaire des fonds se met dans quelque négoce où il faut des especes pour le détail, qui est cause que la Banque ne garde en caisse que le quart ou la sixieme partie de l'argent dont elle fait ses billets. Si la Banque n'avoit pas les fonds de plusieurs de ces capitaux, elle se verroit, dans le cours ordinaire de la circulation, réduite comme les Banquiers particuliers à garder la moitié des fonds qu'on lui met entre les mains, pour faire face; il est vrai qu'on ne peut pas distinguer par les Livres de la Banque ni par ses opérations, la quantité de ces sortes de capitaux qui passent en plusieurs mains, dans les ventes & achats qu'on fait dans *Change-alley*, ces billets sont souvent renouvellés à la Banque & changés contre d'autres dans le troc. Mais [422] l'expérience des achats & ventes de capitaux des fonds fait bien voir que la somme en est considérable: & sans ces achats & ventes, les sommes en dépot à la Banque seroient sans difficulté moins considérables.

670 |25| Cela veut dire que lorsqu'un Etat n'est point endetté, & n'a pas besoin des achats & ventes de capitaux, le secours d'une Banque y sera moins nécessaire & moins considérable.

671 [422] |26| Dans l'année mil sept cent vingt, les capitaux des fonds publics & des *Bublles* qui étoient des attrapes ᵃ& desᵃ entreprises de Sociétés particulieres à Londres, montoient à la valeur de huit cents millions sterlings, cependant les achats & ventes de capitaux si venimeux se faisoient sans peine, par la quantité de billets de toutes especes qu'on mit sur la place, pendant qu'on se contentoit des mêmes papiers [423] pour le paiement des intérêts; mais sitôt que l'idée des grandes fortunes porta nombre de particuliers ᵇà augmenterᵇ leur dépense, à acheter des équipages, des linges & soieries étrangeres, il fallut des especes pour tout cela, je dis pour la dépense des intérêts, & cela mit tous ᶜles systêmesᶜ en pieces.

In the *South-Sea* time, 1720, the capital of *South-Sea* stock was at 1000, and those of the bubbles, at then high rates, were computed to amount to 800 million sterling; and the half-yearly interest of the *South-Sea* capital, at 1000, woul [I, 579, col. 1] have required ten millions sterling, which was, perhaps, more than all the circulating money then in *England*. || Yet credit and paper-circulation kept this mighty fabric up, so long as no more specie was required in circulation than usual; but, when the prospect of so much imaginary wealth made people increase their expenses greatly, and bring in great quantities of foreign commodities for their luxury (both which articles were to be answered by ready money) the nation tumbled in a few months.

|| The Instance of what happened in the Year 1720, both in *France* and *England*, when the Amount of the *English* Bubbles, and that of its National Debts was calculated at a Sum of eight hundred Millions; yet the Purchase and Sale of this prodigious Capital, by the Assistance of Paper-Money was carried on; which demonstrates, what Prodigies this Sort of Riches are capable of affording, when People's Imaginations are heated with the [185] Prospect of Gain: Yet the Moment that real Cash of Gold or Silver is wanted, to supply foreign Aids, and Luxury, that Instant this ficticious Money loses its Credit, and the whole Fabric falls to Pieces, and demonstrates, that nothing but real Bullion is the true Strength and Sinew of a true and permanent Circulation.

669

It is doubtless the origin of these capitals or money deposited in the Bank and drawn out only on rare occasions, such as when an owner of capital engages in some transaction or needs cash for small purchases, which explains why the Bank keeps in reserve only the fourth or sixth part of the silver against which it issues notes. If the Bank had not the funds of many of these capitals it would in the ordinary course of circulation find itself compelled like private banks to keep half its deposits in hand to be solvent. It is true that the Bank books and its dealings do not distinguish those capitals which pass through several hands in the sales and purchases made in Change Alley. These notes are often renewed at the Bank and changed against others in purchases. But the experience of purchases and sales of stock show clearly that the total of them is considerable, and without these purchases and sales the sums deposited at the Bank would be certainly smaller.

670

This means that when a State is not in debt and has no need of purchases and sales of stock the help of a Bank will be less necessary and less important.

671

In 1720 the capital of public stock and of Bubbles which were snares and enterprises of private companies at London, rose to the value of 800 millions sterling, yet the purchases and sales of such pestilential stocks were carried on without difficulty through the quantity of notes of all kinds which were issued, while the same paper money was accepted in payment of interest. But as soon as the idea of great fortunes induced many individuals to increase their expenses, to buy carriages, foreign linen and silk, cash was needed for all that, I mean for the expenditure of the interest, and this broke up all the systems.

a...a: R: 'et'
b...b: R: 'a augmentér A augméntér'
c...c: R: 'Le sistéme'

i. D671 is from the *Dictionary* entry 'Credit' and carries on from D689. See C683.

ii. After A671 the text in the *Analysis* continues directly with the paragraph reproduced in A643. See C627ii.

672 |27| Cet exemple fait bien voir, que le papier & le crédit des Banques publiques & particulieres peuvent causer des effets surprenans dans tout ce qui ne regarde pas la dépense ordinaire pour le boire & pour le manger, l'habillement & autres nécessités des familles: mais que dans le train uniforme de la circulation, le secours des Banques & du crédit de cette espece est bien moins considérable & moins solide qu'on ne pense généralement. L'argent seul est le vrai nerf de la circulation.

This example justifies what has been suggested, that in particular cases, as in that of buying and selling of stocks, banks and credit may produce surprising effects, where the management may not require any additional circulation of species.

‖ If a minister should, by means of the credit of a bank, try to reduce interest in a nation forcibly from 4 to 2, by offering to lend bank notes to all people at 2 *per cent.* he may probably unhinge his whole project; and wheras several in that case, who are diffident of the success, sell out their stock, and call in their specie, they stop the channel of circulation, and cause such a call on the *Bank*, as will soon blow it up. This was the case at *Paris* in 1719 and 1720, though the scheme there was not wholly for reduction of interest; but, the other operations at *Paris* not relating to our present purpose, we shall not now examine the causes of the miscarriage there.

This example shews that the paper and credit of public and private Banks may cause surprising results in everything which does not concern ordinary expenditure for drink and food, clothing, and other family requirements, but that in the regular course of the circulation the help of Banks and credit of this kind is much smaller and less solid than is generally supposed. Silver alone is the true sinews of circulation.

672

i. The phrase '*le boire, le manger, l'habillement*' occurs a number of times in the Rouen manuscript, but is corrected in the print edition of the *Essai*. See C275. The occurrence in E672 is the only place where the phrase appears uncorrected in the print edition. This may be a case of 'editor's fatigue'.

ii. The expression in D672 that creditors by taking out their money may 'blow up' the bank is reminiscent of the expression '*crever la bombe*' in E687 (or '*gare la bombe*' in V687b).

iii. After D672 the entry 'Credit' continues with a quotation from John Locke about the benefits of low interest rates.

673   [424] ‖ **CHAPITRE ªVIIIª.**
Des rafinemens du crédit des Banques générales.

674 |1| La Banque nationale de Londres, est composée
d'un grand nombre d'Actionaires qui choisissent
des Directeurs pour en régir les opérations. Leur
avantage primordial consistoit à faire un partage
annuel des profits qui s'y faisoient par l'intérêt
de l'argent, qu'on prêtoit hors des fonds qu'on
déposoit à la Banque; on y a ensuite incorporé des
fonds publics, dont l'Etat paie un intérêt annuel.

675

[176 continued] The Bank of *England* was established in
the reign of King *William* the III. and consists of two Sets of
Adventurers, the one, a Number of rich Men, who at this Time
when Money was prodigiously scarce, and the Distress of the
Public, in the new Establishment, very great, advanced the
Government, one Million, two hundred thousand Pounds, at
Eight *per Cent.* in Consideration of which, there was granted
to them a Charter to incoporate themselves, into a Body, for the
carrying on this Business of Banking, for thirteen Years, under
the Denomination of the Governors and Company of the bank of
England; this Term of thirteen Years has at different times been
prolonged, in Consideration of further Loans to the succeeding
Government, at lesser Interest, to the Amount of about eleven
Millions.

676

‖ The second Sort of Adventurers, are those who from time to
time, deposit their Money with the Bank, for which they have
Credit [177] given them in the Company's Books, or Bank
Notes payable on Demand: It is the Use and Employment
which this Money is put to, by the Governors and Directors of
this Bank, and the Interest received for the Capitals advanced
to the Government, which enables this Company to pay their
Governors and Directors Appointments, and all other Expences
of carrying on this Business, and a yearly Dividend to the
Proprietors of their Stock, of four and a half and five *per Cent.*
by two half yearly Payments. Some time previous to these half-
yearly Payments, the Governors and Directors of this Company
call a general Meeting of its Stock Proprietors, before whom
they lay the general State of the Company's Affairs, and there
determine the Quantum of what *per Cent.* Half-Year Dividends
can be afforded to the Stockholders out of the Company's Profits;
than which nothing carries the Appearance of fairer Proceeding.
Their Trade consists in circulating certain Government
Securities, advancing Money on the Security of their own Stock,
discounting foreign and inland Bills of Exchange, not exceeding
two Months to run, and once a Week good Notes of Hand, not
exceeding six Weeks to run; and of late Years buying and selling
Gold [178] and Silver Bullion; in the Management of all which
there is all the Caution and Care imaginable taken.

Chapter VIII

Of the refinements of Credit of General Banks

673

The national Bank of London is composed of a large number of shareholders who make choice of Directors to govern its operations. Their primitive advantage consisted in making a yearly distribution of the profits made by interest on the money lent out of the Bank deposits. Later the public debt was incorporated with it, on which the State pays an annual interest.

674

i. A675 follows directly after A641. See C627ii.

ii. A675–A678 offer a much more detailed account of the operations of the Bank of England than E674 and one might argue that some of this is due to Philip Cantillon. However, the account joins up quite seamlessly with A679 to A681 which do have counterparts in E. For this reason this fragment from the *Analysis* (A675–A678) has been included.

675

676

677

|| The Trust and Confidence reposed by the Public, in the Credit and Well-Management of this Company, is prodigious; their Credit is immense; they are not only Cashiers for the Majority of private rich Citizens and Merchants; but also for other rich Companies, and likewise for the Revenue of the State: No other Credit or Paper-Money is received at the Exchequer, and other public Offices, but theirs; this obliges all private Bankers to circulate immense Sums of Bank Notes, and to have them daily by them: But this great Credit, as are the best of all earthly Things, is liable to Corruption, which would be attended, if the Case ever happens, with the most fatal Consequences.

678

|| It is believed, and in Fact certainly ought to be so, that no more Bank Notes are coined and issued out, than what are equal to their Ready-Money Demands. People Without-Doors can make no certain Judgment of the Sum of their Notes issued out in public Circulation, nor of the Amount of their Cash in [179] their Vaults: None but the few of their Governors and Directors (in all Societies the lesser Number govern and command the Voices of the greater) in the Secret, know it; but it is certain, that the Cash with which this Company is intrusted, ought to be employed, so as to be within Call, to make Head and Stand against any sudden Demand or Distrust, which any public Disorder or Exigence of the State may be apt to create.

679 |2|ᵃMalgré un établissementᵃ si solide, on a vu (lorsque la Banque avoit fait de grosses avances à l'Etat, & que les porteurs de billets de banque appréhendoient que la Banque ne fut embarras-[425]sée) qu'on couroit sus & que les Porteurs alloient en foule à la Banque pour retirer leur argent: la même chose est arrivée lors de la chûte de la Mer du Sud, en mil sept cent vingt.

The Misfortunes, consequent to the Schemes of the Year 1720, brought a Run on the Bank;

677

In the eighteenth century the **678**
expression 'People Without-
Doors' was used to indicate
people who are not members
of an official body, for example
Parliament. In A678 it refers to
people who are not governors or
directors of the Bank.

In spite of such a solid foundation   ᵃ...ᵃ: R: 'et   malgré   Cet   The possibility of a run on a bank   **679**
when the Bank had made large   établissémént'   is also mentioned in A631.
advances to the State and the holders
of notes were apprehensive that the
Bank was in difficulties, a run on
the Bank has been seen and holders
of notes went in crowds to the Bank
to draw out money. The same thing
happened on the collapse of the South
Sea Company in 1720.

680 |3| Les rafinemens qu'on apportoit pour soutenir la Banque & modérer son discrédit, ᵃétoient d'abord d'établirᵃ plusieurs Commis pour compter l'argent aux Porteurs, d'en faire compter de grosses sommes en pieces de six & de douze sols, ᵇpour gagnerᵇ du tems, d'en païer quelques parties aux Porteurs particuliers qui étoient-là à attendre des journées entieres pour être païés à leur tour; mais les sommes les plus considérables à des amis qui les emportoient & puis les rapportoient à la Banque ᶜenᶜ cachette, pour recommencer le lendemain le même manége: par ce moïen la Banque faisoit bonne contenance & gagnoit du tems; en [426] attendant que le discrédit se ralentit; mais lorsque cela ne suffisoit pas, la Banque ouvroit des souscriptions, pour engager des Gens ᵈaccrédités & solvablesᵈ, à s'unir pour se rendre garans de grosses sommes ᵉ&ᵉ maintenir le crédit ᶠ&ᶠ la circulation des billets de banque.

the Company to make Head, and in order to stand against this Run, employed a Number of Clerks to tell out the Money which was called for; and other Sums were brought in, and Payments were made (in order to gain Time) in light Six-pences and Shillings, and large Payments were made to particular Friends, who went out with their Bags of Money at one Door, to deliver them to People placed at another, who were let in to pay the same Money to Tellers, who must take Time to count it over; and the Preference of Dispatch was always given to this Sort of People, rather than those who rally called for their Money, to carry it Home. By these Stratagems and Shifts Time was gained, and a Stand [180] made, till a Number of rich Gentlemen and Merchants entered into a Subscription to support the Company,

681 |4| Ce fut par ce dernier rafinement que le crédit de la Banque se maintint en mil sept cent vingt, lors de la chûte de la Mer du Sud; car aussi-tôt qu'on ᵃsutᵃ dans le public que la souscription ᵇfutᵇ remplie par des Hommes riches & puissans, on cessa de courir ᶜàᶜ la Banque, & on y apporta à l'ordinaire des dépôts.

and as soon as the Public had Notice that this Subscription was full, the Run ceased, and Money was brought back again.

682

What happened in the Year 1745, is in every-body's Memory, and therefore needs not to be mentioned; but what results to a thinking man is, that Schemes of this Sort, would destroy the Credit of the best private Banker in the World, and that they are beneath the Dignity and Honour of a great flourishing Company.

‖ I have already observed, that the supposed Advantage, resulting to the Public from the Trade and Business of Banking, is accelerating and facilitating Circulation: In a Country, such as *England*, encumbered with a Load of National Debts, a public Bank is of the greatest Advantage; it facilitates the daily Purchase and Sale of these Debts, at Market; it may be made use of to lower the Interest of these Incumbrances to the Proprietors, by raising their Price at Market.

683

[I, 578, col.2] Let us suppose, upon the existence of a large *sinking fund*, when the interest of the public creditors was 4 *per cent*. that a minister of great abilities has the management of the *Treasury*, and a great influence on the directors of the *Bank of England*, who have a thorough confidence in his veracity, as well as discernment; that he endeavours to reduce the interest of the public creditors, with a view to increase the sinking fund, in order to sink part of the national debts. It the affairs of the nation run smoothly, and without any fears, we conceive such a minister will be able to effect this reduction without bringing any additional sum of money into the nation; that is, without the nation being the richer to induce it to give real cause for such a reduction of interest.

The refinements introduced to support the Bank and moderate its discredit were first to set up a number of clerks to count out the money to those bringing notes, to pay out large amounts in sixpences and shillings to gain time, to pay some part to individual holders who had been waiting whole days to take their turn; but the most considerable sums were paid to friends who took them away and brought them back secretly to the Bank to repeat the same manœuvre the next day. In this way the Bank saved its appearance and gained time until the panic should abate. But when that did not suffice the Bank opened a subscription engaging trusty and solvent people to join as guarantors of large amounts to maintain the credit and circulation of the Bank notes.

[a]...[a]: R: 'Céstoit dabord dEtaler'
[b]...[b]: R: 'pour y gagner'
[c]...[c]: R: 'a'
[d]...[d]: R: 'accredités solvables'
[e]...[e]: R: 'pour'
[f]...[f]: R: 'de'

680

It was by this last refinement that the credit of the Bank was maintained in 1720 when the South Sea Company collapsed. As soon as it was publicly known that the subscription list was filled by wealthy and powerful people, the run on the Bank ceased and deposits were brought in as usual.

[a]...[a]: R: 'scu'
[b]...[b]: 1756b,1769: 'étoit'
[c]...[c]: R: 'sus'

681

i. The first paragraph of A682 is surely an addition by Philip Cantillon: '1745' is a reference to the Jacobite uprising of that year which was accompanied with a sharp fall of stocks in the City, although a run on the Bank was avoided.
ii. The remark 'I have already observed' is a reference to A629, second paragraph.

682

D683 occurs in the long entry 'Credit', *Universal Dictionary* (I, 574–581). This entry was first published in issue 48, which appeared in January or February 1753. Unusually the fragment does not start under a new subheading, but comes at the end of a discussion of the uses of sinking funds. Indeed part of D683 may have been adapted by Postlethwayt to fit in with this discussion. However, the mention of 'a minister of great abilities' in D683 and D684 is reminiscent of E684 and in the following paragraphs other parallels become more obvious.

683

684 |5| Si un Ministre d'Etat en Angleterre, cherchant à diminuer le prix de l'intérêt de l'argent, ou par d'autres vues, fait augmenter le prix des fonds publics à Londres, & s'il a assez de cré-[427]dit sur les Directeurs de la Banque, pour les engager (sous obligation de les dédommager en cas de perte) à fabriquer plusieurs billets de banque, dont ils n'ont reçu aucune valeur, en les priant ᵃde se servirᵃ de ces billets eux-mêmes ᵇpour acheterᵇ plusieurs parties & capitaux des fonds publics; ces fonds ne manqueront pas de hausser de prix, par ces opérations: & ceux qui les ont vendus, voïant ce haut prix continuer, se détermineront peut-être, pour ne point laisser leurs billets de banque inutiles & croïant par les bruits qu'on seme que le prix de l'intérêt va diminuer & que ces fonds hausseront encore, de les acheter à un plus haut prix qu'ils ne les avoient vendus. Que si plusieurs particuliers, voyant les Agens de la Banque acheter ces fonds, se ᶜmêlentᶜ d'en faire autant croïant profiter comme eux, les fonds [428] publics augmenteront de prix, au point que le Ministre souhaitera; & il se pourra faire que la Banque revendra adroitement à plus haut prix tous les fonds qu'elle avoit achetés, à la sollicitation du Ministre, & en tirera non-seulement un grand profit, mais retirera & éteindra tous les billets de banque ᵈextraordinairesᵈ qu'elle avoit fabriqués.

If the minister directs the *Bank* to strike *Bank* notes for large sums (promising, or engaging in name of the legislature, to indemnify the *Bank* in case of any sudden call for ready money) for which no ready money has been deposited, directs these notes to be offered for stock, and effectually proposes good parcels of stock to be bought gradually, the stock will rise in the altercations, and the owners of the stock who sold it, finding the price to continue high, and not being in the channels of commerce to make interest otherwise of their money, will want to buy in again, rather than let their bank notes lie idle.

Let it be supposed, as a Thing possible, that an artful and ingenious Minister of State, well skilled in the Combination of Numbers (such as the once Comp-[181]troller-General of *France*, the famous Mr. *Law* was) and the Nature and Schemes of combining the Imagination of Men, for great Profits, has Interest and Influence with the few, who are in the Secret of the Management of a great Company's Affairs; advises, under Indemnifications, and prevails to have to the Amount of any given large Sum of Bank Notes, coined and filled up, in order to be made use of for the Purchase of South-Sea Old and New Annuities, South-Sea, Bank, and India Stocks: This Money thus employed will certainly raise the Prices of these different Funds, and this Rise still continuing, and the Noise and Expectation from various other Reports, of a further Rise, and the Appearance of rich and opulent Mens daily Purchases, will raise such a dazzling Expectation of Profit, so as to prevail on the very Persons, who in the Beginning, sold out their Funds to re-purchase, rather than let their Bank Notes lie dead: So that the public Price of the Funds may be raised to any Price, and a Necessity raised in the Proprietors of accepting almost any Interest, rather than be payed off; and an Opportunity is given to those who are in the Secret of getting out, and extinguishing these new-coined Bank Notes, and putting into [182] their own Pockets an extraordinary Profit; I say, Schemes of this Sort are possible, but not probable in our Time.

If a Minister of State in England, seeking to lower the rate of interest or for other reasons, forces up the price of public stock in London and if he has enough credit with the Directors of the Bank (under the obligation of indemnifying them in case of loss) to get them to issue a quantity of bank notes without backing, begging them to use these notes themselves to buy several blocks and capitals of the public stock, this stock will not fail to rise in price through these operations. And those who have sold stock, seeing the high price continue, will perhaps decide (so as not to leave their bank notes idle and thinking from the rumours spread about that the rate of interest will fall and the stock go up further in price) to buy it back at a higher price than they sold it for. If several people seeing the agents of the Banks buy this stock step in and do likewise thinking to profit like them, the public funds will increase in price to the point which the Minister wishes. And it may happen that the Bank will cleverly resell at a higher price all the stock it has purchased at the Minister's request, and will not only make a large profit on it but will retire and cancel all the extraordinary banknotes which it had issued.

[a]...[a]: R:'de servir'

[b]...[b]: R: 'en achettent'

[c]...[c]: R: 'melant'

[d]...[d]: R: 'dextraordinaire'

684

i. While E684 and D684 imagine the minister who is competent in financial operations to be active in England, A684 actually names the 'artful and ingenious' minister as John Law. Nowhere in E is Law mentioned by name, but see C508i and ii.

ii. After A684 the *Analysis* continues with the fragment reproduced from A656 onwards. See C627ii.

685 |6| Si la Banque seule hausse le prix des fonds publics en les achetant, elle les rabaissera d'autant lorsqu'elle voudra les revendre pour éteindre ᵃsesᵃ billets extraordinaires; mais il arrive toujours que plusieurs particuliers voulant imiter les Agens de la Banque dans leurs opérations, contribuent à les soutenir; ᵇil y en a mêmeᵇ qui y sont attrapés faute de savoir au vrai ces opérations, où il entre une infinité de rafinemens, ou plutôt de fourberies qui ne sont pas de mon sujet.

686 || They will, perhaps, try to lend out their money upon mortgages; but the notion of a reduction of interest, and the increase of the number of lenders, occasioned by the operation, will make those who mortgage their estates demand money at 4 *per cent*. and all this while there will be no occasion for ready money, but for the interest of the stocks, and of the mortgages (for here we do not suppose new mortgages, but a paying off of old mortgages seems to require ready money, and will increase the number of borrowers, and raise interest) for the capitals in both may be paid in bank bills: and so, while this game is slowly and dexterously managed, the high prices of stock go gradually diminishing the interest of the public creditors; and when the minister has, by these methods, reduced the interest under 4 *per cent*. in the public funds, mortgages and great payments, he will be able to get in the bank notes he ordered to be struck, by selling the stock bought, and leaving it, perhaps, in the hands of the first owners at a higher price.

687 [429] |7| Il est donc constant qu'une Banque d'intelligence avec un Ministre, est capable de hausser & de soutenir le prix des fonds publics, & de baisser le prix de l'intérêt dans l'Etat au gré de ce Ministre, lorsque les opérations en sont menagées avec discrétion, & par-là de libérer les dettes de l'Etat; mais ces rafinemens qui ouvrent la porte à gagner de grandes fortunes, ne sont que très rarement menagés pour l'utilité seule de l'Etat; & les opérateurs s'y corrompent le plus souvent. Les billets de banque extraordinaires, qu'on fabrique & qu'on répand dans ces occasions, ne dérangent pas la circulation, parcequ'étant emploïés à l'achat & vente de fonds capitaux, ils ne servent pas à la dépense des familles, & qu'on ne les convertit ᵃpointᵃ en argent; mais si quelque crainte ou accident imprévu poussoit les [430] Porteurs à demander l'argent à la Banque, on en viendroit ᵇà crever la bombeᵃ, & on verroit que ce sont des opérations dangereuses.

|| By offering reimbursement, the minister may easily bring the proprietors of redeemable funds to take 2 *per cent*. instead of 4 *per cent*. and be satisfied with the same funds at that price. And thus, by increasing the saving fund, he may effectually pay off some part of the capital, and so diminish the debt, and increase the number of lenders.

|| The like ends may be attained by an able minister, if he can, by his own example, and assurances of lowering interest, engage such as have by them large parcels of bank notes, to buy stocks upon such encouragement, and borrow bank bills of others to buy stocks, and keep them in their hands till those who sold them want to buy in again at high prices.

688

       ᵃFIN.ᵃ

If the Bank alone raises the price of public stock by buying it, it will by so much depress it when it resells to cancel its excess issue of notes. But it always happens that many people wishing to follow the Agents of the Bank in their operations help to keep up the price. Some of them get caught for want of understanding these operations, in which there enter infinite refinements or rather trickery which lie outside my subject.

ᵃ...ᵃ: R: 'Ces'

ᵇ...ᵇ: R: 'mais il y en a'

685

686

It is then undoubted that a Bank with the complicity of a Minister is able to raise and support the price of public stock and to lower the rate of interest in the State at the pleasure of this Minister when the steps are taken discreetly, and thus pay off the State debt. But these refinements which open the door to making large fortunes are rarely carried out for the sole advantage of the State, and those who take part in them are generally corrupted. The excess banknotes, made and issued on these occasions, do not upset the circulation, because being used for the buying and selling of stock they do not serve for household expenses and are not changed into silver. But if some panic or unforeseen crisis drove the holders to demand silver from the Bank the bomb would burst and it would be seen that these are dangerous operations.

ᵃ...ᵃ: R: 'pas'

ᵇ...ᵇ: R: 'à Gare la bombe; 1756b, 1769: 'à faire crever la bombe'; M779 has 'à sauve qui peut'

The editor of the print edition may have replaced the uncommon expression '*Gare la bombe*' in R with '*crever la bombe*'. The fact that in M779 we find the alternative expression '*à sauve qui peut*' indicates that readers of R did struggle to make sense of the phrase. Nevertheless, each of these expressions conveys the meaning of something about to blow up. Cf. C672ii.

687

ᵃ...ᵃ: missing in R

688

501

689

All this, I say, an able minister may do by means of credit, without any sensible alteration in the increase, or circulation, of the species of the nation, which will not be much influenced by these operations; only, indeed, here and there some of the specie-lenders of the first class, seeing a general notion of the reduction of interest by the example of that in the funds, will more readily give way to the altercations. But this will not affect the fish-women of *Billingsgate*, who pay a shilling a week interest for a guinea; nor will the wool-merchant sell his wool to the hatter for time the cheaper; and all the lowest undertakers, who are the sources of interest, will continue in our speculation much as they did before; and, by that time the minister's operations are at an end, and the owners of stock set down with them at an interest of 3 *per cent.* the proportion of the specie-lenders and borrowers being not at all altered, the interest of hard money will appear to be still 4 *per cent.* upon good security, and the stocks will consequently return to their proportion, and fall accordingly. For, if interest can be had for specie on good security at 4 *per cent.* the owner of stock, who at this time has but 3 *per cent.* will sell out, and draw in the value of his stock in specie, to lend it; and the sale of stock will consequently fall the price of it.

|| From what has been said it is pretty plain, from the foregoing considerations, that *banks* and *credit* have a vast influence upon the rise and fall of stocks and public funds, where a project is laid for the raising of their price, when there is no additional sum of species required; but they have not so great an influence upon the general circulation, and barter of a nation, which is mostly gathered from minute payments into large sums, and from such sums distributed into minute payments, all which require specie.

689

i. There are a number of phrases in D689 that are reminiscent of ones recurring elsewhere: the 'fish-women of Billingsgate' are also mentioned in E456; 'the wool-merchant [who] sells his wool to the hatter for time' also figures in D446; 'the lowest undertakers, who are the sources of interest' is reminiscent of the views about different classes of borrowers in E460 and D479; for the frequent uses of the term 'altercations', see C248i, for the expression 'general circulation, and barter of a nation', see D303 and for 'minute payments', see C297ii.

ii. The conclusion that banks and credit have a greater influence on the prices of stocks than on 'general circulation' is reminiscent of the views in D655 and E660.

iii. After D689 there is a short fragment that is reproduced in D671 and D672.

References

Abeille, L.-P. 1760. *Corps d'observations 1759–60 de la Société d'Agriculture de Commerce & des Arts de Bretagne*. Paris: La veuve de B. Brunet.

Ananyin, O. 2014. '*Quorum pars magna fui*: On the Cantillon-Marx connection', *The European Journal of the History of Economic Thought*, 21, 6, 950–76.

Anderson, W. 1819. *The London commercial dictionary and sea-port gazetteer*. London: E. Wilson.

Aristotle [4th c. BC] *Politics*, ed. C.D.C Reeve. Indianapolis: Hackett.

Aspromourgos, T. 1989. 'The Theory of Production and Distribution in Cantillon's *Essai*', *Oxford Economic Papers*, 41, 356–73.

Aspromourgos, T. 1996. *On the Origins of Classical Economics. Distribution and Value from William Petty to Adam Smith*. London and New York: Routledge.

Astigarraga Goenaga, J. and Zabalza Arbizu, J. 2007. 'La fortuna del Essai sur la nature du commerce en général (1755), de Richard Cantillon, en la España del siglo XVIII', *Investigaciones de Historia Económica*, 2007, 7, 9–36.

Bauer, S. 1890. Studies on the French Economists, *Quarterly Journal of Economics*. 5, 1, 100–07.

Beausobre, L. de 1791. *Introduction générale à l'étude de la politique, des finances, et du commerce*. Bruxelles: B. Le Franc.

Becagli, V. 1976. 'Hume o Cantillon? A proposito di un errore ricorrente nella pubblicista italiana del Settecento', *Ricerche storiche*, 2, 513–22.

Bellepierre de Neuve-Église, L.J. 1761–63. *L'agronomie et l'industrie, ou les principes de l'agriculture, du commerce et des arts réduits en pratique*. Paris: Despilly.

Bennet, R.J. 2011. 'Malachy Postlethwayt 1707–67: Genealogy and influence of an early economist and "spin-doctor"', *The Genealogists' Magazine*, 30, 6, 187–96.

Berdell, J. 2009. 'Interdependence and independence in Cantillon's *Essai*', *The European Journal of the History of Economic Thought*, 16, 2, 221–49.

Bertholon, P. 1787. *Du commerce et des manufactures distinctives de la ville de Lyon*. Montpellier: Martel ainé.

Bilistein, C.-L. Andreu, baron de. 1762. *Essai sur les duchés de Lorraine et de Bar*. Amsterdam.

Blaug, M. 1997. *Economic Theory in Retrospect* (5th edn). Cambridge: Cambridge University Press.

Boisguilbert, P. Le Pesant de [1697] 1712. *Le détail de la France, la cause de la diminution de ses biens et la facilité du remède en fournissant en un mois tout l'argent dont le Roi a besoin et enrichissant tout le monde*. Bruxelles: G. De Backer.

Boizard, J. 1692. *Traité des monoyes, de leurs circonstances & dépendances*. Paris: J.B. Coignard.

Bordo, M.D. 1983. 'Some Aspects of the Monetary Economics of Richard Cantillon', *Journal of Monetary Economics*, 12, 235–58.

Boyer, A. 1719. *Dictionnaire Royale François-Anglois et Anglois-François*. Amsterdam: P. Humbert.

Brems, H. 1978. 'Cantillon versus Marx: The Land Theory and the Labor Theory of Value', *History of Political Economy*, 10, 4, 669–78.

Brewer, A. 1988. 'Cantillon and the Land Theory of Value', *History of Political Economy* 20, 1, 1–14.

Brewer, A. 1992. *Richard Cantillon. Pioneer of Economic Theory*. London and New York: Routledge.

Brewer, A. (ed.) 2001. *Essay on the Nature of Commerce in General*. New Brunswick, NJ: Transaction Publishers.

Brewer, A. 2005. 'Cantillon, Quesnay and the Tableau Economique', *Bristol University, Economics Department Working Papers*, No. 05/557.

Brian, E. and Théré, C. (eds) 1997. *Richard Cantillon. Essai sur la nature du commerce en général*. Paris: INED. [Reprint of the 1952 edn with additional introductions.]

Brocard, L. 1902. *Les Doctrines économiques et sociales du Marquis de Mirabeau dans l'Ami des Hommes*. Paris: V. Giard & E. Briere.

Brydges, E. (ed.) 1815. *Censura Literaria* (2nd edn). London: Hurst, Rees, Orme and Brown. Vol.5.

Cannan, E. 1895. 'Two Letters of Adam Smith', *The Economic Journal*, 8, 31, 402–04.

Cantillon, R. 1755. *Essai sur la nature du commerce en général*. London: Fletcher Gyles [Paris].

Cantillon, P. 1759. *The Analysis of Trade, commerce, Coin, Bullion, Banks, and Foreign Exchanges*. London [printed for the author].

Carpani, F.M. 1765. *Bilancio dello stato di Milano, con tre prospetti dell'annus racolto de suoi generi*. [Milan.]

Cassius Dio [early 3rd c. AD] *Roman History*. Translation E. Cary, Loeb Classical Library Edition 1917, vol. VI.

Cicero, M. Tullius 70 BC. *Agains Verres*, in C.D. Yonge, ed., *The Orations of M. Tullius Cicero*. London: George Bell & Sons, 1903.

Cochin, H. 1822. *Œuvres complètes de Cochin, Avocat au parlement de Paris*. Paris: L'Éditeur, Fantin, Nicolle. Vol. 6.

Condillac, E. Bonnot de 1776. *Le commerce et le gouvernement, Considérés relativement l'un à l'autre. Ouvrage élémentaire*. Amsterdam [Paris: Jombert & Cellot].

Corps d'Observations de la Société d'Agriculture de Commerce & des Arts, établie par les États de Bretagne. Années 1757 & 1758. 1760. Rennes: J. Vatar.

Cotta, S, and Giolitti, A. (eds) 1955. *Saggio sulla natura del commercio in generale*. Turin: Einaudi.

Croker, T.H., Williams T. and Clark, S. 1765. *The Complete Dictionary of Arts and Sciences*. London.

Davenant, C. 1699. *An essay on the probable methods of making a people gainers in ballance of trade*. London: James Knapton.

Davis, L. and Reymers C. 1768. *A Catalogue of the Libraries of The Rev. Zachary Grey, L.L.D. Author of Notes and Annotations on Hudibras; Malachy Postlethwayte, Esq; Author of the Universal Dictionary of Trade and Commerce; Thomas Cranmer, M.D. A late Learned Mathematician; And several other Persons deceased*. London.

Decker, M. 1744. *An essay on the causes of the decline of the foreign trade, consequently of the value of the lands of Britain, and on the means to restore both*. London: J. Brotherton.

Defoe, D. 1728. *A Plan of the English Commerce. Being a Compleat Prospect of the Trade of this Nation, as well as the Home Trade as the Foreign*. London: C. Rivington.

Descartes, R. 1701. *Regulae Ad Directionem Ingenii*, ed. G. Hefferman 1998. Amsterdam: Atlanta.

Dockès, P. 1969. *L'espace dans la pensée économique du XVIe au xviiie siècle*. Paris: Flammarion.

Du Halde, J.B. 1735. *Description géographique, historique, chronologique, politique, et physique de l'empire de la Chine et de la Tartarie chinoise, enrichie des cartes générales et particulieres de ces pays, de la carte générale et des cartes particulieres du Thibet, & de la Corée; & ornée d'un grand nombre de figures & de vignettes gravées en tailledouce*, Paris: J-B Mercier.

Economic Journal 1896. 'Current Topics', 6, 21, 165.

Edwards, J.R. 2009. 'A business education for "the middling sort of people" in mercantilist Britain', *The British Accounting Review*, 41, 240–55.

Einaudi, L. 2014. *Luigi Einaudi: Selected Economic Essays*, eds Luca Einaudi, Riccardo Faucci, Roberto Marchionatti. Palgrave Macmillan. Vol. 2.

Ekelund, R.B. and Hébert, R.F. 1990. *A History of Economic Theory and Method* (3rd edn). New York: McGraw-Hill.

Eltis, S and Eltis W. 1997. *Commerce and Government, considered in their mutual relationship*. Cheltenham: Edward Elgar. [Translation of Condillac 1776.]

Emery, P.A. and Wooldridge, K. 2011. *St Pancras burial ground. Excavations for St Pancras International, the London terminus of High Speed 1, 2002–3*. London: Gifford.

Fage, A. 1952. 'La vie et l'œuvre de Richard Cantillon' [Reprinted in Brian and Théré 1997, xxiii–xlii].

Fraser, E. 1938. 'Some Sources of Postlethwayt's Dictionary', *Economic History*, 3, 25–32.

Fréron, E.C. 1755. *L'Année littéraire. Année MDCCLV*. Amsterdam [Paris: Lambert]. Vol. V.

Gazetteer and London Daily Advertiser. 1759. Issue 12 February.

Goodacre, M. 2001. *The Synoptic Problem. A Way Through the Maze.* London and New York: T & T Clark International.

Graslin, J.-J.-L. 1767. *Essai analytique sur la richesse et sur l'impôt.* Londres [Nantes].

Graumann, J. P. 1762. *Gesammelte briefe von dem Gelde.* Berlin: C.F. Boss.

Grimm, F.M. [1755] 2006. *Correspondance littéraire,* ed. R. Granderoute. Ferney-Voltaire: Centre internationale d'étude de XVIIIe siècle. Vol. II.

Groenewegen, P.D. 2001. 'Sir James Steuart and Richard Cantillon', in *Eighteenth-century Economics. Turgot, Beccaria and Smith and their contemporaries.* London and New York: Routledge.

Groenewegen, P.D. 2004. 'Postlethwayt, Malachy (1707–1767)', *Oxford Dictionary of National Biography.*

Groenewegen, P.D. 2012. 'A New Translation of Cantillon: Modern Improvement or Anachronistic Rendition into North American English?', *History of Economics Review,* 55, 80–89.

Halicarnassus, D. of, [1st c. AD], *The Roman Antiquities.* Translation E. Cary. Cambridge, MA: Harvard University Press. 1937.

Halley, E. 1693a. 'An Estimate of the Degrees of the Mortality of Mankind, drawn from curious Tables of the Births and Funerals at the City of Breslaw; with an Attempt to ascertain the Price of Annuities upon Lives', *Philosophical Transactions* 17, 192–206, 596–610.

Halley, E., 1693b. 'Some further Considerations of the Breslaw Bills of Mortality', *Philosophical Transactions,* 17, 654–56.

Hamilton, A. [late 1770s] 1961. *Alexander Hamilton's Paybook,* ed. E.P. Panagopoulos. Detroit: Wayne State University Press.

Harris, J. 1757. *An Essay upon Money and Coins.* London: Hawkins.

Hayek, F.A, [1931] 1985. 'Richard Cantillon', *The Journal of Libertarian Studies,* 7, 2, 217–47. [Translation of Hayek's introduction to the German edition of the *Essay.*]

Hayek, F.A. 1932. '[Review of] *Essai sur la nature du commerce en général.* [Higgs ed.]', *The Economic Journal* 42, 165, 61–63.

Hayek, F.A. 1991. *The Trend of Economic Thinking. Essays on Political Economists and Economic History,* eds. W.W. Bartley III and S. Kresge. London: Routledge.

Hayek, H. and Hayek F.A. 1931. *R. Cantillon, Abhandlung über die Natur des Handels im allgemeinen.* Jena: Gustav Fischer.

Hébert, R.F. 1981. 'Richard Cantillon's Early Contributions to Spatial Economics', *Economica,* 48, 1, 71–77.

Hébert, R.F. 1985. 'Was Richard Cantillon an Austrian Economist?', *The Journal of Libertarian Studies,* 7, 2, 69–79.

Hébert, R.F. 2010. 'Foreword' in Saucier and Thornton, *An Essay on Economic Theory,* 5–7.

Higgs, H. 1891. 'Richard Cantillon', *The Economic Journal,* 1, 2, 262–91.

Higgs, H. 1892. 'Cantillon's Place in Economics', *The Quarterly Journal of Economics,* 6, 4, 436–56.

Higgs, H. (ed.) 1931. *Essai sur la nature du commerce en général by Richard Cantillon.* London: Macmillan.

Hone, J. 1944. Richard Cantillon, Economist, Biographical Note, *The Economic Journal,* 54, 96–100.

Hume, D. 1752. *Political Discourses.* Edinburgh: R. Fleming.

Hume, D. 1778. *History of England, from the Invasion of Julius Caesar to the Revolution in 1688.* Vol. 3.

Jevons, W.S. 1881. 'Richard Cantillon and the Nationality of Political Economy', reprinted in Higgs (1931).

Johnson, E.A.J. 1937. *Predecessors of Adam Smith: the growth of British economic thought.* London: P.S. King.

Journal de Commerce. 1760. January, 69–73.

Larrère, C. 2011. 'Montesquieu et Cantillon' in *Montchrestien et Cantillon. Le commerce et l'émergence d'une pensée économique.* Lyon: ENS Éditions. 131–54.

Law, J. 1705. *Money and trade considered, with a proposal for supplying the nation with money.* Edinburgh: Anderson.

Legrand, R. 1900. *Richard Cantillon – un mercantiliste précurseur des physiocrates.* Paris: V. Giard and E. Brière.

Locke, J. 1692. *Some considerations of the consequences of the lowering of interest, and raising the value of money. In a letter to a member of Parliament.* London: Awnsham and Churchill.

Locke, J. 1696. *Several papers relating to money, interest and trade, &c. Writ upon several occasions and published at different times.* London: A. and J. Churchill.

London Evening Post. 1759. Issue 4879, 10–13 February.

Mably, G. Bonnot de. 1757. *Principes des Négociations, pour servir d'introduction au Droit public de l'Europe, fondé sur les traits.* The Hague: n.p.

Mably, G. Bonnot de. 1763. *Entretiens de Phocion, sur le rapport de la morale avec la politique; traduits du grec de Nicoclès; avec des remarques.* Amsterdam: n.p.

Mamroth-Brokman, M. 1908. *Das dictionnaire universel de commerce der gebrüder Savary, als spiegelbild des übergangs der ökonomischen theorien vom merkantilismus zum physiokratischen system.* Wittenberg: Herrosé und Ziemsen.

Mandeville, B. 1725. *The Fable of the Bees: or, Private Vices, Publick Benefits.* London: J. Roberts. Vol. 2.

Marx, K. [1867]. 1977. *Capital. A critique of political economy.* London: Lawrence & Wishart. Vol. 1.

Mauvillon, E. 1756. *Discours Politiques.* Amsterdam: J. Schreuder and Pierre Mortier le jeune. Vol. 3. Reprint 1769.

McCulloch, J.R. 1832. *A dictionary, practical, theoretical and historical, of commerce and commercial navigation.* London: Longman, Rees, Orme, Brown, Green & Longman.

McCulloch, J.R. 1845. *The Literature of Political Economy.* London: Longman, Brown, Green and Longmans.

Meek, R.L. 1962. *The Economics of Physiocracy. Essays and Translations.* Reprint 1993, Fairfield NJ: A.M. Kelley.

Milton, J. 1667. *Paradise Lost. A Poem written in ten books.* London: S. Simmons.

Mirabeau, V. Riquetti de 1756. *L'Ami des hommes, ou Traité de la population.* Avignon: n.p.

Mirabeau, V. Riquetti de 1761. *L'Ami des hommes, ou Traité de la population, Volume 6, part 2: Tableau économique avec ses explications.* Avignon: n.p.

Mirabeau. 1763. *Philosophie rurale ou Économie Générale et Politique de l'Agriculture.* Amsterdam: Les Libraires Associés.

Mizuta, H. 2000. *Adam Smith's Library.* Oxford: Oxford University Press.

Montesquieu, C. de Secondat, de 1748. *De l'esprit des loix ou du rapport que les loix doivent avoir avec la constitution de chaque gouvernement, les moeurs, le climat, la religion, le commerce. &c.* Geneva: Barrillot & fils.

Montlaur, H. de. 1992. *Mirabeau. L'Ami des hommes.* Paris: Perrin.

Morellet, A. 1769. *Prospectus d'un nouveau dictionnaire de commerce.* Paris: Estienne.

Mortimer, T. 1766. *A New and complete dictionary of trade and commerce.* London [printed for the author].

Moureau, F. (ed.) 1993. *De bonne main. La communication manuscrite au XVIIIe siècle.* Oxford: Voltaire Foundation.

Murphy, A. 1985. 'Richard Cantillon – Banker and Economist', *Journal of Libertarian Studies*, 7, 2, 185–216.

Murphy, A. 1986. *Richard Cantillon: Entrepreneur and Economist.* Oxford: Oxford University Press.

Murphy, A. 2009. *The Genesis of Macroeconomics. New Ideas from Sir William Petty to Henry Thornton.* Oxford: Oxford University Press.

Newland, W. 1751. *An Act for Sale of the Estate late of William Newland, Esquire, deceased, in Gatton, Rigate, and Meastham, in the Country of Surrey, for discharging Incumbrances.*

Panagopoulos, E.P. 1961. *Alexander Hamilton's Pay Book.* Detroit: Wayne State University Press.

Patalano, R. 2001. 'Il *Dictionnaire universel de commerce* dei Savary e la fondazione dell'autonomia del discorso economico 1723–1769', *Storia del pensiero economic*, 41, 131–63.

Perrot, J.-C. 1992. *Une histoire intellectuelle de l'économie politique, XVIIe–XVIIIe siècle.* Paris: École des Hautes Études en Sciences Sociales.

Pettus, J. 1670. *Fordinae Regales. Or the History, Laws and Places of the Chief Mines and Mineral Works in England, Wales and the English Pale in Ireland.* London: Thomas Bassett.

Petty, W. 1662a. A *Treatise of Taxes & Contributions.* London: N. Brooke.

[Petty, W.] 1662b. *Natural and Political Observations Mentioned in a following Index, and made upon the Bills of Mortality.* London: John Martin.

Petty, W. 1691a. *The Political Anatomy of Ireland. With the Establishment for the Kingdom when the late Duke of Ormond was Lord Lieutenant. Taken from the Records. To which is added Verbum Sapienti; or an Account of the Wealth and Expences of England, and the Method of raising Taxes in the most Equal manner.* London: D. Brown and W. Rogers.

Petty, W. 1691b. *Political Arithmetick or A Discourse Concerning the Extent and Value of Lands, People, Buildings; [etc.].* London: R. Clavel and H. Mortlock.

Pliny the Elder *c.* AD 77–79. *Natural History*. Translated by H. Rackham, W.H.S. Jones and D.E. Eichholz. Cambridge, MA: Harvard University Press and London: William Heinemann, 1949–54.

Pluquet, F.-A.-A. 1786. *Traité philosophique et politique sur le luxe*. Paris: Barrois.

Plutarch. *c.* AD 96-98. *Lives. The Translation called Dryden's*. Corrected from the Greek and Revised by A.H. Clough, in 5 vols. Boston: Little Brown and Co., 1906.

Ponsard, C. 1958. *Histoire des theories économiques spatiales*. Paris: Armand Colin.

Postlethwayt, M. 1733. *Englishmen's eyes open'd; or all made to see who are not resolv'd to be blind etc*. London: J. Wilford.

Postlethwayt, M. 1734. *A series of Wisdom and Policy, manifested in a Review of our Foreign Negotiations and Transactions for several Years past. Being a complete answer to Politicks on both Sides, etc*. London: J. Roberts.

Postlethwayt, M. [1730s.] *The Accomplish'd Merchant*. [Unpublished pamphlet distributed by the author.]

Postlethwayt, M. 1745. *The African Trade, the great pillar and support of the British Plantation Trade in America*. London: J. Robinson.

Postlethwayt, M. 1746. *The National and Private Advantages of the Africa Trade Considered*. London: John and Paul Knapton.

Postlethwayt, M. 1749. *A Dissertation on the Plan, Use, and Importance, of The Universal Dictionary of Trade and Commerce*. London: John and Paul Knapton.

Postlethwayt, M. 1750. *The British Mercantile Academy or the Accomplished Merchant*. London: John and Paul Knapton.

Postlethwayt, M. 1751–55. *The Universal Dictionary of Trade and Commerce, Translated from the French of the Celebrated Monsieur Savary*. London: John and Paul Knapton. 2 vols.

Postlethwayt, M. 1757. *Great-Britain's True System*. London: Millar, Whiston, White, and Sandby.

Prendergast, R. 1991. 'Cantillon and the Emergence of the Theory of Profit', *History of Political Economy* 23, 3, 419–29.

Pulteney, W. 1734. *The Politicks on both sides with regards to foreign affairs etc*. London: H. Haines.

Quesnay, F. 2005. *Œuvres économiques complètes et autres textes*, eds. C. Théré, L. Charles and J.-C. Perrot. Paris: INED.

Rabelais, F. 1546. *Gargantua et Pantagruel. Le Tiers Livre*. Paris: C. Wechel.

Raynal, G.-T. 1775. *Histoire Philosophique et Politique Des Établissements & du Commerce des Européens dans les deux Indes*. Maestricht: J.-E. Dufour.

Reddick, J. 1996. *The Making of Johnson's Dictionary 1746–1773*. Cambridge: Cambridge University Press.

Redlich, F. 1970. 'The Earliest English Attempt at Theoretical Training for Business: A Bibliographical Note', *History of Political Economy*, 2, 1, 199–204.

Renaudot, E. 1718. *Anciennes Relations des Indes et de la Chine de deux voyageurs mahométans, qui y allèrent dans le neuvième siècle; traduites d'arabe: avec des Remarques sur les principaux endroits de ces relations*. Paris: Coignard.

Rey, A. (ed) 1998. *Dictionnaire Historique de la Langue Française*. Paris: Dictionnaires Le Robert.

Rothbard, M.N. 1995. *Economic Thought Before Adam Smith: An Austrian Perspective on the History of Economic Thought*. Northampton, MA: Edward Elgar.

Rousseau, J.-J. 1932. *Correspondance générale de J.-J. Rousseau*, ed. T. Dufour. Paris: Armand Colin. Vol. 17.

Salleron, L. 1980. 'A Propos de l'édition au Japon d'un manuscrit de l'"Essay" de Cantillon', *Notes et Documents*. Institut National d'Études Démographiques.

Saucier, C. and Thornton, M. 2010. *An Essay on Economic Theory. An English translation of Richard Cantillon's Essai sur la Nature du Commerce en Général*. Auburn, Alabama: Ludwig von Mises Institute.

Savary, P.L. 1723. *Dictionnaire universel de commerce*. Paris: Jacques Estienne

Savary, P.L. 1759. *Dictionnaire universel de commerce*. Copenhagen: C.L. & A. Philibert.

Schumpeter, J. 1954. *History of Economic Analysis*. Reprint 1994. London: Routledge.

Shackle, G.L.S. 1982. 'Cantillon Far Ahead of his Time', in *Homenaje a Lucas Beltran*. Madrid: Editorial Moneda y Crédito. 765–79.

Skinner, A.S., (ed.) 1966. *An Inquiry into the Principles of Political Œconomy by James Steuart*. London and Edinburgh: Oliver & Boyd.

Smith, A. [1776] 1976. *An Inquiry into the Nature and Causes of the Wealth of Nations,* eds R.H. Campbell, A.S. Skinner and W.B. Todd. Oxford: Oxford University Press.

Smith, A. 1978. *Lectures on Jurisprudence,* eds R.L. Meek, D.D. Raphael and P.G. Stein. Oxford: Oxford University Press.

Smith, R.S. 1967. 'A Spanish Edition of Cantillon's *Essai*', *Southern Economic Journal*, 33, 4, 572–73.

Spengler, J.J. 1942. *French Predecessors of Malthus*. Durham, N.C: Duke University Press.

Spengler, J.J. 1954. 'Richard Cantillon: First of the Moderns', *Journal of Political Economy*, 62, 4, 281–95 and 5, 406–24.

Steuart, J. 1767. *An Inquiry into the Principles of Political Œconomy: Being an Essay on the Science of Domestic Policy in Free Nations*. London: A. Millar and T. Cadell.

Swift, J. 1724–25. *Drapier's Letters*. [Dublin: John Harding (first five pamphlets); George Faulkner (last two pamphlets).]

Tatham, W. 1799. *The political economy of inland navigation, irrigation and drainage*. London: R. Faulder.

The Intelligencer or Merchant's Assistant 1738. London: W. Meadows.

Théré, C., Charles, L. and Lefebvre, F. (eds) 2011. *Le cercle de Vincent de Gournay*. Paris: INED.

Thornton, M. 2007. 'Cantillon, Hume and the Rise of Antimercantilism', *History of Political Economy*, 39, 3: 453–80.

Tsuda, T. (ed.) 1979. *Cantillon. Essay de la nature du commerce en général*. Tokyo: Hitotsubashi University.

Turgot, A.R.J. 1766. *Reflections on the Formation and Distribution of Wealth*. Translation in P.D. Groenewegen, *The Economics of A.R.J. Turgot*. 1977. The Hague: Martinus Nijhoff.

van den Berg, R. 2010. 'John Gray's *Essential Principles of the Wealth of Nations*', in N. Allington and N. Thompson eds, *English, Irish and Subversives among the Dismal Scientists. Research in the History of Economic Thought and Methodology*, vol. 28. B. Bingley: Emerald.

van den Berg, R. 2012a. 'Richard Cantillon's Early Monetary Views?', *Economic Thought* ,1, 1, 48–79. Online Journal: et.worldeconomicsassociation.org/article/download/32/13.

van den Berg, R. 2012b. '"Something wonderful and incomprehensible in their œconomy." The English versions of Richard Cantillon's *Essay on the Nature of Trade in General*', *The European Journal of the History of Economic Thought*, 19, 6, 868–907.

van den Berg, R. 2014a. 'Cantillon on Profit and Interest: New Insights from Other Versions of His Writings', *History of Political Economy*, 46, 4, 609–40.

van den Berg, R. 2014b. 'Simple Economic Fictions in Richard Cantillon and Daniel Defoe', paper presented at the 18th ESHET conference in Lausanne, Switzerland, 29–31 May 2014.

Vanderlint, J. 1734. *Money answers all things: or, An essay to make money sufficiently plentiful amongst all ranks of people*. London: T. Cox.

Varro, M. T. [1st c. BC.] *Rerum Rusticarum Libri Tres*. G. Goetz ed. Leipzig: Teuberni 1912.

Vauban, S. Le Prestre de. 1707. *Projet d'une Dixme Royale, qui supprimant la Taille, les Aydes, les Doüanes d'une Province à l'autre, les Décimes du Clergé, les Affaires extraordinaires; [etc.]*. [n.p.]

Vivant de Mezague. 1766. *A general view of England; respecting its policy, trade, commerce, taxes, debts, produce of lands, colonies, manners, &c. &c. Argumentatively stated; from the year 1600 to 1762; in a letter to AMLCD*. London: J. Robson.

Wright, J.K. 1997. *A Classical Republican in Eighteenth-Century France. The Political Thought of Mably*. Stanford: Stanford University Press.

Yeo, R. 2001. *Encyclopaedic Visions: Scientific Dictionaries and Enlightenment Culture*. New York: Cambridge University Press.

Index

For Product Safety Concerns and Information please contact our EU
representative GPSR@taylorandfrancis.com
Taylor & Francis Verlag GmbH, Kaufingerstraße 24, 80331 München, Germany

www.ingramcontent.com/pod-product-compliance
Ingram Content Group UK Ltd.
Pitfield, Milton Keynes, MK11 3LW, UK
UKHW051833180425
457613UK00022B/1232